Microsoft®

Office 2000

8-in-1 Step by Step

Microsoft Press

PUBLISHED BY
Microsoft Press
A Division of Microsoft Corporation
One Microsoft Way
Redmond, Washington 98052-6399

Library of Congress Cataloging-in-Publication Data
Microsoft Office 2000 8-in-1 Step by Step / Catapult, Inc.,
Perspection, Inc., ActiveEducation.
p. cm.
Includes index.
ISBN 1-57231-984-4
1. Microsoft Office. 2. Microsoft Word. 3. Microsoft Excel for Windows. 4. Microsoft PowerPoint (Computer file) 5. Microsoft Access. 6. Microsoft Outlook. 7. Microsoft Publisher. 8. Microsoft Internet explorer. 9. Microsoft FrontPage. 10. Business--Computer programs. 11. Word processing. 12. Electronic spreadsheets. 13. Business presentations--Graphic methods--Computer programs. 14. Database management--Computer programs. 15. Time management--Computer programs. 16. Personal information management--Computer programs. 17. Web sites--Design. 18. Web publishing. 19. Internet (Computer network) 20. World Wide Web (information retreival system) I. Catapult, Inc. II. Perspection, Inc. III. ActiveEducation (Firm)
HF5548.4.M525M52475 1999
005.369--dc21 99-13767
CIP

Printed and bound in the United States of America.

13 QWT 6 5 4 3

Distributed in Canada by H.B. Fenn and Company Ltd.

A CIP catalogue record for this book is available from the British Library.

Microsoft Press books are available through booksellers and distributors worldwide. For further information about international editions, contact your local Microsoft Corporation office or contact Microsoft Press International directly at fax (425) 936-7329. Visit our Web site at www.microsoft.com/mspress. Send comments to *mspinput@microsoft.com.*

Acquisitions Editor: Susanne Forderer
Project Editor: Laura Sackerman
Technical Editor: Helen Letts
Compositor: Frog Mountain Productions

Contents

Finding Your Best Starting Point

Microsoft Office 2000 is a powerful family of integrated programs that you can use to produce sophisticated documents. With *Microsoft Office 2000 8-in-1 Step by Step*, you'll quickly and easily learn how to use Office 2000 to get your work done.

important

This book is designed for use with Microsoft Office 2000 for the Windows and Windows NT operating systems. If your software is not compatible with this book, a Step by Step book matching your software is probably available. Please visit our World Wide Web site at *http://mspress.microsoft.com* or call 1-800-MSPRESS (1-800-677-7377) for more information.

Finding the Best Starting Point for You

This book is designed for readers who are learning Office 2000 for the first time and for more experienced readers who are switching from other programs or earlier versions of Office. Use the following table to find your best starting point in this book.

If you are	Follow these steps
New to computers to graphical (as opposed to text-only) computer programs to Windows to Microsoft Office programs	1. Install the practice files as described in "Using the Microsoft Office 2000 8-in-1 Step by Step CD-ROM." 2. Become acquainted with the Windows operating system and how to use the online Help system. To do this, on the Windows or Windows NT taskbar, click the Start button. On the menu that appears, click Help. In the window that appears, click each topic that you'd like to learn about. 3. Work through the parts of this book in any order.

If you are	Follow these steps
Switching from Lotus SmartSuite from Corel WordPerfect Suite from WordPerfect Office	1. Install the practice files as described in "Using the Microsoft Office 2000 8-in-1 Step by Step CD-ROM." 2. Work through Parts 1 through 8 in any order.

If you are	Follow these steps
Upgrading from Microsoft Office 97	1. Learn about the new features of Office 2000 that are covered in this book by reading through the following section, "New Features in Microsoft Office 2000." 2. Install the practice files as described in "Using the Microsoft Office 2000 8-in-1 Step by Step CD-ROM." 3. Complete the lessons that cover the topics you need. You can use the table of contents to locate information about general topics. You can use the index to find information about a specific topic or feature.

If you are	Follow these steps
Referencing this book after working through the lessons	❶ Use the index to locate information about specific topics, and use the table of contents to locate information about general topics. ❶ Read the Quick Reference at the end of each lesson for a brief review of the major tasks in the lesson. The Quick Reference topics are listed in the same order as they are presented in the lesson.

New Features in Microsoft Office 2000

Microsoft Office 2000 contains new and enhanced features that make it more enjoyable for you to get your job done.

The following table lists the major new features of Microsoft Office 2000 and Microsoft Internet Explorer 5 that are covered in this book and the lesson in which you can learn how to use each feature. You can also use the index to find specific information about a feature or a task that you want to perform.

To learn how to	See
Word 2000	
Use the enhanced Microsoft Office Assistant.	Lesson 1
Navigate expanded menus and truncated toolbars.	Lesson 1
Copy and paste several items at once.	Lesson 2
Use Click And Type to quickly insert justified text anywhere in a document.	Lesson 3
Print multiple pages on a single page.	Lesson 4
Excel 2000	
See the colors and formatting of a workbook even when cells are selected using Excel's new See-Through View.	Lesson 2
Create dates that are year 2000–compatible using new date formats that display years as four digits.	Lesson 4
Outlook 2000	
Find answers to your questions about Microsoft Outlook with the enhanced Office Assistant.	Lesson 1
Customize your Outlook menu options.	Lesson 1
Easily create personal distribution lists of contacts from one or more Contacts folders and the Global Address List.	Lesson 3

To learn how to	See
PowerPoint 2000	
Use the new Normal view.	Lesson 1
Enter text in the Outline, Slide, and Notes panes.	Lesson 2
Access 2000	
Find answers to your questions about Microsoft Access 2000 with the Office Assistant.	Lesson 1
Publisher 2000	
Use the new Catalog.	Lesson 1
Print multiple business cards on a page.	Lesson 2
Drag and drop clip art.	Lesson 4
View new clip art.	Lesson 4
IE 5	
Save Web pages	Lesson 1
Search with the Search Assistant.	Lesson 1
Add and organize Web pages with the Favorites bar.	Lesson 2
FrontPage 2000	
Manage a Web site with FrontPage.	Lesson 1
Create or edit a Web Page with FrontPage's integrated Web page editor.	Lesson 2
Open recently used Webs in FrontPage.	Lesson 3
Use Cascading Style Sheets (CSS) to position items on Web pages.	Lesson 4
Use background spelling checking.	Lesson 5

Corrections, Comments, and Help

Every effort has been made to ensure the accuracy of this book and the contents of the Microsoft Office 2000 8-in-1 Step by Step CD-ROM. Microsoft Press provides corrections and additional content for its books through the World Wide Web at *http://mspress.microsoft.com/support*

If you have comments, questions, or ideas regarding this book or the CD-ROM, please send them to us.

Send e-mail to:

mspinput@microsoft.com

Or send postal mail to:

Microsoft Press
Attn: Step by Step Editor
One Microsoft Way
Redmond, WA 98052-6399

Please note that support for Office 2000 software products is not offered through the above addresses. For help using Office 2000, you can call Office 2000 Technical Support at (425) 635-7070 on weekdays between 6 A.M. and 6 P.M. Pacific Time.

Visit Our World Wide Web Site

We invite you to visit the Microsoft Press World Wide Web site. You can visit us at the following location:

http://mspress.microsoft.com

You'll find descriptions of all of our books, information about ordering titles, notices of special features and events, additional content for Microsoft Press books, and much more.

You can also find out the latest in software developments and news from Microsoft Corporation by visiting the following World Wide Web site:

http://www.microsoft.com/

We look forward to your visit on the Web!

Using the Microsoft Office 2000 8-in-1 Step by Step CD-ROM

The CD-ROM inside the back cover of this book contains the practice files that you'll use as you perform the exercises in the book and multimedia files that demonstrate some of the exercises. By using the practice files, you won't waste time creating the samples used in the lessons—instead, you can concentrate on learning how to use Office 2000. With the files and the step-by-step instructions in the lessons, you'll also learn by doing, which is an easy and effective way to acquire and remember new skills.

important

Before you break the seal on the practice CD-ROM package, be sure that this book matches your version of the software. This book is designed for use with Microsoft Office 2000 for the Windows and Windows NT operating systems. If your program is not compatible with this book, a Step by Step book matching your software is probably available. Please visit our World Wide Web site at *http://mspress.microsoft.com* or call 1-800-MSPRESS (1-800-677-7377) for more information.

Installing the Practice Files

Follow these steps to install the practice files and/or multimedia files on your computer's hard disk so that you can use them with the exercises in this book.

1. If your computer isn't on, turn it on now.
2. If you're using Windows NT, press Ctrl+Alt+Delete to display a dialog box asking for your user name and password. If you are using Windows 95 or Windows 98, you will see this dialog box if your computer is connected to a network. If you don't know your user name or password, contact your system administrator for assistance.

Close

3. Type your user name and password in the appropriate boxes, and then click OK. If you see the Welcome dialog box, click the Close button.
4. Remove the companion CD from the package inside the back cover of this book.
5. Insert the CD in the CD-ROM drive of your computer.
6. On the taskbar at the bottom of your screen, click the Start button.

   The Start menu opens
7. On the Start menu, click Run.

   The Run dialog box appears.
8. In the Open box, type **d:setup** (if your CD-ROM drive is a different letter, be sure to use that letter instead; for example **e:setup**). Don't add spaces as you type.
9. Click OK.

   The Welcome dialog box appears.
10. Click OK.

    The Select Practice And Multimedia Files dialog box appears.
11. When you run the Setup program for the first time, all the items in the Files list are checked by default, so uncheck the items that you do not want installed.

    All checked items will be installed. Remember to scroll down in the Files list to display all the items. If an item is automatically unchecked, it is probably already installed. You may want to install only the items for the parts of the book you will be working on. If you want to install additional items at a later time, you can just run this Setup program again at that time.

tip

If you try to install items that have already been installed, you will receive Confirm File Replace messages. Therefore, if you want to reinstall an item, it is recommended that you first uninstall that item and then run Setup again to install it. See "Uninstalling the Practice and Multimedia Files" later in this section for instructions for installing items.

important

The multimedia files are not required to complete the step-by-step lessons. Therefore, if you have limited hard disk space on your computer, you might choose not to install the multimedia files.

12. From the Drives drop-down list, select the drive you want to install to, and then click the Continue button.

    An installing dialog box appears, indicating the progress of the files being installed on your computer. Once all the selected files have been installed, a Finished dialog box appears.

13. Click OK. Remove the companion CD from your drive and replace it in the package inside the back cover of the book.

During the installation, a new folder was created on your hard disk. The folder is named Office 8in1 Step by Step and it contains all of the practice and multimedia files you chose to install.

tip

In addition to installing the practice and multimedia files, the Setup program created two shortcuts on your desktop. You can double-click the Office 8in1 Step by Step shortcut to view the practice and multimedia files that you copied to your hard disk. If your computer is set up to connect to the Internet, you can double-click the Microsoft Press Welcome shortcut to visit the Microsoft Press Web site. You can also connect to the Web site directly at *http://mspress.microsoft.com*

Using the Practice Files

Each lesson in this book explains when and how to use any practice files for that lesson. When a practice file is needed for a lesson, the book will list instructions on how to open the file. The lessons are built around scenarios that simulate a real work environment, so you can easily apply the skills you learn to your own work. For the scenario in this book, imagine that you're a partner in Impact Public Relations, a small public relations firm. Your company recently installed Office 2000, and you are eager to use it for a variety of business tasks.

Uninstalling the Practice and Multimedia Files

Use the following steps when you want to delete the practice and multimedia files added to your hard disk by the Step by Step setup program.

1. Click Start, point to Settings, and then click Control Panel.
2. Double-click the Add/Remove Programs icon. The Add/Remove Programs Properties dialog box is displayed.
3. Select which item you want to uninstall from the list. The items listed depend on which parts you chose to install with the Setup program.
4. After you have selected a part you want to uninstall, click the Add/Remove button. A confirmation message appears, asking if you want to continue.
5. Click Yes. The files for that part are uninstalled.
6. If you want to uninstall additional parts, repeat steps 3 through 5.
7. When you are finished uninstalling, click the OK button in the Add/Remove Programs Properties dialog box.
8. Close the Control Panel window.

If you would like to delete the Office 8in1 Step by Step and the Microsoft Press Welcome shortcuts on your desktop, follow these steps.

1. On the desktop, click the Office 8in1 Step by Step shortcut to select it.
2. While holding down the Ctrl key, click the Microsoft Press Welcome shortcut to select it as well.
3. Press the Delete key.

   The Confirm Multiple File Delete dialog box appears.
4. Click Yes.

   Both shortcuts are moved to the Recycle Bin.

Need Help with the Practice or Multimedia Files?

Every effort has been made to ensure the accuracy of this book and the contents of the Microsoft Office 2000 8-in-1 Step by Step CD-ROM. If you do run into a problem, Microsoft Press provides corrections for its books through the World Wide Web at:

http://mspress.microsoft.com/support/

We invite you to visit our main Web page at:

http://mspress.microsoft.com

You'll find descriptions of all of our books, information about ordering titles, notices of special features and events, additional content for Microsoft Press books, and much more.

Conventions and Features in This Book

You can save time when you use this book by understanding, before you start the lessons, how instructions, keys to press, and so on, are shown in the book. Please take a moment to read the following list, which also points out helpful features of the book that you might want to use.

Conventions

- Hands-on exercises for you to follow are given in numbered lists of steps (1, 2, and so on). A round bullet (●) indicates an exercise that has only one step.
- Text that you are to type appears in **bold**.
- A plus sign (+) between two key names means that you must press those keys at the same time. For example, "Press Alt+Tab" means that you hold down the Alt key while you press Tab.
- The following icons are used to identify certain types of exercise features:

Icon	Alerts you to
	Skills that are demonstrated in multimedia files available on the Microsoft Office 2000 8-in-1 Step by Step CD-ROM.
	New features in Office 2000.

Other Features of This Book

- You can learn about techniques that build on what you learned in a lesson by trying the optional "One Step Further" exercise at the end of the lesson.
- You can get a quick reminder of how to perform the tasks you learned by reading the Quick Reference at the end of each lesson.
- You can see a multimedia demonstration of some of the exercises in the book by double-clicking the multimedia icons in the Demos folders.

PART 1

Microsoft Word 2000

Creating and Saving Simple Documents

ESTIMATED TIME
25 min.

In this lesson you will learn how to:

- ✔ *Start Microsoft Word 2000.*
- ✔ *Navigate the Word menu bar and toolbars.*
- ✔ *Type and edit a new document.*
- ✔ *Correct mistakes manually and use AutoCorrect.*
- ✔ *Name and save a document.*
- ✔ *Use Microsoft Word Help.*
- ✔ *Create a new toolbar.*

Whether your task is to produce a basic memo, letter, or report, or to design a brochure, newsletter, or Web page, Microsoft Word 2000 provides powerful and easy-to-use tools. It's a snap to cut, copy, and paste text, to format and organize your documents, and to check spelling and grammar—even to correct mistakes as you type.

Using Word to Create Simple Documents

As you work through the exercises in this part of the book, imagine that you are a partner in Impact Public Relations, a small public relations firm that specializes in designing multimedia campaigns for midsize companies. Your duties include writing and editing letters to clients, as well as many other tasks that require efficient word processing skills. In this lesson, you'll create and edit a letter to a potential client, learn how to correct mistakes manually, and work with *AutoCorrect*—a Word feature that automatically corrects some spelling and typographical errors as you type. You'll also learn how to name and save your document to a folder, and how to get help with Word when necessary.

Starting Microsoft Word

There are several ways to start Word. You can start Word from the Office shortcut bar, or you can simply start Word using the Start button on the Windows taskbar.

Start Word from the Windows taskbar

1. On the Windows taskbar, click the Start button.

   The Start menu appears.

2. On the Start menu, point to Programs, and then click Microsoft Word.

   Word 2000 opens, and a new blank document is displayed.

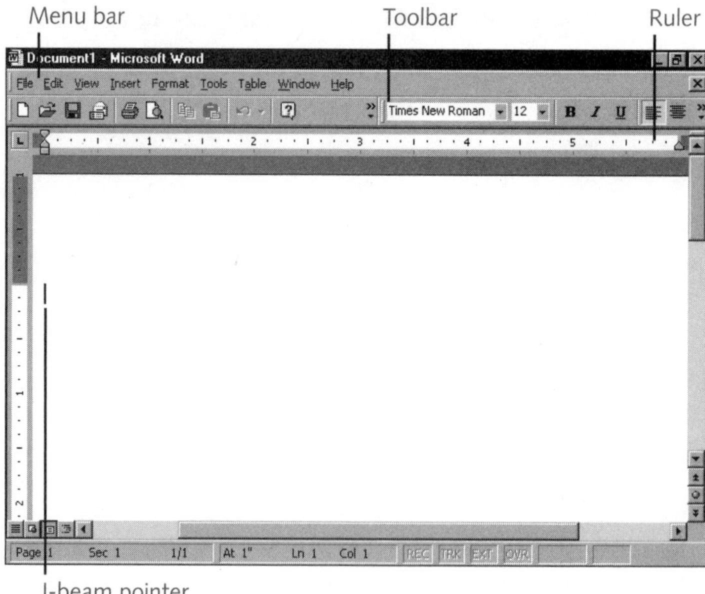

important

If the Office 2000 Registration Wizard appears, you can click Yes to register the product, or you can click No. If you choose to register later, this wizard will appear each time you start Word until you complete the registration.

Using the Office Assistant

When you start Word, an animated character named Clippit appears on your screen. Clippit is an *Office Assistant* who is there to help you produce your documents. Sometimes Clippit will recognize the task you are performing. For example, if you are typing a letter, Clippit will ask you if you would like help writing the letter. If you choose to have help, Clippit will start the Letter Wizard and continue to give you help in completing the task. Otherwise, Clippit will not give you assistance, but will remain on your screen.

You can close the Assistant by pressing the Esc key.

At other times while you're working, Clippit will give you a tip on how to complete a task. Once you have read the tip, you can click OK and Clippit will disappear.

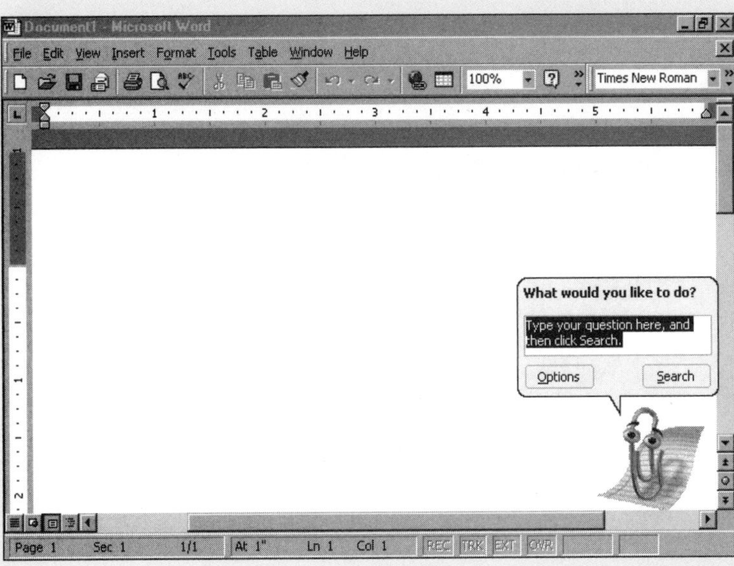

(continued)

continued

You can get help with your task at any time by simply clicking Clippit. When you do, a text box appears, allowing you to type your question. You type a question the same way you would ask someone a question—for example, *How do I save a Word document?*

Once you have asked your question, click Search and Clippit will guide you through the Help topics related to your inquiry. Clippit will remember your last question and search results so that you can easily access other Help topics related to your question. You'll find more information about using Help later in this lesson.

Customizing the Office Assistant

If the Clippit character does not suit your tastes, you can choose another character from the Gallery of Office Assistants if you installed this feature during your Word program installation.

1. Right-click the Office Assistant.

   The Office Assistant shortcut menu appears.
2. Click Choose Assistant.

   The Office Assistant dialog box appears.
3. Click the Gallery tab.
4. Click Next or Back to view the gallery of Office Assistants.
5. Click OK to select an assistant.

Disabling the Office Assistant

If you choose, you can turn off the Assistant so it will not appear on your screen.

1. Right-click the Assistant.

   The shortcut menu appears.
2. Click Options.

   The Office Assistant dialog box appears.
3. Clear the Use The Office Assistant check box.
4. Click OK.

For the purposes of this book, the Office Assistant will not be shown in illustrations. If you choose to disable the Office Assistant, and then want to turn it back on, on the Help menu, click Show The Office Assistant.

Navigating the Word Document Window

When you start Word, a new blank document is displayed in the program window. This window also contains a menu bar and a toolbar to help you quickly and easily turn this blank page into a useful and attractive document.

The Word menu bar organizes commands in a logical manner, making it easy for you to access features you need. For example, all table-related commands are grouped on the Table menu.

> **important**
>
> If this is your first time using Word 2000, you'll notice that when you select a menu, a short list of commands is displayed. As you continue to use Word, the list is automatically customized to your specific work habits. The commands you use most often are added to the short menu. Commands you use less often are still available but hidden until you expand the menu. You can expand the menu in two ways. Click the double arrow at the bottom of the short menu, or just keep your pointer still over the menu for a moment and the menu will expand automatically.

Viewing commands on the Word menu bar

In this exercise, you select a command from the menu.

1. On the Word menu bar, click Format, and then click Theme.
   The Theme dialog box appears.
2. Click Cancel.
   The dialog box closes.

Using Toolbar Buttons

While the Word menu bar displays lists of commands, toolbars display buttons in a horizontal row across the top of the document window. Each button has a picture, or *icon*, on it corresponding to a command.

The Microsoft Word 2000 default setting for toolbars displays the most commonly used buttons from the Standard and Formatting toolbars in one row. By displaying fewer buttons for these two toolbars, Word makes more space available for you to view your work. Once you use a command, its button is added to the toolbar, replacing another button that is less often used.

Clicking one of the More Buttons drop-down arrows gives you access to buttons not currently displayed on the toolbar. There are two of these buttons on the toolbar, one for the Standard toolbar and one for the Formatting toolbar.

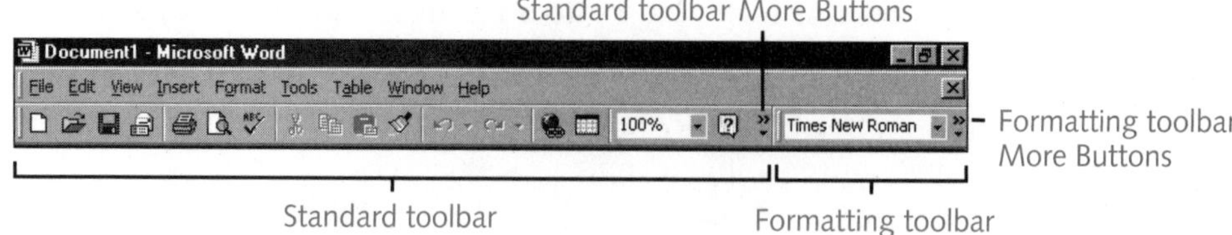

If you do not see a button name on the Tools menu, click Customize. On the Options tab, select Show ScreenTips On Toolbars.

To see the name of any button (which also tells you its function), place your pointer on the button and wait. A ScreenTip appears, showing the button name.

Resetting the Default Toolbar Buttons and Menu Commands

You can quickly reset the toolbar and menu bar to display the default commands. This is particularly useful when you share a computer with others. For example, you may often work with editing commands while a co-worker works with forms commands. You each would reset the toolbars for your own working convenience.

Reset the toolbars and menus

1. On the View menu, point to Toolbars, and then click Customize.
   The Customize dialog box appears.
2. Click the Options tab.
3. Click Reset My Usage Data, and click Yes when prompted.
4. Click Close.

The Customize dialog box closes, and the toolbars and menus are reset to their default settings. If you have adjusted specific settings for any toolbars, those settings will be retained.

When you click the Open button, for example, the Open dialog box appears so you can select a file to open. Clicking some buttons, such as the Bold button on the Formatting toolbar, turns the feature either on or off. When Bold is on, all text you type or select will be formatted in bold. The instructions in this book emphasize using the toolbar buttons whenever possible and displaying the toolbars on one line.

Use a toolbar button

In this exercise, you use a toolbar button.

Open

1. On the Standard toolbar, position the pointer over the Open button.

   A ScreenTip for the button appears, showing the name of the button.
2. Click the Open button.

   The Open dialog box appears.
3. Click Cancel.

Use a toolbar button not currently displayed

In this exercise, you use a command not currently displayed on the toolbar.

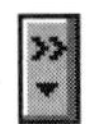

More Buttons

Show/Hide ¶

1. On the Standard toolbar, click the More Buttons drop-down arrow.

   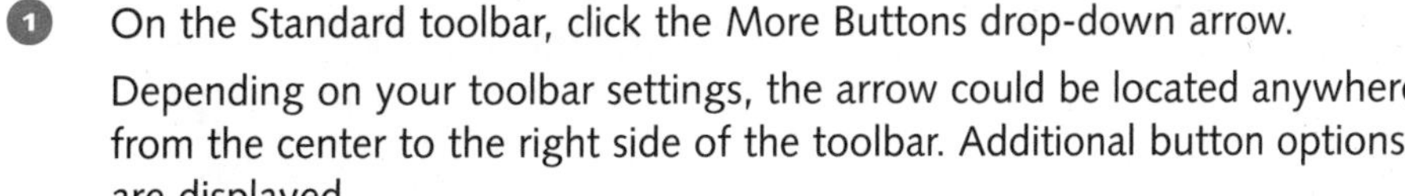

   Depending on your toolbar settings, the arrow could be located anywhere from the center to the right side of the toolbar. Additional button options are displayed.
2. Click the Show/Hide ¶ button.

   The Show/Hide ¶ button is activated and added to the toolbar.
3. On the Standard toolbar, click the Show/Hide ¶ button.

   The command is turned off.

Remove and add toolbar buttons

In this exercise, you remove a button from the Standard toolbar and then add one.

Click a check box to select (activate) or clear (deactivate) a command.

1. On the Standard toolbar, click the More Buttons drop-down arrow.

   The More Buttons menu appears.
2. Click Add Or Remove Buttons.

   The Add Or Remove Buttons menu appears.
3. Clear the Hyperlink check box.

   The button is removed from the Standard toolbar.
4. If an arrow appears at the bottom of the list, point to the arrow.

   Additional toolbar buttons are displayed.

Close

5. Select the Close check box.

   The Close button is added to the end of the Standard toolbar.

6. Click anywhere in the document to close the menu.

Arrange buttons on the toolbar

For a demonstration of how to arrange buttons on the toolbar, open the Office 8in1 Step by Step folder on your hard disk. Then open the Word Demos folder, and double-click the Customize Toolbar icon.

In this exercise, you move the Close button next to the Open button.

1. On the View menu, point to Toolbars, and then click Customize.

   The Customize dialog box appears.

2. Drag the Customize dialog box away from the toolbars by clicking the title bar at the top of the box and, without releasing the mouse button, moving the dialog box. Then, release the mouse button.

3. On the toolbar, drag the Close button to the right of the Open button.

   Your screen should look similar to the following illustration.

Close

When the Customize dialog box is open, Standard and Formatting toolbars are displayed separately, and ScreenTips do not appear.

Close button in new position

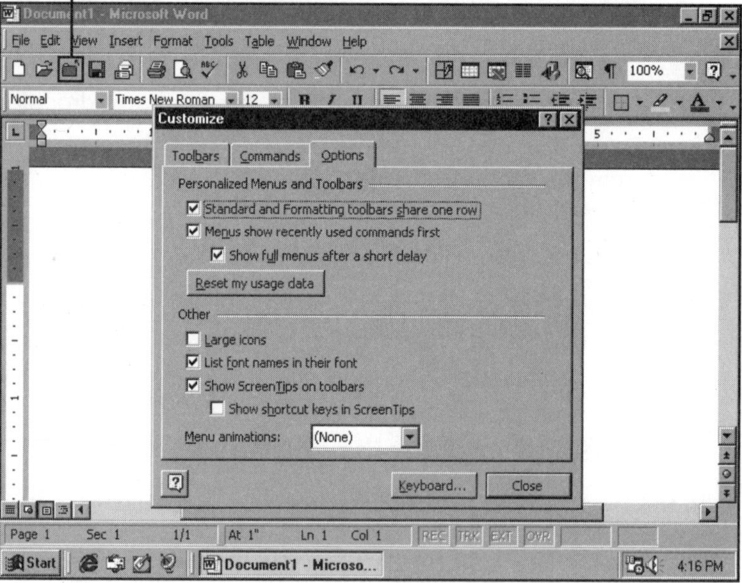

4. In the Customize dialog box, click Close.

Creating and Editing Basic Word Documents

Your responsibilities as a partner in Impact Public Relations require you to keep up regular communications with your clients. Word is an important and efficient tool for this task. To begin a letter, you start typing just as you would with a clean sheet of paper in a typewriter. There are a few things you need to know first, however.

The short, vertical, blinking line at the top of the document is the *insertion point*. The insertion point indicates where text will be entered as you type. As you create a document, you can move the insertion point to edit text anywhere in your document.

When typing long lines of text, you do not have to press Enter each time you want to start a new line. Word will automatically start a new line for you when you reach the right margin. This feature is called *wordwrapping*.

Type text in a letter

In this exercise, you begin a letter to a client, starting with the address block.

New Blank Document

1. Be sure there is a new blank document open. If not, on the Standard toolbar, click the New Blank Document button.
2. Type **Ms. Nina Valerio** and press Enter.

   The insertion point moves down to a new blank line.

A red wavy line under a word means that the automatic Spelling And Grammar Checker is activated, and it recognizes that the underlined word might be misspelled. A green wavy line under a word or sentence indicates a possible grammatical error. You will learn more about the Spelling And Grammar Checker later in this lesson. For now, just ignore any wavy lines.

3. Type **Pacific Books** and press Enter.
4. Finish the address block by typing the following text.

   155 Sashume Street

   San Francisco, CA 94104
5. Press Enter twice to leave two blank lines after the address block.
6. Type **Dear Ms. Valerio:** and press Enter twice.

important

If the Office Assistant is on and it asks you if you want help writing a letter, click Just Type The Letter Without Help. Next, from the menu bar, choose Help, and then click Hide The Office Assistant. Working without the Assistant at this time will let you concentrate on mastering the typing and editing features of Word. For further information on the Assistant, see "Using the Office Assistant," earlier in this lesson.

Type a paragraph in a letter

In this exercise, you continue your letter by typing the following text without pressing Enter.

- Type the following text:

  It was a pleasure speaking with you this morning regarding the upcoming public relations campaign for Pacific Books. As you know, our firm is a full-service public relations agency and works with clients using a team approach. Each team member brings to the client his or her own specialty, giving you a wide range of talents to draw upon. We will assemble your team soon, and we will arrange a meeting for early next week.

Using Delete and Backspace to Edit Text

One of the easiest ways to edit text is to delete and retype. In Word, you can delete text in two ways: with the Delete key and the Backspace key. You use the Backspace key to delete text to the left of the insertion point. The Delete key deletes text to the right of the insertion point. The goal in either case is to place the insertion point at the correct spot to edit the document. Your mouse pointer, which is displayed as an I-beam when placed in the document, is used to move the insertion point.

Move the insertion point

In this exercise, you move the insertion point.

The insertion point is the vertical, blinking line that shows where text will be added when you type.

- Position the pointer before the word *range* and click. The insertion point is now blinking in this new location.

Use Delete and Backspace to edit text

In this exercise, you use both the Backspace and Delete keys to edit your letter.

1. Be sure that the pointer is positioned before the word *range*.
2. Press Delete five times.

   The word *range* is deleted.
3. Type **variety**
4. Click after the word *soon* (before the comma).
5. Press Backspace four times.

   The word *soon* is deleted.
6. Type **shortly**

Correcting Mistakes

You might notice red and green wavy lines under some of your text. These lines flag possible spelling and grammatical errors because the automatic Spelling And Grammar Checker is activated. Once you are finished typing your document, you can go back and edit flagged text. To do this, right-click the flagged word. A shortcut menu is displayed, giving you some correctly spelled words to choose from. You can ignore the suggestions if you like. You can also choose to add the flagged word to a customized dictionary that you build, which can include specialized terms, acronyms, and names that are not included in the standard Word dictionary. If you add the word, it will no longer be underlined as a possible spelling error in later documents.

Use the automatic Spelling And Grammar Checker

In this exercise, you use the automatic Spelling And Grammar Checker to correct spelling errors.

1. Press Ctrl+Home to move to the top of the document.

> **tip**
>
> When you hold down the Ctrl key while pressing Home, you are using a *shortcut key combination*. Doing so moves the insertion point to the top of the document.

2. Right-click the word *Sashume*.

   The automatic Spelling And Grammar Checker shortcut menu is displayed.

3. Click Ignore All.

   The red wavy line disappears. Now the automatic Spelling And Grammar Checker will always ignore the spelling of this word.

4. Right-click the word *Valerio*.

   The automatic Spelling And Grammar Checker shortcut menu is displayed.

5. Click Spelling.

   The Spelling dialog box appears.

6. Click Ignore.

   The Spelling And Grammar Checker will ignore this occurrence of the word. The second occurrence of *Valerio* is still flagged.

7. Click Cancel.

Disable the automatic Spelling And Grammar Checker

In this exercise, you disable the automatic Spelling And Grammar Checker.

1. On the Tools menu, click Options.

   The Options dialog box appears.

2. Click the Spelling & Grammar tab.
3. In the Spelling area, clear the Check Spelling As You Type check box.
4. In the Grammar area, clear the Check Grammar As You Type check box.
5. Click OK.

   The Options dialog box closes, and the automatic Spelling And Grammar Checker is turned off.

Using AutoCorrect

As you type long sections of text in a document, you may be aware of making typographical errors, but when you look at your document after you're finished, these mistakes may have been corrected. This happens because the AutoCorrect feature is activated. This Word feature corrects the most common typographical errors. For example, the most common misspelling of *and* is *adn*. As soon as you type a space or begin a new paragraph after the misspelled word, Word recognizes the misspelling and automatically corrects it.

You can customize AutoCorrect to recognize misspellings you routinely make. You can also delete any entries that you do not want AutoCorrect to change. And you can take AutoCorrect one step further, using it to recognize abbreviations or codes that you create to automate typing certain words—your full name or your company name, for example.

tip

Other corrections Word automatically makes when AutoCorrect is activated include correcting two-initial capitalization (like THis), capitalizing the first word of a sentence and the days of the week, and correcting the accidental use of the Caps Lock key.

View AutoCorrect entries

In the following exercises, you continue working with the document you created in the previous section.

If the AutoCorrect command does not appear on the short Tools menu, wait a moment for the menu to expand.

In this exercise, you view the default list of AutoCorrect entries.

1. On the Tools menu, click AutoCorrect.

   The AutoCorrect dialog box appears.
2. Click the scroll bar arrows to scroll through the list and view the entries.
3. Click Cancel.

Add and delete AutoCorrect entries

In this exercise, you add an AutoCorrect entry to automate insertion of often-used text.

1. On the Tools menu, click AutoCorrect.

   The AutoCorrect dialog box appears.
2. In the Replace box, type **pb** and press the Tab key.
3. In the With box, type **Pacific Books**

   Note the capitalization.
4. Click Add, and then click OK.

Test the new AutoCorrect entry

In this exercise, you continue your letter and test the new AutoCorrect entry.

1. Press Ctrl+End to move to the end of the document.
2. Press Enter three times.

   You should have two blank lines after the first paragraph.
3. Type **The first step to creating a public relations campaign for pb**
4. Press the Spacebar.

   The text *pb* changes to *Pacific Books*.
5. Type **is to research your company image. We believe that this research is the cornerstone of an effective public relations campaign.**

6. Press Enter twice.

   Blank lines are inserted into the document.

Delete an AutoCorrect entry

In this exercise, you delete an AutoCorrect entry.

1. On the Tools menu, click AutoCorrect.

   The AutoCorrect dialog box appears.
2. In the Replace box, type **pb**

   The entry appears at the top of the list.
3. In the Replace box, select the entry.
4. Click Delete.

   The entry is removed.
5. Click OK.

Turn off AutoCorrect

In this exercise, you turn off AutoCorrect.

1. On the Tools menu, click AutoCorrect.

   The AutoCorrect dialog box appears.
2. Clear the Replace Text As You Type check box.

   AutoCorrect is turned off.
3. Click OK.

Working with Formatting Marks

Whenever you type, special characters called *formatting marks* are inserted into the document. The two formatting marks you work with most often are paragraph marks (¶), which are placed in the document each time you press Enter, and space marks (·), which are inserted each time you press the Spacebar. These characters can be displayed on the screen, or hidden, but in either case, they do not show up in the document when it is printed. These formatting marks help you troubleshoot your document during the editing process. You can use these characters to identify extra lines between paragraphs and spaces between words, for example.

Display formatting marks

In this exercise, you turn on the formatting marks.

Show/Hide ¶

- On the Standard toolbar, click the Show/Hide ¶ button.

  Formatting marks are displayed in your open document.

Your screen should look similar to the following illustration.

Show/Hide ¶ button turns formatting marks on and off

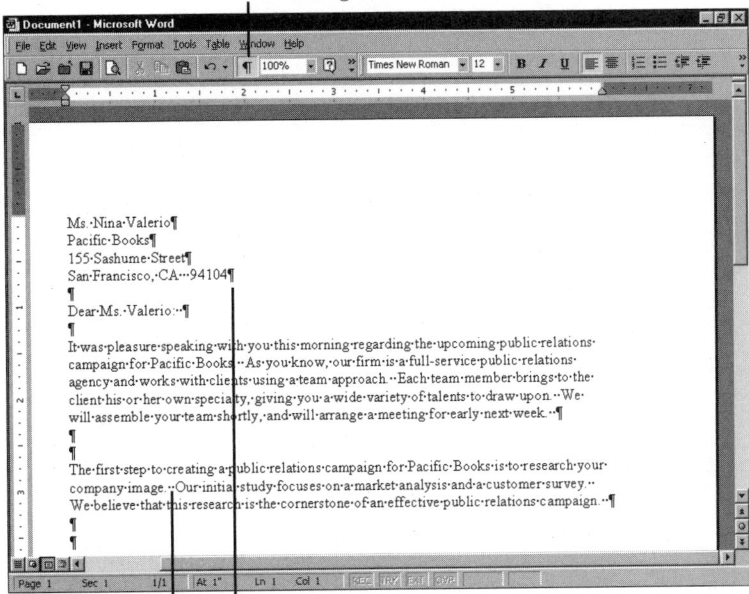

Formatting marks

Delete an extra line between paragraphs

In this exercise, you delete an extra line between two paragraphs in your letter.

1. Be sure that the formatting marks are displayed. If they are not, on the Standard toolbar, click the Show/Hide ¶ button.

2. Click before the first paragraph mark that appears between the two paragraphs.

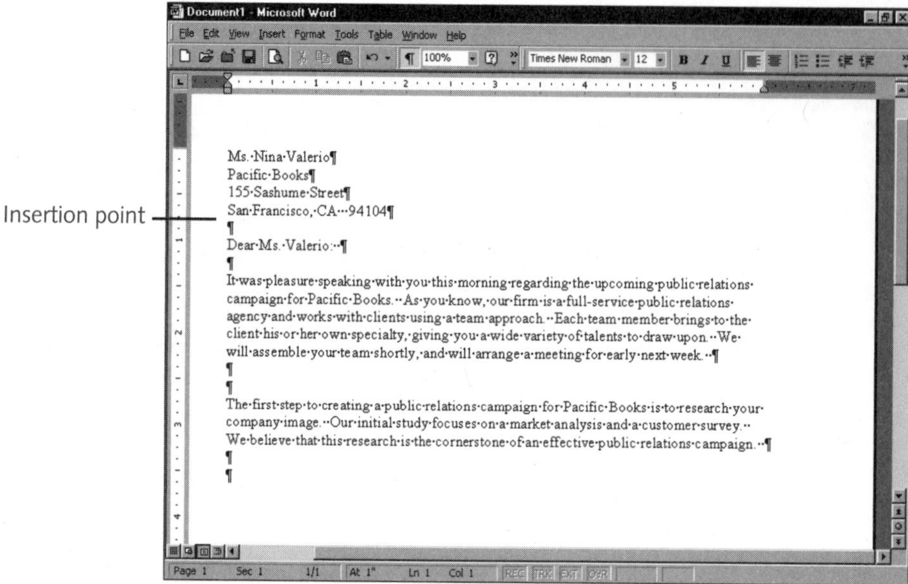

3. Press Delete.

   The paragraph mark is removed, and the lower paragraph moves up one line.

Inserting, Replacing, and Deleting Text

By positioning your insertion point anywhere in your document, you can easily add a word, sentence, or paragraph. You can also quickly select text and delete or replace it.

Insert a sentence in a paragraph

In this exercise, you add an additional sentence to the letter you created in the previous exercises.

1. Click before the sentence beginning *We believe that this research*, and type **This study includes a market analysis and a customer survey.**
2. Press the Spacebar twice to separate the sentences.

Select and replace text in a sentence

In this exercise, you change the sentence you typed in the last exercise.

To drag *means to click the insertion point before text you want to select and then, while holding down the mouse button, moving across the desired text selection.*

1. Click before the sentence beginning *This study includes.*
2. Drag the pointer across *This study includes.*
3. Type **Our initial study focuses mainly on**

   The selected phrase is replaced by the new phrase you just typed.

Delete a word

In this exercise, you select and delete a word in a sentence.

1. In the new sentence, double-click the word *mainly* to select it.

   This selection technique automatically selects the spacing following the selection. This ensures the proper spacing after the text has been deleted.
2. Press Delete to remove the word.

   The remaining text in the document moves to close up the space left by the deleted word.

Saving Documents

If you want to store your document for future use, you must give it a name and save it to a hard disk, a floppy disk, or a network drive. In Word 2000, you also have the option to save documents to Web folders that collect documents that will be published as pages on a Web site.

The first time you save a new document, you will give it a name and specify where you want to store it. After that, Word automatically updates the file in that location each time you save it.

Save a document

In this exercise, you name and save the letter you created in the previous exercises. You will store it in a subfolder of the Word Practice folder on your hard disk.

Save

1. On the Standard toolbar, click the Save button.

   Because this is the first time you have saved this document, the Save As dialog box appears.
2. In the Save In box, click the drop-down arrow and select your hard drive.
3. In the list of folders, double-click the Office 8in1 Step by Step folder. Double-click the Word Practice folder, and then double-click the Lesson01 folder.
4. In the File Name box, select the text and type **Client Letter 01**

> **tip**
>
> File names can be up to 255 characters and can include numbers, spaces, and other characters except the forward slash (/).

5. Click Save to complete the action.

Getting Help

The new Microsoft Word 2000 Help interface makes it easier than ever for you to work with the Microsoft Word Help features. When you start Help, your screen is split into separate windows. Your document appears on the left side of the screen, and the Help window is anchored on the right. This way, both your document and Help screen are clearly visible. There are three ways to search for help in Word. You can:

- Use the Answer Wizard to type a question and let Help find topics related to your inquiry.
- Use the Contents tab to look for information in broad categories.
- Use the Index tab to type a key word about a specific topic.

Ask the Answer Wizard a question

In this exercise, you use the Answer Wizard to find out how to save your document.

1. On the Help menu, click Microsoft Word Help.

   The Microsoft Word Help dialog box appears.

2. Click the Answer Wizard tab.
3. In the What Would You Like To Do? box, type **How do I save my document?**
4. Click Search.

   The Search Results are displayed.
5. In the Select Topic To Display area, click Save A Document if it is not selected already.

Hide

6. On the Help toolbar, click the Hide button.
7. Click the Saving Documents In Microsoft Word Format topic, and then click Save A New, Unnamed Document.
8. Close the Microsoft Word Help window.

Explore the contents of Microsoft Word Help

In this exercise, you use Help to find information on creating documents.

1. On the Help menu, click Microsoft Word Help.

   The Microsoft Word Help dialog box appears.
2. In the Microsoft Word Help dialog box, click the Contents tab.
3. Double-click Creating, Opening, and Saving Documents.

   The topic is expanded.
4. Double-click Creating Documents.
5. Click Create A Memo.

   The instructions for this topic are displayed on the right side of the Help window.

Hide

6. On the Microsoft Word Help toolbar, click the Hide button.

   The Help tabs are hidden, allowing you to work in your document while reading the Help instructions.
7. Close the Microsoft Word Help window.

Use the Microsoft Word Help Index

In this exercise, you use the Help Index to get help creating an envelope for a letter.

1. On the Help menu, click Microsoft Word Help.

   The Microsoft Word Help dialog box appears.

2. In the Microsoft Word Help dialog box, click the Index tab.
3. In the Type Keywords box, type **envelope**
4. Click Search.
5. In the Choose A Topic list, click Create And Print Envelopes.
6. On the Help toolbar, click the Hide button.

   You are ready to follow the directions to create an envelope.
7. Close the Microsoft Word Help window.

One Step Further Creating Your Own Toolbar

As you settle into your routine as a partner in Impact Public Relations, you decide to create your own toolbar displaying commands that you use most often. This toolbar will not change unless you add or remove buttons.

If you are not working through this lesson sequentially, before proceeding to the next step, open the 01A file (Lesson01 folder), and save it as Client Letter 01.

Create a new toolbar

In this exercise, you create a new toolbar and add buttons to it.

1. On the View menu, point to Toolbars, and then click Customize.

   The Customize dialog box appears.
2. Click the Toolbars tab.
3. Click New.

   The New Toolbar dialog box appears.
4. In the Toolbar Name box, type **My Toolbar** and click OK.

   A small toolbar appears in the document. You can reposition either the new toolbar or the Customize dialog box by clicking the title bar and dragging to a new location.

Your screen should look similar to the following illustration.

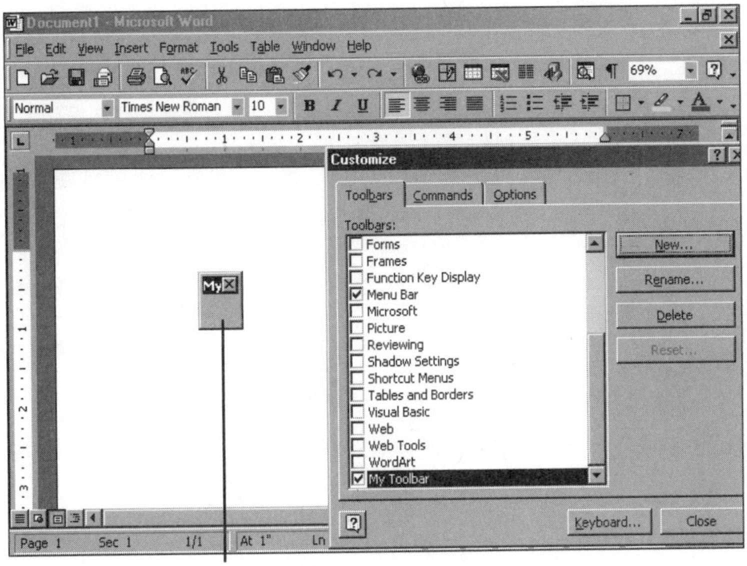

New toolbar

5. In the Customize dialog box, click the Commands tab.

New E-mail Message

6. In the Commands area, drag the New E-mail Message button to the new toolbar.
7. In the Categories area, click Insert, and then in the Commands area, drag the Date button to the new toolbar.

   The toolbar is resized to accommodate the new button.

Date

8. Finish the toolbar by adding any other buttons you want.
9. In the Customize dialog box, click Close.

   The Customize dialog box closes.

Display and use the new toolbar

In this exercise, you move your toolbar and add a date to your letter.

1. Drag the toolbar below the first button on the Standard toolbar.

   Your screen should look similar to the following illustration.

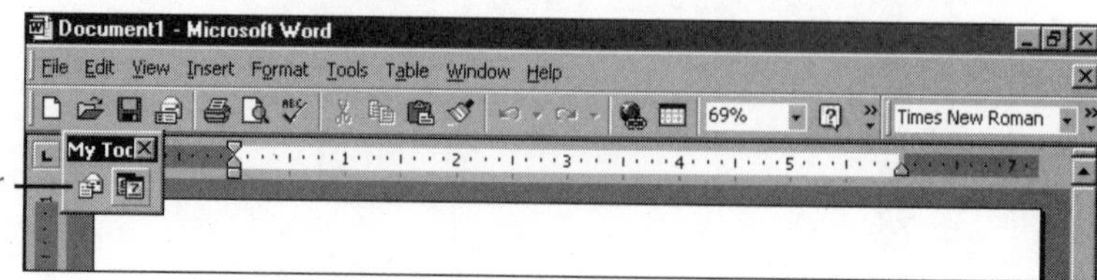

2. Press Ctrl+Home to go to the top of your document.
3. Click the Insert Date button and press Enter twice.

   The date is inserted into the document.

Insert Date

Delete the new toolbar

In this exercise, you delete the toolbar you just created.

1. On the View menu, point to Toolbars, and then click Customize.

   The Customize dialog box appears.
2. In the Customize dialog box, click the Toolbars tab.
3. In the Toolbars list, scroll to view the My Toolbar check box.
4. Select My Toolbar.
5. Click Delete, and then click OK to confirm your action.
6. Click Close.

Finish the lesson

Save

1. On the Standard toolbar, click the Save button

   The changes to your document are saved.
2. On the File menu, click Close.
3. On the File menu, click Exit.

Lesson 1 Quick Reference

To	Do this	Button
Start Word	On the Windows taskbar, click Start. Point to Programs, and then click Microsoft Word 2000.	
Customize the Office Assistant	Right-click the Office Assistant. On the shortcut menu that appears, click Choose Assistant. In the Office Assistant dialog box, click the Gallery tab. Select an Office Assistant, and click OK.	
Disable the Office Assistant	Right-click the Office Assistant. On the shortcut menu, click Options. In the Office Assistant dialog box, clear the Use The Office Assistant check box. Click OK.	
Find a toolbar button not currently displayed	On the Standard toolbar, click the More Buttons drop-down arrow. Select the desired button. On the toolbar, click the button to turn it on and off.	
Add or remove a toolbar button	On the Standard toolbar, click the More Buttons drop-down arrow. Point to Add Or Remove Buttons and select or clear check boxes to add or remove buttons.	
Reset toolbars and menus	On the View menu, point to Toolbars, and then click Customize. On the Options tab, click Reset My Usage Data. Click Yes when prompted, and click Close.	
Arrange buttons on a toolbar	On the View menu, point to Toolbars, and then click Customize. On the toolbar, drag the desired button to a new location. Click Close.	
Remove characters	Position the insertion point, and press Backspace to remove characters to the left. Press delete to remove characters to the right.	

Lesson 1 Quick Reference

To	Do this
Correct a spelling error	Right-click a misspelled word. On the shortcut menu, click Spelling. Choose the appropriate option.
Disable the automatic Spelling And Grammar Checker	On the Tools menu, click AutoCorrect. In the Options dialog box, click the Spelling And Grammar tab. Clear the Check Spelling As You Type and Check Grammar As You Type check boxes. Click OK.
Add an AutoCorrect Entry	On the Tools menu, click AutoCorrect. In the AutoCorrect dialog box, in the Replace box, type a short letter code or abbreviation. In the With box, type the full word or phrase that will replace the code letters. Click Add, and click OK.
Turn off AutoCorrect	On the Tools menu, click Auto-Correct. In the AutoCorrect dialog box, clear the Replace Text As You Type check box. Click OK.
Display formatting marks	On the Standard toolbar, click the Show/Hide button. ¶
Insert a sentence in a paragraph	Click to position the insertion point where you want to insert text, and begin typing.
Save a document	On the Standard toolbar, click the Save button. Be sure the folder in which you want to save your document appears in the Look In box. In the File Name box, type the document name. Click Save.

Lesson 1 Quick Reference

To	Do this
Use Microsoft Word Help	On the Word menu bar, click Help. On the Help menu, click Microsoft Word Help.
Ask the Answer Wizard a question	On the Word menu bar, click Help, and then click Microsoft Word Help. In the Microsoft Word Help dialog box, click the Answer Wizard tab. In the What Would You Like To Do? box, type your question and click Search.
Create a toolbar	On the View menu, point to Toolbars, and then click Customize. In the Customize dialog box, click the Toolbars tab, and then click New. In the New Toolbar dialog box, type the name of the new toolbar. Click OK.

Working with Text

In this lesson you will learn how to:

- ✔ *Open an existing document and save it with a new name.*
- ✔ *Select a view for working in a document.*
- ✔ *Cut, copy, and paste text.*
- ✔ *Undo and redo changes.*
- ✔ *Move multiple text selections at once.*
- ✔ *Link two documents.*

ESTIMATED TIME **30 min.**

After drafting a document, you might decide to move words, sentences, and paragraphs around so that they make better sense or have greater impact.

In this lesson, you'll learn how to open an existing document and make changes to it while preserving the original file. You'll learn how to select text and move it using the mouse and the Cut, Copy, and Paste toolbar buttons. You'll also move multiple items at once with the help of the Microsoft Office Clipboard. You'll work in the Print Layout view and explore other screen display options. As you make changes, you'll also learn how to undo and redo them.

More Buttons

important

The default toolbar setting in Microsoft Word 2000 displays both the Standard and Formatting toolbars in one row, at the top of your document window just below the menu bar. This gives you maximum workspace. While you work through the exercises in this book, toolbar buttons you need may not initially be visible. If a toolbar button is not visible, click one of the two More Buttons drop-down arrows on the toolbar to locate the button you need. When you select a new toolbar button, it is automatically added to the visible portion of the toolbar, replacing one that is not used as often.

Opening Documents

Normally when you open Word, a new blank document window appears. For this lesson, however, you'll open and edit a document that your partner in Impact Public Relations has already begun.

Start Word and open a practice file

In this exercise, you open practice file 02A and then save it with the new name Book Fair 02. By saving the file with a new name, you create a duplicate of the original file that you can edit. The original practice file remains unchanged and available for you to use again if you want to repeat this lesson. This procedure for using practice files is followed throughout the book.

1. On the Windows taskbar, click the Start button.

   The Start menu appears.

2. On the Start menu, point to Programs, and then click Microsoft Word.

   Microsoft Word opens.

Open

In the Open dialog box, you select the folder and document you want to open. The Look In box shows the folder that is currently selected.

3. On the Standard toolbar, click the Open button.

   The Open dialog box appears.

4. Click the Look In drop-down arrow, and then select your hard disk.
5. In the list of folders, double-click the Office 8in1 Step by Step folder. Double-click the Word Practice folder, and then double-click the Lesson02 folder.

   Your screen should look similar to the following illustration.

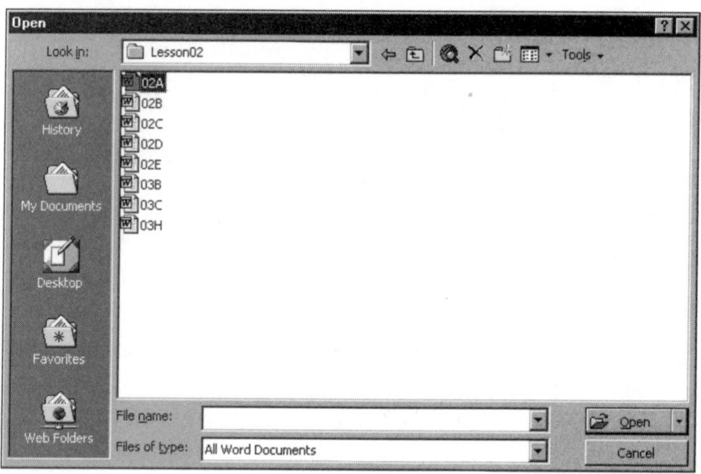

6. In the file list, double-click the 02A file to open it.

   The document opens in the document window.

Saving a File with a New Name

When you save a file, you give it a name and specify where you want to store it. Each time you open a practice file while working through the lessons in this book, you save it with a new name. By doing so, you leave the original practice file unchanged, and you can repeat the exercises as many times as you want.

Save the practice file with a new name

In this exercise, you save the 02A practice file with the name Book Fair 02.

1. On the File menu, click Save As.

   The Save As dialog box appears.
2. Be sure the Lesson02 folder appears in the Save In box.
3. In the File Name box, if the text is not already selected, select it.
4. Type **Book Fair 02**
5. Click Save to save the file and close the dialog box.

   Your file is saved with the name Book Fair 02. When the dialog box closes, your new document is open, and the new document name appears in the title bar. Word automatically closes the original document.

Display formatting marks

To make it easier to edit your document, you can display formatting marks such as paragraph marks and space marks on your screen.

Show/Hide ¶

If the Show/Hide ¶ button is not visible, on the Standard toolbar, click the More Buttons drop-down arrow to locate the button.

- If formatting marks are not currently displayed, on the Standard toolbar, click the Show/Hide ¶ button.

Opening a File from the Documents and File Menus

You can open a document directly using the Documents menu, which you display from the Windows Start menu. You might find this quicker and easier than first opening Word and then opening a file.

Open a file from the Documents menu

1. On the Windows taskbar, click Start.
2. Point to the Documents menu.

   The last 15 documents that you used are displayed in alphabetical order on the menu.
3. Click the document you want to open.

   The associated program opens and displays the document.

Opening a File from the File Menu List

When you are already working in Word, a quick way to open a recently used file is to click the File menu. Listed at the bottom of the File menu are up to nine of the most recently used files. Click a file to open it.

The default number of files listed is four. To change the default number, follow the steps below.

Expand or shorten the File menu list

1. On the Tools menu, click Options, and then click the General tab.
2. In the Recently Used File list, click the arrows to increase or decrease the number.

   The names of the selected number of files will be displayed on the File menu.
3. Click OK.

Selecting a View for Working in a Document

Word provides a range of *views,* or screen displays, you can use to do your work. Which one you choose depends on the type of document you've created and how you want to work with it. The *Normal* view helps you focus on composition, text revisions, and basic formatting such as bold and italic text, without worrying too much about the layout of the page.

When you're applying more elaborate formatting or moving and copying text, it's helpful to work in *Print Layout* view—the default view. This view shows you the page layout and formatting so you can easily see the effects of formatting or how your document looks after you've cut or moved text.

Web Layout view shows you how your Web page will be displayed in a Web browser. *Outline* view lets you focus on document organization by highlighting headings and subheadings. *Document Map* view, discussed later in this lesson, lets you see all document headings on one side of the window. You can move around in your document by clicking the headings. *Full Screen* view fills the window with your document, and no toolbars or controls are displayed.

All of these views can be selected from the View menu. You can also open Normal, Web Layout, Print Layout, and Outline views by using the buttons on the horizontal scroll bar at the bottom left side of the document window. In this lesson, you'll work in Print Layout view.

Work in Print Layout view

Print Layout View

- If you are not already in Print Layout view, click the Print Layout View button, the third button from the left on the horizontal scroll bar.

  Your document should look similar to the following illustration.

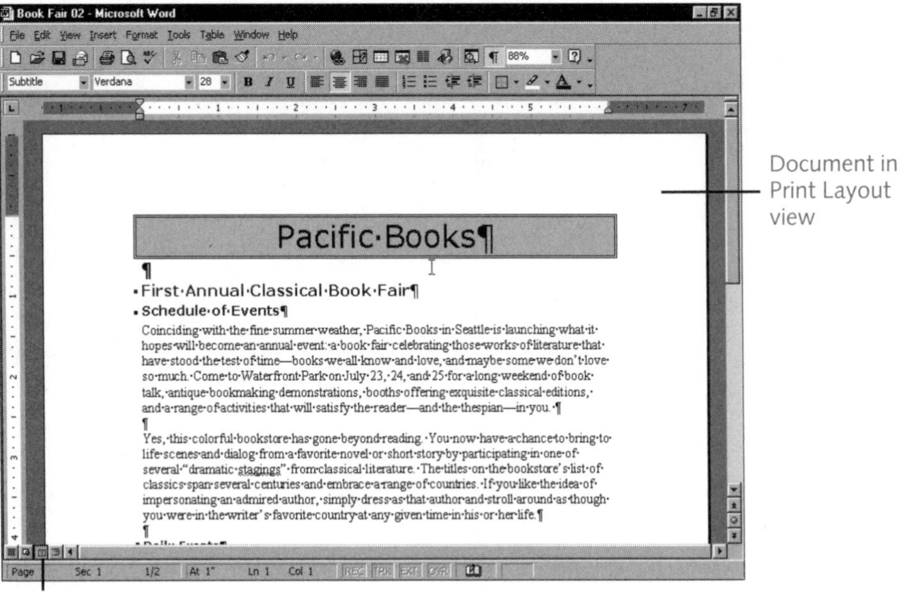

Selecting Text with the Mouse

Most editing actions require you to first select text. Microsoft Word makes text selection quick and easy. Using the mouse, you can select any amount of text, from one character to the whole document. Following is a summary of mouse text selection techniques.

To	Do this
Select a word	Click before the word, hold down the mouse button, and drag the pointer over the word, releasing the mouse button at the end of the word. Or, position the pointer over the word and double-click.
Select more than one word	Select a word, and while holding down the mouse button, drag the pointer over additional text.
Select a line	Position the pointer to the left side of the line you want to select and, when the right-pointing arrow appears, click the mouse.
Select a paragraph	Double-click to select a word, and then quickly click a third time. Or, position the pointer to the left side of the paragraph, and when the right-pointing arrow appears, double-click.
Select a whole document	Position the pointer to the left side of the document and when the right-pointing arrow appears, click the mouse three times.
Select any amount of text	Click where you want the selection to begin. Then, while holding down the Shift key, click where you want the selection to end.

On the left of your document, there's an invisible selection bar. Click there when the right-pointing arrow appears to select a line, a paragraph, or the whole document.

Moving and Copying Text Using the Mouse

The document your partner has asked you to edit already contains several paragraphs and headings, but it still needs a lot of work. You begin to edit the document by moving a heading and copying some text to a new location.

The drag-and-drop feature in Word allows you to use the mouse to pull selected text from one place and put it in another. Dragging text is the most efficient way to move or copy it, as long as you can see the destination for the text on your screen.

Change the magnification

Before moving or copying text, you can change the magnification of your screen to see more of your text within the window.

100%

Zoom

- On the Standard toolbar, click the Zoom drop-down arrow, and then click Page Width.

Select and move a heading

If you are not working through this lesson sequentially, before proceeding to the next step, open the 02B file (Lesson02 folder), and save it as Book Fair 02.

In this exercise, you move a heading in your document.

1. Scroll down so that the headings *Schedule of Events* and *Daily Events* show in the same window.
2. Position the mouse pointer in the selection bar, before the *Schedule of Events* heading.

   The mouse pointer changes to a right-pointing arrow.
3. Click to select the heading.

   The selected text changes to white text on a darker background.

   Your screen should look similar to the following illustration.

Selected heading

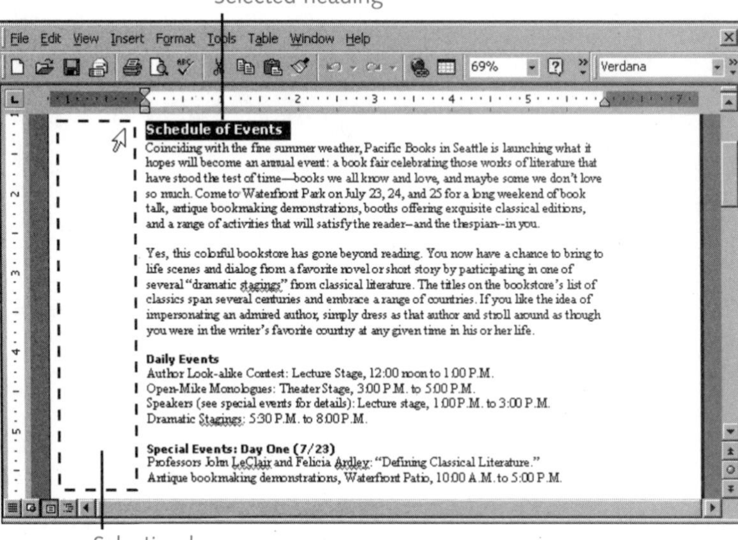

Selection bar

4. Position the mouse pointer over the selected heading.

   The pointer turns into a left-pointing arrow.

5. Click and hold down the mouse button.

   A small, dotted box and a dotted insertion point appear.

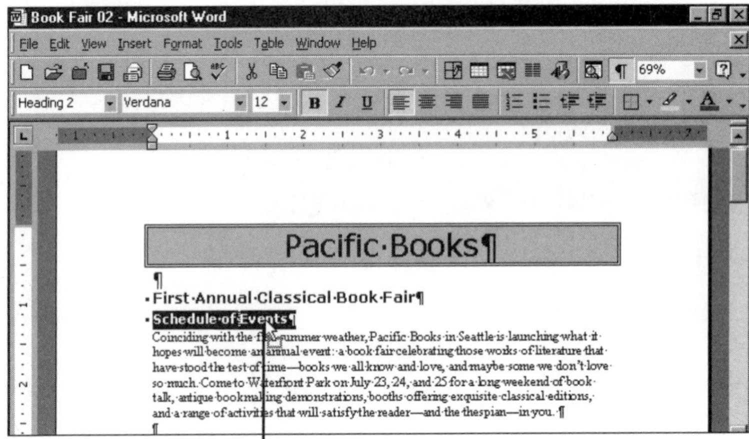

Mouse pointer ready to drag selected text

6. Drag down until the dotted insertion point is before the heading *Daily Events*, and then release the mouse button.

   Your screen should look similar to the following illustration.

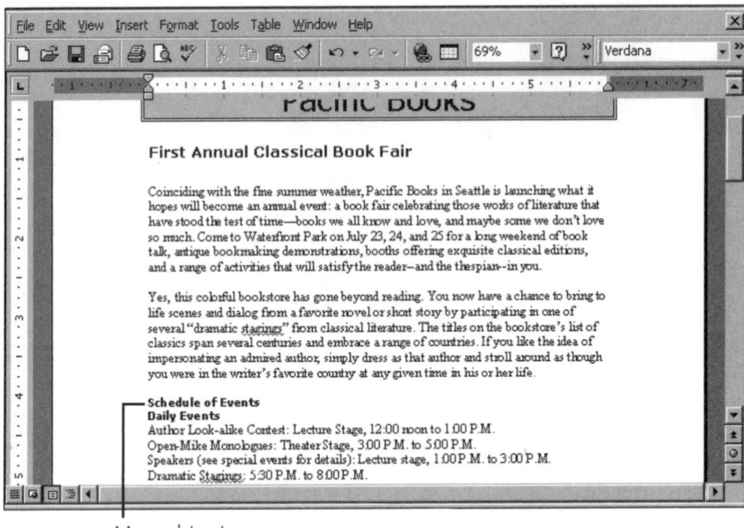

Moved text

7. Click anywhere outside of the selected text to cancel the selection.

Copy text using the mouse

In this exercise, you use the mouse and keyboard to copy text to be repeated in the document.

1. Scroll down until you can see all of the *Daily Events* section.
2. In the line that begins *Open-Mike Monologues*, select the text *Theater Stage* (including the end comma).
3. Hold down the Ctrl key.
4. Point to the selected text, and then hold down the mouse button.
5. Drag to position the dotted insertion point after the text *Dramatic Stagings:* in the *Daily Events* section.
6. Release the mouse button, and then release the Ctrl key.

   A copy of the selected text is inserted. The original text is unchanged.

   Your screen should look similar to the following illustration.

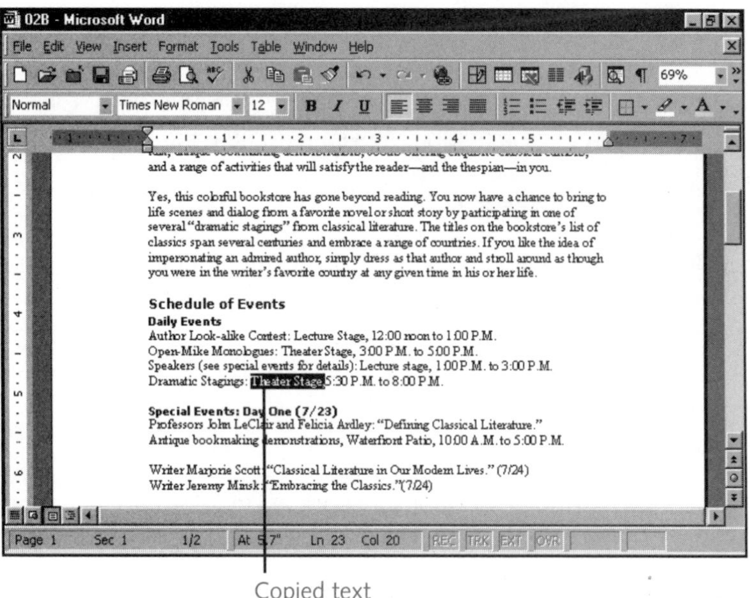

Copied text

7. Click anywhere outside of the selected text to cancel the selection.

Undoing and Redoing Changes

You can undo and redo changes after you make them by using the Undo and Redo buttons on your toolbar. The Undo button reverses your last action. You use the Redo button to reverse an Undo action. For example, if you delete a word and then click Undo, the word will be restored to your document. If you then click Redo, it will be deleted again.

You can also reverse more than one action. When you click the Undo drop-down arrow, you'll see a list of the actions you can reverse. The actions in the Undo list appear with the most recent change at the top of the list and all previous changes below it. Because several changes in sequence often depend on preceding changes, you cannot select an individual action on the list without undoing all the actions that appear above it.

You can undo most Word commands. Commands that cannot be undone include saving, printing, opening, and creating documents.

Undo the last change

Undo

You can also press Ctrl+Z to undo changes.

- On the Standard toolbar, click the Undo button to undo your last change.

  If this action did not remove the text you copied, you might have pressed another key before you clicked the Undo button. Click the Undo button until the new text is removed and the text reads as it did originally.

Redo the change

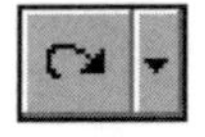

Redo

If the Redo button is not visible, on the Standard toolbar, click the More Buttons drop-down arrow to locate the button.

- On the Standard toolbar, click the Redo button to redo the action you just undid.

  The phrase you copied, *Theater Stage* (including the end comma), should now be replaced to where you first copied it, after *Dramatic Stagings:*

Undo all changes

- On the Standard toolbar, click the Undo drop-down arrow, and then select all the actions.

  All of the changes you made are reversed.

Redo all changes

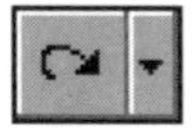

Redo

- On the Standard toolbar, click the Redo drop-down arrow, and then select the top two changes in the list to redo your most recent paste actions.

  Your document should look similar to the following illustration.

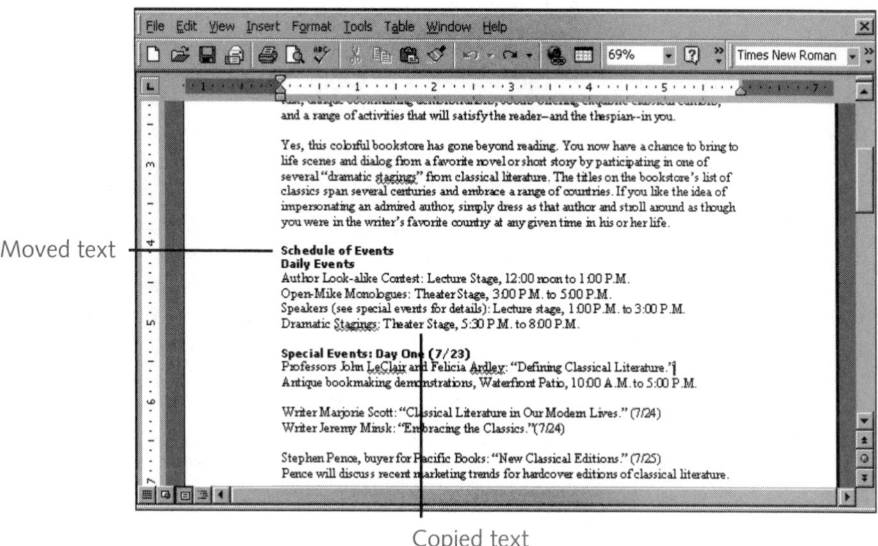

Moving and Copying Text Using Buttons

If you are not working through this lesson sequentially, before proceeding to the next step, open the 02C file (Lesson02 folder), and save it as Book Fair 02.

If you want to move text to a location that is not visible in the document window, you can use the Cut, Copy, and Paste buttons on the Standard toolbar. The Cut button deletes selected text from your document and copies it to the *Windows Clipboard*. The Clipboard is an invisible storage area for text. If you want to copy text from a location in your document, leaving the original text as it is, you use the Copy button. Selected text is again copied to the Windows Clipboard. When you have located the point in the document where you want to move your text, you position your insertion point and then click the Paste button. This moves the text from the Clipboard.

Move text

In this exercise, you move text using the Cut and Paste buttons.

1. Press Ctrl+Home, if necessary, to move the insertion point to the beginning of the document.
2. In the second paragraph, select the last sentence, which begins *If you like the idea of impersonating*. Don't include the ending paragraph mark in the selection.

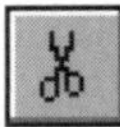

Cut

You can also move selected text to the Clipboard by pressing Ctrl+X.

If a toolbar button you need is not visible, on the toolbar, click the More Buttons drop-down arrow to locate the button.

3. With the text selected, on the Standard toolbar, click the Cut button.

   The text you cut disappears from the paragraph and is moved to the Clipboard.

4. Scroll until you see the heading *Author Look-alike Contests* on page 2.
5. Click at the beginning of the paragraph before the text *The contests will take place.*
6. On the Standard toolbar, click the Paste button to insert the cut text from the Clipboard. Press the Spacebar to separate the sentences. Your screen should look similar to the following illustration.

Paste

You can also paste text by pressing Ctrl+V.

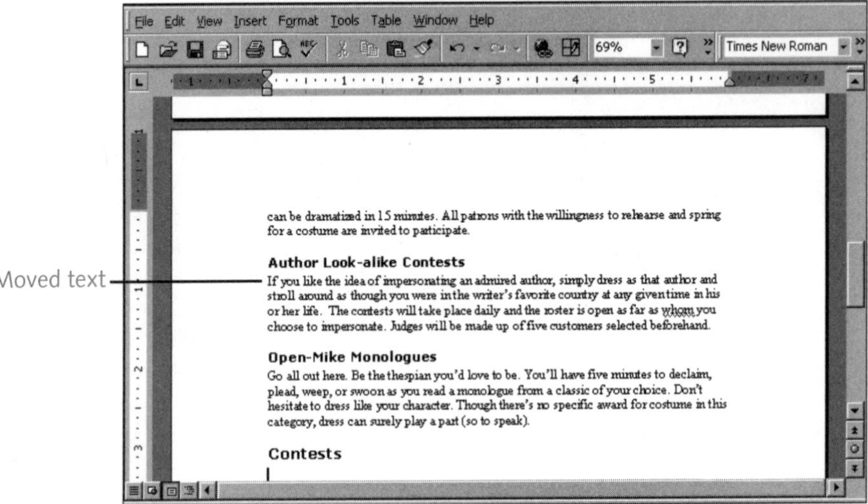

Copy and paste text

In this exercise, you copy and paste text in two places and then edit the headings.

Copy

You can also copy text to the Clipboard by pressing Ctrl+C.

1. Scroll up to the heading *Special Events: Day One (7/23)* on page 1.
2. Select the heading, including the ending paragraph mark.
3. On the Standard toolbar, click the Copy button.

   You see no change in the document, but a copy of the selected text is placed on the Clipboard.

> **tip**
>
> Microsoft Word 2000 introduces an additional type of Clipboard, the *Microsoft Office Clipboard,* that enables you to move or copy up to 12 text items at one time. See "Moving Multiple Items at One Time," later in this lesson, for more information.

Paste

You can also press the F4 key to repeat your last action.

4. Click before the line that begins *Writer Marjorie Scott*.
5. On the Standard toolbar, click the Paste button.

   A copy of the heading is inserted.
6. Click before the line that begins *Stephen Pence*.
7. Click the Paste button again.

   A copy of the heading is pasted a second time.

Edit the new headings

In this exercise, you modify the headings.

1. In the first new heading, above the name *Marjorie Scott*, select *One* and then type **Two**
2. Select the *3* in the date and type **4**

   The text *Two (7/24)* replaces the text *One (7/23)*.
3. In the second new heading, above the name *Stephen Pence*, select *One* and then type **Three**
4. In the *Special Events: Day Three* heading, select the *3* in the date and type **5**

   The text *Three (7/25)* replaces the text *One (7/23)*.
5. In the lines under each of the three *Special Events* headings, delete the dates.

   Your screen should look similar to the following illustration.

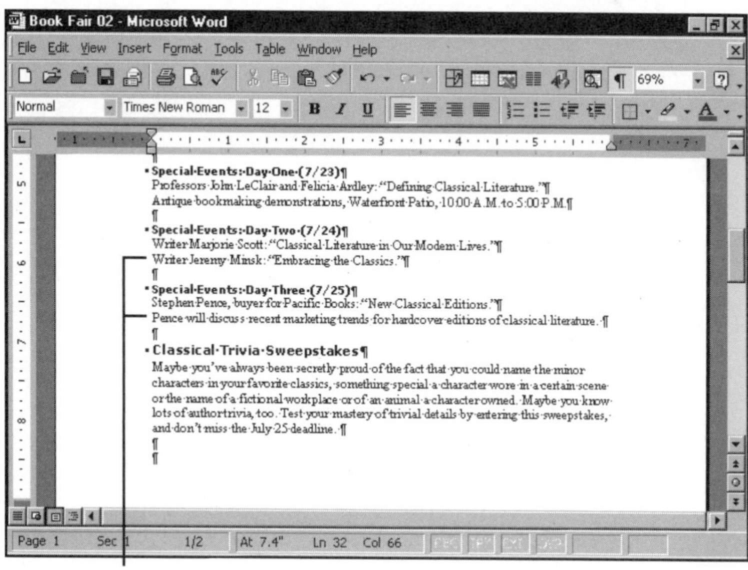

> **important**
>
> When you edit the headings, if the new text you type does not replace the old text, but instead appears next to it, do this: Go to the Tools menu, click Options, and then click the Edit tab. In the Editing Options area, be sure that the Typing Replaces Selection check box is selected.

Moving Text over a Longer Distance

When moving text over many pages in your document, you might find it convenient to work in the Document Map view. This will help you avoid the need to scroll or page up and down excessively. The Document Map view splits the window to show your document headings and subheadings on the left and your document on the right. When you click a heading on the left, the document on the right moves instantly to that heading. You can then place your insertion point in the document and paste the text you have moved or copied. By clicking the plus or minus sign next to a heading, you can expand or collapse the heading to display or hide its subheadings.

In the following exercises, you cut and paste text while in the Document Map view.

> **tip**
>
> In the Document Map view, you may want to turn off the ruler. To do so, on the View menu, click Ruler. If you want to see more of the left side of the window, move the pointer over the border between the two sides. The pointer turns into the two-headed *Resize* arrow. Use it to drag the border. Some headings in the left window may still not be shown completely, but when you place the pointer over one of them, you'll see a ScreenTip that displays the full heading.

Switch to Document Map view

Document Map

- On the View menu, click Document Map, then press Ctrl+Home to move the insertion point to the top of the document.

  Your screen should look similar to the following illustration.

Click here to expand or collapse a heading

Click a heading to move that heading in a document

If the Document Map button is not visible, on the Standard toolbar, click the More Buttons drop-down arrow to locate the button.

Move a block of text

In this exercise, you select text and move it to the bottom of the document.

1. In the left side of the window, click the heading *Schedule of Events*.

   The view jumps to this heading in your document, and you see the heading at the top of your window on the right side, with the insertion point placed before it.

2. In the document, select the entire schedule starting with the heading *Schedule of Events* and including all text through the last special event—the line that ends *editions of classical literature*. Include the ending paragraph mark in the selection.

Cut

3. On the Standard toolbar, click the Cut button.

   The text is removed from the document and stored on the Clipboard.

4. On the left side of the window, click the heading *Essay: My Favorite Classics*.
5. In the document, click before the first paragraph mark under the *Essay* paragraph.

Paste

6. On the Standard toolbar, click the Paste button.

   The Schedule of Events is now the last section in the document.

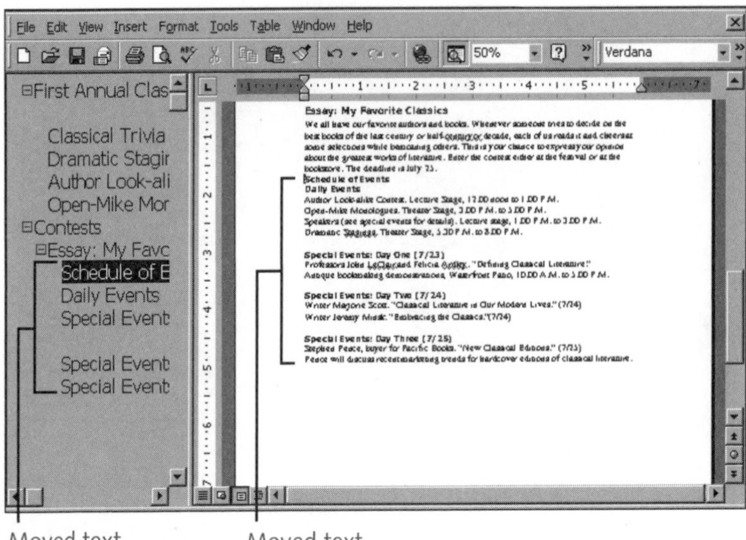

7 To add a line of space between the *Essay* and *Schedule* sections, click before *Schedule* and press Enter. The schedule moves down one line.

Moving Multiple Items at One Time

With the *Collect And Paste* feature in Microsoft Word 2000, you can move or copy up to 12 items to the Microsoft Office Clipboard. You can paste the items in any order into various documents or paste them all in one place, all at one time.

You use the Microsoft Office Clipboard toolbar when you want to collect and paste text. The toolbar displays an icon for each bit of text you have copied onto it. A ScreenTip identifies the copied text, and the text you've moved most recently is stored as the last item on the toolbar. The Microsoft Office Clipboard differs from the Windows Clipboard in that you can copy to it several items at a time rather than only one.

The Clipboard toolbar includes Copy and Paste buttons. If you want to cut the text from your document rather than copy it, use the Cut button on the Standard toolbar. The cut text will be moved to the Clipboard toolbar and cut from your document.

As you continue your edits to the book fair document while working in Document Map view, you'll see how easy it is to organize the document further by collecting and pasting.

Move two blocks of text

For a demonstration of how to move two blocks of text, open the Office 8in1 Step by Step folder on your hard disk. Then open the Word Demos folder, and double-click the Clipboard icon.

In this exercise, you move text to group similar items together.

1. On the View menu, point to Toolbars, and then click Clipboard.

   The Clipboard toolbar appears in the right side of the document window. (Drag the title bar if you need to move the toolbar over.)

2. In the left side of the window, click the heading *Author Look-alike Contests*.

   The *Author Look-alike Contests* heading now shows at the top of the document.

3. Select the heading and the text under it, including the ending paragraph mark.

4. On the Standard toolbar, click the Cut button.

   Cut

   The text is removed from the document and stored on the Clipboard.

5. On the left side of the window, click the heading *Classical Trivia Sweepstakes*.

   The heading is displayed at the top of your document.

6. In the document, select the heading *Classical Trivia Sweepstake*s and the text under it (including the ending paragraph mark), and then, on the Standard toolbar, click the Cut button.

   The Clipboard displays the items you cut from your document.

   Your screen should look similar to the following illustration.

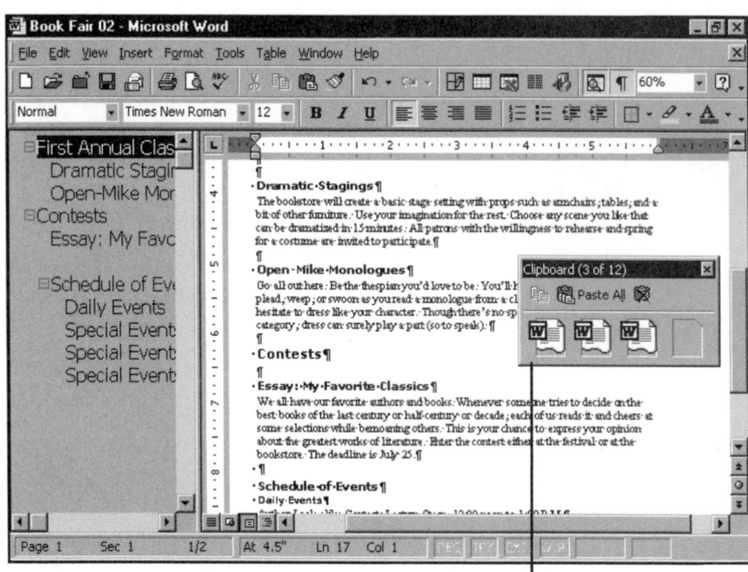

Items moved to the Clipboard and ready to be pasted

7. In the document, click before the paragraph mark above the heading *Essay: My Favorite Classics*, and beneath the heading *Contests*.
8. On the Clipboard, click the text item, *Author Look-alike Contests*.

   The text is pasted above the *Essay* heading.
9. In the document, click in front of the heading *Schedule of Events* on page 2.
10. On the Clipboard, click the text item *Classical Trivia Sweepstakes*.

    The text is pasted below the *Essay* section.

Clear the Clipboard

Clear Clipboard

1. On the Clipboard toolbar, click the Clear Clipboard button.

   Your text items are cleared from the Clipboard.
2. Close the Clipboard.

> **tip**
>
> To paste Clipboard items in a document all at once, in the same order in which they appear on the Clipboard, on the Clipboard toolbar, click the Paste All button.

Close Document Map view

Document Map

- On the Standard toolbar, click the Document Map button.

Save the document

If the Document Map button is not visible, on the Standard toolbar, click the More Buttons drop-down arrow to locate the button.

- On the Standard toolbar, click Save.

  Changes made to the document are saved.

Save

One Step Further

Linking Two Documents

Your partner has created a new logo for your client, Pacific Books. You want to copy the logo in the book fair document. This is a perfect opportunity to use the Word feature called Paste Special. Using Paste Special, you can paste the logo and simultaneously link your book fair document to the source document you copied the logo from. After that, when anyone makes formatting changes to the logo in the source document, those changes will be reflected in your linked document.

In this exercise, you paste the logo into Book Fair 02 using Paste Special to link your document to the source document.

Open a document and save it with a new name

Open

If you are not working through this lesson sequentially, before proceeding to the next step, open the 02D file (Lesson02 folder), and save it as Book Fair 02.

1. On the Standard toolbar, click the Open button.

   The Open dialog box appears.
2. Be sure the Word Practice folder appears in the Look In box.
3. Double-click the Word Practice folder, and double-click the Lesson02 folder.
4. In the file list, double-click the 02E file to open it.

   The document contains a logo for Pacific Books.
5. On the File menu, click Save As.

   The Save As dialog box appears.
6. Be sure the Lesson02 folder appears in the Save In box.
7. In the Save As Type box, be sure Word Document appears. Select and delete any text in the File Name box, and then type **Logo Practice 02**
8. Click Save.

You now have two documents open: Book Fair 02 and Logo Practice 02, with Logo Practice 02 currently displayed. The Windows taskbar shows a button for each open document.

Link two documents using Paste Special

Copy

In this exercise, you copy and paste the logo using the Paste Special command to link two documents.

1. In the Logo Practice 02 document, drag to select the logo and its ending paragraph mark.
2. On the Standard toolbar, click the Copy button.
   The logo is copied to the Clipboard.
3. On the taskbar, click the button for Book Fair 02 to display it.
4. In Book Fair 02, place your pointer in the selection bar next to the heading Pacific Books, and click to select it. Press the Delete key.
5. On the Edit menu, click Paste Special.
   The Paste Special dialog box appears.
6. In the Paste Special dialog box, in the As list, select Formatted Text (RTF) to reflect the type of text you are pasting from the source document.
7. Click Paste Link to create a link in your document to the source document.

Marks the type of text you are pasting

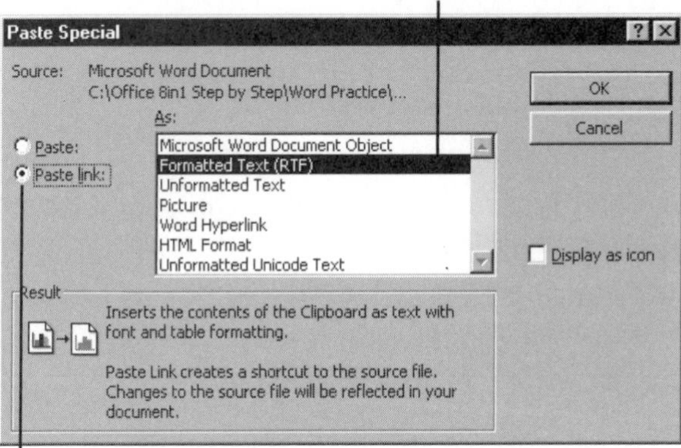

Creates a link to a source document

8. Click OK.
   The new logo replaces the heading in the Book Fair 02 document.

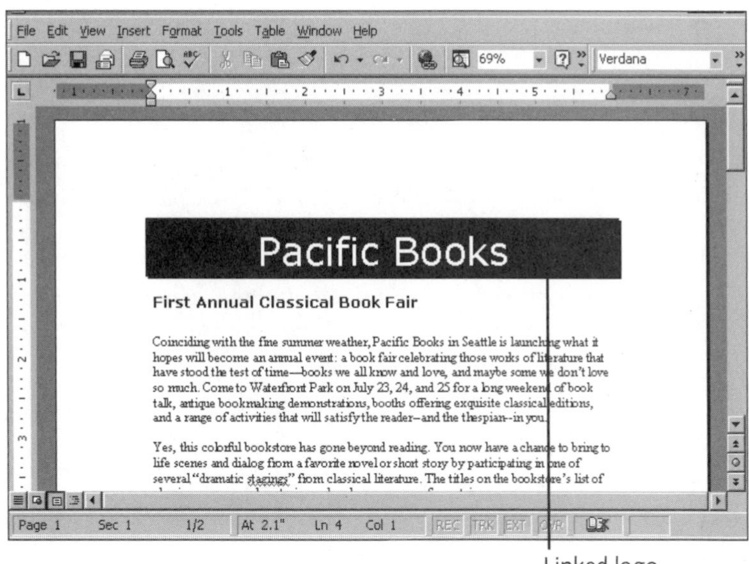

Test the link

In this exercise, you test the link between the two documents.

1. On the Windows taskbar, click Logo Practice 02, and then select the logo.
2. On the Format menu, click Borders And Shading.

   The Borders And Shading dialog box appears.
3. On the Shading tab, in the Fill area, choose a color.

   The Preview area gives a sample of the new color.
4. Click OK.

   Logo Practice 02 is displayed with the new color.
5. Click anywhere outside the selected logo to turn off the selection and view the color.
6. On the Windows taskbar, click Book Fair 02.

   The logo should reflect your change to the background color.

Finish the lesson

Save

1. On the Standard toolbar, click the Save button to save your changes to Book Fair 02.
2. On the File menu, click Close.

3. On the Standard toolbar, click the Save button to save your changes to Logo Practice 02.
4. On the File menu, click Exit.

Lesson 2 Quick Reference

To	Do this	Button
Open an existing document	On the standard toolbar, click the Open button. In the Open dialog box, double-click folders to open and display their contents. When the file you want to open appears in the file list, double-click it.	
Save a document with a new name	On the File menu, click Save As. In the Save As dialog box, type the new file name. Click OK.	
Display a document in a different view	Click the desired view button located to the left of the horizontal scroll bar. Or, on the View menu, select the desired view.	
Adjust the screen magnification	On the Standard toolbar, click the Zoom drop-down arrow, and then select a magnification.	
Move or copy text using the mouse	Select the text. When the mouse pointer becomes a left-pointing arrow, click and hold the mouse button as you drag the text. At the new location, release the button to insert the text.	
Undo a change	On the Standard toolbar, click the Undo button.	
Redo an undone change	On the Standard toolbar, click the Redo button.	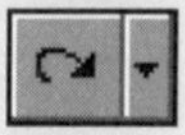
Move or copy text using toolbar buttons	Select the text. On the Standard toolbar, click the Cut or Copy button. Position the insertion point where you want to insert the text, and click the Paste button.	

Lesson 2 Quick Reference

To	Do this	Button
Work in Document Map view	On the Standard toolbar, click the Document Map button.	
Move multiple text items at once	On the View menu, point to Toolbars, and click Clipboard. Cut or copy items to the Clipboard. Position the insertion point and then click an item to paste it.	
Link two documents	Select the item to be linked. On the Standard toolbar, click the Copy button. In the document, click where the item is to be inserted/linked. On the Standard toolbar, click the Edit Paste Special button. In the As box, select an option, and click Paste Link. Click OK.	

Formatting Characters and Paragraphs

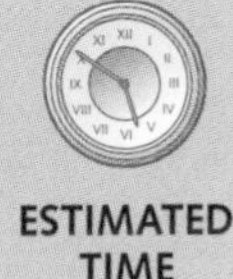

ESTIMATED TIME
35 min.

In this lesson you will learn how to:

- ✔ *Apply formatting to text.*
- ✔ *Copy formatting using the Format Painter.*
- ✔ *Change fonts, font sizes, and font effects.*
- ✔ *Modify the position of paragraphs on a page.*
- ✔ *Add borders and shading to paragraphs.*
- ✔ *Control hyphenation in a document.*
- ✔ *Create a quick logo.*

Learning how to format text will help you improve the impact of your documents. With quick and easy Microsoft Word formatting features, you can emphasize key points and reposition text for greater clarity.

In this lesson, you'll master the use of Word formatting features to enhance a letter to a new client. You'll work with the Format Painter to apply repeated formatting to text, and you'll learn how to align text and apply borders and shading to paragraphs. You'll also learn to use paragraph and line spacing, line breaks, and hyphenation rules to make your work easier.

important

The default toolbar setting in Microsoft Word 2000 displays both the Standard and Formatting toolbars in one row at the top of the document window, just below the menu bar. This gives you maximum workspace. While you work through the exercises in this book, toolbar buttons you need may not initially be visible. If a toolbar button is not visible, click one of the two More Buttons drop-down arrows on the toolbar to locate the button you need. When you select a new toolbar button, it is automatically added to the visible portion of the toolbar, replacing one that is not used as often.

Start Word and open a practice file

In this exercise, you start Word, open a practice file, then save it under a new name.

1. On the Windows taskbar, click the Start button.
   The Start menu appears.
2. On the Start menu, point to Programs, and then click Microsoft Word.
   Microsoft Word 2000 opens.
3. On the Standard toolbar, click the Open button.
   The Open dialog box appears.

Open

4. Click the Look In drop-down arrow, and then select your hard disk.
5. In the list of folders, double-click the Office 8in1 Step by Step folder. Double-click the Word Practice folder, and then double-click the Lesson03 folder.
6. In the file list, double-click the 03A file to open it.
   The document, a letter to a potential client that provides additional information about Impact Public Relations, opens in the document window.
7. On the File menu, click Save As.
   The Save As dialog box appears.
8. Be sure that the Lesson03 folder appears in the Save In box.
9. In the File Name box, select the text, and then type **Client Letter 03**
10. Click Save.

Display formatting marks

To make it easier to edit your document, you can display formatting marks such as paragraph marks and space marks on your screen.

Show/Hide ¶

- If formatting marks are not currently displayed, on the Standard toolbar, click the Show/Hide ¶ button.

Changing the Appearance of Text

You can change the appearance of text by applying formatting attributes, which are available on the Formatting toolbar. Commonly used attributes include bold, italic, and underline.

You can also change the font style and font size with a click of a button. A font is the typeface applied to text, numbers, and punctuation. There are many fonts from which to choose. In Word 2000, the Font list has been enhanced to display the name of the font in its own typeface so that you can preview it before you select it. Word provides other, more complex formats that can be applied from the Format menu.

If you are not working through this lesson sequentially, before proceeding to the next step, open the 03A file (Lesson03 folder), and save it as Client Letter 03.

Apply basic formatting

In this exercise, you enhance a letter to a client with text formatting.

1. In the first sentence of the third paragraph, select the text *Impact Public Relations*.
2. On the Formatting toolbar, click the Bold button, and then click the Italic button.
3. Click anywhere outside of the selected text to cancel the selection. *Impact Public Relations* is now displayed with bold and italic formatting.

   Your screen should look similar to the following illustration.

Bold

Italic

If the toolbar button you need is not visible, on the Formatting toolbar, click the More Buttons drop-down arrow to locate the button.

More Buttons

Bold and italic formatting applied to text

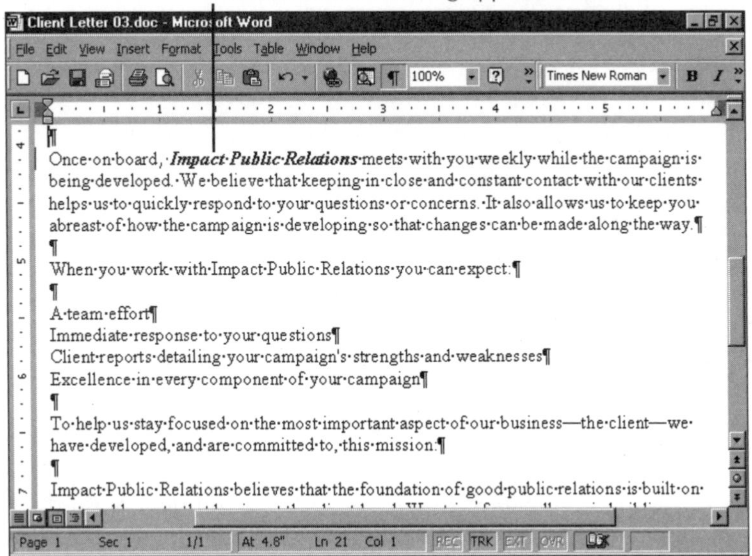

3 Formatting Text

Modify the font and font size

The font size is measured in units called points; there are 72 points in an inch.

In this exercise, you change the font style and font size of your company name.

1. In the first sentence of the third paragraph, select the text *Impact Public Relations*.
2. On the Formatting toolbar, click the Font drop-down arrow to see more options.

   Your screen should look similar to the following illustration.

If the Font button is not visible, on the Formatting toolbar, click the More Buttons drop-down arrow to locate the button.

More Buttons

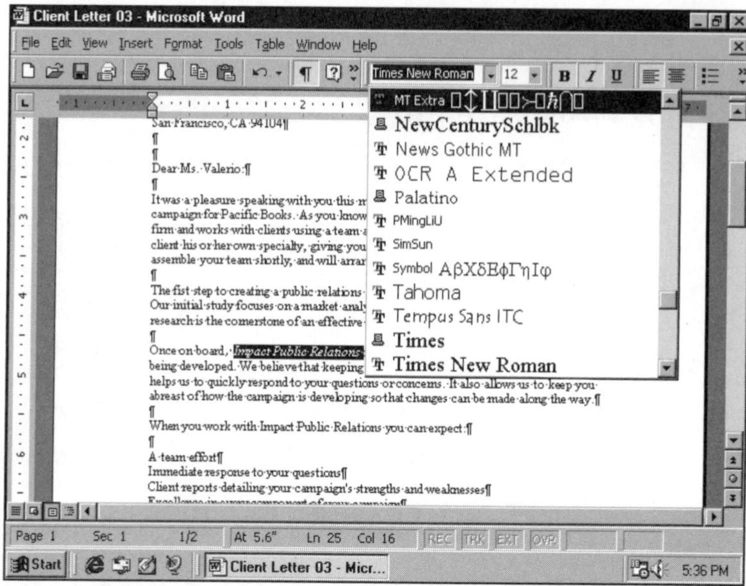

3. In the Font list, scroll down, and click Verdana.

   The selected text is changed to the Verdana font.

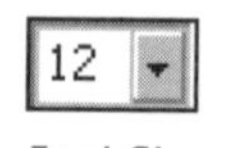

Font Size

4. On the Formatting toolbar, click the Font Size drop-down arrow, and then click 10.

   The size of the selected text changes to 10 points.
5. Click anywhere outside of the selected text to cancel the selection.

Using Additional Text Effects

Not all Word formatting options are available on the Formatting toolbar. You can access additional effects only from the Format menu. Effects used to animate text are also available in Word. To apply these text effects, on the Format menu, click Font, and then click the Text Effects tab. Select from the following text effects.

Text effects	Description
Blinking Background	Background around text flashes on and off.
Las Vegas Lights	Blinking marquee of different colors flashes around text.
Marching Black Ants	Black dashed line moves around text.
Marching Red Ants	Red dashed line moves around text.
Shimmer	Text vibrates on the screen.
Sparkle Text	Text is randomly sprinkled with colored confetti-like shapes.

In the Font dialog box, click the Character Spacing tab to find more ways to enhance your text with these character-spacing rules:

Feature	Description
Scale	Increase and decrease the width of the characters by the percentage selected.
Spacing	Adjust the space between characters. Choose from Normal, Condensed, or Expanded. In the By box, select an exact amount of space, measured in points.
Position	Raises and lowers the selected text position in the line by increments.
Kerning For Fonts	Allows you to specify whether you want the space between characters to be adjusted automatically based on the size of the font.

Apply additional text effects from the Format menu

If you are not working through this lesson sequentially, open the 03B file (Lesson03 folder), and save it as Client Letter 03.

In this exercise, you apply formatting from the Format menu.

1. In the first sentence of the third paragraph, select the text *Impact Public Relations*.
2. On the Format menu, click Font.

   The Font dialog box appears.
3. Click the Font tab, and in the Effects area, select the Small Caps check box.

   The formatting is applied and the result can be seen in the Preview window.
4. Click OK.
5. Click anywhere outside of the selected text to cancel the selection.

Applying Repeated Formatting

If you are not working through this lesson sequentially, before proceeding to the next step, open the 03C file (Lesson03 folder), and save it as Client Letter 03.

The text *Impact Public Relations* appears several times in the letter. Instead of selecting the text and repeatedly applying the formatting, you can use a Word shortcut that copies formatting from text, then pastes, or *paints*, it onto other text selections. This feature is called the *Format Painter*.

To use the Format Painter, first select the text that has the formatting you want to apply to other text selections. Once you activate the Format Painter, all the formatting attributes of the selected text will be attached to your pointer. Double-click the Format Painter button if you're going to copy the formatting to several locations, or just click the button if you're going to copy the formatting only once.

Use the Format Painter

In this exercise, you apply formatting using the Format Painter.

1. In the first sentence of the third paragraph, select the text *Impact Public Relations*.

Format Painter

2. On the Standard toolbar, double-click the Format Painter button, and then move the pointer around in the document.

   The pointer now has a paintbrush attached to it, which indicates that the Format Painter is active. Now any selected text will acquire formatting that matches the formatting of *Impact Public Relations*.

   Your screen should look similar to the following illustration.

If the Format Painter button is not visible, on the Standard toolbar, click the More Buttons drop-down arrow to locate the button.

More Buttons

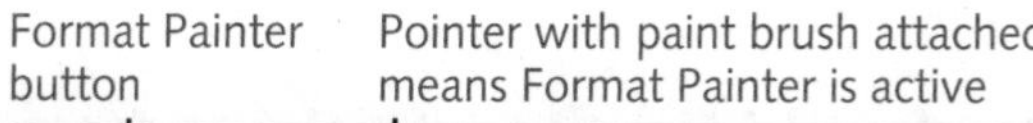

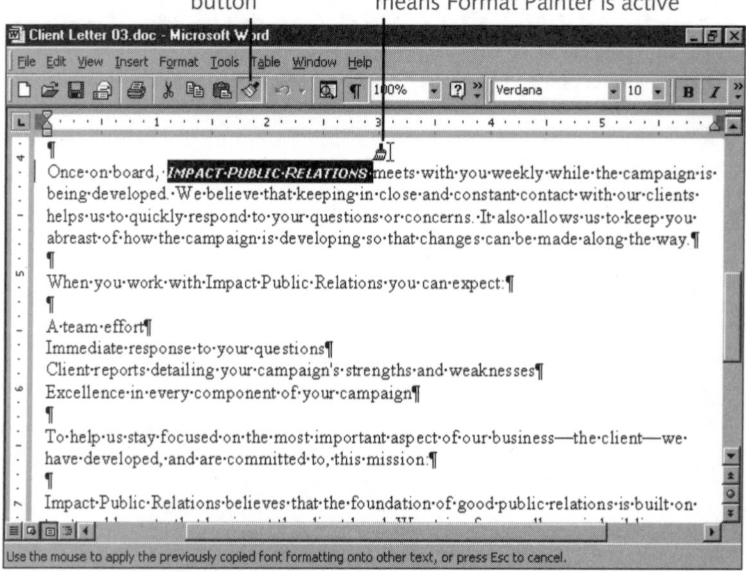

3. In the first sentence of the next paragraph, drag the pointer across the text *Impact Public Relations*.
4. Continue to scroll through the document, dragging the pointer across each occurrence of the text *Impact Public Relations*.

   The Format Painter stays active as you scroll through the document.
5. On the Standard toolbar, click the Format Painter button.

   The Format Painter is turned off.

Changing Paragraph Alignment

If you are not working through this lesson sequentially, before proceeding to the next step, open the 03D file (Lesson03 folder), and save it as Client Letter 03.

Another way to enhance your document is to change the look of paragraphs on the page. One way you can do this is by changing the alignment of the paragraph. Paragraph alignment refers to the position of the paragraph between the left and right margins. There are four ways to align a paragraph. *Align left* means that all lines on the left side of the paragraph are aligned with the left margin, while lines on the right side end at different places. In Word, all paragraphs are aligned on the left unless you specify otherwise. *Align right* is the opposite of align left. Lines on the right side of the paragraph will be aligned with the right margin, while lines on the left side will end in different places. *Center alignment* means text is centered in the middle of the page. Text that is *justified* is aligned with both the left and right margins by spreading the words evenly between the margins. Newspapers typically align text in this way.

tip

If you change the alignment of a single paragraph, you do not need to select the entire paragraph first. Word automatically recognizes that you want to apply an alignment style to that paragraph only. Just position your insertion point anywhere in the paragraph you want to align.

Justify

If the Justify button is not visible, on the Formatting toolbar, click the More Buttons drop-down arrow to locate the button.

Experiment with different alignment techniques

In this exercise, you view the different alignment options.

1. Click anywhere in the first paragraph.
2. On the Formatting toolbar, click the Justify button.

   The paragraph is now justified with both the left and right margins.
3. On the Formatting toolbar, click the Align Left button.

   The paragraph is now back to the default setting.

Use center alignment

In this exercise, you continue designing your letterhead by positioning the company logo.

1. Press Ctrl+Home to move to the top of the document.
2. Click the Impact Public Relations logo to select it.
   The sizing handles appear.
3. On the Format menu, click Picture.
   The Picture dialog box appears.
4. Click the Layout tab, and in the Horizontal area, click Center.
5. Click OK.
   The *Impact Public Relations* logo is centered in the middle of the line.

Center

Justifying Text by Clicking the Insertion Point

With the new *Click And Type* feature in Word 2000, you can set the text justification for new text in your document just by double-clicking anywhere in a blank space. Click And Type can apply left, center, or right alignment, or tabs to text entered in blank areas of your document. This feature allows you to point to any blank area of the document, double-click, and begin typing. This saves you from having to press Enter repeatedly, turn on alignment formatting, or set a tab before typing.

An icon attached to the mouse pointer shows that Click And Type is active and what type of alignment—left, center, or right—will be applied, or where a tab will be set when you double-click.

To use Click And Type to align text, be sure you are in the Print Layout view. Then, position the pointer in a blank area of the document in one of three alignment zones: far left (for left alignment), center (for center alignment), or far right (for right alignment). The pointer displays an icon indicating what alignment will be applied to the new text. Once the correct icon is attached to the pointer, just double-click and begin entering text.

The following illustration shows the mouse pointer icon for left alignment.

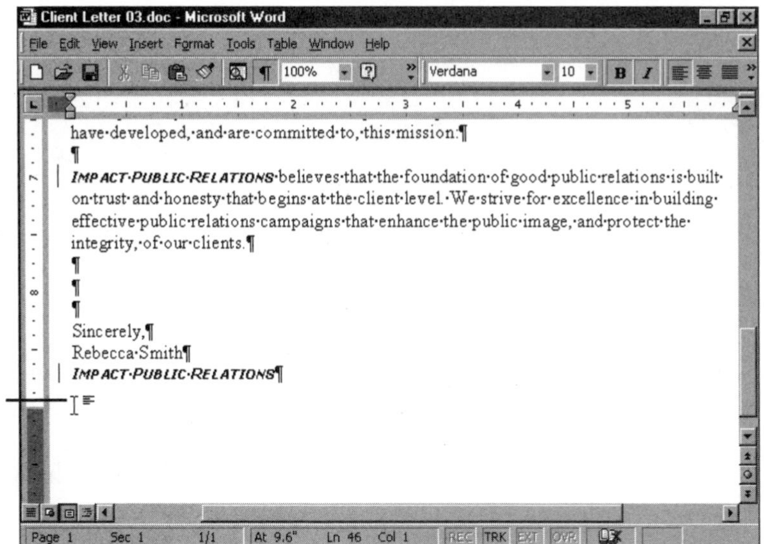

Use Click And Type to insert a date

For a demonstration of how to justify text using Click And Type, open the Office 8in1 Step by Step folder on your hard disk. Then open the Word Demos folder, and double-click the Click And Type icon.

You must be in Print Layout view in order to use Click And Type.

In this exercise, you insert a date using Click And Type.

1. At the half inch vertical ruler marker, double-click in the far right of the document.

   Your screen should look similar to the following illustration.

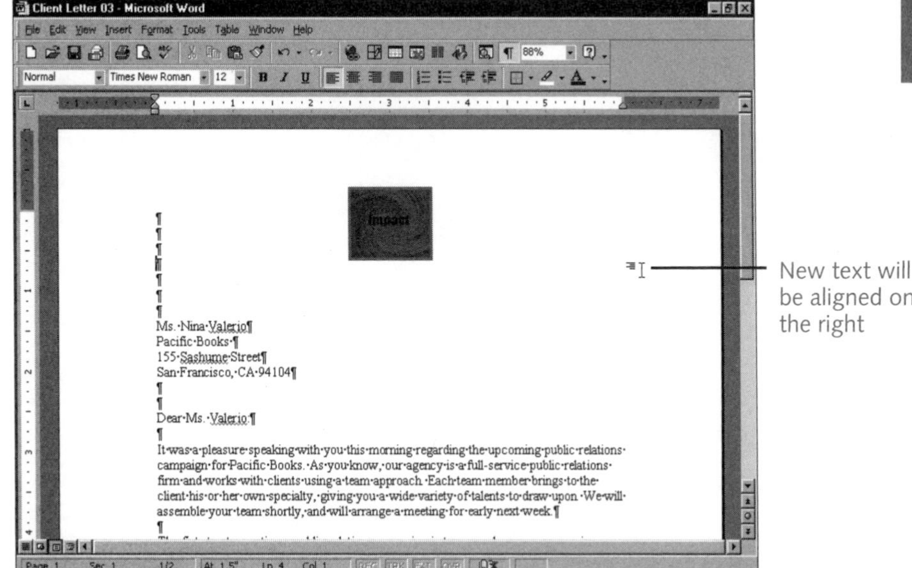

2. Double-click and type today's date.

   The text is right-aligned.

Changing the Spacing of Paragraphs

If you are not working through this lesson sequentially, before proceeding to the next step, open the 03E file (Lesson03 folder), and save it as Client Letter 03.

After you've created a document, you often see ways to improve it by changing paragraph formatting. For example, you might decide that instead of double-spacing a list, one and a half lines between items would look better. You also might decide that even though your final document will be single-spaced, it would be useful to print a double-spaced copy to edit. With Word, it's easy to change the line spacing of your document—temporarily or permanently—by using the Paragraph command. You can also make other changes, such as changing the spacing between paragraphs. For example, although you've selected a font size of 12 points, you might select spacing between paragraphs of 16 points.

Change line spacing

In this exercise, you change the line spacing in a list to make it stand out in your letter.

1. Select the text beginning with *A team effort* through *Excellence in every component of your campaign*.

   Your screen should look similar to the following illustration.

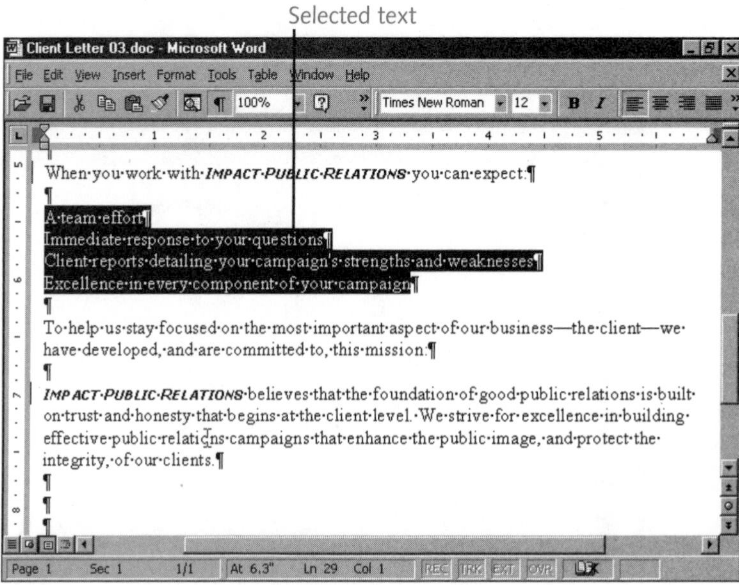

2. On the Format menu, click Paragraph.
3. In the Paragraph dialog box, be sure that the Indents And Spacing tab is selected.
4. In the Line Spacing area, click the drop-down arrow, and then click 1.5 lines.

   Your screen should look similar to the following illustration.

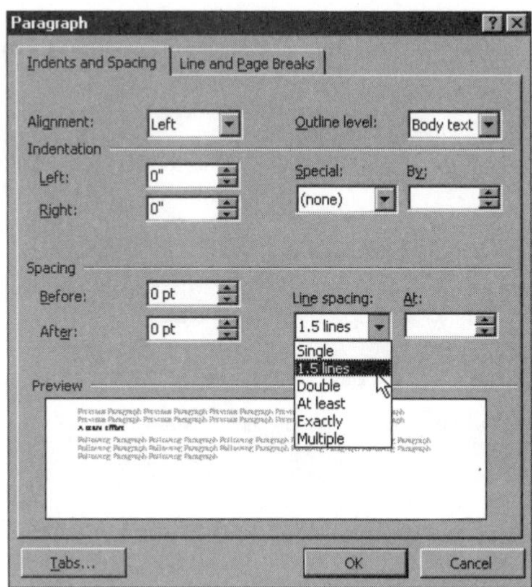

5. Click OK.

   The Paragraph dialog box closes, and the list spacing changes to 1.5 lines.

   Your screen should look similar to the following illustration.

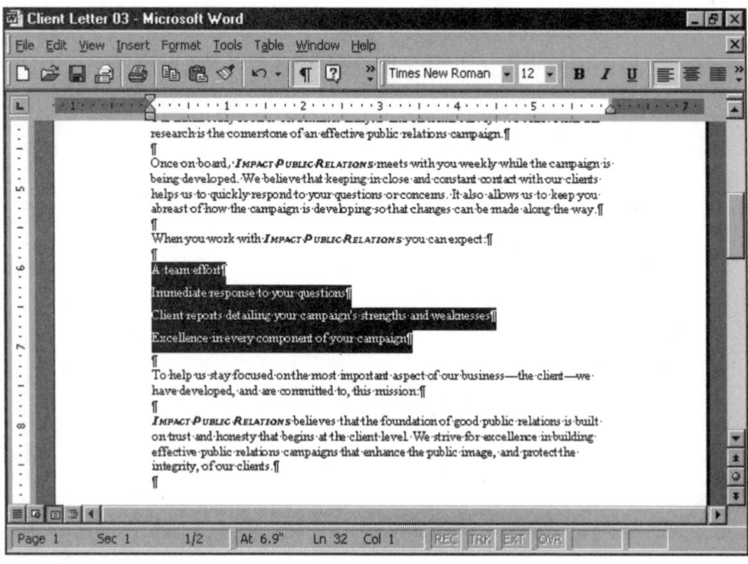

Change paragraph spacing

In this exercise, you set your own paragraph spacing and remove the paragraph marks.

1. Select the first three paragraphs of the letter.

   Your screen should look similar to the following illustration.

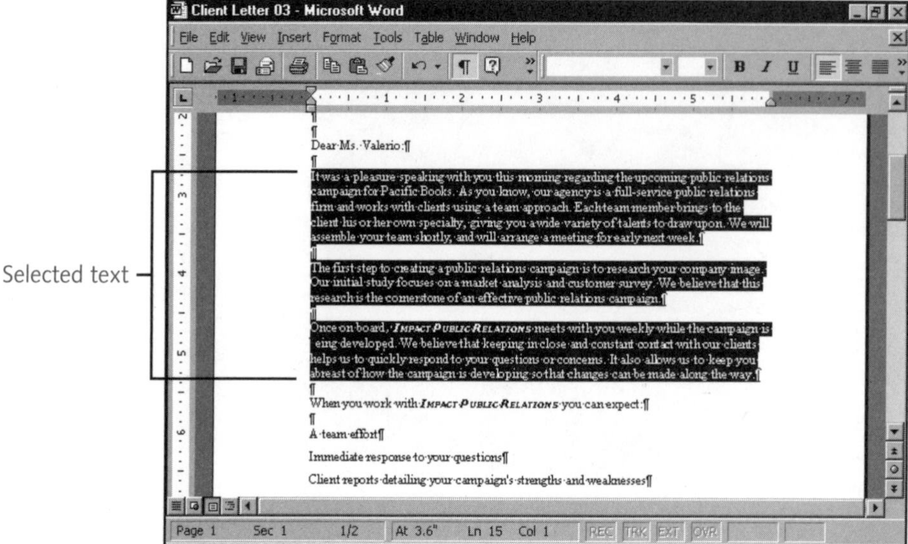

2. On the Format menu, click Paragraph.
3. In the Spacing Before box, click the up arrow until 18 pt shows in the box.
4. In the Spacing After box, click the up arrow until 18 pt shows in the box.

   Your screen should look similar to the following illustration.

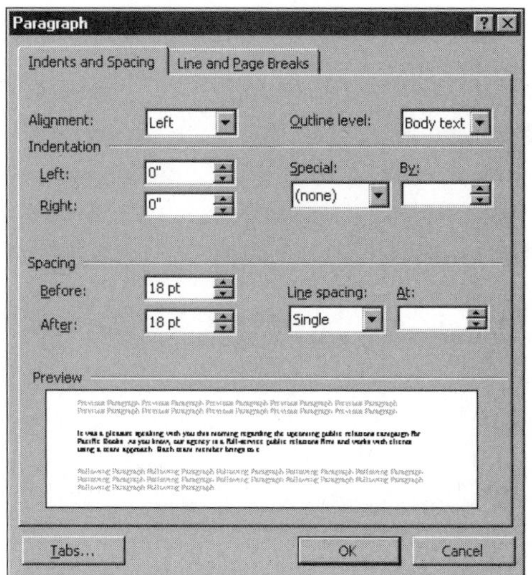

5. Click OK.

   The Paragraph dialog box closes, and the spacing before and after paragraphs changes to 18 points.

6. Click anywhere outside of the selected text to cancel the selection.

Delete paragraph marks

In this exercise, you delete unnecessary paragraph marks between each paragraph.

1. Press Ctrl+Home to move the insertion point to the beginning of the document.

2. Click before the paragraph mark below the text *Dear Ms. Valerio* and press the Delete key.

   The paragraph mark is removed. There is still space between the salutation and first paragraph.

3. Scroll down and delete the paragraph mark between the first and second paragraphs.

5. Scroll down and delete the paragraph mark between the third and fourth paragraphs.

Setting Additional Paragraph Rules

When you come to the end of a page in a document, Word starts a new page by automatically placing a page break in your document. This is called a *soft page break*. Word ensures that a single line of a paragraph is not printed on a page by itself. This default feature is called *Widow And Orphan Control*. However, beyond this control of single lines, Word automatically splits paragraphs when the end of a page is reached. You can further modify the way a paragraph is printed by setting text flow options found in the Paragraph dialog box.

By selecting the Keep Lines Together option, for example, you ensure that text you want to keep on one page is not separated by a soft page break. This option is particularly useful when working with tables because it ensures that they do not get split across two pages. Besides the Keep Lines Together option, there are other paragraph rules you can apply by clicking the Line And Page Breaks tab in the Paragraph dialog box. These options are summarized as follows.

Option	Description
Widow/Orphan Control	Prevents the last line of a paragraph from being printed at the top of a new page (widow) or the first line of a paragraph from being printed at the bottom of a page (orphan).
Keep Lines Together	Keeps all lines of a paragraph on the same page.
Keep With Next	Keeps two paragraphs on the same page.
Page Break Before	Forces a page break before a specified paragraph.
Suppress Line Numbers	Suppresses line numbering when the Line Numbering feature is active.
Don't Hyphenate	Ensures that words are not hyphenated at the end of a line.

Keep lines together

If you are not working through this lesson sequentially, before proceeding to the next step, open the 03F file (Lesson03 folder), and save it as Client Letter 03.

In this exercise, you set line and page break options to keep a paragraph together.

1. On the View menu, click Normal.

   Your view is changed from Print Layout to Normal.

tip

When you are working with text longer than two pages, it is easier to work in the Normal view. This is because the Normal view simplifies the display of the document by not showing the top and bottom margins. As a result, all text is displayed continuously, with dotted lines indicating where pages will break when the document is printed.

2. Select the paragraph beginning with the text *Impact Public Relations believes that the foundation of*.

   Your screen should look similar to the following illustration.

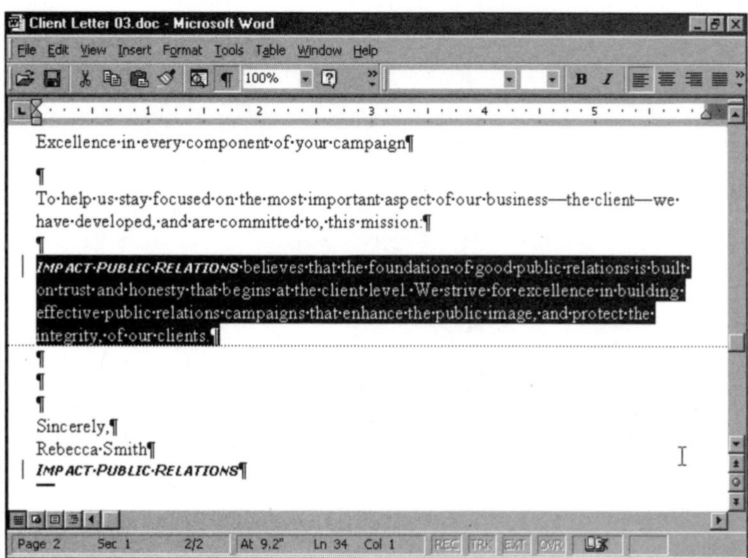

For more about setting page breaks, see Lesson 4, "Previewing and Printing a Document."

3. On the Format menu, click Paragraph.
4. In the Paragraph dialog box, click the Line And Page Breaks tab.
5. Select the Keep Lines Together check box, and click OK.

   The entire paragraph is moved to the next page.
6. On the View menu, click Print Layout.

Adding Borders and Shading to Paragraphs

Once you have positioned paragraphs where you want them on the pages, you can apply borders and shading. This formatting helps draw attention to text in your document. Word has more than 20 different border styles you can choose from, and each can be displayed in line weights (thickness) ranging from ¼ point to 6 points. You can also choose from a variety of border colors. As you create borders, they are added to the Line Style list, making them available for future use in your document.

Do not add a border to a paragraph that must split across two pages, however, because the page break will split the border between two pages. Using the Keep Lines Together option can help prevent this.

Controlling Hyphenation

By default, Word will not hyphenate text at the end of a line. Instead, it will move the whole word down to the next line. However, if a hyphenated word occurs at a normal line break, Word will maintain that hyphenation and put the first part of the word on one line, and the last part on the next line.

There are certain circumstances when you would not want Word to follow the default hyphenation rules. These include occurrences of phone numbers and hyphenated names falling at the end of a line. When you want to ensure that hyphenated text does not break across two lines, you can specify a *nonbreaking hyphen.*

To do this, click where you want to insert the nonbreaking hyphen, and press Ctrl+Shift+Hyphen. Your hyphenated text will be moved to the next line.

To ensure that proper names are not separated over two lines, you can specify a *nonbreaking space.*

Insert a nonbreaking space

1. Position your pointer between the two words you want to keep together.
2. Select the space mark between the two words.
3. Press Ctrl+Shift+Spacebar.

If you decide that you do not want Word to hyphenate under any circumstances, you can specify that rule in the Paragraph dialog box. On the Format menu, click Paragraph. In the Paragraph dialog box, click the Line And Page Breaks tab. Select the Don't Hyphenate check box, and click OK. Word will no longer hyphenate text in your document.

Display the Tables And Borders toolbar

If you are not working through this lesson sequentially, before proceeding to the next step, open the 03G file (Lesson03 folder), and save it as Client Letter 03.

In this exercise, you prepare to add a border and shading around your company mission statement.

- On the View menu, point to Toolbars, and then click Tables And Borders. The Tables And Borders toolbar appears. If necessary, drag it to a position directly under the Formatting toolbar.

Apply a border

In this exercise, you add a border around your company mission statement.

1. Click the paragraph starting with the text *Impact Public Relations believes that the foundation of*.

Outside Border

2. On the Tables And Borders toolbar, click the Outside Border button.

   The paragraph is surrounded by an outside border.

   Your screen should look similar to the following illustration.

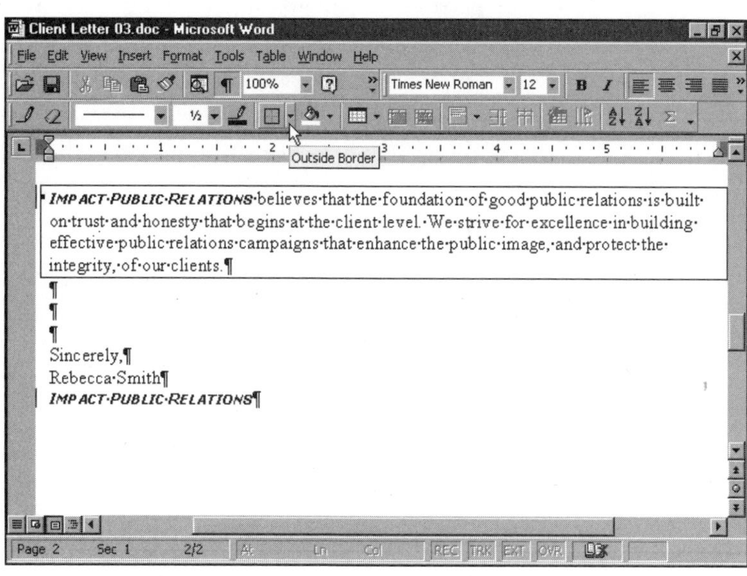

Change the border

In this exercise, you change the border style and then the line weight.

1. Click at the beginning of the paragraph beginning with *Impact Public Relations believes*.

Line Style

2. On the Tables And Borders toolbar, click the Line Style drop-down arrow to see more options.
3. Scroll to the bottom of the Line Style list and click the line style that is third from the bottom.

   Your screen should look similar to the following illustration.

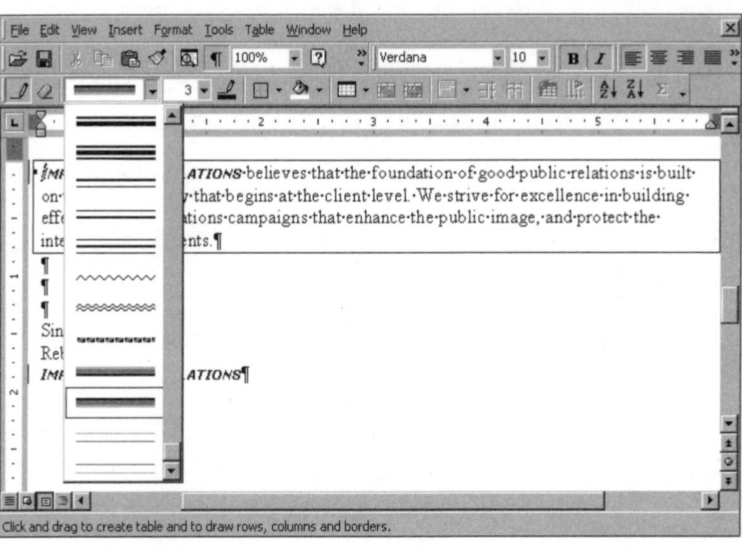

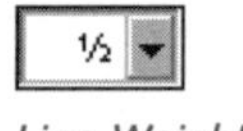

Line Weight

Border Color

4. On the Tables And Borders toolbar, click the Line Weight drop-down arrow to see more options, and then select 1 ½ pt.
5. On the Tables And Borders toolbar, click the Border Color button, and then click Dark Blue.

Outside Border

6. Click the Outside Border button.

   The border is updated. If you display the Line Style list, you will see that this new border style has been added.

Apply shading to a paragraph

In this exercise, you add shading around the company mission statement.

1. Click at the beginning of the paragraph starting with the text *Impact Public Relations believes that the foundation of*.

Shading Color

2. On the Tables And Borders toolbar, click the Shading Color drop-down arrow to see more options.
3. Click Gray-5%.

   The paragraph is filled with gray 5% shading.

   Your screen should look similar to the following illustration.

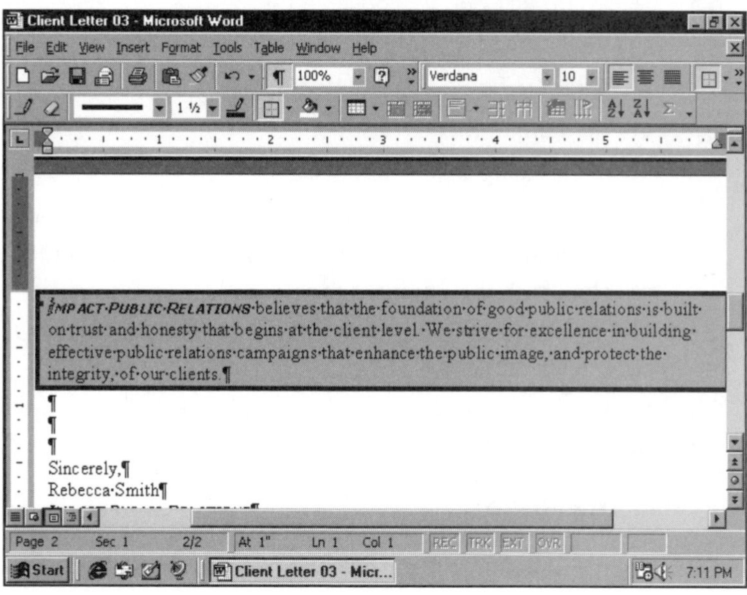

4. On the View menu, point to Toolbars, and then click Tables And Borders. The Tables And Borders toolbar is removed from view.

One Step Further: Creating a Quick and Colorful Logo

If you are not working through this lesson sequentially, before proceeding to the next step, open the 03H file (Lesson03 folder), and save it as Client Letter 03.

There are many creative ways to use the Borders And Shading feature. In this exercise, you create a logo for your new client, Pacific Books.

Create a logo

1. Click to the left of the second paragraph marker below the mission statement, and type **As per your request, I have created a logo for Pacific Books. This logo will be used everywhere, including your new Web site.** Press Enter twice.
2. Type **Pacific Books**, and press Enter.
3. Select the text *Pacific Books*.
4. On the Formatting toolbar, click the Center button.

   The text *Pacific Books* is centered.

Center

You can also press Ctrl+E to center the text.

5. On the Format menu, click Font.

   The Font dialog box is displayed.
6. In the Font list, click Verdana. In the Size list, click 36, and click OK.
7. On the Format menu, click Borders And Shading, and then, if not already selected, click the Borders tab.
8. In the Setting area, click Shadow. In the Color list, click Dark Blue, and then click the Shading tab.
9. In the Fill palette, click Dark Blue, and click OK. Click anywhere outside of the selected text to cancel the selection.

Finish the lesson

Save

1. On the Standard toolbar, click the Save button.

   Changes made to Client Letter 03 are saved.
2. On the File menu, click Close.
3. On the File menu, click Exit.

Lesson 3 Quick Reference

To	Do this	Button
Format text in bold and italic	Select the text to be formatted. On the Formatting toolbar, click the Bold button, and then click the Italic button.	B I
Modify fonts and font size	Select the text to be modified. On the Formatting toolbar, click the Font drop-down arrow. Select a font. Click the Font Size drop-down arrow, and select a point size.	
Use the Format Painter	Select the text containing the formatting you want to copy. On the Standard toolbar, double-click the Format Painter button. Drag across the new text you want to format. On the Standard toolbar, click the Format Painter button to turn it off.	
Center text	Select the text, or click in the paragraph to be centered. On the Formatting toolbar, click the Center button.	
Use Click And Type	Be sure you are in Print Layout view. Double-click in a blank space in the document. Note the mouse pointer icon to determine how text will be aligned. Begin typing.	
Change line spacing	Select the paragraphs to be formatted. On the Format menu, click Paragraph. In the Paragraph dialog box, be sure that the Indents And Spacing tab is selected. Click the Line Spacing drop-down arrow, click the desired line spacing, and click OK.	

Lesson 3 Quick Reference

To	Do this	Button
Change paragraph spacing	Select the paragraphs to be formatted. On the Format menu, click Paragraph. In the Paragraph dialog box, click the Spacing Before arrow until the desired point size is displayed in the box. Click the Spacing After arrow until the desired point size is displayed. Click OK.	
Keep lines together	Select a paragraph. On the Format menu, click Paragraph. In the Paragraph dialog box, click the Line And Page Breaks tab. Select the Keep Lines Together check box. Click OK.	
Create a nonbreaking hyphen	Click before the hyphenated word and press Ctrl+Shift+Hyphen.	
Insert a nonbreaking space	Click between the two words to be kept together. Select the space mark between the two words. Press Ctrl+Shift+Spacebar.	
Apply a border	Click at the beginning of the paragraph to be formatted. On the Tables And Borders toolbar, click the Border drop-down arrow, and choose an outside border style. Click the Outside Border button.	
Apply shading to a paragraph	Position the insertion point at the beginning of the paragraph to be formatted. On the Tables And Borders toolbar, click the Shading Color button drop-down arrow. Click the desired shading.	

Lesson 3 Quick Reference

To	Do this	Button
Create a logo	Select the text to be used as a logo. On the Formatting toolbar, click Center. On the Format menu, click Font. In the Font dialog box, select a font and font size. On the Format menu, click Borders And Shading, and then click the Borders tab. In the setting area, select a setting. In the Color list, select a color. On the Shading tab, from the Fill palette, select a color. Click OK.	

4

Previewing and Printing a Document

In this lesson you will learn how to:

- ✔ *Preview how your document will look when printed.*
- ✔ *Insert page breaks.*
- ✔ *Adjust margins using the ruler.*
- ✔ *Print a whole document or just a part.*
- ✔ *Print an envelope.*
- ✔ *Shrink a document to fit on one page.*

ESTIMATED TIME
20 min.

After organizing, editing, and formatting a document, you will probably want to print it. Before you do, you can make adjustments to it in *Print Preview*. This document view helps you avoid wasted print jobs, as you can see your work before printing it. In this lesson, you view the layout of a Word document before you print it; then you edit it and adjust the margins and the text flow across pages. Finally, you print the whole document, as well as just one page.

More Buttons

important

The default toolbar setting in Microsoft Word 2000 displays both the Standard and Formatting toolbars in one row, at the top of the document window, just below the menu bar. This gives you maximum workspace. While you work through these exercises, toolbar buttons you need may not initially be visible. If a toolbar button is not visible, click one of the two More Buttons drop-down arrows on the toolbar to locate the button you need. The new button you select will be added to the visible portion of the toolbar, replacing one that is not used as often.

Start Word and open a practice file

To begin this lesson, be sure Word is started. Follow the instructions to open a practice document named 04A, and then save it with the new name Book Fair 04.

1. On the Standard toolbar, click the Open button.
   The Open dialog box appears.
2. Click the Look In drop-down arrow, and then select your hard disk.
3. In the list of folders, double-click the Office 8in1 Step by Step folder. Double-click the Word Practice folder, and then double-click the Lesson04 folder.
4. In the file list, double-click the 04A file to open it.
   The document opens in the document window.

Open

5. On the File menu, click Save As.
   The Save As dialog box appears.
6. Be sure that the Lesson04 folder appears in the Save In box.
7. In the File Name box, select the text, and then type **Book Fair 04**
8. Click Save.

Display formatting marks

To make it easier to edit your document, you can display formatting marks such as paragraph marks and space marks on your screen.

Show/Hide ¶

- If formatting marks are not currently displayed, on the Standard toolbar, click the Show/Hide ¶ button.

Previewing Documents

If you are not working through this lesson sequentially, before proceeding to the next step, open the 04A file (Lesson04 folder), and save it as Book Fair 04.

To see exactly how your document will look when printed, use the Print Preview command. The Print Preview window shows you where lines of text break on the page and where page breaks occur. If you don't like the layout, you can make adjustments before you print, which might prevent a wasted print job.

As a partner at Impact Public Relations, you've created a document for your client, Pacific Books, that will become the basis for a newsletter and will later be part of the client's Web site. You've added headings and a logo, and included a schedule. Now you'd like to see how it will look when printed, and you want to show your partner a draft.

Preview a document

In this exercise, you preview a document before printing it.

Print Preview

If the Print Preview button is not visible, on the Standard toolbar, click the More Buttons drop-down arrow to locate and select the button.

- On the Standard toolbar, click the Print Preview button.

  The Print Preview window opens and the first page of your document is displayed. The Print Preview toolbar appears, and the Word menu bar remains unchanged.

  Your screen should look similar to the following illustration.

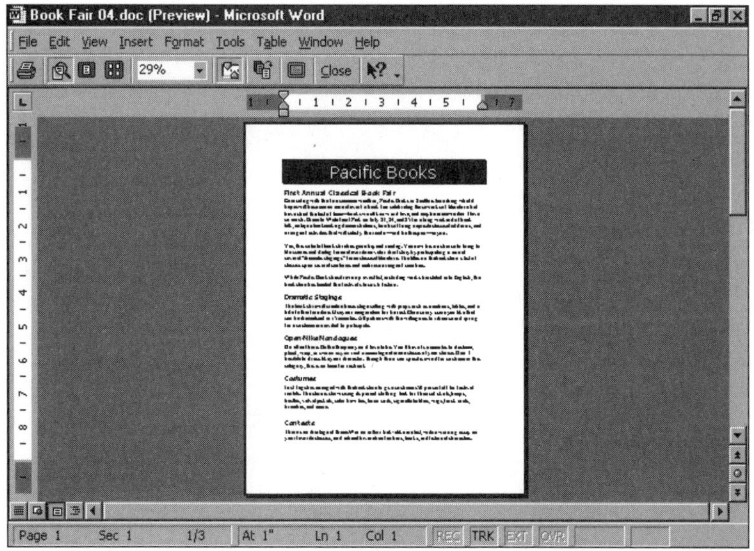

View Ruler

One Page

tip

If your screen does not match this illustration, on the Print Preview toolbar, click the View Ruler button to display the ruler. Click the One Page button if you see more than one page of the document.

View all pages

In this exercise, you view all pages of your document in Print Preview.

Multiple Pages

- On the Print Preview toolbar, click the Multiple Pages button, move the pointer across the three boxes in the top row to select them, and then click.

  Your three-page document is displayed in full.

  Your screen should look similar to the following illustration.

Multiple pages in Print Preview

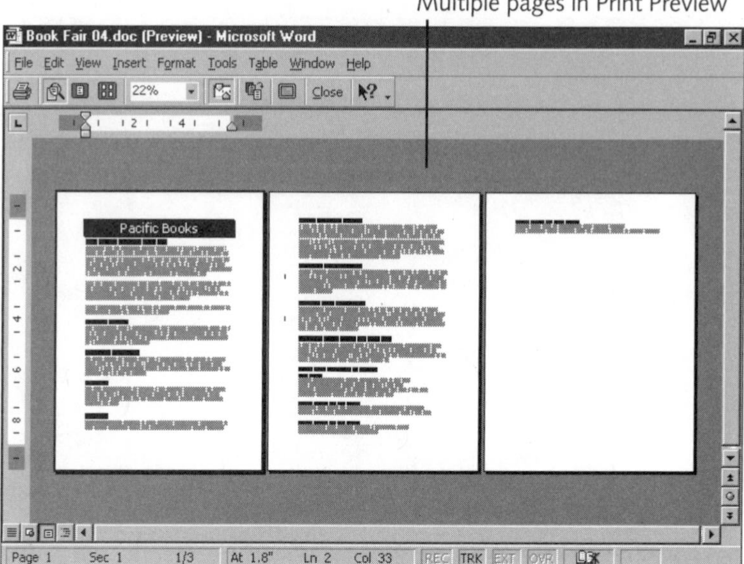

Editing While in Print Preview

If you are not working through this lesson sequentially, before proceeding to the next step, open the 04A file (Lesson04 folder), and save it as Book Fair 04.

While viewing your document in Print Preview, you might think of text changes you'd like to make. You don't have to switch to Print Layout view or another document view to do this; you can make the changes in the Print Preview window. However, if your text or formatting changes are extensive, you might find it easier to edit using Normal, Print Layout, or Web Layout view.

As you look over Book Fair 04, you remember that there's a quotation you intended to add in the first section. To make this addition, you use the magnifier to enlarge text so you can see it more clearly, and then you add the new text. The Magnifier button is activated by default when you open the Print Preview window.

Add text in Print Preview

In this exercise, you use the magnifier to enlarge text, and then you add a quotation.

1. In the Print Preview window, move your pointer to the first page of the document.

   The pointer now looks like a magnifying glass.

Magnifier

2. On Page 1, place the pointer before the third paragraph, and click.

   The text is magnified.

   Your screen should look similar to the following illustration.

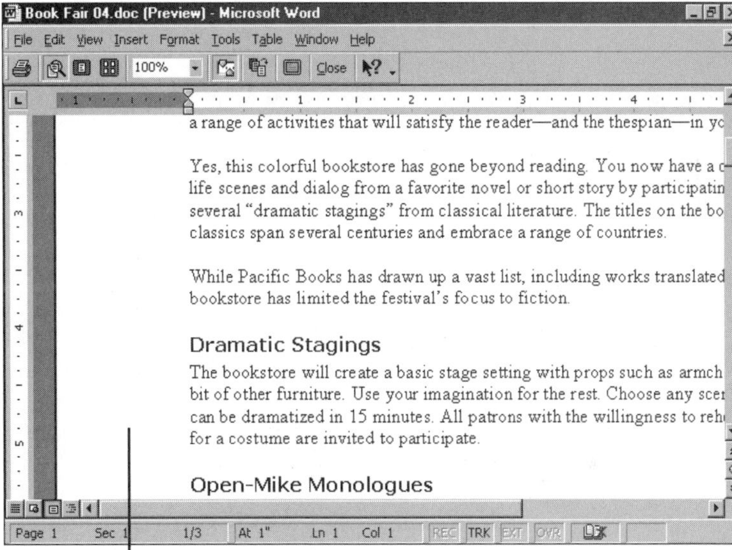

Magnified view of text in Print Preview

3. Scroll until you can see the full width of the text.
4. On the Print Preview toolbar, click the Magnifier button.

   The magnifier is turned off, and the pointer becomes the insertion point.

5. Click after the word *fiction* in the third paragraph (after the period).
6. Press the Spacebar and type **Erica Thomas, manager of the Seattle store, says, "It might seem like a crime to exclude poetry, but we've already established our fall poetry festival, and we decided it was fiction's turn."**

Inserting Page Breaks

If you are not working through this lesson sequentially, before proceeding to the next step, open the 04B file (Lesson04 folder), and save it as Book Fair 04.

As you type text in Word, page breaks are inserted automatically when you reach the end of a page. These are called soft page breaks. If you add or delete text on the page, the soft page break moves automatically to accommodate the increased or decreased amount of text.

Soft page breaks are shown in Normal view as a single dotted line across the page. In Print Layout view, you see the actual end of the page on your screen. You cannot move or delete soft page breaks except by editing the text. You can, however, create a page break exactly where you want one by inserting a hard page break. After you insert a hard page break, Word repaginates the document and changes soft page breaks appropriately.

In Normal and Print Layout views, a hard page break is shown as a dotted line with the label *Page Break*. Neither the line nor the label appears in a printed document.

When you insert a hard page break, information below the break will always start at the top of a new page. You might use the hard page break to keep certain paragraphs of your document together, or to divide text more evenly across pages. It's best to insert hard page breaks only when your document is nearly final, to avoid a wasted print job.

You can also control how the text breaks across pages by setting line and page break options found in the Paragraph command on the Format menu. Lesson 3, "Formatting Characters and Paragraphs," discusses this subject further.

Insert a page break

In this exercise, you insert a hard page break.

100%

Zoom

1. On the Print Preview toolbar, click the Zoom drop-down arrow, and then click Page Width.
2. Scroll to the heading *Contests*, at the bottom of the first page, and then click before the heading.

You can also insert a hard page break by pressing Ctrl+Enter.

3. On the Insert menu, click Break.

   The Break dialog box appears.
4. Be sure Page Break is selected in the Break dialog box, and click OK.

   A hard page break is inserted, and the text following the break moves to the next page.

Multiple Pages

5. On the Print Preview toolbar, click the Multiple Pages button, move the pointer across the first three boxes in the top row to select them, and then click.

   Your document appears with its new page breaks.
6. On the Print Preview toolbar, click Close.

7. Scroll up to see the new page break at the bottom of page 1.

   Your screen should look similar to the following illustration.

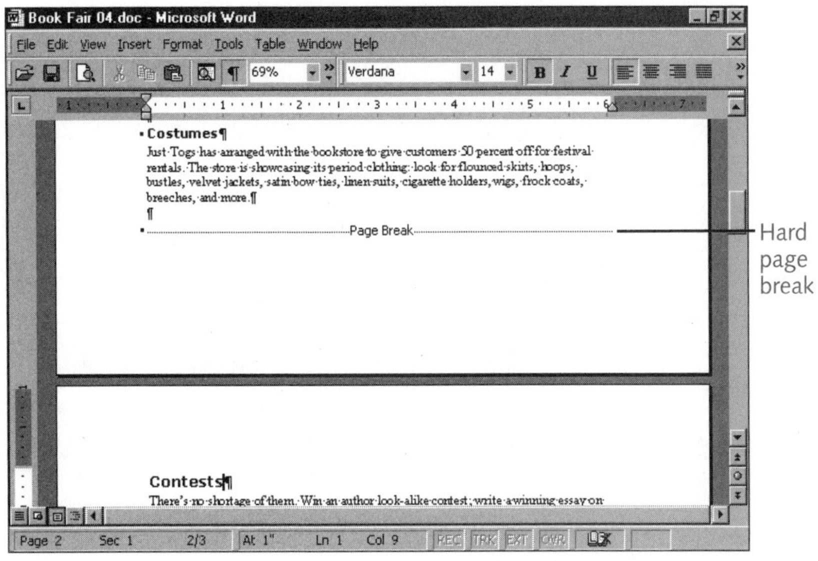

8. Save the document.

Adjusting Margins with the Ruler

Although you can use the Page Setup command and dialog box to specify a variety of settings for your margins, you can also adjust margins quickly by using the ruler.

If you are not working through this lesson sequentially, before proceeding to the next step, open the 04C file (Lesson04 folder), and save it as Book Fair 04.

In the next exercise, you adjust the left margin to match the right margin in the Book Fair 04 document.

> **tip**
>
> On the Print Preview toolbar, you can click the Ruler button to display or hide the ruler. Also, on the View menu, you can click Ruler to accomplish the same task.

Change the left margin with the ruler

In this exercise, you use the ruler to adjust the left margin.

1. Press Ctrl+Home to move the insertion point to the top of the document.

2. Position the pointer on the left margin marker (on the left edge of the ruler). When the pointer changes to a double-headed arrow, click and hold while you press the Alt key.

   Left and right margin measurements are displayed.

3. Keeping the mouse button and the Alt key depressed, drag to the right until the width of the left margin measures 1.25 inches.

   Your screen should look similar to the following illustration.

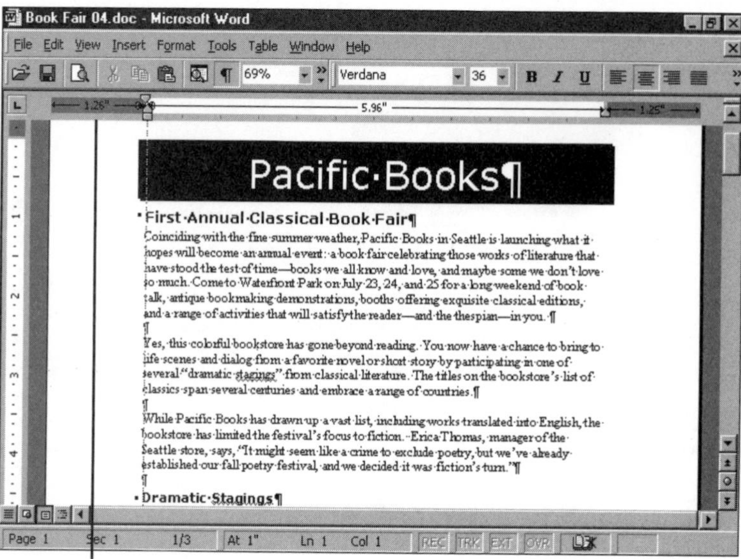

Left margin measurement

4. Release the mouse button and the Alt key.

   The left margin is now the width of the right margin on each page in the document.

Save

5. On the Standard toolbar, click the Save button.

   Changes made to your document are saved.

tip

To check to see that a margin adjustment hasn't altered any soft page breaks, view the entire document in Print Preview again before saving it. If you find that narrowing your margin has bumped text to a new page, you can either return to Print Layout view and readjust the margin, or alter the margin while in Print Preview, by using the mouse button and Alt key. The new margins you set will apply to all pages. You might find it more difficult to hit exact measurements in Print Preview.

Setting Mirrored Margins in a Document

The Page Setup dialog box in Word enables you to set margin widths and other related options, including mirror margins. This option adjusts margins for facing pages when a document is printed or photocopied on both sides of the paper, or back-to-back.

When you print a document, you might need to leave a bit of space along one edge of the pages to accommodate binding. The space along the edge is called the gutter margin. To set a gutter margin, in the Page Setup dialog box, click the Margins tab. Set the gutter margin as wide as necessary to accommodate binding. For documents that read left to right, the binding is usually along the left edge of the pages.

When you're printing or copying back-to-back, you must also turn on Mirror Margins to tell Word to place the gutter margin on facing pages rather than on the left side of every page. Set the gutter position to Left. On even-numbered pages, Word will flip the widths of the left and right margins set for odd-numbered pages so that even-page margins mirror odd-page margins.

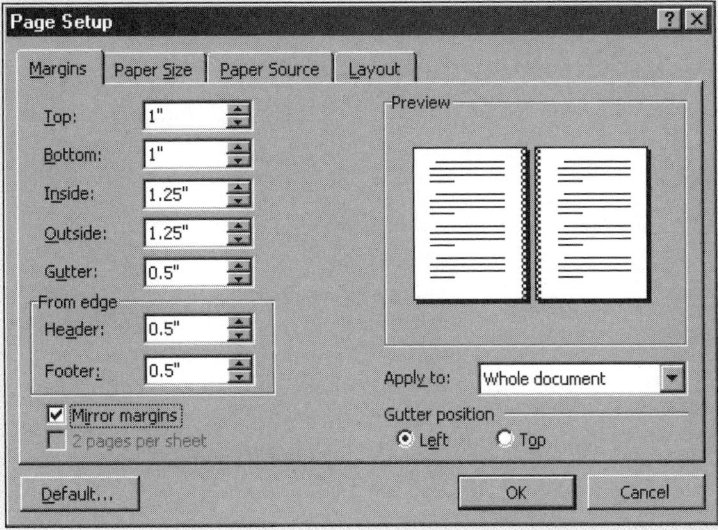

The preview area shows the gutter margin as a checkerboard on the pages. The preview shows you approximately how much of the page Word gives to the gutter margin.

Printing Documents

Another way to print the currently selected document, is to click the Print button on the Print Preview toolbar. Default print settings will apply.

The quickest and easiest way to print a document is to click the Print button on the Standard toolbar. This prints the whole document using default settings. If you are connected to multiple printers, the Print button activates the default printer.

To print only certain pages or multiple copies, or to otherwise alter the default settings, use the File menu. On the File menu, click Print to display the Print dialog box, and then select specific options.

If your computer is not connected to a printer, you can skip to the end of this lesson.

> **tip**
>
> The Microsoft Windows 95, Windows 98, and Windows 2000 operating systems enable you to continue working in Word or another program as your document prints in the background—you don't have to wait for the printer to finish first. To ensure that you have background printing enabled in Word, on the Tools menu, click Options, click the Print tab, and then verify that Background Printing is selected.

If you are not working through this lesson sequentially, before proceeding to the next step, open the 04D file (Lesson04 folder), and save it as Book Fair 04.

Print the entire document

In this exercise, you print the Book Fair 04 document.

1. Be sure that the printer is on.
2. On the Standard toolbar, click the Print button.
   The document is printed.

Print

Print one page of the document

In this exercise, you fix a typo in the document, and then reprint just one page.

1. On the left side of the status bar, double-click the page-number display.
   The Find And Replace dialog box appears, and the Go To tab is selected.

2. On the Go To tab, type **2** in the Enter Page Number box, click Go To, and then click Close.

   Page 2 of Book Fair 04 is displayed on the screen.

3. Click after the word *decad*, in the second line of the paragraph.

Save

4. Type the letter **e** to fix the typo, and then, on the Standard toolbar, click the Save button.

5. On the File menu, click Print.

   The Print dialog box appears.

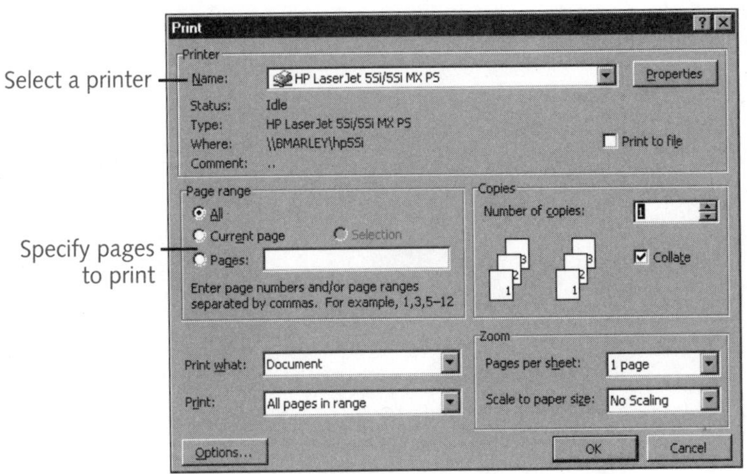

6. In the Page Range area, click Current Page.

7. Click OK to begin printing.

8. After the page has printed, on the Standard toolbar, click the Save button.

9. On the File menu, click Close.

Additional Printing Options

In the Print dialog box, you can select a variety of options affecting the way your document is printed. Among your choices is a new zoom feature that prints multiple pages on one page and allows you to scale a document to fit various paper sizes. For example, if your document page is set up for legal-sized paper, but you're printing on letter-sized paper, select Letter 8½ x 11 in the scaling list. To set your printer to adjust to a letter-sized page, on the Tools menu, click Options, and then on the Print tab, select Allow A4/Letter Paper Resizing. The following options are some of those available from the Print dialog box. To open the Print dialog box, on the File menu, click Print.

Print a few pages of a long document

1. In the Print dialog box, in the Page Range area, click Pages.
2. In the Pages area, type page numbers or a page range, separated by commas (for example, *10-14, 17, 20*) and click OK.

Print selected text

1. In the document, select the text you want to print.
2. On the File menu, click Print to display the Print dialog box.
3. In the Page Range area, click Selection, and click OK.

Print and collate several copies

1. In the Print dialog box, in the Number of Copies area, type a number.
2. Select the Collate check box, and click OK.

Print multiple pages on one page

1. In the Print dialog box, in the Zoom area, select a number of pages per printed sheet. (For example, if you want two pages to print on a single page, select 2 Pages.)
2. Click OK.

Scale a document for larger or smaller paper

1. In the Print dialog box, in the Zoom area, select a paper size in the Scale To Paper Size list.
2. Click OK.

Printing Envelopes

Open

With Word, it's easy to address and print an envelope as long as your printer will accept envelopes. On the Tools menu, click Envelopes And Labels. In the Envelopes And Labels dialog box, specify the size of envelope or brand of label you want to print.

In the following exercises, you open the 04E practice file and save it as Client Letter 04. Then you print an envelope.

Open a letter and save it with a new name

In this exercise, you open a letter and save it with a new name.

1. On the Standard toolbar, click the Open button.
   The Open dialog box appears.
2. Click the Look In drop-down arrow, and then select your hard disk.
3. In the list of folders, double-click the Office 8in1 Step by Step folder. Double-click the Word Practice folder, and then double-click the Lesson04 folder.
4. In the file list, double-click the 04E file to open it.
   This is a letter from your firm to a client, Pacific Books.
5. On the File menu, click Save As.
   The Save As dialog box appears.
6. Be sure that the Lesson04 folder appears in the Save In box.
7. In the File Name box, select the text, and then type **Client Letter 04**
8. Click Save.

tip

The default envelope size is a standard #10 business envelope. To print an envelope of a different size, on the Tools menu, click Envelopes And Labels. In the Envelopes And Labels dialog box, click Options. In the Envelope Options dialog box, click the Envelope Options tab. In the Envelope size area, select the appropriate size. To position your envelope for printing, consult the documentation that came with your printer. If your envelope isn't printed correctly, click the Feed area of the Envelopes And Labels dialog box and see the default settings and other position options that Word offers.

Print an envelope

In this exercise, you print an envelope.

1. Select the recipient's address at the top of the letter.
2. Place an envelope in your printer.
3. On the Tools menu, click Envelopes And Labels.

   The Envelopes And Labels dialog box appears.
4. In the Envelopes And Labels dialog box, be sure that the recipient's address and the return address are correct. The return address is based on information you entered when you installed the software. If either address is wrong, type the corrections.
5. Click Print.

   Your printer prints the addressed envelope.

> **tip**
>
> To avoid having to add the return address each time you print an envelope, on the Tools menu, click Options. On the User Information tab, type the name and address information that you always want to use as your return address. Click OK.

One Step Further Shrinking a Document to Fit

If you are not working through this lesson sequentially, before proceeding to the next step, open the 04E file (Lesson04 folder), and save it as Client Letter 04.

When you view a document in the Print Preview window, you see that the last page contains only a small amount of text. You might decide that the document would look better if all the text were on one page. Rather than editing your text, you can use the Shrink To Fit feature in Print Preview to reduce the number of pages by one. Word does this by reducing the document font sizes.

> **important**
>
> To undo a Shrink To Fit command, on the Edit menu, click Undo Tools Shrink To Fit. If you have saved and closed the document after using Shrink To Fit, you will have to manually restore the document to the original font sizes.

Shorten the letter by one page

In this exercise, you use Shrink To Fit to reduce the length of a letter by one page.

Print Preview

1. On the Standard toolbar, click the Print Preview button.

Multiple Pages

2. On the Print Preview toolbar, click the Multiple Pages button, move your pointer over the first and second boxes to display both pages of the letter, and then click.

Shrink To Fit

3. On the Print Preview toolbar, click the Shrink To Fit button.

   The letter shrinks to fit on one page.
4. Close the Print Preview window to return to Print Layout view.
5. Scroll through the letter to view the changes.

Save

6. On the Standard toolbar, click the Save button. Changes made to Client Letter 04 are saved.

Finish the lesson

1. On the Standard toolbar, click Save.

   Changes made to Book Fair 04 are saved.
2. On the File menu, click Close.
3. If you want to quit Word for now, on the File menu, click Exit.

Lesson 4 Quick Reference

To	Do this	Button
Display a document in Print Preview	On the Standard toolbar, click the Print Preview button.	
Change from single-page view to multiple-page view	On the Standard toolbar, click the Print Preview button. On the Print Preview toolbar, click the Multiple Pages button and select the number of pages you want to display.	
Magnify text for editing in Print Preview	On the Standard toolbar, click the Print Preview button. In the Print Preview window, position the mouse pointer on the document. When the pointer changes to a magnifying glass, click the area of the document you want to magnify.	

Lesson 4 Quick Reference

To	Do this	Button
Edit text in Print Preview	On the Standard toolbar, click Print Preview. On the Print Preview toolbar, click the Magnifier button to turn the magnifying glass into the insertion point.	
Insert a page break	Click where you want the page break, and on the Insert menu, click Break. In the Break dialog box, select Page Break, and then click OK.	
Adjust margins using the ruler	Place the pointer on the edge of the ruler, where the margin marker is, and wait for the pointer to change into a double-headed arrow. Press Alt and then drag to change the margins.	
Print a whole document	On the Standard toolbar, click the Print button. Or, on the Print Preview toolbar, click the Print button.	
Print part of a document using dialog box options	On the File menu, click Print. Select the options you want in the Print dialog box. Click Print.	
Print an envelope	Open a letter file and select the recipient's address. On the Tools menu, click Envelopes And Labels. Position the envelope in your printer. In the Envelopes And Labels dialog box, click Print.	
Shrink a document to fit on one page	On the Standard toolbar, click the Print Preview button. On the Print Preview toolbar, click the Multiple Pages button, display both pages, and then click the Shrink To Fit button.	

PART 2

Microsoft Excel 2000

LESSON

1

Working in the Excel Environment

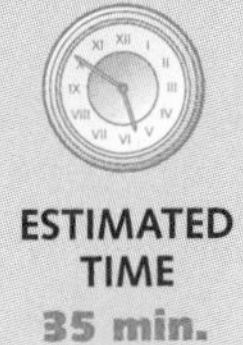

ESTIMATED TIME
35 min.

In this lesson you will learn how to:

- ✔ *Open and save a workbook.*
- ✔ *Move around in a workbook.*
- ✔ *Enter and edit text and numbers manually and automatically.*
- ✔ *Undo and redo changes.*
- ✔ *Check spelling.*
- ✔ *Customize Excel 2000.*

Microsoft Excel 2000 offers features that make working in a spreadsheet environment fast and easy. In this part of the book, you will work with Excel and see for yourself what a powerful analysis tool it is. You will also learn about features new to Excel 2000 and how they can enhance your work.

You can get faster results with the new streamlined menus and toolbars that help you navigate easily through the features that you most often use. Excel 2000 also provides an improved Office Assistant to provide help by answering your questions and offering tips.

As you use this book, imagine that you are a partner in Impact Public Relations, a small public relations firm. Your company recently installed Office 2000 and is about to begin developing several electronic templates, using Excel 2000. You have assumed the responsibility for creating the templates which will be used by employees for invoicing, reporting business expenditures, and other similar tasks. Your first task, however, is to become familiar with the basic features of Excel 2000.

More Buttons

important

If you don't see a button on your toolbar, click the More Buttons drop-down arrow for that toolbar to display a list of additional toolbar buttons. In this list, click the toolbar button that you want to use. This executes the command and adds the button to the toolbar, replacing one that has not been used for a while. If you want to display the Standard and Formatting toolbars separately, on the View menu, point to Toolbars, and then click Customize. In the Customize dialog box, on the Options tab, clear the Standard And Formatting Toolbars Share One Row check box, and click Close. For more information on the new Excel 2000 personalized toolbar and menu features, see the One Step Further section, "Customizing Excel," at the end of this lesson.

Getting Started with Excel 2000

Each new Excel workbook consists of three blank, individual worksheets.

You are ready to get started with Excel 2000. When the program opens, you see that the Excel workspace consists of five areas: the workbook window, the menu bar, the Standard and Formatting toolbars, the formula bar, and the status bar.

A *workbook* is Excel's basic working environment. This is where you work and store your data. When opened, a new workbook window displays a blank worksheet. Each workbook can contain multiple *worksheets* that are used to organize various kinds of related information in a single workbook file (for example, an expense workbook entitled YearToDate.xls could contain 12 worksheets—a January worksheet, a February worksheet, a March worksheet, and so on). All worksheets for a single workbook are stored together as a convenient single file. In the following exercises, you will open an existing workbook file—the 01A.xls practice file provided—and save it with a new filename.

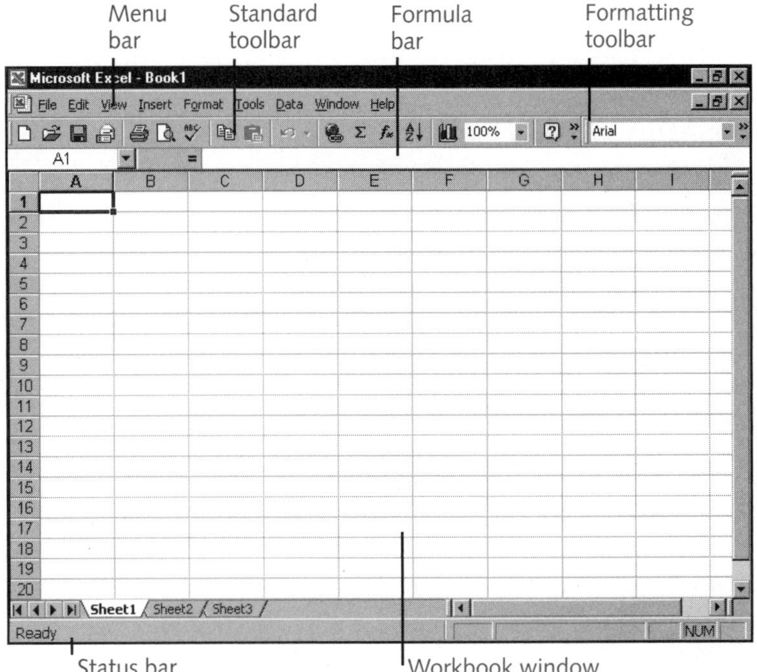

Open an existing workbook

In this exercise, you start Microsoft Excel 2000 and open an existing Excel workbook using the practice file 01A.xls.

1. On the taskbar at the bottom of your screen, click the Start button.

   The Start menu appears.

2. On the Start menu, point to Programs, and then click Microsoft Excel.

   Microsoft Excel 2000 opens.

Open

3. On the Standard toolbar, click the Open button.

   The Open dialog box appears.

4. In the Look In drop-down list, select your hard disk.

   The names of all folders and files on your hard disk are displayed in the Open dialog box.

5. Scroll down, if necessary, to locate the Office 8in1 Step by Step folder, and double-click it. Then double-click the Excel Practice folder.

   The names of all folders in the Excel Practice folder are displayed in the Open dialog box.

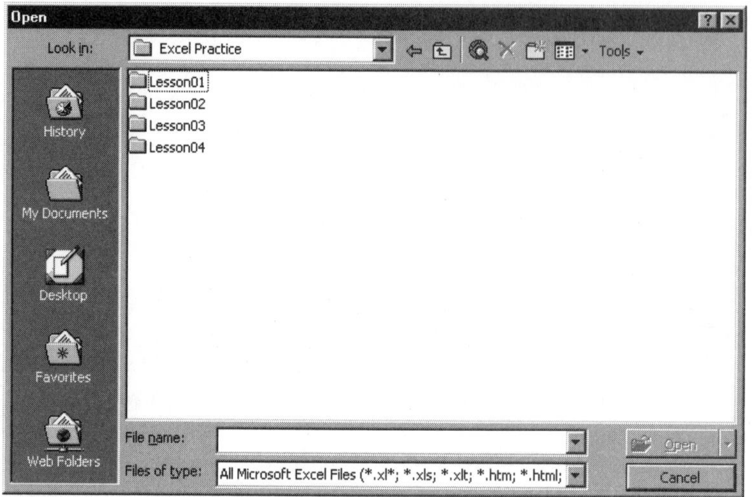

6. Double-click the Lesson01 folder.

   The names of all files in the Lesson01 folder are displayed in the Open dialog box.

7. Double-click the 01A.xls file.

   The Open dialog box closes, and the 01A.xls workbook opens.

Meet the Office Assistant

By now, the Office Assistant has probably made an appearance on your screen, so now is a great time to introduce it. If it did not appear, you can easily reach it—on the Help menu, click Show The Office Assistant.

The default Office Assistant for Office 2000 is Clippit the paper clip, an animated character that appears on your screen to offer help.

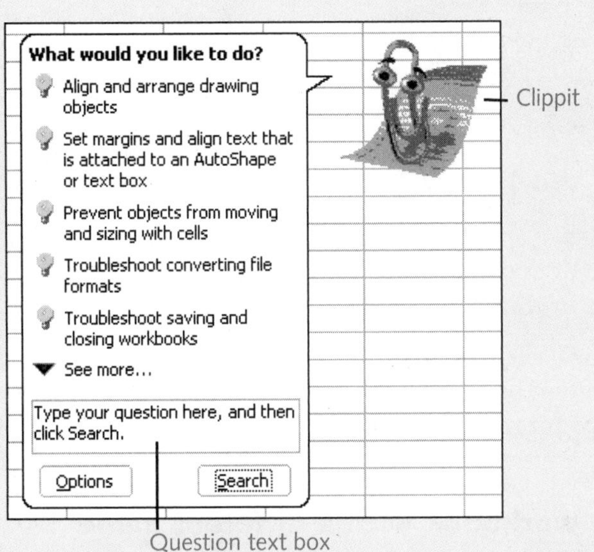

To get help from the Office Assistant, simply click in the Type Your Question Here, And Then Click Search box, and then type your question. Then click the Search button or press Enter. After a few moments of pondering, the Office Assistant displays a list of possible topics relating to your question. You can check out these topics by clicking your choice.

From time to time as you work, the Office Assistant automatically appears with a light bulb overhead. When this happens, the Office Assistant has a tip about the action that you are performing. Simply click the light bulb to display the helpful information.

If you receive the message **The Selected Assistant Character Is Not Available...**, *click No, and then click Cancel.*

You can specify the type of assistance that you want from the Office Assistant for both help and tips. To do so, right-click the Office Assistant, and then on the shortcut menu, click Options. This opens the Office Assistant dialog box. On the Options tab, customize the Office Assistant by selecting the check boxes for those options you want turned on or by clearing the check boxes for those that you want turned off. You can also turn off the Office Assistant entirely by simply clearing the Use The Office Assistant check box.

If the Open dialog box is on the screen, the Office Assistant's Options command will be inactive.

You can even select a different animated character as your Office Assistant—for example, Rocky, the Dot, the Genius, or Mother Nature. To do so, on the bottom of the Office Assistant dialog box, click the Options button. Then, on the Gallery tab, scroll through the characters using the Back and Next buttons. When you see the one you'd like, click OK.

important

For the purposes of this book, the Office Assistant should not appear on your screen. On the Help menu, click Hide The Office Assistant.

Saving a Workbook File

When you save an existing file with a different name, you actually create a duplicate of the original file on your computer's hard disk. This allows the original file to remain unchanged.

When saving a file, you need to specify two things: the new name for the file, and the location on your computer's hard disk or the Internet/intranet server where you want to store the new file. For the purposes of this book, you are going to save files in the Excel Practice folder on your hard drive.

Save the workbook with a different name

In this exercise, you save 01A.xls with a different filename.

1. On the File menu, click Save As.

   The Save As dialog box appears and the current filename is selected.

If you are not working through this exercise sequentially, navigate to the Office 8in1 Step by Step folder on your hard disk, double-click the Lesson01 folder, and open the 01A.xls workbook.

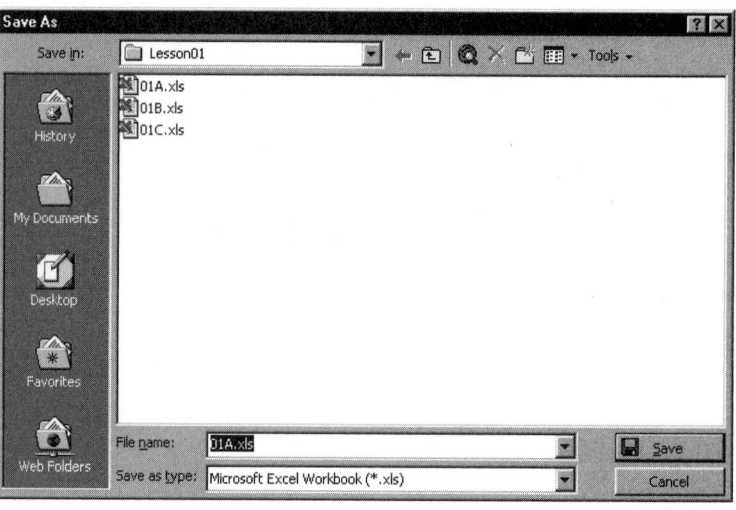

2. In the File Name box, type **Getting_Started**.

tip

When you type a new filename in the File Name box of the Save As dialog box, it is not necessary to type the .xls file extension at the end. Simply type the filename without the file extension, and then click Save. Excel automatically assigns the appropriate file extension to the filename based on the format designated in the Save As Type box.

3. Click the Save button.

   The Save As dialog box closes, and the file is saved with the new name as shown in the title bar.

Navigating Easily in a Workbook

So that you can easily move around in a workbook to view its contents, Excel provides several easy-to-use navigating tools. These navigating tools always appear at the bottom of the workbook window in the form of sheet tabs and sheet tab scroll buttons.

Sheet tabs represent the separate worksheets within a workbook and are displayed as tabs at the bottom of the workbook window. They resemble the index divider page tabs in a three-ring binder. When you click a sheet tab, the corresponding worksheet is displayed in the window and becomes the *active sheet*.

Sheet tab scroll buttons—located at the bottom of a workbook window in the lower-left corner—also help you navigate through a workbook. The two sheet tab scroll buttons in the middle move the tabs one worksheet at a time in the direction indicated. The two outermost tab scroll buttons give you the ability to view the first or last tab in the workbook, depending on which direction you choose. Hence, they are called the First Tab button and the Last Tab button. Unlike sheet tabs, tab scroll buttons do not activate a sheet. They only allow you to scroll through workbook sheet tabs to view the tab titles. Once you click a sheet tab, that worksheet becomes the active sheet.

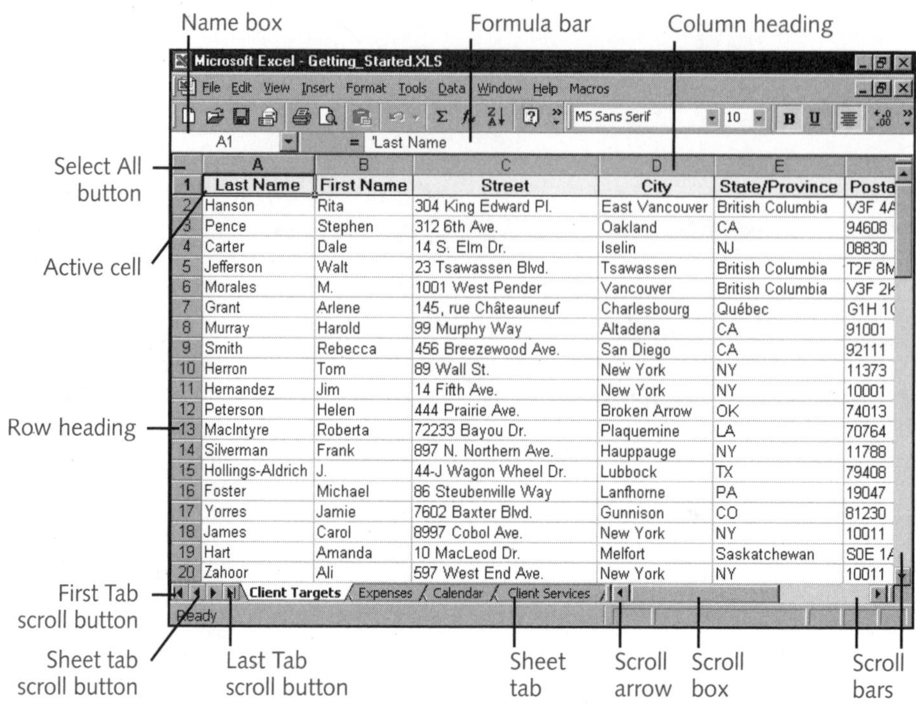

Select individual worksheets

If you are not working through this lesson sequentially, open the file 01A.xls from the Lesson01 folder before you continue.

At first glance, you can see that the workbook has at least four worksheets. In this exercise, you select different sheets and scroll through the workbook to view all of its contents.

1. In the workbook, click the Recap sheet tab.

   The Recap worksheet becomes the active sheet.

2. Click the First Tab scroll button and then click the Client Targets sheet tab.

   The Client Targets worksheet becomes the active sheet.

3. Click the Last Tab scroll button.

   You move to Sheet16, the last sheet tab in the workbook. However, Sheet16 does not become the active sheet; Client Targets is still the active sheet.

You can press Ctrl+Page Up to move to the previous worksheet or Ctrl+Page Down to move to the next worksheet in a workbook.

4. Click the Sheet16 tab.

   Sheet16 becomes the active sheet.

5. Right-click any sheet tab scroll button.

   A shortcut menu lists the names of all of the worksheets in the workbook; Sheet16 is checked as the active sheet.

6. On the shortcut menu, click Client Targets.

   The Client Targets sheet becomes the active sheet.

Navigating Easily in a Worksheet

A worksheet is like an automated ledger sheet consisting of columns and rows. *Columns* run vertically in a worksheet. The gray area at the top of each column is called a *column heading*. Each column heading contains a unique letter that identifies that column. *Rows* run horizontally in a worksheet. The gray area at the left of each row is called a *row heading*. Each row heading contains a unique number that identifies that row.

Select single or multiple columns and rows in a worksheet

In this exercise, you select rows and columns in the Client Targets worksheet.

If you are not working through this lesson sequentially, open the file 01A.xls from the Lesson01 folder before you continue.

To select your entire worksheet, click the Select All button in the upper-left corner where the column and row headings intersect, or press Ctrl+A.

1. Click column heading A, click column heading C, and then click column heading E.

   Each of these columns is selected when you click its column heading.
2. Click column heading A, hold down the Shift key, and then click column heading D.

   All columns from A through D are selected.
3. Click column heading A, and then drag to column heading D.

   All columns from A through D are selected.
4. Click column heading A, hold down the Ctrl key, and then click the column C and column E headings.

   Only columns A, C, and E are selected.
5. Click row heading 5, click row heading 10, and then click row heading 15.

   Each of these rows is selected when you click its row heading.
6. Click row heading 5, hold down Shift, and then click row heading 10.

   All rows from 5 through 10 are selected.
7. Click row heading 2 and then drag through the row headings to row heading 10.

   All rows from 2 through 10 are selected.
8. Click row heading 1, hold down Ctrl, and then click row headings 5 and 10.

   Only rows 1, 5, and 10 are selected.

Cells and Ranges of Cells

The box where a row and column intersect is called a *cell*. Each cell has a *cell reference,* the unique name or address assigned to the cell based on its column and row location in the worksheet. For example, the cell reference for the cell that intersects column A and row 1 is A1.

The mouse pointer is properly positioned for selecting a cell or range of cells when it appears as a white plus sign.

Before you can work with a cell, you must first select it. Once selected, it becomes the *active cell,* and its reference is displayed in the Name box at the left end of the formula bar. Although only one cell can be active at a time, you can select a group of cells, called a *range*.

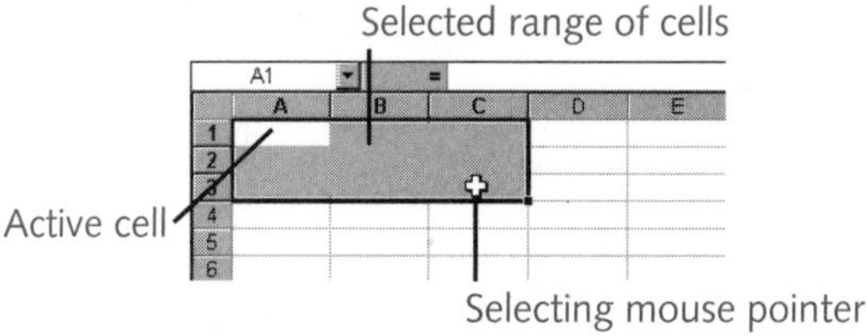

Select a cell or ranges of cells

In this exercise, you select a single cell and a range of cells in the Client Targets worksheet.

1. In the Client Targets worksheet, click cell A3.

   Cell A3 becomes the active cell; its reference is displayed in the Name box, and its contents are displayed in the formula bar. The headings for column A and row 3 are bold and raised.

2. Click cell A2 and drag to cell E5.

   Cell A2 is the active cell within the selected range of cells, and the column and row headings in the range are bold and raised.

3. Press and hold down Ctrl, click cell A11, and then drag to cell E12.

   Two rectangular ranges of cells are selected, and cell A11 is the active cell.

Using Quick Features

In Excel, there might be more than one way to quickly and easily perform the same task. Learning some of the quick ways to select a cell using your mouse pointer, a menu option, or the keyboard can save you time when working in a large worksheet.

Learning quick ways to move around your worksheet can also save you time. One way is by using the *scroll bars* along the right side and bottom of the workbook window. Each scroll bar has *scroll arrows* at either end. These allow you to move through the worksheet one column or row at a time. Located within the scroll bar itself is a *scroll box* that indicates the position of the window over the worksheet.

D	E	
City	State/Province	Posta
East Vancouver	British Columbia	V3F 4A
Oakland	CA	94608
Iselin	NJ	08830
Tsawassen	British Columbia	T2F 8M
Vancouver	British Columbia	V3F 2K
Charlesbourg	Québec	G1H 1(
Altadena	CA	91001
San Diego	CA	92111
New York	NY	11373
New York	NY	10001
Broken Arrow	OK	74013
Plaquemine	LA	70764
Hauppauge	NY	11788
Lubbock	TX	79408
Lanthorne	PA	19047
Gunnison	CO	81230

NUM

Scroll box

Scroll bar

Scroll arrows

Scroll box

In these two exercises, you use some of Excel's quick and easy features to select cells and move around a large worksheet.

Use quick features to activate a cell

In this exercise, you use some of Excel's timesaving features to quickly select cells in the Client Targets worksheet.

1. At the left end of the formula bar, click inside the Name box.

   The cell reference displayed in the Name box is highlighted.

2. In the Name box, type **G58** and press Enter.

   The screen scrolls down, and cell G58 becomes the active cell.

3. On the Edit menu, click Go To.

   The Go To dialog box appears.

To quickly display the Go To dialog box, press Ctrl+G.

To instantly move the active cell back to the beginning of the worksheet, press Ctrl+Home.

4. In the Reference box, type **A1** and click the OK button.

   Cell A1 becomes the active cell.

5. Double-click the bottom border of cell A1 with the white arrow mouse pointer.

   The cell at the very bottom of the list becomes the active cell.

6. In the active cell at the bottom of your list, double-click the top border.

   The first cell at the top of the list becomes the active cell.

Use quick features to move around a worksheet

In this exercise, you use Excel's scroll bars to quickly and easily view different parts of the Client Targets worksheet.

The Name box always displays the active cell reference, regardless of where you scroll the window.

1. In the vertical scroll bar, slowly drag the scroll box downward.

   Your screen should look similar to the following illustration.

You can use ScreenTips to help position the scroll box precisely.

The ScreenTip that appears as you drag the scroll box displays the name of the row that appears at the top of the window when you release the mouse button.

2. On the vertical scroll bar, click the upper scroll arrow several times to move back to the top of the worksheet, one row at a time.
3. On the horizontal scroll bar, click the right or left scroll arrow to scroll the worksheet to the right or left, one column at a time.

To quickly move back to the active cell, press Ctrl+ Backspace.

Entering Information

You can make two basic types of entries in a cell—*constants* and *formulas.*

A constant is an entry that is either a numeric value, text value, or date or time value. A numeric value includes only numerals. A text value includes any other character and can include an entry such as *89 Main Street.*

A formula is a mathematical operation that always begins with an equal sign (=) and performs a calculation using other existing values in a worksheet.

You'll learn more about working with formulas in Lesson 3, "Adding Formulas."

When you begin typing an entry in a cell, three buttons appear on the *Formula bar* at the top of the workbook window. The Enter button (the green check mark) and the Cancel button (the red X) perform a function similar to pressing Enter and Esc on your keyboard, respectively. The Edit Formula button—the equal sign—opens the Formula palette to assist you in constructing a formula.

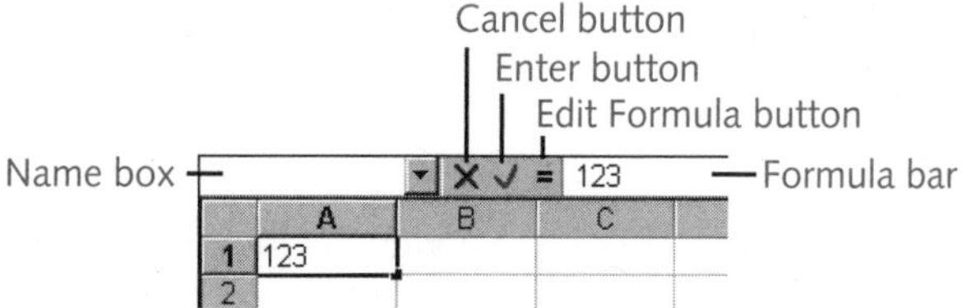

You can enter information either directly in a cell in your worksheet or in the formula bar itself. For the purpose of the exercises in these lessons, you enter information directly in the cells in the worksheet.

You select the cell in which you want to enter information and then begin typing. Either press Enter to enter what you typed and activate the cell directly below, or press the Tab key to enter what you typed and activate the cell to the immediate right. You can also press any arrow key or click another cell to activate it and type information in it.

In these exercises, you learn how to enter data in cells and use some of Excel's automated features to save time.

Enter text and numbers manually

If you are not working through this lesson sequentially, open the file 01A.xls from the Lesson01 folder before you continue.

In this exercise, you record some of next year's planned expenses in the Expenses worksheet.

1. Click the Expenses sheet tab.

   The Expenses worksheet becomes the active sheet.

2. Click cell B17, type **$346** and then press Tab.

   Your entry is displayed in cell B17, and C17 becomes the active cell.

Text that is too long to be displayed in a single cell overlaps adjacent cells. However, the text is stored only in the original cell.

3. In cell C17, type **Office 2000 upgrade** and press Enter.

   Your entry is displayed in cell C17. Cell B18 becomes the active cell because Excel's AutoReturn feature automatically recognizes a pattern in the way in which you are entering data.

4. Move the mouse pointer to the border between column C and column D in the column headings area.

   Your mouse pointer changes to a double-headed arrow.

   Your screen should look similar to the following illustration.

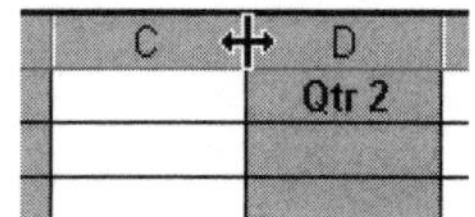

5. Double-click the divider line between column C and column D.
   Column C widens to fit the *Office 2000 upgrade* entry.

Saving Time Using Quick Features

Sometimes, when setting up a new worksheet, you need a series of column or row headings—for example, dates, days of the week, months of the year, or quarters. Excel's AutoFill and Fill Series features can save you lots of time entering series data. For example, a client list worksheet might contain columns for services and the name of a client rep. Excel's AutoComplete and Pick From List features help cut down the amount of typing that you do and increase the accuracy of your entries. AutoComplete scans all of the entries for the column in which you are entering data to determine whether there is a match. If there is, AutoComplete finishes the entry you are typing with the unique match it located in that same column. Pick From List allows you to select an entry from a drop-down list box for the column in which you are entering data.

Save time using AutoFill

In this exercise, you use AutoFill to begin creating a simple calendar that includes a series, the days of the week from Monday through Friday.

1. Click the Calendar sheet tab.

   The Calendar worksheet becomes the active sheet.
2. Click cell B1, type **Monday**, and press Enter.

   Cell B2 becomes the active cell.
3. Click cell B1, and then place the mouse pointer in the lower-right corner of the cell.

   The pointer becomes a small black plus sign. This is called an *AutoFill pointer*.

   Your screen should look similar to the following illustration.

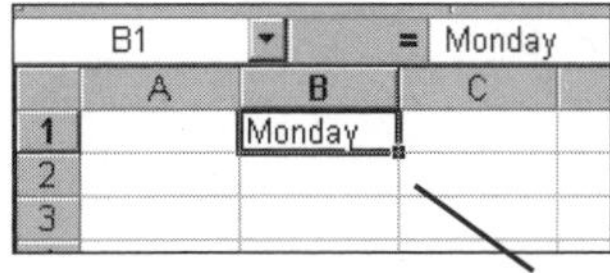

4. From cell B1, drag the AutoFill pointer to cell F1.

   Excel completes the text series with the days of the week.
5. Double-click the divider line between column heading D and column heading E.

   Column D widens to fit the *Wednesday* entry.

Save time using Fill Series

In this exercise, you use Fill Series to complete the calendar by adding a series of hours spaced at half-hour increments.

1. Click cell A2, type **9:00** and press Enter.

   Cell A3 becomes the active cell.
2. In cell A3, Type **9:30** and press Enter.
3. Click cell A2, and then drag to cell A3.

   Cells A2 and A3 are selected.
4. Position the mouse pointer so that the plus sign appears over the AutoFill handle in the lower-right corner of the selected range.
5. Hold down the right mouse button (be sure that it's the right mouse button), drag the AutoFill handle downward to cell A9, and then release the mouse button.

6. On the shortcut menu, click Fill Series.

   Excel completes the number series in half-hour increments.

   Your screen should look similar to the following illustration.

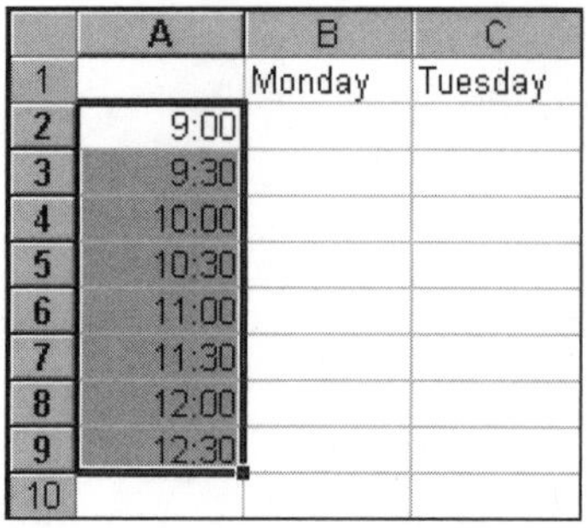

	A	B	C
1		Monday	Tuesday
2	9:00		
3	9:30		
4	10:00		
5	10:30		
6	11:00		
7	11:30		
8	12:00		
9	12:30		
10			

Save time using AutoComplete

In this exercise, you use AutoComplete to enter data in a list.

> **tip**
>
> If AutoComplete doesn't work, it probably isn't turned on. To use AutoComplete, on the Tools menu, click Options. On the Edit tab, select the Enable AutoComplete For Cell Values check box.

1. Click the Client Services sheet tab.

   The Client Services worksheet becomes the active sheet.
2. In the Name box, type **A26** and press Enter.

   Cell A26, at the bottom of the worksheet, becomes the active cell, in which you will enter a new client named *Market Florist*.
3. In cell A26, type **Mar** and then watch what happens in cell A26.

   Margo Tea Company, the unique match in the Company Name column, is displayed in cell A26.
4. Continue typing **ket Florist** and then press Tab.

   Cell B26 becomes the active cell.
5. In cell B26, type **R** and then watch what happens in cell B26.

   Radio ad development, the unique match in the Services column, is displayed in cell B26.

6. Because *Radio ad development* is the correct entry, press Tab to accept that entry.

   Cell C26 becomes the active cell.

Save time by using Pick From List

In this exercise, you use Pick From List to enter data in a list.

1. Ensure that the mouse pointer shaped like a large white plus sign is over cell C26.
2. Right-click the cell, and on the shortcut menu, click Pick From List.

   All unique entries in the Client Rep column are displayed.
3. Click Rita, and then press Tab.

   The word *Rita* is displayed in cell C26, and D26 becomes the active cell.

Save time by using Ctrl+Enter

You can quickly enter the same data into several cells at once by using two keys on your keyboard—Ctrl+Enter.

1. Click the Calendar sheet tab.

   The Calendar worksheet becomes the active sheet.
2. Click cell B8, and then drag to cell F9.

   Cell B8 is the active cell within the selected range.
3. Type **Lunch**

   The word *Lunch* is displayed in cell B8.
4. Press Ctrl+Enter.

   The word *Lunch* is displayed in all cells in the range.

Changing and Correcting Information

It is always a good idea to review your worksheet for accuracy. If your document is small enough, manually correcting a few errors can be done quickly. However, whether your document is large or small, you can use automated Excel features to make the job easier.

In this section, you use Excel's Undo, Redo, and the Spelling Checker commands to make corrections to a worksheet.

Undoing and Redoing

Sometimes you might make errors during the process of correcting errors, or you might decide not to keep a revision that you just made. The Undo and Redo commands help you quickly recover from editing mistakes without having to reenter data.

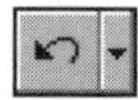

Undo

The Undo button on the Standard toolbar lets you undo your previous action by simply clicking the button. It stores the last 16 actions that you performed and allows you to undo each of those as well. Your last 16 actions are displayed in a list. To access this list, on the Standard toolbar, click the small down arrow next to the Undo button. Then select those actions that you want to undo in order to undo them simultaneously.

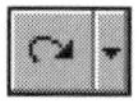

Redo

The Redo button on the Standard toolbar operates in the same way as the Undo button, only in reverse. Each time that you undo an action using the Undo button, that action is transferred to the Redo button drop-down list. You can redo your last undone action by clicking the button itself, or you can redo up to the last 16 undone actions.

Change entries using Undo and Redo

If you are not working through this lesson sequentially, open the file 01B.xls from the Lesson01 folder before you continue.

In this exercise, you make changes and corrections to the Calendar worksheet. Then you undo some of those changes using the Undo and Redo commands.

1. Click the Calendar sheet tab, if necessary.

   The Calendar worksheet becomes the active sheet.
2. Click cell B1, and then drag to cell F1.

   A rectangular range of cells is selected.
3. Press the Delete key.

   The contents of the range are deleted.
4. Click cell A2, and then drag to cell A9.

   A rectangular range of cells is selected.
5. Press Delete.

   The contents of the range are deleted.
6. On the Standard toolbar, click the Undo button.

   Your previous action is undone; the time entries reappear in cells A2 through A9. The Redo button on the Standard toolbar is now active.
7. On the Standard toolbar, click the down arrow next to the Redo button, and then click Clear.

   The entries in cells A2 through A9 are deleted again.

More Buttons

Click More Buttons on the Standard toolbar to locate the Redo button.

You can quickly undo an action in your worksheet by pressing Ctrl+Z.

8. On the Standard toolbar, click the down arrow next to the Undo button. In the list, drag downward to select both Clear actions, and then click.

   All of your previous deletions are undone.

9. Click cell A1, and then drag to cell F9.

10. Right-click within the range of cells, and on the shortcut menu, click Clear Contents.

    The entries in the range of cells are deleted.

Spelling Checker

Spelling

The Spelling Checker is another feature that you can use to correct typing and spelling errors. When you click the Spelling button on the Standard toolbar, the Spelling dialog box appears.

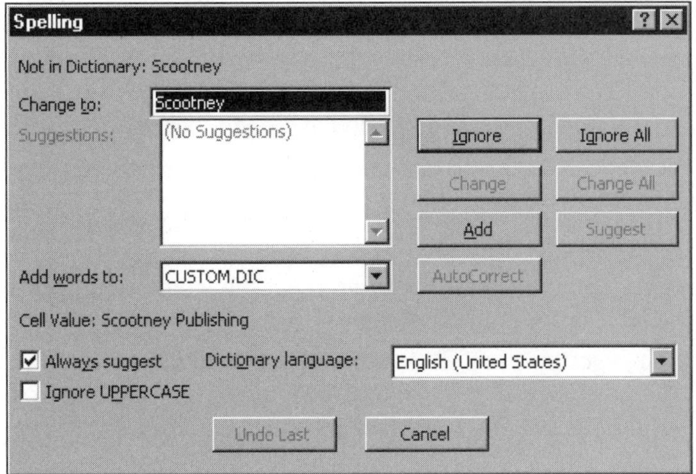

What is checked during a spelling check depends on what you select in your worksheet. If a range of cells is selected, only the range is checked. If a single cell is selected, the Spelling Checker scans the entire worksheet—all cells, comments, graphics, and page headers and footers. If you start the Spelling Checker in the middle of your worksheet, a dialog box prompts you to continue checking at the beginning of the worksheet. Once the spelling check is finished, a message appears with one of two statements, whichever is applicable: *The spelling check is complete for the selected cells* or *The spelling check is complete for the entire sheet.*

Correct entries using the Spelling Checker

In this exercise, you learn how to eliminate spelling errors using the Spelling Checker.

1. Click the Recap sheet tab.

   The Recap worksheet becomes the active sheet, and cell A1 is the active cell.

Spelling

2. On the Standard toolbar, click the Spelling button.

   The Spelling dialog box appears, informing you that the word *YTD*, the entry in cell F3, is not in the dictionary. Because Excel does not recognize *YTD*, the Suggestions box is inactive.

3. Click Ignore.

   The entry in cell F3 remains unchanged. The spelling check continues, and the Spelling dialog box informs you that the word *Equippments*, the entry in cell A18, is not in the dictionary.

   Excel displays *Equipments*—what it guesses the spelling should be—in the Change To box. Alternate words are displayed in the Suggestions box. Because the word is supposed to be *Equipment*, neither option is helpful.

You can manually enter the correct spelling of a word in the Change To box.

4. In the Change To box, click the mouse pointer after the *s* in the word *Equipments*.
5. Press Backspace, and click Change.

   The Spelling dialog box informs you that the word *Maintanence*, the entry in cell A32, is not in the dictionary.

6. In the Suggestions box, click Maintenance, and then click Change.

   The misspelled word in cell A32 is corrected, and a message informing you that the spelling check is complete for the entire sheet is displayed.

7. Click OK.

   The spelling check is complete.

One Step Further: Customizing Excel

Excel menus logically group Excel commands together, making it easy to perform a specific task. For example, if you want to change the formatting of a cell or a column, you can easily find the formatting commands grouped under the Format menu. To access a particular menu, simply point to it on the menu bar and click. Initially, the most frequently used features are displayed as menu commands. However, if you leave the mouse pointer still for a moment, the menu expands and the full selection of commands is displayed.

You can also expand a menu by clicking the down arrows at the bottom of the short menu. Once one expanded menu is displayed on the menu bar, all other menus that you click display their expanded menus, as well.

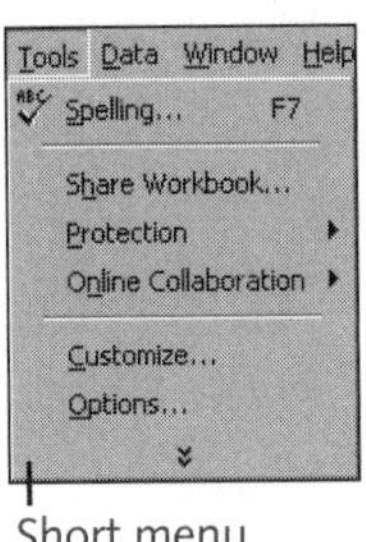

Short menu

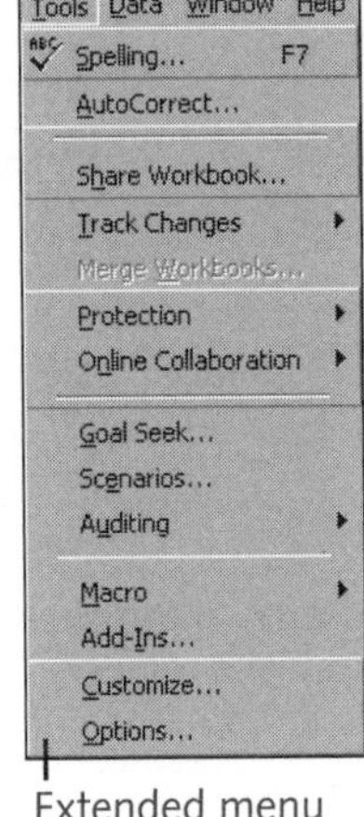

Extended menu

Perhaps you decide that you don't like the way Excel expands a menu when you leave your pointer over it for a moment. You want to be able to click the down arrows at the bottom of the menu yourself, or you might even decide that you don't want to use expanding menus at all. In this exercise, you customize this feature to your preference.

Customize Excel's expanding menus

New

1. On the Standard toolbar, click the New button.

   A new Excel document opens.
2. On the Tools menu, click Customize.

   The Customize dialog box appears.
3. Click the Options tab.

   Your screen should look similar to the illustration on the following page.

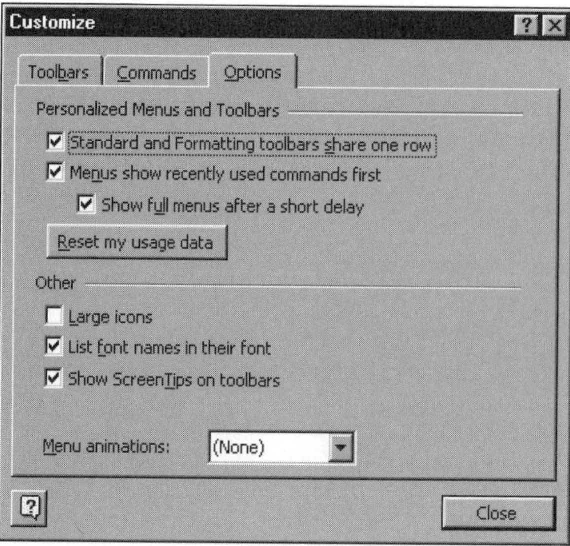

The Options tab lets you customize menus to show recently used commands first or to show full menus after a short delay.

4. Clear the Show Full Menus After A Short Delay check box, and then click Close.
5. Click the Tools menu and leave your pointer over the menu for a moment.

   Notice that the Tools menu does not display the additional menu options.
6. At the bottom of the Tools menu, click the down arrows.

   The Tools menu expands to show all commands.
7. On the Tools menu, click Customize.

   The Customize dialog box appears.
8. On the Options tab, clear the Menus Show Recently Used Commands First check box, and then click Close.
9. Click the Tools menu.

   The Tools menu expands to show all commands.

important

If you keep your menus at the settings made in this section, the illustrations in this book might not look the same as those on your screen. In addition, some of the procedures using the menus might differ. To return your menu to the default settings, on the Tools menu, select Customize. Click the Options tab, and then select the Menus Show Recently Used Commands First and the Show Full Menus After A Short Delay check boxes. Click the Reset My Usage Data button. Click Yes to confirm the reset request, and then close the dialog box.

Finish the lesson

1. To continue to the next lesson, close all open workbooks. When you are prompted to save the changes you made to the new workbook opened in the One Step Further section, click No. When you are prompted to save the changes you made to your Getting_Started workbook, click Yes.
2. If you are finished using Excel for now, on the File menu, click Exit.

Lesson 1 Quick Reference

To	Do this	Button
Open an existing workbook	On the Standard toolbar, click the Open button. Locate the folder in which your file is saved, and then double-click the filename.	

To	Do this
Save an existing workbook with a different name	On the File menu, click Save As. Locate the folder in which you want to save the file. In the File Name box, type the new filename, and then click Save.
Select a worksheet	Click the sheet tab of the worksheet that you want to use.
Select a single column	Click the column heading of the column that you want.
Select multiple adjacent columns or rows	Click the column or row heading for the first column that you want to select, hold down Shift, and then click the column heading for the last column that you want to select.
Select multiple nonadjacent columns or rows	Hold down Ctrl, and then click each nonadjacent column or row heading.
Select a cell	Click the cell you want.
Select a range of cells	Click the first cell of the range, hold down mouse button, and then drag through the cells to the opposite diagonal corner of the range that you want to select.
Enter text and numbers manually	Select a cell. Type the text or numbers that you want, and then press Tab or Enter.

Lesson 1 Quick Reference

To	Do this
Enter text and numbers using AutoReturn	Click a cell in a new row of a list to activate it. Type data in the cell, and then press Tab to accept the entry and activate the next cell. Repeat this process across the row until the last cell in the row is activated. In the last cell, type the entry and press Enter (not Tab).
Enter text and numbers automatically using AutoFill	Click a cell, type the entry for the series you want to begin creating, and press Enter. Click the cell again and place the mouse pointer in the lower-right corner of the cell. Drag the AutoFill handle to select the ranges that you want to contain the information.
Enter text and numbers automatically using Fill Series	Click a cell, type an entry for the series that you want to begin creating, and press Enter. Click the cell again to select it and place the mouse pointer in the lower-right corner of the cell to display the AutoFill handle. Hold down the right mouse button and drag the AutoFill handle to a cell that you want. Release the mouse button, and on the shortcut menu, select Fill Series.
Enter text automatically using AutoComplete	Click a cell in a list and begin typing your entry. Press Tab or Enter to accept the suggested entry.
Enter text automatically using Pick From List	Click a cell in a list to activate it. Right-click the cell, and on the shortcut menu, select Pick From List. In the drop-down list box, click the entry that you want, and then press Tab or Enter to accept the entry and activate the next cell.
Enter text in multiple cells simultaneously	Select a range of cells. In the active cell, enter the text. Press Ctrl+Enter.
Change information manually	Click the cell containing the information that you want to change. Type the correct information and press Enter or Tab, or click another cell.

Lesson 1 Quick Reference

To	Do this	Button
Undo a previous action or up to 16 previous actions	On the Standard toolbar, click the Undo button to undo the last action, or click the Undo drop-down arrow to undo a series of previous actions.	
Redo an undone action or up to 16 previous undone actions	On the Standard toolbar, click the Redo button to redo the previously undone action, or click the Redo drop-down arrow to redo a series of previously undone actions.	
Check spelling	On the Standard toolbar, click the Spelling button.	
Customize expanding menus so that all menu options are displayed	On the Tools menu, click Customize. In the Customize dialog box, on the Options tab, clear the Menus Show Recently Used Commands First check box, and then click Close.	

Setting Up a Worksheet

ESTIMATED TIME **30 min.**

In this lesson you will learn how to:

- ✔ *Add a keyword to the workbook properties.*
- ✔ *Name worksheets.*
- ✔ *Enter labels and adjust the layout.*
- ✔ *Add comments and set data validation.*
- ✔ *Change cell alignment and wrapping.*
- ✔ *Preview and print a worksheet.*
- ✔ *Add a picture to a worksheet.*
- ✔ *Format an inserted picture.*

In this lesson, you will begin creating a new online invoice for Impact Public Relations. You will open a new workbook and format it by adding and positioning text entries, adding instructions for other employees, and setting rules so that only the appropriate data can be entered in specific cells. You'll then preview and print a copy of the new invoice. This invoice, which you'll continue to build in future lessons, will be the basis for the *template* that you'll create in Lesson 4, "Dressing Up a Worksheet."

Templates are like stencils; you use the same basic pattern over and over again, and just change the color of paint to create a different look. Like stencils, templates let you reuse the same basic invoice structure, so you don't have to redo the formatting work the next time you need to create an invoice. Creating an invoice in the form of a template will save you time and make you a more productive partner at Impact Public Relations.

Setting Up a New Workbook

In this exercise, you take the first steps in creating an invoice for Impact Public Relations, save it with a keyword so that it's easy to find later, and then name individual worksheets in the invoice workbook.

When you open Microsoft Excel, a new, blank workbook opens on your screen, and you can start using it right away. Because you are going to use this workbook many times for billing Impact's customers, you want to save this blank workbook with a descriptive filename indicating that it is to be used as the invoice template. Then you add a *keyword* to the *file properties* of your Impact Public Relations invoice. File properties include the document title, subject, author, and keywords that help distinguish each file that you create. You can add keywords to your file properties to help you find a specific file among the hundreds that can accumulate in your folders.

To learn more about formulas, turn to Lesson 3, "Adding Formulas."

If a workbook contains several pages (or *worksheets*), the names on the sheet tabs are important for identifying each sheet and helping you to quickly locate the sheet with which you want to work. For example, a new, blank workbook opens with three worksheets, which are named Sheet1, Sheet2, and Sheet3. More descriptive names for each worksheet save you time when you're looking for specific data. A descriptive sheet tab name might also be used in a formula, and it provides the default header for the printed page.

More Buttons

important

If you don't see a button on your toolbar, click the More Buttons drop-down arrow for that toolbar to display a list of additional toolbar buttons. In this list, click the toolbar button that you want to use. This executes the command and adds the button to the toolbar, replacing one that has not been used for a while. If you want to display the Standard And Formatting toolbars separately, on the View menu, point to Toolbars, and then click Customize. In the Customize dialog box, on the Options tab, clear the Standard And Formatting Toolbars Share One Row check box, and click Close. For more information on the new Excel 2000 personalized toolbar and menu features, see the One Step Further section, "Customizing Excel," in Lesson 1.

Create and save a new workbook

In this exercise, you open and name a new workbook, and then you save it in your Excel Practice folder.

1. On the taskbar at the bottom of your screen, click the Start button.

   The Start menu appears.

2. On the Start menu, point to Programs, and then click Microsoft Excel.

   Microsoft Excel 2000 opens to a new, blank workbook.

New

3. On the Standard toolbar, click the New button.

   A new workbook appears.

Save

4. On the Standard toolbar, click the Save button.

   The Save As dialog box appears.

5. In the Save In drop-down list, select your hard disk, and then double-click the Office 8in1 Step by Step folder. Double-click the Excel Practice folder.

   The original filename is displayed in the File Name box.

6. In the File Name box, double-click, and then type **IPR_Invoice**
7. Click Save.

   The file is saved in the Excel Practice folder, and the new filename is displayed in the title bar.

Understanding File Properties

You can search for a file using one of the many file properties that are recorded for each file that you create. Some properties, such as Author and Date Last Saved, are automatically recorded by Excel. Other file properties, such as Keyword and Subject, must be entered manually. For example, if you create monthly revenue workbooks, you can add the keyword *revenue* to each of these files. Later, when you search for the word *revenue*, Excel finds all the files that have that keyword as a file property.

Add a keyword

In this exercise, you add the keyword *invoice* to your invoice worksheet. When you create a template from this worksheet, all copies of the template contain this keyword. This makes finding and organizing customer invoices much easier.

1. On the File menu, click Properties.

   The IPR_Invoice Properties dialog box appears.

2. On the Summary tab, click inside the Keywords box, and then type **Invoice**

   The Properties dialog box should look similar to the following illustration.

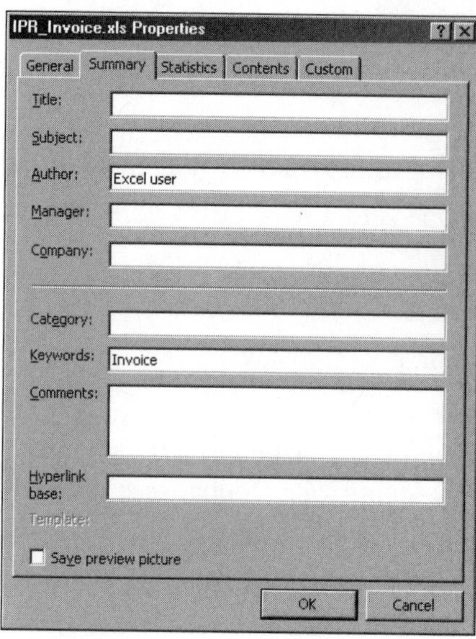

3. Click OK.

Save

4. On the Standard toolbar, click the Save button.

   The new keyword is saved in the file properties.

Name the worksheets in the workbook

In this exercise, you name the invoice worksheet *Invoice*, a more meaningful name than the default name, *Sheet1*.

To change a worksheet name, you can also right-click the worksheet tab and then, on the shortcut menu, click Rename.

1. At the bottom of the page, double-click the Sheet1 sheet tab.

   The sheet name on the tab is selected and ready to be edited.

   Your worksheet should look similar to the following illustration.

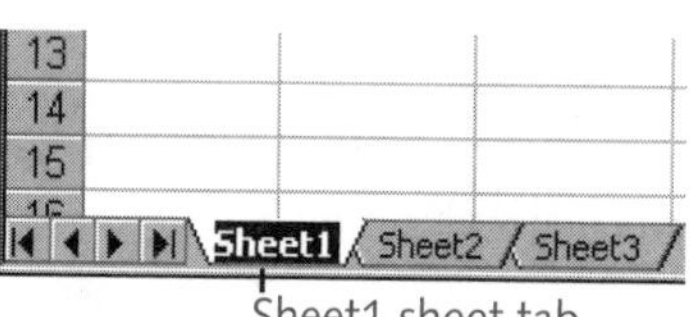

2. Type **Invoice** and press Enter.

   The sheet is renamed *Invoice*, as shown on the sheet tab. Your worksheet should look similar to the following illustration.

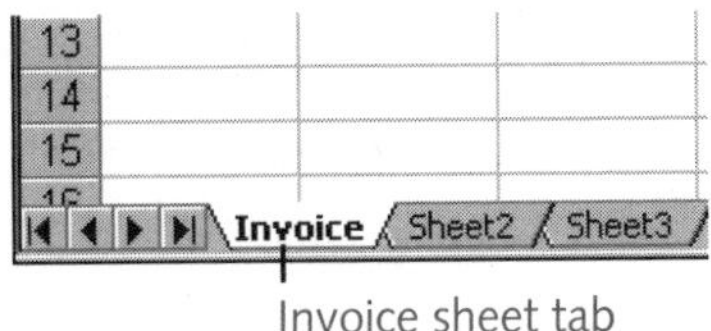

Invoice sheet tab

Setting Up an Invoice

Your Invoice worksheet is to be a standard form that the Impact Public Relations sales staff can fill out online, print, and then mail or fax to customers. You create the Invoice worksheet in stages. Next you build the foundation of the invoice by entering and arranging labels. In later lessons, you add formulas to the worksheet so that your calculations are automatic, and then you apply formatting to the worksheet to give the invoice a professional look.

Enter labels on an invoice

In this exercise, you enter labels for various areas of the invoice.

If you are not working through this lesson sequentially, open the file 02A.xls from the Lesson02 folder before you continue.

1. In cell A1, type **Account Name** and press Enter.
2. In cell A2, type **Address** and press Enter.
3. In cell A3, type **City and State** and press Enter.
4. In cell A4, type **Zip + 4** and press Enter.
5. In cell A5, type **Work Performed** and press Enter.
6. In cell A6, type **Task Name** and then press Tab.
7. In cell B6, type **Description** and then press Tab.
8. In cell C6, type **$ Billed** and press Enter.

Your worksheet should look similar to the following illustration.

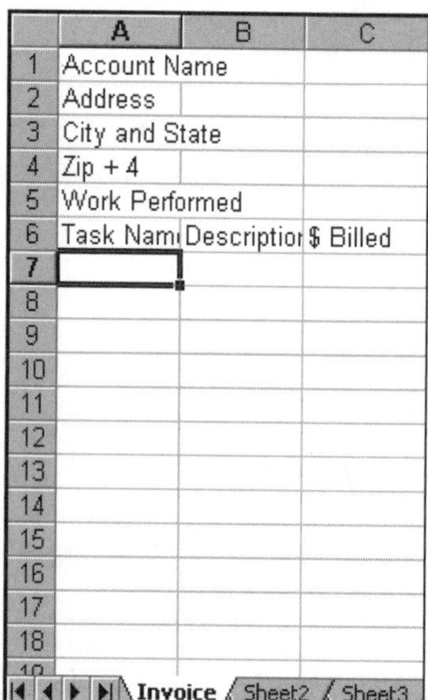

Adjust the layout

In this exercise, you merge cells and adjust column widths to organize your worksheet and make the best use of the page space. You also change the text alignment to improve the look of the invoice.

Merge And Center

1. Select cells A1 through G1. Then on the Formatting toolbar, click the Merge And Center button.

   The text is aligned in the center of the merged cells.
2. Repeat this step for cells A5 though G5.
3. Drag the right border of the column A heading until the entries in cells A2 through A6 fit within the column.

   As you drag a column border, a ScreenTip appears indicating the column width.
4. Select cells A2 through A4, hold down the Ctrl key, and then click cell A6.

   You have selected a nonsequential range.

Center

5. On the Formatting toolbar, click the Center button.

   Your worksheet should look similar to the following illustration.

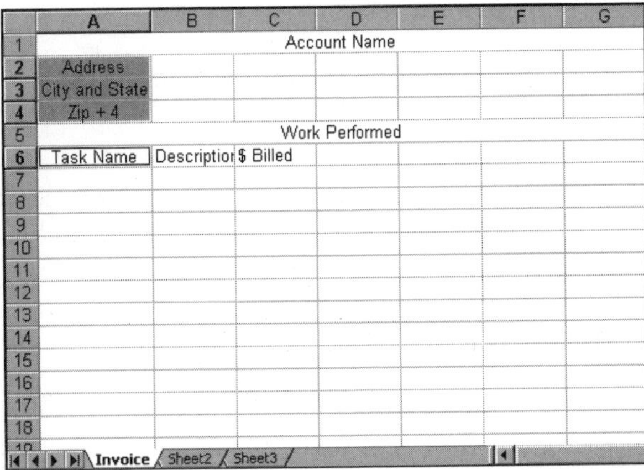

Add a promotional message

In this exercise, you enter a promotional message in the Invoice worksheet to encourage future business.

Merge And Center

1. In cell A10, type **We help your business make an Impact!** and press Enter.

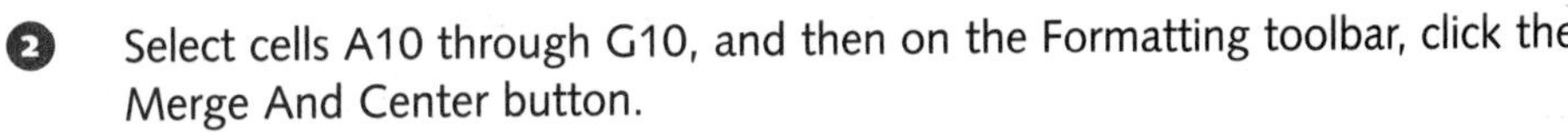

2. Select cells A10 through G10, and then on the Formatting toolbar, click the Merge And Center button.

   The text in cells A10 through G10 is aligned in the center of the merged cells.

   Your worksheet should look similar to the following illustration.

	A	B	C	D	E	F	G
1				Account Name			
2	Address						
3	City and State						
4	Zip + 4						
5				Work Performed			
6	Task Name	Descriptior	$ Billed				
7							
8							
9							
10				We help your business make an Impact!			
11							
12							
13							
14							
15							
16							
17							
18							

Invoice / Sheet2 / Sheet3

Previewing the Invoice and Making Additional Adjustments

If you are not working through this lesson sequentially, open the file 02B.xls from the Lesson02 folder before you continue.

You're about to print your Invoice worksheet. But before you do, it's a good idea to preview your worksheet to see how it is going to look in print. This way, you get a clear view of the layout of the printed page, and you can find and fix small errors before printing the worksheet.

Preview the invoice

Print Preview

1. On the Standard toolbar, click the Print Preview button.

   The Preview window appears, letting you see what the worksheet is going to look like when you print it.

2. Move the mouse pointer over any part of the preview page. When the pointer takes the shape of a magnifying glass, click the preview page.

   A close-up of the area you clicked appears.

Adjust a column width in Print Preview

You notice that the column for Description is too narrow. In this exercise, you adjust it in Print Preview.

The gridlines are visible on your worksheet, but not in Print Preview. To be sure the gridlines are printed, on the File menu, click Page Setup. On the Sheet tab, select the Gridlines check box.

1. On the toolbar in Print Preview, click the Margins button.
2. Scroll to the top of the page.
3. Place the mouse pointer on the third vertical margin marker from the left. Then drag it to the right until the label, Description, fits in the column.
4. Click Close.

   Your worksheet reappears.

Add a row

When you return to the worksheet, you realize that the invoice doesn't contain a row for customer phone numbers. In this exercise, you add that row.

To delete a column or row, right-click the column or row heading. Then on the shortcut menu, click Delete.

1. Right-click the heading for row 5.

   Row 5 is selected, and a shortcut menu appears.
2. On the shortcut menu, click Insert.

   The new row appears above row 5. All of the following rows are renumbered.
3. In cell A5, type **Phone Number** and press Enter.
4. If necessary, readjust the width of column A by dragging the right border of the column A heading until all entries in that column fit.

Adding Other Useful Features to an Invoice

Because your invoice is to be used by several people at Impact Public Relations, you want to add some instructions and data validation to ensure that the invoice is used correctly. Data *validation* prevents other users from entering inaccurate data, such as text in a cell that should contain a number value. This reduces errors and helps you maintain control over the data entered in the invoice.

Add comments to an invoice

In this exercise, you add a comment to help your co-workers enter information into the invoice.

If you are not working through this lesson sequentially, open the file 02C.xls from the Lesson02 folder before you continue.

1. In the Invoice worksheet, select cell A7 (Task Name).
2. On the Insert menu, click Comment.

   A comment box labeled with your user name appears in the worksheet.

> **tip**
>
> To change the way your name appears in the comment box, on the File menu, click Properties. In the Properties dialog box, click the Summary tab. In the Author box, type your name as you'd like it to appear, and click OK.

3. Type **Enter each task name on a separate row.**

   Your worksheet should look similar to the following illustration.

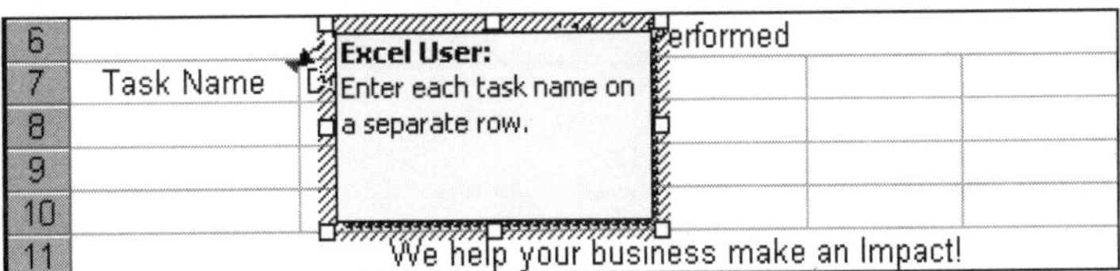

4. Click anywhere outside the comment box.

   The comment box closes.
5. Place the mouse pointer over cell A7.

   Your comment appears.

Add a feature to control data entry in an invoice

1. Select cells C8 through C10.
2. On the Data menu, click Validation.

   The Data Validation dialog box appears.
3. On the Settings tab, in the Allow drop-down list, select Whole Number.
4. In the Data drop-down list, select Greater Than Or Equal To.
5. In the Minimum box, type **100**

   The Data Validation dialog box should look similar to the following illustration.

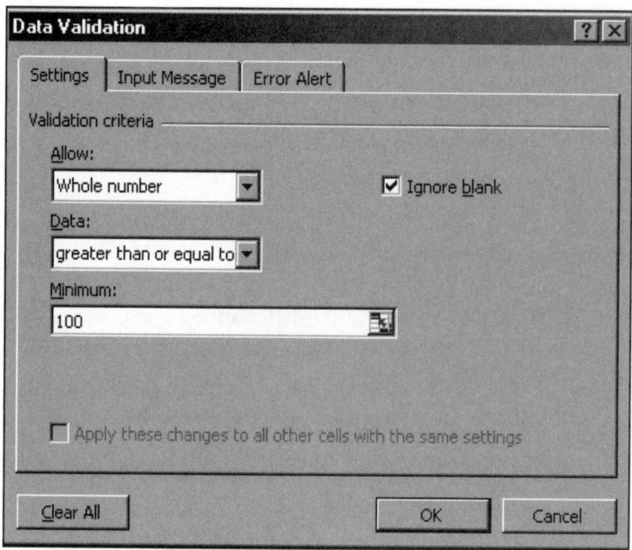

6. Click the Error Alert tab.
7. Be sure that the Show Error Alert After Invalid Data Is Entered check box is selected.
8. In the Style drop-down list, select Warning.
9. In the Title box, type **Invalid Entry**

10. In the Error Message box, type the following:

    You must enter a whole number greater than or equal to 100.

    The Data Validation dialog box should look similar to the following illustration.

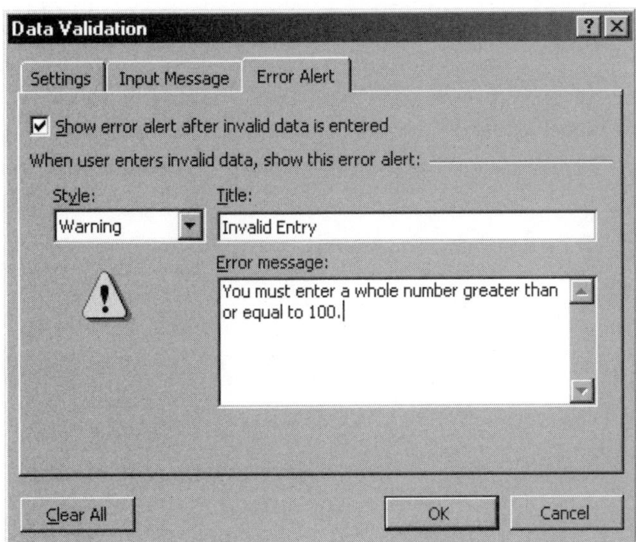

11. Click OK.
12. Select cell C8, type **50** and press Enter.

    An error message appears containing the warning that you entered in the Data Validation dialog box.
13. Click No to change the entry; then type **100** and press Enter.

    Your entry is accepted.

Because you used a warning and not a stop message, you can choose to continue. If you had entered a stop message, you would not be allowed to proceed with the invalid entry.

Changing Cell Alignment and Wrapping

Your business partner walks by and you decide to show off your new Invoice worksheet. After some discussion, the two of you notice that there are a few other things you could change to make it easier to enter data in the invoice.

Apply text wrapping to cells

If you are not working through this lesson sequentially, open the file 02D.xls from the Lesson02 folder before you continue.

In this exercise, you make additional column width adjustments and wrap the text to make data fit into certain cells.

1. Place the mouse pointer on the right border of the column B heading, and then drag the right border of column B until 36.00 is displayed in the ScreenTip.

   Column B widens to accommodate data entry in the Work Performed portion of the worksheet.

   Your screen should look similar to the following illustration.

ScreenTip

	A	B	C	D	E
1		Account Name			
2	Address				
3	City and State				
4	Zip + 4				
5	Phone Number				
6		Work Performed			
7	Task Name	Description	$ Billed		
8			100		
9					
10					
11		We help your business make an Impact!			

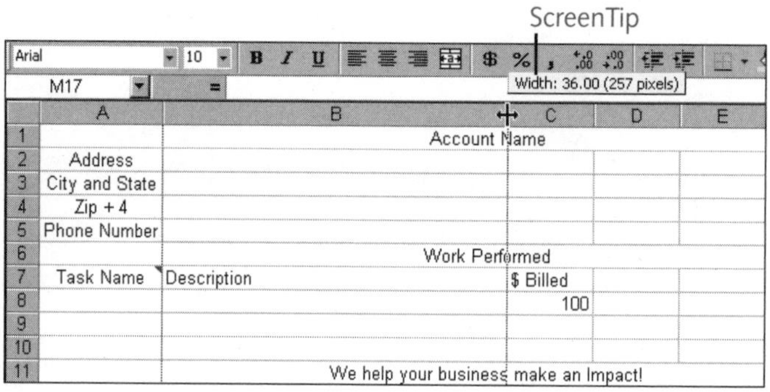

2. Select cell B8 and type the following:

   Study demographics and determine the most effective advertising medium and press Enter.

3. Select cells B8 through B10, and then right-click the selected cells.

   A shortcut menu appears.

4. On the shortcut menu, click Format Cells.

   The Format Cells dialog box appears.

The Wrap Text feature prevents the text from overlapping the adjacent cell.

5. On the Alignment tab, select the Wrap Text check box, and click OK.

   The wrapping option is applied to cells B8 and B10. Now, when you create a multiline text entry in cells B8 through B10, after you press Enter, the text automatically wraps and the row height is adjusted to accommodate the entry.

   Your worksheet should look similar to the following illustration.

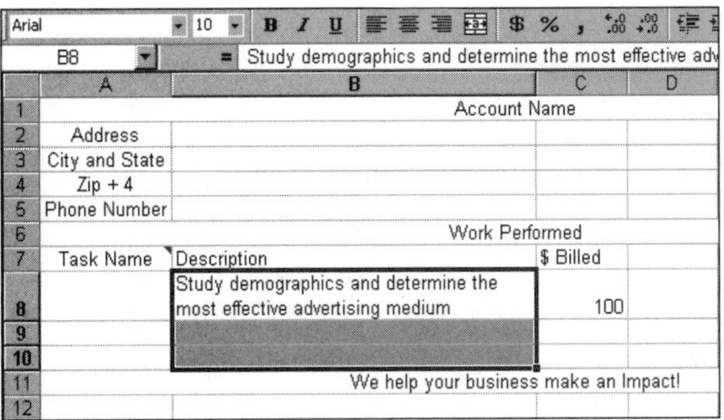

Change cell alignment

In this exercise, you adjust the text alignment in the cells where you've applied wrapping. This makes the first line of text in these cells always align at the top of the cell.

1. Select cells A8 through C10.
2. Right-click in the selected area, and then on the shortcut menu, click Format Cells.

   The Format Cells dialog box appears.
3. On the Alignment tab, in the Vertical drop-down list, select Top, and click OK.

   The text alignment in cells A8 though C10 is reset. Notice that when multiple lines of text are entered in cell B8, the entry in C8 is aligned at the top of the cell.

   Your worksheet should look similar to the following illustration.

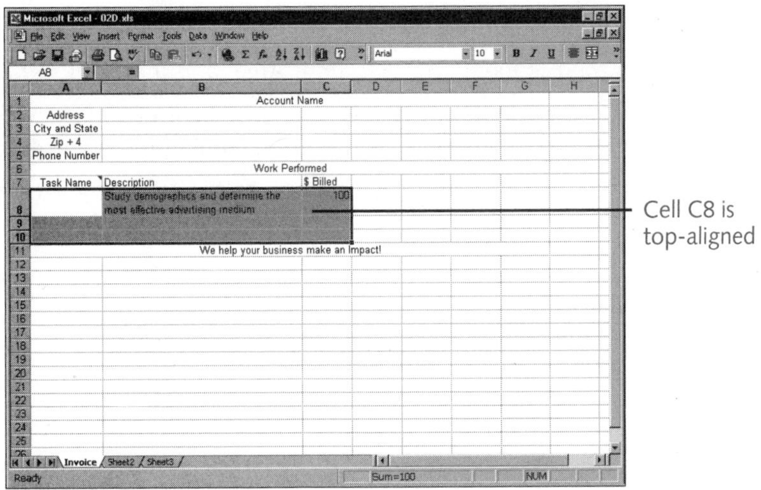

Printing an Invoice

You can print your worksheet using the *default* print settings. These are the settings your printer uses unless you set it differently. To print only those areas of your worksheet that contain specific data or text, you can define a print area. Once you set a print area, this portion of your worksheet is printed automatically the next time you print. As your invoice grows with added information, you can define a new print area so that all of the relevant data is printed. Conversely, you might want to print only selected portions of your worksheet—for example, in order to keep certain information confidential.

important

For the following exercises, be sure that your computer is properly connected to a printer and that the printer is turned on.

Quickly print a copy of an invoice

In this exercise, you use the Print button to quickly print a single copy of the active worksheet using the default print settings.

If you are not working through this lesson sequentially, open the file 02E.xls from the Lesson02 folder before you continue.

- On the Standard toolbar, click the Print button.

  Your worksheet is printed.

Define a print area

In this exercise, you define a print area in your worksheet.

1. Select cells A1 through G11.

   Only the cells that you want to print are selected.

2. On the File menu, point to Print Area, and then click Set Print Area.

   The designated print area is highlighted with Excel's new See-Through View. You can see the text and formatting behind the highlighting.

   Your worksheet should look similar to the following illustration.

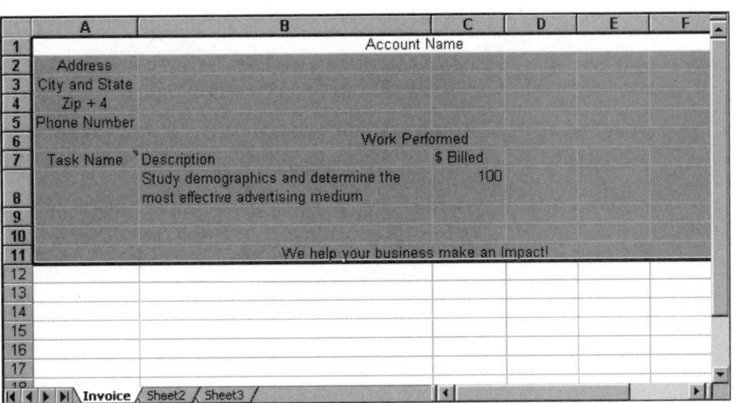

Print

3. On the Standard toolbar, click the Print button.

   The selected area of your worksheet is printed.

One Step Further: Adding a Picture to the Worksheet

Because your invoice is to be sent to Impact Public Relations' customers, it needs to look professional and attractive. You decide to improve the invoice appearance by adding the company logo to the invoice.

Create a space on an invoice

In this exercise, you create a space for the logo using the Insert command on the shortcut menu.

If you are not working through this lesson sequentially, open the file 02F.xls from the Lesson02 folder before you continue.

1. On the invoice worksheet, right-click the row 1 heading.

   Row 1 is selected, and the shortcut menu appears.
2. On the shortcut menu, click Insert.

   A new row is inserted at the top of the worksheet, above row 1.

Insert the logo

In this exercise, you locate the logo on your hard disk and insert it in the invoice.

1. Click cell A1.
2. On the Insert menu, point to Picture, and then click From File.

   The Insert Picture dialog box appears.

Dragging different handles to enlarge a picture produces different results.

3. In the Look In drop-down list, select your hard disk. Double-click the Office 8in1 Step by Step folder, and then double-click the Excel Practice folder. Double-click the Lesson02 folder, and then double-click the 02G.wmf file.

   The Impact Public Relations company logo is pasted into the upper-left corner of the worksheet.

   Your worksheet should look similar to the following illustration.

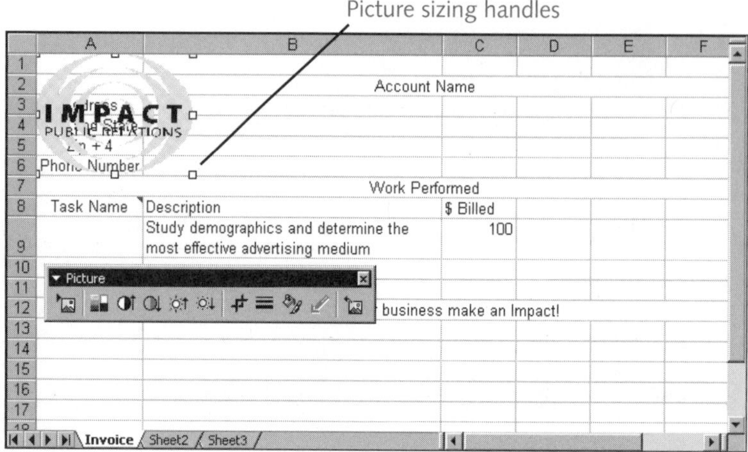

Make final adjustments

In this exercise, you set formatting specifications for the logo and increase the row height to accommodate the logo.

1. Right-click the logo, and then on the shortcut menu, click Format Picture.

   The Format Picture dialog box appears.

2. In the Format Picture dialog box, click the Colors And Lines tab.
3. In the Line area, in the Color drop-down palette, click the Blue color box.
4. In the Style drop-down list, click the 3-point line, and click OK.

   A thick, blue border appears around the logo.

5. Place the mouse pointer between the row 1 and 2 headings.

   You'll know you are at the right spot when the mouse pointer changes to a double-headed arrow.

When you use the corner handles, the logo stays in proportion as you resize it.

6. Drag the row border downward until the logo fits comfortably in row 1. Your worksheet should look similar to the following illustration.

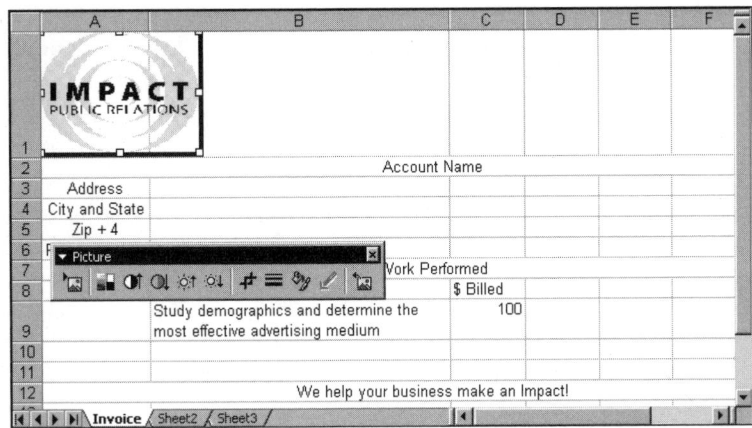

Save

7. Save your work.

Finish the lesson

1. To continue to the next lesson, close all open windows.
2. If you are finished using Microsoft Excel for now, on the File menu, click Exit.

Lesson 2 Quick Reference

To	Do this	Button
Open a new workbook	On the Standard toolbar, click the New button.	
Save a new workbook	On the File menu, click Save As. Open the folder in which you want to save the file. In the File Name box, type the new filename, and click Save.	
Add a keyword to the file properties	On the File menu, click Properties. On the Summary tab, in the Keywords box, enter a keyword, and click OK. On the Standard toolbar, click Save.	
Name worksheets in a workbook	At the bottom of the worksheet, double-click the sheet tab. Type the desired name and press Enter.	

Lesson 2 Quick Reference

To	Do this	Button
Enter labels on a worksheet	Select a cell, type the desired label, and press Enter.	
Merge and center text in cells	Select the relevant cells and then on the Formatting toolbar, click the Merge And Center button.	
Adjust column width	Drag the right border of the column to the right or left until it is the correct width.	
Center text in cells	Select the cells, and then on the Formatting toolbar, click the Center button.	
Preview the worksheet before printing	On the Standard toolbar, click the Print Preview button.	
Adjust column width in Print Preview	On the toolbar in Print Preview, click the Margin button. Drag the margin marker in the desired direction. Click Close.	
Add a row	Right-click the row heading, and then on the shortcut menu, click Insert.	
Add comments to a worksheet	Select the cell, and then on the Insert menu, click Comment. Enter your comment, and click outside the comment box to close it.	
Control data entry in a worksheet	Select the cells, and then on the Data menu, click Validation. Enter the data limitations. Click the Error Alert tab and enter the desired warning level. Click OK.	
Apply text wrapping to cells	Right-click the selected cells, and then on the shortcut menu, click Format Cells. When the Format Cells dialog box appears, click the Alignment tab. Select the Wrap Text check box, and click OK.	

Lesson 2 Quick Reference

To	Do this	Button
Change cell alignment	Right-click the selected cells, and then on the shortcut menu, click Format Cells. When the Format Cells dialog box appears, click the Alignment tab. In the Horizontal or Vertical list, select the desired alignment style, and click OK.	
Quickly print a copy of a worksheet	On the Standard toolbar, click the Print button.	
Define a print area	Select the cells you want to print. On the File menu, point to Print Area, and click Set Print Area. On the Standard toolbar, click the Print button.	
Add a picture to a worksheet	Click the cell where you want to insert a picture. On the Insert menu, point to Picture, and then click From File. In the Insert Picture dialog box, in the Look In list, browse to find the file for the picture you want to insert, and then double-click the file.	
Format an inserted picture	Right-click the inserted picture, and on the shortcut menu, click Format Picture. In the Format Picture dialog box, click the tab of the formatting you want to apply to the picture, and then set formatting specifications. Click OK.	

Adding Formulas

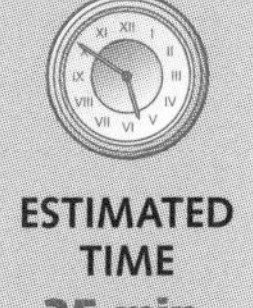

ESTIMATED TIME **25 min.**

In this lesson you will learn how to:

- ✔ *Open an existing workbook using its file properties.*
- ✔ *Name a cell or range of cells.*
- ✔ *Add calculation formulas to a worksheet.*
- ✔ *Copy a formula to another cell.*
- ✔ *Calculate a total using the SUM function.*
- ✔ *Display special messages on invoices.*

You and your business partner are working on an invoice for Impact Public Relations. You want to include areas showing a subtotal, the sales tax, and the total charges for services. So that you don't have to do manual calculations each time, you will add formulas to your invoice to make the process fast, easy, and accurate.

A *formula* is a calculation or procedure performed by Microsoft Excel 2000 to determine a value in a particular cell in your worksheet using values already entered in other cells. Excel also includes some predefined calculations—called *functions*—that are already named for easy use.

All formulas in Excel begin with an equal sign (=). Without the equal sign, the cell entry is interpreted as regular data—that is, as text, numbers, or a combination of the two. A formula can be written to include a *cell reference*, which is the unique location of a cell based on its column and row intersection—for example, A1.

In a formula, the cell reference is either *relative* or *absolute*. A relative cell reference changes depending on where it is placed. In other words, if you copy or move a formula that contains a relative cell reference from one cell to another, the cell reference in the formula automatically changes to that of the new cell. For example, if a formula containing the cell reference A1 is copied and pasted into cell D3, the cell reference in the formula automatically changes to D3.

An absolute cell reference does not change when copied or moved to another cell. In other words, if you copy or move a formula that contains an absolute reference from one cell to another, the formula still calculates using the original cell reference.

Using formulas can be even faster and easier when you assign a name to a cell or range of cells. By using the assigned name, you don't have to remember column and row labels when writing a formula. Another advantage is that a cell name can be used in a formula in any worksheet within the same workbook—for example, the entry in cell A4 of Sheet1 can be used in a formula in Sheet6.

In this lesson, you will open a file by searching the file properties for a keyword. Then you will add formulas to the Impact Public Relations invoice in order to speed calculations and save time preparing client invoices. To do this, you will name cells and ranges of cells, write formulas using cell references and cell names, and copy those formulas into other cells.

More Buttons

important

If you don't see a button on your toolbar, click the More Buttons drop-down arrow for that toolbar to display a list of additional toolbar buttons. In this list, click the toolbar button that you want to use. This executes the command and adds the button to the toolbar, replacing one that has not been used for a while. If you want to display the Standard and Formatting toolbars separately, on the View menu, point to Toolbars, and then click Customize. In the Customize dialog box, on the Options tab, clear the Standard And Formatting Toolbars Share One Row check box, and click Close. For more information on the new Excel 2000 personalized toolbar and menu features, see the One Step Further section, "Customizing Excel," in Lesson 1.

Opening an Existing Workbook Using Its File Properties

For more information on adding a keyword to your workbook file properties, see Lesson 2, "Setting Up a Worksheet."

You're ready to open the invoice worksheet, but you can't remember its exact filename. However, you know that when you saved it, you added the keyword *invoice* to its file properties, so you want to search using the keyword to open the invoice. Once the workbook is open, you can save it in your Excel Practice folder with a new name.

Open an existing workbook

1. On the taskbar at the bottom of your screen, click the Start button.

   The Start menu appears.

2. On the Start menu, point to Programs, and then click Microsoft Excel.

   Microsoft Excel 2000 opens.

3. On the Standard toolbar, click the Open button.

   The Open dialog box appears.

Open

4. In the Open dialog box, click Tools, and then click Find.

   The Find dialog box appears.

   Your screen should look similar to the following illustration.

You can also access the Find dialog box by pressing Ctrl+F.

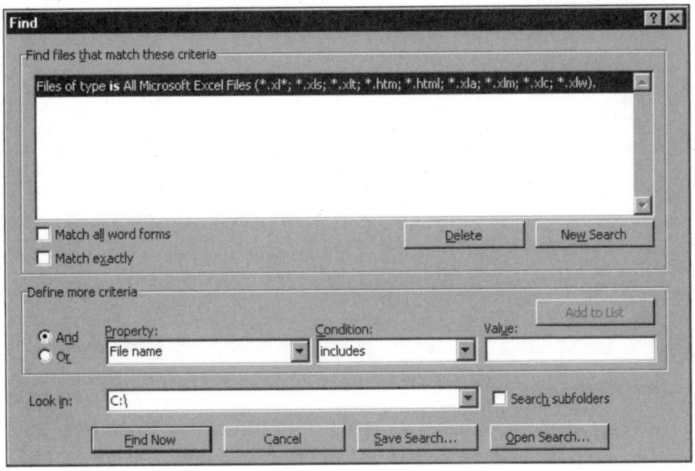

5. In the Property drop-down list, select Keywords.
6. In the Condition drop-down list, be sure that the words *Includes Words* are displayed.
7. In the Value box, type **Invoice** and then click the Add To List button.

   The additional search criterion item is added to the Find Files That Match These Criteria list.
8. In the Look In drop-down list, select your hard disk.
9. Select the Search Subfolders check box, and then click the Find Now button.

   Excel searches your entire hard disk for all files with the keyword *Invoice*. Search results are displayed in the Open dialog box.

   Your screen should look similar to the following illustration.

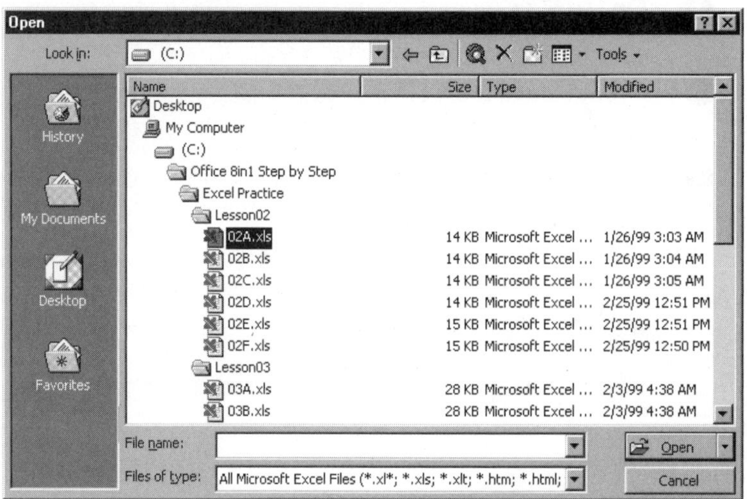

10. Scroll down the list, if necessary, and double-click the 03A.xls file.

    The 03A.xls workbook opens.

Save a workbook with a different name

In this exercise, you save the 03A.xls practice file with a different name, *Impact_Invoice*.

1. On the File menu, click Save As.

   The Save As dialog box appears. The original filename, 03A.xls, is displayed in the File Name box.

2. In the File Name box, type **Impact_Invoice**, and click Save.

   The new filename, Impact_Invoice.xls, is displayed in the worksheet title bar.

Making Formulas Easier to Understand and Use

Your business partner suggests naming the cells or ranges of cells that you know you're going to use in the formulas. This will make writing a formula much easier.

There are several ways to name a cell, and you can choose the method that makes the most sense to you relative to the specific task that you are performing. For example, you can use the column or row labels, which might most accurately describe the adjacent data. Or you can create a descriptive name that helps you more easily understand the formula in which the name is to be included.

Naming Cells and Ranges

Here are some things to keep in mind when naming cells or ranges of cells:

- A name must begin with a letter.
- A number can be used as long as it follows a letter or underscore. Note that if you begin a name with a number, Excel automatically inserts an underscore before the name.
- A space between words and/or numbers in a name is indicated with an underscore—for example, Practice_Files.
- A name cannot resemble a cell reference—for example, *A2*.
- Single letters, except *R* and *C*, can be used as a name.

Name a cell or range of cells using adjacent cell labels

In this exercise, you name the cells that you want to contain the subtotal, sales tax, and total due calculations in the invoice.

If you are not working through this lesson sequentially, open the file 03A.xls from the Lesson03 folder before you continue.

1. Select cells D24 through E26.

   A rectangular range of cells is selected.

2. On the Insert menu, point to Name, and then click Create.

The Create Names dialog box appears.

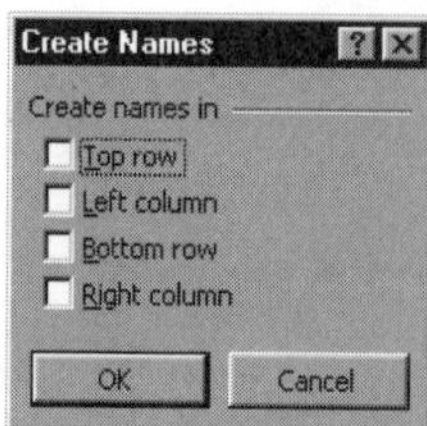

3. Select the Left Column check box, and click OK.
4. Click cell E24.

   Notice that the cell name *Subtotal* is displayed in the Name box at the left end of the formula bar.

Excel 2000 automatically recognizes labels that are located in the left column of the selected range.

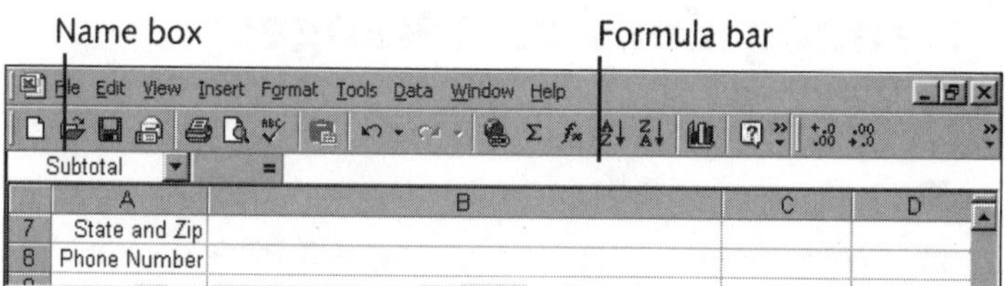

5. Click cell E25, and then click E26.

   Notice that each cell name shown in the Name box corresponds to the label in the adjacent cell to the left.

Name a range of cells using Define Name

In this exercise, you give a range of cells a new descriptive name.

1. Select cells D11 through D23.

   A rectangular range of cells is selected.
2. On the Insert menu, point to Name, and then click Define.

   The Define Name dialog box appears.

You can display the Define Name dialog box quickly by pressing Ctrl+F3.

3. In the Names In Workbook box, type **Rate** and click OK.

   The range name *Rate* is displayed in the Name box at the left end of the formula bar.

Name a cell or range of cells using the Name box

In this exercise, you name a range of cells using the Name box.

Although a range of cells can have a name, the Name box on the formula bar contains only the cell reference of the selected cell within that range.

1. Click cell E11, and drag downward to cell E23.

   A rectangular range of cells is selected.

2. Click the Name box.

   The cell reference of the first cell selected, E11, is displayed in the Name box.

3. In the Name box, type **Billed** and press Enter.

   The range of cells is named *Billed*.

4. Click the Name box drop-down arrow to display a list of all of your defined names.

   Your screen should look similar to the following illustration.

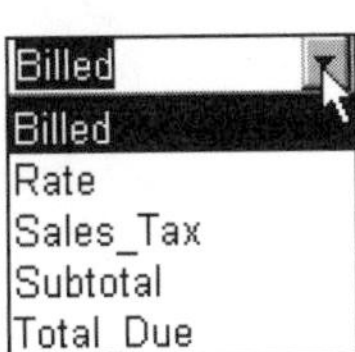

5. In the Name box drop-down list, select Total_Due.

   The cell named *Total_Due* becomes the active cell.

Entering Calculation Formulas

In Excel 2000, a formula can use values in cells to perform such operations as addition, multiplication, division, and subtraction. Formulas need a *mathematical operator*—either the plus sign (+), the minus sign (-), the multiplication sign (*), or the division sign (/)—in order to perform a calculation.

A formula can also contain a *function,* a predefined set of instrucitons that saves time when you write formulas. A function helps describe the operation being performed and usually precedes one or more *arguments.* An argument provides the information that tells the function what data to calculate and what operations to perform. For example, the SUM function—the most common function performed using Excel—adds all of the numbers in a range of cells. The arguments in a SUM function specify what cells are to be added together: =SUM(A1:A2). In the following exercises, you will write a simple formula to multiply the values in several cells of your invoice. Then you will copy the formula to other cells and use the SUM function to add several values in your invoice.

Write a formula

If you are not working through this lesson sequentially, open the file 03B.xls from the Lesson03 folder before you continue.

In this exercise, you create a simple formula to discuss with your business partner. To figure the amount to bill a client, you write a formula that multiplies the number of hours billed by the billing rate.

1. Click cell A11, type **Update Web site** and then press Tab.
2. In cell B11, type **Two promotional ads for the Festival & Feast 2000 celebration** and then press Tab.
3. In cell C11, type **5** and then press Tab.
4. In cell D11, type **26** and then press Tab.

   In cell D11, *$26* is displayed.
5. In cell E11, type = (an equal sign) to begin writing the formula.
6. Click cell C11, and then notice what is displayed in cell E11.

   In cell E11, the cell reference C11 appears after the equal sign.

   Your screen should look similar to the following illustration.

The practice file cells are formatted to show dollar signs. You will learn how to do this in Lesson 4, "Dressing Up a Worksheet."

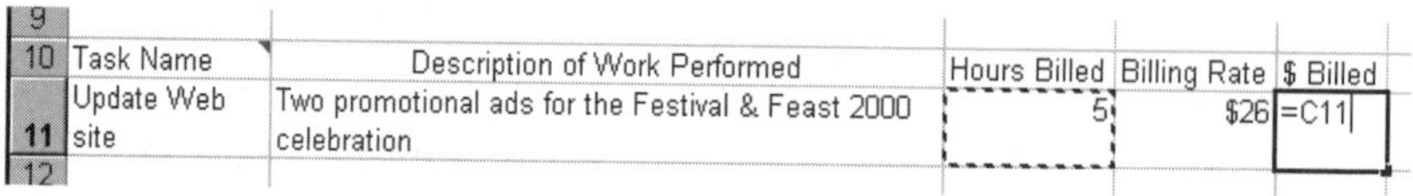

9					
10	Task Name	Description of Work Performed	Hours Billed	Billing Rate	$ Billed
11	Update Web site	Two promotional ads for the Festival & Feast 2000 celebration	5	$26	=C11
12					

7. With the insertion point still in cell E11, type * (an asterisk), the mathematical operator for multiplication.
8. Click cell D11, and notice that the cell reference D11 appears after the asterisk in cell E11. Press Enter.

   In cell E11, the result of the operation, $130, replaces the formula.

9. Click cell E11, and then look at the formula bar.

   The formula is displayed in the formula bar, but *$130* remains in cell E11.

   Your screen should look similar to the following illustration.

	Task Name	Description of Work Performed	Hours Billed	Billing Rate	$ Billed
9					
10	Task Name	Description of Work Performed	Hours Billed	Billing Rate	$ Billed
11	Update Web site	Two promotional ads for the Festival & Feast 2000 celebration	5	$26	$130
12					

Copy the formula to other cells

In this exercise, you use AutoFill to copy the formula you wrote in the previous exercise to other cells in your invoice.

1. Be sure that cell E11 is the active cell.
2. Place the mouse pointer in the lower-right corner of cell E11 until a small black plus sign appears over the AutoFill handle.
3. Drag the AutoFill handle downward in the worksheet to cell E23.

   The AutoFill handle is used to copy data in the selected cell to a different cell or range of cells.

   The formula in cell E11 is copied to each cell in the selected range.

   Your screen should look similar to the following illustration.

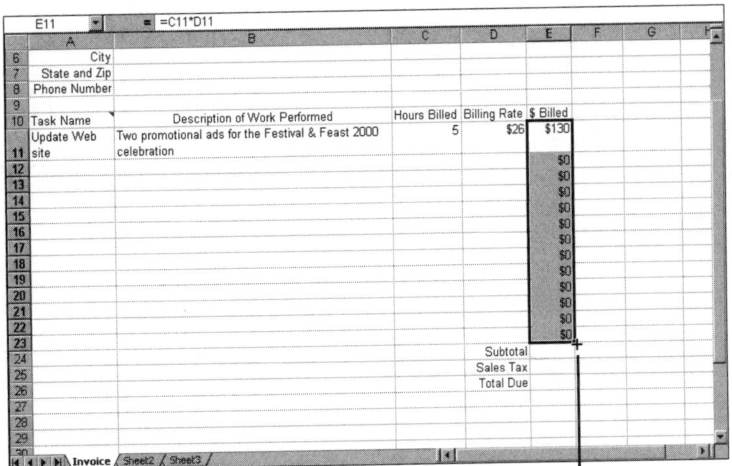

When placed over the AutoFill handle, the mouse pointer changes to a plus sign

4. Click cell E12, and then look at the formula bar.

   The cell references within the formula use the values from the new cell, E12, rather than the values from the original cell, E11.

> ## tip
>
> To copy a cell containing a formula to another cell in your worksheet, point to the border of the cell with the formula, hold down the Ctrl key, and then drag to the other cell.

The AutoSum button on the Standard toolbar makes the SUM function even easier to use.

AutoSum

Add a formula to calculate a total using SUM

In this exercise, you add a formula to your invoice using the AutoSum button.

1. In the Name box drop-down list, select Subtotal.

   Cell E24, the cell to the right of the cell labeled Subtotal, becomes the active cell.

2. On the Standard toolbar, click the AutoSum button.

   A moving border appears around the cells used in the formula. Cell E24 contains the formula SUM(Billed).

   The argument portion of the formula automatically displays the name that you assigned to the range of cells—*Billed*—rather than the cell references E11 through E23.

   Your screen should look similar to the following illustration.

IF | =SUM(Billed)

	A	B	C	D	E	F
9						
10	Task Name	Description of Work Performed	Hours Billec	Billing Rate	$ Billed	
11	Update Web site	Two promotional ads for the Festival & Feast 2000 celebration	5	$26	$130	
12					$0	
13					$0	
14					$0	
15					$0	
16					$0	
17					$0	
18					$0	
19					$0	
20					$0	
21					$0	
22					$0	
23					$0	
24				Subtotal	=SUM(Billed)	
25				Sales Tax		
26				Total Due		
27						
28						
29						
30						

Invoice / Sheet2 / Sheet3

3. Press Enter.

   In cell E24, the result of the operation, $130, replaces the formula.

Add a formula to calculate a specific tax rate

In this exercise, you write a formula to calculate sales tax at 8.5 percent, the rate for your area. Then you write a formula to total your invoice.

You can also type 8.5% instead of .085.

1. Click cell B25, type **Tax rate:** (be sure to type the colon), and press Tab.
2. In cell C25, type **.085** and press Enter.
3. In the Name box drop-down list, select Sales_Tax.

   Cell E25, the cell named *Sales_Tax*, becomes the active cell.
4. Type = and then click cell E24.

   The cell name *Subtotal* is displayed in the formula.

   Your screen should look similar to the following illustration.

		$0	
		$0	
	Subtotal	$130	
0.085	Sales Tax	=Subtotal	
	Total Due		

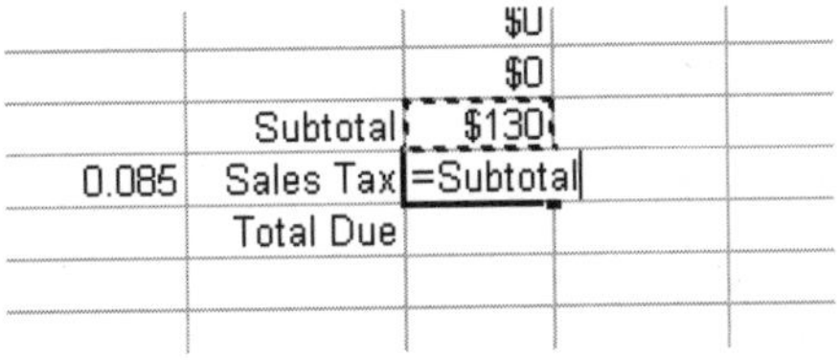

5. Type * and then click cell C25.

   The tax rate in cell C25 is added to the formula.

   Your screen should look similar to the following illustration.

		$0	
		$0	
	Subtotal	$130	
0.085	Sales Tax	=Subtotal*C25	
	Total Due		

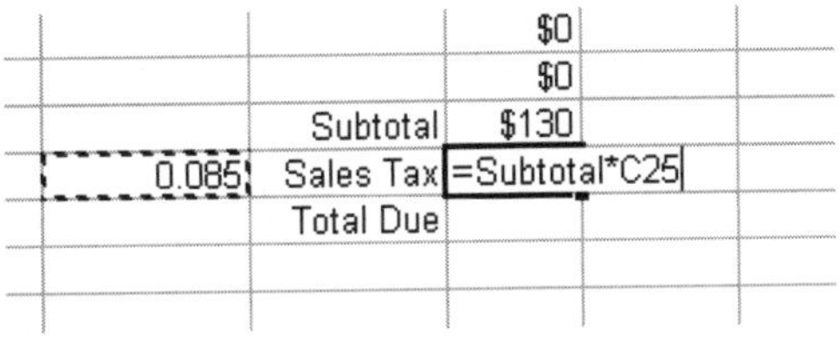

6. Press Enter.

   The sales tax is calculated, and the result of the operation, $11.05, replaces the formula.

7. Type = and then click cell E24.

   The cell name *Subtotal* is displayed in the formula.

8. Type + (a plus sign), and then click cell E25.

   The cell name *Sales_Tax* is displayed after the plus sign in the formula.

   Your screen should look similar to the following illustration.

		$0	
		$0	
	Subtotal	$130	
0.085	Sales Tax	$11.05	
	Total Due	=Subtotal+Sales_Tax	

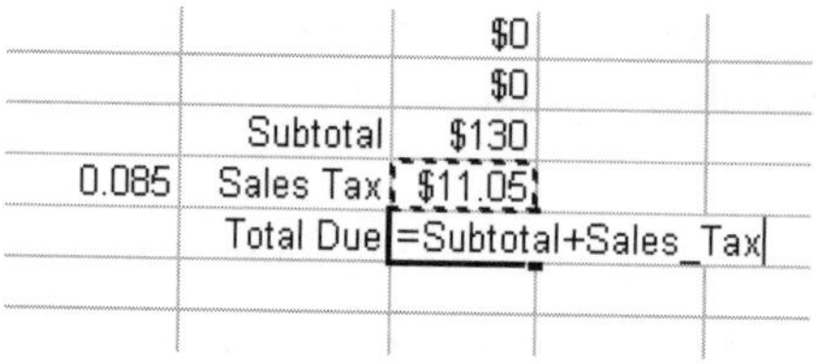

9. Press Enter.

   The result of the operation, $141.05, replaces the formula.

10. Double-click the border between E and F.

    Column E widens to fit $141.05.

    Your screen should look similar to the following illustration.

	A	B	C	D	E
9					
10	Task Name	Description of Work Performed	Hours Billed	Billing Rate	$ Billed
11	Update Web site	Two promotional ads for the Festival & Feast 2000 celebration	5	$26	$130
12					$0
13					$0
14					$0
15					$0
16					$0
17					$0
18					$0
19					$0
20					$0
21					$0
22					$0
23					$0
24				Subtotal	$130
25		Tax rate:	0.085	Sales Tax	$11.05
26				Total Due	$141.05
27					
28					

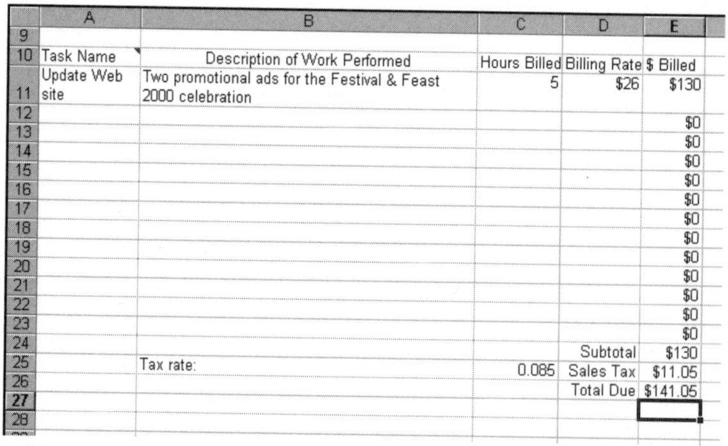

One Step Further — Displaying Special Messages on Invoices

If you are not working through this lesson sequentially, open the file 03C.xls from the Lesson03 folder before you continue.

You and your business partner decide to include another function in the invoice template. Impact Public Relations gives a 2 percent discount for prompt payment on invoices over $5,000, and you want to add a message reminding customers. In the following exercise, you create a formula that adds a message to only those invoices with a balance greater than $5,000.

Write a formula to automatically insert a message

In this exercise, you will use the IF function to create a formula that automatically inserts a message in invoices totaling more than $5,000.

1. Select cells A30 through cell E30.
2. On the Formatting toolbar, click the Merge And Center button.

   The cells are merged and centered.

Merge And Center

3. On the Formula bar, click the Edit Formula button.

   The formula palette appears. At the left end of the formula bar, the Functions box is displayed.

Edit Formula

4. In the Functions drop-down list, click IF.

   The formula palette enlarges to help you create the arguments for your IF formula.

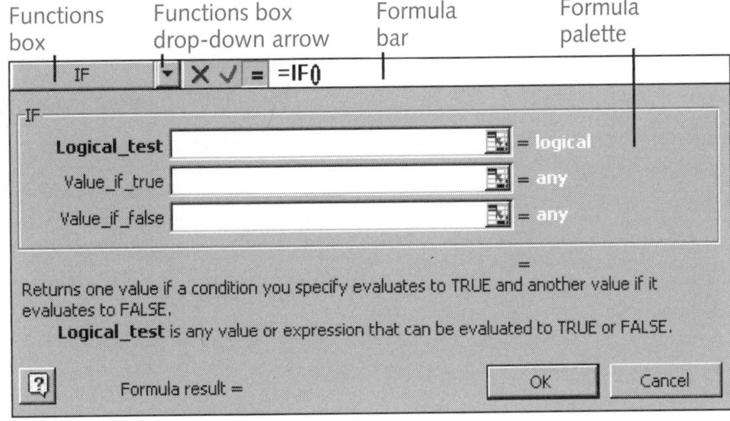

5. Click cell E26.

   In the Logical_Test box, the cell name *Total_Due* is displayed.

6. Type **>5000** and then press Tab.

7. In the Value_If_True box, type **"Invoices over $5,000 are discounted 2 percent if paid within 30 days."** (Be sure to include the quotation marks.) Then press Tab.

In a formula, the greater-than sign (>) requires that a certain action take place when the value in a cell exceeds the value following the greater-than sign.

8. In the Value_If_False box, type "" (a set of quotation marks with no spaces between them).

   Your screen should look similar to the following illustration.

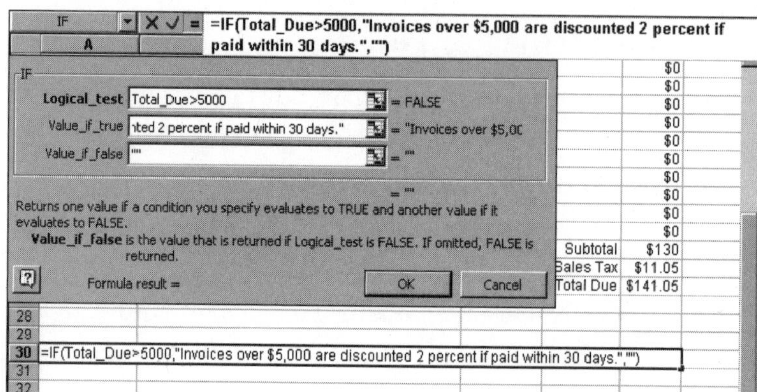

9. Click OK.

   When the invoice total in cell E26 is over $5,000, your message will automatically be displayed on line 30.

Finish the lesson

1. To continue to the next lesson, close any open windows.
2. If you are finished using Microsoft Excel for now, on the File menu, click Exit.

Lesson 3 Quick Reference

To	Do this	Button
Open an existing workbook using a keyword	On the Standard toolbar, click the Open button. Click Tools, and then click Find. In the Property drop-down list, click Keywords. Type the keyword in the Value box, and then click the Add To List button. In the Look In drop-down list, click your hard disk, and then select the Search Subfolders check box. Click Find Now.	
Save an existing workbook using a different name	On the File menu, click Save As. In the Save In drop-down list, locate the folder in which you want to save the file. In the File Name box, type the new filename, and then click Save.	
Name a cell or range of cells using the label in the adjacent cell	Select the labeled cell or range of cells, and then drag to select the adjacent cells to be named. On the Insert menu, point to Name, and then click Create. Be sure that the correct Create Names In check box is selected, and click OK.	
Name a cell or range of cells	Select the cell or range of cells being named. On the Insert menu, point to Name, and then click Define. In the Names In Workbook box, type the name, and click OK.	
Write a formula to multiply values in a worksheet	Click the cell in which you want to create the formula. Type =, and then click the first cell to be multiplied. Type *, click the second cell to be multiplied, and press Enter.	
Copy a formula to other cells	Click the cell containing the formula. Drag the AutoFill handle downward through the cells to be included.	
Write a formula using the AutoSum button	Click the cell in which you want to create the SUM formula. On the Standard toolbar, click the AutoSum button, select the range of cells to be added, and then press Enter.	Σ

Lesson 3 Quick Reference

To	Do this	Button
Write a formula to display text in a cell if a particular condition exists	On the formula bar, click the Edit Formula button. In the Functions box, click IF. Click the cell in which the condition could occur, and then in the Logical_Test box, type the comparison operator and value of the condition. In the Value_If_True box, within quotation marks, type the text that you want to display if the value in that cell meets the condition you typed in the Logical_Test box. In the Value_If_False box, within quotation marks, type the text that you want to display if the value in that cell doesn't meet the condition you typed in the Logical_Test box. Click OK.	

4

Dressing Up a Worksheet

ESTIMATED TIME **30 min.**

In this lesson you will learn how to:

- ✔ *Format cells manually and with styles.*
- ✔ *Format numbers, including four-digit year 2000 date formats.*
- ✔ *Add custom headers and footers.*
- ✔ *Save an invoice as a template.*
- ✔ *Edit a template.*

In this lesson, you will format an invoice to give it a professional look. Then you'll save it as a template so that others at Impact Public Relations can use it for their work.

Formatting is important for making your worksheet easy to read and use. You can group data logically using cell borders and cell shading, make labels stand out using font styles and alignment, and make numbers more intelligible by defining the way they are displayed. You can also create headers and footers that are printed on every page and assign settings that automatically print the current date or number of pages.

One way to make formatting easier is to use *styles*. Styles are a collection of formatting attributes that you can create and use over and over. You can also change them as needed to save time when you want to format a group of cells.

More Buttons

> **important**
>
> If you don't see a button on your toolbar, click the More Buttons drop-down arrow for that toolbar to display a list of additional toolbar buttons. In this list, click the toolbar button that you want to use. This executes the command and adds the button to the toolbar, replacing one that has not been used for a while. If you want to display the Standard and Formatting toolbars separately, on the View menu, point to Toolbars, and then click Customize. In the Customize dialog box, on the Options tab, clear the Standard And Formatting Toolbars Share One Row check box, and click Close. For more information on the new Excel 2000 personalized toolbar and menu features, see the One Step Further section, "Customizing Excel," in Lesson 1.

Formatting Cells to Create a Professional Look

In the following exercises, you format fonts and change the look of your invoice with borders and cell shading. You also learn how to use styles to save time when changing cell formatting and how to set page margins so that the invoice fits in the center of a single page.

Open and save the practice file

1. On the taskbar at the bottom of your screen, click the Start button.
   The Start menu appears.
2. On the Start menu, point to Programs, and then click Microsoft Excel.
   Microsoft Excel 2000 opens.
3. On the Standard toolbar, click the Open button.
   The Open dialog box appears.

Open

4. In the Look In drop-down list, select your hard disk.
5. In the list of folders, double-click the Office 8in1 Step by Step folder, and then double-click the Excel Practice folder. Double-click the Lesson04 folder.

6. Double-click the 04A.xls file.

   The 04A.xls workbook opens.

7. On the File menu, click Save As.

   The Save As dialog box appears.

8. In the Save In drop-down list, select your hard disk. Double-click the Office 8in1 Step by Step folder, and then double-click the Excel Practice folder.

   The original filename, 04A.xls, is displayed in the File Name box.

9. In the File Name box, type **Template**

10. Click Save.

Format the attributes of a cell

In this exercise, you format cells by changing fonts, font sizes, and font attributes.

1. On the Invoice worksheet, select cell A2 (which is merged through cell E2).

2. On the Formatting toolbar, in the Font drop-down list, select Impact.

   The font changes from Arial to Impact. Notice that Excel 2000 displays an example of each font in the font list.

3. On the Formatting toolbar, in the Font Size list, select 16.

   The words *Client Invoice* change to a larger font size.

Bold

4. On the Formatting toolbar, click the Bold button.

   The words *Client Invoice* become bold.

Italic

5. Select cells A4 through A8, hold down the Ctrl key, and then select A10.

6. On the Formatting toolbar, in the Font Size drop-down list, select 12.

Align Right

7. On the Formatting toolbar, click the Bold button, click the Italic button, and then click the Align Right button.

   Notice that you need to adjust the column width so each label fits within the column.

8. Double-click the border between columns A and B.

   Column A widens to fit the longest cell in the column.

   Your worksheet should look similar to the following illustration.

	A	B	C	D
1	IMPACT PUBLIC RELATIONS			
2		Client Invoice		
3				
4	Account Name			
5	Address			
6	City			
7	State and Zip			
8	Phone Number			
9		Work Performed		
10	Task Name	Description of Work Performed	Hours Billed	Billing Rate

Format cells with borders

In this exercise, you use different types of borders to group the client information and the billing information.

1. Select cells A4 through E8.

   The cells containing client information are selected.

2. On the Formatting toolbar, click the Borders button drop-down arrow.

   The Borders palette appears.

Borders

3. Click the Thick Box Border button.

   A thick outline border is applied to the selected range.

Thick Box Border

4. Select cells B4 through E4.

5. On the Formatting toolbar, click the Merge And Center button.

   The cells in the selected range are merged.

Merge And Center

6. Following the same procedure, merge and center cells B5 through E5, B6 through E6, B7 through E7, and B8 through E8.

> **important**
>
> Be sure that you don't select all the cells from B4 through E8 as a single range and then click the Merge And Center button, because this makes the entire range become a single cell.

7. Select cells A10 through A13, and then drag to select cells E10 through E13.

8. On the Formatting toolbar, click the Borders button drop-down arrow.

   The Borders palette appears.

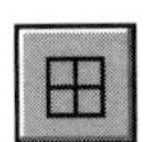

All Borders

To place borders around multiple ranges at the same time, hold down Ctrl, select all of the individual ranges, and then insert borders around them all at once.

9. On the Borders palette, click the All Borders button.
   Your worksheet should look similar to the following illustration.

2	**Client Invoice**				
3					
4	*Account Name*				
5	*Address*				
6	*City*				
7	*State and Zip*				
8	*Phone Number*				
9	Work Performed				
10	*Task Name*	Description of Work Performed	Hours Billed	Billing Rate	$ Billed
11					
12					
13					
14	We help your business make an Impact!				

Apply shading

In this exercise, you apply shading to the cells that contain billing information as a visual reminder to users not to enter information in those cells.

1. Select cells D10 through D13, and then drag to select cells E10 through E13.
2. On the Formatting toolbar, click the Fill Color button drop-down arrow.
   The Fill Color palette appears.
3. In the middle of the bottom row, click the Light Turquoise box.
   The selected range is now shaded.

Fill Color

You can also drag the Fill Color palette onto the worksheet so that it's closer to the area that you are formatting.

Using Styles

A *style* is a collection of formatting attributes, such as font, font size, bold type, italic type, cell shading, or color. Styles are easy to create, apply, and change. When you apply a style to a cell, all of the formatting attributes contained in the style are applied to the cell. When you change a formatting attribute in a style (such as a font), that attribute automatically changes in all cells to which the style has been applied.

Using a style is a great way to apply the same formatting to several worksheets without taking the time to change each one individually. Suppose that you have several worksheets that all have the same type of labels, and you need to change the formatting of all the labels. Applying a style saves a lot of time because you can simply change the style definition instead of reformatting each cell.

All documents sent to customers of Impact Public Relations must use a uniform style. To change formatting more easily, you've decided to use styles in the invoice so that future modifications can be done quickly. This way, you won't have to worry about making many small changes to hundreds of cells.

Format cells using styles

If you are not working through this lesson sequentially, open the file 04B.xls from the Lesson04 folder before you continue.

In this exercise, you create a style based on existing cell formatting and then apply the style to several cells.

1. On the Invoice worksheet, select cell A2.
2. On the Format menu, click Style.

   The Style dialog box appears with the style name highlighted. The dialog box lists the attributes associated with the style shown in the Style Name box.
3. In the Style Name box, type **Main Label** and click OK.

   The formatting applied to cell A2 is now available as a style named *Main Label*.
4. Select cells A4 through A8.

   The account information labels are selected.
5. On the Format menu, click Style. In the Style Name box, type **Secondary Label** and click OK.

   The formatting applied to cell A4 through A8 is now available as a style named *Secondary Label*.

Format cells using Format Painter

In this exercise, you use Format Painter to make formatting cells even easier.

Format Painter

1. On the Invoice worksheet, select cell A2. Then on the Standard toolbar, click the Format Painter button.

   The mouse pointer changes to a paintbrush similar to the one on the Format Painter button, and an animated line of dashes marks the source cell.
2. Click cell A14.

   The Main Label style is applied to the promotional message in the selected cell. The Format Painter automatically turns off.

Your worksheet should look similar to the following illustration.

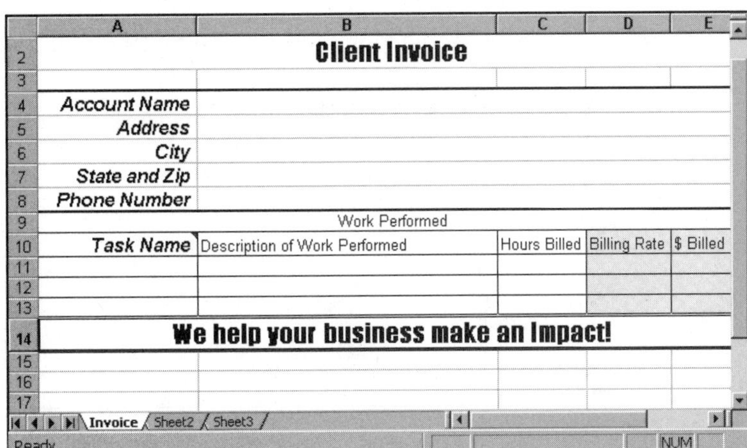

3. Select cell A8, and then on the Standard toolbar, quickly double-click the Format Painter button.

   The Format Painter will now stay on until you turn if off.

4. Click cell B10.

   The Secondary Label style is applied to cell B10.

5. Click cell C10, then click cell D10, and then click cell E10.

   The Secondary Label style is applied to each cell that you click.

6. Click the Format Painter button.

   Format Painter turns off.

7. Adjust the column widths as necessary so that text fits neatly into the cells.

Center

8. Select row 10 by clicking the row 10 heading. Then click the Center button.

   The text aligns in the center, and the cells remain formatted in Secondary Label style. Notice that parts of the heavy border from the account information cells are copied into row 10.

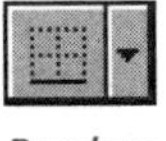

Borders

9. Select cells A10 through E10, and then click the Borders button drop-down arrow.

   The Borders palette appears.

Thick Box

10. On the Borders palette, click the Thick Box Border button.
    A thick outline border is applied to the selected range.

    Your worksheet should look similar to the following illustration.

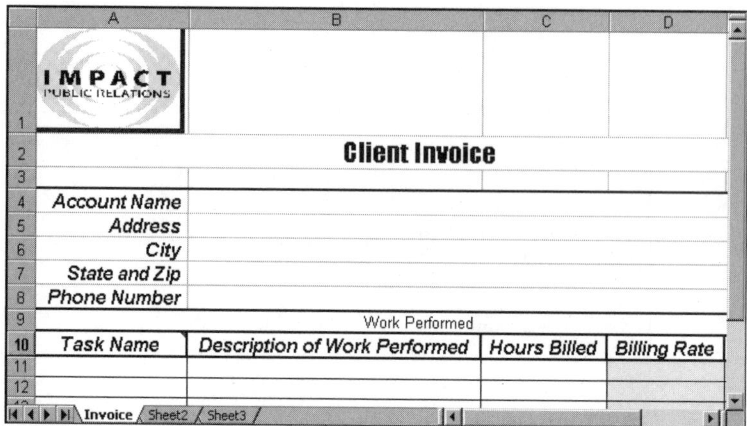

Formatting Numbers to Create a Professional Look

When you format numbers, you define how number values are displayed in a worksheet. Number formats include dollar signs, comma separators in numbers larger than 1000, decimal places, dates, times, and percentages. You can even format cells so that Zip Codes, phone numbers, and Social Security numbers are automatically formatted. In addition, you can customize formatting to meet your own needs—for example, you can add text to show that an invoice amount is billed by the hour. Number formatting takes effect only when a cell contains a number.

By default, all cells in a worksheet use the General number format: extra zeros to the right of the decimal point are left out, all calculated decimal places are shown, and numbers are aligned on the right.

Format numbers automatically as a phone number

If you are not working through this lesson sequentially, open the file 04C.xls from the Lesson04 folder before you continue.

In this exercise, you format cells as phone numbers using special formatting.

1. On the Invoice worksheet, select cell B8.
2. Right-click the cell, and then on the shortcut menu, click Format Cells.
   The Format Cells dialog box appears.

3. On the Number tab, select Special in the Category list.

   The Type list appears in the Format Cells dialog box.
4. In the Type list, select Phone Number, and click OK.
5. In cell B8, type **4255551234** and press Enter.
   The phone number is properly formatted as (425) 555-1234.

Format numbers automatically as a date

In this exercise, you format a cell as a date using a new four-digit date format that is year 2000–compatible.

1. Select cell A3.
2. Right-click the selected cell, and then on the shortcut menu, click Format Cells.

   The Format Cells dialog box appears.
3. On the Number tab, in the Category list, select Date.

   The Type list appears in the Format Cells dialog box.
4. In the Type list, select 3/14/98, and click OK.
5. In cell A3, type **April 25, 2000** and press Enter.
   The date is properly formatted as 4/25/00.

Format numbers automatically as a dollar amount

In this exercise, you format cells as dollar amounts.

1. Select cells E11 through E13.
2. Right-click the selected range, and then on the shortcut menu, click Format Cells.

   The Format Cells dialog box appears.
3. On the Number tab, in the Category list, select Currency.

   Three lists appear in the Format Cells dialog box.
4. In the Decimal Places list, click the down arrow until 0 is displayed.
5. In the Symbol list, be sure the dollar sign ($) is displayed, and click OK.
6. In cell E11, type **910.80** and press Enter.
   The dollar sign appears in front of the number in cell E11. The entry rounds up to the nearest whole number, 911, with no decimal places.

Your worksheet should look similar to the following illustration.

B	C	D	E
Client Invoice			
(425) 555-1234			
Work Performed			
Description of Work Performed	***Hours Billed***	***Billing Rate***	***$ Billed***
			$911
We help your business make an Impact!			

Format numbers using a custom format

In this exercise, you include the words *per hour* after entries in the Billing Rate column.

1. Select cells D11 through D13, right-click the selected range, and then on the shortcut menu, click Format Cells.

   The Format Cells dialog box appears.

2. On the Number tab, in the Category list, select Custom.

   The Type list appears in the Format Cells dialog box.

3. In the Type list, select 0.
4. In the Type box, place the insertion point in front of the 0, and then type **$** and a space.
5. Place the insertion point after the 0, and then type a space and **"per hour"** (be sure to include the quotation marks).

   Your entry should look like the entry in the following illustration.

The quotation marks in the Type box tell Excel what to insert in the cells, but they don't actually appear in the worksheet.

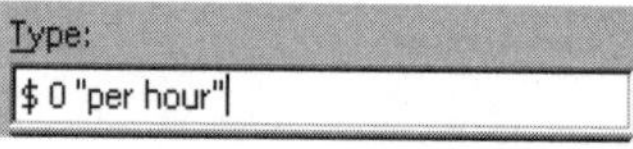

6. Click OK.

   The Custom number format is applied and saved.

7. Select cell D11, type **18** and press Enter.

   Your entry is correctly formatted as $18 per hour, as shown in the following illustration.

Billing Rate	*$ Billed*
$ 18 per hour	$911

Format numbers using a conditional format

In this exercise, you create a conditional format to apply blue shading to a cell entry in the $ Billed column to indicate that the total is less than the amount budgeted.

If a cell contains formula results or other cell values that you want to monitor, you can identify the cells by applying conditional formatting.

1. Select cell E11.
2. On the Format menu, click Conditional Formatting.

   The Conditional Formatting dialog box appears.
3. In the Condition 1 area, be sure that *Cell Value Is* is selected in the box on the left. In the middle drop-down list, select *Less Than*. In the box on the right, type **1000**

   The value $1,000 is set as the amount budgeted for Task 1.
4. Click Format.

   The Format Cells dialog box appears.
5. Click the Color box drop-down arrow.

   The Color palette appears.
6. Click the Blue box in the lower-right corner, and click OK.
7. In the Conditional Formatting dialog box, click OK.

   Since the number in cell E11 is less than the budgeted amount of $1,000 for this task, the value is highlighted in blue.

   Your worksheet should look similar to the following illustration.

Billing Rate	*$ Billed*
$ 18 per hour	$911

Conditional formatting indicated by color

Adding Custom Headers and Footers

Headers or footers are useful for keeping track of page numbers, different versions of a worksheet, when the worksheet was revised or printed, and other information to help you keep your files organized. Headers and footers can only be viewed in Print Preview mode or when the worksheet is printed. You can easily create and customize a header or footer, as is demonstrated in the following exercise.

Create a custom header

If you are not working through this lesson sequentially, open the file 04D.xls from the Lesson04 folder before you continue.

In this exercise, you add a header to your invoice.

1. On the Invoice worksheet, on the File menu, click Page Setup.

   The Page Setup dialog box appears.

2. On the Header/Footer tab, click Custom Header.

   The Header dialog box appears. Notice that you can enter different information in the left, middle, and right sections of the header.

3. In the Center Section box, type **Impact Invoice**

Font

4. Select the text you just typed, and then click the Font button.

   The Font dialog box appears.

5. In the Font Style box, select Bold. Then, in the Size box, select 14, and click OK.

   The font dialog box closes.

   Your screen should look similar to the following illustration.

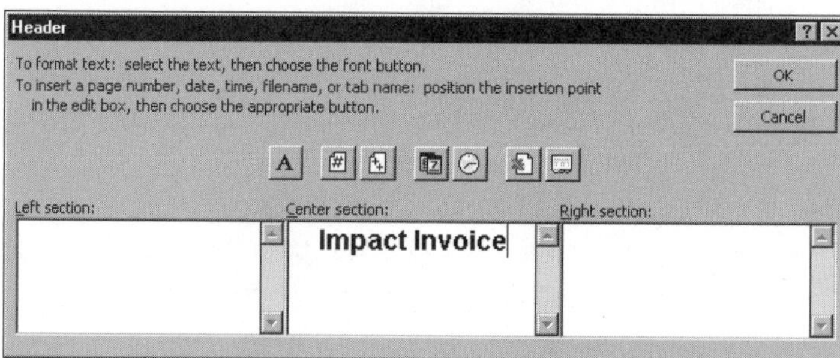

6. In the Header dialog box, click OK.

   The Header dialog box closes. Notice the changes to your header in the Header/Footer tab. Keep the Page Setup dialog box open for the next exercise.

Create a custom footer

In this exercise, you create a footer that displays the print date, the filename, and the page number.

1. In the Page Setup dialog box, on the Header/Footer tab, click Custom Footer.
2. Click inside the Right Section box, and then click the Date button.

Date

3. Select the text in the Right Section box, and then click the Font button.

   The Font dialog box appears.

4. In the Size box, select 12, and click OK.

   The Font dialog box closes.

File Name

Page Number

5. Click inside the Center Section box, and then click the File Name button. Press Enter, and then click the Page Number button.
6. Select the text in the Center Section box, and then click the Font button.
7. In the Font dialog box, in the Font Style list, select Bold. Then in the Size box, select 12, and click OK.
8. In the Footer dialog box, click OK.

   The Footer dialog box closes. Notice the changes to your Footer in the Header/Footer tab.

   Your screen should look similar to the following illustration.

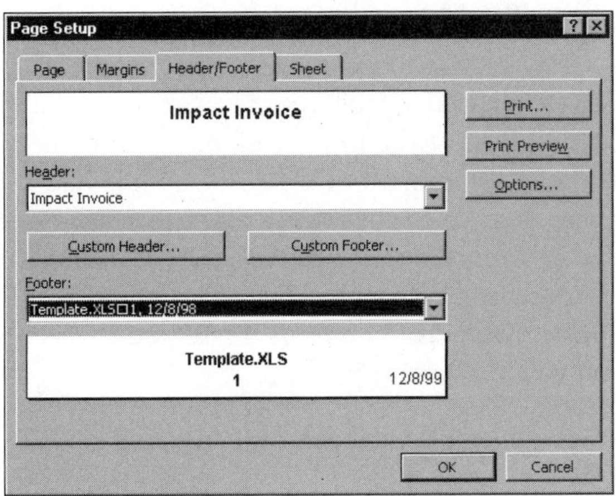

9. In the Page Setup dialog box, click OK.

   Your custom header and footer are now in place.

Changing Page Margins

A *margin* is the area on a page between the text and the edge of the paper. You can adjust the worksheet margins to make all of the text fit on one page and to center text on a page, which makes your printed worksheet easier to read. To be sure that your worksheet fits on the page and looks good, you adjust the margins in Page Setup.

Center the worksheet on the page

In this exercise, you use Page Setup to change the page margins so that the Impact invoice fits and is centered on the page.

If you are not working through this lesson sequentially, open the file 04E.xls from the Lesson04 folder before you continue.

1. On the Invoice worksheet, on the File menu, click Page Setup.

   The Page Setup dialog box appears.
2. On the Margins tab, double-click in the Left box, and then type **.5**
3. In the Right box, double-click, and then type **.5**
4. In the Center On Page area, select the Horizontally check box.
5. Click OK.

   The worksheet will be centered on the page when it is printed.

Saving an Invoice as a Template

You're almost ready to save your Impact Invoice as a template so that other employees can use it.

A *template* is a preformatted worksheet that is ready to be filled with specific data. You could simply save the Impact Invoice you've been working on as a document instead of a template, but then your employees could not benefit from all the work you've done to format the invoice. In addition, they would have to create a new invoice from scratch each time they want to use it. You will therefore save your Impact Invoice as a template in the Spreadsheet Solutions folder. Your employees can then make copies of it and add their data in the rows and columns that you've already set up.

First, you need to make some final adjustments to make it easier to use. Then, when you have saved it, any Impact employee who has access to your templates folder can use it for their work.

Make some final adjustments

If you are not working through this lesson sequentially, open the file 04F.xls from the Lesson04 folder before you continue.

In this exercise, you delete Sheet2 and Sheet3, since you're not using them.

1. On the Invoice worksheet, click the Sheet2 tab, hold down the Shift key, and then click the Sheet3 tab.

   Sheets 2 and 3 are selected.

To select non-adjacent sheets, select the first sheet, hold down Ctrl, and click other sheets as needed.

2. On the Edit menu, click Delete Sheet.

   A warning message appears.

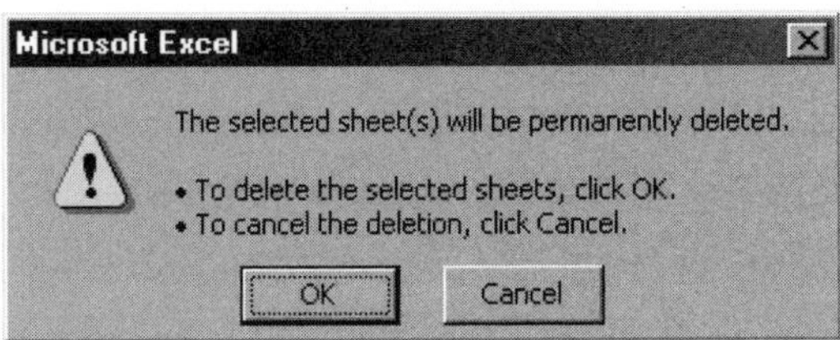

3. Click OK.

   Sheets 2 and 3 are permanently deleted.

Save the invoice as a template

In this exercise, you save your invoice as a template.

1. On the File menu, click Save As.
2. In the Save As Type drop-down list, select Template.
3. In the File Name box, double-click to select the old filename, and then type **IPR_Invoice** and click Save.

   The workbook is saved as a template in the Templates folder.
4. Close the workbook window.

Be sure that the invoice is available as a template

Now that the template is complete, you ensure that the invoice opens correctly and looks the way you want.

1. On the File menu, click New.
2. On the General tab, double-click the IPR_Invoice icon.

   A copy of your invoice, temporarily named *IPR_Invoice1*, opens and is ready to be filled out and saved with a permanent name.
3. Close the IPR_Invoice1 file. If a dialog box asking if you want to save your changes appears, click No.

One Step Further Editing a Template

Open the template

If you are not working through this lesson sequentially, open the file 04G.xls from the Lesson04 folder. Then skip to the "Edit the Template" exercise.

Because so many employees will be using your template, you want it to be perfect. In the following exercises, you make some refinements to the template so it's as close to perfect as possible.

In this exercise, you open the original IPR_Invoice template so that you can edit it.

1. On the File menu, click Open, and then locate the Templates folder on your hard disk in your Windows Templates subfolder.
2. Double-click the IPR_Invoice file.

   The actual template, and not a copy, opens. The name *IPR_Invoice.xlt* is displayed in the title bar.

tip

If you are not able to find the IPR_Invoice.xlt template in the Templates folder from the file menu, click the Start button at the bottom of your screen, point to Find, click Files Or Folders, and in the Find: All Files dialog box, search for the file on your hard drive.

Edit the template

In this exercise, you edit the footer information in the template.

1. On the File menu, click Page Setup.

   The Page Setup dialog box appears.
2. On the Header/Footer tab, click Custom Footer.
3. Click inside the Center Section box, select the text *[&(File]*, and then click Delete.
4. To remove the blank line, click Delete again.
5. In the Footer dialog box, click OK.

   The Footer dialog box closes. You can see the changes to your footer in the Header/Footer tab of the Page Setup dialog box.

6. Click OK.

   The Page Setup dialog box closes.

7. Save your work.

Finish the lesson

1. Close any open windows.
2. If you are finished using Microsoft Excel for now, on the File menu, click Exit.

Lesson 4 Quick Reference

To	Do this	Button
Change fonts	Select the cell contents. On the Formatting toolbar, in the Font drop-down list, select the font you want.	
Change the size of a font	Select the cell or cell contents. On the Formatting toolbar, in the Font Size drop-down list, select the size you want.	
Change the attributes of a font	Select the cell or cell contents. On the Formatting toolbar, click the Bold or Italic button.	B I
Add a border	Select the range of cells you want. On the Formatting toolbar, click the Borders button drop-down arrow, and then select the border type you want.	
Apply shading	Select the range of cells you want. On the Formatting toolbar, click the Fill Color button drop-down arrow, and then select the color you want.	
Name a style	Select the cell or cell range of cells, and then, on the Format menu, click Style. In the Style dialog box, enter the style name you want, and click OK.	
Use Format Painter	Click the cell that is formatted with the style you want, and then, on the Standard toolbar, click the Format Painter button. Click the target cell to apply the style.	

Lesson 4 Quick Reference

To	Do this
Format numbers	Select the cell or cell range. Right-click the selection. On the shortcut menu, click Format Cells. In the Format Cells dialog box, click the Number tab, and then select the style you want. Click OK.
Add headers and footers	On the File menu, click Page Setup. In the Page Setup dialog box, click the Header/Footer tab, and then click either the Custom Header or Custom Footer button. Enter the information you want, and click OK.
Change margin settings	On the File menu, click Page Setup. In the Page Setup dialog box, click the Margins tab, and then enter the desired values in the margin measurement boxes. Click OK.
Center the worksheet	On the File menu, click Page Setup. In the Page Setup dialog box, click the Margins tab. In the Center On Page area, select the Horizontally check box. Click OK.
Delete unnecessary sheets	Select the tabs of the unneeded sheets. On the Edit menu, select Delete Sheet. In the warning message box, click OK.
Save a worksheet as a template in the Templates folder	On the File menu, click Save As. In the Save As Type drop-down list, select Template. In the list of folders, double-click the Templates folder, and then click Save.
Open the new template	On the File menu, click New. Click the General tab, and then double-click the appropriate icon.
Edit a template	On the File menu, click Open. In the Open dialog box, browse to locate the template you want to edit. Double-click the template file. Edit the template. On the File menu, click Save.

PART 3

Microsoft Outlook 2000

LESSON

1

Jumping into Your E-mail

ESTIMATED TIME
45 min.

In this lesson you will learn how to:

- ✔ *Start Microsoft Outlook 2000.*
- ✔ *Navigate in the Outlook Bar.*
- ✔ *Review e-mail messages and attachments.*
- ✔ *Reply to and forward e-mail messages.*
- ✔ *Save e-mail messages and check sent messages.*
- ✔ *Format and print a copy of e-mail messages.*
- ✔ *Use Notes as a reminder.*
- ✔ *Customize your Inbox.*

Managing personal communications and information is essential for success in today's business world. With Microsoft Outlook 2000, you have complete command over your business communications and schedule. You can:

- Send and forward e-mail messages.
- Add attachments to e-mail messages.
- Mark messages as confidential or urgent.
- Route files for feedback.
- Track your appointments on your calendar.
- Create an appointment from an e-mail message.
- Reschedule and edit appointments.
- Keep track of your personal and business contacts.

Workgroup

You can configure Outlook to work in a workgroup environment or over the Internet.

In a Workgroup environment, your computer is connected to a server. Other computers in your organization can also be connected to the same server or to other servers connected together into a network. You communicate with others in your workgroup and access the Internet via this network of servers.

Internet Only

In an Internet-only environment, which is more typical for home computers, your computer is connected via modem to an Internet service provider (ISP). Your ISP provides access to the Internet.

Starting Outlook 2000, the Gateway to Your E-mail

The screen you see when you start Outlook has several parts.

- The large area beneath the folder banner is called the Information viewer. Your e-mail, calendar, and other information are displayed in this window.
- Above the Information viewer are the Standard and Advanced toolbars. These contain buttons for the commands that you will use most frequently. You can customize the toolbars to make them more useful by adding your own favorite buttons or removing ones you don't use. You can hide one or both of the toolbars, or compress them onto a single row, by using the Toolbar commands in the View menu.
- The vertical column of shortcuts to the left of the Information viewer is the Outlook Bar. Each shortcut on the Outlook Bar will take you directly to the contents of an Outlook folder. Shortcuts eliminate the need to type complicated path names to reach the files you want. Each Outlook folder contains the programs and files for a particular Outlook feature, such as Inbox or Contacts. Outlook folders that do not have an associated shortcut can be opened directly from the Folder List.

- The shortcuts on your Outlook Bar are organized in groups. When you install Outlook, the Outlook Shortcuts, My Shortcuts, and Other Shortcuts groups of shortcuts are automatically created. You can create new groups and place new shortcuts within those groups. You can also add shortcuts to groups that already exist.

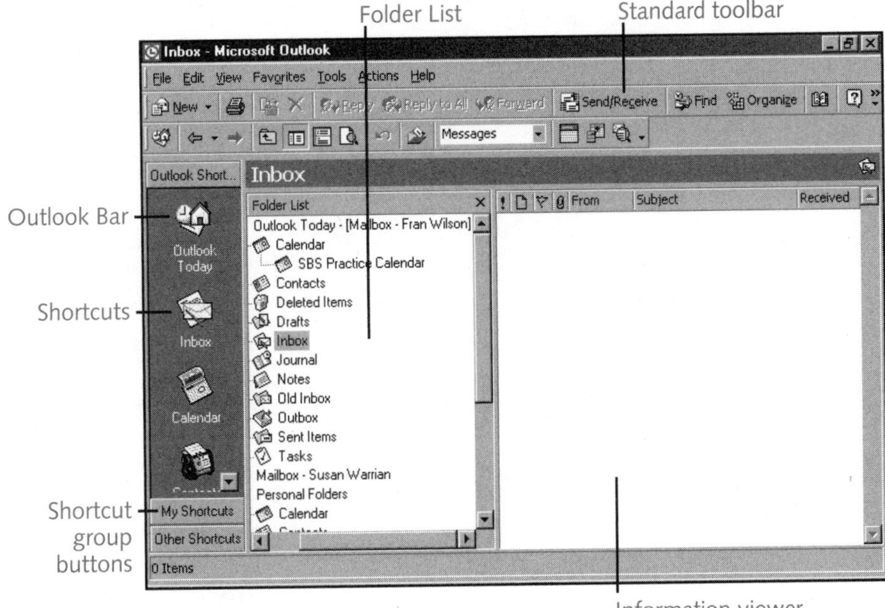

Internet Only

The following table shows the different groups and shortcuts included in the standard installation of Outlook 2000. Other configurations may show different shortcuts, depending on how you set up your program.

Group	Shortcut	Description
Outlook Shortcuts	Outlook Today	Opens the "day-at-a-glance" view with an overview of your Calendar, e-mail messages, and tasks.
	Inbox	Opens the Inbox folder, which contains your e-mail messages.
	Calendar	Opens the Calendar folder, which displays your appointments.
	Contacts	Opens the Contacts folder, which stores the names, phone numbers, and addresses of the important people in your life.
	Tasks	Opens your Task list, which displays a to-do list.
	Notes	Opens the Notes folder, which stores general information, such as ideas, reminders, lists and directions, in the form of notes.
	Deleted Items	Opens the Deleted Items folder, which temporarily stores the items you delete until you permanently delete them.
My Shortcuts	Drafts	Opens the Drafts folder, which stores e-mail messages that you have created but have not sent.
	Outbox	Opens the Outbox folder, which holds e-mail messages that you are sending until you are connected to your mail server.
	Sent Items	Opens the Sent Items folder, which stores copies of e-mail messages you have sent.
	Journal	Opens the Journal folder, which displays a history of your recorded activities in a timeline format.
Other Shortcuts	My Computer	Provides access to the drives, folders, and files on your computer.
	My Documents	Provides access to the My Documents folder on your hard disk.
	Favorites	Opens the Favorites folder, which stores shortcuts to your favorite Internet addresses or to other items on your computer.

E-mail is now the preferred method of communication for business and many other purposes. It combines the immediacy and informality of a phone call with the benefits of written correspondence.

As a new account manager at Impact Public Relations, your daily tasks include reading and responding to e-mail messages, some of which have important documents attached. Because you are busy with several clients at once, you also need an effective way to record and organize miscellaneous ideas and information as you think of them. In this lesson, you begin using Outlook 2000 to manage your e-mail and create electronic notes.

You begin by starting Microsoft Outlook 2000, and then open Outlook Today for an overview of your day. The Outlook Today pane displays your calendar for up to seven days, your list of tasks, and whether you have any e-mail messages—all on one screen. In order to have a more realistic experience accessing e-mail messages, you then create a practice Inbox and copy messages into it from the Outlook Practice folder on your hard disk that is created during Setup. Using this practice Inbox ensures that these exercises will not interfere with your actual Inbox and e-mail messages.

Start Outlook 2000

Outlook

1. On the desktop, double-click the Microsoft Outlook 2000 icon.
   The Microsoft Outlook 2000 startup screen appears.
2. Click Next.
3. In the E-Mail Service Options area, select either the Internet Only or the Corporate Or Workgroup option, depending on your setup.
4. Click Next.
   Outlook's configuration will be tailored to your work needs.
5. Click Yes to make Outlook your default manager for Mail, News, and Contacts.
6. The first time you open Outlook, Clippit, the default Office Assistant, and the Welcome To Microsoft Outlook Help balloon appear. Click Start Using Microsoft Outlook.

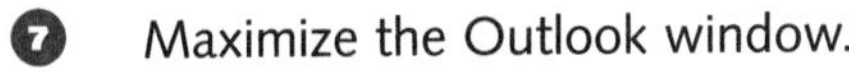

7. Maximize the Outlook window.

Maximize

Meet the Office Assistant

If you have started Microsoft Outlook 2000 before, some of the opening screens described here might not appear.

The Office Assistant probably just popped up on your screen. So, now is a great time to introduce it. If it did not appear, you can easily reach it—on the Help menu, click Show The Office Assistant.

The default Office Assistant for Office 2000 is Clippit the paper clip, an animated character that automatically appears on your screen to offer help.

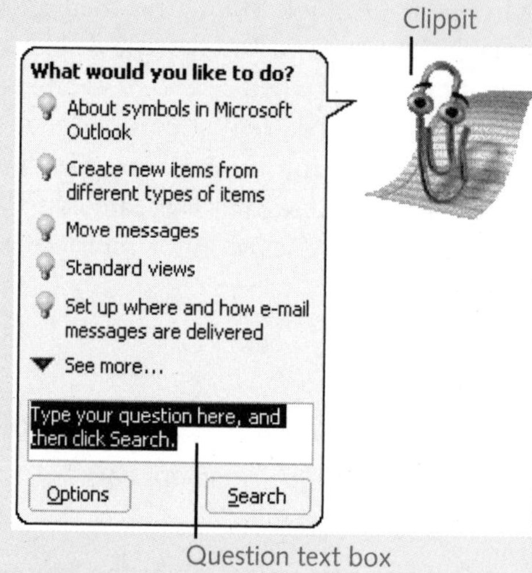

To get help from the Office Assistant, simply click in the Type Your Question Here, And Then Click Search box, and then type your question. Then click the Search button or press Enter. After a few moments of pondering, the Office Assistant displays a list of possible topics relating to your question. You can check out these topics by clicking your choice.

From time to time as you work, the Office Assistant automatically appears with a light bulb overhead. When this happens, the Office Assistant has a tip about the action that you are performing. Simply click the light bulb to display the helpful information.

If you receive the message "The selected Assistant character is not available... Would you like to install it now?" click No, and then click Cancel.

You can specify the type of assistance that you want from the Office Assistant for both help and tips. To do so, right-click the Office Assistant, and then on the shortcut menu, click Options. This opens the Office Assistant dialog box. On the Options tab, customize the Office Assistant by clearing the check boxes for those options that you want turned off (by default, all check boxes should already be selected). You can also turn off the Office Assistant entirely by simply clearing the Use The Office Assistant check box.

You can even select a different animated character as your Office Assistant—for example, Rocky, the Dot, the Genius, or Mother Nature. To do so, on the bottom of the Office Assistant box, click the Options button. Then, on the Gallery tab, scroll through the characters using the Back and Next buttons. When you see the one you'd like, click OK.

important

For the purposes of this book, the Office Assistant should not appear on your screen. On the Help menu, click Hide The Office Assistant.

Open Outlook Today for an overview of your day

Outlook Today provides a quick overview of the day's appointments, tasks, and the number of e-mail messages you have. In this exercise, you open Outlook Today and make it your *default* page, the first screen you see when you start Outlook.

Outlook Today

1. On the Outlook Bar, click the Outlook Today shortcut.

   The Outlook Today screen appears. Your screen should look similar to the illustration below.

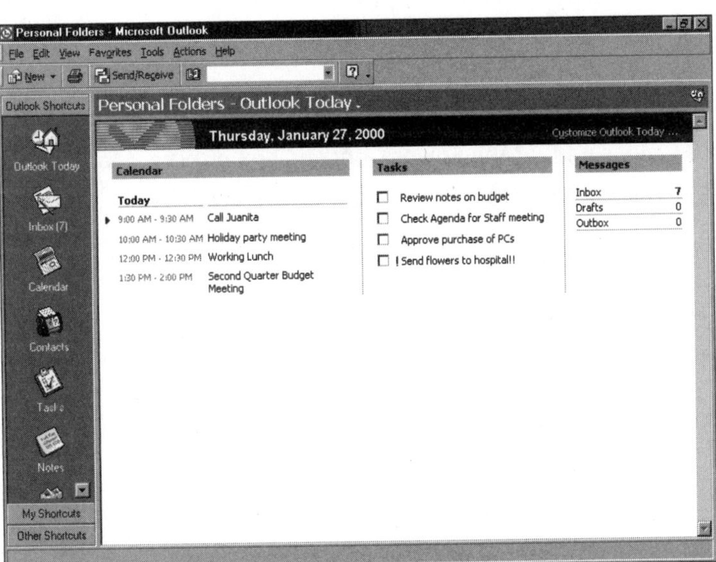

2. Scroll, if necessary, and then click the Customize Outlook Today link.

   The Outlook Today options for Startup, Messages, Calendar, Tasks, and Styles appear in the Information viewer.

3. In the Startup area, be sure that the When Starting, Go Directly To Outlook Today check box is selected.

4. Click the Save Changes button.

   The Outlook Today screen reappears.

Clicking a folder in the Folder List displays the files or subfolders that it contains.

5. If the Folder List is not displayed, on the View menu, click Folder List.

   The Folder List appears.

More Buttons

> **important**
>
> If you don't see a button on your toolbar, click the More Buttons drop-down arrow for that toolbar. Point to the Add Or Remove Buttons drop-down arrow to display a list of additional toolbar buttons. In this list, click the button that you want to use. This executes the command and adds the button to the toolbar, replacing one that has not been used for a while.

Create an SBS Practice Inbox

In order to begin your work, you'll need to set up a practice Inbox to access your e-mail messages.

Inbox

1. On the Outlook Bar, click the Inbox shortcut.
2. Be sure that the Folder List is displayed.
3. On the Standard toolbar, click the New Mail Message button drop-down arrow, and then click Folder.

   The Create New Folder dialog box appears.

New Mail Message

4. Be sure that the Folder Contains box displays Mail Items.
5. In the Name box, type **SBS Practice Inbox** and click OK. You'll create the shortcut to it in step 8.

6. If you are prompted to add the shortcut to the Outlook Bar, click No.

   The SBS Practice Inbox folder appears in the Folder List as a subfolder of your Inbox.

7. On the Standard toolbar, click the New Mail Message button drop-down arrow, and then click Outlook Bar Shortcut.

   The Add To Outlook Bar dialog box appears.

8. In the Folder List, click the plus sign (+) next to the Inbox folder to display the subfolders, click the SBS Practice Inbox folder, and click OK.

   The new SBS Practice Inbox shortcut appears at the bottom of the Outlook Bar.

To quickly add a shortcut to the Outlook Bar, right-click the folder in the Folder List and click Add To Outlook Bar.

Set up practice e-mail

In real life, e-mail messages arrive over the Internet or your office network and pop up automatically in your Inbox. In these lessons, you won't be working with real e-mail messages. Instead, you will drag e-mail messages from the Outlook Practice folder into your SBS Practice Inbox folder.

1. Click the Start button, point to Programs, and then click either Windows Explorer or Windows NT Explorer, whichever is on your computer.

   The Windows Explorer or Windows NT Explorer window opens on top of your Outlook window.

2. Browse through the folders on your hard disk until you locate the Office 8in1 Step by Step folder, and double-click it.

3. Double-click the Outlook Practice folder.

   The contents of the folder are displayed.

4. Open the Lesson01 folder.

   The contents of the folder are displayed.

5. Right-click a blank area on the taskbar (the horizontal bar across the bottom of the screen), and then click Tile Vertically if you have Windows 95, or Tile Windows Vertically if you have Windows 98 or Windows NT.

   The Explorer and SBS Practice Inbox windows are now arranged side by side.

To select all three messages at once, click the first message, and then hold down the Shift key while clicking the last message.

6. Drag the practice e-mail message files, indicated by envelope icons, from the Lesson01 folder in the Outlook Practice folder to your SBS Practice Inbox folder in the Folder List.

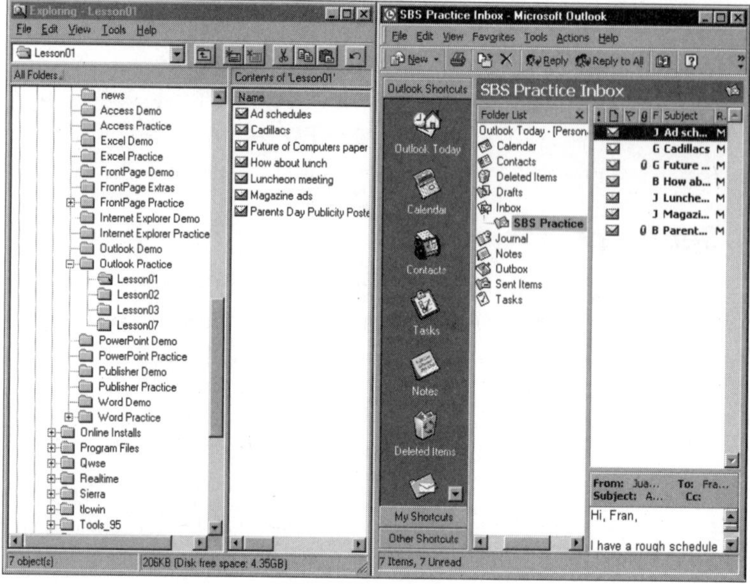

Close

7. In the Explorer window, click the Close button.
8. Maximize Outlook.

   The e-mail messages are displayed in the Information viewer.

Reviewing Your E-mail Messages and Attachments

You have arrived early for work one Tuesday morning at Impact Public Relations. Looking at your Inbox, you discover several e-mail messages, including some from Five Lakes Publishing, Awesome Computers, and the DaVinci School of Arts and Crafts, three of your client accounts.

With Outlook 2000, you can quickly preview e-mail messages without actually opening them so that you can identify and deal with the urgent ones immediately and save the rest for later. One especially useful feature of e-mail is that documents can be attached to and sent with messages. An attached document remains in the format in which it was created, such as Microsoft Word. If you have the application that was used to create the attachment, you can open and edit it directly. Even without that particular application, if the attachment is in almost any standard format, it can be converted into text that can be read and edited.

In the following exercises, you open, read, reply to, and forward messages, and save an e-mail attachment to use later.

Open and read a message

1. If the SBS Practice Inbox is not open, on the Outlook Bar, click the SBS Practice Inbox shortcut.
2. In the Information viewer, double-click the Magazine Ads message from Juanita Rivera.

   The text of the message appears in the Message form. In the header, the names of the sender and the recipients, and the date and time of the message, appear.

   Your screen should look similar to the following illustration.

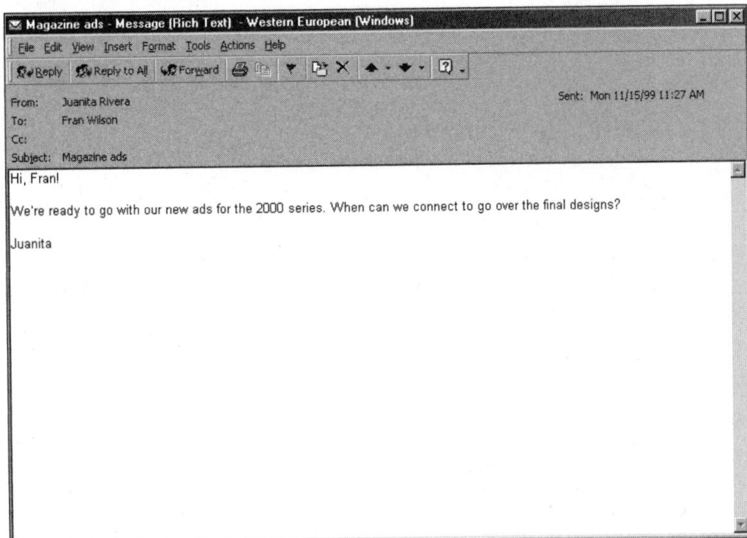

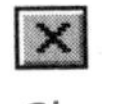
Close

3. After reading the e-mail message, on the Message title bar, click the Close button.

   Your message closes and the envelope icon changes from closed to open to indicate that the message has been read.

Save time by previewing messages

You have an important company meeting this morning, and no time to read all of your e-mail messages. You know that at least some of them require immediate attention. You need to preview them to find out which ones are urgent.

In this exercise, you practice two ways to preview your messages. First, with AutoPreview, you can see the first few lines of all of your unread messages. Second, using the Preview pane, you can see the complete text of a selected message without opening it.

AutoPreview

AutoPreviewed messages are still flagged as unread—the envelope icon is still sealed—which is useful for sorting them later.

1. On the View menu, click AutoPreview.

   The first few lines of all messages are displayed. Your screen should look similar to the following illustration.

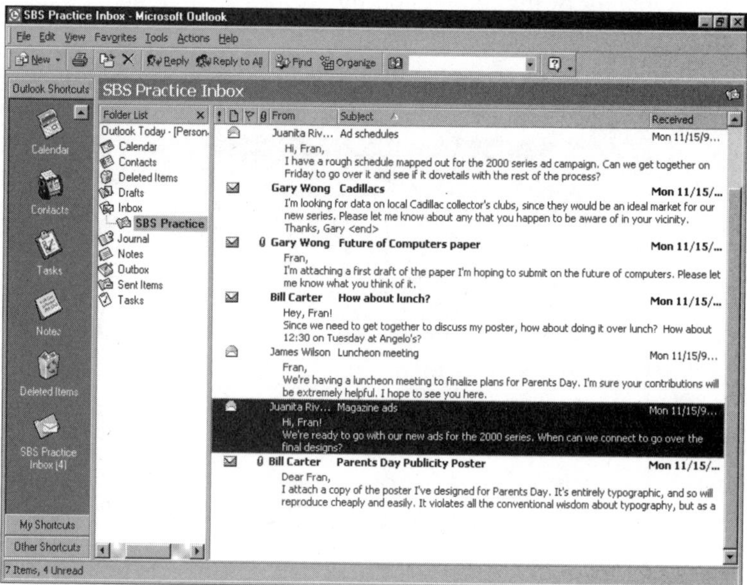

2. Click a message in order to select it.
3. On the View menu, click Preview Pane.

   The Preview pane opens in a separate window at the bottom of the Information viewer, and you can read the complete text of the message.

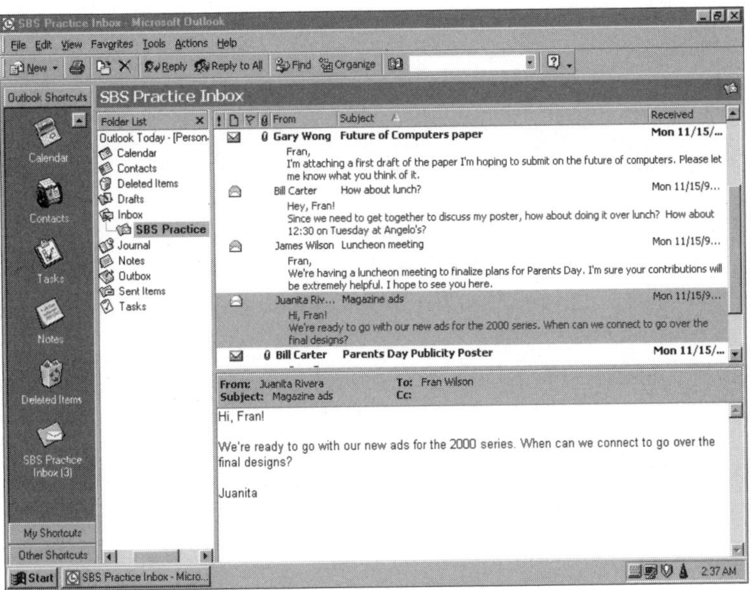

4. On the View menu, click AutoPreview.

   A standard list of e-mail messages appears.

> **tip**
>
> You can choose to be notified as soon as new e-mail messages arrive. On the Tools menu, click Options. On the Preferences tab, click the E-Mail Options button, and then select the Display A Notification Message When New Mail Arrives check box. Click OK twice to close all open dialog boxes. Now, when a new e-mail message arrives, a message appears on your screen to let you know.

Open and save an attachment

Your colleague at the DaVinci School, Bill Carter, has created a publicity poster for the upcoming Parents Day at the school and he has sent you a copy of it as an attachment to his e-mail message. In this exercise, you open the poster and decide to save it to a folder on your hard disk in case you need to use it later.

1. Double-click the Parents Day Publicity Poster message from Bill Carter.

   The message is displayed, and an attachment shortcut similar to the one shown below appears at the bottom of the message window.

To quickly save an attached file without opening it, right-click the attachment. On the shortcut menu, click Save As.

Attachments are deleted only when the e-mail message is deleted or when you manually delete the attachment from the message and save the changes.

2. Double-click the attachment icon.

   The attachment opens in Microsoft Word or, if you don't have Word, in WordPad. You can now read, change, and save the document, and print copies of it.

3. On the File menu, click Save As.

   The Save As dialog box appears.

4. In the Save As dialog box, in the Save In drop-down list, select a folder on your hard disk. In the File Name box, select the current filename, type **Parents day poster** and click the Save button.

   Bill's poster has been saved in your folder. The original attachment is still attached to the e-mail message and can be opened again later.

5. Quit Microsoft Word (or WordPad).
6. Close the message.

Close

Outlook Menus Automatically Customize Your Options

Outlook menus logically group commands together, making it easy to access a feature. For example, all formatting commands are grouped on the Format menu. To access a particular menu, simply point to it on the menu bar and click. Initially, the most frequently used features are displayed as menu commands. However, if you hold the mouse pointer still for a moment, the menu expands and the full selection of commands is displayed. You can also expand a menu by clicking the arrows at the bottom of the menu. Once one full menu is displayed on the menu bar, all other menus that you click display their expanded menus as well. As shown in the following illustration, when fully expanded, a menu always indicates infrequently used commands by displaying them against a lighter, recessed background.

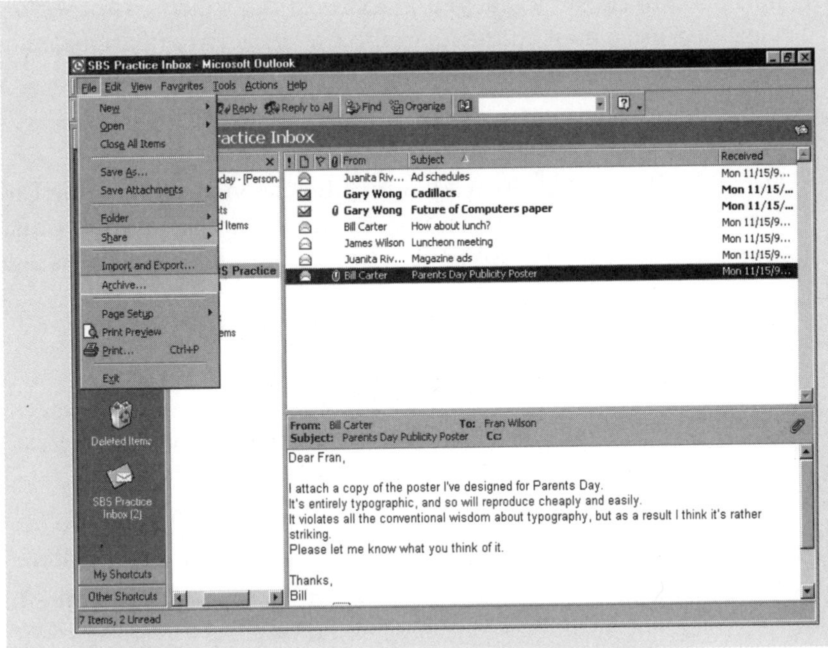

Replying to E-mail Messages

Outlook provides three different methods to respond to messages. You can choose to send your reply to the sender alone or to the sender *and* to everyone else listed in that message's Cc and Bcc boxes. You can also choose to forward the message, along with any attachments, to the sender, to other recipients, or to another person. Knowing how to apply each of these three methods will provide great flexibility in your e-mail communications.

One difference between replying to a message and forwarding a message is this: if the original message included an attachment, the attachment is not sent back if you use Reply or Reply To All. To include the attachment in your reply or to send the e-mail message to someone who was not on the original recipient, Cc, or Bcc lists, you must forward the message.

If you don't see a Bcc box in your Message form, on the View menu, click Bcc Field.

tip

If you need to ensure that other people see a copy of an e-mail message, on the Message form, type their e-mail addresses in the Cc (courtesy copy) box. You can also send a blind courtesy copy by typing their addresses in the Bcc box. When you send a blind copy, the recipients in the To and Cc boxes are unaware of the copy that was sent to the people listed in the Bcc box.

In the following exercises, you practice all three methods of replying to a message. Because e-mail addresses in these exercises are fictitious, all replies will be returned as undeliverable and can be deleted at your leisure.

Reply to a message

Dr. James Wilson has invited you to a luncheon meeting at the DaVinci School. Attending the meeting promises to be both a pleasant social occasion and useful for your role as the school's publicist. You decide to accept his e-mail invitation.

SBS Practice Inbox

1. If it is not open already, on the Outlook Bar, click the SBS Practice Inbox shortcut.

   The SBS Practice Inbox appears.

2. In the SBS Practice Inbox Information viewer, double-click the message from James Wilson.

   The message appears.

To enter the meeting in your Calendar, see Lesson 2, "Learning the Basics of Scheduling."

3. On the Message form Standard toolbar, click the Reply button.

   The Reply form appears. James Wilson already appears in the To box as the recipient.

4. In the message area of the Reply form, type the following:

   Dr. Wilson: I'd be honored to attend your luncheon. I'll see you there.

5. Click the Send button.

   The Reply form disappears, and your message is sent.

Internet Only

   If you are working in an Internet-only environment, after you click the Send button on the Message form Standard toolbar, your message is placed in the Outbox. To send the message, on the Standard toolbar, click Send/Receive. If you are not presently connected to the Internet, you may be prompted to connect. Complete the instructions from your Internet service provider to access the Internet.

Close

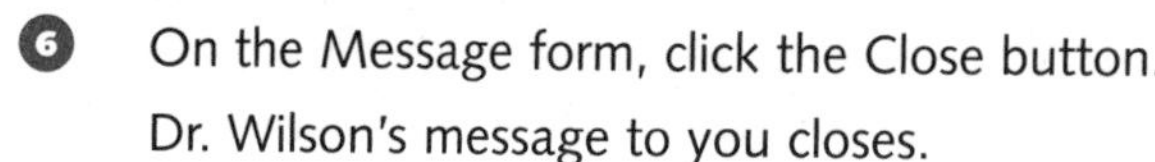

6. On the Message form, click the Close button.

   Dr. Wilson's message to you closes.

Reply to everyone who received a message

Gary Wong is the sales manager for Five Lakes Publishing, which publishes a series of books about classic American cars. He has sent out a request to various colleagues for information about Cadillac collectors clubs. Since you happened across a new club at the county fair last weekend, you suspect that he and the others might be interested. In this exercise, you send your reply to everyone who received Gary's message.

1. In the SBS Practice Inbox Information viewer, open the message from Gary Wong entitled Cadillacs.

   The message appears.
2. On the Message form Standard toolbar, click the Reply To All button.

   The Reply form appears.
3. Type the following response:

   Check out the King County Classic Cadillac Collector's Club.
4. Click the Send button.

   The Reply form disappears, and your message is sent to Gary Wong and to everyone listed in the Cc box in his message.

   Internet Only

   If you are working in an Internet-only environment, after you click the Send button on the Message form Standard toolbar, your message is placed in the Outbox. To send the message, on the Standard toolbar, click Send/Receive. If you are not presently connected to the Internet, you may be prompted to connect. Complete the instructions from your Internet service provider to access the Internet.

   Close
5.  On the Message form, click the Close button.

Forward a message

Let's suppose that Bill Carter at the DaVinci School wants to have your advice before he shows his poster to Dr. Wilson. You tell Bill that the poster is not only professional, but also attractive, and you offer to forward it to Dr. Wilson.

1. In the SBS Practice Inbox Information viewer, open the message from Bill Carter entitled Parents Day Publicity Poster.
2. On the Message form Standard toolbar, click the Forward button.
3. In the To box, type Dr. Wilson's e-mail address: **Jamesw@davinci.davinci**

4. In the message window, type your praise of Carter's poster:

   Dr. Wilson:

   I am very impressed with Mr. Carter's efforts here. I think this will provide excellent exposure for the school.

5. Click the Send button.

   The message window closes. In addition to your message, the attachment containing a copy of Bill's poster is now sent to Dr. Wilson.

Internet Only

   If you are working in an Internet-only environment, after you click the Send button on the Message form Standard toolbar, your message is placed in the Outbox. To send the message, on the Standard toolbar, click Send/Receive. If you are not presently connected to the Internet, you may be prompted to connect. Complete the instructions from your Internet service provider to access the Internet.

Close

6. On the Message form, click the Close button.

   The message from Bill Carter closes.

Saving and Checking Your Sent Messages

When you send an e-mail message, you do not necessarily lose the information contained in the message. You can store a copy of any e-mail message that you send in the Sent Items folder, where you can later review it. If you decide that you no longer need a message, you can delete it from the Sent Items folder. Even then, you still retain a copy of the item in the Deleted Items folder; these items remain until you permanently remove them. This system of backup copies helps you avoid losing important information.

Keep copies of your sent e-mail messages

You can choose whether or not to have copies of all your e-mail messages stored in the Sent Items folder. In this exercise, you retain the option of keeping your e-mail messages stored in Sent Items so that later exercises proceed correctly.

1. On the Tools menu, click Options.

   The Options dialog box appears.

2. In the Options dialog box, on the Preferences tab, click the E-Mail Options button.

   The E-Mail Options dialog box appears.

3. Be sure the Save Copies Of Messages In Sent Items Folder check box is selected.
4. In the E-Mail Options dialog box, click OK.
5. In the Options dialog box, click OK.

Locate a message you've already sent

Suppose that you want to double-check exactly what you wrote to Bill Carter. In this exercise, you learn how to navigate in My Shortcuts to review messages you've already sent.

1. On the bottom of the Outlook Bar, click My Shortcuts.

   The shortcuts to the Drafts, Outbox, Sent Items, and Journal folders appear.

Sent Items

2. Click the Sent Items shortcut.

   A list of the e-mail messages that you have sent appears in the Information viewer.

3. Double-click the message you sent to Bill Carter.

   The message opens.

4. After reading what you wrote, close the message.

You can preview these e-mail items with AutoPreview or in the Preview pane, just as with any other e-mail messages.

> **tip**
>
> After deleting items from Outlook folders, a copy still remains in the Deleted Items folder until you empty it. Items deleted from the Deleted Items folder are permanently deleted. To free space on your hard disk and to more quickly and easily locate your important items, empty your Deleted Items folder regularly. To permanently delete items, click the Deleted Items shortcut, select all the items you want to remove, and then on the Standard toolbar, click the Delete button. A warning box appears prompting you for confirmation. Click OK.

Deleted Items

Formatting and Printing Copies of E-mail Messages

Sometimes you need hard copy of an e-mail message, for example, to distribute at a meeting. You can format and print copies of the e-mail messages you receive and the ones you send, just as you can with any other document.

Format and print an e-mail message

In this exercise, you make changes in the formatting of an e-mail message, and then print a copy of the result.

To make the message easier to read, you can click the Actual Size button on the Print Preview toolbar.

1. If the SBS Practice Inbox is not open, on the Outlook Bar, click the SBS Practice Inbox shortcut.
2. In the Information viewer, click the message from James Wilson.

Print

> **tip**
>
> If no changes are needed in the format or layout of the e-mail message, you can print the message immediately by clicking the Print button on the Standard toolbar.

Print Preview

3. On the File menu, click Print Preview.

   In the Print Preview window, you now see an image of the message as it will appear when printed.
4. On the Print Preview toolbar, click the Page Setup button.

   The Page Setup dialog box appears.
5. On the Format tab, in the Fonts area, click the Font button next to the Fields box.

   The Font dialog box appears. The current font size and style choices are displayed in the Sample box.
6. In the Font list, select Times New Roman.
7. In the Size list, type or select 12.

   The text has now been reformatted to be displayed in 12-point Times New Roman font.
8. In the Font dialog box, click OK, and then in the Page Setup dialog box, click OK.
9. In the Print Preview dialog box, click the Print button.

   The Print dialog box appears with Memo Style selected as the print style.
10. In the Print dialog box, click OK.

    The message is printed.

Using Notes to Store Information

Many people jot down notes—ideas, messages, chores, and reminders—on notepads or bits of paper as they think of them during the course of a day. In Outlook, you can capture these spontaneous thoughts in electronic form. Outlook's Notes takes the place of sticky notes. The note will stay on your screen when Outlook is minimized, and when you click the note on the taskbar, it will reappear on your screen no matter what Microsoft Office 2000 program you are running.

In the following exercise, you write yourself a reminder to get together with Bill Carter to discuss printing and distributing his poster, and then you save the reminder for later use.

Create a note

Notes

New Note

1. On the Outlook Bar, scroll if necessary to bring the Notes shortcut into view. Click the Notes shortcut.
2. On the Standard toolbar, click the New Note button.

   A new blank note form appears that looks like a yellow sticky note.
3. Type **Call Bill about getting together re poster**

   The note should look similar to the following illustration.

Close Note

4. On the note, click the Close Note button.

   Your note closes, and a shortcut appears in the Information viewer with the first few words of the content listed underneath.
5. Double-click the note.

   The complete note reappears on the screen.
6. On the note, click the Close Note button.

You can access your note while in another Microsoft Office 2000 program. Clicking Note on the taskbar makes it reappear on your screen.

Views in Notes

As your notes accumulate, you will want to organize them. This is easily done in Outlook. To use any of the views below, on the Outlook Bar, click the Notes shortcut. On the View menu, point to Current View, and then click the view you want.

(continued)

continued

Click this view	To see notes
Icons	Represented by icons arranged from left to right by creation date.
Notes List	In a list sorted by creation date.
Last Seven Days	In a list created during the last seven days.
By Category	In a list grouped by categories and sorted by creation date within each category.
By Color	In a list grouped by color and sorted by creation date for each color.

One Step Further

Customizing Your Inbox

You can rearrange the way your Inbox is set up and how it handles your e-mail to better suit your personal work style. You can change how your incoming e-mail is displayed, in which font it appears, and where it is automatically filed when you are finished with it, all of which can contribute to your efficiency at Impact Public Relations. In this exercise, you set your e-mail to automatically open the next item in your Inbox after deleting the previous one, thus saving you a step in reading your mail.

Automatically open the next item after a message is deleted

1. On the Tools menu, click Options.

   The Options dialog box appears.

2. On the Preferences tab, click the E-Mail Options button.

   The E-Mail Options dialog box appears.

Advanced E-Mail Options give you even more opportunities to customize your Inbox.

3. In the After Moving Or Deleting An Open Item box, click the drop-down arrow, and then select Open The Next Item.

   Your screen should look similar to the following illustration.

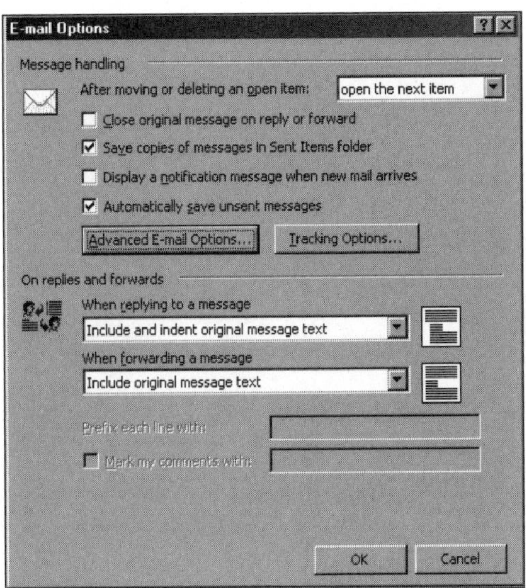

4. In the E-Mail Options dialog box, click OK, and then in the Options dialog box, click OK.

Finish the lesson

Calendar

1. If you want to continue on to the next lesson, on the Outlook Bar, click the Calendar shortcut.
2. If you have finished using Outlook for now and are working in a Workgroup environment, click File, and then click Exit And Log Off. If you are working in an Internet-only environment, click File, and then click Exit.

Lesson 1 Quick Reference

To	Do this	Button
Start Outlook 2000	On the desktop, click the Outlook 2000 shortcut.	
Open Outlook Today	On the Outlook Bar, click the Outlook Today shortcut.	
Make Outlook Today your default screen	On the Outlook Bar, click the Outlook Today shortcut. Click the Customize Outlook Today link, select the When Starting, Go Directly To Outlook Today check box, and then click the Save Changes button.	

Lesson 1 Quick Reference

To	Do this
Read an e-mail message	In the Inbox Information viewer, double-click the message.
Partially preview all e-mail messages	On the View menu, click AutoPreview.
Preview a complete message	On the View menu, click Preview Pane.
Open an attachment	Open the e-mail message, and then double-click the attachment shortcut.
Save an attachment	Double-click the attachment icon, and on the File menu, click Save As. Find the folder that you want to use, type a name for the file in the File Name box, and then click the Save button.
Reply to the sender of an e-mail message	Open the message, click the Reply button, type your response, and then click the Send button. In an Internet-only environment, on the Standard toolbar, click the Send/Receive button.
Reply to the sender of an e-mail message and all who received it	Open the message, click the Reply To All button, type your response, and then click the Send button. In an Internet-only environment, on the Standard toolbar, click the Send/Receive button.
Forward a message	Open the message and click the Forward button. Type e-mail addresses in the To and Cc boxes, and then click Send. In an Internet-only environment, on the Standard toolbar, click the Send And Receive button.
Keep copies of all your sent e-mail messages	On the Tools menu, click Options. In the Options dialog box, on the Preferences tab, click the E-Mail Options button. Select the Save Copies Of Messages In Sent Items Folder check box. In the E-Mail Options dialog box, click OK. In the Options dialog box, click OK.
Locate a message you have sent	On the bottom of the Outlook Bar, click My Shortcuts. Click the Sent Items shortcut. Double-click the message you want.
Delete an item from the Sent Items folder	Drag the item to the Deleted Items folder.

Lesson 1 Quick Reference

To	Do this	Button
Format and print an e-mail message	Open the message and then click the Print button; or, on the File menu, click Print Preview, and then click the Page Setup button. In the Page Setup dialog box, select or clear the formatting or other options, and click OK. In the Print Preview dialog box, select or clear options, click the Print button, and click OK.	
Create a note	On the Outlook Bar, click the Notes shortcut. On the Standard toolbar, click the New Note button. Type the note.	
Customize your Inbox	On the Tools menu, click Options, and then click the E-Mail Options button. Select or clear your preferred settings. Click the Advanced Options button for additional choices. Click OK twice to close the dialog boxes.	

Learning the Basics of Scheduling

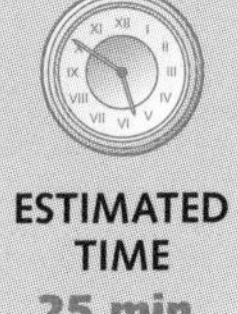

ESTIMATED TIME **25 min.**

In this lesson you will learn how to:

- ✔ *Navigate in your Calendar.*
- ✔ *Open and view Calendar items.*
- ✔ *Add appointments to your Calendar.*
- ✔ *Delete Calendar items.*
- ✔ *Format and print a copy of your schedule.*
- ✔ *Create an appointment from an e-mail message.*

Microsoft Outlook 2000 helps you manage all your time commitments. You can view your schedule one day at a time, one week at a time, or for an entire month. You can search for or sort appointments, and you can customize your Calendar to display the information in a way that's convenient for you.

As the Impact Public Relations account manager, you have appointments with many different clients, and many meetings and events to attend. In this lesson, you begin to gain control of your schedule by practicing how to add and delete Calendar items, how to format your Calendar to your own preferences, and how to print a copy of your schedule in several different formats.

Getting Ready for the Lesson

In this exercise, you start Outlook 2000 and prepare the practice folders and files that you need. You create a practice Calendar folder, add a shortcut to the Outlook Bar, and then copy the files to the folder.

Start Outlook and copy the practice files

In this exercise, you start Outlook and set up the special files and folders needed for this lesson. This keeps the lesson materials separate from your own daily work.

Microsoft Outlook

Calendar

For a detailed example of how to copy practice files to a practice folder, see the exercise "Set Up Practice E-mail" in Lesson 1.

SBS Practice Calendar

1. On the desktop, double-click the Microsoft Outlook icon.

   Outlook 2000 opens.
2. If necessary, maximize the Outlook window.
3. On the Outlook Bar, click the Calendar shortcut.

   Your Calendar appears with today's date displayed in the Appointment area.
4. If necessary, on the View menu, click Folder List to display the Folder List.
5. Select the Calendar folder in the Folder List.
6. On the File menu, click New, and then click Folder.

   The Create New Folder dialog box appears.
7. Be sure that the Folder Contains box displays Appointment Items.
8. In the Name box, type **SBS Practice Calendar** and click OK.

   A Calendar folder called SBS Practice Calendar is created.
9. If you get the message Add Shortcut To Outlook Bar? click No. You'll create the shortcut to it in step 9.
10. On the Standard toolbar, click the New Appointment button drop-down arrow, and then click Outlook Bar Shortcut.

    The Add To Outlook Bar dialog box appears.
11. Click the plus sign (+) next to the Calendar folder, click SBS Practice Calendar, and click OK.

    An SBS Practice Calendar shortcut is added to the bottom of the Outlook Bar.
12. Drag the practice Calendar files, indicated by calendar icons, from the Lesson02 folder in the Outlook Practice folder on your hard disk to your SBS Practice Calendar folder in the Folder List.
13. On the Outlook Bar, click the SBS Practice Calendar shortcut.

    The SBS Practice Calendar appears in the Information viewer.

Navigating in Calendar

When you open Calendar, the Information viewer displays the Appointment area, the TaskPad, and the Date Navigator.

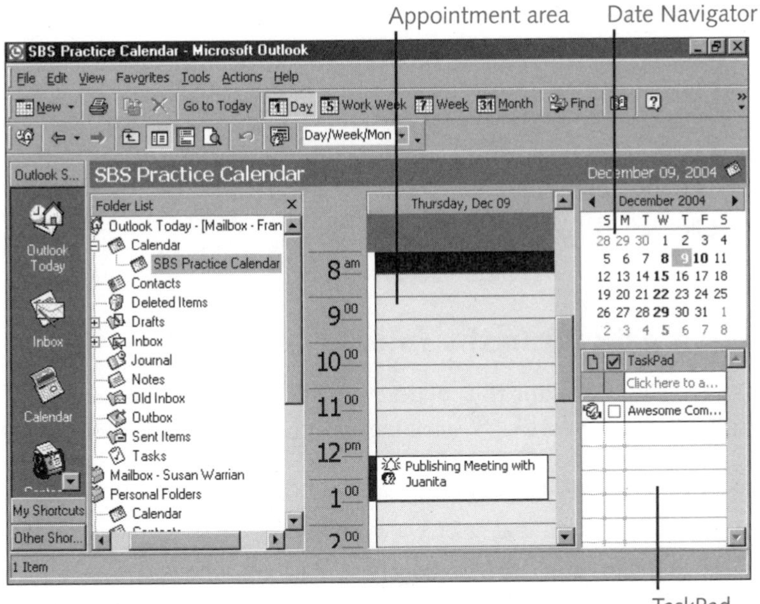

The Appointment area is divided into half-hour time slots. The schedule is highlighted from 8:00 A.M. to 5:00 P.M., but you can enter appointments for other times as well. You can also customize the schedule to display a week at a time or a month at a time. By using the Left and Right arrow keys on the keyboard, you can scroll forward and backward through your daily schedule one day at a time.

The small monthly calendar in the upper-right corner of the Information viewer is the *Date Navigator*. Instead of scrolling through your Calendar day by day to get to a specific date, you can use the Date Navigator to go directly there. By dragging the Date Navigator's left border to the left or right, you can choose to display either one or two monthly calendars at once. By clicking the right and left arrows next to the name of the month, you can scroll month by month. By clicking a specific date in the Date Navigator, the schedule jumps directly to that date, which then is displayed in your Appointment area. You can also tell instantly whether you have anything scheduled for a specific day by scrolling through the Date Navigator to the appropriate month. Dates displayed in boldface type have at least one scheduled event.

Below the Date Navigator is the TaskPad, which shows a quick overview of the tasks that are currently on your Task list.

Go directly to a date

As a busy account manager, you sometimes need to schedule appointments far in advance.

1. On the Date Navigator, click the right scroll arrow twice to move forward two months.
2. Click any date.

   The page for that date appears in your Appointment area.

Go to a date far in the future

Let's say that you want to schedule a trade show for the year 2005. You can go quickly to that date without scrolling month by month through the Date Navigator.

1. On the View menu, point to Go To, and then click Go To Date.

   The Go To Date dialog box appears.
2. In the Date box, type or select the date **09-17-05** and click OK.

   The Appointment area and the Date Navigator now display the date: Saturday, September 17, 2005.

You can type the date as 09-17-05 or as Sept 17, 2005, or in any other form; AutoDate converts the information into the correct form.

Using Ordinary Phrases to Set the Date and Time

Calendar's AutoDate feature allows you to type ordinary phrases and abbreviations for a specific date or time and converts them to a numerical date format. Examples of phrases that you can type in the Go To Date dialog box (and in other date boxes in Outlook) include: *first of October*, *from Friday to Wednesday*, *in three weeks*, *July twenty-third*, *last Saturday*, *next Friday noon*, *one week from today*, *six weeks ago*, *ten days from now*, *the week ending next Saturday*, *this Friday*, *tomorrow*, *until June sixth*, and *yesterday*. Examples of phrases that you can type in time boxes include: *eight am*, *midnight*, *noon*, and *six-fifteen*.

Outlook interprets ordinary phrases based on today's date. For example, if the current date is Monday, October 1, and you type *this Thursday*, Outlook's Calendar jumps to Thursday, October 4; but if you type *next Thursday*, the Calendar jumps to Thursday, October 11.

Open a Calendar item

In this exercise, you've been asked to speak to a group of prospective clients on December 10, 2004. You check to see if you are available on that date.

1. On the Date Navigator, click the left arrow until you locate the month of December 2004.

   The calendar for December 2004 is displayed on the Date Navigator with the date for December 10 in boldface type.
2. Click December 10.

   Holiday Shopping appears in the schedule. You decide that your clients are more important than the shopping.
3. Double-click the Holiday shopping entry.

   The Holiday Shopping appointment form appears.
4. Select the text in the Subject field, and type the following:

   Meet with colleagues from publishing companies
5. Click Save And Close.

   A warning dialog box appears.
6. Click Yes to accept the changes.

   The new appointment appears in your schedule. Your screen should look similar to the following illustration.

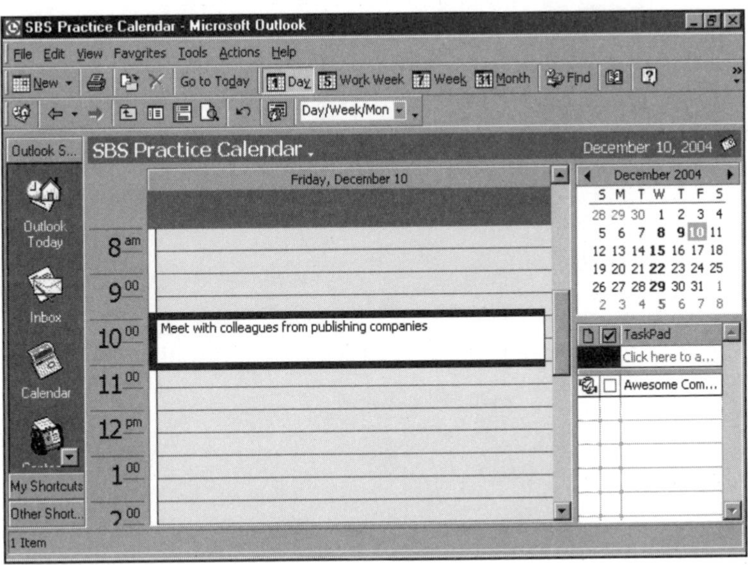

View your future appointments

As an account manager, you must always stay on top of your schedule; being aware of your existing commitments helps you realistically manage your workload. In this exercise, you take a look at your future appointments.

1. On the Date Navigator, scroll to the second week in December 2004, and then click a date that appears in boldface type. The daily schedule for that date appears in the Appointment area.
2. On the Date Navigator, click the following day.

   The schedule for the following day appears in the Appointment area.
3. On the Standard toolbar, click the Week button to view your schedule for the week.

   A one-week calendar showing all of your appointments appears in the Appointment area.

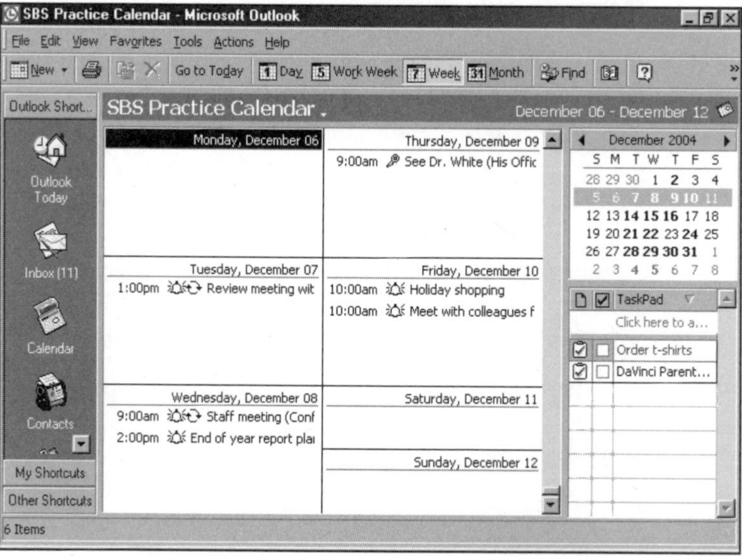

4. On the Standard toolbar, click the Month button to see your schedule for the month.

A one-month calendar showing all of your appointments appears in the Appointment area.

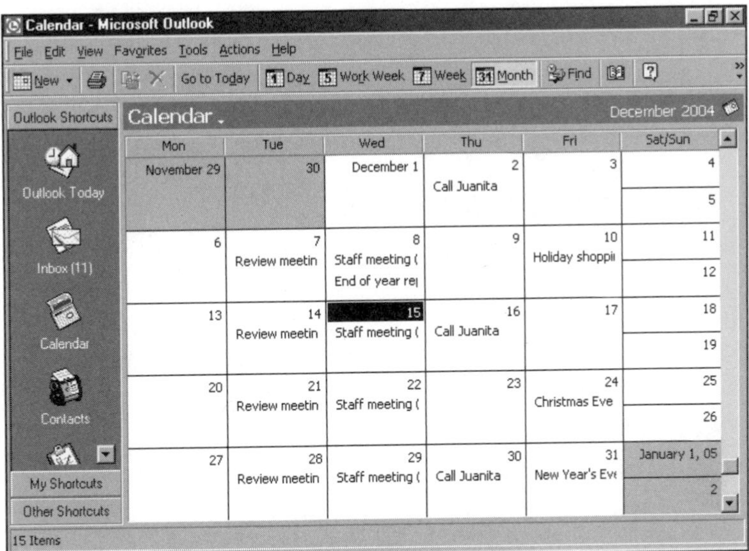

5. On the Standard toolbar, click the Day button to return to the daily view.

Adjusting Your Schedule

Keeping on top of your time commitments may mean making frequent adjustments to your schedule. The electronic schedule is as easy to use as a desktop calendar. In this exercise, you add an appointment to the Calendar and then delete an appointment that has been canceled.

Add an appointment directly to your Calendar

In this exercise, you schedule an appointment to meet with your colleague Jim for lunch.

1. On the Standard toolbar, click the Go To Today button.

   Today's schedule appears in the Appointment area.

2. On the keyboard, press the Right arrow key to scroll forward to tomorrow's schedule, and then click the 12 P.M. time slot.

   The 12 P.M. time-slot area is highlighted.

3. Type **Meet Jim for lunch** in the time slot, and press Enter.

   As your entry appears, the time slot becomes white with a blue border.

> **tip**
>
> You can type appointment information, such as duration and location, directly into your appointment record. To do this, double-click the new appointment when you have completed the entry in your schedule. (You can also right-click the appointment, and then click Open.) When the Appointment form appears, enter your data, and then click the Save And Close button.

Delete an appointment

The Delete key on the keyboard deletes only the displayed text, and not the appointment itself.

Sometimes your colleagues cancel appointments, which must then be deleted from your schedule.

1. Be sure that Calendar is open, and then go to tomorrow's schedule showing the noon appointment with Jim for lunch.
2. Click the 12 P.M. appointment to select it.
3. On the Standard toolbar, click the Delete button.

   The appointment is deleted from your Calendar.

Delete

Making a Printed Copy of Your Schedule

Because you have many meetings and events to attend with your clients or on their behalf, you are not always at your computer. Nevertheless, you must keep careful track of your schedule in order not to miss important appointments and commitments. One way to accomplish this is to bring your schedule with you. Outlook 2000 can produce a printed schedule in many different formats. The options available in the Print dialog box allow you to choose:

For additional printing options, on the File menu, click Print, and then scroll through the list in the Print Styles box.

- Whether your daily schedule is printed on one page or on two.
- Whether entries from your Task list and an area for notes are included.
- How many hours of the day are shown.
- What fonts are used for printing.
- Whether to add headers and footers.
- Whether to show a day, a week, or a month on each page.
- Whether to print only those days that have entries and eliminate days that are blank.
- Whether to start a new page every day, every week, or every month.

Choose how your printed schedule looks

Press Ctrl+G to go directly to the Go To Date dialog box.

1. On the Outlook Bar, click the SBS Practice Calendar shortcut.
2. On the View menu, point to Go To, and then click Go To Date, type (or click the drop-down arrow and select) **January 4, 2005**, and click OK.

   The daily schedule for that date appears in the Appointment area.

Print

3. On the Standard toolbar, click the Print button.

   The Print dialog box appears, with Daily Style selected in the Print Style box.
4. In the Print Style area, click Page Setup.

   The Page Setup: Daily Style dialog box appears.
5. On the Format tab, in the Options area, click the Layout drop-down list and select 2 Pages/Day. Click OK.

   The Page Setup: Daily Style dialog box closes.

You must have a printer connected to your computer for this exercise to work.

6. In the Print dialog box, click OK.

   A two-page daily schedule is printed.

One Step Further: Creating New Calendar Items from Other Types of Outlook Items

When you receive an e-mail message asking for an appointment or meeting, you do not need to retype that information into your Calendar. Outlook can do that for you.

You have received an e-mail message from your colleague Bill Carter. He wants to get together for another working lunch on the DaVinci School of Arts and Crafts Parents Day campaign. In this exercise, you use Mr. Carter's e-mail message as the basis for automatically creating an appointment.

Create an appointment from an e-mail message

SBS Practice Inbox

1. On the Outlook Bar, click the SBS Practice Inbox shortcut.

   The SBS Practice Inbox appears in the Information viewer.
2. If the Folder List is not displayed on your screen, on the View menu, click Folder List.

   The Folder List appears.

The Subject box of the Appointment form is automatically derived from the subject of the e-mail message. Edit it as necessary.

3. In the Information viewer, select Mr. Carter's How About Lunch? e-mail message, and then drag it onto the SBS Practice Calendar folder in the Folder List.

   An Appointment form appears, with some information from the e-mail message filled in.

4. On the Appointment form, in the Subject box, select the text and type **Lunch with Bill**. In the Start Time box, click the drop-down arrow and select December 9, 2004. In the next box, change the time to 12:00 P.M., and then click Save And Close.

   The e-mail message is saved as an appointment.

5. To view the new appointment in your schedule, click the SBS Practice Calendar shortcut. On the View menu, point to Go To, and then click Go To Date. In the Date box, select the current date and type **December 9, 2004**

   The new appointment appears in the Appointment area of your schedule.

> **tip**
> Most Outlook items can be turned into other kinds of Outlook items by dragging them onto the Outlook Bar shortcut representing the type of item that you'd like to create. An e-mail message can be turned into an appointment, or a contact, or even a task. Contact information can be turned into an e-mail, and so on.

Finish the lesson

SBS Practice Inbox

1. If you want to continue on to the next lesson, on the Outlook Bar, click the SBS Practice Inbox shortcut.
2. If you have finished using Outlook for now and are working in a Workgroup environment, on the File menu, click Exit And Log Off. If you are working in an Internet-only environment, on the File menu, click Exit.

Lesson 2 Quick Reference

To	Do this
Go directly to a date in Calendar	On the Date Navigator, scroll to the target month, and then click the target date.
Go to a date in Calendar without scrolling	On the View menu, point to Go To, click Go To Date, type or select a new date in the Date box, and click OK.

Lesson 2 Quick Reference

To	Do this	Button
Open a Calendar item	Double-click the item.	
View appointments for a different date	On the Date Navigator, click the date.	
View appointments for a week	On the Date Navigator, click a date in the week that you want to view, and then on the Standard toolbar, click Week.	
View appointments for a month	On the Date Navigator, click a date in the month that you want to view, and then on the Standard toolbar, click Month.	
Add an appointment directly to your Calendar	On the Date Navigator, click the day you want, and then in the appointment area, click the time you want. Type the appointment data in the time slot.	
Delete an appointment	In the Appointment area, click the time slot for the item, and then on the Standard toolbar, click the Delete button.	X
Print your schedule	On the Date Navigator, click a date, and then on the Standard toolbar, click the Print button, and click OK.	
Create an appointment from an e-mail message	On the Outlook Bar, click the Inbox shortcut. On the View menu, click Folder List. In the Information viewer, select an e-mail message, and drag it onto the Calendar folder in the Folder List. On the Appointment form, edit and complete the information, and then click the Save And Close button.	

LESSON

3

Creating and Sending E-mail Messages

ESTIMATED TIME
40 min.

In this lesson you will learn how to:

- ✔ *Compose and send messages.*
- ✔ *Use the Address Book.*
- ✔ *Add attachments to messages.*
- ✔ *Mark messages confidential or urgent.*
- ✔ *Retrieve messages sent in error.*
- ✔ *Route files for feedback.*

E-mail is a quick, convenient way to communicate with people both at your workplace and at other locations. Your messages are received almost instantly, and you can attach files and embed Internet links. You can also duplicate many of the formatting features of other written correspondence.

Suppose that you are the account manager at Impact Public Relations. You are responsible for dozens of clients, and you also need to communicate internally with your management and staff. In this lesson, you practice creating and sending e-mail messages and attachments to your clients. After you draft a message, you address it using the Address Book, and then you format the message, mark it confidential and urgent, enclose attachments, and send it. You also learn how to retrieve a message that you've sent by mistake.

Getting Ready for the Lesson

In this exercise, you start Outlook 2000 and prepare the practice files and folders that you need. This keeps the lesson materials separate from your own daily work. If you haven't already done so, you create a practice Inbox, add a shortcut to the Outlook Bar for your practice files folder, and then copy the files to the folder.

Start Outlook and copy the practice files

1. On the desktop, double-click the Microsoft Outlook 2000 icon.

   Outlook 2000 opens.

Maximize

2. If necessary, maximize the Outlook window.

See Lesson 1, "Jumping into Your E-mail."

> **important**
>
> Before proceeding to the next step, you must have created an SBS Practice Inbox folder and shortcut.

For more detailed information on copying practice files to this practice folder, see Lesson 1, "Jumping into Your E-mail."

3. Click the SBS Practice Inbox shortcut.
4. Drag the practice e-mail message files, indicated by envelope icons, from the Lesson03 folder in the Outlook Practice folder to your SBS Practice Inbox folder in the Folder List.
5. Drag the practice Contacts files, indicated by address card icons, from the Lesson03 folder in the Outlook Practice folder to your Contacts folder in the Folder List.

   The three Microsoft Word practice documents should not be copied.

Creating New E-mail Messages

You have just received details about a new sales initiative that must be communicated immediately to your client base. Your support staff must be kept in the loop without your clients' being aware of their behind-the-scenes involvement. Because your client base is geographically diverse and your support staff is organized into geographic units, you need to be especially careful that the internal copies are routed accurately.

In this exercise, you compose and address an e-mail message to one of your clients and then use it as a template for a mass mailing to others in your client base.

Compose a new e-mail message

You begin by drafting the e-mail message to your first client, Dale Carter, with copies to the appropriate internal support staff.

New Mail Message

1. On the Outlook Bar, click the SBS Practice Inbox shortcut.
2. On the Standard toolbar, click the New Mail Message button.

   A blank Message form appears. Your screen should look similar to the following illustration.

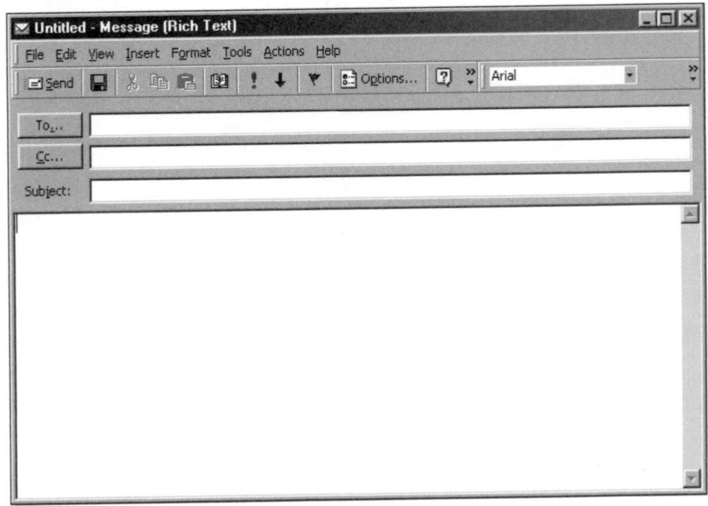

See the following section, "Using the Address Book to Enter E-Mail Recipients," to learn how to use the Address Book to address e-mail messages.

To enter more than one address into the To, Cc, or Bcc box, type an address, insert a semicolon, and then type the next address.

> **important**
>
> Throughout this book, you send e-mail to fictitious people. After you send the message, you will receive a screen message telling you that your message is non-deliverable. You can ignore this message and continue with the lesson.

3. In the Message form, in the To box, type Dale Carter's e-mail address **dalec@millertextiles.millertextiles**, and press Tab.
4. Type **pstout@ipr.ipr** in the Cc box, and press Tab.

tip

If you want to send a person a copy without others' being aware of it, use the Bcc feature. Click the Cc button, type the address in the Bcc portion of the Select Names dialog box, and click OK. The address then appears in the Bcc box of the message form.

Completing the Subject box is a courtesy that lets readers know what your message is about before they open and read it.

5. In the Subject box, type **New Sales Initiative** and press Tab.

   The Message form title bar changes to reflect the subject matter.

6. Type the following in the message area of the form:

   Dale—We have a new sales program that I would like to review with you as soon as possible.

Save an unfinished draft of your e-mail message

Already late for a meeting, you decide to finish the message after you return to your desk. Outlook 2000 allows you to save your work in the Drafts folder for later use.

Save

If your Folder List is not visible on the screen, on the View menu, click Folder List.

1. On the Standard toolbar, click the Save button, and then close the message.
2. To retrieve the saved draft of your message, in the Folder List, click the Drafts folder.

   The Information viewer displays a list of saved drafts. Your screen should look similar to the following illustration.

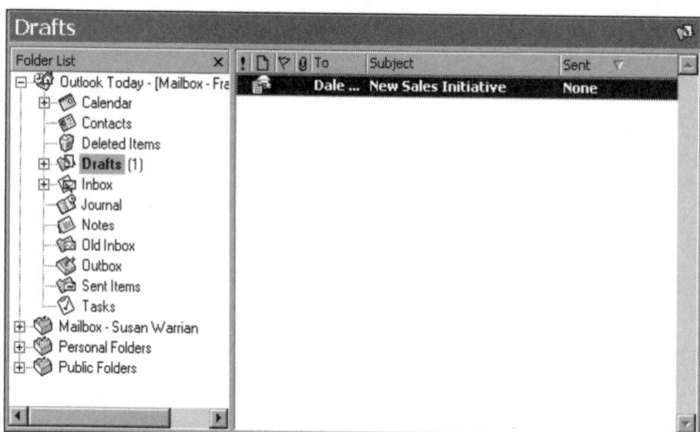

3. Double-click the New Sales Initiative message. Move the insertion point to the end of the text and then type the following:

   I will call you tomorrow to discuss this in greater detail.

Check your spelling

To give the message one last quality check before sending it, you run a spelling check.

1. On the Tools menu, click Spelling.

   If the Spelling feature detects a potential problem, the Spelling dialog box appears.
2. If a word or group of words are highlighted in boldface type in the dialog box, correct them as appropriate.
3. When the spelling check is complete, click OK, and then click the Minimize button in the upper-right corner of the New Sales Initiative—Message form.

   The New Sales Initiative—Message form is reduced to a button on the taskbar. (Later in this lesson, you maximize the New Sales Initiative—Message form again.)

Minimize

If you do not see the Message form on the taskbar, click the Start button, point to Settings, and then click Taskbar. Select the Always On Top check box.

> **tip**
>
> To set Outlook 2000 to check the spelling in your e-mail messages automatically, on the Tools menu, click Options. In the Options dialog box, click the Spelling tab, and then select the Always Check Spelling Before Sending check box.

Using the Address Book to Enter E-mail Recipients

The stack of business cards you brought from a recent trade show provides a good mailing list for prospective clients. Some of the cards represent new contacts; others represent existing contacts already in your database that have relocated to new companies or locations. Since you want to send several of them information on the new sales initiative, you decide to add the new records and change the existing records in your Address Book. Then you use the Address Book to address an e-mail message to one of your new prospects.

Add new contacts to the Address Book

With your stack of business cards in hand, you add information about a new contact, Rob Kahn, to your Address Book.

Address Book

1. On the Outlook Bar, click the SBS Practice Inbox shortcut.
2. On the Standard toolbar, click the Address Book button.

   The Address Book dialog box appears.

New Entry

3. In the Address Book dialog box, click the New Entry button.

   The New Entry dialog box appears.

4. In the Select The Entry Type area, be sure New Contact is selected, and click OK.

   The Untitled—Contact form appears, displaying several tabs.

If you use Outlook 2000 in an Internet-only environment, some of these dialog boxes and forms may look different.

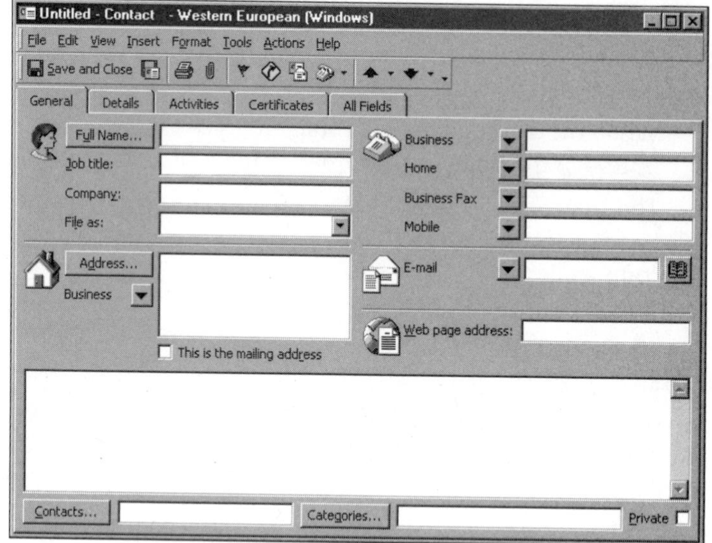

To enter additional information, click the applicable tab and follow the same procedure.

5. On the General tab, in the Full Name box, type **Rob Kahn** and then press Tab.

   The contact name is automatically recorded as Kahn, Rob in the File As box.

6. In the E-mail box, type **robertk@litware.litware**

7. Click the Save And Close button.

   The Rob Kahn—Contact form closes, and Rob Kahn is added to your Contact list.

Change information in the Address Book

The next card in your stack is for an existing contact, Sue Kennedy, who has changed employers. You update your Address Book to reflect her new e-mail address.

1. In the Address Book dialog box, in the Show Names From The drop-down list, select Contacts.

2. In the name list, double-click Sue Kennedy.

   The Sue Kennedy—Contact form appears.

> **tip**
>
> You can also select the contact name by typing the first few letters of the person's name in the Type Name Or Select From List box. Outlook 2000 locates the name in the list and selects it for you. Double-click the name, and then type the new information where appropriate.

To change additional information, click the appropriate tab and follow the same procedure.

3. On the General tab, in the E-mail box, update her e-mail address to **skennedy@wcoastsales.wcoastsales**
4. On the Contact Standard toolbar, click the Save And Close button.

   Sue Kennedy's updated file is saved and the form closes.

Create distribution lists in the Address Book

You regularly send important e-mail messages about the new sales initiative to certain staff members. To save time and to ensure that no staff member is inadvertently left out, in this exercise you create a *distribution list,* a handy collection of contacts grouped under a single name.

If you use Outlook 2000 in an Internet-only environment, some of these dialog boxes and forms may look different.

1. In the Address Book dialog box, click the New Entry button.

   The New Entry dialog box appears.
2. In the New Entry dialog box, in the Select The Entry Type area, select New Distribution List, and click OK.

   The Distribution List form appears with the Members tab active.
3. On the Distribution List form, in the Name box, type **New Sales Initiative Team**, and then press Enter.

   Your screen should look similar to the following illustration.

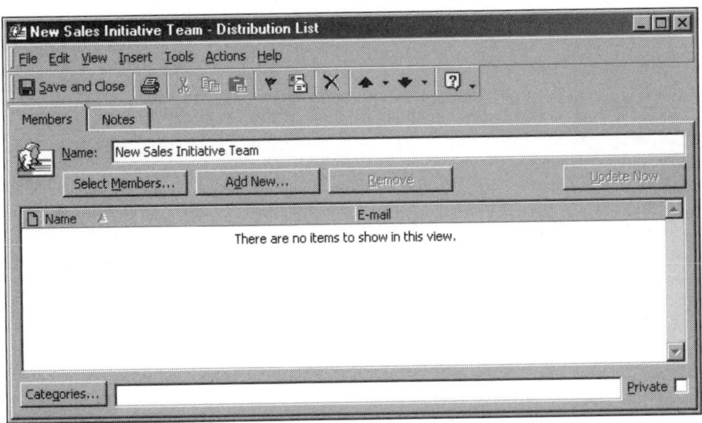

To add a contact not yet in the Address Book to the distribution list, on the Members tab, click the Add New button.

4 Click the Select Members button.

The Select Members dialog box appears.

5 In the Select Members dialog box, in the Show Names From The drop-down list, select Contacts.

6 In the list of contact entries, click Peter Stout, and then click the Add button.

7 Repeat steps 5 and 6 for Susan Warrian.

8 In the Select Members dialog box, click OK.

The Select Members dialog box closes and the New Sales Initiative Team—Distribution List form appears.

9 Click the Save And Close button.

The group appears in the Contact list identified by a group icon and the group name in boldface type.

Close

10 Click the Close button.

tip

To remove a person from the distribution list, double-click the group name in the Contact list. Click the group member's name in the group member list box, click the Remove button, and then click the Save And Close button.

Enter e-mail addresses from the Address Book

Now that you have correct e-mail addresses for your clients in the Address Book, you can quickly and accurately address your e-mail messages.

1 Click the New Sales Initiative—Message button on the taskbar.

The Message form reappears on your screen.

2 In the New Sales Initiative—Message form, click the To button.

The Select Names dialog box appears.

tip

To insert a person from the Address Book in the Cc or Bcc box, click the Cc button, select the person's name, and then click the Cc or Bcc button as applicable. Click OK.

3 In the Show Names From The drop-down list, select Contacts.

4. In the name list, select George Ruter and then click the To button.

   The name is added after Dale's name in the Message Recipients list.

5. Click OK.

   The Select Names dialog box closes and you can now continue working on your message, amending the greeting to read **Dale and George—**

Adding Attachments to Messages

For a demonstration of how to address and attach files to your e-mail message, double-click the Office 8in1 Step by Step folder on your hard disk. Then double-click the Outlook Demos folder, and double-click the Mail icon.

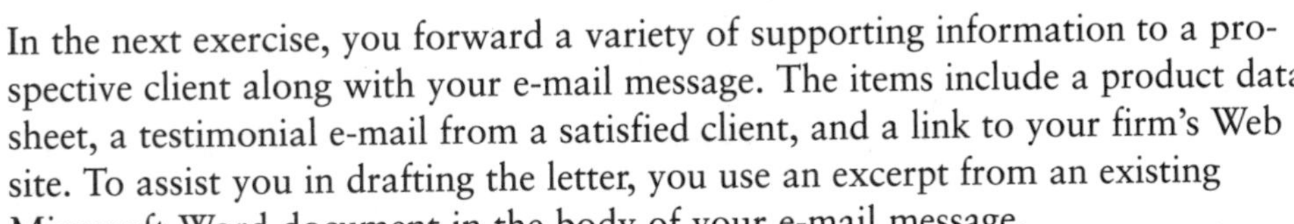

In the next exercise, you forward a variety of supporting information to a prospective client along with your e-mail message. The items include a product data sheet, a testimonial e-mail from a satisfied client, and a link to your firm's Web site. To assist you in drafting the letter, you use an excerpt from an existing Microsoft Word document in the body of your e-mail message.

Send files with e-mail messages

To send the product data sheet, which is a Microsoft Word document, you attach the file to the e-mail message.

1. In the New Sales Initiative—Message form, move the insertion point to the end of the text, and press Enter.

   A blank line is added.

Insert File

2. On the Message form Standard toolbar, click the Insert File button.

   The Insert File dialog box appears.

3. In the Insert File dialog box, locate the Outlook Practice folder and double-click it.

   The contents of the folder are displayed.

4. Double-click the Lesson03 folder, and then double-click the Product Data Sheet document.

   An icon representing the attached Word file appears in the message area at the insertion point or at the bottom of the screen.

Workgroup

> **tip**
>
> In a Workgroup environment, coworkers on the same server can access your attachment using a shortcut that you send to them. To send a shortcut, click the Insert File button, select the file you want to attach, click the Insert drop-down arrow, and then select Insert As Shortcut. A shortcut linking your message to the appropriate file on the server appears in the message area.

Attach other e-mail messages

Over time, you have collected a wonderful set of e-mail messages from satisfied clients. In this exercise, you attach a testimonial e-mail message to your original e-mail message.

1. On the Message form, click the Insert menu, and then click Item.

   The Insert Item dialog box appears.

2. In the Insert Item dialog box, in the Look In list, click the plus sign (+) next to the Inbox folder, and then click the SBS Practice Inbox folder.

   The contents of the SBS Practice Inbox folder are displayed in the Items list. Your screen should look similar to the following illustration.

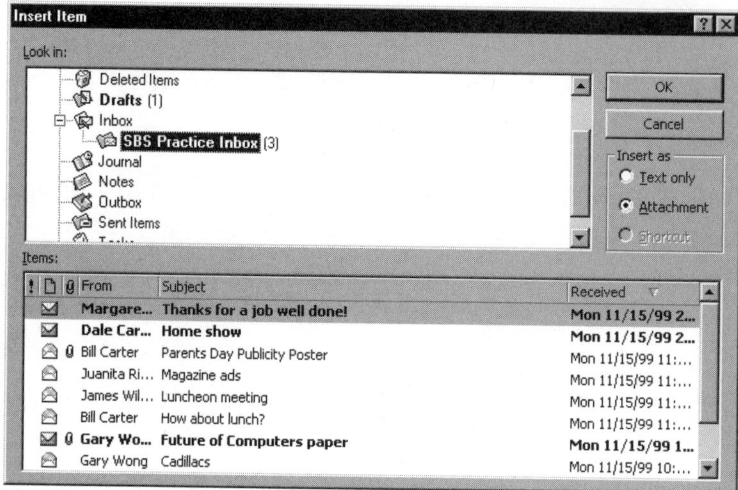

3. In the Insert As area, be sure that Attachment is selected.

4. In the Items list, double-click the Thanks For A Job Well Done! message.

   The Insert Items dialog box closes, and an icon for the e-mail message is added to the New Sales Initiative message.

To insert more than one e-mail message file, repeat steps 2 through 4 until all the files you want are attached.

Embed a hyperlink in your message

The finishing touch is to add a hyperlink to your message, so that your client has ready access to your firm's Web site. To visit the Web site, all your client has to do is to click the hyperlink.

The hyperlink will be easily identified by your e-mail recipients, because the address will be underlined and colored.

1. Type the following sentence and Internet address for your firm's Web site at the end of your message:

   You can also access our homepage on the Internet at http://microsoft.com

   The sentence appears in the message area, and the Internet address is formatted as a hyperlink.

2. On the Message form Standard toolbar, click the Save button.

   The message is saved.

3. On the Message form, click the Close button.

   The message closes.

Close

Customizing the Appearance of Your E-mail Messages

Outlook provides three formatting options for sending your e-mail messages—plain text, rich text, and HTML. Plain text, the simplest of the three options, is readable by all e-mail recipients, but does not enable you to use standard word processing formatting features in your messages, such as bold type, italics, font variations, and bulleted lists. Rich text and HTML enable you to use these standard formatting features, maximizing the impact of your e-mail messages and making them look as professional as your other business communications; but not all e-mail recipients can read this format. HTML format is becoming the formatting standard for e-mail messages and provides the richest set of formatting options for users.

You can also choose to use Microsoft Word as your *e-mail editor*. By using Word to help create your e-mail messages, you can use many of Word's features such as automatically checking your spelling as you type, adding bullets and numbering, and more. If the message recipient is not using Word, however, some formatting may be converted to plain text.

In addition to formatting, you can customize the appearance of your e-mail messages and save typing time by automatically adding a *signature*. A personal signature is a predefined block of text that appears at the end of your e-mail messages. It may include information such as your name, title, and company name, or anything else that you want to include. You can create multiple signatures to choose from, such one for formal and another for informal e-mail messages, and, if you are using rich text or HTML formatting, you can format the signature to look professional.

Format e-mail using Outlook 2000 rich text, HTML, or plain text

You set your messages to use HTML format.

1. On the Tools menu, click Options.

   The Options dialog box appears. Your screen should look similar to the following illustration.

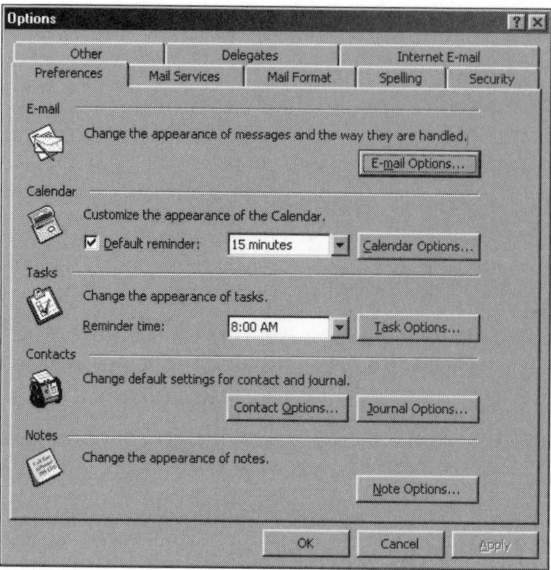

2. In the Options dialog box, click the Mail Format tab, and then, in the Send In This Message Format drop-down list, select HTML.

important

In the Message Format area, select the Use Microsoft Word To Edit E-mail Messages check box to use Word as your e-mail editor.

Use steps 1 through 3 to select the Microsoft Outlook rich text or plain text formats.

3. Click OK.

   The Options dialog box closes.

tip

To personalize your message by selecting your own e-mail stationery, click the SBS Practice Inbox shortcut. On the Actions menu, point to New Mail Message Using, and then click More Stationery. When the Select A Stationery dialog box appears, select the stationery that you want to use, and click OK. If you want a larger selection of e-mail stationery to choose from, click the Get More Stationery button and you will be connected to a Web site where you can review and download from a larger selection.

Add your electronic signature

In this exercise, you create an electronic personal signature and add it to the Signature list so that all new messages will automatically include your name and contact information.

1. On the Tools menu, click Options.

   The Options dialog box opens with the Preferences tab active.

2. In the Options dialog box, click the Mail Format tab.

   The Mail Format tab becomes active.

3. On the Mail Format tab, in the Signature area, click the Signature Picker button.

   The Signature Picker dialog box opens.

4. In the Signature Picker dialog box, click the New button.

   The Create New Signature dialog box opens.

5. In the Create New Signature dialog box, in the Enter A Name For Your New Signature box, type **Formal Signature** and then click the Next button.

   The Edit Signature dialog box opens.

6. In the Edit Signature dialog box, type and format the information that you would like to include as your personal signature.

   Your screen should look similar to the following illustration.

7. In the Edit Signature dialog box, click the Finish button, and then in the Signature Picker dialog box, click OK.

   The Edit Signature dialog box and the Signature Picker dialog box close.

8. In the Options dialog box, click OK.

   The Options dialog box closes.

9. On the Outlook Bar, click the My Shortcuts button, and then click the Drafts shortcut.

   The Drafts Information viewer appears.

Your signature will appear by default in newly created e-mail messages. Since this message is in draft form, you must insert your signature into it.

10. In the Drafts Information viewer, double-click the New Sales Initiative message.

    The New Sales Initiative message opens.

11. Position the insertion point in the message box, press Ctrl+End to move to the end of the text, and then press the Enter key.

12. On the Insert menu, point to Signature, and then click Formal Signature.

    Your electronic signature is added to the bottom of your message.

tip

If you are using Word as your e-mail editor, type and select your desired signature on a message form. On the Insert menu, point to AutoText and then click New In the Create AutoText dialog box. Type a name for the signature, and click OK. To insert the signature at the end of your message, on the Insert menu, point to AutoText, point to Normal, and then click the signature you want.

Setting Your Send Options

Outlook 2000 provides several options for *flagging* or *marking* your messages to let the recipient know the message content's status at a glance. You can mark a message as private, personal, or confidential, or you can mark the importance level as high or low. You can flag a message with a variety of flags to indicate the type of response needed. Since the message you need to send contains sensitive pricing information, you flag your message as both urgent and confidential by changing the default send options.

Set the importance level

Because your client must see this message as soon as possible, you mark it as urgent. This way, it arrives flagged and listed at the top of his new messages.

Importance: High

- On the Message form Standard toolbar, click the Importance: High button.

  The recipient will now be able to see that the message is urgent because the Importance: High symbol will appear next to the message in his Inbox.

Importance: Low

> **tip**
>
> To send the message with low importance, on the Message form Standard toolbar, click the Importance: Low button.

Set the sensitivity level

Because the message contains proprietary company information that you do not want shared with your competitors, you also mark the message as confidential.

1. On the Message form Standard toolbar, click the Options button.

   The Message Options dialog box appears.

2. In the Message Settings area, in the Sensitivity drop-down list, select Confidential. Your screen should look similar to the following illustration.

Close

3. In the Message Options dialog box, click the Close button.

   The Message Options dialog box closes and the sensitivity setting will appear in the recipient's Comment area of the message.

> **important**
>
> Selecting one of the enhanced sensitivity features alerts the recipient to the special nature of the message content. It does not prevent the recipient from forwarding, printing, or otherwise disclosing the content.

Sending Your E-mail Messages

Now that your message is complete, you send it over the Internet to your client, and over your company's network to the support staff on your Cc list. Unfortunately, moments after you send the message, a message appears on your own screen telling you that your e-mail was not delivered because of a faulty e-mail address. After correcting the address, you resend the message.

Send a message over the Internet and within your workgroup

In this exercise, you send your message to your client over the Internet and to the internal staff through your firm's network.

> **important**
>
> Throughout this book, you send e-mail to fictitious people. After you send the message, you will receive a screen message telling you that your message is nondeliverable. You can ignore this message and continue with the lesson.

Internet only

1. On the Message form Standard toolbar, click the Send button.

   If you work in a Workgroup or if you work in an Internet-only environment and are connected to the Internet, your message is sent automatically.

2. If you are not connected to the Internet, your message is placed in the Outbox. To send the message, on the Standard toolbar, click the Send/Receive button. Complete the instructions from your Internet service provider to access the Internet.

   Your message is sent.

Resend a message

Internet only

Shortly after you send your e-mail message, a message appears in your Inbox telling you that your e-mail message is not deliverable, so you recheck the client's e-mail address, correct it, and resend the message.

1. In the Folder List, click the Sent Items folder.

   The contents of the Sent Items folder appears in the Information viewer.

2. In the Sent Items Information viewer, click the New Sales Initiative message.

   The New Sales Initiative message opens.

3. On the Message form, on the Actions menu, click Resend This Message.

   The New Sales Initiative message reappears, with the Send button option now available.

4. In the To box, click Dale's e-mail address and type **dcarter@millertextiles.millertextiles**

5. On the Message form Standard toolbar, click the Send button.

   The message is sent to the new address. The original New Sales Initiative message reappears.

6. On the original New Sales Initiative—Message form, click the Close button.

Close

Retracting an E-mail Message That You've Sent by Mistake

You're having a tough day. The message you sent to Dale Carter also contains an error in the content. If Dale Carter hasn't already opened it, you can retrieve the message.

Workgroup

Recall an e-mail message

To correct your error, you quickly retrieve the message.

1. In the Folder List, click the Sent Items folder.

   The contents of the Sent Items folder appears in the Information viewer.

2. In the Sent Items Information viewer, double-click the most recent New Sales Initiative message.

   The message appears.

3. On the Message form Standard toolbar, click the Actions menu, and then click Recall This Message.

   The Recall This Message dialog box appears.

4. In the Are You Sure You Want To area, click Delete Unread Copies Of This Message, and click OK.

   The dialog box closes.

5. On the Message form, click the Close button.

Close

important

You must act quickly, because the message can be retrieved only if the recipient has not yet received it.

One Step Further Routing Files to Contacts and Coworkers for Feedback

Workgroup

In this exercise, you work in a Workgroup environment and have finished a draft of your new sales initiative outline. You want feedback from three key people in operations and sales. You also want to be able to identify the person making the comments so that you can follow up with them later. To do this, you set up a routing file.

Create a routing file

To route your document to the appropriate staff members, you need to set up a routing file so that Peter Stout, Susan Warrian, and Sue Kennedy each receive the document in that order.

1. On the Windows taskbar, click Start, point to Programs, and then click Microsoft Word.

   Microsoft Word opens.

Open

2. On the Microsoft Word Standard toolbar, click the Open button.

   The Open dialog box appears.

3. Locate the Outlook Practice folder and open it.

   The contents of the folder are displayed.

4. Open the Lesson03 folder, and then double-click the New Sales Initiative document.

   The New Sales Initiative Word document opens.

5. Click the File menu, point to Send To, and then click Routing Recipient.

   The Routing Slip dialog box appears.

6. Click the Address button.

   The Address Book dialog box appears. Your screen should look similar to the following illustration.

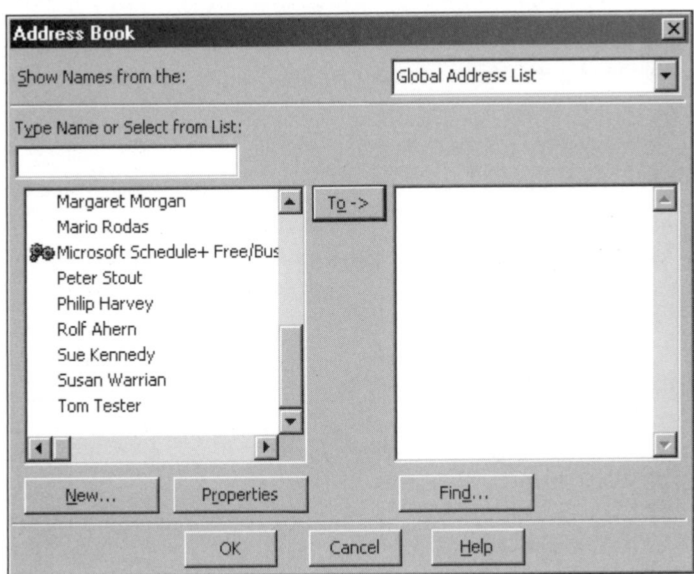

7. In the Show Names From The drop-down list, select Contacts.
8. In the name list, click Peter Stout, the first person to receive the document, and then click the To button.

   The name appears in the To box.
9. Repeat this process with Susan Warrian and Sue Kennedy, and click OK.

   The Routing Slip dialog box appears, listing all three names in the To box.
10. In the Message Text area, type the following:

    Please review the attached report and return your feedback to me by next Wednesday.
11. At the bottom of the Routing Slip dialog box, in the Route To Recipients area, be sure that the One After Another option is selected and that the Return When Done and Track Status check boxes are also selected.
12. In the upper-right corner of the dialog box, click the Add Slip button.

    The Routing Slip dialog box closes.

13. On the File menu, click Exit.

    The Route Document dialog box appears, asking if you want to begin routing the document.

14. In the Route Message dialog box, click No, and then in the message box prompting you to save your changes, click No.

    Word closes and Outlook reappears.

important

Since this exercise was not a real scenario, you clicked No in the dialog boxes in step 14. To actually route the document, you must click Yes in the Route Document dialog box.

Finish the lesson

1. To continue to the next lesson, click the SBS Practice Inbox shortcut on the Outlook Bar.
2. If you have finished using Outlook for now and are working in a Workgroup environment, click File, and then click Exit And Log Off. If you are working in an Internet-only environment, click File, and then click Exit.

Lesson 3 Quick Reference

To	Do this	Button
Create a new e-mail message	On the Standard toolbar, click the New Mail Message button, and then complete the heading and message areas.	New
Save an e-mail draft	On the Standard toolbar, click the Save button, and then on the Message form, click the Close button.	
Check spelling	On the Tools menu, click Spelling. If a word or group of words is highlighted in the dialog box, correct as appropriate. When the spelling check is complete, click OK.	

Lesson 3 Quick Reference

To	Do this	Button
Add a new contact to the Address Book	On the Standard toolbar, click the Address Book button, and then click the New Entry button. In the New Entry dialog box, be sure New Contact is selected, click OK, and then on the Contact form, type the contact information for each tab.	 
Update an Address Book entry	On the Standard toolbar, click the Address Book button. In the Address Book dialog box, in the Show Names From The drop-down list, select Contacts. In the name list, double-click the contact that you want to change. In the Contact form, click the tab containing the information that you want to change, make the change, and then on the Contact Standard toolbar, click the Save And Close button.	
Create a distribution list in the Address Book	On the Standard toolbar, click the Address Book button and then click the New Entry button. In the New Entry dialog box, select New Distribution List, and click OK. In the Distribution List form, type the group name. Click the Select Members button, and then in the Select Members dialog box, select Contacts. Select the name you want from the list, and then click the Add button, repeating this process for each name you want to add to the distribution list. Click OK, and then click the Save And Close button.	

Lesson 3 Quick Reference

To	Do this	Button
Enter an e-mail address from the Address Book	On the Message form Standard toolbar, click either the To, Cc, or Bcc button, as necessary. In the Select Names dialog box, select either Global Address List or Contacts, as necessary. Select the name you want from the list, and then click either the To, Cc, or Bcc button. When all names have been added, click OK.	
Attach a file to an e-mail message	Open an e-mail message. In the message area, position the insertion point at the end of the text. On the Message form Standard toolbar, click the Insert File button and then select the correct file from the list.	
Attach an e-mail message to another e-mail message	Open an e-mail message, and then in the message area, position the insertion point at the end of the text. On the Insert menu, click Item. In the Look In drop-down list, select the Inbox (or Outbox) folder, and then double-click the e-mail message to be attached.	
Embed a hyperlink in an e-mail message	Type the Internet address in the body of your message where desired, and a formatted hyperlink is automatically inserted.	
Format e-mail messages using HTML, Outlook 2000 rich text, or plain text	On the Standard toolbar, click the Tools menu, and then click Options. Click the Mail Format tab to activate it, and then in the Message Format area, in the Send In This Format drop-down list, click the drop-down arrow and select the format you want. Click OK.	

Lesson 3 Quick Reference

To	Do this	Button
Add an electronic signature	On the Tools menu, click Options, and then click the Mail Format tab. In the Signature area, click the Signature Picker button, and then click the New button. In the Create New Signature dialog box, type a name for your signature, and then click the Next button. In the Edit Signature dialog box, type and format the information for the signature, and then click the Finish button. Click OK twice to close the dialog boxes. To insert the signature, open the message, and then position the insertion point at the end of the text in the message area. On the Insert menu, point to Signature, and then click the signature name you want.	
Set the importance level of a message	On the Message form Standard toolbar, click either the Importance: High button or Importance: Low button as appropriate.	! ↓
Set the sensitivity level of a message	On the Message form Standard toolbar, click the Options button. In the Message Settings area, in the Sensitivity box, click the drop-down arrow and select the setting from the list.	
Resend a message	In the Folder List, click the Sent Items folder, and then double-click the message to resend. On the Actions menu, click Resend This Message, edit as needed, and then click the Send button. On the original Message form, click the Close button.	

Lesson 3 Quick Reference

To	Do this
Recall a message sent in error	In the Folder List, click the Sent Items folder, and then double-click the message to recall. On the Actions menu, click Recall This Message, and click OK.
Create a routing file	On the Windows taskbar, click Start, point to Programs, and then click Microsoft Word. On the Word Standard toolbar, click the Open button. Scroll as necessary to locate the file you want from the list, and then double-click the file. Click the File menu, point to Send To, and then click Routing Recipient. In the Routing Slip dialog box, click the Address button. Select the name from the list of the first person to receive the document, and then click the To button. Repeat as necessary for each additional name. In the Message Text area, type a message to the recipients and then click the Add Slip button. On the File menu, click Exit. In the Routing Message dialog box, click Yes.

Managing Your Calendar

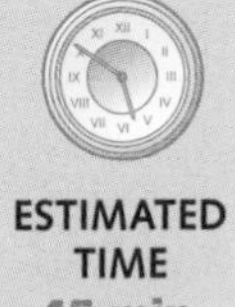

ESTIMATED TIME
45 min.

In this lesson you will learn how to:

- ✓ *Schedule different types of appointments and events.*
- ✓ *Move and edit appointments.*
- ✓ *Manage appointments by setting reminders and assigning categories.*
- ✓ *Save an appointment in vCalendar format to share on the Internet.*
- ✓ *Customize your Calendar to meet your personal needs.*
- ✓ *Export Outlook data to the Timex Data Link Watch.*

In Lesson 2, "Learning the Basics of Scheduling," you learned how to enter appointments in your Calendar. In this lesson, you learn about meetings and events and practice using advanced techniques to organize your schedule to meet specific work and personal needs.

The Outlook Calendar provides a variety of ways to manage your schedule. You can enter details about an appointment to help you remember important information, such as what you are to discuss and with whom you are meeting. You can set up reminders to alert you about upcoming meetings or attach documents, such as an agenda or background material, to an appointment. Appointments can be organized by the same categories you use to manage your messages, tasks, and contacts. You can also block out time for all-day events and create appointments that recur at specified intervals.

If you use Outlook in a Workgroup environment, you can share your Calendar with whichever coworkers you choose at various viewing levels. For example, at the default viewing level, your colleagues are able to see just the times when you are busy or free without seeing the details of your schedule.

To share your Calendar with colleagues who use different scheduling programs or who use Outlook in another organization, you can save your appointments as a *vCalendar*, a technology standard for the exchange of scheduling information. The vCalendar format creates a file that others can import into any scheduling program that supports the vCalendar standard.

As Fran Wilson, Impact Public Relations account manager, one of your responsibilities is to attend trade shows for such clients as Awesome Computers and Ramona Publishing. In this lesson, you block out time for a trade show and set it as a recurring event. You save an appointment in vCalendar format to share with a colleague. You also organize your Calendar information by category and create your own categories so that you can manage your time as efficiently as possible.

Getting Ready for the Lesson

In this exercise, you start Outlook 2000 and prepare the practice files and folders that you need.

Start Outlook and copy the practice files

Microsoft Outlook

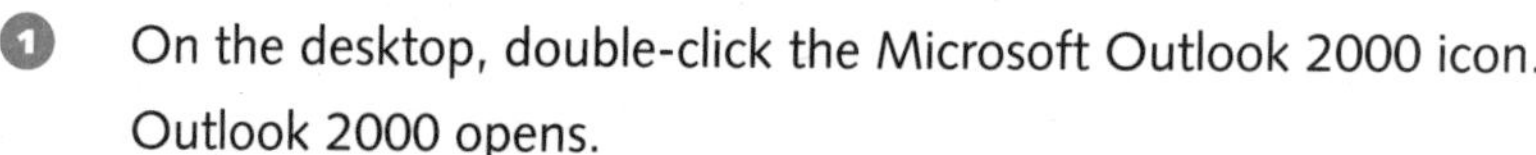

1. On the desktop, double-click the Microsoft Outlook 2000 icon.
   Outlook 2000 opens.
2. If necessary, maximize the Outlook window.

Maximize

> **important**
>
> To continue with this lesson, you must have created an SBS Practice Calendar folder and shortcut, and an SBS Practice Contacts folder and shortcut. If you have not yet done so, see Lesson 2, "Learning the Basics of Scheduling."

SBS Practice Calendar

3. On the Outlook Bar, click the SBS Practice Calendar shortcut.

4. Drag the practice Calendar files, indicated by calendar icons, from the Lesson04 folder in the Outlook Practice folder to your SBS Practice Calendar folder in the Folder List.
5. Drag the practice Contacts file, indicated by an address card icon, from the Lesson04 folder in the Outlook Practice folder to your SBS Practice Contacts folder. The Microsoft Word document should remain in the Lesson04 folder.

For more detailed information on copying practice files to this practice folder, see Lesson 1, "Jumping into Your E-mail."

Scheduling Appointments

In Lesson 2, you practiced how to enter an appointment directly into your Calendar by typing it in a time slot. Outlook provides other ways to enter more complex appointments into your Calendar. For example, you can schedule:

- Recurring appointments for activities such as weekly staff meetings. You can easily set your appointments to recur automatically by defining a number of recurrences or until a given date.
- Appointments that contain detailed information to help you stay on top of your commitments. Outlook enables you to create such a record by entering information such as the location and duration of an appointment and comments describing the purpose on the Appointment form.
- Private appointments that appear on your Calendar but which hide the details of the appointment, even from those with permission to view your schedule.

In this section, you enter detailed information about an appointment, schedule an appointment classified as private, schedule an event, create a recurring appointment and delete one occurrence, move an appointment to a new date, and edit appointment information that has changed.

Appointments, Meetings, and Events

For optimum use of Outlook, you need to know how the terms *appointment, meeting,* and *event* are defined in Calendar.

Appointments are activities that you can schedule in Outlook that do not involve inviting other people or reserving resources, such as a conference room.

(continued)

continued

Meetings are activities to which you invite other people or for which you reserve resources. When you create a meeting, you identify the people to invite and the resources to reserve, and you pick a meeting time. Then you send meeting requests via Outlook for a face-to-face or online meeting. Responses to your meeting requests appear in your Inbox.

Events are activities that last 24 hours or longer. Events can include conventions, holidays, birthdays, or the company picnic. Events do not occupy blocks of time in the Appointment area of Calendar; rather, the name of the event appears in a banner above the time slots on the specified date.

Schedule a detailed appointment

You need to call Juanita at Ramona Publishing in preparation for the American Booksellers Association meeting. To be sure that you don't forget any of the details of the meeting, you enter complete information on the Appointment form.

New Appointment

1. On the Outlook Bar, click the SBS Practice Calendar shortcut, and then on the Standard toolbar, click the New Appointment button.

   A blank Appointment form appears.

> **tip**
>
> You can open a blank form for a new appointment, contact, task, journal entry, or message from any window in Outlook 2000. For example, you do not have to be in a Calendar folder to open a new Appointment form. From any window you have open, on the File menu, point to New, and then click Appointment.

2. On the Appointment form, in the Subject box, type the following:

   Call Juanita at Ramona Publishing
3. In the Location box, type **My office**
4. In the Start Time boxes, select the contents and type **Mon 5/23/2005** and **9 am**
5. In the End Time boxes, select the contents, type the same date, and type **10 am**
6. In the Comment area, type the following:

   Finalize plans for the ABA: how many posters should we bring?

7. Click the Save And Close button.

   The new appointment appears in the 9:00 A.M. to 10:00 A.M. time slots on your Calendar for May 23, 2005.

tip

To see the comments about your appointments, on the Standard toolbar, click the View menu, point to Current View, and then click Day/Week/Month View With AutoPreview. The entry for the appointment will display the location and comments from the Appointment form.

Schedule a private appointment

There are some appointments that you do not want others in your organization to know about. In this exercise, you schedule an appointment and flag it as private, for your eyes only.

New

New Appointment

1. In the Date Navigator, scroll to December 2004, and then click December 9.

   December 9, 2004, is displayed in the Appointment area.
2. In the Appointment area, select the 9:00 A.M. to 10:00 A.M. time slots.
3. On the Standard toolbar, click the New Appointment button.

   The Appointment form appears. The date and time boxes are already filled in.
4. On the Appointment form, in the Subject box, type **See Dr. White**
5. In the Location box, type **His office**
6. In the Comment area, type **Annual physical exam**
7. On the Appointment form, in the lower-right corner, select the Private check box.

Private

8. On the Appointment form Standard toolbar, click the Save And Close button.

   The Appointment form closes. Your Calendar reappears, displaying the new appointment entry with a key icon to indicate that the appointment is private.

Schedule an event

A trip to the annual convention of the American Booksellers Association will keep you out of the office for about a week. You need to enter this event in your Calendar to be sure that it does not conflict with commitments to your other clients.

To schedule events lasting more than one day, clear the All Day Event check box. Then complete the End Time information you want.

1. Be sure that the SBS Practice Calendar Appointment area is displayed.
2. On the Actions menu, click New All-Day Event.

   A blank Event form appears.
3. On the Event form, in the Subject box, type **American Booksellers Association**
4. In the Location box, type **Miami**
5. In the Start Time box, select the current text and type **May 27, 2005**
6. In the End Time box, select the current text and type **May 31, 2005**
7. In the Comment area, type the following:

   Distribute Ramona Publishing posters to press, TV, reviewers, and readers
8. On the Event form Standard toolbar, click the Save And Close button.

   The Event form closes.

To indicate that you are out of the office, in the Show Time As drop-down list, select Out Of Office.

9. On the View menu, point to Go To, and then click Go To Date. In the Go To Date dialog box, in the Date box, select the current text if necessary, and type **May 27, 2005**
10. In the Show In drop-down list, select Week Calendar, and click OK.

The days dedicated to the convention are now entered as events in your Calendar. They appear on your Calendar as a banner above the other appointments for each day. Your time during those days is flagged as free. You can still enter any appointments you might have while at the convention. In Week view, your screen will look similar to the following illustration.

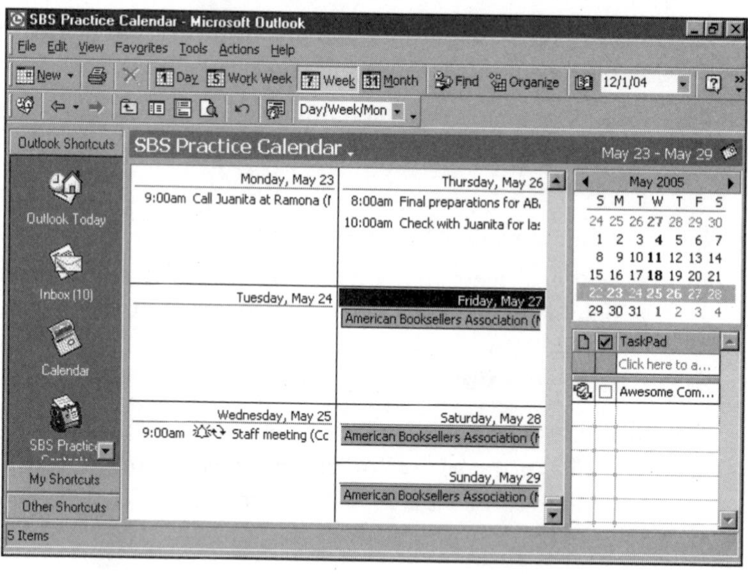

Free and Busy Time

On the Appointment form, you can designate whether your time is free or busy by selecting one of several options (Free, Tentative, Busy, or Out Of Office). The option you choose is important for others who have access to your Calendar and may want to schedule a meeting with you. Events are automatically designated as free time, since you might want to schedule appointments or meetings at the event. To block out an entire day during which you are unavailable, you would enter it in Calendar as an all-day appointment, since appointment time is designated as busy.

Schedule an all-day appointment

To prepare for the American Booksellers Association convention, you schedule an appointment for an entire day during which you do not want to be disturbed.

You can also open an Appointment form by selecting and then right-clicking the time slot. On the shortcut menu, click New Appointment.

1. On the Standard toolbar, click the Day button.

   The Appointment area displays the time slots for a single day.
2. In the Date Navigator, scroll to May 2005, and then click May 26.

   May 26, 2005, is displayed in the Appointment area.
3. Double-click the 8:00 A.M. time slot.

   The Appointment form appears with the date and times filled in.
4. In the Subject box, type **Final preparations for ABA**
5. On the Appointment form, in the second End Time box, select the text and type **5:00 p.m.**
6. On the Appointment form Standard toolbar, click the Save And Close button.

   The appointment now fills the Appointment area.
7. Select and double-click the 10 A.M. time slot.

   An Appointment form opens.
8. In the Subject box, type **Check with Juanita for last-minute problems** and then click Save And Close.

   The Appointment area is now divided into two columns.

Your screen should look similar to the following illustration.

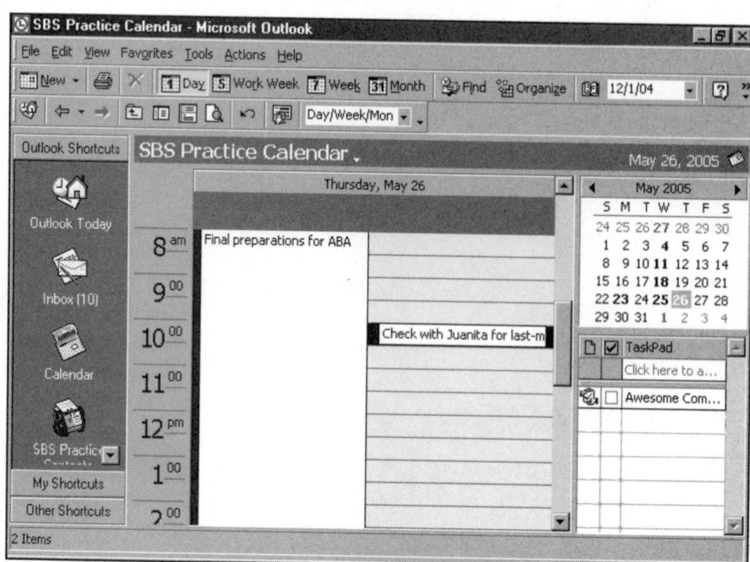

tip

To change your appointment status from free to busy or busy to free, open the Appointment form for the item, and in the Show Time As box, click the drop-down arrow, and then select the option that you prefer.

Schedule a recurring appointment

Because you attend the American Booksellers Association convention every year, you decide to enter a recurring appointment in your Calendar for a day of preparation prior to the event.

1. In the Date Navigator, click May 16, and then double-click any time slot.

   A new Appointment form appears, with the date and times filled in.
2. On the Appointment form Standard toolbar, click the Recurrence button.

   The Appointment Recurrence dialog box appears.
3. In the Appointment Time area, in the Duration box, click the drop-down arrow, and then select 1 Day.
4. In the Appointment Recurrence dialog box, in the Recurrence Pattern area, select Yearly, and then click the option that displays Third, Monday, and May in the three side-by-side boxes.

   The option now reads The Third Monday Of May.

5. Click OK.

   The Appointment Recurrence dialog box closes. The Appointment form appears with the recurrence pattern listed below the location.

6. On the Recurring Appointment form, in the Subject box, type **Preparations for the ABA**

7. In the Location box, type **Varies**

8. On the Appointment form Standard toolbar, click the Save And Close button.

   You now have a preparation day scheduled to occur two weeks before every Memorial Day weekend.

9. To view the next occurrence of your ABA preparation day, in the Date Navigator, scroll to May 2006, and then double-click the third Monday.

   Recurring

   Your ABA preparation day appears in the Appointment area. The appointment is displayed with a circular arrow icon to indicate a recurring appointment.

Make an existing appointment recurring

In this exercise, you decide to make an existing appointment to call Juanita Rivera into a series of recurring appointments that occur monthly for five months prior to the ABA convention.

1. In the Date Navigator, scroll to May 2005, click May 23, and then double-click the 9:00 A.M. appointment to call Juanita.

   The Call Juanita At Ramona Appointment form appears.

2. On the Appointment form Standard toolbar, click the Recurrence button.

   The Appointment Recurrence dialog box appears.

3. In the Appointment Recurrence dialog box, in the Recurrence Pattern area, select Monthly, and then click the option that displays Fourth, Monday, and 1 in the three side-by-side boxes.

   The option reads The Fourth Monday Of Every 1 Month(s).

4. In the Range Of Recurrence area, select the existing Start date and type **1/24/05**

5. In the Range Of Recurrence area, click the End After option, and then in the box, select the current text, and then type **5**

6. Click OK.

   The Appointment Recurrence dialog box closes, and the recurrence pattern appears on the Appointment form below the location.

7. On the Appointment form, in the Subject box, change the text to read: **Annual Preparations for the ABA: monthly phone conference with Ramona Publishing**

If you get a warning message at this point, you can ignore it.

8. Click the Save And Close button.

   Five monthly phone conferences are now scheduled prior to the ABA trade show (scheduled for late May) on your Calendar.

9. On Date Navigator, scroll to January 2005, and then click the fourth Monday.

   The first monthly appointment appears in the 9:00 A.M. time slot. The fourth Mondays in February, March, April, and May show the same appointment.

Move or copy an appointment

You sometimes have to change your appointments. But with Outlook you don't have to delete them in one place and then retype them in another; instead, you can move or copy appointments to their new times. In this exercise, you reschedule your physical exam with Dr. White.

1. In the Date Navigator, scroll to December 2004, and then click December 9.

   December 9, 2004, is displayed in the Appointment area.

2. Click the left border (the move bar) of the Dr. White appointment scheduled for 9:00 A.M. to 10:00 A.M.

   The pointer becomes a four-headed arrow.

3. Drag the appointment to December 16 in the Date Navigator.

   The date changes to December 16. The Appointment area for that day appears, with Dr. White's rescheduled appointment retaining its original start and end times.

To move an appointment to another time on the same date, click its left border and drag it to the new time slot.

Edit a recurring appointment

Sometimes people's schedules change so much that the time of a regular, recurring meeting becomes inconvenient and must be rescheduled. Because of a new conflict, you decide to change your weekly meetings with Chris from 9:00 A.M. on Wednesday to 10:00 A.M. on Monday.

1. In the Date Navigator, scroll to January 2005, and then click January 26.

   January 26, 2005, appears in the Appointment area of your Calendar.

2. Double-click the Review Meeting With Chris appointment at 8:00 A.M.

   Because this is a recurring appointment, the Open Recurring Item dialog box appears, prompting you to open either the single occurrence of the meeting or the series of meetings.

3. In the Open Recurring Item dialog box, click the Open The Series option, and click OK.

   The Recurring Appointment form appears.

4. On the Recurring Appointment form Standard toolbar, click the Recurrence button.

   The Appointment Recurrence dialog box appears.

5. In the Appointment Recurrence dialog box, in the Appointment Time area, change the Start Time box to 10:00 A.M., and then in the Recurrence Pattern area, change the day from Wednesday to Monday.

If you get a warning message at this point, you can ignore it.

6. Click OK.

   The Appointment Recurrence dialog box closes.

7. On the Appointment form Standard toolbar, click the Save And Close button.

   Now during the first five months of 2005, your monthly conference will occur on the fourth Monday of the month at 10:00 A.M., rather than on the fourth Wednesday at 9:00.

> **tip**
>
> If you want to change only one appointment in a series of recurring appointments, in the Open Recurring Item dialog box, select the Open This Occurrence option, and then make your changes on the Appointment form.

Delete a recurring appointment

Juanita Rivera has phoned and reported that she may not always be available for a phone conference at 9:00 A.M. on the fourth Monday of every month to prepare for the ABA convention, so you decide to delete the series of meetings.

1. In the Date Navigator, scroll to January 2005, and then click January 24.

   January 24, 2005, is displayed in the Appointment area.

2. In the Appointment area, click the 9:00 A.M. appointment.

   The 9:00 A.M. time slot is selected.

Delete

3. On the Standard toolbar, click the Delete button.

   The Confirm Delete dialog box appears, prompting you to delete either the entire series or only this one occurrence.

4. In the Confirm Delete dialog box, click the Delete All Occurrences option, and click OK.

   The series of appointments is deleted.

Delete

tip

Pressing the Delete key on the keyboard erases only the text for the selected appointment, but the appointment still remains on your Calendar. To delete the appointment itself, you must click the Delete button on the Standard toolbar.

Managing Appointments

Effective time management depends on knowing when you need to be somewhere and exactly how you are spending your time. Outlook provides features that help you manage your time better, such as finding appointments, setting reminders, attaching documents to appointments, sharing appointments electronically with others, and categorizing appointments.

- You can easily find when an appointment is scheduled to occur by using Find to search for words or other data that appear in your Outlook Calendar.
- You can set up a reminder for a single appointment as far ahead as you choose, and you can even have Outlook routinely remind you of all of your upcoming commitments. A reminder notice is a small box that pops up on your screen, even if you're using another application, alerting you to the appointment.
- You can electronically attach documents for an appointment to the appointment itself so that they will be instantly available when you need them.
- You can share your schedule with others who do not use the same scheduling program by saving an appointment in vCalendar format. If your colleagues are using Outlook or another scheduling program compatible with vCalendar technology, they will be able to import the files directly into their schedules.
- You can assign your appointments to several default categories or to customized categories that you create to better understand how you are allocating your time. This allows you to view appointments in only certain categories.

Find an appointment

In this exercise, you practice finding an appointment dealing with preparations for the American Booksellers Association convention.

1. On the Standard toolbar, click the Find button.

   The Find Items In SBS Practice Calendar panel appears.

2. In the Find Items In SBS Practice Calendar panel, in the Look For box, type **ABA** and click the Find Now button.

   The items containing the term *ABA* are displayed in a table under the Find Items In SBS Practice Calendar panel.

Close button

Close

3. In the Find Items In SBS Practice Calendar panel, click the Close button.

   The panel closes.

Set up a reminder notice

Some appointments are so important that you want to be sure that you don't miss them. You can set up a reminder to alert you about all your appointments as far ahead of time as you choose.

1. On the View menu, point to Current View, and be sure that Day/Week/Month is selected.
2. In the Date Navigator, scroll to December 2004, and then click December 16.

   December 16, 2004, appears in the Appointment area.

3. In the Appointment area, double-click the Dr. White appointment.

   The See Dr. White Appointment form appears.

4. On the Appointment form, select the Reminder check box.
5. In the Reminder box, click the drop-down arrow and select 30 minutes.

   The reminder is now set to pop up on your screen 30 minutes prior to the appointment with Dr. White.
6. On the Appointment form Standard toolbar, click the Save And Close button.

   Since reminders will not function in subfolders such as the SBS Practice Calendar folder, a message box prompts you for an OK.
7. In the message box, click Yes.

   The message box closes and then the Appointment form closes. An alarm icon appears in the See Dr. White appointment, indicating a reminder notice has been set.

Reminder Notices

When a reminder notice appears on your screen, you can perform one of three actions:

- Click the Dismiss button to close the Reminder dialog box.
- Click the Snooze button to reschedule the reminder. If you click the Snooze button, the reminder will be repeated in another five minutes, unless you change the amount of time in the Click Snooze To Be Reminded Again drop-down list.
- Click the Open Item button to open the Appointment form and review its contents.

When a Reminder dialog box appears, your screen will look similar to the following illustration.

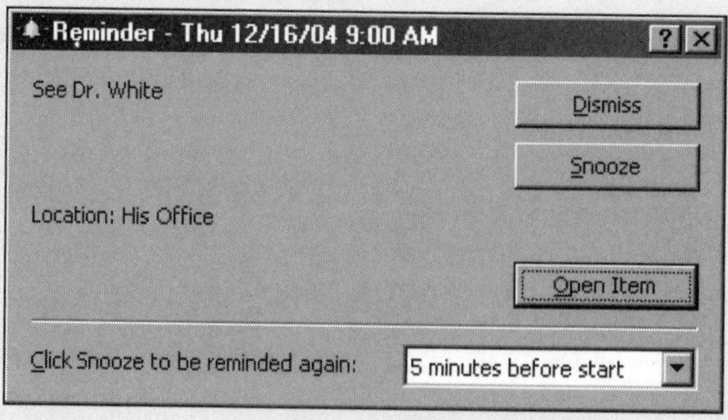

Set reminder options for all new appointments

Rather than decide case-by-case which appointments should have reminders, you can set up Calendar to always remind you of upcoming commitments.

1. On the Tools menu, click Options.

   The Options dialog box appears.
2. On the Preferences tab, in the Calendar area, select the Default Reminder check box, and then in the Default Reminder box, select 10 Minutes.

   A reminder will automatically appear on your screen 10 minutes before any appointment is scheduled to start.
3. Click OK.

> **tip**
>
> If you do not want to be reminded of items in your Calendar, in the Options dialog box, on the Preferences tab, in the Calendar area, clear the Default Reminder check box.

Attach a document to an appointment

Outlook allows you to electronically "staple" any documents you need to the appointment. In this exercise, you attach the promotional literature that will be considered at a meeting to the appointment for that meeting.

1. On the View menu, point to Current View, and be sure that Day/Week/Month is selected.
2. In the Date Navigator, scroll to January 2005, and then click January 24.

   January 24, 2005, is displayed in the Appointment area.
3. In the Appointment area, select the 1:00 P.M. to 2:00 P.M. time slots.
4. On the Standard toolbar, click the New Appointment button.

   New Appointment

   A blank Appointment form appears with the start and end times filled in.
5. On the Appointment form, in the Subject box, type **Five Lakes promotional campaign** and then, in the Location box, type **Conference room**
6. On the Appointment form Standard toolbar, click the Insert File button.

   Insert File

   The Insert File dialog box appears.
7. In the Look In drop-down list, browse to find the Outlook Practice folder and then double-click it.

   You can attach any type of file to an appointment.

   The contents of the folder are displayed.

8. Double-click the Lesson04 folder, and then double-click the Five Lakes Promotion document.

   The Five Lakes Promotion icon is inserted in the Comment area on the Appointment form. Your screen should look similar to the following illustration.

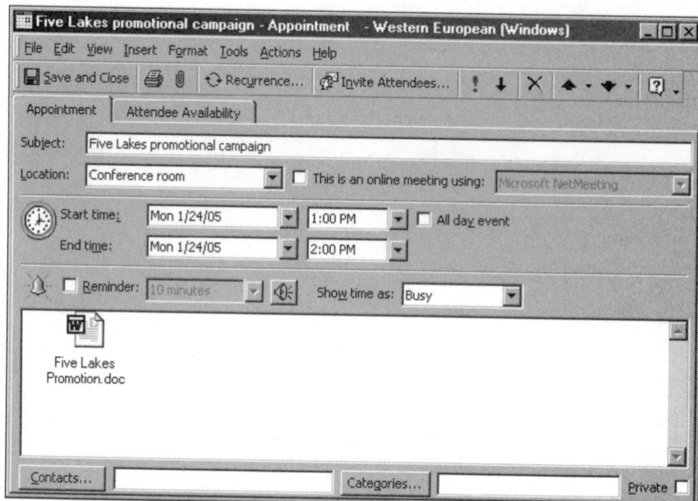

9. On the Appointment form, click the Save And Close button.

   The Appointment form closes.

Save an appointment in vCalendar format

Now that you've set up your Five Lakes appointment, in this exercise you save it in vCalendar format. Once it is in this format, you send the appointment as an e-mail attachment to your colleagues so that they know your schedule.

1. In the Appointment area, click the Five Lakes appointment.
2. On the File menu, click Save As.

   The Save As dialog box appears.
3. In the Save As dialog box, in the Save In drop-down list, locate the folder where you want to save the file.
4. In the File Name box, type a name for the file.
5. In the Save As Type box, click the drop-down arrow, and then select vCalendar Format.
6. Click the Save button.

   Your appointment is saved in vCalendar format.

Organizing with Categories

To help organize and keep track of your appointments, meetings, and events, you can assign them to various *categories*. Categories are assigned to all types of Outlook items from the *Master Category List,* an alphabetical list of categories that includes the set of default categories provided by Outlook in addition to categories you create to suit your particular needs. After assigning one or more categories to an appointment, meeting, or event, you can use the categories in two ways.

You can organize different types of Outlook items, such as messages, contacts, and your appointments, into related groups while still maintaining them in separate Outlook folders. For example, the messages, contacts, and appointments related to your international customers can be stored in separate folders but grouped by assigning them to the International category found in the Master Category List.

You can organize similar items, such as appointments, into different groups without having to store them in different folders. For example, you may want to view only those appointments related to your activities with a community group with which you volunteer. You can create a custom category to group these appointments and view them separately from the rest of your Calendar.

Assign appointments to categories

You decide to organize your Calendar so that you can view your personal and business appointments separately. In this exercise, you assign several appointments to the Business category and an appointment to the Personal category.

> **tip**
> Assigning an appointment to the Personal category is not the same as selecting the Private check box on the Appointment form. The Private check box prevents others who might have access to your Calendar from seeing the details of the appointment. You might select a Business appointment as Private if it dealt with sensitive matters, such as a personnel problem.

1. In the Date Navigator, scroll to December 2004, and then click December 8.

   December 8, 2004, is displayed in the Appointment area.

2. On the Standard toolbar, click the Organize button. If it is not visible, click the More Buttons drop-down arrow, and then click the Organize button.

   The Ways To Organize SBS Practice Calendar panel appears.

More Buttons

For a demonstration of how to assign appointments to categories and view related groups, double-click the Office 8in1 Step by Step folder on your hard disk. Then double-click the Outlook Demos folder, and double-click the Categories icon.

3. On the Ways To Organize SBS Practice Calendar panel, click the Using Categories link.

   The Using Categories page opens.

4. On the Using Categories page, in the Add Appointments Selected Below To list, select Business.
5. In the Appointment area, select the 9:00 A.M. staff meeting, press and hold down the Ctrl key, and then select the 2:00 P.M. End Of Year Report Planning meeting.
6. In the Ways To Organize SBS Practice Calendar panel, click the Add button.

   Done! is displayed next to the Add button.

7. In the Add Appointments Selected Below To list, select Personal.
8. In the Appointment area, click December 10, select the 10 A.M. Holiday Shopping appointment, and then click the Add button.

   Done! is displayed next to the Add button.

9. On the Ways To Organize SBS Practice Calendar panel, click the Using Views link.

   The Using Views page opens.

10. On the Using Views page, in the Change Your View list, select By Category.

    The headings for the groups of appointments are displayed in the Information viewer. Your screen should look similar to the following illustration.

Close Organize button

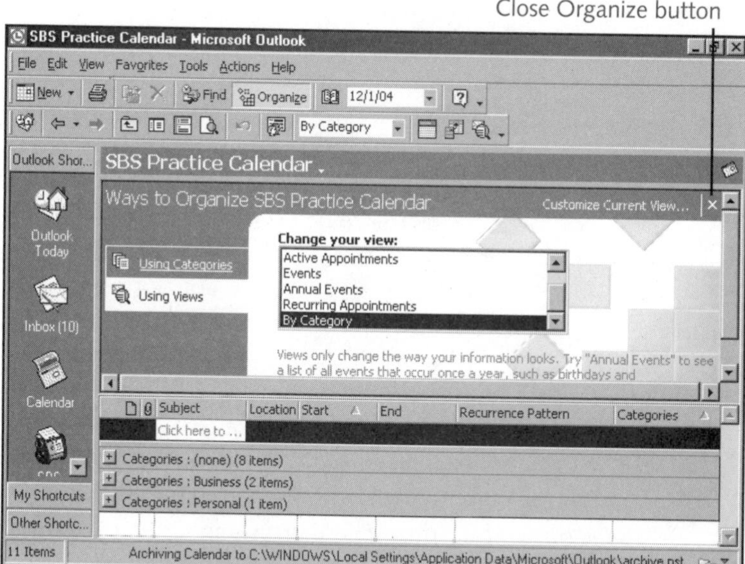

11. In the Information viewer, click the plus sign (+) next to the Business and Personal categories.

    The appointments in each group are displayed.

Close

12. On the Ways to Organize SBS Practice Calendar panel, click the Close button.

Personalizing Your Calendar

Unlike that of a desk calendar, the format of Outlook's Calendar can be changed to suit your needs. It provides five basic *views* or formats, each of which can be further modified to let you see your time commitments and tasks in the way most useful to you. Each view, except Day/Week/Month, displays the subject, start and end times, the location, and categories. Each view can also display symbols to show whether there's an attachment or whether the item is a recurring appointment.

About Calendar Views

Outlook provides a variety of ways to view your Calendar.

Click this view	To see
Day/Week/Month	Appointments, events, and meetings for days, weeks, or a month. Also includes a list of tasks. This view looks like a paper calendar or planner.
Day/Week/Month With AutoPreview	Same as the Day/Week/Month view, except that the first lines of the text appear in each Calendar item.
Active Appointments	A list of all appointments and meetings beginning today and going into the future, with details.
Events	A list of all events, with details.
Annual Events	A list of events that happen once a year, with details.
Recurring Appointments	A list of recurring appointments, with details.
By Category	A list of all Calendar items grouped by category, with details.

(continued)

continued

Change the period of time that is displayed

You can choose how much time is displayed in the Day/Week/Month Calendar views.

1. On the View menu, point to Current View, and then click Day/Week/Month.
2. On the Standard toolbar, click the button for the amount of time that you want to view.

To view Calendar items for	Do this
One day	Click the Day button.
Seven days	Click the Week button.
Five days, Monday through Friday	Click the Work Week button.
One month	Click the Month button.

Set the days and hours for your work week

Not everyone works the same hours, days, or weeks. Your schedule at Impact Public Relations is to work four 10-hour days. In this exercise, you set up your Calendar to reflect your actual work schedule, a four-day work week.

1. On the View menu, point to Current View, and be sure that Day/Week/Month is selected.
2. On the Tools menu, click Options.

   The Options dialog box appears.
3. On the Preferences tab, click the Calendar Options button.

   The Calendar Options dialog box appears.
4. In the Calendar Options dialog box, be sure that the check boxes next to only Monday, Tuesday, Wednesday, and Thursday are selected.

5. In the Start Time box, click the drop-down arrow, and then select 7:00 A.M.
6. In the End Time box, click the drop-down arrow, and then select 6:00 P.M.
7. In the First Day Of Week box, click the drop-down arrow, and then select Monday.
8. In the Calendar Options dialog box, click OK, and then in the Options dialog box, click OK.
9. On the Standard toolbar, click the Work Week button.

   The Appointment area displays a four-day week, beginning with Monday, with daily work hours from 7 A.M. to 6 P.M.

Display appointments with end times and as clocks

Some people like to see when their appointments both begin and end. Also, some people can visualize their schedules more easily if their appointments are presented in the form of a clock. In this exercise, you customize your Calendar by adding end times in your appointment entries and by displaying both start and end times in the form of a clock.

1. In the Date Navigator, scroll to December 2004, and then click December 6.

   December 6, 2004, is displayed in the Appointment area.
2. On the View menu, point to Current View, and then click Customize Current View.

   The View Summary dialog box appears.
3. In the View Summary dialog box, click the Other Settings button.

   The Format Day/Week/Month View dialog box appears.
4. In the Format Day/Week/Month View dialog box, in the Week and Month areas, be sure that the Show End Time check boxes are selected.
5. In the Week and Month areas, select the Show Time As Clocks check boxes.
6. In the Format Day/Week/Month View dialog box, click OK, and in the View Summary dialog box, click OK.
7. On the Standard toolbar, click the Week button.

   A seven-day week is displayed in the Appointment area. The start and end times for your appointments are indicated to the left of each entry by clock graphics.

Your screen should look similar to the following illustration.

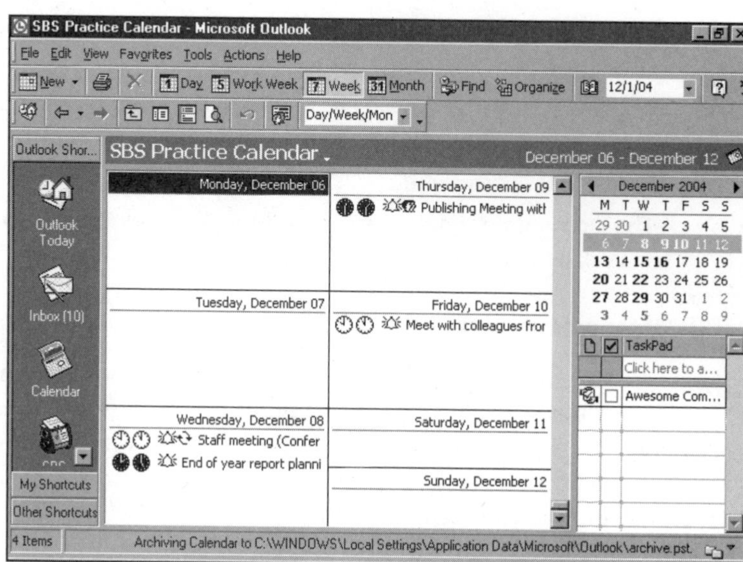

Change the current time zone

When you travel across times zones, reconciling your schedule can be tricky. In this exercise, you change your current time zone in Outlook.

> **important**
>
> Changing your current time zone in Outlook is equivalent to changing it in Microsoft Windows Control Panel. Any change in Outlook affects the time displayed in other Windows-based programs.

1. On the Standard toolbar, click the Day button.
2. On the Tools menu, click Options.

   The Options dialog box appears.
3. In the Options dialog box, click the Preferences tab, and then click the Calendar Options button.

   The Calendar Options dialog box appears.

If you already work in New York, substitute Los Angeles, and choose Pacific Time.

4. In the Calendar Options dialog box, in the Calendar Options area, click the Time Zone button.

   The Time Zone dialog box appears.

5. In the Time Zone dialog box, in the Label box, type **New York**
6. In the Time Zone box, click the drop-down arrow, and then select Eastern Time.
7. To set your computer clock to automatically adjust for daylight saving time changes, select the Adjust For Daylight Saving Time check box.
8. In the Time Zone dialog box, click OK; in the Calendar Options dialog box, click OK; and then in the Options dialog box, click OK.

   The three dialog boxes close. The Appointment area reappears, displaying the label *New York* above the time bar. Your appointment times have now been adjusted to reflect the new time zone.

tip

To quickly change the time zone on your computer, on the Standard toolbar, click the Day button. In the Appointment area, right-click anywhere on the gray time bar, and then on the shortcut menu, click Change Time Zone.

Show an additional time zone in Calendar

In this exercise, you add a second time zone, Greenwich Mean Time, next to the original time zone in the Appointment area.

1. On the Standard toolbar, click the Day button.
2. On the Tools menu, click Options.

   The Options dialog box appears.
3. On the Preferences tab, click the Calendar Options button.

   The Calendar Options dialog box appears.
4. In the Calendar Options dialog box, click the Time Zone button.

   The Time Zone dialog box appears.
5. In the Time Zone dialog box, select the Show An Additional Time Zone check box.
6. In the Label box, type **Greenwich Mean Time**
7. In the Time Zone box, click the drop-down arrow, and then select Greenwich Mean Time: Dublin, Edinburgh, Lisbon.
8. In the Time Zone dialog box, click OK; in the Calendar Options dialog box, click OK; and then in the Options dialog box, click OK.

   The three dialog boxes close. Greenwich Mean Time appears as a second time bar.

Your screen should look similar to the following illustration.

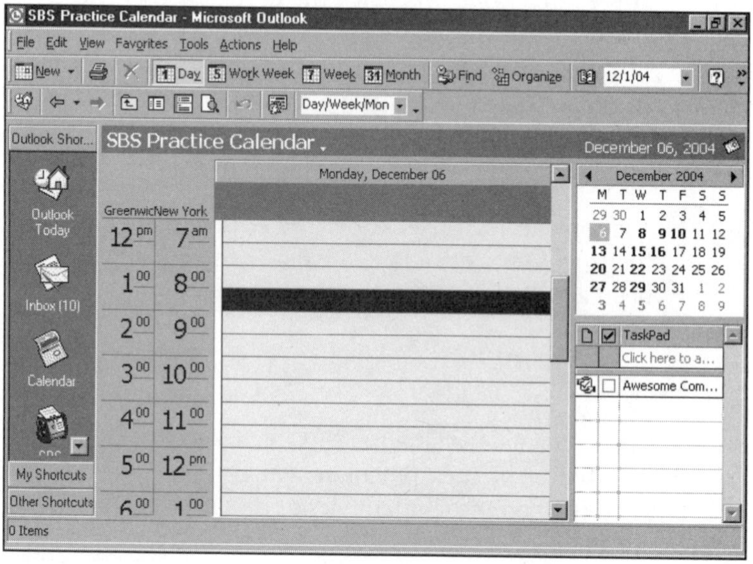

tip

You can quickly switch between the two time zone columns displayed in your daily Appointment area. For example, if you regularly commute between Seattle and Dublin, set your current time zone to Seattle time and your second time zone to Dublin time. When you fly to Dublin, click Swap Time Zones so that the Dublin time zone column is located next to your appointments. To switch your current time zone with the second time zone, on the Tools menu, select Options, and then on the Preferences tab, click the Calendar Options button. In the Calendar Options dialog box, click the Time Zone button, click the Swap Time Zones button, and then click OK three times to close the dialog boxes. The second time zone column will appear in the Appointment area next to the time slots, adjusting the times for your appointments.

To remove the second time zone, right-click the time bar on the left edge of the Appointment area. Click Change Time Zone, and then clear the Show An Additional Time Zone check box. Click OK to close the dialog box.

Add a country's holidays to your Calendar

Holidays are considered all-day events or appointments.

To keep up with the holidays that might be important to a key Canadian client, you decide to add Canadian holidays to your Calendar.

1. On the Tools menu, click Options.

   The Options dialog box appears.

2. On the Preferences tab, click the Calendar Options button.

   The Calendar Options dialog box appears.

You can add holidays for most of the major countries and religious communities of the world.

3. In the Calendar Options dialog box, click the Add Holidays button.

   The Add Holidays To Calendar dialog box appears.

tip

Individual holidays can be copied to Calendar by opening a holiday folder and then dragging each appointment to Calendar.

4. In the Add Holidays To Calendar dialog box, in the list of countries, select the check box next to Canada.
5. In the Add Holidays To Calendar dialog box, click OK.

   An Import-Holidays dialog box appears while the holidays are added.
6. In the Calendar Options dialog box, click OK; and then in the Options dialog box, click OK.

   The dialog boxes close. Calendar is now set up to display Canadian holidays on the appropriate dates.
7. In the Date Navigator, scroll to July 2001, and then click July 1.

   Canadian Independence Day is displayed for that date in the Appointment area.

tip

To remove holidays for a country from your Calendar, on the View menu, point to Current View, and then click Events. A list of events in your Calendar is displayed in a table view. In the list of events, select the holiday that you want to remove, and then on the Standard toolbar, click the Delete button. Repeat until each holiday that you want to remove is deleted.

One Step Further: Using the Timex Data Link Watch

The Timex Data Link Watch produced by Timex Corporation receives information exported from Outlook and other similar programs, including Microsoft Schedule+. The Outlook Timex Data Link Watch Wizard makes it easy to export any of the following to the watch: appointments, tasks, phone numbers, anniversaries, reminders, and current time and time zone information.

Copy Outlook information to the Timex Data Link Watch

important

Before you can follow this procedure, you must have the Timex Data Link Watch and have installed the Timex Data Link Watch files from your Office 2000 installation CD-ROM or from the network location that you used to set up the program. If you didn't install Office from a CD-ROM, you can download the files you need over the Internet. To access the Internet, in Outlook, click the Help menu, and then click Office On The Web.

1. Install the software included with your Timex Data Link Watch onto your hard disk.
2. Start Outlook, and then on the File menu, click Import And Export.

   The Import And Export Wizard dialog box appears.
3. In the Choose An Action To Perform box, select Export To The Timex Data Link Watch, and then click the Next button.

   The Timex Data Link Watch Wizard dialog box appears. The default check boxes for the data to be exported are selected. Your screen should look similar to the following illustration.

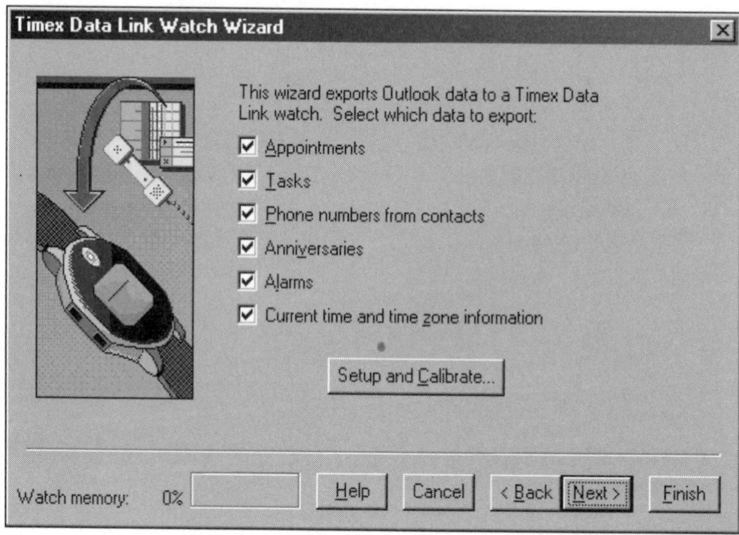

4. Continue to click the Next button to move through the Import And Export Wizard and specify more export options.

5. Click the Finish button.

   The Export To Watch dialog box appears.

6. Hold the watch in front of the screen as directed, and click OK.

   The data is exported to the watch, and a message appears asking if the export was successful.

7. If the export was successful, click Yes.

   The message and the Timex Data Link Watch Wizard dialog box close.

8. If the export was unsuccessful, try again or see the Timex Data Link Watch troubleshooting instructions.

Finish the lesson

1. To continue to the next lesson, on the File menu, click the Close button.
2. If you have finished using Outlook for now and are working in a Workgroup environment, on the File menu, click Exit And Log Off. If you are working in an Internet-only environment, on the File menu, click Exit.

Lesson 4 Quick Reference

To	Do this	Button
Schedule a detailed appointment	On the Outlook Bar, click the Calendar shortcut, and then click the New Appointment button. On the Appointment form, type information in the appropriate boxes, select options, and then on the Appointment form Standard toolbar, click the Save And Close button.	New
Schedule a private appointment	Select and double-click the time slot you want. On the Appointment form, type information in the appropriate boxes. In the lower-right corner, select the Private check box, and then click the Save And Close button.	
Schedule an event	On the Actions menu, click New All-Day Event. On the Event form, type information in the boxes, and then click the Save And Close button.	

Lesson 4 Quick Reference

To	Do this
Schedule an all-day appointment	Select and double-click the time slot you want. On the Appointment form, change the start and end times to show a full workday. Type any additional information, and then click the Save And Close button.
Schedule a recurring appointment	Select the appropriate time slot. Double-click the time slot. On the Appointment form, click the Recurrence button. On the Appointment Recurrence form, select the options that you want, and click OK. On the Appointment form, type additional information in the boxes, and then click the Save And Close button.
Make an existing appointment recurring	Double-click an appointment. On the Appointment form, click the Recurrence button. On the Appointment Recurrence form, select the options that you want, and click OK. On the Appointment form, type additional information in the boxes, and then click the Save And Close button.
Move or copy an appointment	Click the left border of the appointment that you want to move, and then drag the appointment to a new date in the Date Navigator. If the appointment needs to be on the same date at a different time slot, drag it to the new time slot.

Lesson 4 Quick Reference

To	Do this	Button
Edit or move a recurring appointment	Open the appointment that you want to edit or move. In the Open Recurring Item dialog box, select Open The Series. On the Recurring Appointment form, click the Recurrence button. Change the time and date as needed, and click OK. On the Appointment form, click the Save And Close button.	
Delete a recurring appointment	Select the appointment to delete. On the Standard toolbar, click the Delete button. In the Confirm Delete dialog box, click Delete All Occurrences, and click OK.	X
Find an appointment	On the Standard toolbar, click the Find button. In the Look For box, type a keyword, and then click the Find Now button.	
Set up a reminder notice	Double-click the appointment you want to be reminded about. On the Appointment form, select the Reminder check box, and then in the next box, click the drop-down arrow and select the amount of time prior to the appointment that you want the reminder to appear. Click the Save And Close button.	
Set reminder options for new appointments	On the Tools menu, click Options, and then click the Preferences tab. In the Calendar area, select the Default Reminder check box, and then enter how long before the appointment you want the reminder to occur. Click OK.	

Lesson 4 Quick Reference

To	Do this	Button
Attach a document to an appointment	Double-click the time slot you want for the appointment. On the Appointment form, type the appropriate information. On the Appointment form Standard toolbar, click the Insert File button. Locate and double-click the file that you want to attach. Click the Save And Close button.	
Save an appointment in vCalendar format	Select the appointment that you want to save in vCalendar format. On the File menu, click Save As. In the Save As dialog box, in the Save In drop-down list, locate the folder where you want to save the file. In the File Name box, type the file name. In the Save As Type box, click the drop-down arrow, select vCalendar, and then click the Save button.	
Add appointments to categories	On the Standard toolbar, click the Organize button, and then click the Using Categories link. In the Add Appointment Selected Below To drop-down list, select a category. In the Appointment area, select an appointment, and then click the Add button. Select other categories or appointments as needed, and click the Add button each time. To view related groups of appointments, on the Ways to Organize Your Calendar panel, click the Using Views link. On the Using Views page, in the Change Your View list, select By Category. Click the plus sign (+) next to the category you want to view.	

Lesson 4 Quick Reference

To	Do this
Set up your work week days and hours	On the Tools menu, click Options, and then click the Preferences tab. Click the Calendar Options button, and select the options for days and times that you want. Click OK twice to close the dialog boxes.
Display appointments with end times or as clocks	On the View menu, point to Current View, and then click Customize Current View. Click the Other Settings button, and then in the Week and Month areas, be sure that the Show End Time and the Show Time As Clock check boxes are selected. Click OK twice to close the dialog boxes.
Change the current time zone	On the Tools menu, click Options, and then click the Preferences tab. Click the Calendar Options button, and then click the Time Zone button. In the Current Time Zone area, type a description in the Label box, then in the Time Zone box, click the drop-down arrow, and select the time zone that you want to view. To adjust your computer clock to automatically adjust for daylight saving time changes, select the Adjust For Daylight Saving Time check box. Click OK three times to close the dialog boxes.
Add an additional time zone in Calendar	On the Tools menu, click Options, and then click the Preferences tab. Click the Calendar Options button, and then click the Time Zone button. Select the Show An Additional Time Zone check box. In the Label box, type a description. In the Time Zone box, click the drop-down arrow, and then select the time zone that you want to add. Click OK three times to close the dialog boxes.
Add a country's holidays to your Calendar	On the Tools menu, click Options, and then click the Preferences tab. Click the Calendar Options button, and then click the Add Holidays button. Select the check box next to each country whose holidays you want to add, and click OK three times to close the dialog boxes.

Lesson 4 Quick Reference

To	Do this
Copy Outlook information to the Timex Data Link Watch	Install the software included with the Timex Data Link Watch on your hard disk. Start Outlook, and then on the File menu, click Import And Export. In the Choose An Action To Perform box, select Export To The Timex Data Link Watch, and then click the Next button. Continue to click the Next button to move through the Import And Export Wizard and specify export options. Click the Finish button. Hold the watch in front of the screen as directed, and click OK. If the export was successful, in the message box that appears, click Yes. If the export was unsuccessful, try again or see the Timex Data Link Watch troubleshooting instructions.

PART 4

Microsoft PowerPoint 2000

LESSON

1

Creating a Presentation

ESTIMATED TIME
20 min.

In this lesson, you will learn how to:

- ✔ *Start PowerPoint.*
- ✔ *Use the AutoContent Wizard.*
- ✔ *Move around in a presentation.*
- ✔ *Change text in the Outline pane.*
- ✔ *Change and add text in the Slide pane.*
- ✔ *Change presentation views.*
- ✔ *Preview slides in Slide Sorter view.*
- ✔ *Save a presentation.*

With Microsoft PowerPoint you can create overhead slides, speaker's notes, audience handouts, and an outline, all in a single presentation file. PowerPoint offers powerful wizards to help you create and organize your presentation step by step.

As the Vice President of Sales for Impact Public Relations, you're responsible for developing a new employee training program. The president of Impact has asked you to create a brief presentation to describe the project at the annual stockholders' meeting.

In this lesson, you'll learn to start PowerPoint, use the AutoContent Wizard to create a presentation, and change and insert text. You'll edit text, move around in your presentation, look at your content in different views, and save your work.

Starting PowerPoint

Office Assistant

There are several ways to start PowerPoint and all your other applications; one way is to use the Start button on the taskbar. When you run PowerPoint for the first time, it displays the Office Assistant shown in the margin. The Office Assistant answers your questions, offers tips, and provides help on a variety of PowerPoint 2000 program features.

Start Microsoft PowerPoint

Start

1. On the taskbar, click the Start button.

   The Start menu appears.
2. On the Start menu, point to Programs.

   The Programs menu appears, displaying all the programs on your hard disk drive, including Microsoft PowerPoint.
3. Click the Microsoft PowerPoint icon to start PowerPoint.
4. Click the Start Using Microsoft PowerPoint option button or right-click the Office Assistant, and then click Hide Clippit on the shortcut menu to continue.

   The PowerPoint Startup dialog box appears, giving you a choice of how to begin PowerPoint.

Understanding the PowerPoint Startup Dialog Box

When you first start PowerPoint, the PowerPoint Startup dialog box appears. This dialog box gives four options for beginning your PowerPoint session. Note that you can click the check box at the bottom of the dialog box so that the Startup dialog box will not appear again.

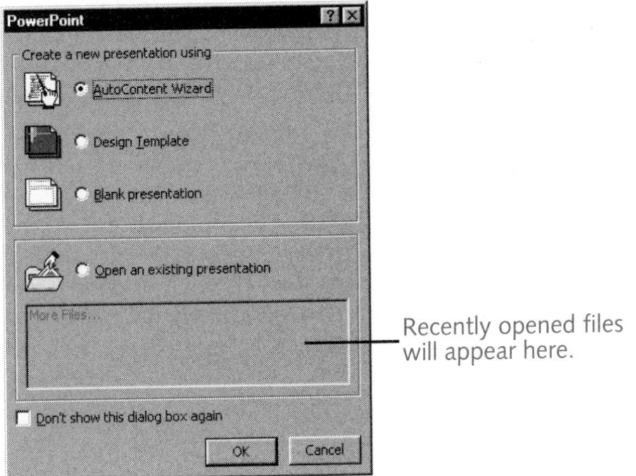

To begin your PowerPoint session, choose from one of four options to create a new presentation or open an existing one in the PowerPoint Startup dialog box. The following table describes the available options.

Select	To	Toolbar button
AutoContent Wizard	Create a new presentation using the AutoContent Wizard, which prompts you for a presentation title and information about your presentation. Choose a presentation style and type, and then PowerPoint provides a basic outline to help guide you in organizing your content into a professional presentation.	
Design Template	Create a new presentation based on a design template, which is a presentation with predefined slide colors and text styles. The New Presentation dialog box appears, in which you can choose a template.	

Select	To	Toolbar button
Blank Presentation	Create a new blank presentation. The New Slide dialog box appears with 24 predesigned slide layouts from which you can choose to create a new slide.	
Open An Existing Presentation	Open an existing PowerPoint presentation. A list of recently opened files appears below the option button. If the file you want is not in the list, click More Files, and then click OK. The Open dialog box appears.	

Using the AutoContent Wizard

If you are not working through this lesson sequentially, before proceeding to the next step, start PowerPoint.

If you have trouble writing the content for your presentation, let PowerPoint help you get started with the AutoContent Wizard. Creating a presentation can be much easier with the AutoContent Wizard because it saves you time by helping to organize your presentation. It takes you through a step-by-step process and prompts you for some of the information for your presentation, including information for the *title slide*, the first slide in your presentation.

Select the AutoContent Wizard

1. Click the AutoContent Wizard option button.
2. Click the OK button.

tip

If PowerPoint is already running, you can start the AutoContent Wizard by selecting New from the File menu, clicking the General tab, and then double-clicking the AutoContent Wizard icon.

Read the AutoContent Wizard introduction

The AutoContent Wizard dialog box opens displaying the Start screen. On the left side of the dialog box is a list of the screens in the wizard.

- Read the introduction, and then click the Next button.

  The second screen in the AutoContent Wizard appears, and the square next to Presentation Type on the left on the dialog box turns green to indicate that this is the current screen.

Choose a presentation type

First the AutoContent Wizard prompts you to select a presentation type. To help you identify presentation types quickly, the wizard organizes presentations by category.

1. Click the Projects button.
2. In the list box on the right, click Project Overview if it is not selected already.

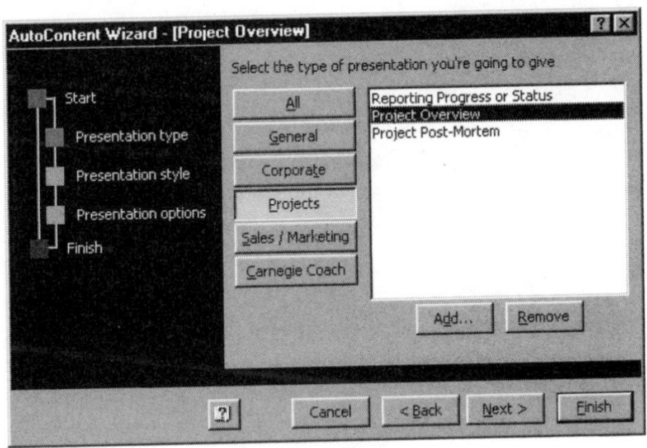

3. Click the Next button.

Choose a presentation style

The AutoContent Wizard now prompts you to select the media type for your presentation.

1. Click the On-screen Presentation option button to select that presentation type if it is not already selected.
2. Click the Next button.

Enter presentation title slide information

In the steps throughout this book, bold type indicates text that you should type exactly as it appears; italics indicates text that you supply.

The AutoContent Wizard now prompts you to enter information for the title slide and for footer information to be included on each slide. If you make a mistake as you type the information, press the Backspace key to delete the error, and then type the correct text.

1. Click in the Presentation Title box, type **New Employee Training Program** and then press the Tab key.
2. In the Footer box, type **Impact Public Relations**

3. Make sure the Date Last Updated and the Slide Number check boxes are selected.

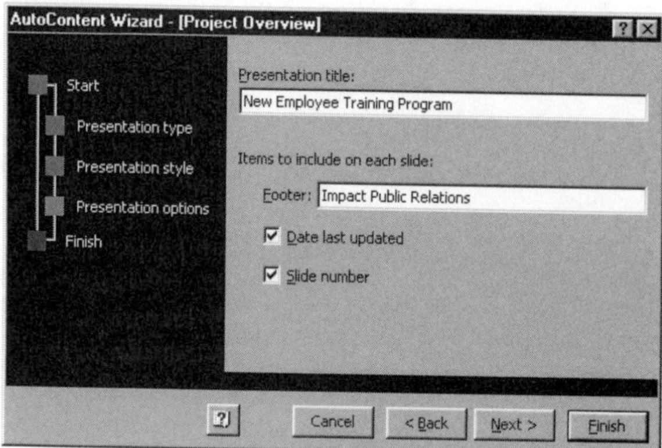

4. Click the Next button.

Finish the AutoContent Wizard

If you want to change any of the information you previously entered, you can click the Back button. Otherwise, the AutoContent Wizard will now create your presentation.

- Click the Finish button.

  The PowerPoint presentation window appears with content provided by the AutoContent Wizard in outline form on the left and the title slide on the right. The name on the title slide is the name of the registered user.

Understanding the Presentation Window

The *presentation window* is the canvas on which you type text, draw shapes, create graphs, add color, and insert objects. Along the top of the presentation window are the menus and buttons you'll use to perform the most common presentation tasks; another row of buttons may appear along the left side and on the bottom of the screen. The buttons you see are organized on *toolbars*. Toolbar buttons are shortcuts to commonly used menu commands and formatting tools. Simply click a button on the appropriate toolbar for one-step access to tasks such as formatting text and saving your presentation. Your toolbars may have different buttons visible than the ones shown in the figure on the following page. At the bottom of the presentation window are view buttons that allow you to look at your presentation in different ways.

The default view, Normal, is made up of three panes: the Outline, Slide, and Notes panes. In the Outline pane, a slide icon appears to the left of each slide's title. The paragraph text underneath each title appears indented with bullets. The Slide pane shows the slide as it will appear in the presentation. The Notes pane is where you enter speaker notes. Note that your name (or the registered user's name), the presentation title, the company name, and the current date and slide page number appear on the first slide. You can resize any of the panes by dragging the gray bar that separates them.

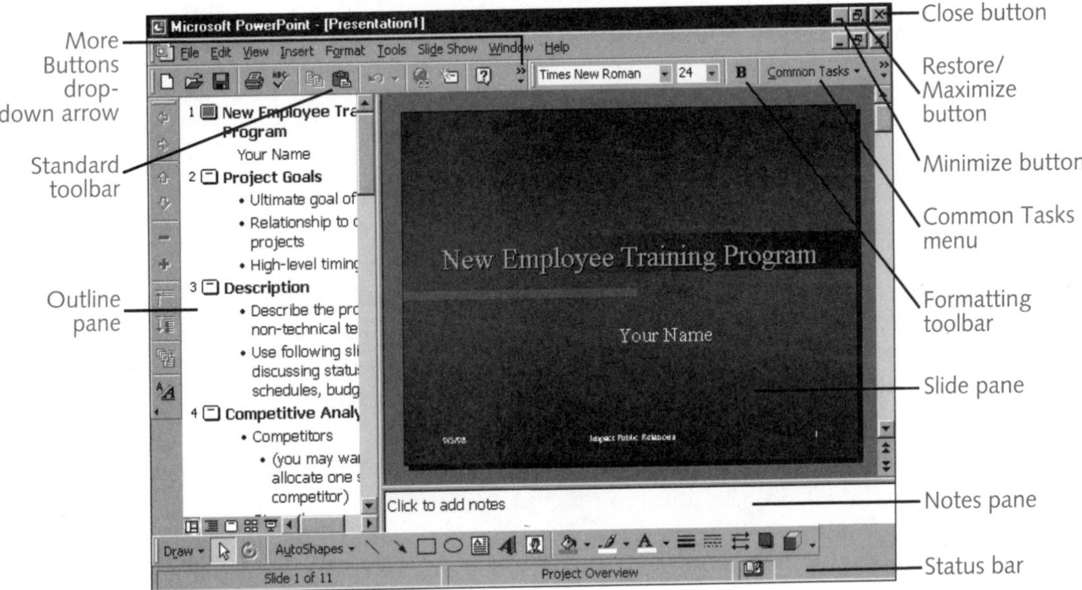

As with any Windows program, you can adjust the size of the PowerPoint and presentation windows with the Minimize and Restore/Maximize buttons, and you can close Microsoft PowerPoint or the presentation window with the Close button.

tip

If your presentation window is minimized or resized, your screen may look different from the above illustration. From this point on, all illustrations of the presentation window will be shown in their own window; that is, the presentation window is not maximized.

ScreenTips and the Status Bar

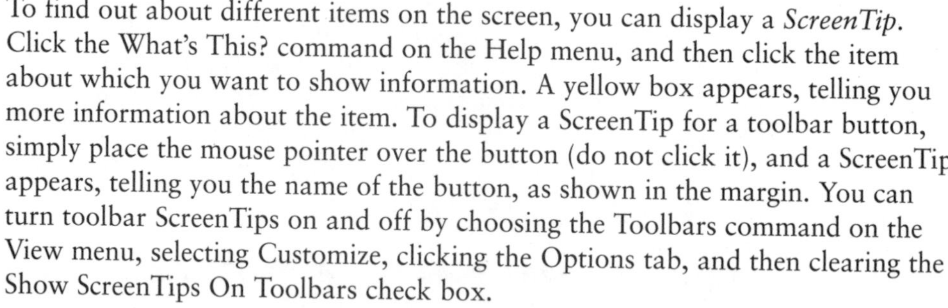

To find out about different items on the screen, you can display a *ScreenTip*. Click the What's This? command on the Help menu, and then click the item about which you want to show information. A yellow box appears, telling you more information about the item. To display a ScreenTip for a toolbar button, simply place the mouse pointer over the button (do not click it), and a ScreenTip appears, telling you the name of the button, as shown in the margin. You can turn toolbar ScreenTips on and off by choosing the Toolbars command on the View menu, selecting Customize, clicking the Options tab, and then clearing the Show ScreenTips On Toolbars check box.

Messages appear at the bottom of the window in an area called the *status bar*. These messages describe what you are seeing and doing in the PowerPoint window as you work.

Moving Around in a Presentation

You can move around in a presentation in several ways in PowerPoint. You can click the scroll arrows to scroll line by line, click either side of the scroll box to scroll window by window, or drag the scroll box to move immediately to a specific slide. In the Slide pane or Notes pane, you can click the Next Slide and Previous Slide buttons located at the bottom of the vertical scroll bar. And you can also press the Page Up or Page Down keys to scroll window by window. If you use these keys, the slides in the Slide pane will change also.

Scroll in the Outline pane

To scroll in the Outline pane, you use the scroll bars.

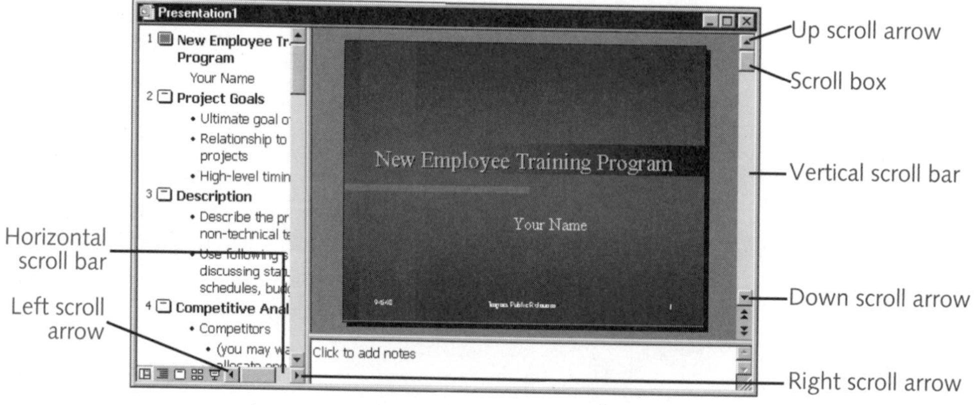

1. Click the down scroll arrow in the Outline pane a few times to see the text below the current pane.

   Each time you click a scroll arrow, PowerPoint changes the screen to show you one more line.

2. Click below the scroll box in the scroll bar in the Outline pane.

   The next window of information in the outline appears. When you click below or above the scroll box, PowerPoint scrolls window by window.

3. Drag the scroll box to the bottom of the scroll bar—you cannot drag it off the scroll bar.

   The end of the outline appears. With this method, you can quickly jump to the beginning, middle, or end of an outline, or anywhere in between.

Move from slide to slide in the Slide pane

If you are not working through this lesson sequentially, before proceeding to the next step, open PowerPoint.

To move from slide to slide in the Slide pane and in Slide view, you can use the scroll bars or the Next Slide and Previous Slide buttons.

1. Click below the scroll box in the vertical scroll bar in the Slide pane.

   Slide 2 appears in the Slide pane. Notice that the Outline pane jumps to slide 2 as well, and the slide icon next to slide 2 in the Outline pane is gray to indicate that this is the current slide.

Previous Slide

2. Click the Previous Slide button.

   Slide 1 appears in the Slide pane. Now you'll use the Next Slide button to look at the slides in your presentation.

Next Slide

3. Click the Next Slide button until you reach the end of the presentation.

   As you can see, each slide contains suggestions for how you might develop and organize your presentation.

4. Drag the scroll box up the vertical scroll bar to view slide 3, but don't release the mouse button.

Your presentation window should look like the following illustration:

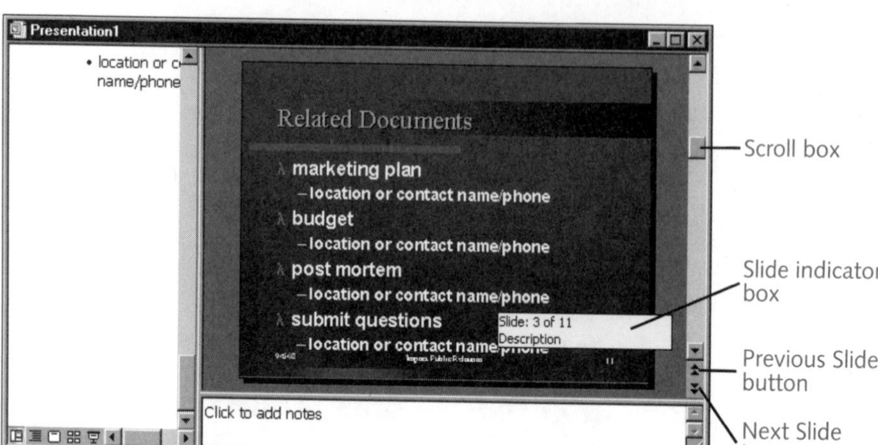

A slide indicator box appears, telling you the slide number and title of the slide to which the scroll box is pointing. The scroll box indicates the relative position of the slide in the presentation on the scroll bar.

5. Release the mouse button.

   The status bar changes from *Slide 11 of 11* to *Slide 3 of 11*.

> **tip**
>
> You can click the slide icon next to a slide in the Outline pane. The Slide pane will jump to the slide you clicked.

Changing Text in the Outline Pane

If you are not working through this lesson sequentially, before proceeding to the next step, open PowerPoint.

The AutoContent Wizard helps you get started with a suggested presentation outline. Now your job is to modify and delete the outline text to meet your specific needs. When working with the text outline, you'll find that the Outline pane is the most useful pane in which to work.

Change text in the Outline pane

I-beam pointer

1. In the Outline pane, scroll up to slide 2 and position the pointer (which changes to an I-beam) to the right of the text *Project Goals* in slide 2 and double-click to select the title text.

PowerPoint highlights the selected text, so that once you've selected it, the subsequent text you type—regardless of its length—replaces the selection.

2. Type **Program Overview**

   If you make a typing mistake, press the Backspace key to erase it. Notice that the text changes in the Outline pane also.

Four-headed arrow pointer

3. Position the I-beam pointer (which changes to a four-headed arrow) over the bullet in the Outline pane next to the text *Ultimate goal of project* in slide 2 and click to select the bulleted text.
4. Type **Impact's Goals**
5. In slide 2, click the bullet next to the text *Relationship to other projects* and type **Training Sessions**
6. In slide 2, click the bullet next to the text *High-level timing goals* to select the bulleted text.
7. Press the Delete key.

Previous Slide

8. Click the Previous Slide button in the Slide pane to move back to slide 2.

   Your presentation window should look like the following illustration:

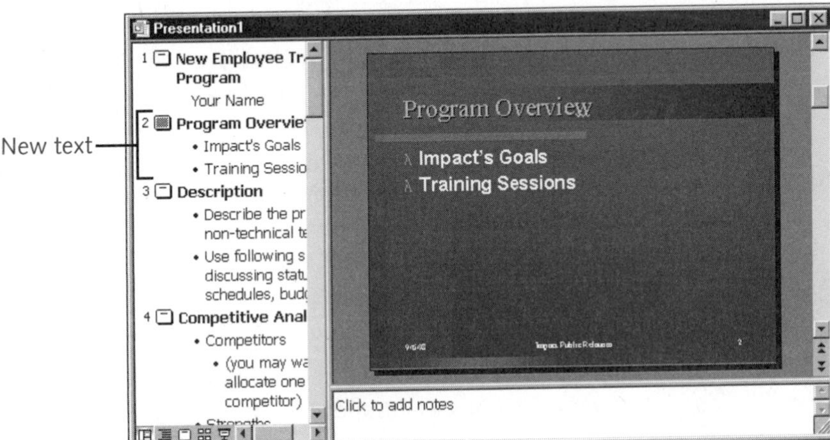

Changing Your Mind

If you are not working through this lesson sequentially, before proceeding to the next step, open PowerPoint.

A handy feature in PowerPoint is the Undo command on the Standard toolbar or Edit menu, which reverses up to your last 20 actions. For example, choosing the Undo command now will restore the text you just deleted. Whenever something happens that is not what you intended, click Undo to reverse your previous actions one at a time. If you decide that the undo action is not what you wanted, you can click the Redo button or click Redo on the Edit menu to restore the undone action.

You must undo or redo your actions in the order in which you performed them. That is, you cannot undo your fourth-previous action without first reversing the three actions that precede it. To undo a number of actions at the same time, you can use the Undo drop-down menu.

Use the Undo and Redo commands

1. On the Standard toolbar, click the Undo button to reverse your last action.
2. On the Standard toolbar, click the down-arrow next to the Undo button.

   The Undo drop-down menu appears.

Undo button with arrow

3. Click the second item in the list, *Typing*.

   The second bullet in slide 2 reverts back to the AutoContent Wizard's text.
4. On the Standard toolbar, click the Redo button.

Redo button with arrow

tip

If you don't see a toolbar button on your toolbar, click the More Buttons drop-down arrow for that toolbar to display additional toolbar buttons. Click the toolbar button you want to use from the list. This executes the command and adds this button to the toolbar, replacing one that has not been used for a while.

More Buttons

5. On the Standard toolbar, click the Redo button drop-down arrow, and then click the first item in the list, *Clear*, to restore the changes you just undid.

tip

You can change the number of actions the Undo command will undo by adjusting the number of Undo actions that appear on the Undo list. To do this, click Options on the Tools menu, and then click the Edit tab and change the maximum number of undos at the bottom of the dialog box.

If you are not working through this lesson sequentially, before proceeding to the next step, open PowerPoint.

Changing and Adding Text in the Slide Pane

You can work with your presentation's text in the Slide or Outline pane. In the Slide pane, you work with one slide at a time.

Change text in the Slide pane

Next Slide

1. Click the Next Slide button in the Slide pane.
2. Position the pointer (which changes to the I-beam) over the title text in slide 3 and click to select the title box.

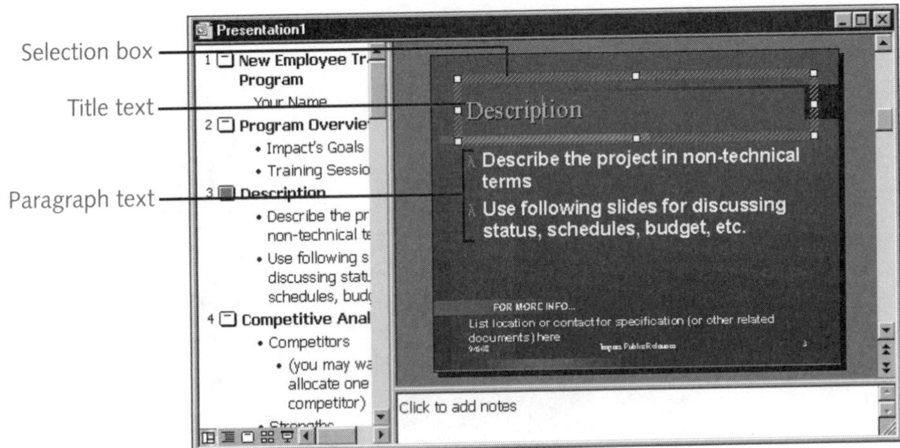

The text is surrounded by a rectangle of slanted lines called a *selection box*, with the blinking insertion point placed in the text. The selection box lets PowerPoint know what object you want to change on the slide. An object containing slide text is called a *text object*. A typical slide contains a title, called *title text*, and the major points beneath the title, called *paragraph* or *bullet text*.

3. Double-click the title text *Description* to select it.
4. Type **Training Session Development**

I

I-beam pointer

5. Position the pointer (which changes to an I-beam) over any of the bulleted text in slide 3 and click.
6. Drag to select all the text in the first bullet *Describe the project...* .
7. Type **Content development stage**

✥

Four-headed arrow pointer

8. Position the pointer over the bullet next to the text *Use the following slides...* in slide 3 so it changes to the four-headed arrow pointer, and then click to select the bulleted text.
9. Type **Lining up speakers for video**

Add text in the Slide pane

To add more bulleted text to the text object, you place the insertion point at the end of a line of text, press Enter, and then add another line of text.

1. Press Enter to create a new bullet.

   A new bullet automatically appears in the slide. The new bullet appears black until you add text.

2. Type **Program will be ready in two weeks**

3. Click outside of the selection box to deselect the text object.

   Your presentation window should look like the following illustration:

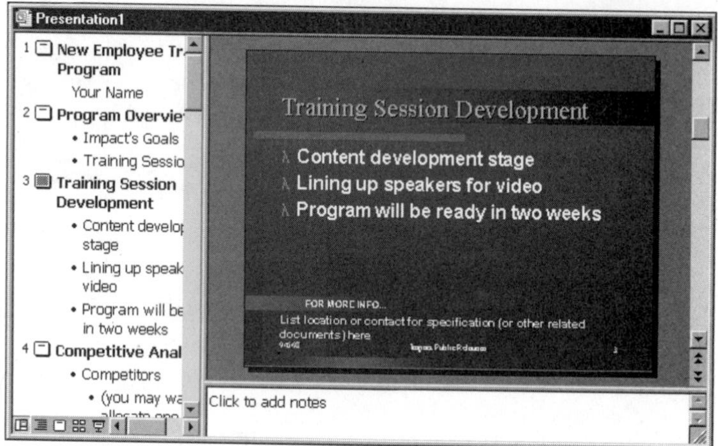

Understanding PowerPoint Views

For a demonstration of how to work in PowerPoint views, open the Office 8in1 Step by Step folder on your hard disk. Then open the PowerPoint Demos folder and double-click the Choose A View icon.

PowerPoint has six views to help you create, organize, and display your presentation. You have been working in *Normal view*. In *Slide view*, the Slide pane is resized to fill almost the whole presentation window. *Outline view* is similar to using the Outline pane in Normal view, but the Outline pane is resized so it is much larger and the Slide and Notes panes are resized smaller. *Slide Sorter view* allows you to organize the order and status of the slides in your presentation. *Notes Page view* differs from the Notes pane slightly; you can add speaker's notes in the Notes pane, but if you want to add graphics as notes, you must be in Notes Page view. *Slide Show view* allows you to preview your slides as they will be displayed as an electronic presentation. Slide Show view displays your slides as you would see them in Slide view, but the slides fill the entire screen. You can switch views using the view buttons at the bottom of the presentation window. Illustrations of Slide, Outline, Slide Sorter, and Notes Page view are shown on the following page.

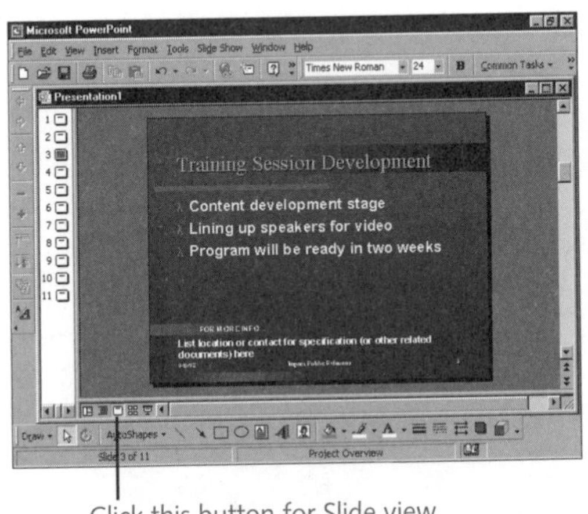

Click this button for Slide view.

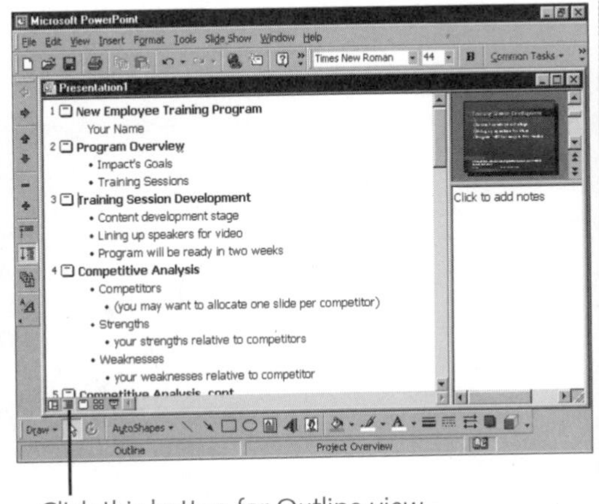

Click this button for Outline view.

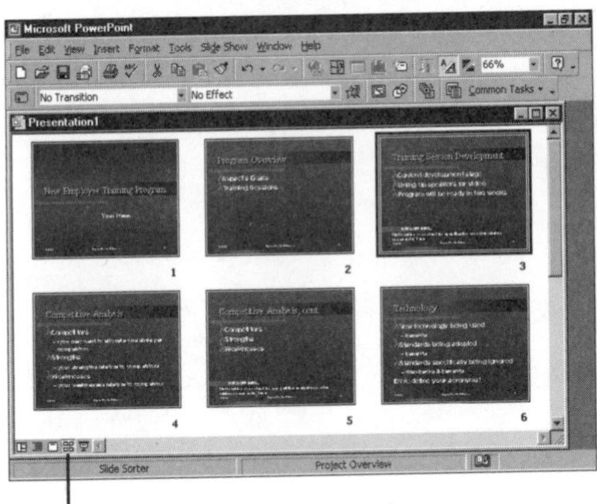

Click this button for Slide Sorter view.

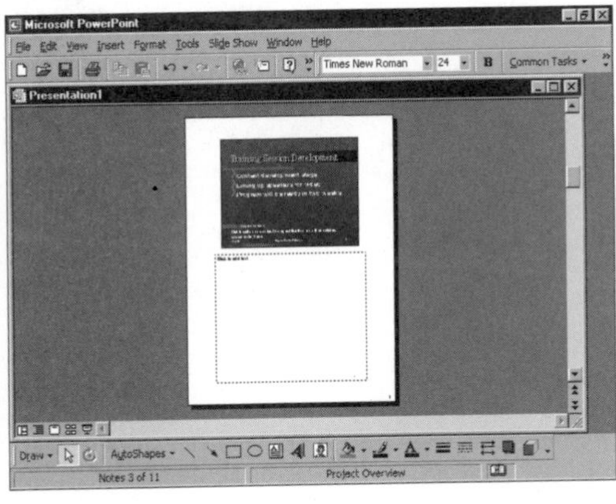

Notes Pages view

Changing Presentation Views

If you are not working through this lesson sequentially, before proceeding to the next step, open PowerPoint.

The view buttons at the bottom of the presentation window let you switch between the different views. All of these view commands are also available on the View menu except for the Slide and Outline view commands. There is no button to switch to Notes Page view; you must use the command on the View menu. Changes to the text that you make in one view appear in the other views.

Change to Slide view

You can change to Slide view and look more closely at the slide you just changed.

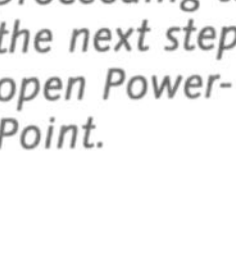

Slide View

- Click the Slide View button.

Your presentation window should look like the following illustration:

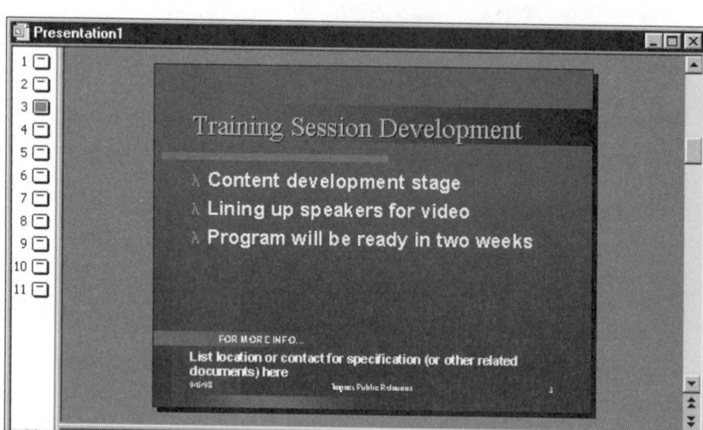

Slide view is the Slide pane from the Normal view enlarged to fill the presentation window. You change text and scroll in Slide view the same way you did in the Slide pane.

Previewing Slides in Slide Sorter View

If you are not working through this lesson sequentially, before proceeding to the next step, open PowerPoint.

Another way to view your presentation is to use Slide Sorter view. Slide Sorter view allows you to preview your entire presentation as slide miniatures—as if you were looking at photographic slides on a light board. In this view as well as in Outline view, you can easily rearrange the order of the slides in your presentation. To quickly switch back to the view you were in before you switched to Slide Sorter view, you can double-click a slide miniature to display that slide in the previous view.

Change to Slide Sorter view and preview slides

Slide Sorter View

1. Click the Slide Sorter View button.

   All the slides now appear in miniature on the screen, and the slide you were viewing (the one with the insertion point) in Slide view is surrounded by a dark box, indicating that the slide is selected. You can scroll through the slides in Slide Sorter view to view all the slides in your presentation.
2. Drag the scroll box in the scroll bar to see the slides at the end of the presentation.
3. Drag the scroll box to the top of the scroll bar.

   The beginning slides of the presentation appear.

Your presentation window should look like the following illustration:

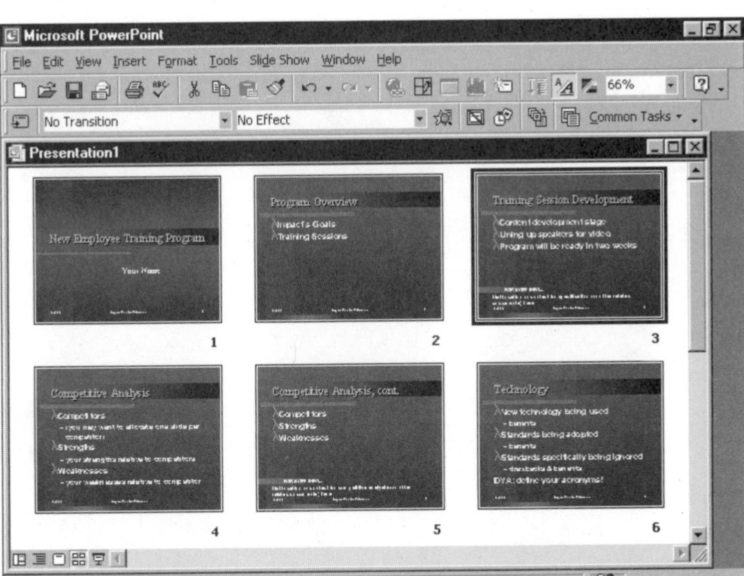

Note that your screen may display a different number of slides than shown in the illustration.

When slides are displayed formatted in Slide Sorter view, titles may be hard to read. PowerPoint allows you to suppress the slide formatting in order to read the slide titles.

4 Hold down the Alt key, and click an individual slide.

The formatting for the slide disappears and the title appears clearly. When you release the mouse button, the display format reappears.

Change to a specific slide in the previous view

Try switching back to Slide view.

- Double-click slide 1.

  The presentation view changes back to Slide view showing slide 1.

Saving a Presentation

The work you've completed thus far is stored only in your computer's temporary memory. To save your work for further use, you must give the presentation a name and store it on a hard disk drive.

The first time you save a new presentation, the Save As dialog box opens when you choose the Save command. Once you have named your presentation, clicking the Save button on the Standard toolbar or selecting Save on the File menu saves the changes you just made to your presentation. In other words, the newer version overwrites the original version. If you want to keep both your original file and the new version, you can use the Save As command on the File menu to save the new version with a new name.

Save a presentation

Save

1. On the Standard toolbar, click the Save button.

   PowerPoint displays the Save As dialog box.

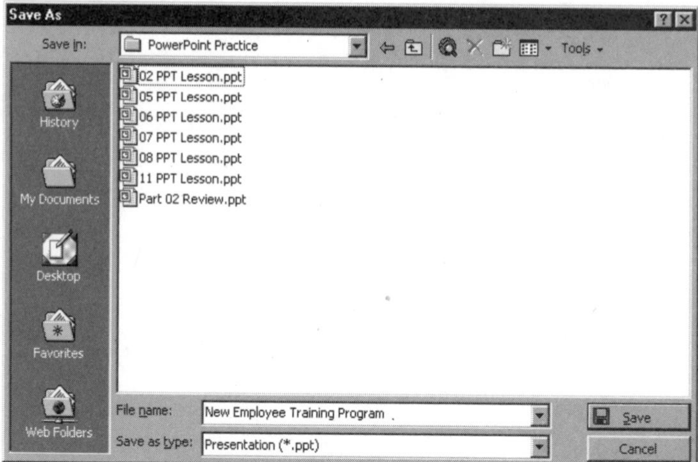

2. In the File Name text box, double-click to select the existing text, and then type **Impact Employee Training Report Pres 01**

   The word *Pres* in the filename is an abbreviation for Presentation.

3. In the Save In box, click the drop-down arrow and navigate to the PowerPoint Practice folder in the Office 8in1 Step by Step folder.
4. In the list of file and folder names, double-click the PowerPoint Practice folder.

tip

You can save a slide as an overhead picture to use in other programs. Display or select the slide that you want to save, and then click Save As on the File menu. In the Save As Type box, click Windows Metafile, and click the Save button. Now you can insert it as you would any picture.

5. Click the Save button or press Enter to save the presentation.

   The title bar name changes from *Presentation1* to *Impact Employee Training Report Pres 01.*

One Step Further Changing Presentation Properties

If you are not working through this lesson sequentially, before proceeding to the next step, open PowerPoint.

In this lesson, you have learned how to start PowerPoint and use the AutoContent Wizard to enter your ideas into a PowerPoint presentation. In addition, you have learned how to enter and change text in the Slide and Outline panes, how to move from slide to slide, how to switch between views, and how to preview and save your presentation.

With PowerPoint's Presentation Properties dialog box, you can enter information about your presentation that will help you find the file if you forget its name or location. You can use the property information to search for your presentation by its content, keyword, or date.

Add presentation properties

1. On the File menu, click Properties.

   The Presentation Properties dialog box appears displaying summary information. Generally, you should enter keywords that would help you identify the file later.
2. Click the Summary tab, and then in the Category text box, type **Progress Report**, and then press Tab.
3. In the Keywords text box, type **Training Sessions**

   You can click other tabs in the Presentation Properties dialog to display other information about your presentation.
4. Click the OK button.

Finish the lesson

Close

1. On the File menu, click Exit or click the Close button in the program title bar.
2. If a dialog box appears, asking whether you want to save the changes you made to your presentation, click the Yes button.

Lesson 1 Quick Reference

To	Do this	Button
Create a presentation using the AutoContent Wizard	In the PowerPoint Startup dialog box, click the Auto-Content Wizard option button, or, on the File menu, click New, click the General tab, and then double-click the AutoContent Wizard icon.	
Scroll in a window	Click a scroll arrow or drag the scroll box in the vertical or horizontal scroll bar.	
Move from slide to slide	Click the Next Slide or Previous Slide button.	
Change text in the Outline and Slide panes	Select the text and then make the changes you want.	
Add text in the Outline and Slide panes	Click to place the insertion point at the end of a bulleted item, press Enter, and type.	
Reverse an action	On the Edit menu, click Undo, or click the Undo toolbar button.	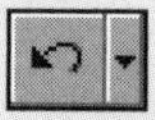
Redo an undo action	On the Edit menu, click Redo, or click the Redo toolbar button.	
Change presentation views	Click any of the view buttons, or click one of the view commands on the View menu.	
Preview slide miniatures	Click the Slide Sorter View button.	
Save a new presentation or changes to an existing one	On the File menu, click Save, or click the Save toolbar button.	
Save a presentation with a different name	On the File menu, click Save As.	
Enter presentation properties	On the File menu, click Properties, and then type text in the appropriate text box.	
End a PowerPoint session	On the File menu, click Exit, or click the Close button on the program title bar.	

Working with a Presentation

In this lesson you will learn how to:

- ✔ *Start a new presentation using a design template.*
- ✔ *Enter text in the Slide pane.*
- ✔ *Create a new slide.*
- ✔ *Enter text in the Outline pane.*
- ✔ *Edit text in Normal view.*
- ✔ *Enter text in the Notes pane.*
- ✔ *Use Notes Page view.*
- ✔ *Insert slides from other presentations.*
- ✔ *Rearrange slides in Slide Sorter view.*
- ✔ *Show slides in Slide Show view.*

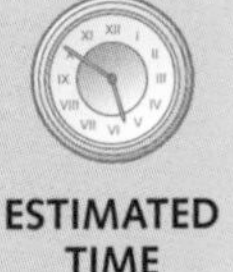

ESTIMATED TIME
20 min.

To work efficiently with Microsoft PowerPoint, you will need to become familiar with the important features of the product. In the previous lesson, you learned how to create a presentation using the AutoContent Wizard, change title and paragraph text, change views, move from slide to slide, preview slides, and save your presentation.

After quickly and easily creating a progress report presentation for the employee training program at Impact Public Relations, you decide to use PowerPoint to develop the program content. The next step is to start a new presentation and develop the content for the first training session, "Recruiting New Clients." Your Sales Manager has given you several slides to include in the presentation.

In this lesson, you'll learn how to start a new presentation with a design template, enter slide text, create new slides, insert slides from other presentations, rearrange slides in Slide Sorter view, enter speaker's notes, and show your slides in Slide Show view.

Starting a New Presentation Using a Design Template

In addition to starting a presentation with sample text from the AutoContent Wizard as you did in Lesson 1, you can also start a new presentation without having PowerPoint insert any text. You can choose a preformatted or blank design. To start a new presentation, you use the New command on the File menu. You can choose a different layout for each slide to create a specific design look, such as a slide with a graph. To see more layouts, you can scroll down the list. You choose a layout by clicking it in the AutoLayout gallery list. The layout title for the selected AutoLayout appears to the right of the gallery list.

Start a new presentation with a presentation design

1. If you quit PowerPoint at the end of the last lesson, restart PowerPoint now.
2. If you just started PowerPoint, click the Design Template option button in the PowerPoint Startup dialog box, and then click the OK button.

   or

   If PowerPoint is already running, from the File menu, click New.

   The New Presentation dialog box appears. From the General tab in the New Presentation dialog box, you can start a blank presentation or the AutoContent Wizard. The templates listed on the Presentations tab are the same ones the AutoContent Wizard uses.
3. Click the Design Templates tab.

   This tab contains a list of presentation designs.
4. Click the Sunny Days icon (you may have to scroll right to see it).

   A sample slide appears in the Preview box.

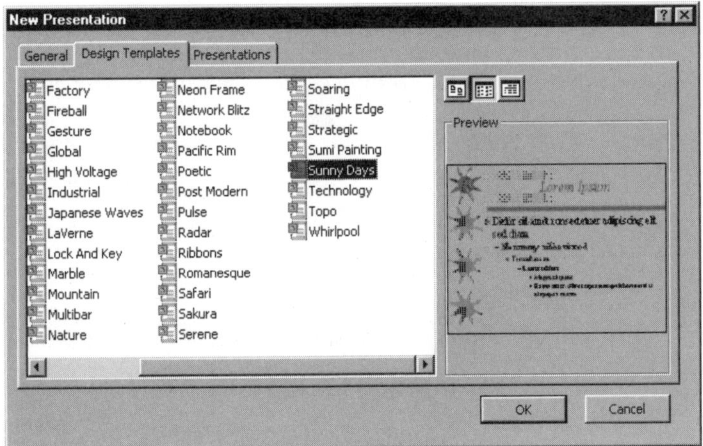

5 Click the OK button.

The New Slide dialog box appears.

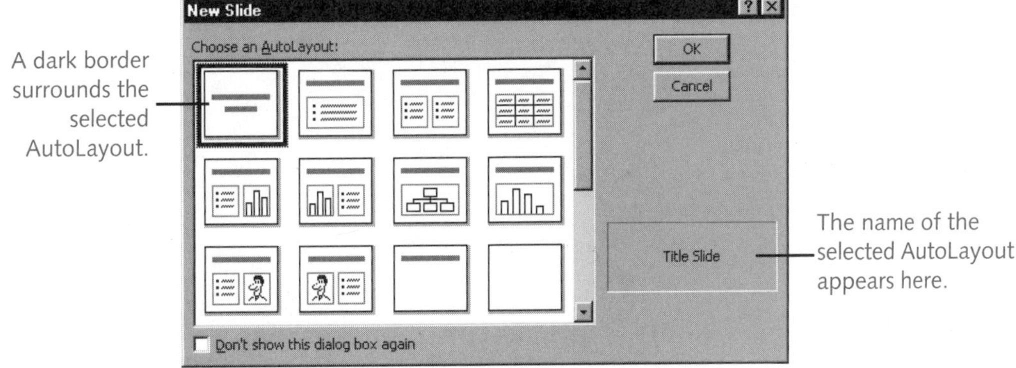

6 Click the OK button to use the default Title Slide AutoLayout.

The title slide appears in the presentation window.

Entering Text in the Slide Pane

If you are not working through this lesson sequentially, before proceeding to the next step, open PowerPoint.

To add text to your presentation, you can enter text into either the Slide or the Outline pane in Normal view, or in Slide or Outline view. The Slide pane in the new presentation window includes two text boxes called *text placeholders*. The box at the top is a placeholder for the slide's title text. The lower box is a placeholder for the slide's subtitle text. After you enter text into a placeholder, the placeholder becomes a *text object*.

Type title and subtitle text in Slide view

To give your slide a title, you click the title placeholder and start typing.

1. In the Slide pane, click in the text placeholder *Click to add title*.

   A selection box surrounds the placeholder, indicating that the placeholder is ready to enter or edit text. The placeholder text disappears and a blinking insertion point appears.
2. Type **Recruiting New Clients**

   Notice that the text appears in the Outline pane at the same time.
3. Click in the text placeholder *Click to add subtitle*.

   The title object is deselected, and the subtitle object is selected.
4. Type **Your Name** and press Enter.
5. Type **Impact Public Relations**

   Your presentation window should look like the following illustration:

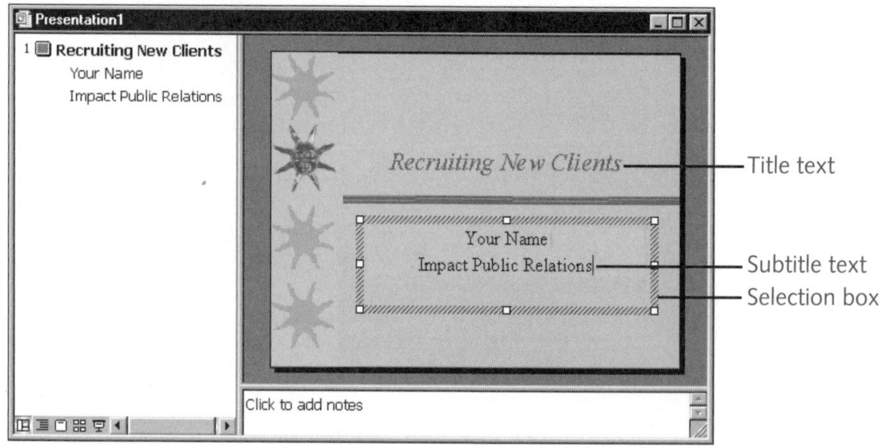

If you are not working through this lesson sequentially, before proceeding to the next step, open PowerPoint.

Creating a New Slide

You can create a new slide in your presentation using the New Slide button on the Standard toolbar, the New Slide command on the Insert menu, or the New Slide command on the Common Tasks menu button.

New Slide

Create a new slide

1. On the Standard toolbar, click the New Slide button.

   The New Slide dialog box appears.

2. Click the OK button to use the default Bulleted List AutoLayout.

   A new empty slide is added after the current slide in the Slide pane and a new slide icon is created in the Outline pane. The status bar displays *Slide 2 of 2*.

> **tip**
>
> To add a new slide that has the same layout as the current slide, hold down Shift and click the New Slide button. This shortcut eliminates the need to select the same AutoLayout from the New Slide dialog box.

Enter text in a new slide

If you start typing on an empty slide without having first selected a placeholder, PowerPoint enters the text into the title object.

- Type **Develop a Plan**

  Notice that the new slide and new title appeared in the Outline pane when you created them in the Slide pane.

  PowerPoint lets you work directly in the Slide or Outline panes, as well as in Slide and Outline views, to enter your ideas. Now you'll switch to the Outline pane to complete this slide.

Entering Text in the Outline Pane

The Outline pane shows your presentation text in outline form just as if you had typed the text in Microsoft Word 2000. In the Outline pane, however, a slide icon appears to the left of each slide's title. To enter text in the Outline pane, click to position the insertion point where you want the text to start and begin typing. The body text underneath each title appears indented one level.

Enter paragraph text

In this section, you'll change a paragraph text indent level, and type paragraph text to complete slide 2. If you make a typing error, press the Backspace key to delete the mistake and then type the correct text.

I

I-beam pointer

1. Position the pointer, which changes to the I-beam pointer, to the right of the title in slide 2 in the Outline pane and click.

   A blinking insertion point appears.

2. Press Enter.

   PowerPoint adds a new slide, and a new slide icon is added in the Outline pane with the blinking insertion point next to it. To add paragraph text to slide 2 instead of starting a new slide, you'll need to change the outline level from slide title to a bullet.

3. Press the Tab key.

   Pressing the Tab key indents your text to the right one level and moves the text from slide 3 back to slide 2. The slide icon changes to a small gray bullet on slide 2 in the Outline pane.

4. Type **Develop a list of contacts** and press Enter.

   A new bullet is added at the same indent level. Notice that once you press Enter after typing bullet text, the bullet becomes black.

5. Type **Schedule periodic phone calls to prospective clients** and press Enter.

   Also note that the text automatically wrapped to the next line in the Outline pane without your having to press Enter.

6. Type **Re-evaluate your strategy regularly**

Create a new slide and enter text

With the insertion point after the word *regularly*, you create a new slide from an indented outline level using a toolbar button and a keyboard command.

1. Press Enter.
2. On the Outlining toolbar, click the Promote button.

Promote

> **important**
>
> If the Outlining toolbar is not visible on your screen, on the View menu, point to Toolbars, and then click Outlining.

   A new slide is created with the insertion point to the right of the slide icon. Next you'll type title and paragraph text.

3. Type **Make the Client Number One** and press Enter.
4. Press Tab.

   A new indent level is created for slide 3. Now, using that indent level, you'll enter the following three bulleted points under slide 3 to finish the slide.

5. Type **Be creative** and press Enter.
6. Type **Stay positive** and press Enter.
7. Type **Be tenacious**

   Next you'll create a new slide using a keyboard command.
8. Hold down the Ctrl key and press Enter.
9. Type **Summary**, press Enter, and then press Tab.

   A new indent level is created for slide 4.
10. Type **Create a plan suitable to your temperament** and press Enter.
11. Type **Try to avoid cold calls** and press Enter.
12. Type **Keep current with the client's industry trends**

    Your presentation window should look like the following illustration:

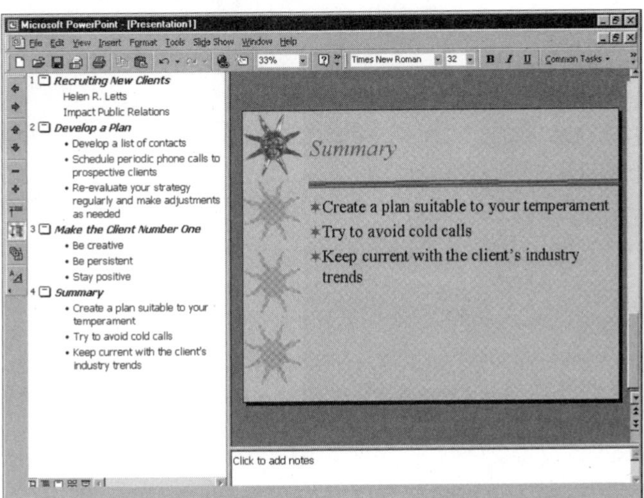

Editing Text in Normal View

Once you have created slides and entered text, you can easily modify the text in your presentation. You can insert new text anywhere in the Outline and Slide panes. If you want to edit text, you will need to select it first. You can select individual characters, sentences, paragraph text, or title text in either the Outline or Slide panes. Selecting text in PowerPoint works just as it does in Microsoft Word 2000.

Once text is selected, you can replace it or rearrange it. You can rearrange title and paragraph text in both the Outline and Slide panes. Also in the Outline pane, you can rearrange text among slides or rearrange a group of slides.

Insert new text

1. In the Outline pane, position the I-beam pointer just after the word *regularly* in slide 2 and click.

   This places the blinking insertion point where you want to begin typing, as shown in the following illustration:

I-beam pointer

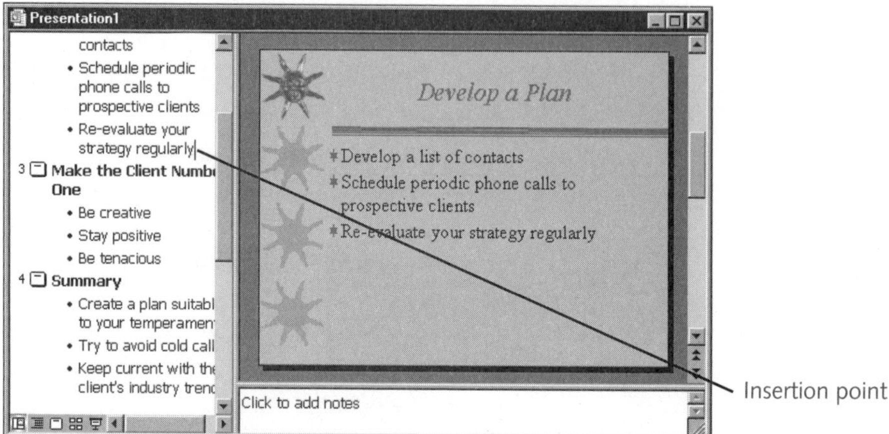

> **important**
>
> If the insertion point is not where you want it, reposition the I-beam pointer and click again to place the insertion point in the desired location.

2. Press the Spacebar and type **and make adjustments as needed**

   PowerPoint makes room in the outline for the new text.

Select and replace text

To select one or more words or characters, you can also drag the pointer over the text you want to select.

In this exercise, you select and replace text in the Outline pane.

1. In the Outline pane, position the I-beam pointer over any part of the word *tenacious* in the third bullet point of slide 3.

2. Double-click to select the word.

   Your presentation window should look like the following illustration:

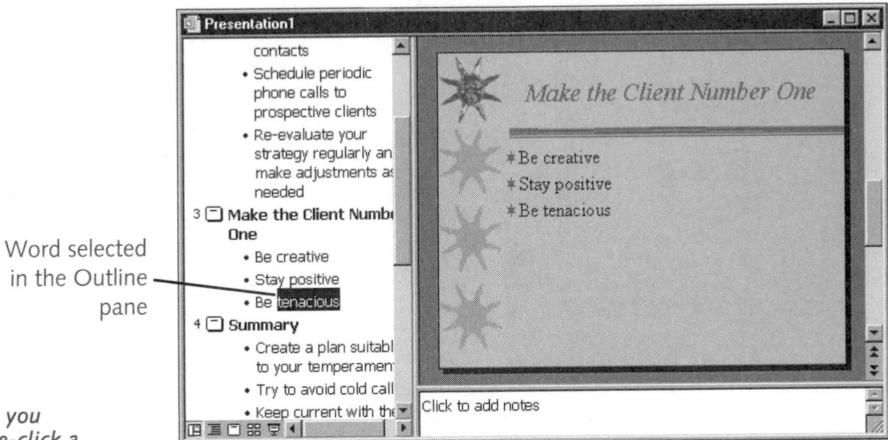

When you double-click a word, PowerPoint also selects the space that follows. Once you've selected text, the next text you type—regardless of its length—replaces the selection.

   The text is now highlighted, indicating it has been selected.

3. Type **persistent**

   The new word replaces the text in the both the Outline and Slide panes.

Select and rearrange text

To select paragraph text or an individual slide in the Outline pane, you click the associated bullet or slide icon to its left.

1. Move the pointer over the bullet next to *Be persistent* in slide 3.

   The pointer changes to a four-headed arrow.

2. Click the bullet to select the entire line.

3. Drag the selected item up until a horizontal line appears above the bullet entitled *Stay positive*, but do not release the mouse button yet.

   The horizontal line indicates where the selected text will go. The mouse pointer changes to a two-headed arrow.

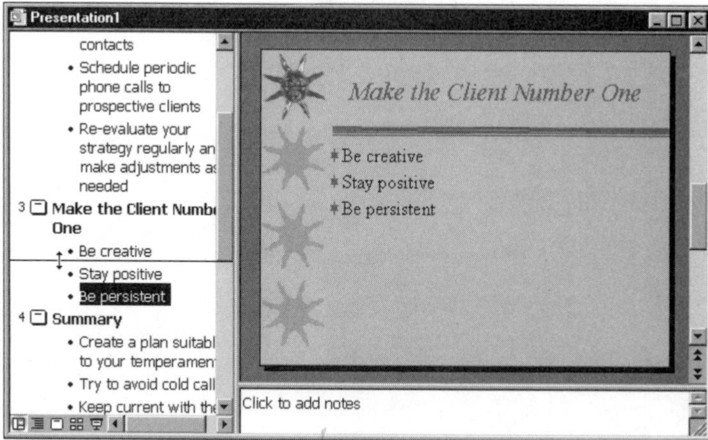

4. Release the mouse button.

   The entire line moves up one level.

Entering Text in the Notes Pane

If you are not working through this lesson sequentially, before proceeding to the next step, open PowerPoint.

In the Notes pane, you can create speaker's notes for your presentation that appear on separate notes pages. Each slide in your presentation has a corresponding notes page. To enter speaker's notes in the Notes pane, click in the Notes pane and begin typing. Entering and changing text in the Notes pane works the same as it does in the Slide and Outline panes. You can also enter speaker notes in Notes Page view by clicking Notes Page on the View menu.

Enter text in the Notes pane

1. Click in the Notes pane in slide 3.

   The notes placeholder text disappears and a blinking insertion point appears. Your presentation window should look like the following illustration:

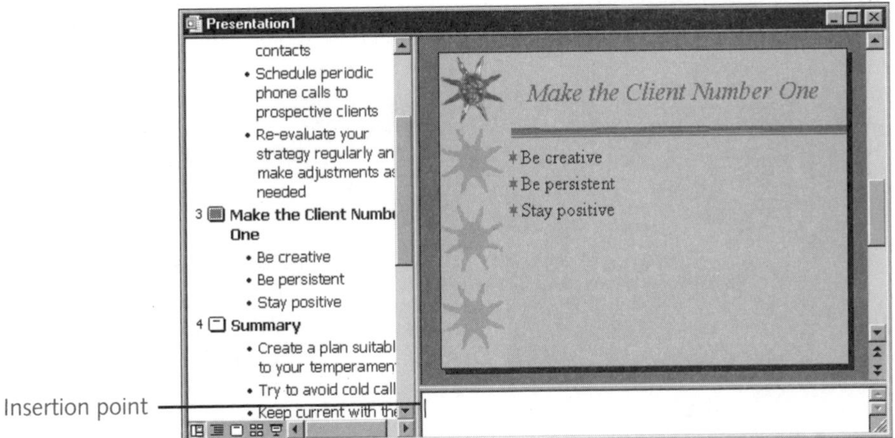

2. Type the sentence below, but do not press the Enter key. If you make a mistake, press the Backspace key to delete the mistake, and type the correct text.

   Being persistent without being annoying is a skill you will need to perfect.

Using Notes Page View

If you want to read all your speaker's notes, it might be easier to switch to Notes Pages view, in which you can move from notes page to notes page the same way as in Slide view.

Move from notes page to notes page in Notes Page view

1. From the View menu, click Notes Page.

   Notes Page view appears at approximately 30% view on most screens to display the entire page. Your view scale might be different depending on the size of your monitor.

The presentation window should look like the following illustration:

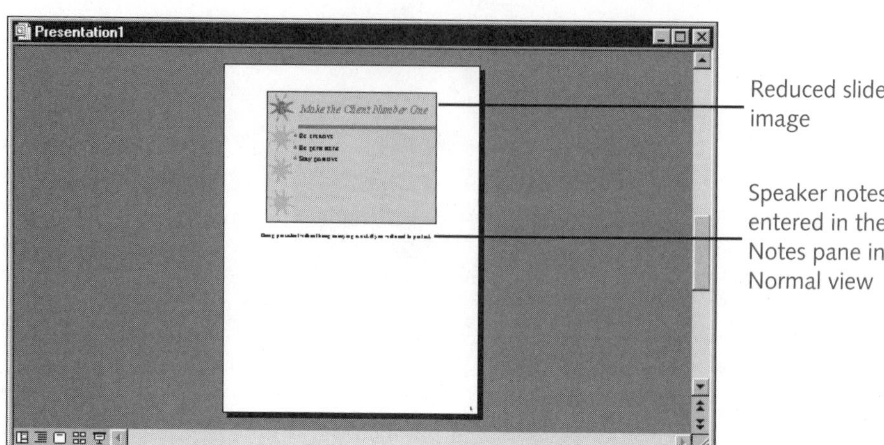

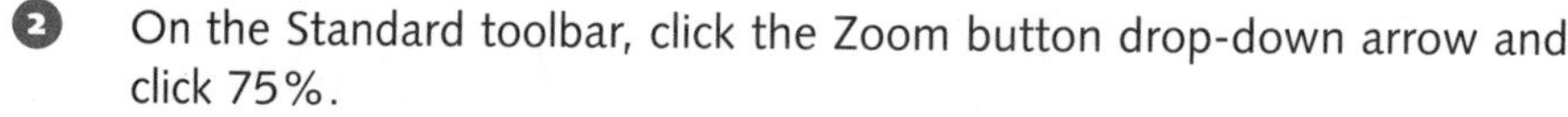

2. On the Standard toolbar, click the Zoom button drop-down arrow and click 75%.

   The view scale increases to 75%.

Next Slide

3. Click the Next Slide button.

   The status bar displays *Notes 4 of 4*.

4. Click the Notes placeholder to select it.

   The selection box surrounds the area that contains the Notes text.

5. Type **Experienced sales reps will lead a question and answer session immediately following this presentation.**

6. On the Standard toolbar, click the Zoom drop-down arrow and click Fit.

Normal View

7. Click the Normal View button.

Inserting Slides from Other Presentations

You can save time creating a presentation by using work that has already been done by you or a coworker. When you insert slides from another presentation, the new slides conform to the color and design of your current presentation, so you don't have to make many changes.

Insert slides into your presentation

1. From the Insert menu, click Slides From Files.

   The Slide Finder dialog box appears.

2. Click the Browse button.

   The Browse dialog box appears.
3. In the Look In box, click the drop-down arrow and navigate to the PowerPoint Practice folder in the Office 8in1 Step by Step folder.
4. In the list of file and folder names, double-click the PowerPoint Practice folder.
5. In the list of file names, click the file titled 02 PPT Lesson, and then click the Open button.

   The Slide Finder dialog box reappears.
6. Click slide 2, click slide 3, click the right scroll arrow, and then click slide 4 to select the slides you want to insert.

   The Slide Finder dialog box should look like the following illustration:

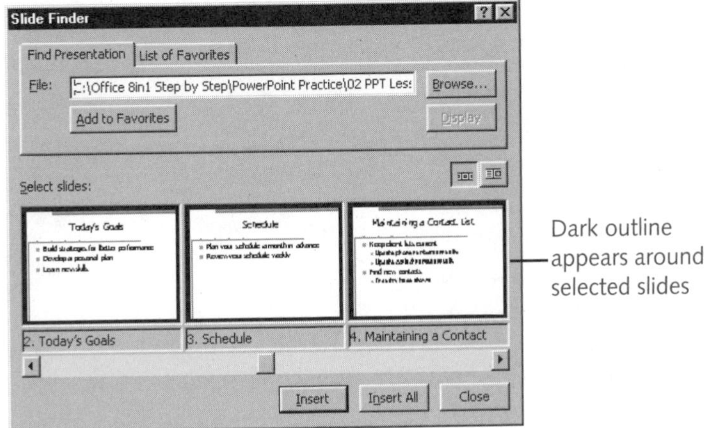

7. Click the Insert button.

   PowerPoint inserts the slides into your presentation after the current slide.
8. Click the Close button.

   The last inserted slide appears in the Slide pane.

Rearranging Slides in Slide Sorter View

After copying slides from another presentation into your current one, you'll want to rearrange the slides into the order that most effectively communicates your message. This is best done in Slide Sorter view.

Move a slide in Slide Sorter view

In Slide Sorter view, you can drag one or more slides from one location to another.

Slide Sorter View

1. Click the Slide Sorter View button.

   Your presentation window should look like the following illustration. Notice that the Slide Sorter toolbar appears above the presentation window.

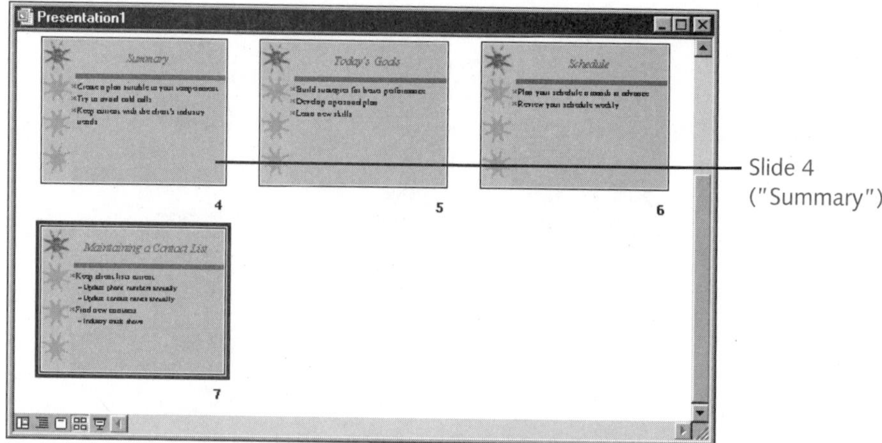

2. Click slide 4 ("Summary").
3. Drag the slide to the empty space after slide 7 ("Maintaining a Contact List").

   Notice that the mouse pointer changes to the drag pointer when you begin to drag. When you release the mouse button, slide 4 is moved to its new position and the other slides in the presentation are automatically repositioned and renumbered.

Drag pointer

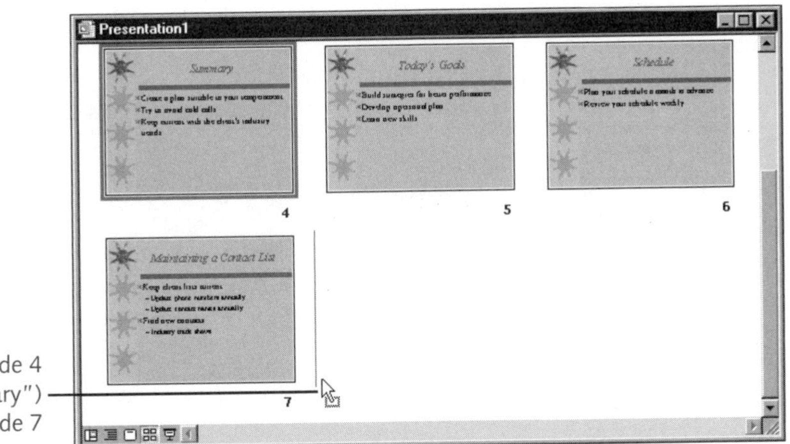

Dragging slide 4 ("Summary") after slide 7

4. Drag the scroll box to the top of the vertical scroll bar, and click the newly renumbered slide 4 ("Today's Goals").
5. Drag slide 4 between slides 1 and 2. Switch to Normal view so that PowerPoint saves your presentation in Normal view instead of Slide Sorter view.
6. Double-click slide 1 to return to the previous view, Normal view.

> **tip**
> In Slide Sorter view, you can also move slides between two or more open presentations. Open each presentation, switch to Slide Sorter view, and click Arrange All on the Window menu. Drag the slides from one presentation window to the other.

Save the presentation

Save

For information about saving a presentation, see Lesson 1, "Creating a Presentation."

1. On the Standard toolbar, click the Save button.

   PowerPoint displays the Save As dialog box, in which you can type a new name for your presentation.
2. In the File Name box, type **IPR Recruiting Pres 02**

   The "02" at the end of the presentation file name matches the lesson number.
3. In the Save In box, ensure that the PowerPoint Practice folder is selected.

4. Click the Save button.

   PowerPoint saves the presentation with the new name IPR Recruiting Pres 02, which now appears in the presentation window title bar.

Showing Your Slides in Slide Show View

Now that you have saved your presentation, review the slides for accuracy and flow. You can review your slides easily in Slide Show view. Slide Show view displays your slides using the entire screen as an on-screen presentation on your computer.

Use slide show view

Slide Show

1. Make sure slide 1 appears in the Slide pane.
2. Click the Slide Show button.

   PowerPoint displays the first slide in the presentation.
3. Click the mouse button to advance to the next slide.
4. Click one slide at a time to advance through the presentation.

   After the last slide in the presentation, PowerPoint returns to the current view.

tip

To end a slide show before you reach the last slide, press the Esc key.

One Step Further Customizing PowerPoint

You have learned how to open a presentation, insert and rearrange text, copy and paste slides between presentations, and rearrange slides in Slide Sorter view. You can customize certain features of PowerPoint by using the Options dialog box. For example, you can open recently used files by accessing them on the File menu. With the Options command, you can change the number of recently used files that appear on the File menu.

Change PowerPoint options

1. On the Tools menu, click Options, and then click the General tab.

   The Options dialog box appears with the General tab open.
2. Click the Recently Used File List up arrow twice to reach 6 entries.
3. Click the OK button.
4. Click the File menu to see the expanded list of recently used files, and then press the Esc key to cancel the menu.

Finish the lesson

1. From the File menu, click Exit.
2. If a dialog box appears, asking whether you want to save the changes you made to your presentation, click the Yes button.

Lesson 2 Quick Reference

To	Do this	Button
Start a new presentation using a design template	From the File menu, click New, and then click the Design Templates tab. Double-click a presentation icon.	
Type title or subtitle text on a slide	Click the title placeholder or subtitle placeholder and begin typing.	
Create a new slide	Click the New Slide button on the Standard toolbar, or click New Slide on the Insert menu or on the Common Tasks menu.	
Enter text in the Outline pane	Click in the Outline pane where you want to insert text and start typing.	
Edit text in the Outline and Slide panes	Select the text you want to edit, and then type to replace it or drag to rearrange it.	
Enter text in the Notes pane	Click in the Notes pane and start typing.	
Enter text in Notes Page view	On the View menu, click Notes Page. Click the placeholder and type.	
Insert slides from a presentation file	On the Insert menu, click Slides From Files. Click Browse to select a file. Type the full path name of the presentation file in the File box. Click Display to show all files in the presentation. Click the slides you want to insert. Click insert, and then click close.	

To	Do this	Button
Rearrange slides in Slide Sorter view	Select slides in Slide Sorter view. Drag the slides to the new location.	
Show slides in Slide Show view	Click the Slide Show button. Click each slide to move through the slide show.	
Change PowerPoint options	On the Tools menu, click Options.	

LESSON

3

Applying and Modifying Templates

In this lesson you will learn how to:

- ✔ *Change the display using the master.*
- ✔ *Modify master placeholders.*
- ✔ *Format master text.*
- ✔ *Adjust master text indents.*
- ✔ *Reapply a slide layout.*
- ✔ *Save a presentation as a template.*

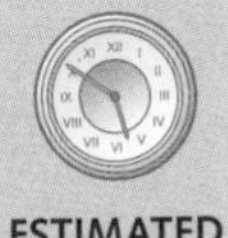

ESTIMATED TIME
20 min.

A *template* is a presentation file that has a predefined set of color and text characteristics. You can create a presentation from a template or you can apply a template to an existing presentation. When you apply a template to a presentation, the slides in the presentation take on the characteristics of the template, so you can maintain a uniform design. To make maintaining a uniform design even easier, Microsoft PowerPoint uses masters that control the look of the individual parts of the presentation, including formatting, color, graphics, and text placement. Every presentation has a set of masters, one for each view.

As the Vice President of Sales for Impact Public Relations, you have been working on a general presentation that can be customized for new clients. After adding and modifying the text in the previous lesson, you're ready to apply a presentation design template.

In this lesson, you'll learn how to apply a PowerPoint template, change the display for master objects, modify and format the master text, reapply a layout from the master, and save a presentation as a template.

Start the lesson

Follow the steps below to open the practice file called 03 PPT Lesson, and then save it with the new name IPR Company Pres 03. If you haven't already started PowerPoint, do so now.

1. If you just started PowerPoint, click the Open An Existing Presentation option button in the PowerPoint Startup dialog box, click More Files in the list box, and then click the OK button.

   or

   Open

   If PowerPoint is already running, click the Open button on the Standard toolbar.

   The Open dialog box opens.
2. In the Look In box, ensure that the PowerPoint Practice folder is open.
3. In the file list box, double-click the file named 03 PPT Lesson to open it.
4. On the File menu, click Save As.

   The Save As dialog box opens. Be sure the PowerPoint Practice folder appears in the Save In box.
5. In the File Name box, type **IPR Company Pres 03**
6. Click the Save button.

   The presentation is saved and the title bar changes to the new name.

Understanding and Applying Templates

PowerPoint comes with a wide variety of templates that are professionally designed to help you achieve the look you want. When you apply a template to your presentation, PowerPoint copies the information from each master in the template to the corresponding masters in your presentation. All slides in your presentation will then acquire the look of the template.

You can use one of many templates that come with PowerPoint, or you can create your own from existing presentations. Moreover, you can apply different templates throughout the development process until you find the look you like best.

Apply a template

To apply a template to an existing presentation, you can open the presentation and then use the Apply Design dialog box to locate and select the template you want. For the presentation, you'll apply a company template created by one of your employees in the Marketing department.

If you are not working through this lesson sequentially, before proceeding to the next step, open the 03 PPT Lesson file.

1. On the Formatting toolbar, click the Common Tasks menu button, and then click Apply Design Template.

   The Apply Design Template dialog box appears.

2. In the Look In box, ensure that the PowerPoint Practice folder is open.
3. In the list of file and folder names, click 03 PPT Template.

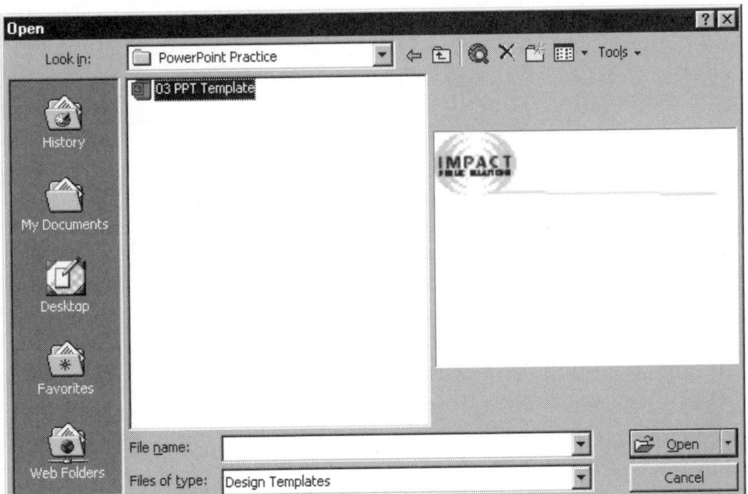

4. Click the Apply button.

   The information from the template file 03 PPT Template is applied, or copied, to the masters in your presentation. The text style and format, slide colors, and background objects change to match the template. Your content remains the same.

Your presentation window should look like the following illustration:

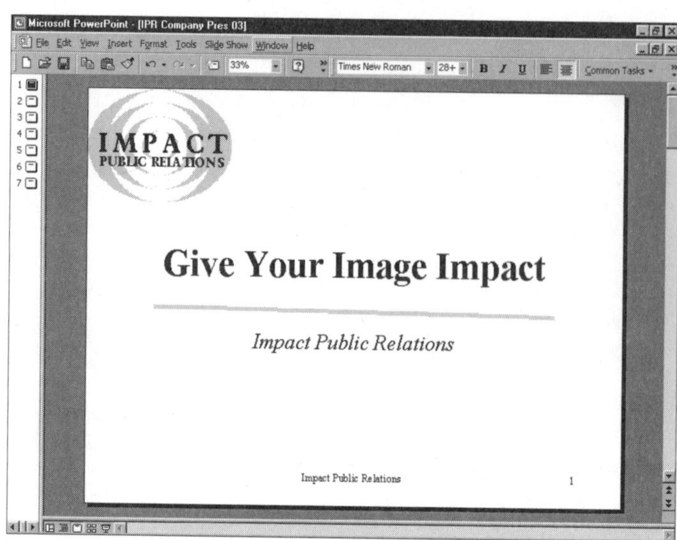

Understanding PowerPoint Masters

PowerPoint comes with two special slides called *masters*. The *Slide Master* controls the properties of every slide in the presentation. All the characteristics (background color, text color, font, and font size) of the Slide Master appear on every slide in the presentation. When you make a change on the Slide Master, the change affects every slide. For example, if you want to have your company logo, other artwork, or the date appear on every slide, you can place it on the Slide Master.

The Slide Master contains master placeholders for title text, paragraph text, the date and time, footer information, and the slide number. The master title and text placeholders control the text format for every slide in your presentation. For example, when you change the master title text format to italic, the title on each slide changes to italic to follow the master. If, for a particular slide, you want to override the default settings on the Slide Master, you can use commands on the Format menu. For example, if you want to omit background graphics on a slide, you can use that option in the Background dialog box.

The title slide has its own master, the *Title Master.* Changes you make to the Title Master affect only the title slide of the presentation. The Title Master contains placeholders similar to the Slide Master. The main difference between the Slide Master and the Title Master is the Title Master's use of a master subtitle style instead of the master text style.

PowerPoint also comes with a handout master and a notes pages master, where you can add the items you'd want to appear on each of those pages.

When you view a master, the Master toolbar appears. This toolbar contains only two buttons: the Slide Miniature button and the Close button. If you click the Slide Miniature button, a slide miniature appears so you can see the effect of changes you make to the Slide Master. You click the Close button to return to the view you were in before you opened the Master.

View the Slide Master

If you are not working through this lesson sequentially, before proceeding to the next step, open the 03 PPT Lesson1 file.

Your presentation has a new look now that you've applied a different template, but now you'd like to make some changes to the Slide Master.

- On the View menu, point to Master, and then click Slide Master.

  The Slide Master appears along with the Master toolbar. Your screen should look like the following illustration:

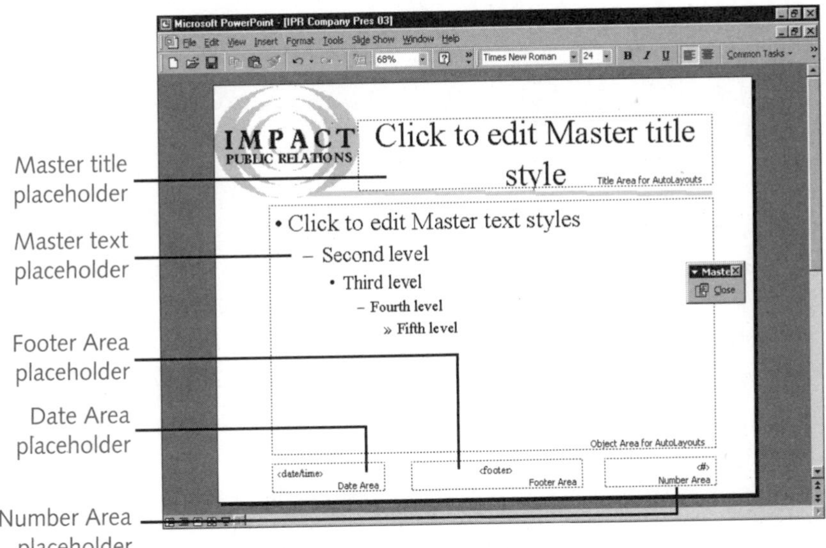

View the Title Master

Now you'll view the Title Master.

- On the View menu, point to Master and then click Title Master.

The Title Master slide appears, as shown in the following illustration:

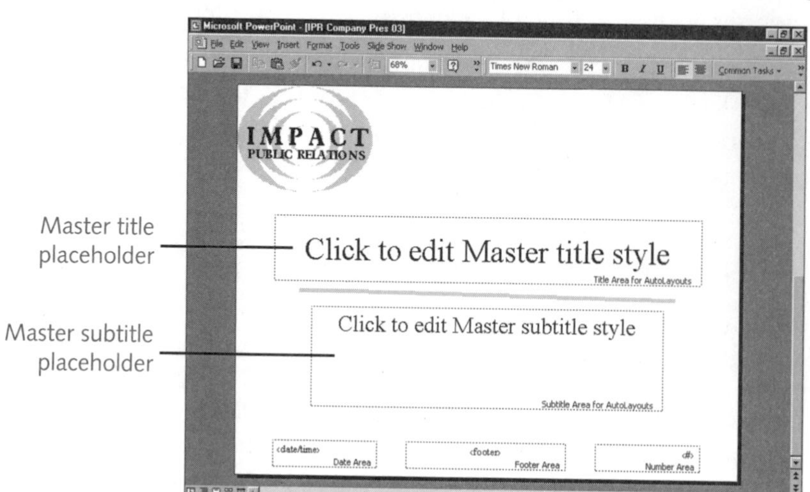

tip

If you don't have a Title Master, you can create one by switching to the Slide Master and clicking New Title Master on the Insert menu.

Switch between the Title Master and the Slide Master

1. In Title Master view, drag the scroll box up on the vertical scroll bar.

   The Slide Master appears.
2. On View menu, point to Master, and then click Title Master.

   The Title Master appears again.

Switch to Handout Master and Notes Master

1. On the View menu, point to Master, and click Handout Master.

   The Handout Master and Handout Master toolbar appear. Using the Handout Master toolbar, you can show the positioning of two, three, four, six, or nine slides per page.
2. On the Handout Master toolbar, click the Show Positioning Of 3-Per-Page Handouts button.

   The master changes to show three handouts.
3. On the View menu, point to Master, and then click Notes Master.

   The Notes Master appears, showing the slide and speaker note text positioning for the notes pages.

4. On the Master toolbar, click the Close button.

   PowerPoint returns you to the first slide in your presentation in Slide view.

Changing the Display Using the Master

Each master contains placeholders where you can add background objects, such as text and graphics, that will appear on every page. Examples of objects you may want to include are your company name, logo, or product name.

Remove the footer from the title slide

The footer information on the title slide for the Impact Public Relations presentation already appears in the subtitle of the slide, so you'll remove the duplicate information from the title slide in this exercise.

If you are not working through this lesson sequentially, before proceeding to the next step, open the 03 PPT Lesson1 file.

1. On the View menu, click Header And Footer.

   The Header And Footer dialog box appears.

2. Click the Don't Show On Title Slide check box.

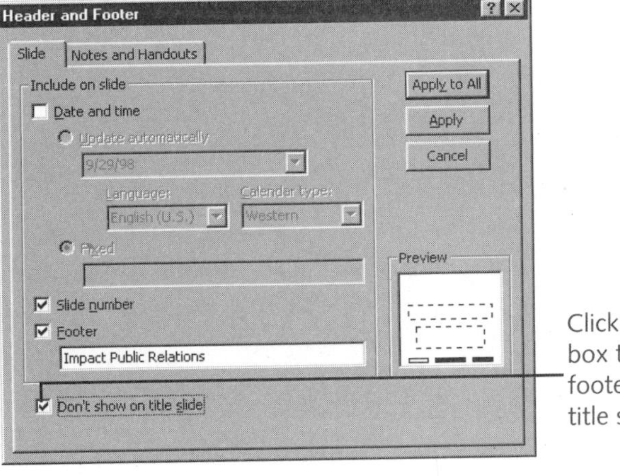

Click this check box to hide the footer on the title slide.

3. Click the Apply To All button.

   The slide footer information disappears from the title slide.

4. Click the Next Slide button to view slide 2.

   The slide footer information remains on the rest of the slides in the presentation.

Next Slide

3 Modifying Templates

Modifying Master Placeholders

If you are not working through this lesson sequentially, before proceeding to the next step, open the 03 PPT Lesson2 file.

You can modify and arrange placeholders for the date and time, footers, and slide numbers on all of the master views.

Edit master placeholders

The footer, date and time, and slide number appear on the Slide Master in the default position. For your presentation, you'll customize the position of the placeholders.

Slide View

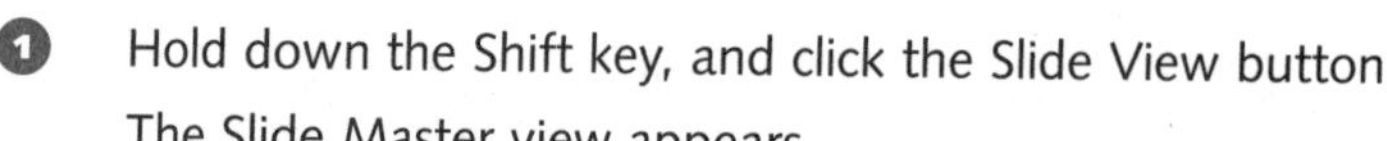

1. Hold down the Shift key, and click the Slide View button.

   The Slide Master view appears.

   Holding down the Shift key and clicking a view button switches you to the corresponding master view. With the title slide displayed, the Slide View button becomes the Title Master View button. With any of the other slides displayed, the Slide View button becomes the Slide Master View button.
2. Click the border of the Date Area placeholder in the bottom-left corner.

   Be sure you click the placeholder border so the dotted selection box appears. If the slanted-line selection box appears, click the edge of it.
3. Press the Delete key.

> **tip**
>
> If you delete a placeholder by mistake, you can click Master Layout on the Format menu, click the appropriate placeholder check box, and then click the OK button to reapply the placeholder, or you can click the Undo button.

4. Click the border of the Footer Area placeholder to select it with the dotted selection box.
5. Hold down the Shift key, and drag the Footer Area placeholder to the left until the edge of the placeholder aligns with the edge of the master text placeholder.

   Holding down the Shift key while you drag a PowerPoint object constrains the movement of the object horizontally or vertically. That is, the object stays in the same plane. In this case, the footer will remain aligned with the number area placeholder.
6. Click a blank area of the slide to deselect the placeholder.

Formatting Master Text

Formatting the placeholders in Slide Master view provides consistency to your presentation. The master placeholders for the title, bulleted text, date and time, slide number, and footer determine the style and position of those objects. To format master text, you select the text placeholder and alter the format to look the way you want. To format bulleted text, you have to place the insertion point in the line of the bulleted text you want to change.

In addition to formatting text, PowerPoint allows you to customize the bullets in your presentation for individual paragraphs or entire objects. You can replace the bullet with a different font, with a picture from the Picture Bullet Gallery, or with a number.

Format master text attributes

If you are not working through this lesson sequentially, before proceeding to the next step, open the 03 PPT Lesson3 file and switch to Slide Master view.

In this exercise, you'll format the text in the Footer Area and Number Area placeholders for your presentation.

1. Hold down the Shift key, click the Footer Area placeholder, and then click the Number Area placeholder to select both objects.
2. On the Formatting toolbar, click the Font Size drop-down arrow, and click 20.
3. Hold down the Shift key, and click the Footer Area placeholder.

   The Footer Area placeholder is deselected.

Italic

4. On the Formatting toolbar, click the Italic button.

   The Number Area placeholder becomes italic.

Slide View

5. Click the Slide View button.

   Your presentation window should look like the following illustration:

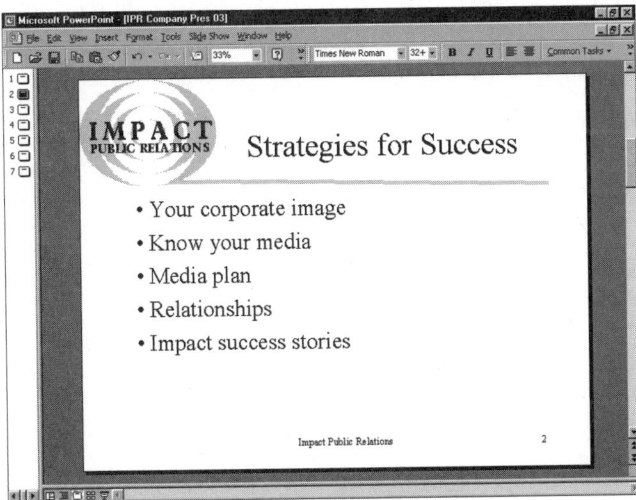

Format master title and bulleted text

Slide Master View

Italic

1. Hold down the Shift key and click the Slide Master View button.
2. In the master text placeholder, position the I-beam cursor to the right of the text *Second level* and click.
3. On the Formatting toolbar, click the Italic button.

   The Second level text becomes italic.
4. Click a blank area outside the master text placeholder to deselect it.

   Your Slide Master should look like the following illustration:

If the Master toolbar does not appear on your screen, click the View menu, point to Toolbars, and then click Master.

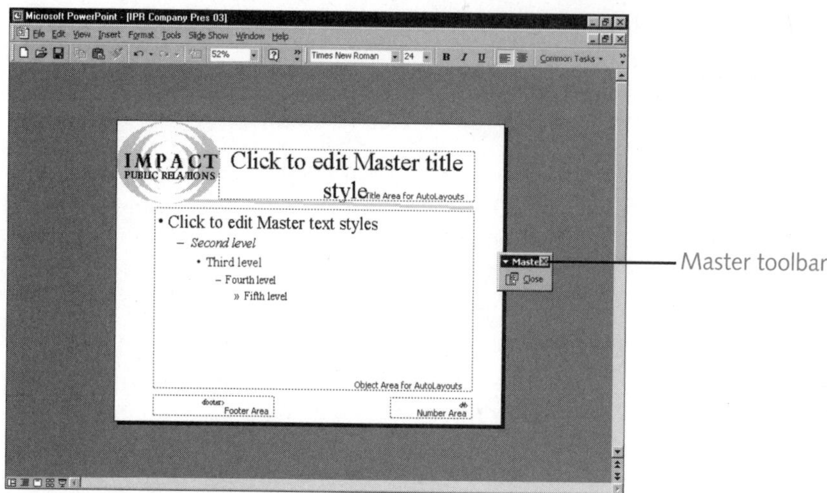

Format master bullets

1. On the Slide Master, click the first line of text titled *Click to edit Master text styles* in the master text placeholder.

   The insertion point is placed in the text.
2. On the Format menu, click Bullets And Numbering.

   The Bullets And Numbering dialog box appears, with the current bullet symbol selected. You can click a different bullet color in the Color drop-down list, adjust the size percentage in the Size box, change the symbol by selecting another one from this dialog box or by using the Picture or Character command, or change the bullets to numbers using the Numbered tab.

3. Click the Character button. The Bullet dialog box opens.
4. Click the Bullets From drop-down arrow, and then scroll down and click Wingdings.
5. In the dialog box, click the diamond bullet, as shown in the following illustration:

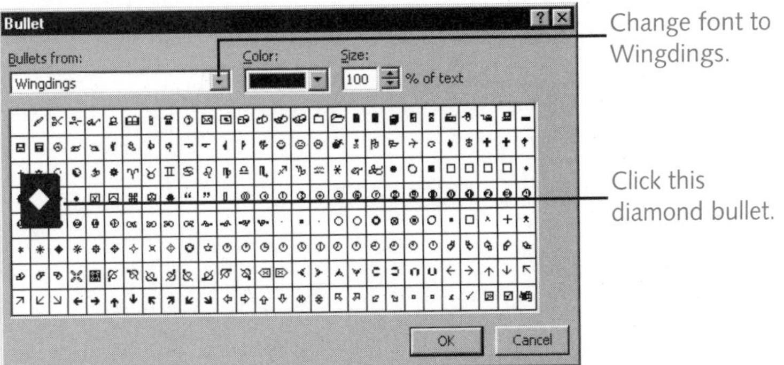

Change font to Wingdings.

Click this diamond bullet.

6. Click the Color drop-down arrow and click the purple color.
7. Click the Size down arrow until 85 appears.

   The new bullet size is reduced by 15 percent on the slide.
8. Click the OK button.

   The purple diamond bullet appears in the first line of text.

Format master bullets using a picture

1. Right-click the second line of text titled *Second level* in the master text placeholder.

   The insertion point is placed in the text and a pop-up menu appears.
2. Click Bullets And Numbering on the pop-up menu.
3. Click the Picture button.

   The Picture Bullet dialog box opens with the Pictures tab on top. This dialog box is part of the Clip Gallery. It contains pictures you can use as bullets.
4. Click the down scroll arrow twice, click the blue diamond bullet in the second row, and then click Insert Clip on the pop-up menu.

Insert Clip

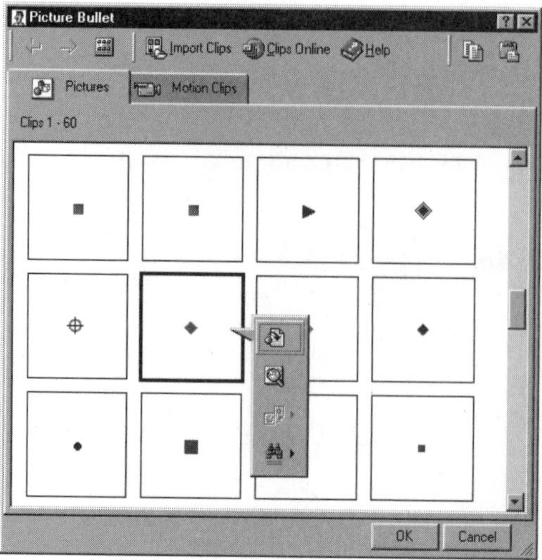

5. Click the OK button.

Slide View

Next Slide

6. Click the Slide View button, and then click the Next Slide button.

   The new bullets appear on slide 3 as shown in the following illustration:

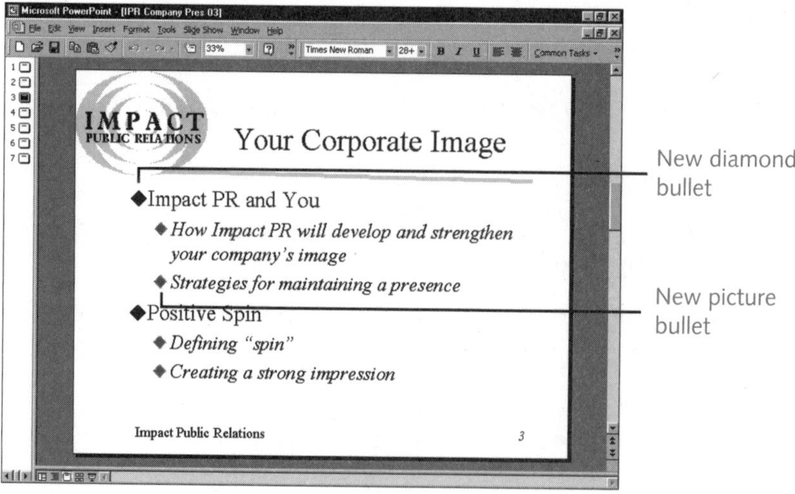

7. Click the Save button on the Standard toolbar.

tip

You can use a scanned image or other photograph to replace a bullet. In the Picture Bullet dialog box, click Import Clips, select the image you want to import in the Add Clip To Clip Gallery dialog box, and then click Import. The image will appear as one of the choices on the Pictures tab.

Adjusting Master Text Indents

If you are not working through this lesson sequentially, before proceeding to the next step, open the 03 PPT Lesson4 file.

PowerPoint uses indent markers to control the distance between bullets and text. Adjusting indents in PowerPoint works the same way it does in Microsoft Word 2000. To change the distance between a bullet and its corresponding text, you first display the ruler, which shows the current bullet and text placement.

Display the ruler

Slide Master View

1. Hold down the Shift key and click the Slide Master View button.

   The Slide Master appears.

2. Click the line of text titled *Click to edit Master title style.*
3. On the View menu, click Ruler.

   Your presentation window should look like the following illustration:

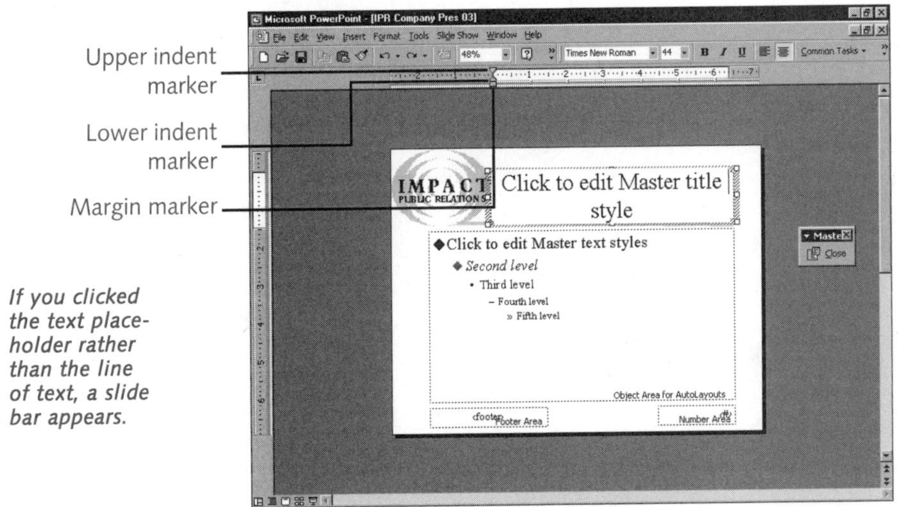

If you clicked the text placeholder rather than the line of text, a slide bar appears.

About Setting Indent Markers

Indent markers

Margin marker

The indent markers on the ruler control the indent levels of the master text object. Each indent level consists of two triangles, called *indent markers*, and a small box, called a *margin marker.* The upper indent marker controls the first line of the paragraph; the lower indent marker controls the left edge of the paragraph. Each indent level is set so that the first line extends to the left of the paragraph, with the rest of the paragraph "hanging" below it. This indent setting is called a *hanging indent.*

For a demonstration of how to adjust indents, open the Office 8in1 Step by Step folder on your hard disk. Then open the PowerPoint Demos folder and double-click the Adjust Text Indents icon.

To adjust an indent marker, you move the triangle on the ruler to a new position. You can move the entire level—the bullet and text—by using the margin marker.

Adjust indent markers

In the IPR company presentation, the diamond bullet in the first indent level appears too close to the text. In this exercise, you'll adjust the indent markers to add space between the bullet and the text.

1. Click the line of text titled *Click to edit Master text styles* in the master text placeholder.

   The ruler adds indent markers for each level of text represented in the bulleted list. Five indent markers appear.

2. Drag the lower indent marker of the first indent level to the left margin of the ruler, as shown in the following illustration:

Move the lower indent marker to here.

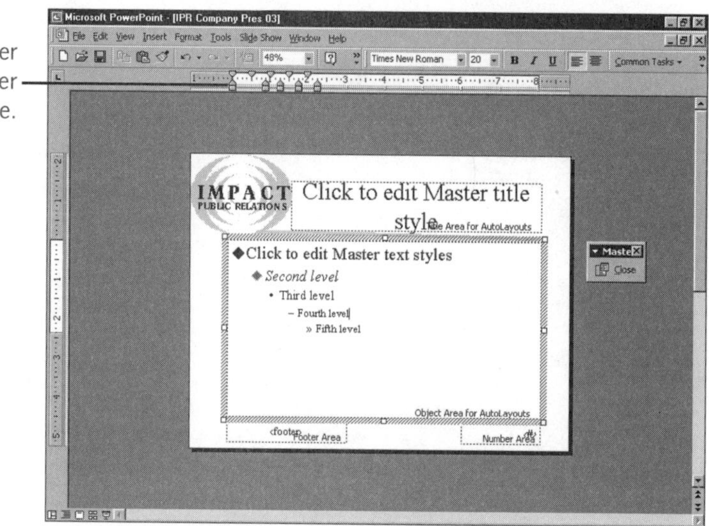

When you release the mouse button, the text for the first indent level moves next to the bullet on the left margin.

Adjust the margin level

1. Slowly drag the margin marker of the first indent level to the left margin of the ruler.

   Both the bullet and text move to the left margin.

> **important**
>
> If you drag an indent level or margin marker into another indent level, the first indent level (or marker) pushes the second indent level until you release the mouse button. To move an indent marker back to its original position, drag the indent level's margin marker or click the Undo button.

Your presentation window should look like the following illustration:

Move the margin marker to here.

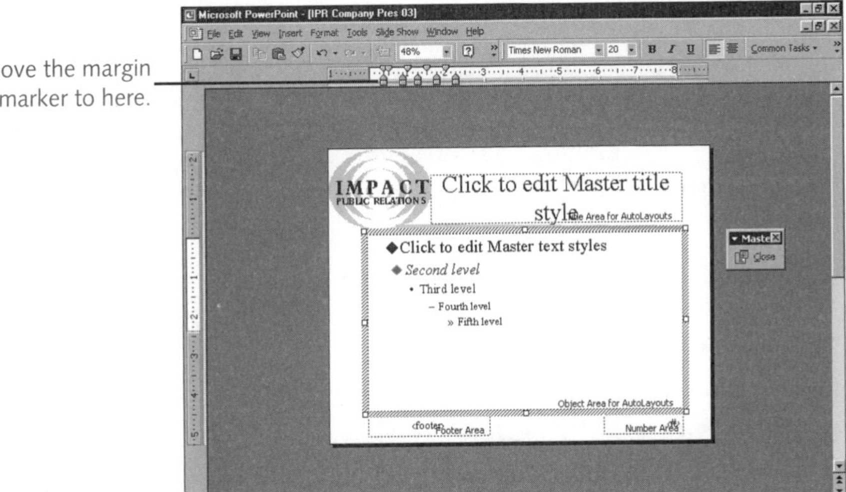

Moving the first indent marker repositions the left margin of the master text object to the 0.5 inch mark. (Notice the first text level in the master text object.)

> **tip**
>
> If the ruler on your screen looks different from the one in the illustration, you may not have moved the margin marker. If the indent markers are not aligned over one another, drag one of the markers back to the other. Also, depending on the size of your monitor, indent changes may be subtle and hard to detect.

2. Drag the upper indent marker of the first indent level to the left edge of the ruler.

   The first indent level of the ruler is formatted again as a hanging indent. Your presentation window should look like the following illustration:

Move the upper indent marker to here.

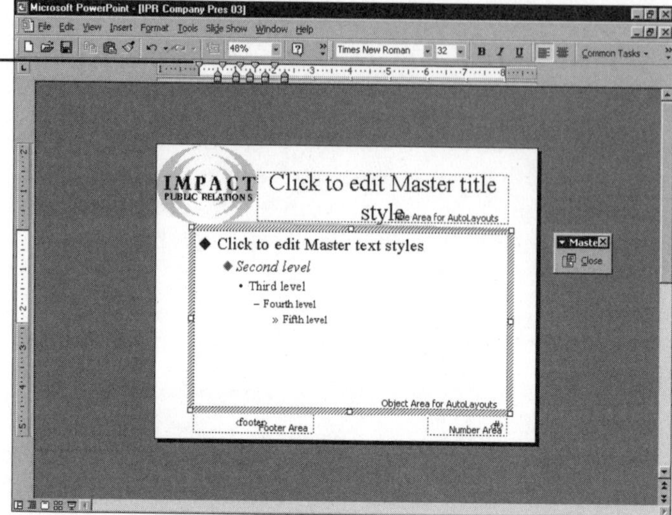

3. In a blank area of the Slide Master, click the right mouse button and then click Ruler.

   The ruler closes.

Slide View

4. Click the Slide View button.

   PowerPoint returns you to slide 3.

Reapplying a Slide Layout

If you make changes to the layout of a slide but then decide you would rather use the original slide layout, you can reapply the slide layout to that slide using the Slide Layout command. You can also change the current layout of a slide by selecting a new layout from the Slide Layout dialog box.

If you are not working through this lesson sequentially, before proceeding to the next step, open the 03 PPT Lesson4 file.

Apply a slide layout

1. On slide 3, click the edge of the title object to select it with the dotted-line selection box.
2. Drag the title object to the right edge of the slide.

Your presentation window should look like the following illustration:

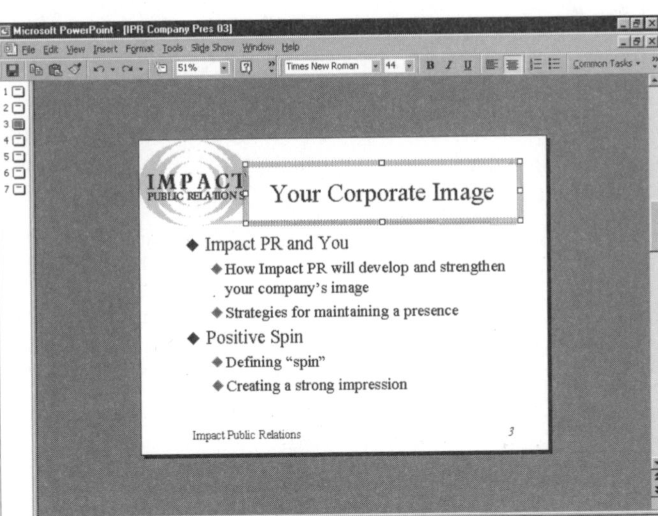

3. On the Formatting toolbar, click the Common Tasks menu button, and then click Slide Layout.

   The Slide Layout dialog box appears with the current slide layout style selected.

4. Click the Reapply button.

   PowerPoint uses the slide layout to reposition the title object to its original position on the slide.

Save the presentation

Save

- On the Standard toolbar, click the Save button.

  No dialog box appears because the presentation is already named. The current information in your presentation is saved with the same name.

Saving a Presentation as a Template

If you are not working through this lesson sequentially, before proceeding to the next step, open the 03 PPT Lesson4 file.

After customizing the masters, you can save the presentation as a new template, which you can apply to other presentations.

Save the presentation as a template

1. On the File menu, click Save As.

   The File Save dialog box appears. IPR Company Pres 03 appears in the File Name box.

2. In the File Name box, type **IPR Company Template**
3. Click the Save As Type drop-down arrow and click Design Template.

   PowerPoint displays the Templates folder. To include your new template with the others that are included with PowerPoint, you need to save the template in one of the corresponding folders. A new template icon will appear in the New Presentation dialog box. For the purposes of this lesson, save this template with the rest of your practice files.
4. In the Save In box, ensure that the PowerPoint Practice folder is open.
5. Click the Save button.

   The template is saved in the PowerPoint Practice folder.

One Step Further Hiding Master Objects

If you are not working through this lesson sequentially, before proceeding to the next step, open the 03 PPT Lesson3 file.

In this lesson you have learned how to apply a template, view and switch to a master, change the master title and master text of your presentation, change bullets, adjust margin indents, reapply a slide layout, and save a presentation as a template.

For individual slides, you may want to hide background objects, such as date and time, header and footer, and slide number placeholders, graphics, shapes, and lines, so they do not appear on the screen. In this exercise, you'll try hiding the master objects from slide 4.

Hide master objects on a slide background

Next Slide

1. Click the Next Slide button to move to slide 4.
2. In a blank area of the slide, click the right mouse button, and click Background.

   The Background dialog box appears. This dialog box is also available from the Format menu.
3. Click the Omit Background Graphics From Master check box.

   The Omit Background Graphics From Master option is turned on.
4. Click the Apply button.

   The background objects are omitted from the slide.

Finish the lesson

1. On the File menu, click Exit.
2. If a dialog box appears, asking whether you want to save the changes to your presentation, click the Yes button.

Lesson 3 Quick Reference

To	Do this	Button
Apply a template	On the Formatting toolbar, click the Common Tasks menu button, and then click Apply Design Template.	
Switch to master views	On the View menu, point to Master, and then click the view you want, or hold down the Shift key and click the Slide View button.	
Change the display using the master	Display the master, and then add or modify the objects on the master.	
Modify master placeholders	Display the master, and then select the placeholder object and drag it to its new position.	
Format the master text	Select the master text object, and then click the formatting effects you want on the Formatting toolbar.	
Change the bullet format	Display the master, and then click a line of text. On the Format menu, click Bullets And Numbering. Click a new bullet symbol; click the Numbered tab and click a numbering style; click Character, and then choose a new font and bullet; or click Picture and choose a picture to use as a bullet.	
Display the text object ruler	Select a line of text. On the View menu, click Ruler or click the right mouse button and click Ruler on the shortcut menu.	
Set the indent for the first line of text	Drag the upper triangle on the ruler.	
Set the indent for a paragraph other than the first line of text	Drag the lower indent marker on the ruler.	

Lesson 3 Quick Reference

To	Do this	Button
Adjust a paragraph margin	Drag the margin marker on the ruler.	
Reapply a slide layout	Display the slide, click the Common Tasks menu button on the Formatting toolbar, then click Slide Layout. Select a layout, then click the Reapply button.	
Save a presentation as a template	On the File menu, click Save As. Click the Save As Type drop-down arrow, click Design Template, then click the Save button.	
Hide master objects on a slide background	On the Format menu, click Background. Click the Omit Background Graphics From Master check box, then click the Apply button.	

Producing a Slide Show

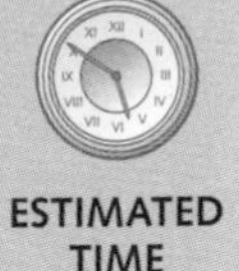

ESTIMATED TIME
20 min.

In this lesson you will learn how to:

- ✔ *Navigate in Slide Show view.*
- ✔ *Annotate slides during a slide show.*
- ✔ *Set slide transitions.*
- ✔ *Animate slide text.*
- ✔ *Animate slide objects.*
- ✔ *Animate chart objects.*
- ✔ *Hide a slide during a slide show.*
- ✔ *Create and edit a custom show.*

In Microsoft PowerPoint you can display your presentations on your computer monitor using Slide Show view. The Slide Show feature uses your computer like a projector to display your presentation on your monitor full-screen or, using special hardware, on an overhead screen. A slide show can also operate continuously, unattended, to show a presentation.

As Vice President of Sales at Impact Public Relations, you have been working on a company presentation. With your slides in place, you are ready to set up your slide show for Mary Anne Kobylka, the CEO, who wants to see it before you give the presentation at next month's meeting of department heads.

In this lesson, you'll learn how to give a slide show, draw on a slide during a slide show, add slide transitions, add text and object slide animation, hide a slide from a slide show, and create and edit a custom slide show.

Start the lesson

Follow the steps below to open the practice file called 04 PPT Lesson, and then save it with the new name IPR Company Pres 04. If you haven't already started PowerPoint, do so now.

1. If you just started PowerPoint, click the Open An Existing Presentation option button in the PowerPoint Startup dialog box, click More Files in the list box, and then click the OK button.

   or

   If PowerPoint is already running, click the Open button on the Standard toolbar.

   Open

   The Open dialog box opens.
2. In the Look In box, ensure that the PowerPoint Practice folder is open.
3. In the file list box, double-click the file named 04 PPT Lesson to open it.
4. On the File menu, click Save As.

   The Save As dialog box opens. Be sure the PowerPoint Practice folder appears in the Save In box.
5. In the File Name box, type **IPR Company Pres 04**
6. Click the Save button.

   The presentation is saved and the title bar changes to the new name.

Navigating in Slide Show View

If you are not working through this lesson sequentially, before proceeding to the next step, open the 04 PPT Lesson file.

PowerPoint has several options for navigating through your slide show presentation. You can click, press keys on the keyboard, or use commands on the Show Popup menu in Slide Show view to move from slide to slide. With the Slide Navigator, you can jump to slides out of sequence.

You can also start a slide show with any slide by selecting the slide in another view, and then clicking the Slide Show button. To end a slide show at any time, click the End Show command on the Show Popup menu or press the Esc key.

Navigate through your slide show presentation

In this exercise, you use the Slide Navigator on the Show Popup menu to navigate through your presentation in Slide Show view.

Slide Show

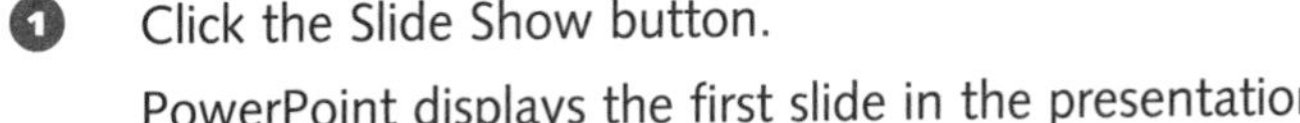

1. Click the Slide Show button.

   PowerPoint displays the first slide in the presentation.

2. Click the left mouse button or press the Spacebar.

   The slide show advances to the next slide.

3. Move the mouse to display the pointer.

   The Show Popup menu button appears in the lower-left corner of the screen, as shown in the margin.

Show Popup

4. Click the Show Popup menu button.

   The Show Popup menu appears, showing slide show navigation controls.

5. On the Show Popup menu, click Next.

   The slide show advances to slide 3.

Clicking the Show Popup menu button and right-clicking the screen both display the Show Popup menu.

6. Click the right-mouse button, and then click Previous on the Show Popup menu.

   Slide 2 appears in Slide Show view.

tip

During a slide show, you can press the Right arrow key, the Page Down key, or the N key to advance to the next slide, and you can press the Left arrow key, the Page Up key, or the P key to return to the previous slide.

7. Click the right mouse button, point to Go, and then click Slide Navigator.

   The Slide Navigator dialog box appears, showing a list of slides in your presentation with the current slide selected.

8. In the list of slide names, click slide 9.

The Slide Navigator dialog box should look like the following illustration:

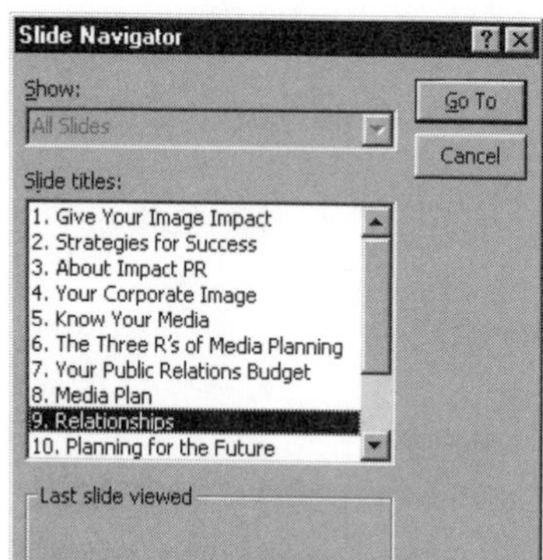

9. Click the Go To button.

   Slide 9 appears in Slide Show view.

Using the By Title command is an alternative to using the Slide Navigator dialog box.

10. Right-click the screen, point to Go on the Show Popup menu, point to By Title, and then click 14 Impact PR.

    Slide 14 is the last slide in the presentation.

11. Click the left mouse button.

    A black slide appears that informs you that you have reached the end of the slide show.

12. Click the left mouse button.

    Slide 1 appears in Normal view.

Start a slide show on any slide

1. Click the slide icon for slide 3 in the Outline pane.
2. Click the Slide Show button.

   The slide show starts by displaying slide 3.

3. Press the Spacebar to advance to slide 4.

End a slide show on any slide

- Click the right mouse button and click End Show, or press the Esc key.

  Slide 4, the current slide in the slide show, appears in Normal view.

Annotating Slides during a Slide Show

If you are not working through this lesson sequentially, before proceeding to the next step, open the 04 PPT Lesson file.

During a slide show presentation, you can annotate slides by drawing freehand lines and shapes to emphasize your message. To do this, choose the pen tool from the Show Popup menu and then draw. You can change the pen color at any time during the presentation by choosing a new color from the Show Popup menu.

Draw a freehand line

In this exercise you underline your slide title during a slide show using the pen tool.

Slide Show

Pen Tool

You can also press Ctrl+P to display the pen tool.

1. Drag the scroll box to slide 8, and then click the Slide Show button.

   PowerPoint displays the current slide in the presentation.

2. Click the right mouse button, point to Pointer Options, and then click Pen.

   The pointer changes to the pen tool. Now you are ready to draw on the slide.

> **important**
>
> When the pen tool is active in Slide Show view, clicking the mouse button doesn't advance the slide show to the next slide. You need to change the pen tool back to the pointer to advance using the mouse button.

3. Draw a line under the bulleted point *Creation*.
4. Click the right mouse button, point to Screen, and then click Erase Pen.

   The annotation is erased. You can also press the E key to erase annotations.

Change the pen color

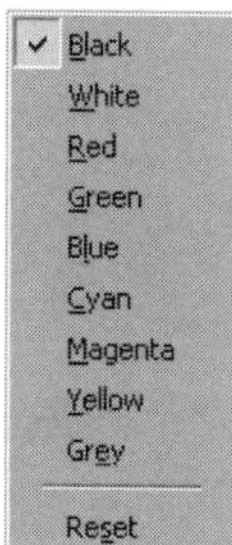

1. Click the Show Popup menu button, point to Pointer Options, and then point to Pen Color.

   The Pen Color menu appears as shown in the margin, showing a selection of different colors.
2. On the Pen Color menu, click Cyan.
3. Draw a line under the bulleted item *Production*.
4. Click the right mouse button, point to Pointer Options, and click Automatic.

   The pen tool changes back to the pointer. Now you can click the mouse button to advance to the next slide.

> **tip**
>
> To make the pointer visible all the time, press Ctrl+A, or right-click to display the Show Popup menu, point to Pointer Options, and then click Arrow.

5. Press the Esc key.

   The slide show ends and slide 9 is displayed in Normal view.

Setting Slide Transitions

If you are not working through this lesson sequentially, before proceeding to the next step, open the 04 PPT Lesson file.

A slide transition is the visual effect given to a slide as it moves on and off the screen during a slide show. Slide transitions include such effects as Checkerboard Across, Cover Down, Cut, and Split Vertical Out. You can set a transition for one slide or a group of slides by selecting the slides in Slide Sorter view and applying the transition. You can also set transition speeds. The Slide Transition Effects drop-down arrow on the Slide Sorter toolbar is the fastest and easiest way to apply a slide transition effect. To set the transition speed, you need to use the Slide Transition dialog box.

Apply a slide transition effect

Slide Sorter View

1. Click the Slide Sorter View button, drag the scroll box up to the top of the scroll bar, and then click slide 1 to select it.
2. On the Slide Sorter toolbar, click the Slide Transition Effects drop-down arrow, scroll down, and click Dissolve.

   The transition effect is previewed on the slide miniature for slide 1, and PowerPoint places a transition symbol below the lower-left corner of slide 1. This tells you a slide transition effect has been applied to this slide.

Transition symbol

3. Click the transition symbol below slide 1.

   The Dissolve transition effect is demonstrated on the slide 1 miniature.

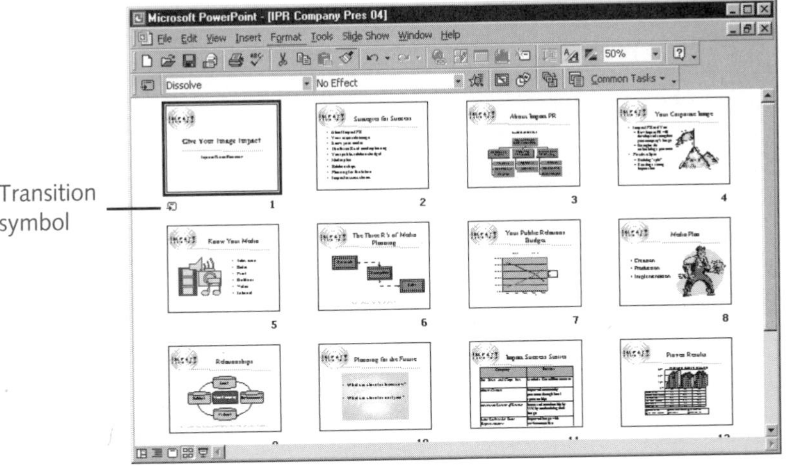

Slide Show

4. Click the Slide Show button.

   Slide Show view displays slide 1 with the Dissolve transition effect.

5. Press the Esc key to stop the slide show.

Apply multiple transitions and change transition speed

In this exercise, you apply a transition effect to the rest of the slides and then change the transition speed.

1. On the Edit menu, click Select All.

   All the slides in the presentation appear selected. You'll need to deselect slide 1 since it already has a slide transition.

2. Hold down the Ctrl key, and click slide 1 to deselect the slide.

Slide Transition

3. On the Slide Sorter toolbar, click the Slide Transition button, or on the Tools menu, click Slide Transition.

   The Slide Transition dialog box appears.

4. Click the Effect drop-down arrow, and then scroll down and click Random Bars Horizontal.

   The preview box demonstrates the transition effect.

5. Click the Medium option button to set the transition speed.

The Slide Transition dialog box should look like the following illustration:

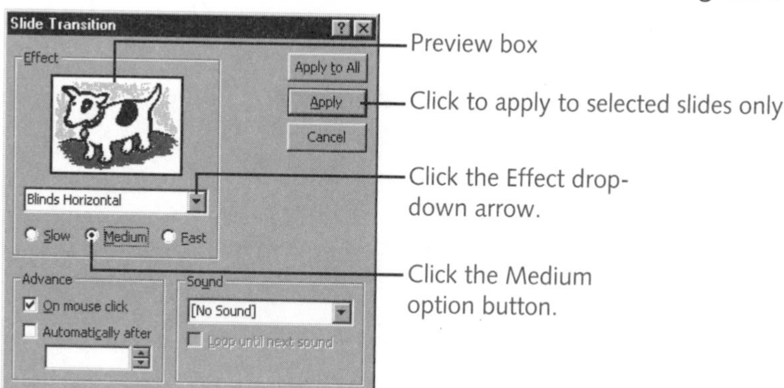

6. Click the Apply button.

   The transition effect is applied to the selected slides. Notice that all the slides now have a transition symbol below their left corners.

Slide Show View

7. Click the Slide Show View button.

   Slide Show view displays slide 2 with the Random Bars Horizontal effect.

8. Click the mouse button several times to advance through the slides, watch the transition effect, and then press the Esc key to end the slide show.

   PowerPoint returns you to Slide Sorter view with the last slide presented in slide show selected.

9. Press Ctrl+A, on the Slide Sorter toolbar, click the Slide Transition Effects drop-down arrow, click No Transition, and then click in a blank area of the presentation window.

Animating Slide Text

During a slide show, you can have slide text appear on the screen one paragraph, word, or letter at a time. A slide with text that you set to appear incrementally is called a *text animation slide*. You can apply animation effects in Slide Sorter view, in the Slide pane in Normal view, and in Slide view. If you apply an animation effect in Slide Sorter view, the effect is applied to every object on the slide except the title and background objects. If you apply it in Normal or Slide view, you need to select the objects on the current slide that you want to animate and then apply the effect.

The easiest way to apply animation effects is to use the Animation Effects toolbar. The Animation Effects toolbar contains basic effects, such as Laser Text, Drive-In, Flying, Camera, Typewriter Text, Drop-In Text, and Flash Once. Most of these have a sound connected to the animation. Another quick method

For a demonstration of how to change animation settings, open the Office 8in1 Step by Step folder on your hard disk. Then open the PowerPoint Demos folder and double-click the Animate Slide Objects icon.

of applying animation effects is to point to Preset Animation on the Slide Show menu and then click an effect on the menu. In Slide Sorter view, you can also click the Preset Animation button drop-down arrow on the Slide Sorter toolbar and click one of the options on the list. Finally, in Normal and Slide views, you can also customize the animation of an object by selecting the Custom Animation command on the Slide Show menu.

If you apply both a transition and an animation effect to a slide, the transition will occur first, and then the transition effect will be displayed.

View the Animation Effects toolbar

- Right-click any toolbar, and then click Animation Effects.

  The Animation Effects toolbar appears as a floating toolbar in the presentation window.

Animate title slide text

If you are not working through this lesson sequentially, before proceeding to the next step, open the 04 PPT Lesson file.

1. In Slide Sorter view, click slide 1.
2. On the Animation Effects toolbar, click the Animate Title button.

   Clicking the Animate Title button applies the Drop-In animation effect to the title of the slide. An animation symbol appears below slide 1.

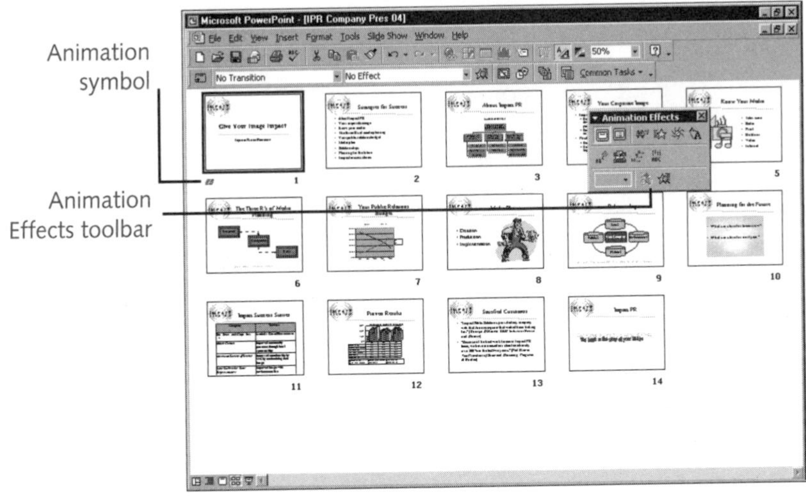

Camera Effect

Animate Slide Text

3. On the Animation Effects toolbar, click the Camera Effect button.

   The Animate Slide Text button on the Animation Effects toolbar now appears pushed in. The Preset Animation button on the Slide Sorter toolbar changes to Box Out. The Camera effect is the same as the Box Out effect on the Slide Sorter toolbar, but it includes the sound of a camera shutter.

Producing a Slide Show 4

4. Click the animation symbol below slide 1.

   The title flies down from the top, and the subtitle text appears with the camera sound.

Animate text for multiple slides

1. Click slide 2, hold down the Shift key, and then click slides 3 and 4.

   Slides 2, 3, and 4 are selected.
2. On the Slide Sorter toolbar, click the Preset Animation button drop-down arrow, and then click Fly From Left.

   The animation effect is demonstrated in the slide 2 miniature.

Slide Show

3. Click the Slide Show button.

   Slide 2 appears without the bulleted text.
4. Click the mouse button.

   The first bulleted item flies across the screen from the left. A whoosh sound is applied with the Fly From Left effect.
5. Click the mouse button as many times as necessary to display all of the bulleted items on slide 2, the object on slide 3, and the clip art and two bulleted items on slide 4.
6. Press the Esc key to end the slide show.

Change text animation slide settings

Instead of animating all of the objects on a slide at once, you can animate the text one word at a time. To change this setting, you need to open the Custom Animation dialog box.

Slide View

Custom Animation

1. Click slide 1, and then click the Slide View button
2. On the Animation Settings toolbar, click the Custom Animation button, or on the Slide Show menu, click Custom Animation.

   The Custom Animation dialog box appears. The top box lists all of the objects, excluding background objects, on the slide. Items with a check mark are listed below in the Animation Order list. This list shows the order in which animated objects will appear during the slide show.
3. In the Animation Order list, click the Text 2.

   The subtitle text object appears selected in the preview box.
4. Click the Effects tab.
5. In the Introduce Text area, click the top drop-down arrow, and then click By Word.

The option sets the text to be animated one word at a time. The Custom Animation dialog box should look like the following illustration:

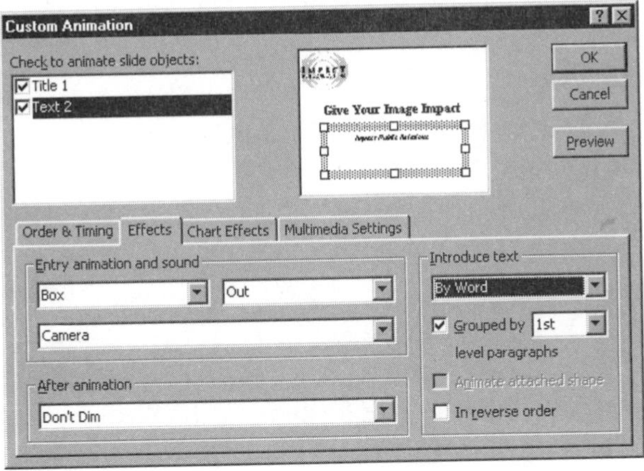

6. Click the OK button.

   Start the slide show to demonstrate the new animation effect.

Slide Show

7. Click the Slide Show button.

   The title drops in.

8. Click the mouse button to display the subtitle.

   The subtitle appears one word at a time.

9. Press the Esc key.

Change text animation levels for a slide

You can determine what text indent levels you want to animate. For example, in slide 4 there are two levels of bulleted text. You can customize the animation so that the levels of text in each bulleted item animate separately.

Next Slide

Custom Animation

1. Click the Next Slide button three times to advance to slide 4.
2. On the Animation Settings toolbar, and click the Custom Animation button, or on the Slide Show menu, click Custom Animation.

   The Custom Animation dialog box appears with current animation settings and a preview of the current slide. Notice that the slide title is not animated.

3. In the Animation Order box, click Text 2 and then click the Effects tab.

   The bulleted text object appears selected in the preview box. In the Introduce Text area, the Grouped By 1st Level Paragraphs animation setting is turned on.

4. In the Introduce Text area, click the Grouped By drop-down arrow, and then click 2nd.

   The option sets the text to animate the first and second level paragraph lines separately.

5. Click the Preview button.

   In the preview box, each level of the bulleted text flies across the screen from the left one at a time.

6. Click the OK button.

tip

If you print a presentation that contains slides with animation, you can click the Include Animations check box in the Print dialog box to print each stage of animation on the slide on a separate page.

Animating Slide Objects

If you are not working through this lesson sequentially, before proceeding to the next step, open the 04 PPT Lesson file.

In addition to animating text in a slide show, you can customize the animation of slide objects, such as drawn objects. As with text, to set custom animation effects, you must be in the Slide pane of Normal view or in Slide view.

To animate objects with text, you can animate the text and the object separately or together. The default is for the object and its text to be animated at the same time. If you like, you can animate only the text in an object.

Another way you can customize object animation on a slide is to change the order of appearance for text or shapes on the screen during a slide show.

Animate slide object text

1. In Slide view, drag the scroll box to slide 6.

   You can work in Normal view if you prefer.

2. Drag to draw a selection marquee around the three shapes and the connectors.

Custom Animation

3. On the Animation Settings toolbar, click the Custom Animation button, or on the Slide Show menu, click Custom Animation.

   The Custom Animation dialog box appears showing the Effects tab. The three objects and two connector lines are selected in the preview box and in the selection list at the top of the dialog box.

4. In the Entry Animation And Sound area, click the top-left drop-down arrow, and then click Peek.

   The default for the Peek animation effect is From Bottom, as listed in the box to the right of the Peek effect. The selected objects now have a check mark next to them in the list at the top of the dialog box.

5. Click the Preview button.

   The three objects appear one at a time, and then the connector objects appear.

Change the animation order

1. In the Custom Animation dialog box, click the Order & Timing tab.
2. In the Animation Order box, click *4. Shape 6*.

   The top connector appears selected in the preview box.

3. Click the up arrow button above the word Move twice.

   The Shape 6 animation order changes from fourth to second.

4. In the Animation Order box, click *4. Text 5*, and then click the down arrow button below the word Move.

   The Text 5 animation order changes from fourth to fifth.

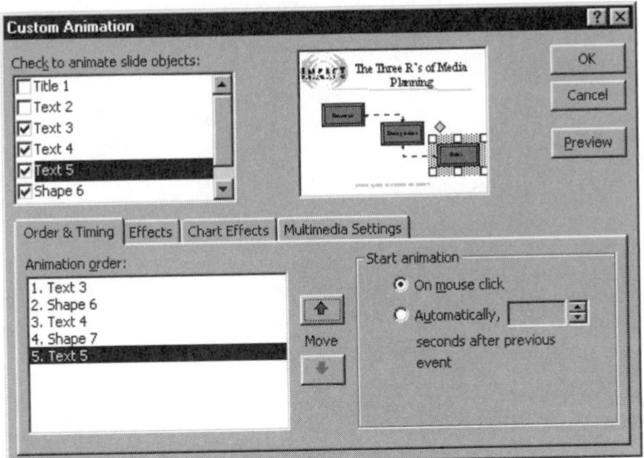

5. Click the Preview button.

   The objects and connector lines appear one after another from top to bottom.

6. Click the OK button.

If you are not working through this lesson sequentially, before proceeding to the next step, open the 04 PPT Lesson file.

Animating Chart Objects

Charts that you create with Microsoft Graph or import from Microsoft Excel can also be animated. For example, you can animate each data series in your chart to appear at a different time.

Animate a chart

Custom Animation

1. In the Outline pane, click the slide icon for slide 12.
2. Click the chart object to select it, and then on the Animation Settings toolbar, click the Custom Animation button, or on the Slide Show menu, click Custom Animation.

   The Custom Animation dialog box appears with the Effects tab on top.
3. Click the Chart Effects tab.
4. In the list at the top of the dialog box, click the Chart 2 check box.
5. Click the Introduce Chart Elements drop-down arrow, and then click By Series.
6. In the Entry Animation And Sound area, click the top-left drop-down arrow, and then click Blinds.

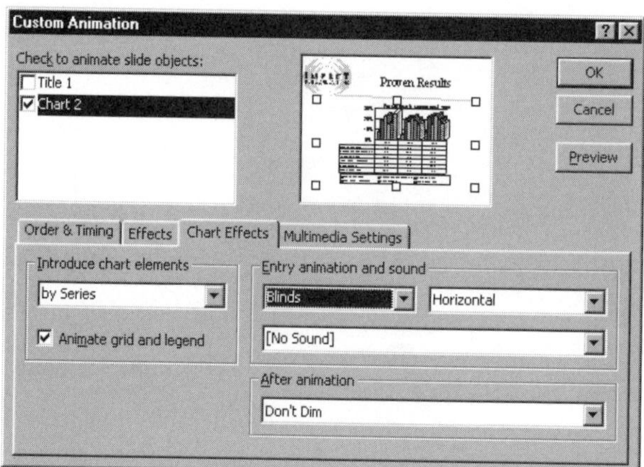

Slide Show

7. Click the OK button.
8. Click the Slide Show button, and then click the mouse button eight times to view the animation.
9. Press the Esc key.
10. If the Animation toolbar is visible, click the Close button on the Animation Effects toolbar.

If you are not working through this lesson sequentially, before proceeding to the next step, open the 04 PPT Lesson file.

Hiding a Slide during a Slide Show

You might want to customize an on-screen presentation for a specific audience. With PowerPoint, you can hide the slides you don't want to use, but still want to keep, during a slide show by using the Hide Slide command.

Hide a slide during a slide show

Slide Sorter View

Hide Slide

1. Click the Slide Sorter View button.
2. Click slide 10 to select it.
3. On the Slide Sorter toolbar, click the Hide Slide button.

   A hide symbol appears over the slide number, as shown in the following illustration:

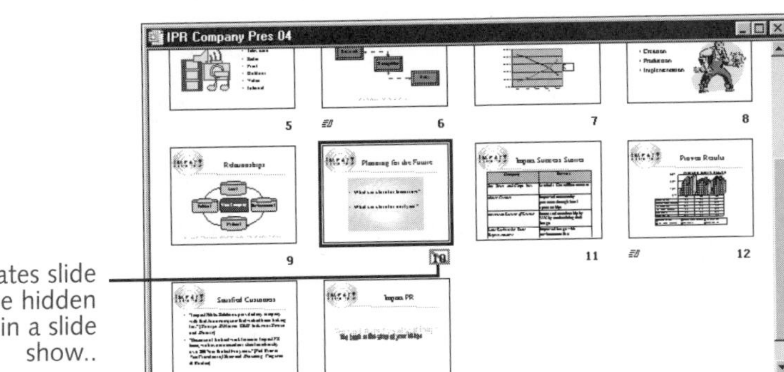

Indicates slide will be hidden in a slide show..

Slide Show

4. Click slide 9 to select it.
5. Click the Slide Show button and then click the mouse button.

   The slide show hides slide 10 and displays slide 11.
6. Press P to go back to slide 9.
7. Click the right mouse button, point to Go, point to By Title, and then click (10) Planning for the Future, or press the H key to show the hidden slide.

   The hidden slide appears in Slide Show view.
8. Press the Esc key to end the slide show.

Creating and Editing a Custom Show

If you are not working through this lesson sequentially, before proceeding to the next step, open the 04 PPT Lesson1 file.

You can create a custom slide show from any view.

With PowerPoint you can create a presentation within a presentation. Instead of creating multiple, nearly identical presentations for different audiences, you can group together and name the slides that differ and then jump to these slides during your presentation.

Create a custom show

1. In Slide Sorter view, on the Slide Show menu, click Custom Shows.

   The Custom Shows dialog box appears.
2. Click the New button.

   The Define Custom Show dialog box appears. The default custom show name appears selected in the Slide Show Name box.
3. In the Slide Show Name box, type **IPR Custom Show 04**
4. In the Slides In Presentation box, click Slide 1, and then click the Add button.

   Slide 1 appears in the Slides In Custom Show box on the right.
5. Select and add slides 3, 4, 6, 8, 13, and 14 to the custom slide show to match to the following illustration:

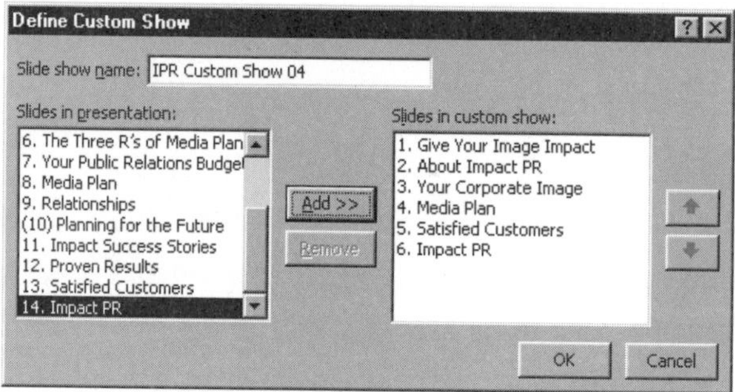

6. Click the OK button.

   The Custom Shows dialog box appears.
7. Click the Show button.
8. Click to complete the slide show.

   Slide Sorter view appears.

Edit a custom show

1. On the Slide Show menu, click Custom Shows.
   The Custom Shows dialog box appears.
2. Click IPR Custom Show 04, and then click the Edit button.
   The Define Custom Show dialog box appears.
3. In the Slides In Custom Show box, click slide 2.
   To change the order of the selected slide, click the up arrow button or the down arrow button. To remove the selected slide, click the Remove button.
4. Click the Remove button.
   Slide 2 is removed from the custom show.
5. Click the OK button.
   The Custom Shows dialog box appears.
6. Click the Close button.

Save the presentation

Save

- On the Standard toolbar, click the Save button.
  No dialog box appears because the presentation already has a name. The current information in your presentation is saved with the same name.

One Step Further Dimming Animation Text

If you are not working through this lesson sequentially, before proceeding to the next step, open the 04 PPT Lesson file.

You have learned to produce and present a slide show in PowerPoint using Slide Navigator, transitions, and text and object animations. You also learned to hide a slide and create and edit a custom slide show.

In addition to the animation slide settings you practiced, you can also dim out or hide animation text after displaying it. PowerPoint dims out animation text by changing its color.

Dim out animated text

For the company presentation, you set the animation text so that each animated text paragraph dims out once you've shown it.

1. Display slide 13 in Slide view.
2. Click a word in the bulleted text to place the insertion point.
3. On the Slide Show menu, click Custom Animation.

   The Custom Animation dialog box appears with Text 2 selected in the list at the top of the dialog box.
4. In the Entry Animation And Sound area, click the top-left drop-down arrow, scroll down, and click Wipe.
5. Click the After Animation drop-down arrow and click the light blue color box.

   After an animated text paragraph transition, the previous animated text will change to the light blue color.
6. Click the OK button.
7. Click the Slide Show button.
8. Click the mouse button twice to display the animation effect.
9. Press the Esc key to end the slide show.

Slide Show

Finish the lesson

1. On the File menu, click Exit.
2. If a dialog box appears, asking whether you want to save the changes to your presentation, click the Yes button.

Lesson 4 Quick Reference

To	Do this	Button
Run a slide show	Click the Slide Show button, and then click the mouse button or press the Spacebar to move through the show.	
Navigate in a slide show	Click the Slide Show button. Right-click the screen and click Next, Previous, or Go.	
Start a slide show with any slide	In any view, go to the slide from which you want to start the slide show, and then click the Slide Show button.	

Lesson 4 Quick Reference

To	Do this	Button
Stop a slide show	Press the Esc key.	
Annotate slides during a slide show	Press Ctrl+P or right-click to display the Show Popup menu, point to Pointer Options, and then click Pen. Draw on the slide. To stop, press Ctrl+A or right-click, point to Pointer Options, and then click Automatic or Arrow.	
Change the pen color	Right-click to display the Show Popup menu, point to Pointer Options, point to Pen Color, and click a color.	
Set slide transitions	Select the slides in Slide Sorter view. On the Slide Sorter toolbar, click the Slide Transition Effects drop-down arrow, and then select a transition, or on the Slide Sorter toolbar, click the Slide Transition button to open the Slide Transition dialog box.	
Apply text animations to slides	In Slide Sorter view, select one or more slides. On the Animation Effects toolbar, click an animation effect.	
Apply object animations to slides	On the Animation Effects toolbar, click an animation effect.	
Change the animation order	On the Animation Effects toolbar, click the Animation Order button.	
Hide a slide during a slide show	In Slide Sorter view, select one or more slides. On the Slide Sorter toolbar, click the Hide Slide button.	
Create a new custom slide show	On the Slide Show menu, click Custom Shows, and then click the New button.	
Dim out animated text	On the Animation Effects toolbar, click the Custom Animation button. Select an animation effect, click the After Animation drop-down arrow, and then click a gray color.	

PART 5

Microsoft Access 2000

LESSON

1

Using Forms

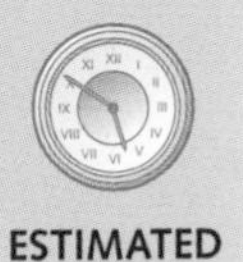

ESTIMATED TIME
40 min.

In this lesson you will learn how to:

- ✔ *Open a database.*
- ✔ *Enter and update data using a form.*
- ✔ *Navigate between records in a form.*
- ✔ *Use the Microsoft Access editing tools.*
- ✔ *Find and remove data in a form.*
- ✔ *Replace data that meets certain criteria.*

The key to juggling many items, whether they are bowling pins, carpooling schedules, or other complex data, is to organize the items so that you can find them quickly and easily. Your chosen method may be as simple as a wallet calendar or as complex as an enterprise-wide computer system, but the principle is the same: assemble the information you need in one place, and keep it handy.

The information that you store for future reference is called *data,* and one place in which you can store the data is a *database*. In Microsoft Access, data can be dates, sums of money, graphical images, words, entire files, and almost anything else that can be stored on a computer disk. For example, among the data that you'll work with in these lessons are bonbon pictures, recipes, and chocolate sales information.

In an Access database, data is entered and manipulated in a *form,* and stored in a *table.* Forms resemble familiar paper forms; an interactive text box, often referred to as a *field,* takes the place of each printed box on the paper form. All the fields on a form make up a *record.* This lesson focuses on the basics of forms in Access, and on entering data into forms.

The Office Assistant

Have you met your new assistant yet? As you begin working with Microsoft Office 2000 programs, the animated *Office Assistant,* Clippit, jumps in to offer helpful messages as you work. You can type any question to your Office Assistant in the Assistant balloon, and then click Search. Clippit will guide you through Access Help. Clippit also remembers your last question and search results so that you can quickly find additional Help topics related to your question.

You can close any Office Assistant tip or message by pressing the Esc key.

Clippit is ready with Help topics and tips on your tasks as you work, telling you what you need to know, just when you need to know it. Clippit displays a light bulb to indicate that it has a tip about the action that you're currently performing. Click the light bulb to see the tip.

Office Assistant

The Assistant appears whenever you:

- Click the Office Assistant button on any Access toolbar.
- Choose Microsoft Access Help on the Help menu, or press F1.
- Click certain commands or try new tasks.

important

For simplicity and clarity, the Office Assistant won't appear in any other illustrations in this book. If you want to match the illustrations, right-click the Office Assistant, and then click Hide. If you want to leave the Office Assistant displayed, but find it getting in your way, simply drag it to another area of the screen.

Imagine that you're a partner at Impact Public Relations, a small public relations firm that specializes in designing multimedia campaigns for midsize companies. Impact represents Sweet Lil's Chocolates, Inc., a rapidly growing gourmet chocolate company. Sweet Lil's has recently decided to start using Access 2000 to improve its information management and to help take its business worldwide. You'll be designing its international campaign.

The marketing department at Sweet Lil's has accepted your proposal for a worldwide campaign, using Access 2000 to handle the resulting data needs. You'll be assisting the Sweet Lil's staff in implementing the systems you've proposed.

As the first phase of the marketing campaign, Impact has just completed a survey of people in selected locations around the world concerning their chocolate preferences. To verify that the new data entry system is functioning properly, you open the Sweet Lil's database and spot-check the new Chocolate Preferences form by adding and updating a few entries yourself.

Opening a Database

If you're just starting to use Access 2000 with this lesson, follow these steps for starting Access and opening a database.

Start Microsoft Access 2000

1. On the taskbar, click the Start button.
2. Point to Programs, and then click Microsoft Access.
   The Microsoft Access dialog box appears.

From here, you can either open an existing database or create a new database.

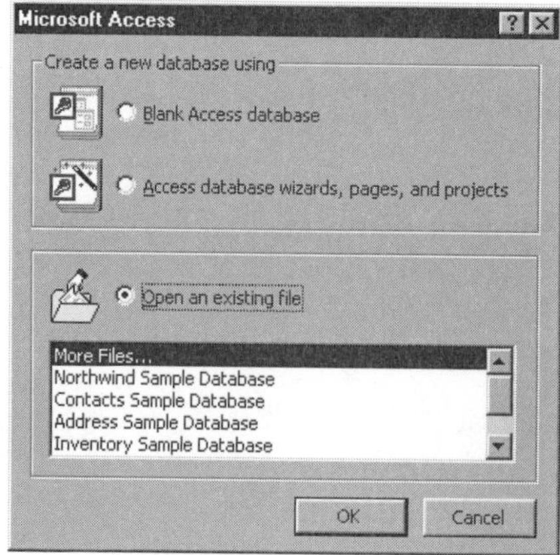

Open a database

In this exercise, you open the Sweet Lil's database.

You can use the Database window to open and work with any object in the database.

1. In the Microsoft Access dialog box, be sure that the Open An Existing File option is selected, and click OK.

   The Open dialog box appears.

2. In the Look In box, click the drop-down arrow and navigate to the Access Practice folder in the Office 8in1 Step by Step folder.

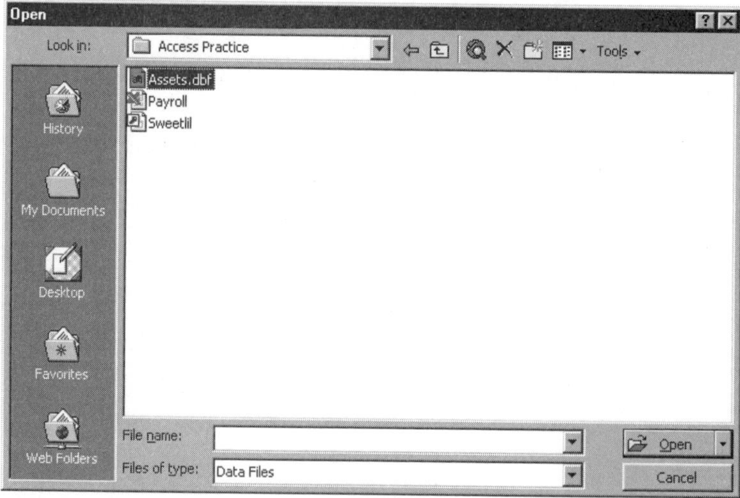

3. Click Sweetlil and then click Open.

The Database window for the Sweet Lil's database opens. On the left side of the Database window is the Objects bar, which you can use to view the tables, queries, forms, reports, pages, macros, and modules of the open database.

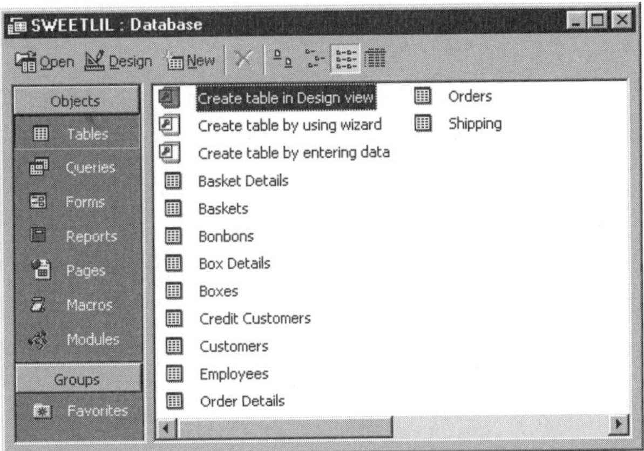

tip

Once you've opened a database, you can take advantage of two shortcuts. The next time you start Access 2000, you'll see that same database filename listed in the Microsoft Access dialog box. You can then open the database quickly: just double-click the database filename to open the database from the Microsoft Access dialog box.

Short and Expanded Menus

If this is your first time using Access 2000, you'll notice that when you select a menu, it displays a short list of commands. The commands that appear on the *short menu* the first time you use Access 2000 are the default commands for that menu.

If you rest your pointer on the menu for a moment, the menu expands to display the full selection of commands available to you for that menu. This is called an *expanded menu*. Another quick way to view the full selection of commands is to move your mouse pointer down the menu and click the double arrows at the bottom.

Each time you select a command from the expanded portion of the menu, that command automatically gets shifted up to the short menu of default commands. In this way, over time the short menus become tailored to your particular usage patterns.

To have an expanded menu appear at all times, right-click the menu bar and then click Customize. In the Customize dialog box, click the Options tab and then clear the Menus Show Recently Used Commands First check box. Close the dialog box.

Understanding Forms

Access 2000 stores data in tables, but the most common way to work with data is with a form. Like a paper form, the Access 2000 form contains text boxes, the fields into which you type the appropriate information.

Every element in an Access 2000 database is a graphical object. Graphical objects that accept, display, or locate data are called controls. Any field that contains or accepts data on a form is actually a control. In addition to text boxes, which are your windows into the database, a form has other controls, such as option buttons and command buttons, for working with the database.

As your business needs change, so do your information needs—and so must any database that you use to track your information. You'll want to add records to your database, as well as locate records that need to be changed or deleted. Using forms is the best way to perform all these actions.

Entering and Updating Data

Now that you've opened the Sweet Lil's database, you can open the Chocolate Preferences form and begin checking the data entry system.

Open a form

1. In the Database window, click Forms on the Objects bar to open the forms list.

   A list of forms is displayed in the Database window.
2. Double-click Chocolate Preferences.

   The Chocolate Preferences form opens.

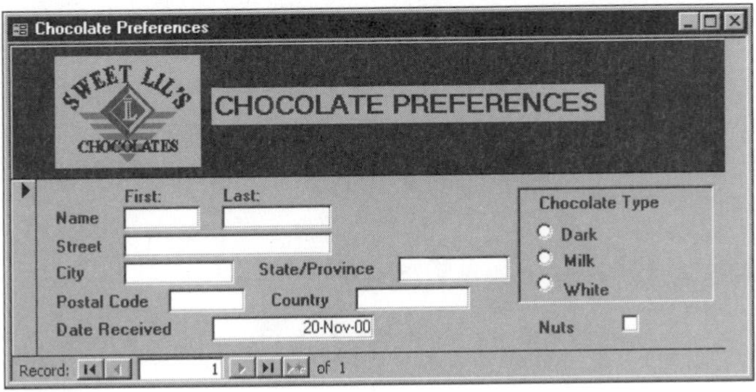

Enter data using a form

You use the blank Chocolate Preferences form you just opened to enter the information for a respondent from Canada.

If you make a mistake, just press Backspace to erase, and then retype.

1. Type **Amanda** in the First Name field of the Chocolate Preferences form.

   As you begin typing, a small triangle symbol in the left margin of the form changes to a pencil, indicating that information is being changed.
2. Press the Tab key to move the insertion point to the Last Name field.
3. Type **Hart** in the Last Name field.

You can press F2 to place the insertion point at the end of the field.

 Type the following address information, pressing Tab to move from field to field.

Street:	**10 MacLeod**
City:	**Melfort**
State/Province:	**Saskatchewan**
Postal Code:	**S0E 1A0**
Country:	**Canada**

When you press Tab after entering Canada in the Country field, the insertion point disappears, and a dotted line appears around the Dark option in the Chocolate Type option group.

> **tip**
>
> Some fields are automatically filled with predetermined data. In the Chocolate Preferences form, for example, the Date Received field is filled with the current date. Access skips over these fields automatically as you move from field to field.

Selecting Dialog Box Options

In the Chocolate Preferences form, Chocolate Type is an *option group,* a set of mutually exclusive option button controls. The Nuts field contains a *check box,* which requires a yes-or-no response.

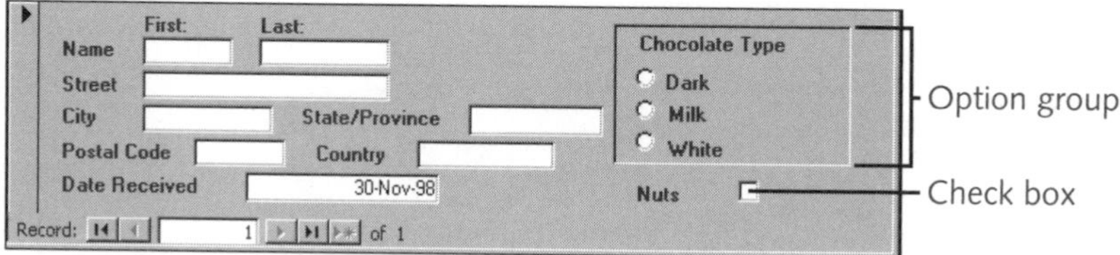

Select an option button

You can also press the Down Arrow key or the Up Arrow key to select Milk.

Amanda Hart enjoys milk chocolate, so you select the Milk option button for her.

- Select the Milk option button.

  A dot appears in the Milk option button, indicating that the option is selected.

Select a check box

You can also press the Spacebar to select or clear a check box.

In this form, a check mark in the check box means yes (nuts are fine); an empty box means no (I don't like nuts in my chocolates). Amanda Hart likes nuts in her milk chocolate, so you select the Nuts check box for her.

- Select the Nuts check box.

  A check mark appears in the Nuts check box.

Modify records in a form

Each set of fields on a form represents a separate record. When you get to the end of the form, which in this case is the Nuts check box, pressing Tab again takes you to the next record.

> **important**
>
> Whenever you move the insertion point out of a record, Access 2000 automatically saves any changes you made to the record. This differs from how you save documents in Microsoft Word; for example, in a database form or table, you don't need to save new data manually as you work.

1. In the form, while still in the Nuts check box, press Tab.

   The insertion point appears in the First Name field of the next form.
2. Type **Rita** in the First Name field.
3. Enter the following information, pressing Tab to move from field to field.

It's a good idea to proofread your entries after adding information.

Last Name:	**Corquette**
Street:	**300 Locust Avenue**
City:	**Thousand Oaks**
State/Province:	**CA**
Postal Code:	**91320**
Country:	**USA**
Chocolate Type:	**Dark**
Nuts:	**No**

Update an existing record

Looking over your data entries, you notice that you didn't type the word *Drive* in Amanda Hart's street address. You try returning to the previous record and updating it now.

Previous Record

1. Click the Previous Record button on the navigation bar.
2. In the Street field of Amanda Hart's record, click after the *d* in MacLeod to return to the end of that field.

   The insertion point appears where you click.

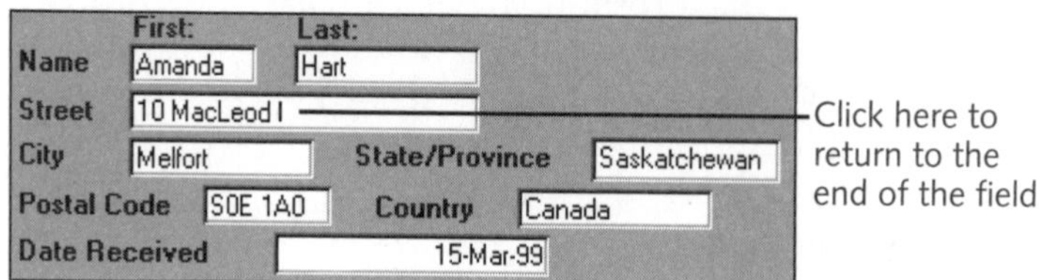

3. Press the Spacebar to insert a space after MacLeod, and then type **Drive**

   As you begin typing, the triangle symbol in the margin changes to a pencil.
4. Click the Next Record button.

   The change to the first record is saved. The pencil symbol disappears.

Next Record

Close a form

You've successfully opened the Chocolate Preferences form and used it to enter and update records in the database. All that remains is to close the form.

Close

- Click the Close button to close the Chocolate Preferences form.

important

Be sure that you click the Close button on the form window only. Do not click the Close button on the Database window or the Microsoft Access window, or you will close the database prematurely. As soon as you close the form, the record you're working in is saved.

Navigating Between Records

Wherever a Microsoft Access 2000 window shows a series of data, a *navigation bar* appears on the bottom edge of the form. You've just seen an example of a navigation bar in the Chocolate Preferences form. The navigation bar shows which record is currently being displayed; it also includes navigation buttons that allow you to move quickly among the records. You can move forward or backward one record at a time, to the beginning or end of the records, or to a particular record. You can also add a new record from the navigation bar.

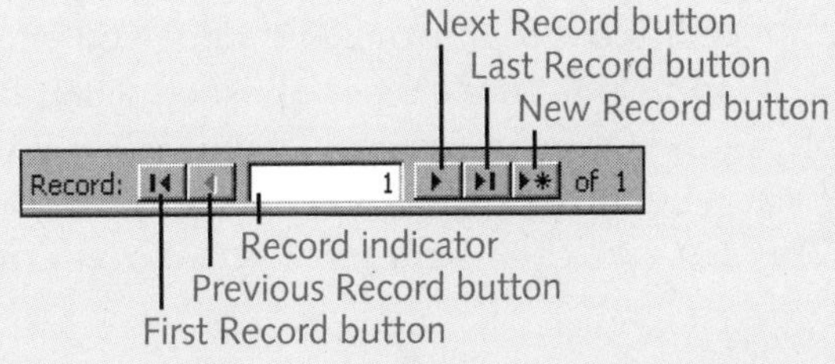

On the keyboard, press Ctrl+Home for the first record, the Page Up and Page Down keys for the previous and next records, and Ctrl+End for the last record.

The First Record button takes you immediately to the first record. The Previous Record button moves you back one record at a time. The record indicator displays the number of the current record and allows you to enter a record number and move to that record immediately. The Next Record button moves you forward one record at a time. The Last Record button takes you immediately to the last record. The New Record button generates a new, blank record.

Entering Data Efficiently and Correctly

Forms can help make data entry faster and more accurate by letting you choose values from a list and by letting you know when you've entered incorrect values into a field.

The Bonbons form presents two different kinds of lists from which you can select a value. Chocolate Type is a *list box* control, which displays only predetermined values that are always visible. A related control is the *combo box,* in which the predetermined values are not fully visible. A combo box has a *drop-down arrow* on the right side to open and close the list. Filling Type and Nut Type are both combo boxes.

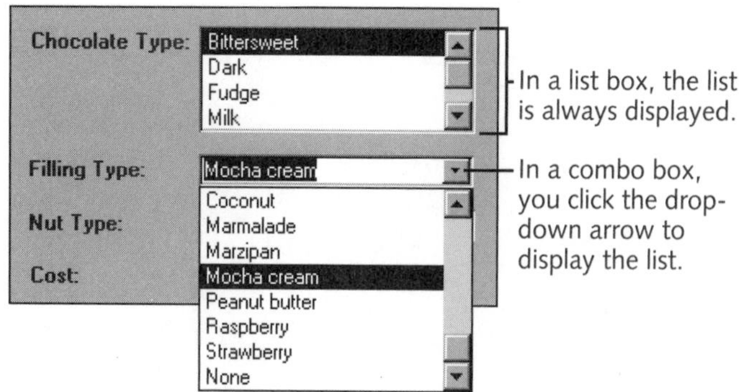

In a list box, the list is always displayed.

In a combo box, you click the drop-down arrow to display the list.

To ensure accurate data entry, Access 2000 can also display a message when you enter incorrect information into a form. The value you enter in a field is checked against a *validation rule* that was established when the form was created. For example, in the Orders form, you cannot enter an order date that is later than the current date. If the value you enter breaks a validation rule, a message appears. You can't exit the field until you correct or delete the invalid data.

Because sales of Candlelight Ecstasy bonbons dropped last year, Sweet Lil's has altered that recipe, changing the Candlelight Ecstasy filling from raspberry to marzipan. The marketing department has asked you to demonstrate how to reflect this change in the database.

Select a value from a combo box

1. In the Database window, ensure that Forms is selected on the Objects bar. Double-click the Bonbons form in the forms list.

   The Bonbons form opens to the first record, which is for the Candlelight Ecstasy bonbon.
2. In the Filling Type combo box, click the drop-down arrow to display the list.

   This list shows all the fillings that Sweet Lil's uses in its bonbons.
3. In the Filling Type combo box, type **Marzipan** or select the word from the list.

You can type just marz *instead; because* Marzipan *is the only value that starts with those four letters, it is selected.*

Enter a new price in a field

Marzipan is a more expensive filling than Mocha cream, so the marketing department asks you to change the price from $0.30 to $1.35.

1. Press Tab twice to move to the Cost field, and then type **1.35**

   The entry $0.30 is replaced.

2. Press Tab.

   A message tells you that the value you entered is too high.

3. Click OK.

   You check with the marketing department; there's been a mistake. The cost should be $0.35.

4. Delete 1.35 by pressing the Backspace key, and then type **.35**

5. Press Tab.

   Access accepts this price, adds a dollar sign, and moves the insertion point to the Bonbon ID field.

6. Close the Bonbon form.

Efficient Editing Tools

Many convenient editing features are available to help you keep your database accurate and up-to-date.

You can get an introduction to editing features by scanning and using the Edit menu. Next to each command name, you'll see the corresponding toolbar button face (left side) and keyboard shortcut (right side). These visual cues are an excellent tool for learning to associate the buttons and key combinations with the commands you use most often.

Most people find that using a toolbar button is faster than clicking a menu command. If you'd rather use the keyboard, the keyboard shortcuts can be even faster. Find the method that works best for you.

Another helpful editing tool is the *Microsoft Office Clipboard* toolbar, which appears the first time you cut or copy more than one item. This toolbar allows you to collect and paste up to 12 different items or objects at a time. ScreenTips display the first few words of each item to identify what's on the Clipboard. Close the Clipboard toolbar to cut or copy a single item at a time.

When you quit Access 2000, you may get a message noting a large amount of information on the Clipboard and asking whether you want to share it with other programs. Unless you plan to paste it elsewhere, click No.

Finding Records

Information doesn't do you any good unless you can lay your hands on it quickly and easily. Of the many features that Access 2000 provides, the most important is finding the needle you want amid the haystack of information that you've gathered. Often you know what you're searching for; sometimes you need to do a little detective work. Either way, Access 2000 can help you.

Find the record you want

Sweet Lil's is starting to receive calls from customers who've recently completed the Chocolate Preferences marketing questionnaire and want to confirm that their information has been received. You decide to test the questionnaire data entry system yourself by taking the next call, from a customer named Claudia Hemshire. In this exercise, you look up Claudia Hemshire in the Customers table using the View Customers form.

1. In the Database window, double-click the View Customers form in the forms list.

   The View Customers form opens.

2. On the View Customers form, click in the Last Name field.

Find

3. On the Form View toolbar, click the Find button.

   The Find And Replace dialog box appears, with the Find tab active. The contents of the Find What box, the Look In list, and the Match list reflect the last search you performed.

For a case-sensitive search (to find Polish *but ignore* polish*), click More, and then select the Match Case check box.*

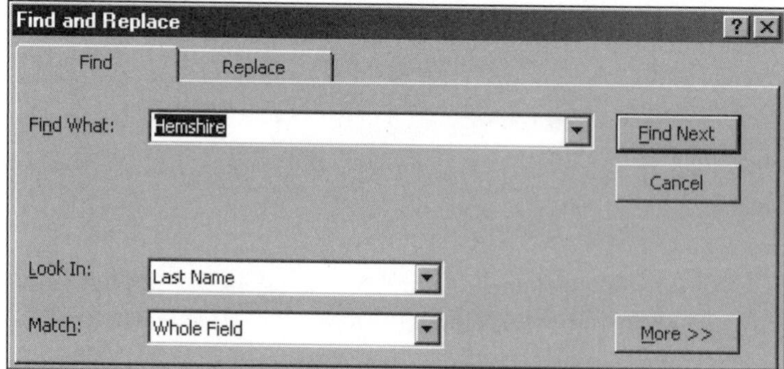

If the Find And Replace dialog box is hiding the View Customers form, drag the dialog box off to the side.

4. Click the title bar of the Find And Replace dialog box and drag it to a new location that enables you to view both it and the View Customers form.

5. In the Find What box, type **Hemshire**
6. In the Look In list, select Last Name if it isn't displayed already.
7. In the Match list, select Whole Field if it isn't displayed already.
8. Click Find Next.

   The record for a Claudia Hemshire appears in the View Customers form. This appears to be the record you want, but you must be sure there aren't any other customers with the same name.
9. Click Find Next again.

   A message appears, confirming that there are no other matches.
10. Click OK, and then click Cancel to close the Find And Replace dialog box.

Wildcard Characters

There will be times when you don't know quite which records you need. For example, you might find that some database entries were misspelled or otherwise entered incorrectly, so searching for the correct spelling fails to find these entries. To find and replace erroneous data, you'll have to be able to search for a mixture of known and unknown text.

Wildcard characters are special symbols that represent unknown characters in a word or term. The question mark (?) represents any single unknown character, and the asterisk (*) represents one or more unknown or unspecified characters within a word or term. For example, a search for *?ouse* would match *douse*, *house*, *louse*, *mouse*, *rouse*, and *souse*; the character in the first position can be anything, but the second character must be an *o*, the third a *u*, the fourth an *s*, and the fifth an *e*.

The asterisk wildcard character is especially useful, as it allows you to find almost anything for which you can approximate a match. For example, if you're trying to find someone whose name is unknown other than it sounds like *Newman*, you could search for *N*man** and find the records for *Newman*, *Newmann*, *Neuman*, and *Neumann*.

Find a record when you're missing details

Occasionally the Sweet Lil's shipping department can't make out the address on a shipping label. Fred Mallon, the shipping coordinator, just asked you to help out with a tough case—all that's left on the label he's holding is a partial street name, *rose*. In this exercise, you teach him to use wildcard characters to find the customer information he needs to fulfill this order.

1. On the View Customers form, click anywhere in the Street field.

Find

2. On the Form View toolbar, click the Find button.

   The Find And Replace dialog box appears. The contents of the Find What box and the Match list reflect the last search you performed. The contents of the Look In list automatically changed to Street.

3. In the Find What box, type **rose**

   The previous entry is replaced.

4. In the Match list, click Any Part Of Field.

   Because *rose* is only part of the street name, you want to search for it no matter where it occurs in the field.

You don't have to go back to the first record of the database; Find searches the entire table from any record.

5. In the Find And Replace dialog box, click Find Next.

   A record appears with the word *Parkrose* in the address. You note the customer's name, address, and phone number.

6. Click Find Next again.

   Another record appears, this time with *Montrose* in the address. Again you note the customer's name, address, and phone number.

7. Click Find Next one more time.

   A message appears, confirming that there are no other matches.

8. Click OK, and then click Cancel to close the Find And Replace dialog box.
9. Close the View Customers form.

You have found two possible candidates. The shipping coordinator now has all the information he needs to contact the two customers, determine which one placed the order, and recreate the illegible label.

Adding and Removing Record Text

The marketing department at Sweet Lil's often needs to alter bonbon descriptions in response to changes in customer preferences or the availability of ingredients. Mary Culvert, Sweet Lil's marketing vice president, has asked you to make these changes.

In the following exercises, you'll add new record text, modify existing records, undo changes you've made, and delete records.

Using the Form View Toolbar

The toolbars that appear beneath the Access 2000 menu bar are dynamic, changing as you move from the Database window to another window. When the Database window is active, Access 2000 displays the Database toolbar, with toolbar buttons that are specific to database administration. When you open a form, the Form View toolbar replaces the Database toolbar.

Some toolbar buttons become available only when certain database objects are being viewed. For example, the OfficeLinks and New Object toolbar buttons are available when you're viewing the tables and queries lists in the Database window, but they're not when you're viewing the forms list. And some toolbar buttons are available only in a particular context; for example, the Paste button is unavailable until you've used Copy or Cut.

The Form View toolbar has buttons that are specific to forms, along with general purpose buttons for text editing. The toolbar buttons that you will use to train the marketing department are Save, Cut, Copy, Paste, Undo, Find, New Record, and Delete Record.

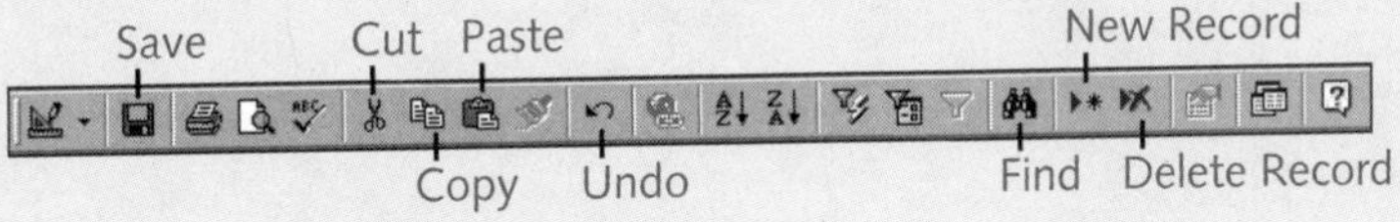

Adding Text in a Form

Mary Culvert first asks you to promote sales of all bonbons with hazelnuts, the most expensive nut ingredient, by adding a bit more local color to the descriptions of those bonbons. In this exercise, you make this change by adding the phrase *Pacific Northwest* in front of the word *hazelnut* in bonbon descriptions.

Add text to a field

1. In the Database window, ensure Forms is selected on the Objects bar. Double-click the Bonbons form in the forms list.

   The Bonbons form opens.
2. Click in the Nut Type field.

Find

3. On the Form View toolbar, click the Find button.

   The Find And Replace dialog box appears. The contents of the Find What box and the Match list reflect the last search you performed. The contents of the Look In list automatically changed to Nut Type.
4. In the Find What box, type **hazelnut**
5. In the Match list, select Whole Field.
6. Click Find Next.

   The first record to highlight Hazelnut in the Nut Type field is record 8: Hazelnut Bitters.

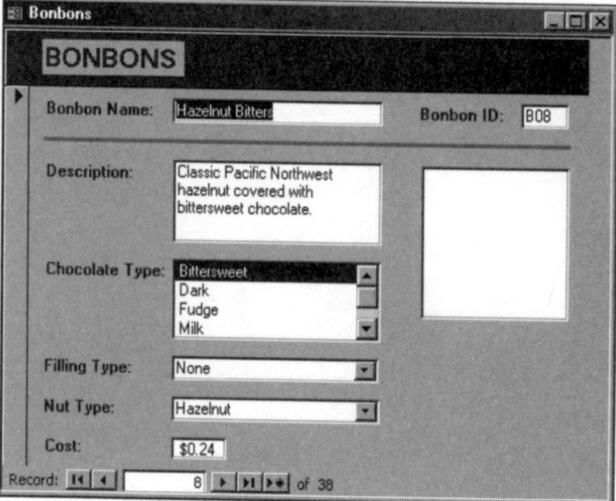

7. Click Cancel to close the Find And Replace dialog box.
8. In the Description field for the Hazelnut Bitters bonbons, click just to the left of the word *hazelnut.*

   The insertion point appears where you click.
9. Type **Pacific Northwest** and then press the Spacebar to insert a space before the word *hazelnut.*

Copy text from one field to another

Rather than retyping the phrase *Pacific Northwest* again and again, in this exercise you copy it to the Description fields of the remaining hazelnut bonbon records.

1. In the Description field for the Hazelnut Bitters bonbons, select the phrase *Pacific Northwest* including the trailing space.

Copy

2. On the Form View toolbar, click the Copy button.

   A copy of the selected text is placed on the Clipboard.

3. Click the Nut Type field.
4. On the Form View toolbar, click the Find button.

   The Find And Replace dialog box appears, with the correct settings from the previous procedure.

5. In the Find And Replace dialog box, click Find Next.

   The next record to indicate Hazelnut should be record 13: Hazelnut Supreme.

Paste

6. In the Description field for the Hazelnut Supreme bonbons, click just to the left of the word *hazelnut*. On the Form View toolbar, click the Paste button.

   The insertion point appears just in front of *hazelnut*, and the phrase *Pacific Northwest* is copied from the Clipboard to the field.

7. Click Find Next one more time.

   A message appears, confirming that there are no other matches.

8. Click OK, and then click Cancel to close the Find And Replace dialog box.

tip

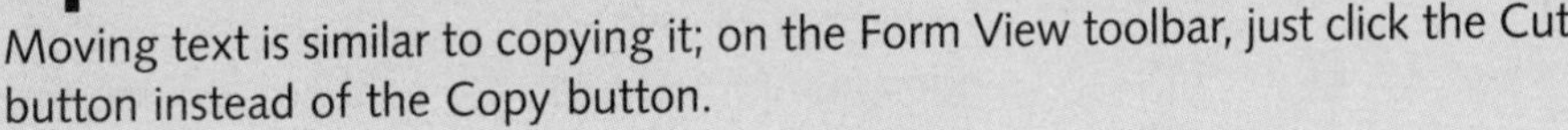

Moving text is similar to copying it; on the Form View toolbar, just click the Cut button instead of the Copy button.

Cut

Add another record using the toolbar

Because a number of respondents to the questionnaire indicated a preference for dark chocolate with nuts, Mary asks that you add another bonbon style. In this exercise, you enter a record for a new Chocolate Kiwi bonbon.

New Record

1. On the Form View toolbar, click the New Record button.

   A new, blank record appears in the Bonbons form.
2. Enter the following information.

Bonbon Name:	**Chocolate Kiwi**
Description:	**Brazil nut surrounded by dark chocolate, cross-sectioned like a kiwi fruit.**
3. Select the appropriate values—Dark, None, and Brazil—in the Chocolate Type, Filling Type, and Nut Type fields, respectively.
4. In the Cost field, type **.29**
5. In the Bonbon ID field, type **D12**

Undoing Changes in a Record

The Undo button on the Form View toolbar is handy for going back to the previous stage of the current field or record. The ToolTip and menu command for the Undo button change to reflect the current reversible action. For example, the Undo button ToolTip and menu command display *Undo Typing* if your last change was typing a word, and *Undo Delete* if you just deleted a word. Once the record has been saved, however, you can no longer undo any of the changes.

Undo your most recent action

Previous Record

1. On the navigation bar, click the Previous Record button until you reach the record for the Calla Lily bonbon.
2. In the Description box for the Calla Lily bonbon, position the insertion point to the left of the word *in* and use the Backspace key to delete the word *sculpted*.
3. Position the insertion point between the word *lily* and the period at the end of the description. Press the Spacebar and type **pad**

Undo

You can also press Ctrl+Z to undo your most recent action.

4. On the Form View toolbar, rest the mouse over the Undo button.

   The ToolTip displays *Undo Typing* to describe your most recent change.

5. On the Form View toolbar, click the Undo button.

   The word *pad,* your most recent change, is deleted.

Undo all edits in the current field or record

You realize that the original text in that field was better after all, so you try Undo again.

The action of the Undo feature itself has altered, because you undid your most recent change in the previous exercise. Rather than restore the original text one change at a time, Undo now undoes all edits that you made in the current field.

1. On the Form View toolbar, rest the mouse over the Undo button.

   The ToolTip displays *Undo Current Field/Record* because you undid your most recent change in the previous exercise.

2. On the Form View toolbar, click the Undo button.

   All your previous edits are discarded. The Undo button is then disabled, and the ToolTip changes to *Can't Undo* when you rest the mouse over it.

Delete an entire record in a form

Because no customer who responded to the questionnaire indicated a preference for white chocolate with nuts, in this exercise you delete the record for the Broken Heart bonbon.

1. Click in the Bonbon Name field.
2. On the Form View toolbar, click the Find button.

   The Find And Replace dialog box appears.

Find

3. In the Find What box, type **Broken Heart**
4. In the Look In list, verify Bonbon Name is selected.
5. In the Match list, verify Whole Field is selected.

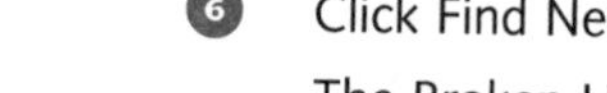

6. Click Find Next.

   The Broken Heart record appears.

Delete Record

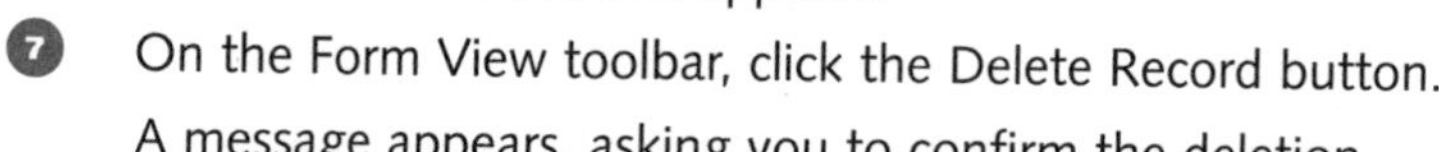

7. On the Form View toolbar, click the Delete Record button.

   A message appears, asking you to confirm the deletion.

8. Click Yes.

   The record is now deleted. The record indicator on the navigation bar reflects the change to the number of records in the database.

9. Click Cancel to close the Find And Replace dialog box.
10. Close the Bonbons form.

important

Do not confuse Delete with Delete Record. Delete is a key on the keyboard and removes only selected text or objects. Delete Record is a button on the Form View toolbar and removes an entire record. Both are listed as commands on the Edit menu, but they do not look the same. Delete has a keyboard shortcut just to its right, and Delete Record has the same face as the toolbar button just to its left.

One Step Further Replacing Data

You'll encounter many situations in which you'll want to find information in the database and then replace it with more current information. The Replace feature quickly replaces any information that meets your criteria. For example, if you know that a customer address or an internal company term has changed, you can combine finding and replacing that data in a single step.

Replace data that meets known criteria

As part of its move to worldwide sales, Sweet Lil's has merged its marketing and sales departments. All employees of both departments are now members of the marketing department. To update the database to reflect this change, you must replace every occurrence of *Sales* in the Department Name field of the Employees database table with *Marketing*. In this exercise, you do so using the Employees form.

1. In the Database window, double-click Employees in the forms list.

   The Employees form opens.

2. On the Employees form, click in the Department Name field.

Find

3. On the Form View toolbar, click the Find button.

   The Find And Replace dialog box appears.

4. In the Find And Replace dialog box, click the Replace tab.

   The Replace tab is identical to the Find tab, with the addition of a Replace With box (currently empty), a Replace button, and a Replace All button.

You can also click Replace on the Edit menu, or press Ctrl+H.

5. In the Find What box, type **Sales**
6. In the Replace With box, type **Marketing**
7. In the Match list, verify Whole Field is selected.

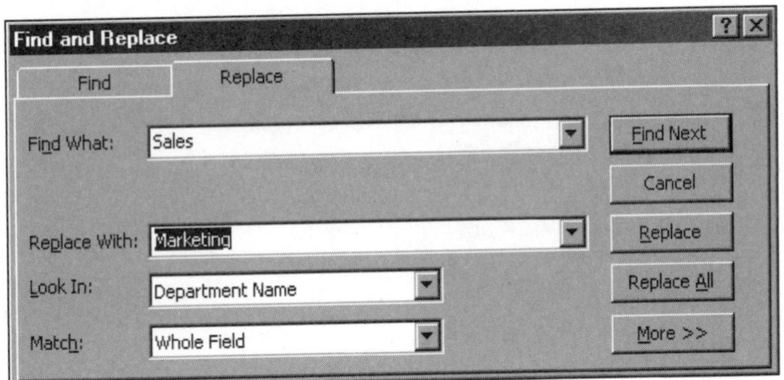

8. Click Replace All.

   A message appears, warning you that you won't be able to undo this Replace operation.

9. Click Yes.

   All occurrences of *Sales* are changed to *Marketing* in the Department Name field throughout the Employees table.

10. Close the Find And Replace dialog box.
11. Close the Employees form.

How the Year 2000 Affects Computers

Much has been said about "The Year 2000 Problem" and its effect on computers worldwide. But what exactly does this mean for computers in general, and how is Access 2000 affected?

There are two main issues concerning the year 2000 and your computer.

The first issue relates to how computers store dates and make calculations using dates. The most common method used to store dates in software is to save just the last two digits of the year, based on the assumption that the first two digits are *19*. As a result, computers read the date *2000* as *00;* lacking the first two digits, they incorrectly use the year 1900.

A second problem relates to leap year. Many computer systems and programs do not recognize the year 2000 as a leap year. This causes all dates after February 29, 2000, to be off by one day.

Access 2000 has been carefully tested against the Microsoft Year 2000 Compliance Standard and has been rated in its top category: Compliant. That means Access 2000 will recognize the year 2000 on January 1, 2000; will correctly display leap day, February 29, 2000; and will continue to display the correct date on March 1, 2000. It also means that any date calculations using the year 2000 (and beyond) will be correct.

Finish the lesson

1. To continue to the next lesson, on the File menu, click Close.
2. If you are finished using Access 2000 for now, on the File menu, click Exit.

Lesson 1 Quick Reference

To	Do this
Open a database	In the Microsoft Access dialog box, double-click the database name.
Open a form	In the Database window, click Forms on the Objects bar, and then double-click the form name.
Update an existing record	Click within the field at the place you want to insert text, and then begin typing.

Lesson 1 Quick Reference

To	Do this	Button
Move among records	On the navigation bar, click the navigation buttons.	
Move directly to a specific record	Type the record number in the record indicator on the navigation bar, and then press Enter.	
Find a record	Click in the field containing text you want to find. Click the Find button on the Form View toolbar. Enter the text you want to find, and then click Find Next.	
Add another record	Click the New Record button on the Form View toolbar.	
Copy text to another record	Select the text to copy, and use the Copy and Paste buttons on the Form View toolbar.	
Save your work	Data is saved automatically when you move to to another record or window, close a form, or exit the program.	
Undo your most recent action	Click the Undo button on the Form View toolbar.	
Undo all edits in the current field or record	Click the Undo Current Field/Record button on the Form View toolbar.	Undo Current Field/Record
Delete an entire record	Click anywhere in the record you want to delete. Click the Delete Record button on the Form View toolbar.	
Replace text in records	Click the Find button on the Form View toolbar. Click the Replace tab, enter the text you want to find and the text you want to replace it with, and then click Find Next. Then click Replace.	

Using Tables and Subforms

In this lesson you will learn how to:

- ✔ *Open a database table.*
- ✔ *Present a datasheet effectively.*
- ✔ *Update multiple records using a table.*
- ✔ *View multiple tables with a subform.*
- ✔ *Freeze and hide columns in a datasheet.*

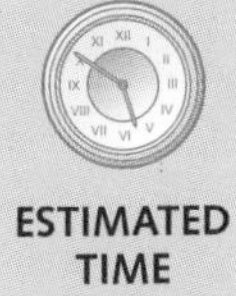

ESTIMATED TIME
25 min.

Behind every good form there stands a good table. This paraphrased adage is probably not applicable in all situations, but it is true of any well-constructed database. A table is where your data is stored, and a form is the most common vehicle for viewing and changing that data. The View Customers form that you used in Lesson 1, for example, is a convenient way of viewing and manipulating data in the *underlying* Customers table, the table that the View Customers form is based on. There are situations, however, where working with data directly in a table is the better option.

A typical Microsoft Access 2000 database contains a number of tables. The rows and columns of each table house the data for one topic; the Bonbons table, for example, contains the specifics about each bonbon in the Sweet Lil's product line. Each row of the table is a separate record, and each column of the table is a field in the record. In each record of the Bonbons table, there are eight fields: Bonbon Name, Bonbon ID, Bonbon Description, Chocolate Type, Filling Type, Nut Type, Bonbon Cost, and Picture.

To generate interest in Sweet Lil's new Bonbon Baskets line, Impact Public Relations has set up a promotional campaign in which sample baskets of bonbons are mailed to Sweet Lil's customers four times during the next calendar year.

In this lesson, you make use of tables, forms, and subforms to present information about the different sample baskets to the marketing department at Sweet Lil's. In the process, you open an existing database table and arrange the table to make it easier to use. You also use a main form and subform to examine records from multiple tables at one time.

Start Microsoft Access 2000 and reopen the database

- If Access 2000 isn't started yet, start it. Open the Sweet Lil's database. If the Microsoft Access window doesn't fill your screen, maximize the window.

  If you need help opening the database, see Lesson 1, "Using Forms."

Viewing Data

In Access 2000, data in a table, form, report, or query may be presented in several ways, called *views*.

For a table or a form, *Datasheet view* displays all the data in a tabular format, each row a record and each column a field. When you open a table, it always appears first in Datasheet view, because Datasheet view is the *default view* of a table. Both tables and forms in Datasheet view are usually called datasheets.

If a form has already been created based on a table, *Form view* for either the table or the form displays the table data within the associated form. Form view presents only the fields required for a given task, arranged to show each individual record to its best advantage. (When you open a form, it always appears first in Form view, which is the default view of a form.)

In *Table Design view* the table is displayed as a list of fields and their associated properties, which may be changed as well as viewed. *Form Design view* lets you create a new form or revise the structure of an existing one. Design view is never a default view. Instead, you must switch to Design view from another view.

View

To switch between Design view and the default view, just click the View button. When you change views, the View button face switches to show the alternate view. With the View button you can also switch almost as easily to another view: click the drop-down arrow next to the View button, and then click the view you want from the list.

Form view is generally the easiest and safest view to use, because it has the most safeguards and fewest complications. There are times, however, when you need to see multiple records at the same time or view a table for which no form has been developed. Datasheet view lets you see the database table as a table and work directly with the data it contains.

Viewing a Datasheet

Most of the tables in the Sweet Lil's database can be viewed through forms. For example, you never actually need to show the Sweet Lil's marketing department the entire Bonbons table when you demonstrate how to alter bonbon descriptions; instead, you work in the Bonbons form, modifying fields that show information about individual records in the underlying Bonbons table.

A database table works much like a spreadsheet, so a table viewed in this row-and-column format is often referred to as a *datasheet*—a database spreadsheet. The datasheet displays every record and every field in a table. In large tables, some columns might contain a lot of text, and there are probably many fields, so you might not be able to view all the table data at once. There are therefore several strategies available for making large datasheets easier to work with.

In these exercises, you open the Bonbons table to become more familiar with the Sweet Lil's product line. You rearrange the fields for optimum viewing of fields, using the record and field selectors.

Open a table

1. In the Database window, click Tables on the Objects bar to open the tables list.

   A list of tables is displayed in the Database window.

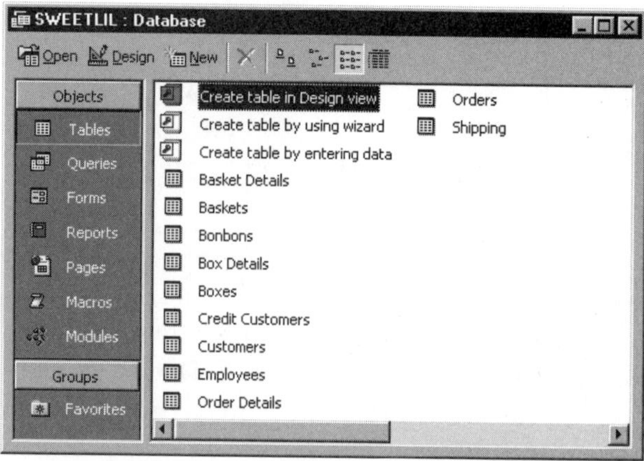

2. In the tables list, double-click Bonbons.

   The Bonbons table opens in Datasheet view.

When you first open a table, it is displayed with each row as a record and each column as a field. A triangular pointer appears to the left of the first record, indicating that it is the current record. The first field of the first record is selected, indicating that it is the current field.

Selecting Records Within a Table

The triangular pointer that indicates the current record is the *record indicator.* It appears in a column of gray boxes that runs along the left side, called *record selectors.* A similar set of *field selectors* runs across the top row of the table. The field selectors include the field name.

Field selector

Record selector

Record indicator

Bonbons : Table

Bonbon Name	Bonbon ID	Chocolate Type	Nut Type	Filling Type
Candlelight Ecstasy	B01	Fudge	Cashew	Mocha cream
Bittersweet Blueberry	B02	Bittersweet	None	Blueberry
Marzipan Oakleaf	B03	Bittersweet	None	Marzipan
Bittersweet Strawberry	B04	Bittersweet	None	Strawberry
Bittersweet Raspberry	B05	Bittersweet	None	Raspberry
Bittersweet Marmalade	B06	Bittersweet	None	Marmalade
Bittersweet Cherry	B07	Bittersweet	None	Cherry, whole
Hazelnut Bitters	B08	Bittersweet	Hazelnut	None
Almond Supreme	D01	Dark	Almond	None
Heart on a Sleeve	D02	Dark	None	Cherry cream
Cashew Supreme	D03	Dark	Cashew	None
Almond Fudge Mocha	D04	Dark	Almond	Amaretto

Record: 6 of 38

The record indicator shows where you are in the table. You can click a record selector to select an entire row of fields, which is by definition a single record. You can click a field selector to select an entire column. You can also select several field or record selectors at once to make a change to multiple columns or rows. Only adjacent fields or rows can be selected.

Change the row height of a table

Field text wraps when a row has enough height to fit more than one line of text.

With the Bonbons table open in Datasheet view, only a partial view of the Bonbon Description field appears. Right now there's just enough height to see one line per row, which is fine for most fields, but not for the descriptions of bonbon in the Bonbon Description field. By increasing the row height, you're able to view all lines of the Bonbon Description field at once.

Maximize

1. Verify that the Microsoft Access window and the Bonbons datasheet are maximized.

   The datasheet for the Bonbons table expands to fill the Microsoft Access window.

2. Position the mouse pointer on the border between any two record selectors.

   The mouse pointer becomes a double-headed arrow.

Bonbon ID	Bonbon Name	Chocolate Type	Nut Type
B01	Candlelight Ecstasy	Dark	Cashew
B02	Bittersweet Blueberry	Bittersweet	None
B03	Marzipan Oakleaf	Bittersweet	None
B04	Bittersweet Strawberry	Bittersweet	None
B05	Bittersweet Raspberry	Bittersweet	None

Position the mouse pointer here.

A single row can't be sized differently from the other rows.

3. Drag the border down to make the row immediately above it grow taller.

   All rows are resized.

4. Scroll to the right and adjust the row height until you can read the entire text of the Bonbon Description field.

Change the column width of a table

Now you go on to make the Nut Type and Bonbon ID columns narrower, so that you can see additional table fields.

1. Position the mouse pointer on the border between the field selectors for the Nut Type and Filling Type fields.

   The mouse pointer becomes a double-headed arrow.

To view additional fields without resizing, use the horizontal scroll bar to scroll to the right.

Position the mouse pointer here.

Nut Type	Filling Type
Almond	Amaretto
Hazelnut	None
None	Cherry, whole

You can resize columns independently of one another.

2. Double-click the border between the Nut Type and Filling Type field selectors.

   The Nut Type column is resized to match the width of the widest entry in the field, including the complete field name at the top of the column.

3. Drag the right border of the Bonbon ID column to the left until it's just slightly larger than the three-character Bonbon ID entries.

Save

4. On the Datasheet View toolbar, click the Save button.

   The Bonbons table will now retain its current layout in Datasheet view.

5. Close the Bonbons table.

Records are automatically saved as you move from record to record, but you must manually save your changes to the layout of a table or form, so that it appears this way every time you use it.

Updating Data Using a Table

For a review of Access editing tools, see Lesson 1, "Using Forms."

Many of the editing tools that you use in Form view are also available in Datasheet view, including Find, Cut, Copy, Paste, New Record, and Delete Record.

It's often helpful to view multiple records using Datasheet view. Updating records directly in a table should be done with caution, however. Fewer data validation tools are available in Datasheet view, so you increase the chance of introducing errors into your data. And if you do spot an error, the Undo command can undo only the changes you've made since your most recent save.

It's best to use Form view to perform update operations.

Viewing Multiple Tables with a Subform

Think of a *subform* as a form within a form. A subform lets you work with records from several separate tables within a single form. The fields of the main form reflect data from one table, while the data in the subform reflects the other table—or tables. This makes the data both easier to use and more reliable, because information from the various tables is kept separate, while the relationship is maintained.

Now that you've reviewed descriptions of the bonbons, it's time to look over information about the various baskets that have been set up for the promotional mailing. To do so, you use the Baskets form, which includes a subform called Basket Details.

The Baskets table, viewed through the Baskets form, stores information about the various basket types in which bonbons are packaged. The Basket Details subform displays selected fields from the Basket Details and Bonbons tables. With this structure, the form displays information about the basket itself (name, ID number, and a general description of its contents) in the main form and information about the basket's contents (what types of bonbons it contains and details about each bonbon type) in the subform. The subform provides a direct connection between one set of records, defining baskets, and another, defining basket contents. Using the form and subform together, you can add and delete bonbon types to define the contents of a new basket, until you've assembled a basket that holds the exact mix that you want.

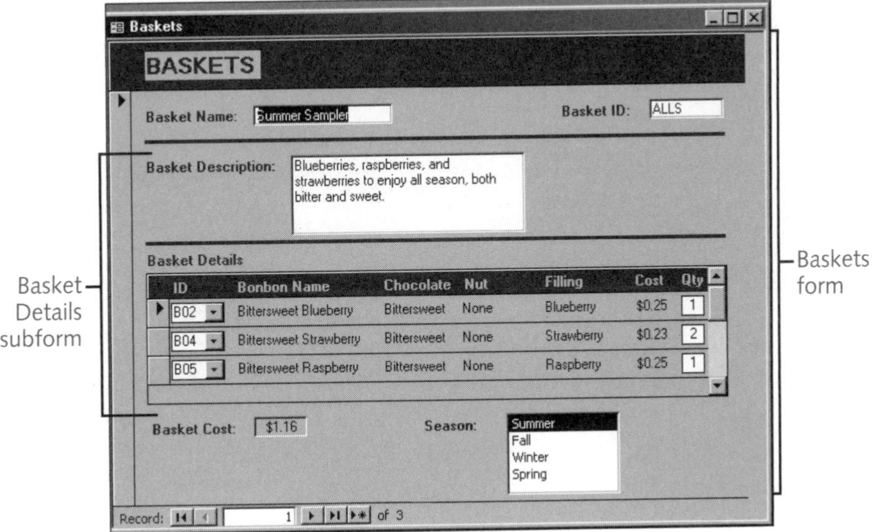

In these exercises, you use the Baskets form and its Basket Details subform to create a new basket for the winter promotional mailing.

If not looking through this lesson sequentially, open the Sweetlils database.

Add a record in a main form

1. In the Database window, click Forms on the Objects bar to display the forms list.
2. In the forms list, double-click Baskets.

   The Baskets form opens, displaying the first record of the Baskets table in the main form, and its associated Basket Details subform below.

New Record

3. On the Form View toolbar, click the New Record button.

   A new, blank record appears, with the insertion point in the Basket Name box.
4. Type the following information into the appropriate fields of the main form.

   Basket Name: **By The Fire**

   Basket ID: **WINT**

   Basket Description: **Nuts and berries coated with chocolate and fudge for those long winter evenings.**
5. Press the Tab key to move to the subform.

   The insertion point appears in the ID field of the Basket Details subform.

Add records in a subform

In this exercise, you define the contents of the By The Fire basket, selecting the ideal combination of bonbon types for this basket. Each bonbon you select will be saved as a separate record in the Basket Details table. The records will be linked, however, to the record for the By The Fire basket in the Baskets table.

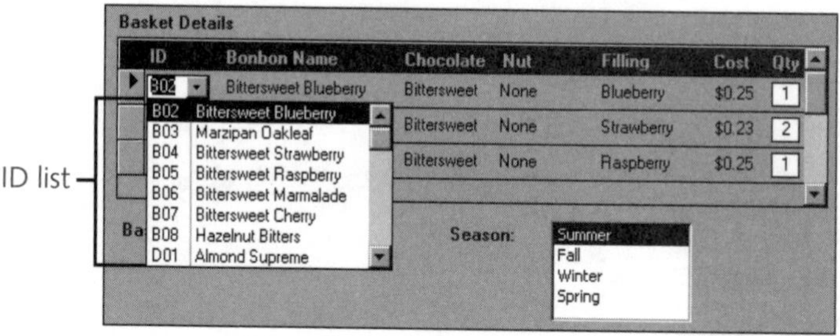

1. In the ID field of the Basket Details subform, click the drop-down arrow of the first ID cell, and then select B02 Bittersweet Blueberry.

   B02 appears in the field, and the Bonbon Name, Chocolate, Nut, Filling, and Cost fields are filled in with corresponding values. A new, blank record appears below the first record.
2. Press Tab to move to the Qty field.
3. In the Qty field, type **1** and press Tab.

   Access 2000 saves the first record in the subform.
4. Type the following records into the subform.

ID	Bonbon Name	Qty
B05	**Bittersweet Raspberry**	**1**
D03	**Cashew Supreme**	**1**
F01	**Walnut Fudge Mocha**	**2**

   The Basket Cost field on the main form changes as each new record is added to the subform. The main form automatically calculates the cost of the basket based on its contents, as defined in the subform.
5. Scroll back through the subform to check your work. Be sure that each record is correct before continuing.
6. In the last record in the subform, press Ctrl+Tab.

   The insertion point moves from the subform to the Season field in the main form.

Pressing Ctrl+Tab and Ctrl+Shift+Tab moves the insertion point from the subform to the next and previous fields, respectively, in the main form.

Complete the main form

To complete the By The Fire basket, all you need to do is select the season during which it will be mailed.

1. In the Season field, select Winter and press Tab.

   Access saves the completed record and opens a new, blank record.
2. Press Shift+Tab to return to the previous main form and subform.

   Access returns to the record you just entered and discards the blank record.
3. Close the Baskets main form.

   The Sweetlil database window is displayed.

One Step Further Refining Datasheet Views

Datasheet view can be difficult to use when there are a large number of fields. You often get lost in the Bonbons datasheet, even after resizing the fields and columns, due to the size and complexity of the table. Two strategies for refining the Datasheet view come in handy now: freezing the most useful column and hiding an unnecessary column.

Freeze a datasheet column

The Bonbon Name field provides a reference point for the table, identifying which row of data belongs to which bonbon. You freeze the entire Bonbon Name column so that it remains visible on the left, no matter how many fields you scroll through on the right.

1. Click Tables on the Objects bar. In the tables list, double-click Bonbons.
2. Click the Bonbon Name field in any row.
3. On the Format menu, click Freeze Columns.

   The Bonbon Name column now is positioned as the first column in the table. A bold vertical line appears along the right border of the column, which is now frozen and can't be scrolled.

To unfreeze columns at any time, click Unfreeze All Columns on the Format menu.

You drag the horizontal scroll box back and forth a few times to test this. Sure enough, the Bonbon Name column remains frozen on the left as all the other columns scroll freely back and forth.

Hide a datasheet column

The Picture field is a good choice for a column to hide. Its bonbon graphics aren't currently visible because the table is too large to fit on the screen without scrolling, so the Picture field isn't useful to you at the moment. In this exercise, you hide the Picture field and make the datasheet less cluttered.

To reveal any hidden columns, click Unhide Columns on the Format menu, and then select the appropriate check boxes.

Drag from here...

...to here.

Bonbon Name	Bonbon Cost	Picture
Candlelight Ecstasy	$0.30	Bitmap Image
Bittersweet Blueberry	$0.25	Bitmap Image
Marzipan Oakleaf	$0.40	Bitmap Image
Bittersweet Strawberry	$0.23	Bitmap Image
Bittersweet Raspberry	$0.25	Bitmap Image
Bittersweet Marmalade	$0.17	Bitmap Image
Bittersweet Cherry	$0.26	Bitmap Image
Hazelnut Bitters	$0.24	Bitmap Image

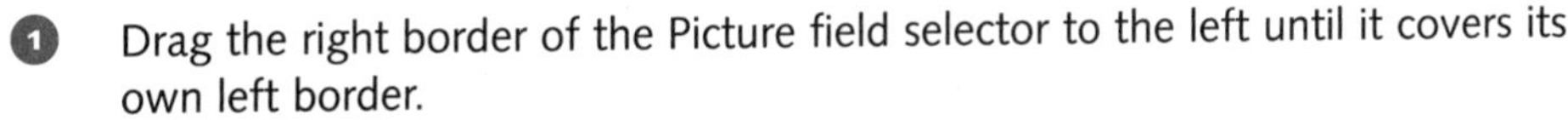

1. Drag the right border of the Picture field selector to the left until it covers its own left border.

   The Picture column is hidden.

Save

2. On the Table Datasheet toolbar, click the Save button.

   The Bonbons table will now retain its current layout in Datasheet view.

3. Close the Bonbons table.

Finish the lesson

1. To continue to the next lesson, on the File menu, click Close.
2. If you're finished using Access 2000 for now, on the File menu, click Exit.

Lesson 2 Quick Reference

To	Do this	Button
Open a table	In the Database window, click Tables on the Objects bar, and then double-click the table name.	
Resize all datasheet rows	Drag the border between record selectors.	
Resize a datasheet column	Drag the right-hand border of the field selector for the column you want to resize.	
Switch views	Click the View drop-down arrow on the Datasheet, Form, or Design View toolbar, and then select the view you want.	
Add a new record in a main form	Click the New Record button on the Form View toolbar.	
Add a new record in a subform	In the subform, click the first drop-down arrow, and select an item.	
Move from a form to a subform	Click in the field to which you want to move.	
Freeze a column	Click anywhere in the column, and then click Freeze Columns on the Format menu.	
Hide a column	Drag the right border of the field selector over the left border of the field selector.	
Unhide a hidden column	On the Format menu, click Unhide Columns, and then select the hidden field in the Unhide Columns dialog box.	

LESSON

3

Using Filters and Reports

ESTIMATED TIME
40 min.

In this lesson you will learn how to:

- ✔ *Sort records.*
- ✔ *Extract specific information by using a filter.*
- ✔ *Report only the information you need.*
- ✔ *Preview report details.*
- ✔ *Print all or part of a report.*
- ✔ *Create mailing labels.*

The sheer volume of information in a database can be overwhelming. In most cases, you're not interested in the bulk of the information, just the information you need at the moment. You want to focus on the information you're after, without wading through distracting data, and share that information quickly and easily with others or preserve it for future reference. You can do that by using the Microsoft Access 2000 sorting, filtering, and reporting tools.

The sales department at Sweet Lil's has collected a year's worth of records about the orders they've filled. Now the department needs to make sense of that data and put it to good use. In this lesson, you help rearrange and refine the data to extract needed information, and demonstrate how to open, preview, and print reports, including mailing labels.

Start Microsoft Access 2000 and reopen the database

- If Access isn't started yet, start it. Open the Sweet Lil's database. If the Microsoft Access window doesn't fill your screen, maximize the window.

  If you need help opening the database, see Lesson 1, "Using Forms."

Viewing Only the Information You Need

Access allows you to change your view of the data in a database without affecting the actual physical arrangement of the database itself, so you can organize the data to make it more meaningful. The two most useful techniques for organizing data are sorting and filtering.

Sorting is simply rearranging the records into a specific order based on the contents of a given field or fields. You can sort records alphabetically, by number, by date, or by a specified characteristic, such as being male or female. Records can be sorted in ascending (A–Z and 0–9) or descending (Z–A and 9–0) order.

Filtering is screening out all records that do not match a given set of criteria defined in a *filter*. A filter makes it possible to view a particular group of records exclusively. For example, you could apply a filter to view only those orders that were placed on a certain date.

Sorting and filtering can be done in either Form view or Datasheet view. Neither sorting nor filtering change the actual data; each process simply adjusts your view of the data. When you sort a form, the sort order is saved automatically, so that when you reopen the form, the records are displayed in the order in which you last sorted them. When you sort a table, Access gives you the option of saving the sort order. Filters, however, are *not* saved along with the form or table and must be reapplied each time you want to see the filtered view.

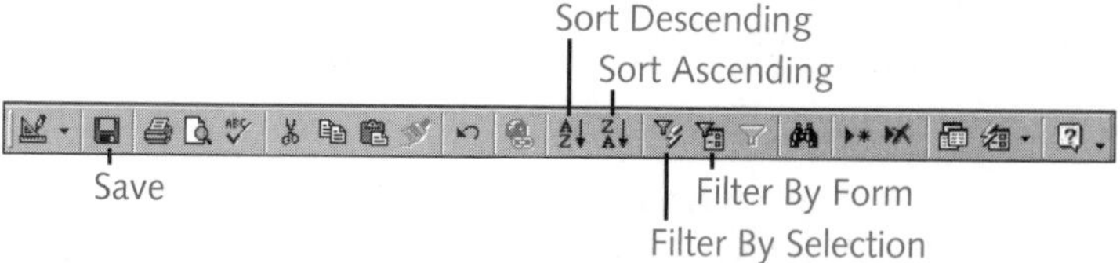

Sorting Records

To make sense of Sweet Lil's candy orders, it's not enough simply to list them in the order in which they were placed. You also need to group the records together in various ways to see how they're related. For example, grouping the records in the Orders table by customer name might help you determine who the "best" customers are and how much repeat business they're doing.

There's no one ideal arrangement or order for records in a database, because people consult a database in response to a wide range of needs. Rowen Gilbert, vice-president of planning for the sales department, typically needs to know how orders are distributed geographically, so the best arrangement for him is usually by region. Liz Yarrow, an administrative assistant for the operations department, always needs to find the most recent orders as quickly as possible, so the best arrangement for her is by order number, in reverse chronological order. Robin Saito, a shipping clerk, needs all orders listed by their unique ID numbers.

Switching Between Views

Access allows you to switch quickly and easily between available views. In a form, you have the option of switching between Form, Datasheet, and Design views, and in a table you can switch between Datasheet and Design views. You have three view options in Form view because a table exists independent of any forms that may be created from it, but a form is dependent on an underlying table.

To switch between views, click the drop-down arrow next to the View button, and then click the view you want from the list. When you select the view you want, the View button face changes to show the view that will be displayed if you click the button. The toolbar button always toggles between Design view and the default view of the object with which you're working, such as a table, a query, a form, a report, or a page.

In general, it's best to stay in Form view for most of your work, switching to Datasheet view (and thus the underlying table) only when necessary and switching back to Form view immediately thereafter. You must open a table directly if you intend to change its design, however, because each database object has its own distinct Design view.

To sort by multiple fields, select the fields you want to sort by before clicking a Sort button.

To see the records grouped together in different ways, you can sort them by different fields using the Sort Ascending and Sort Descending toolbar buttons. In this exercise, you show Rowen, Liz, and Robin how to sort the Orders records to suit their different needs. Sorting is so quick and easy in Access that you can help all three get their answers at once.

Sort records on a specific field

1. In the Database window, click Forms on the Objects bar to display the forms list.
2. In the forms list, double-click Orders, and then maximize the Orders form window.

   The Orders form opens in Form view. Notice the Order ID number for record 1.

View

3. On the Form View toolbar, click the View drop-down arrow, and then click Datasheet View.

   The Orders form reappears in Datasheet view. The arrangement of the records is more apparent in Datasheet view.
4. On the Orders datasheet, use the horizontal scroll bar to scroll to the right until you can see the ShipStateOrProvince field, and then click the ShipStateOrProvince field selector.

   When the mouse pointer passes over the field selector, the pointer becomes a downward-pointing arrow. Now when you click the field selector, the entire column is selected.

Sort Ascending

5. On the Form View toolbar, click the Sort Ascending button.

   All the records are rearranged so that the states and provinces are listed in ascending alphabetical (A–Z) order. Rowen can now see how the orders are distributed by state.
6. On the Datasheet View toolbar, click the View drop-down arrow, and then click Form View.

   The displayed record has changed to Order ID 228.
7. Click Order ID 228.

   Now that Rowen has the information he needs, you can help Liz sort the records by order ID.

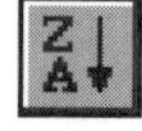

Sort Descending

8. On the Form View toolbar, click the Sort Descending button.

   The record changes from Order ID 228 to Order ID 413. Records are now sorted in descending numerical order by order ID. Order ID 413 is now the first record in the table.

You can sort records in either Form view or Datasheet view, but the results are more apparent in Datasheet view.

9. On the Form View toolbar, click the View drop-down arrow, and then click Datasheet View.

   Liz can now see the records in reverse chronological order, with the most recent order first.
10. In the Orders datasheet, select the Order ID field.

    Robin also needs to see the records sorted by order ID, but in chronological order.

Sort Ascending

11. On the Form View toolbar, click the Sort Ascending button.

    All the records are grouped by order ID, in ascending numerical order. Robin can now see the original sequence in which the orders were placed.

Refining Your View of the Data

Sorting is very useful for quick reference, but it has its limitations. Sorting records displays a table in a more helpful arrangement, but you still have to view all the records in the table. No matter how you sort the records, you can't screen out records in which you have no interest. To do that, you must use a filter.

This morning, Rowen Gilbert arrives at your desk with an urgent request: he needs you to find out how many orders have been shipped to Canada. You show him how easy it is to set up a filter for just this kind of question.

Filtering a Form by Selection

Filter By Selection works much like a sort, except that it matches against the *contents* of the field and allows only matching records to pass through. The Filter By Selection feature allows you to filter selectively by a single criterion per field, that criterion being the contents of the field at the time you select it. The field and contents you select serve as an *example* of the information you want to see.

Filter by selection

You can also filter by multiple fields by selecting the fields you want before clicking the Filter By Selection button.

In this exercise, you use Filter By Selection to display just the Canadian orders for Rowen.

1. Be sure the Orders form is open in Datasheet view.
2. In the Orders datasheet, scroll right until you can see the ShipCountry column, and then click any ShipCountry field containing the word *Canada.*

   This sets, by example, the criterion for the filter: a ShipCountry field with the word *Canada* in it.

Filter By Selection

3. On the toolbar, click the Filter By Selection button.

   The filter displays only the records with the word *Canada* in the ShipCountry field. The word *(Filtered)* appears on the navigation bar, indicating that this is a filtered view. The Apply Filter toolbar button becomes the Remove Filter toolbar button.

Orders

PostalCode	ShipCity	ShipStateOrProvince	ShipPostalCode	Country	ShipCountry	Acco
26502	Toronto	Ontario	M9W 6A6	USA	Canada	
G1R 5E9	Québec	Québec	G1R 5E9	Canada	Canada	
B0P 1R0	Kingston	Nova Scotia	B0P 1R0	Canada	Canada	
04657	10 Mile	British Columbia	T2F 8M4	USA	Canada	
K1S 4C9	Ottawa	Ontario	K1S 4C9	Canada	Canada	
R0A 0J0	Winnipeg	Manitoba	R0A 0J0	Canada	Canada	
17033	Ottawa	Ontario	K1S 4C9	USA	Canada	
37150	Ft. Smith	Yukon Territory	X0E 0P0	USA	Canada	
11788	Ottawa	Ontario	K2A 3L2	USA	Canada	
B0P 1K0	Coldbrook	Nova Scotia	B0P 1K0	Canada	Canada	
A1A 3W5	St. John's	Newfoundland	A1A 3W5	Canada	Canada	
76102	Kanata	Ontario	K2K 1K4	USA	Canada	
H2G 2V8	Montréal	Québec	H2G 2V8	Canada	Canada	
94538	Sydney	Nova Scotia	B1P 4Z6	USA	Canada	
R3E 5X2	Calgary	Alberta	R3E 5X2	Canada	Canada	
G3J 1R4	Anjou	Québec	H1M 1X5	Canada	Canada	
03038	Peterborough	Ontario	K9J 7B1	USA	Canada	
M1T 3J9	Scarborough	Ontario	M1T 3J9	Canada	Canada	
A1A 3G7	St. John's	Newfoundland	A1A 3G7	Canada	Canada	

Record: 1 of 89 (Filtered)

Filtering by Form

The Filter By Form feature allows you to filter selectively by more than one criterion per field. Like Filter By Selection, it sets criteria by example. But where Filter By Selection simply applies the current contents of a particular field, Filter By Form allows you to select any one of the possible items in a particular field.

Filter by form

Sweet Lil's accepts three major credit cards: World Credit, Elite Fund, and Select Card. Rowen now asks you to find out how many of those Canadian orders were paid for with an Elite Fund credit card. In this exercise, you use the Filter By Form feature to further filter the results, displaying only the Canadian orders that were placed using the Elite Fund credit card.

Filter By Form

1. On the toolbar, click the Filter By Form button.

   The view collapses to a single row of fields. An arrow appears by the ShipCountry field and the word *Canada* is highlighted in the ShipCountry list.

2. Scroll to the right until you see the Credit Card field.
3. On the Orders Filter By Form grid, click the Credit Card field, click the drop-down arrow, and then select 2.

Because the Credit Card field is an option group on the Orders form, the credit card type is stored as a number. The Elite Fund credit card is the second choice in the option group, so it has been assigned the number 2.

Apply Filter

4 Click the Apply Filter button.

The filter displays only the records with *Canada* in the ShipCountry field and in the Credit Card field. The Apply Filter button changes to the Remove Filter button.

5 Click the Remove Filter button.

The normal Datasheet view reappears, with all records displayed.

6 Close the Orders datasheet. If you are asked to save changes, click No.

Preserving Your View in a Report

After you've gotten the desired view of your data, you might want to share that view with others at Sweet Lil's or Impact Public Relations. You can do this by using a *report*. A report is similar to a form in that they both extract specific information from the database and organize it in a meaningful fashion. Forms, however, are used primarily for data manipulation, whereas reports are used for data presentation. Reports can be printed on paper, saved in your local directory, sent via e-mail, posted to a shared folder for use by a workgroup, published to an intranet to reach an entire corporation, or published on the Internet to reach as wide an audience as possible.

Sweet Lil's newest marketing agent, Nora Bromsler, has taken the lead in mastering Access. To assist the marketing department, she has created the Sales By Box report, which displays sales records for any range of dates in calendar year 1998.

You set criteria by example for a filter, but you enter parameter values manually to set criteria for a report.

Sales By Box is an interactive report: it prompts the user for a start and end date for the period to be covered in the report. These dates are the *parameter values* or report criteria. The Sales By Box report then extracts and presents only the records that meet those criteria. The range of dates can vary from a single day to the entire year.

Sweet Lil's marketing vice president, Mary Culvert, needs to review sales for the first two weeks of June 1998, the beginning of the traditional summer season. In the following exercises, you help Mary open, preview, and print the information she needs using the Sales By Box report.

Open a report

When the Sales By Box report is opened, it requests the start and end dates for the period to be covered. Entering the report criteria is thus a part of opening the report.

1. In the Database window, click Reports on the Objects bar to display the reports list.
2. In the reports list, double-click Sales By Box.

   The message *Enter Parameter Value* appears, prompting for the start date of the period Mary wants the report to cover.

Access 2000 accepts date entries in a number of formats, but you must clearly distinguish the month, day, and year.

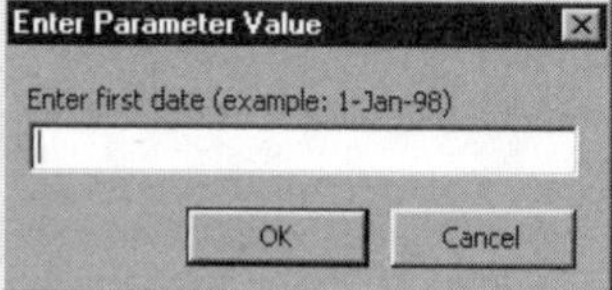

3. In the Enter Parameter Value text box, type **1-Jun-98** and press Enter.

   The Enter Parameter Value message prompts for the end date of the period Mary wants covered.
4. Type **June 15, 1998** and press Enter.

   Mary's report opens in Print Preview view. The Print Preview toolbar replaces the Database toolbar.

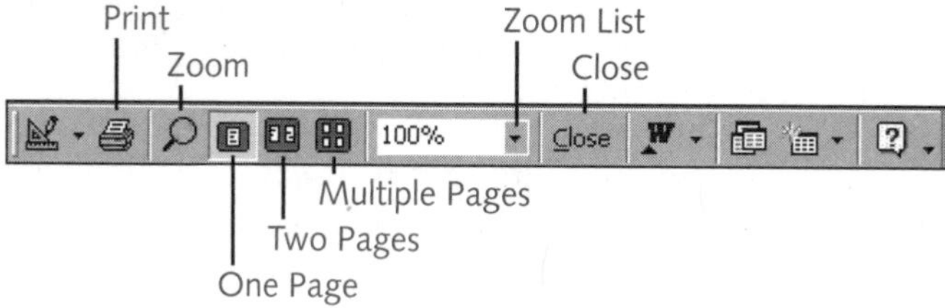

Microsoft Windows Regional Settings

Microsoft Windows 95, Windows 98, and Window NT use regional settings to determine how to interpret numeric dates. For example, the numeric date *1/2/98* is interpreted as month-day-year (January 2, 1998) if the regional settings are for United States English, and as day-month-year (1 February 1998) if the regional settings are for British English.

Access recognizes a number of ways to enter dates, but you must clearly distinguish the month from the day. When you enter the month alphabetically, either abbreviated (Jan) or in full (January), Access recognizes and accepts it regardless of the month and day order. When you enter a date numerically, however, Access looks to your regional settings to determine the month and day order.

For example, Access recognizes both *13/1/98* and *1/13/98* as January 13, 1998—there are only 12 months in a year, so the date isn't ambiguous. But both *12/1/98* and *1/12/98* can be interpreted as either January 12, 1998 or December 1, 1998, depending on your regional settings.

Some regional settings put the year first, so other dates are also ambiguous in an international environment. For example, *3/2/1* can be January 2, 2003 or February 1, 2003 or February 3, 2001 or March 2, 2001.

Previewing a Report

The Print Preview view includes a navigation bar similar to that of a form or a datasheet for moving among pages.

A report is automatically saved and opened in Print Preview view the moment it is created. The view of the information contained in a report serves as a snapshot of that view, which you can view or print. Reports were originally designed with printing in mind, however, so the layout you see is dependent upon the default printer settings of your computer.

When you open a report, it appears at full magnification so you can clearly read the information it contains. The mouse pointer becomes a magnifying glass with a minus sign (-) when it passes over any part of the report page. The degree of magnification is displayed in the Zoom box on the Print Preview toolbar.

Preview a report

You can select the degree of magnification from 10% to 200% or select Fit in the Zoom box.

To help Mary Culvert learn more about reports, you want to show her the many ways to view both the contents and the layout of a report in the Print Preview view.

You can also use the arrow keys and the Page Up, Page Down, Home, and End keys to move through the page.

1. Click anywhere in the fully magnified report page.

   The view zooms out to show you the entire page, and the minus sign (-) on the mouse pointer becomes a plus sign (+). On the Print Preview toolbar, the Zoom box now displays *Fit.*

You can use the Multiple Pages toolbar button to view the layout of up to six pages at a time.

2. Click anywhere in the zoomed-out report page.

   The view zooms in to 100 percent magnification centered on the point you clicked, and the mouse pointer plus sign becomes a minus sign. On the Print Preview toolbar, the Zoom box now displays *100%.*

3. Use the vertical scroll bar to move up and down the page, and use the horizontal scroll bar to move from side to side.

Two Pages

4. On the Print Preview toolbar, click the Two Pages button.

   The view zooms out to show two pages, side by side. On the Print Preview toolbar, the Zoom box now displays *Fit* again.

One Page

5. On the Print Preview toolbar, click the One Page button.

   All but the first page disappears.

Print a report

A printer must be selected before you can print a report.

By just viewing the report in Print Preview view, Mary learned everything she needed to know, but she also wants a printed copy for an upcoming meeting. She notices that the default quarter-inch left margin is too narrow and would like to widen it to a full inch. Mary asks you to adjust the page setup, print a single "proof page" for her approval, and then print the entire report in time for her meeting.

1. On the File menu, click Print.

   The Print dialog box appears.

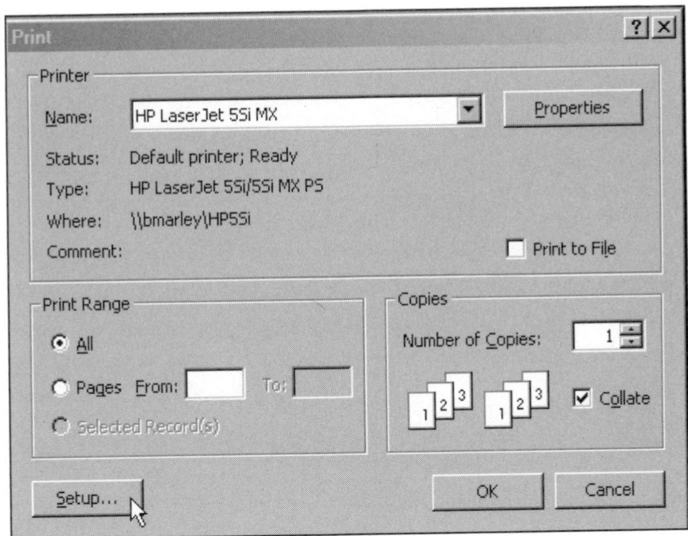

2. In the Print dialog box, click Setup.

   The Page Setup dialog box appears, with the Margins tab active.

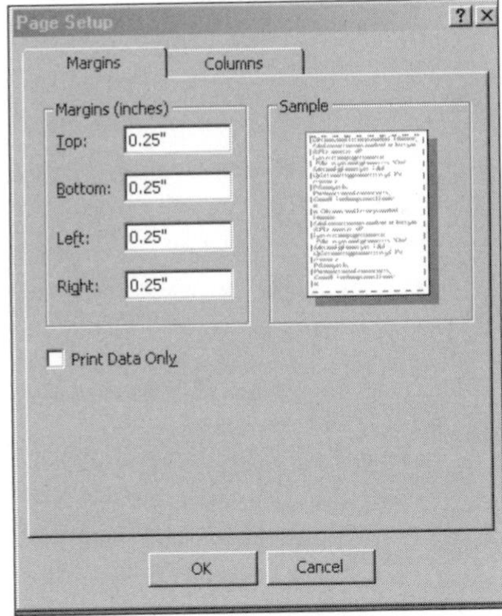

When you make a change to the page setup, the change is saved and becomes the new default setting.

3. Double-click the Left Margin box, and then type **1**

   The left margin changes from the default 0.25 inches to one inch. In the Sample preview picture, the left margin of the report shifts to the right.

4. Click OK.

   The Page Setup dialog box closes. The left margin of the report is now set to one inch. All future Sales By Box reports will also have one-inch left margins, until the page setup is changed again.

5. In the Print Range area of the Print dialog box, select Pages.

   When you select the Pages option, the insertion point appears in the From box. You want to print page 1 of the report as a proof page for Mary.

6. In the From box, type **1**, and then press Tab.

7. In the To box, type **1** and press Enter.

   Only the first page (range 1 to 1) of the Sales By Box report is printed. This proof page confirms that the report will indeed be printed as expected, and Mary approves final printing of the entire report.

Print

8. On the Print Preview toolbar, click the Print button.

   Access prints the entire Sales By Box report, exactly as you see it in Print Preview view. This is the most convenient way to print a report once the page layout has been checked.

Close

9. On the Print Preview toolbar, click the Close button.

   The Sales By Box report closes, and the Database window reappears.

> **tip**
>
> When you double-click a report in the Database window reports list, Access 2000 opens it in Print Preview view. To print a report without opening it first, just click the report in the Database window, and then click the Print button on the Database window toolbar. To specify how many copies to print and whether to collate the copies, click Print on the File menu.

Creating Mailing Labels

At Impact's suggestion, Sweet Lil's plans to promote its newest bonbon, Chocolate Kiwi, by mailing a free sample to all of its customers. Henry Czynski, the senior shipping clerk, needs to create a set of mailing labels of a suitable size and layout to fit on a single-serving candy box; the labels must be sorted by postal code so that all the boxes addressed to the same area can be shipped out together.

In Access 2000, a set of mailing labels is simply a specialized report whose layout matches that of your label stock. This mailing label report extracts the names and mailing addresses from the database, sorts them into a specified order, and arranges them in whatever label format you choose. The Label Wizard steps you through the process of creating a mailing label report.

Your mailing label report contains the design of the mailing labels—text appearance, layout, and sorting order—but not the actual names and addresses to be printed on the candy box labels. These remain stored in the Customers table of the database, which is updated as needed in the normal course of Sweet Lil's business. Each time the mailing label report is used, Access extracts the current information from the database. The design is saved and reused, but the data will always be current.

In these exercises, you show Henry how to use the Label Wizard to design and print the single-serving candy box labels that he needs, sorted by postal code. He loads the label stock into the printer, and sits down to watch you create his labels.

Start the Label Wizard

1. In the Database window, be sure the reports list is displayed.
2. On the Database window toolbar, click the New button.

   The New Report dialog box appears.

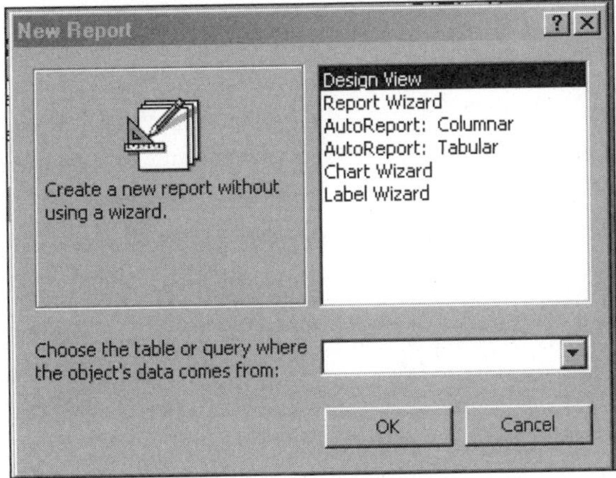

3. In the list at the top of the New Report dialog box, select Label Wizard.

4. In the list at the bottom of the New Report dialog box, click the drop-down arrow and select Customers.

   The Customers table contains all of Sweet Lil's customer information, including names and addresses.

5. Click OK.

   The first page of the Label Wizard appears.

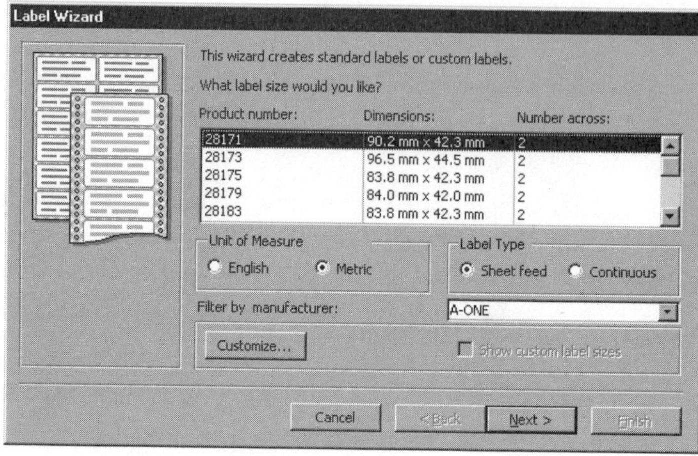

Select a standard mailing label

If none of the listed labels meets your needs, you can define a custom label in the dimensions that match your label stock.

Access comes with an extensive library of standard label formats, listed by manufacturer and dimensions in either English (inch) or metric (millimeter) measurements, for both sheet feed and continuous feed printing.

Henry Czynski tells you that the Avery 5160 1-inch by 2⅝-inch sheet-feed label, with three columns of labels per sheet, is the most suitable label stock for the Sweet Lil's single-serving candy box.

1. In the Filter By Manufacturer list box, select Avery.
2. Click English as the unit of measure.
3. Select product number 5160.
4. Click Next.

The second page of the Label Wizard appears.

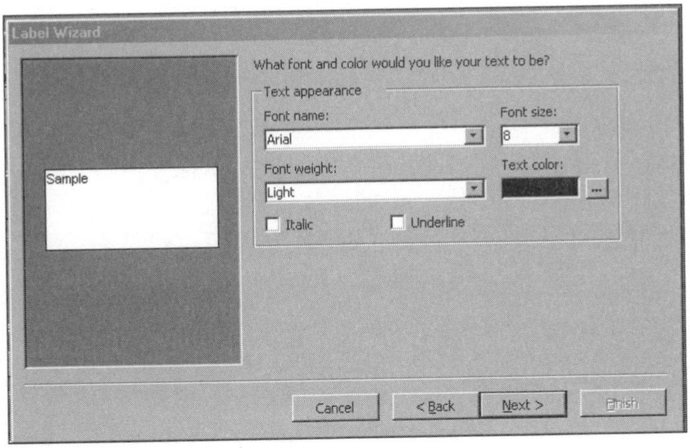

Refining the Look of Labels

For your labels, you can select any font available on your computer and any color available on your default printer. The font selection may vary, depending on the capabilities of the default printer; for example, some printers provide a wider range of point sizes or formatting options, such as bold or italic, for the same font than other printers do.

Define the text appearance of labels

To make the mailing labels look as distinctive and friendly as possible, befitting Sweet Lil's image, Henry suggests using an italic, 9-point Century Gothic Light font.

1. On the second page of the Label Wizard, select Century Gothic Light in the Font Name list.

   The font of the word *Sample* in the sample box changes to Century Gothic Light.

> **important**
>
> Century Gothic Light is a standard font in Microsoft Windows 98. If you don't find it in your font list, substitute a font that is available on your computer.

2. In the Font Size list, select 9.

   The font size of the word *Sample* in the sample box changes to 9 points.

3. Select the Italic check box.

   The font style of the word *Sample* in the sample changes to italic text.

4. Click Next.

   The third page of the Label Wizard appears.

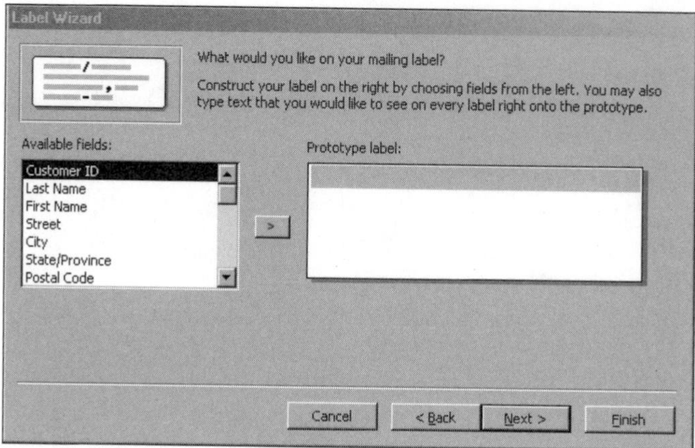

Define the layout of labels

You can select any field from the Customers table and place it on the Label Wizard's prototype label in the order that you want the corresponding information to be printed. Henry confirms that the Sweet Lil's shipping department uses a four-line layout consisting of the customer's full name, followed by a standard two-line address, and the country name. You reproduce that layout here. A shaded bar shows you the line of print you'll be filling in on the label.

> **tip**
>
> The Sweet Lil's layout requires only four lines of text, but the Avery 5160 label holds five lines of 9-point text. This gives you a margin of error, should one of the four lines exceed the length of the smaller-than-usual label format when filled in with the corresponding information.

You can also select the field name, and then click Add.

1. On the third page of the Label Wizard, double-click FirstName in the Available Fields list.

   The FirstName field is added to the first line of the prototype label, and the insertion point appears at the end of the field.

2. Press the Spacebar.

   A blank space appears after the FirstName field on the prototype label.

If you make a mistake, select the line on the prototype label and press Backspace to remove your typing.

3. In the Available Fields list, double-click LastName.

   The LastName field is added after the FirstName field on the first line of the prototype label, with a space between the two fields.

4. At the end of the first line of the prototype label, press Enter.

   The insertion point and shaded bar move to the second line of the prototype label.

5. On the second line, add the Street field and then press Enter.
6. On the third line, add the City, StateOrProvince, and PostalCode fields. Type a comma and space between the City and StateOrProvince fields and a space between the StateOrProvince and PostalCode fields. Press Enter.
7. On the fourth line, add the Country field.
8. Click Next.

   The fourth page of the Label Wizard appears.

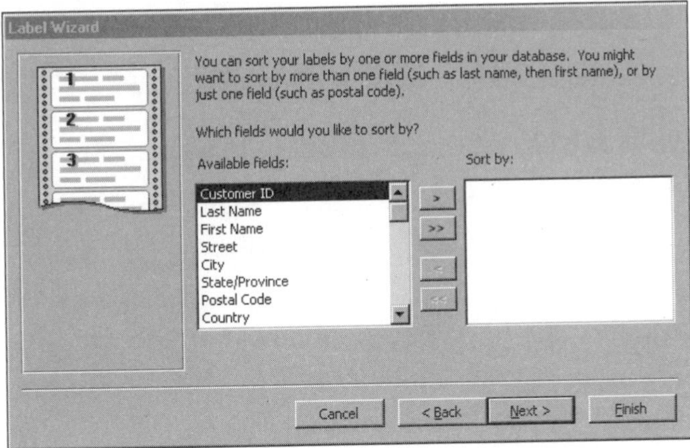

Sorting Labels by Fields

You can sort by any field in the Customers table. You can even sort by multiple fields. For example, you could sort by last name and then first name, to get all the labels in alphabetic order by last name and all the labels with the same last name in alphabetic order by first name.

Sort mailing labels

To group together all the boxes addressed to the same area, as Henry requested, you sort the labels by their postal code.

1. On the fourth page of the Label Wizard, double-click PostalCode in the Available Fields list.

   The PostalCode field is added to the Sort By list.

2. Click Next.

   The final page of the Label Wizard appears. Access 2000 suggests a name, *Labels Customers,* for the mailing labels report and gives you the option of previewing the mailing labels or modifying the label design.

Create a label report and print labels

Now that he's helped to create a label design, you show Henry that he can save the design and print the labels at any time.

1. On the final page of the Label Wizard, be sure the See The Labels As They Will Look Printed option is selected and click Finish.

   The mailing label report is saved as Labels Customers and is displayed in Print Preview.

Print

2. On the Print Preview toolbar, click the Print button.

   Access prints the Labels Customers report directly onto the label stock Henry has loaded into the printer.

Close

3. On the Report window, click the Close button to close the report.

One Step Further Creating More Complex Filters

Six months ago, Impact Public Relations launched a Sweet Lil's marketing campaign in Canada. Now it's time to evaluate how successful it's been, before deciding whether to expand the campaign into the United States. To do this, you can use filters to set criteria for just the Canadian orders that have been placed since the marketing campaign began.

Create a complex filter using Advanced Filter/Sort

The Canadian campaign began on November 15, 1998. To see only the records relevant to the campaign, you must create a filter that shows only Canadian customers added on or after November 15, 1998.

1. In the Database window, click Forms on the Objects bar to display the forms list.
2. In the forms list, double-click Customer Review.

   The Customer Review form opens in Form view.

Filter By Form

Filter By Form works differently in Form view than in Datasheet view.

3. On the Form View toolbar, click the Filter By Form button.

   The Filter By Form dialog box appears, with the Look For tab active. The Filter/Sort toolbar replaces the Database toolbar.
4. Click the Country field, click the drop-down arrow, and then select Canada.

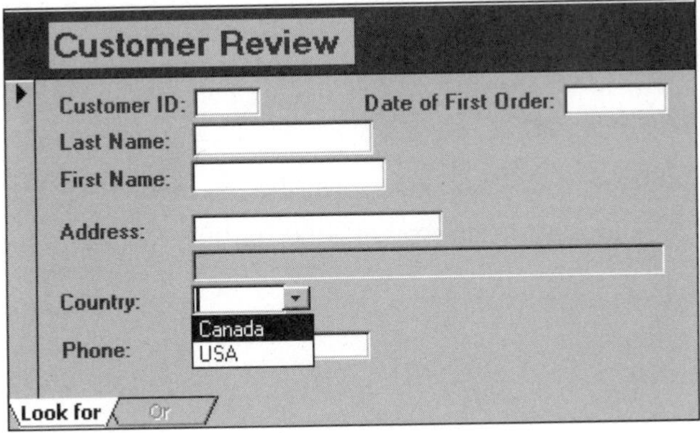

Canada appears as a criterion in the Filter By Form dialog box. You could run a simple filter now by clicking the Apply Filter button on the Filter/Sort toolbar, but you first must add another criterion and set a sort order to get the specific information that you need for your evaluation of Canadian sales data.

5. On the Filter menu, click Advanced Filter/Sort.

   The Filter window opens, displaying the filter criteria you set in the Filter By Form dialog box. Now you can add a filter for the order date, and sort the filtered records into reverse chronological order.

6. Move to the first empty field in the Filter criteria grid. Click the Field drop-down arrow, and then select DateOfFirstOrder.

An expression is a formula that calculates a value.

7. Click in the Sort cell of the DateOfFirstOrder column.
8. Click the Sort drop-down arrow, and then select Descending.
9. In the Criteria cell of the DateOfFirstOrder column, type the expression **>=15-Nov-98** and then press Enter.

   This expression means *on or after November 15, 1998.* After you enter the expression, Microsoft Access converts it to >=*#11/15/98#* to indicate that it's a date/time value.

Apply Filter

10. Click the Apply Filter button.

    In the filtered view you see only the new orders placed in Canada during the campaign.

11. Close the Customer Review form.

    Advanced filter criteria are saved for future reference. These criteria will be displayed the next time you use Advanced Filter/Sort. You may accept them or delete them and apply other criteria at that time.

Based on the disappointingly low number of orders in response to the Canadian campaign, you decide not to expand the campaign into the United States.

Finish the lesson

1. To continue to the next lesson, on the File menu, click Close.
2. If you're finished using Access 2000 for now, on the File menu, click Exit.

Lesson 3 Quick Reference

To	Do this	Button
Sort records in a filter	Select a field, and then click the appropriate Sort button.	
Set criteria for a filter	Select an example of the criteria on the form or datasheet.	
Set criteria for an advanced filter	In the Filter criteria grid, select a field and enter an expression.	
Apply a filter by selection	Set one criterion per field in the form or datasheet, and then click the Filter By Selection button on the Datasheet View toolbar.	
Apply a filter by form	Set one criterion per field in the form or datasheet, and then click the Filter By Form button on the Datashet View toolbar. Select one item in a field or fields, and then click the Apply Filter button on the Filter/Sort toolbar.	
Remove a filter by form after applying it	Click Remove Filter on the Datasheet View toolbar.	
Open a report	Click Reports on the Objects bar of the Database window, and then double-click the report you want.	
Zoom in or out on a report	Click anywhere in the Print Preview view.	
View two pages	Click the Two Pages button on the Print Preview toolbar.	
Print an entire report	Click the Print button on the Print Preview toolbar.	
Print specific report pages	On the File menu, click Print, and then enter the page numbers you want to print.	
Create mailing labels	Click Reports on the Objects bar of the Database window. Click the New button on the Database window toolbar, select Label Wizard, and follow the instructions.	

Managing Database Change

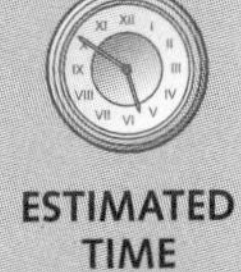

ESTIMATED TIME **45 min.**

In this lesson you will learn how to:

- ✔ *Determine when a new table is needed.*
- ✔ *Create a table with the Table Wizard.*
- ✔ *Design and modify a table.*
- ✔ *Define the fields in a table.*
- ✔ *Change field properties.*
- ✔ *Create database relationships.*
- ✔ *Combine data from several related tables.*

The only thing that remains constant is change. Over time, your needs and interests shift as you grow and develop. Information that was once of great importance may become unnecessary or even distracting, while information that was once of no use or interest may suddenly become vital. As the amount of information in your life or business increases, you may need to reorganize or redistribute it in order to keep track of it all. You may find that you must purchase a new bookcase, new file folders, or even an entire set of new file cabinets to cover a new area of interest.

The same is true of your database. When you begin one, the data can be managed almost at a glance, but as the data grows, you must change views or apply filters to make sense of it. When something changes significantly, you may have to modify a portion of the database to track that change. For example, you might have an address table that lists names, street addresses, phone numbers, and fax numbers. It will prove inadequate after you start making contacts through the Web, unless you can add new fields for e-mail addresses and Web sites.

Sweet Lil's has grown to the point that it's having trouble meeting customer needs. The management has identified the problem, but needs you to implement the solution. In this lesson, you'll create a new database table, define its fields, add and modify fields to meet changing needs, and create new relationships within a database.

Start Microsoft Access 2000 and reopen the database

- If Access 2000 isn't started yet, start it. Open the Sweet Lil's database. If the Microsoft Access window doesn't fill your screen, maximize the window.

  If you need help opening the database, see Lesson 1, "Using Forms."

Modifying Database Tables

When your database doesn't include information that you need to track, it's time to expand it. This may be as simple as adding a new field or even just a single new record to an existing table. It might, however, involve the creation of an entirely new table.

Often, you'll add a new table to an existing database in response to some new or unforeseen need. In most cases, the nature of the need dictates the organization of the new information.

For example, the Sweet Lil's database is currently organized into 11 tables, each of which covers a different topic or entity within the database—basket details, baskets, bonbons, box details, boxes, credit customers, customers, employees, order details, orders, and shipping. Each record in each table describes an individual unit or unique item of that entity, such as a particular customer or a certain type of bonbon. Each field in each record describes a different characteristic or attribute of that item—the name of a particular customer or the filling in a certain type of bonbon.

Whenever you create a table, ideally you should already have the entity it represents clearly in mind, along with a concise definition of all the fields needed for each record. Each record should contain all the information needed to describe the item it represents. You will be designing a better table by defining the fields needed, determining the type of data you want to store, and thinking about special restrictions or field properties.

Sweet Lil's is growing rapidly, but so are customer demands. Customers expect gift orders to be delivered within two or three days. To meet these demands, Sweet Lil's must speed up delivery.

The shipping coordinator, Fred Mallon, determined that the main bottleneck in delivery was the reliance on a single shipping company. He has made arrangements with two more companies, both offering air delivery service, to eliminate the bottleneck and expedite deliveries. Fred has been using a Shipping table to store each company's shipping costs to various regions, but there's currently no address information on the companies themselves. Adding that information to the existing Shipping table would be inefficient, because one carrier can have many different shipping charges depending on where the item is shipped, so the same address information would have to be entered many times. This indicates that the information Fred needs is not directly relevant to the Shipping table—what he needs is a new table.

Fred requires the new table for tracking information on the three shipping companies Sweet Lil's now uses. This new Carriers table should be linked to the existing Shipping table so that cost information is available if needed, without compromising the existing table.

In the following exercises, you'll show Fred how to create the new Carriers table using the Table Wizard and working in Design view. You will also show him how to create a relationship between the Carriers and Shipping tables.

Using the Table Wizard

Access 2000 can help you create a new table. Using the Table Wizard is a quick way to add a new table to an existing database. You can select the fields that reflect the attributes of each item in the new table. If you don't think of all the fields you need while working in the Table Wizard field list, you can add them later in Design view.

Standard Field Naming Convention

Although Access 2000 allows spaces and punctuation in field names, there's a standardized naming convention to which your field names must conform if you plan to use your data in other database programs. Since you can't be sure when you might need to share data, you should only use letters and numbers, without spaces or punctuation, in field names.

For database programs (like Access) that allow mixed uppercase and lowercase letters, multiple-word field names use capitalization to distinguish words in a field name. For example, First Name would be FirstName, with the two words in the field name distinguished by capitalization. For database programs that only use uppercase letters, multiple-word field names use the underscore (_) character to separate words in a field name. For example, First Name would be FIRST_NAME, with the two words in the field name separated by an underscore instead of a space.

The name that appears on the form label or datasheet column heading does not need to be the same as the field name. Each field has a Caption property, which determines the name that's displayed as a label or column heading. For example, a CustID field with a Caption property set to Customer ID will display Customer ID on forms and datasheets, but will still use CustID as the actual field name for queries and relationships.

Create a table using the Table Wizard

In this exercise, you show Fred how to use the Table Wizard to add a Carriers table to the Sweet Lil's database. Fred has prepared for creating the new table by listing the relevant attributes that describe a shipping company's address: the company's name, a street address, a city, a state or province, and a postal code. With this clear definition in hand, you are now ready to create the new Carriers table for Fred.

1. In the Database window, click Tables on the Objects bar to display the tables list.

2. In the tables list, double-click Create Table By Using Wizard.

   The first page of the Table Wizard appears.

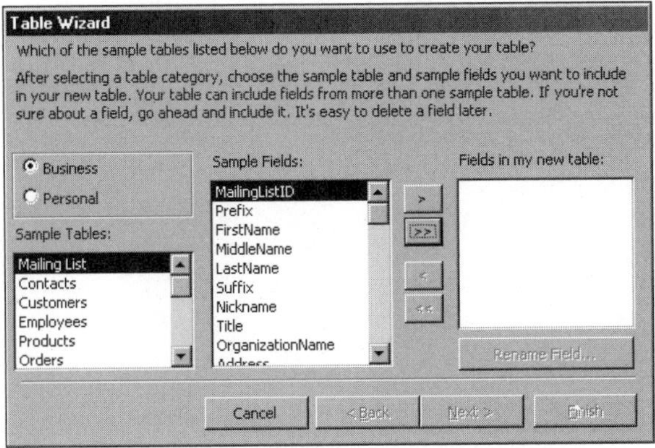

3. On the first page of the Table Wizard, be sure the Business option is selected, and in the Sample Tables list, select Suppliers.
4. In the Sample Fields list, double-click the fields that most closely match Fred's list.

Fred's List	Sample Field
Carrier Name	SupplierName
Street Address	Address
City Address	City
State Address	StateOrProvince
Postal Code	PostalCode

   As you select each field, it appears in the Fields In My New Table list.
5. In the Fields In My New Table list, select SupplierName, and then click Rename Field.

   The Rename Field dialog box appears.
6. In the Rename Field dialog box, type **CarrierName** and then press Enter.

   The Rename Field dialog box closes.

7. Repeat steps 5 and 6, changing the StateOrProvince field name to **State**
8. Click Next.

   The second page of the Table Wizard appears, with Suppliers selected in the What Do You Want To Name Your Table? box.

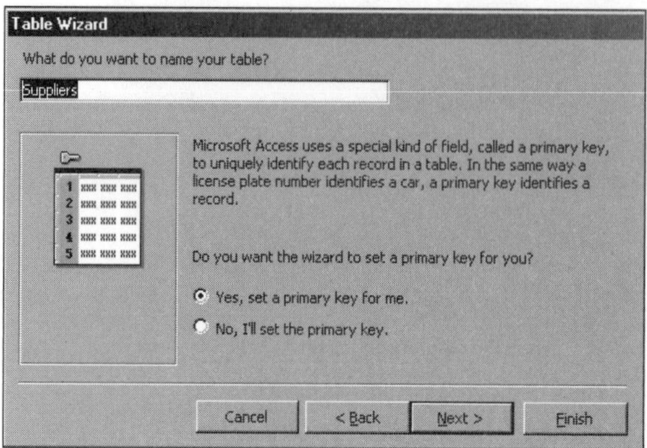

9. In the What Do You Want To Name Your Table? box, type **Carriers**
10. Be sure the Yes, Set A Primary Key For Me option is selected, and then click Next.

    The third page of the Table Wizard dialog box appears. You tell Fred that at this point the Carriers table doesn't require any relationship with any other table.

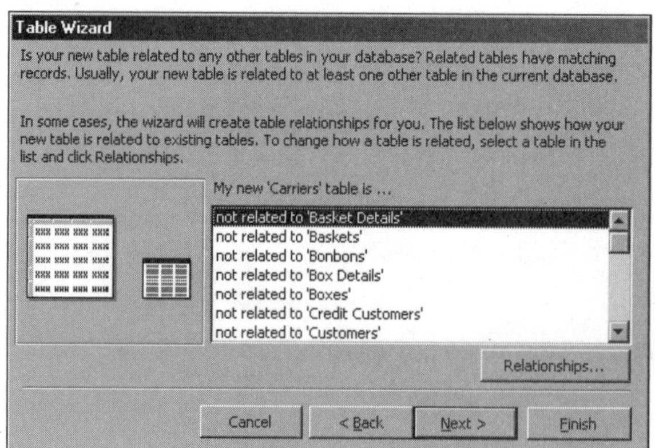

11. Click Next again, and when the last page of the Table Wizard appears, click Finish.

    The Carriers table opens in Datasheet view. The new table contains all the fields you selected, plus an automatically numbered CarriersID field, which is set as the primary key. Every record will now have a unique identification number, represented by the contents of the CarriersID field.

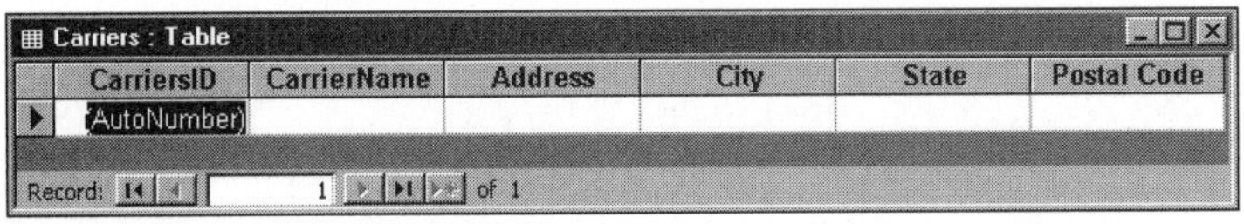

    Carriers : Table

CarriersID	CarrierName	Address	City	State	Postal Code
(AutoNumber)					

    Record: 1 of 1

12. Close the Carriers table.

The Primary Key

A *primary key* is a field or group of fields that uniquely identifies each record in a table. No two records in a given table can have the same value in their primary key field. An employee identification number is often used as a primary key in accounting systems because every employee must have one, and every one is unique.

Primary key fields serve a number of purposes. Because the primary key field uniquely identifies each record in the table, the primary key is used to create a *relationship* between tables, allowing all the records in one table to be matched to the records in another. In the absence of a specific sort order, records in a table are sorted by the primary key field.

A primary key can consist of one or more fields. Multiple-field primary keys are used when the value in the field chosen as the primary key can't be unique. For example, the Shipping table lists each carrier more than once because each carrier has a different charge for each area, so the carrier doesn't uniquely identify a record. But, because there's only one delivery route from a given carrier to a given area, the combination of carrier and area does uniquely identify a record.

Access 2000 has an *AutoNumber* feature that assigns a unique number to each record as it's created. AutoNumber fields are thus well suited for use as primary keys. It's usually easiest and safest to let Access 2000 use the AutoNumber field as the primary key.

Changing a Table in Design View

With Access, you have a number of ways to create new tables—letting the Table Wizard guide you, using Design view, and even typing directly into a blank datasheet. No matter which approach you take, at some point you will probably need to change a table design. The best place to make these changes is in Design view.

Now that you have finished creating the Carriers table using the Table Wizard, Fred has asked you to show him how to add a field that will indicate whether the shipping company provides air delivery service. In the following exercises, you show Fred how to add the AirDelivery field in Design view.

Add a field in Design view

1. In the Database window, verify Tables on the Objects bar is selected.
2. In the tables list, verify Carriers is selected, and then click the Design button on the Database window toolbar.

   The Carriers table opens in Design view, with the names and data types of the Carriers table fields listed in the grid in the upper portion of the window. The properties of the selected field are shown in the Field Properties in the lower portion of the window. The Table Design toolbar replaces the Database toolbar.

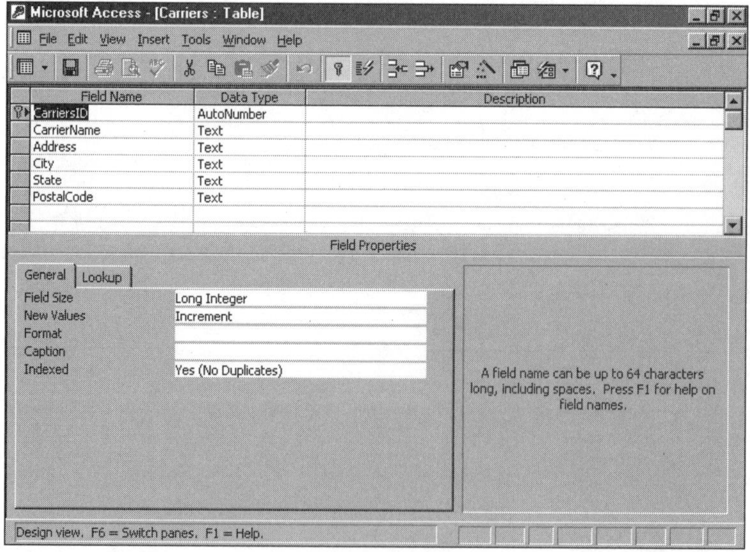

3. In the grid, click the Field Name cell of the first empty row.

   The triangular record indicator appears in the record selector.

4. Type **AirDelivery** and then press Tab.

   When you press Tab, the highlighted word *Text* and a drop-down arrow appear in the Data Type cell of that row. Information about that field also appears in the property sheet.

5. In the Data Type cell of the AirDelivery row, click the drop-down arrow, and then select Yes/No.

   The data type changes to Yes/No. The change is reflected in the property sheet.

Save

6. On the toolbar, click the Save button.

   The changes are saved, but you want to show them to Fred.

View

7. Click the View button to switch to Datasheet View.

   The new field, Air Delivery, containing a check box, now appears in the datasheet. You may need to scroll to the right to see the new field.

Entering Data Using an AutoForm

With the Carriers table now complete, Fred is ready to enter the data he's compiled for the first three carriers. You remind him that data should always be entered using a form, and you tell him that data entry forms are easy to create. Because his form is very basic, requiring no special formatting or controls, he can use the AutoForm feature to create the form.

> **important**
>
> In the following exercise, you can edit as much as necessary within a record, but be careful not to delete a record and begin it all over again. If you enter one record, delete it, and then reenter it, the CarrierID number will be different than intended. Understanding the data type of autonumber will explain this. An autonumber data type does the work of entering a unique, sequential number into a field. It increments by 1 for each record and never reuses a value once it is deleted. In the Carriers table, the CarrierID uses the autonumber data type. Since CarrierID is also the primary key field for the record, it is the unique identifier. When relating tables, the primary key field is used to link two tables that share a common field. The contents of the common field must be identical. For this reason, be careful in the following exercise not to delete a record in the Carriers table.

Create an AutoForm and enter data

New Object: AutoForm

1. On the Table Datasheet toolbar, click the New Object: AutoForm button.

   The new Carriers form appears with (AutoNumber) already selected in the CarriersID field. The Table Datasheet toolbar becomes the Form View toolbar, and the Formatting (Form/Report) toolbar appears below it. On the Form View toolbar, the New Object: AutoForm button becomes the New Object: Table button.

> **tip**
>
> The New Object toolbar button can create any Access 2000 object: AutoForm, AutoReport, AutoPage, table, query, form, report, page, macro, module, or class module. Like the View toolbar button, the New Object button and the corresponding ToolTip change when you change views.

Because the CarriersID is already assigned in the Shipping table, the carriers must be entered in the same order to create a match.

2. Press Tab to move to the CarrierName field, and type **Wild Fargo Carriers**

   When you start typing, the CarriersID field is filled in automatically.

3. Fill out the rest of the form, pressing Tab to move from field to field. (For this record, leave the AirDelivery check box clear to indicate No; press Tab twice to skip over it and start a new record.)

Address:	**410 NE 84th Street**
City:	**Chicago**
State:	**IL**
PostalCode:	**606574512**
AirDelivery:	**No**

   The predefined PostalCode field is already formatted for ZIP+4—the numbers are automatically separated into two groups.

4. Enter the information for the two remaining carrier records. To select the AirDelivery check box, press the Spacebar.

CarrierName:	**Grey Goose Express**	**Pegasus Overnight**
Address:	**100 Day Street**	**45908 Airport Way**
City:	**New York**	**Dallas**
State:	**NY**	**TX**
PostalCode:	**123781701**	**786545908**
AirDelivery:	**Yes**	**Yes**

AutoForm allows you to create a form whenever you need one. You can discard the AutoForm when you're finished with it.

5. Close the new Carriers form.

   A message appears, confirming that you want to save the changes to the new form.

6. Click No.

   The new Carriers form closes, and the Carriers table reappears in Datasheet view.

Refresh the table data

Fred is impressed with the AutoForm feature, but when the new Carriers form closes he's puzzled—the Carriers table is still empty! Where are the three new records you just entered?

You explain that because the Carriers table was still open while you were entering the data, the table displayed on the screen is no longer current. The simplest way to update the data in the table is to close and open the table.

1. Close the Carriers table.
2. In the tables list of the Database window, double-click Carriers.

   The Carriers table appears, displaying three new records.

3. Close the Carriers table.

Improving Data Entry and Display

Access 2000 sets *properties*, or attributes, of a field to define the characteristics of the field and how data is entered and displayed in the field. When you create a table using the Table Wizard or a form using the Form Wizard or AutoForm, Access 2000 sets many of the field properties for you. For example, when you selected the predefined PostalCode field from the Table Wizard, the field was already formatted for ZIP+4. The most visible properties of a field are its data type and its display format.

The *data type* is another kind of attribute. It establishes the kind of data that the field can accept—text, numbers, dates and times, yes-or-no data, monetary amounts—or whether it can accept user-entered data at all. For example, the AutoNumber data type fills the field with a predetermined number that can't be changed.

Each data type has a set of associated properties. For example, the Text and Number data types have a Field Size property that sets the maximum number of letters or the type of number that you can store in the field. The Yes/No data type doesn't have a Field Size property, however, because it can accept only two values.

The *display format* determines how the data is displayed and printed. This format is often associated with the data type. For example, the Text, Memo, Number, Currency, Date/Time, and Yes/No data types have predefined formats that are also associated with the regional settings determined in Control Panel. These predefined formats may be changed at any time or overridden entirely by changing the properties of the field in which the data is displayed. For example, by changing the Format field property, a Yes/No text box can be made to display True and False or On and Off instead.

Other properties might also affect the display format. For example, a field with a Yes/No data type can be displayed as a check box, a text box, or a combo box by changing the Display Control field property.

important

Changing the Display Control field property changes only the format of the data as it is entered into the form. The format in which data is presented to or accepted from the user is independent of the format in which Access 2000 processes it. For example, the currency format displays an entry as a monetary value of $4.81 even if it was entered as 4.8142. Access stores the value as entered and displays it according to the format.

Set field properties

Fred has a problem with the new Carriers table: it's too easy to accidentally select or clear the AirDelivery check box with a stray click of the mouse. He likes the idea of an either-or control, but he'd prefer that at least two steps be required to change it, not just a single mouse click. He'd also prefer to see the words *Yes* and *No* when looking up the information. In this exercise, you help Fred turn the check box into a combo box by changing the Display Control field property.

1. Verify that the Carriers table is displayed in Datasheet view.
2. Click the View button on the Table Datasheet toolbar.
3. In the grid, click anywhere in the AirDelivery row.

   The AirDelivery field properties appear in the property sheet.

4. In the Field Properties, click the Lookup tab.

   Check Box appears in the Display Control property box.

5. Click in the Display Control property box, click the drop-down arrow, and then select Combo Box.

   After you have set the Display Control property to Combo Box, the default control in the table and on any new forms based on the table becomes a combo box. The Field Properties reflects this change, displaying nine other properties that apply to combo boxes (and not to check boxes).

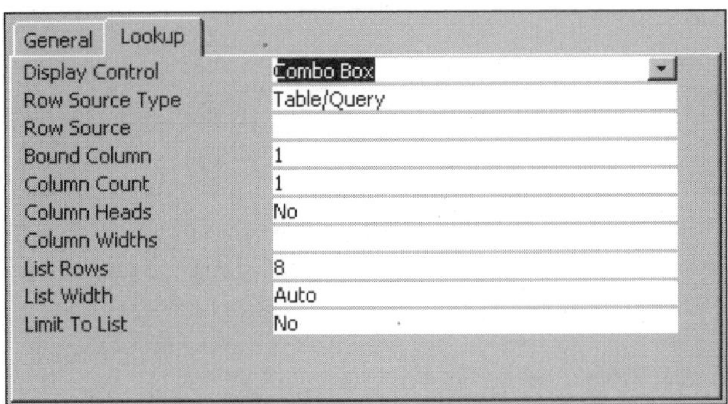

6. Click in the Row Source Type property box, click the drop-down arrow, and then select Value List.

   This tells Access 2000 to use a predefined list of values in the combo box.

7. In the Row Source property box, type **No;Yes**

   This creates the predefined list of values for the combo box: No or Yes, with No as the default value.

View

8. Save your changes, and then click the View button on the Table Design toolbar to switch to Datasheet view.

   The words *Yes* and *No* now appear in the AirDelivery field. You may need to scroll to the right to view the field.

New Object: AutoForm

9. On the Table Datasheet toolbar, click the New Object: AutoForm button to create a form for testing the new AirDelivery combo box in Form view.

   The AirDelivery field is now a combo box that lets you select Yes or No.

10. Close the Carriers table.

Connecting a New Table to a Database

When you add a new table, it's important that you understand how the new table will interact with existing tables. For the data in the table to be useful, you must incorporate it into the database by establishing logical links or *relationships* to other tables. Relationships are used to collect data from several tables and place them in a single form, report, or query. Once you do create a relationship between specific tables, you can use the relationship to combine data from one table with data in the other table, following the lines of that relationship.

For example, the relationships between the Bonbons, Basket Details, and Baskets tables allow information from the Bonbons and Basket Details tables to be combined into the Baskets subform and added to the Baskets form. When a bonbon ID for a given basket is selected in the Baskets subform, the corresponding bonbon name, chocolate type, filling type, nut type, and cost are drawn from the related Bonbons table, and the corresponding quantity is drawn from the related Basket Details table. The BonbonCost and Quantity fields are then used to calculate the total basket cost on the Baskets form.

Understanding Table Relationships

Access 2000 creates *relational databases:* databases that combine data from multiple tables. It does this by means of relationships between the various tables of a database. After you create tables and let Access 2000 set a primary key for each table, you can create relationships between the tables to collect data from several tables and place it all in a single form, report, or query.

Between two tables, you can create one of two types of relationship: one-to-many or one-to-one.

The most common relationship is the *one-to-many* relationship, in which one record in one table can be related to many records in another table. For example, one customer can place many orders; each record in the Customers table can therefore be related to many records in the Orders table. In a one-to-many relationship, the table on the "one" side is termed the *primary table,* and the table on the "many" side is the *related table*. In the above example, the Customers table is the primary table and the Orders table is the related table.

A table can be the related table in one relationship and the primary table in a different relationship.

The primary table in the relationship can have many matching records in the related table. Creating a link between the primary key field in the primary table and a field that has a matching value—called a *foreign key* field—in the related table is what establishes the relationship between the two. For example, the CarriersID field in the Carriers table matches the CarriersID field in the Shipping table, so a relationship can be made between the two tables. One carrier can have many different shipping charges, depending on where the item is being shipped, so the Carriers table is the primary table in a one-to-many relationship with the related Shipping table.

In the far less common one-to-one relationship, one record in the primary table can have only one matching record in the related table. For example, a new table of bonbon recipes could only have a *one-to-one* relationship with the existing Bonbons table, because the recipe for each bonbon is unique.

Access 2000 uses a system of rules to create *referential integrity* between tables, which ensures that relationships between records in related tables are valid and that you don't accidentally delete or change related data. For example, you must match a carrier in the Carriers table for every shipping charge in the Shipping table to enable the relationship between the two tables to work properly. Referential integrity prohibits any changes to the primary table that would invalidate records in the related table. Referential integrity also prevents the entry of a related record that doesn't have an associated primary record. For instance, it prevents the entry of an order record for a customer that does not exist in the database. A record without an associated primary record is called an *orphan*.

After you create a relationship between two tables, you can't modify or delete the fields on which the relationship is based without first deleting the relationship.

Creating a Relationship

The primary tool for creating and managing relationships in Access 2000 is the Relationships window. It lets you create simple relationships, and is ideally suited for creating complex relationships, especially when:

- Referential integrity is required.
- The primary key includes more than one field.
- There's no matching field common to the two tables.

The Relationships window allows you to join matching fields that have either the same or different names, and to see the relationships that you create in a graphical, "big picture" overview.

The Shipping table has information about the cost to ship from one region to another and the Carriers table has information about the shipping companies. To find out how much it costs to deliver a box of bonbons, you must know where and by whom it's being shipped. Since the shipping charge is the amount charged by a given carrier to ship to a given area, and each carrier ships to more than one area, the procedure for finding the charge is to look up the carrier, then the area, and then the charge. Each carrier serves many areas, with a different charge for each area, so there's a one-to-many relationship between the Carriers information and the Shipping information.

To combine the new information about the carriers with the existing information about the shipping charges, Fred must establish a relationship between the new Carriers table and the existing Shipping table. In the following exercises, you help Fred create a one-to-many relationship between the Carriers and Shipping tables, using the Relationships window and Relationship toolbar.

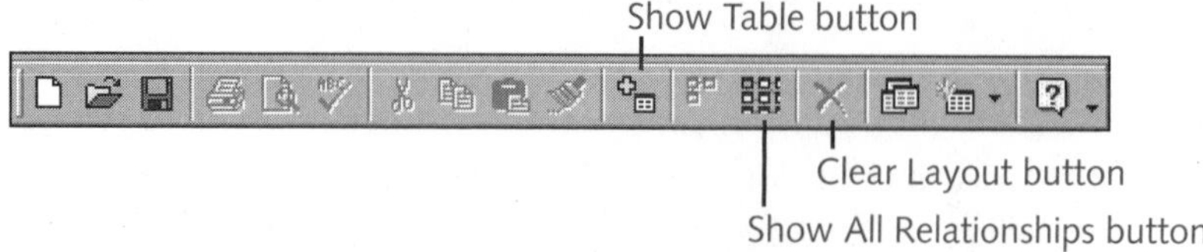

Lay out tables in the Relationships window

Before Fred adds, alters, or deletes a relationship between the Carriers and Shipping tables, he needs to know what relationships (if any) already exist. In this exercise, you show Fred how to open the Relationships window and lay out the Carriers and Shipping tables. The Relationships window will show him how the two tables are related.

1. Verify that all tables and forms are closed.

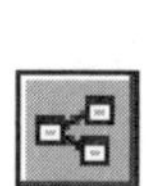

Relationships

2. On the Database toolbar, click the Relationships button.

   The Relationships window opens. The Relationship toolbar replaces the Database toolbar.

Clear Layout

3. If anything appears in the Relationships window, click the Clear Layout button on the Relationship toolbar, and then click Yes in the confirmation message.

   The Relationships window should be empty before you begin.

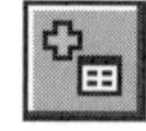

Show Table

4. On the Relationship toolbar, click the Show Table button.

   The Show Table dialog box appears.

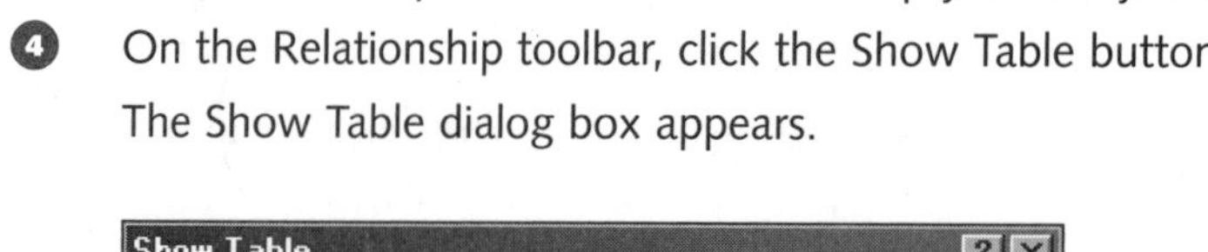

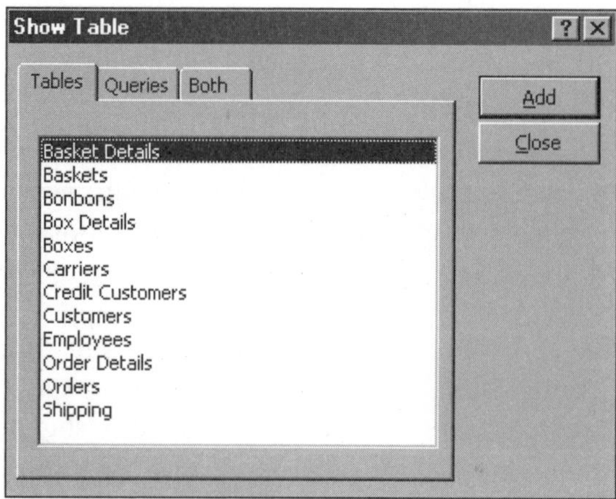

5. In the Show Table dialog box, be sure the Tables tab is active, and then double-click Carriers in the tables list.

   The Carriers field list appears in the Relationships window, with the CarriersID primary key field selected.

6. In the Show Table dialog box, double-click the Shipping table.

   The Shipping field list appears in the Relationships window, with the CarriersID primary key field selected. (This field will be the foreign key in this relationship.) If the table is not visible, drag the Show Table dialog box aside.

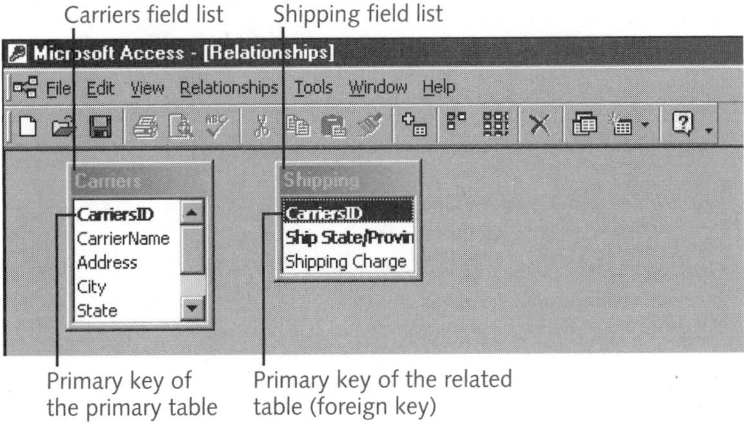

7. Close the Show Table dialog box.

Create a relationship between two tables

To combine the new information about the carriers with the existing information about the shipping charges, Fred must establish a relationship between the new Carriers table and the existing Shipping table. In this exercise, you show Fred how to relate the Carriers and Shipping tables.

> **important**
>
> In this exercise, the direction in which you drag the key field determines which is the primary table and which is the related table. The table from which you drag the field is always set as the primary table, and the table to which you drag the field is always set as the related table.

1. In the Relationships window, drag the CarriersID field from the Carriers field list to the CarriersID field in the Shipping field list.

   The Edit Relationships dialog box appears, and One-To-Many appears in the Relationship Type box.

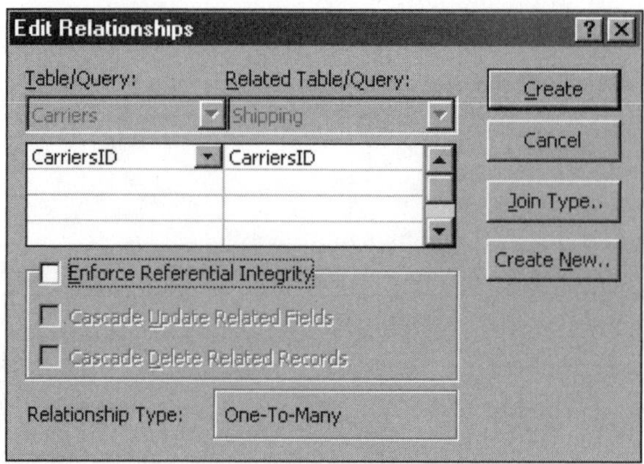

Referential integrity prevents orphan records.

2. In the Edit Relationships dialog box, select the Enforce Referential Integrity check box.
3. Click Create.

   The Edit Relationships dialog box closes. The Carriers table is now related to the Shipping table, as indicated by a line linking the matching fields in both tables. Near the line, the *1* beside the Carriers field list and the ∞ (infinity symbol) beside the Shipping field list show that it's a one-to-many relationship. The relationship remains intact until you delete it.

To delete a relationship, click the join line linking the related fields, and then press Delete.

The layout in the Relationships window is a visual aid. Saving or deleting the layout has no effect on the database.

4. Close the Relationships window.

   A message appears, confirming that you want to save changes to the Relationships layout.

 Click Yes.

The layout you just created is saved and will reappear whenever you open the Relationships window, until you clear or modify the layout and save those changes.

Relate a multiple-field primary key to a matching key

Now that he's created a relationship between the Carriers and Shipping tables, Fred realizes that a similar relationship between the Shipping table and the Orders table would make it possible to automate the process of looking up an order's shipping charge. The CarriersID and ShipStateOrProvince fields in the Orders table can be used to find the related carrier name in the Carriers table and the related shipping charge in the Shipping table.

To create a relationship between the Shipping and Orders tables, you must relate the primary key of the Shipping table to the related key in the Orders table. The primary key of the Shipping table consists of *two* fields—CarriersID and ShipStateOrProvince—because the primary key has to be unique. Shipping charges are based on both the carrier and the delivery area, so both must be included in the key. The Shipping table lists the same carrier and the same delivery area multiple times because each carrier has a different charge for each area. But because there's only one delivery route from a given carrier to a given area, the combination of carrier and area is unique.

To create a relationship when the primary table has a multiple-field primary key, you must relate all the fields of the primary key in the primary table to matching fields in the related table. (The related table must already have fields that match those of the primary table key.)

In this exercise, you show Fred how to create a relationship between the multiple-field primary key of the Shipping table and the matching data in the Orders tables.

1. On the Database toolbar, click the Relationships button.

Show Table

2. On the Relationships toolbar, click the Show Table button.

   The Show Table dialog box appears.

3. In the Show Table dialog box, click the Tables tab, double-click the Orders table, and then close the Show Table dialog box.

   The Orders field list appears in the Relationships window, with the OrderID primary key selected.

Fields with different names can be related as long as their data type and field size are the same.

4. In the Relationships window, drag the CarriersID field from the Shipping field list to the CarriersID field in the Orders field list.

   The Edit Relationships dialog box appears, and Indeterminate appears in the Relationship Type box.

5. In the Table/Query list, click the first empty field below the CarriersID field.

   A drop-down arrow appears next to the empty field.

You can relate any number of matching fields between the primary and related tables.

6. Click the drop-down arrow next to the empty field, and then select ShipStateOrProvince from the list.
7. In the Related Table/Query list, click the first empty field below the CarriersID field.
8. Click the drop-down arrow and then select ShipStateOrProvince from the list.

   One-To-Many appears in the Relationship Type box.

Because it's impossible to maintain full correspondence between the ShipStateOrProvince fields in both tables here, Enforce Referential Integrity should not be selected.

9. Click Create.

   The Edit Relationships dialog box closes. The CarriersID and ShipStateOrProvince fields in the Shipping table are now related to the matching fields in the Orders table. You may have to scroll through or resize the Orders list to view the relationship between the two fields.

10. Close the Relationships window and click Yes at the message to save the layout.

One Step Further Combining Data from Related Tables Using a Query

For more information about creating and using queries, see Lesson 5, "Using Queries."

Fred has created a relationship between the Carriers and Shipping tables and another relationship between the Shipping and Orders tables. Because of the interrelationships among these three tables, he can now automate the process of looking up a shipping charge by drawing upon information in all three tables simultaneously using a *query*. A query works much like a filter, showing only the fields that contain information of interest, but a query can combine fields from two or more tables by following the chain of relationships between them.

To automatically look up the appropriate shipping charge for a given order, Fred must create a query that combines related information from the Carriers, Shipping, and Orders tables. The query can use the CarrierID and ShipStateOrProvince fields in the Orders table to find the related carrier name in the Carriers table and the related shipping charge in the Shipping table.

Use a query to combine data from related tables

In this exercise, you show Fred how to combine data from the Carriers, Shipping, and Orders tables, using a query.

1. In the Database window, click Queries on the Objects bar to open the queries list.
2. In the queries list, double-click Create Query By Using Wizard.

   The first page of the Simple Query Wizard appears.

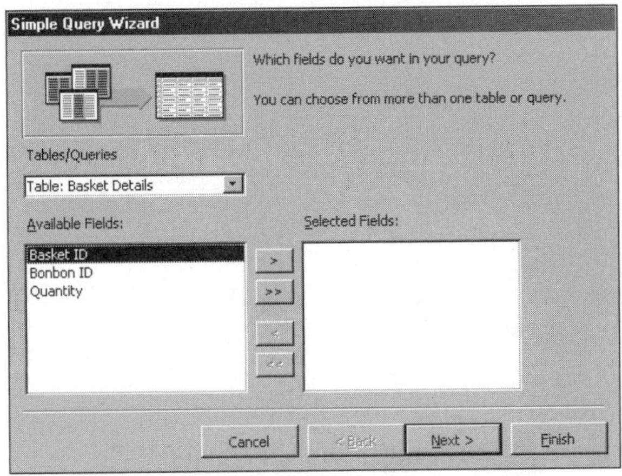

3. In the Tables/Queries list of the Simple Query Wizard, click the drop-down arrow and then select Table: Orders.

   The fields of the Orders table appear in the Available Fields list.
4. In the Available Fields list, double-click OrderID.

   The OrderID field from the Orders table appears in the Selected Fields list.
5. In the Tables/Queries list, select Table: Carriers, and then in the Available Fields list, double-click CarrierName.

   The CarrierName field from the Carriers table appears in the Selected Fields list.
6. In the Tables/Queries list, select Table: Shipping, and then in the Available Fields list, double-click ShippingCharge.

   The ShippingCharge field from the Shipping table appears in the Selected Fields list.

Access 2000 uses the relationships you created to combine the fields from all of the related tables.

7 Click Next.

The second page of the Simple Query Wizard appears.

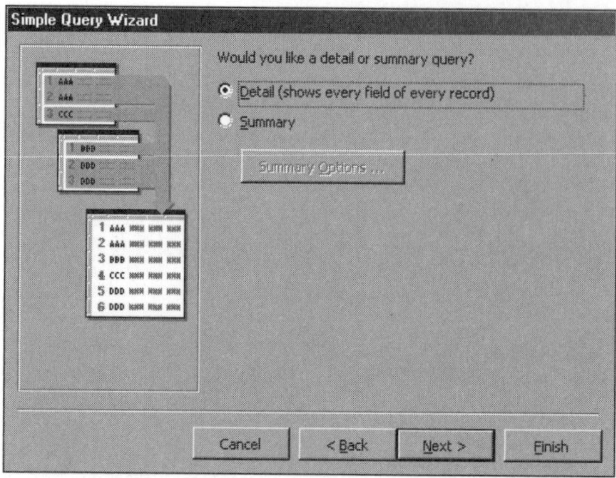

8 Be sure the Detail (Shows Every Field Of Every Record) option is selected, and then click Next.

The third page of the Simple Query Wizard appears.

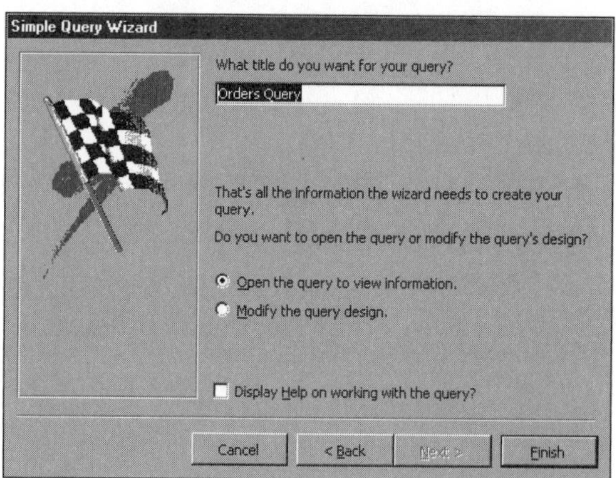

9 Be sure the Open The Query To View Information option is selected. In the What Title Do You Want For Your Query? box, type **Carriers Information** and then click Finish.

The new Carriers Information query opens, displaying the order ID, carrier name, and shipping cost for every order in the Orders table.

10. Close the Carriers Information query.

    The query was saved automatically when it was created, so the Carriers Information query will appear in the queries list of the Database window.

Finish the lesson

1. To continue to the next lesson, on the File menu, click Close.
2. If you're finished using Access 2000 for now, on the File menu, click Exit.

Lesson 4 Quick Reference

To	Do this	Button
Create a table	In the Database window, click Tables on the Objects bar, double-click Create Table By Using Wizard, and follow the instructions.	
Add a field	Open the table in Design view, type a field name in the first empty row, and then select a data type.	
Create an AutoForm to add data to a new table	With the table in Datasheet view, click the New Object: AutoForm button on the Datasheet toolbar.	
Set a field property	In Design view, select a field in the grid, and then change the setting in the appropriate property box of the property sheet.	
Create a relationship between two tables	Click the Relationships button on the Database toolbar. Click the Show Table button on the Relationship toolbar. In the Show Table dialog box, add the primary and related tables. In the Relationships window, drag the primary key field from the primary table to the matching key field of the related table. In the Edit Relationships dialog box, select the Enforce Referential Integrity check box, and then click Create.	
Delete a relationship between two tables	In the Relationships window, click the line connecting the tables, and then press Delete.	
Combine data from related tables using a query	In the Database window, click Queries on the Objects bar. Double-click Create Query By Using Wizard, and follow the instructions.	

LESSON

5

Using Queries

- ✔ *Use the Query Wizard to simplify your search.*
- ✔ *Create and modify a query in Design view.*
- ✔ *Set criteria for queries.*
- ✔ *Sort data and hide fields in a query.*
- ✔ *Use a query to combine data from multiple tables.*
- ✔ *Refine the results of a query.*

ESTIMATED TIME **25 min.**

For a review of creating and using filters, see Lesson 3, "Using Filters And Reports."

You have organized detailed information about Sweet Lil's into a series of easily managed tables. You now want to know how to use the information to your best advantage. There are many possible reasons why you might want to retrieve only certain data from your tables. You might want to be able to predict sales trends, or the marketing department may be considering a sales campaign by region. You might also want to track sales trends by season, area, or type of item. When the key ingredient of a certain bonbon changes, you might want to quickly locate the nearest supplier of that ingredient.

Microsoft Access 2000 offers flexible methods of data retrieval that allow you to find the information you need to answer specific questions. The two most useful methods are filters and queries. *Filters* allow you to exclude irrelevant data, giving you a clear view of the data you want. *Queries* work much the same as filters, showing only the fields that contain information of interest, but queries can draw information from more than one table and preserve that view permanently.

Mary Culvert, vice president of marketing at Sweet Lil's, takes a look at the company's quarterly report and realizes the company needs to cut expenses in order to increase its profit margin in time for the annual report. She wants to review the data on the highest priced bonbons to help her determine how best to reduce overall costs. Among the data Mary needs to find is pricing information, information on the distribution of the highest priced bonbons, and sales data on baskets and boxes that include those bonbons.

In this lesson, you show Mary how to create queries, set query criteria, use the Query Wizard, sort data within query fields, and refine the results of queries, and print query results.

Understanding Queries

Posing questions as simple as "How many boxes and baskets of bonbons were sold in New York in May?" can help you learn how to make sense of the raw data available in tables. Queries are questions that you pose in Access 2000, such as asking "What data meets these criteria?" Queries can help you find the specific information you need.

Access 2000 offers two methods for creating queries. The first method is to use query wizards, step-by-step guides that take you through the process of creating a query. There are four Access 2000 query wizards: the Simple Query Wizard, the Crosstab Query Wizard, the Find Duplicates Query Wizard, and the Find Unmatched Query Wizard. The Simple Query Wizard is the easiest to use and is covered in this lesson.

Working directly in Query Design view, the second method for writing queries, allows you to develop a query from scratch and to modify existing queries. While the query is open in Query Design view, you can add new fields, insert criteria, set parameters, define sort order, and total the information in fields.

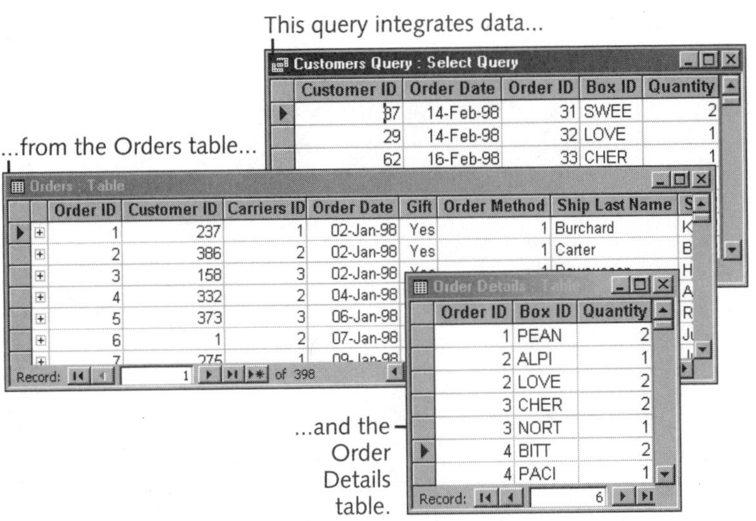

While filters can extract details from one table, queries allow you to extract information from several different tables at the same time. Queries can also be saved and used again.

Start Microsoft Access 2000 and reopen the database

- If Access 2000 isn't started yet, start it. Open the Sweet Lil's database. If the Microsoft Access window doesn't fill your screen, maximize the window.

  If you need help opening the database, see Lesson 1, "Using Forms."

Creating a Query with the Query Wizard

The easiest way to construct a new query in Access 2000 is to use the Simple Query Wizard. You simply choose the table you want to work with, and then select the fields that contain the information you need. The Simple Query Wizard collects the information you request and presents it to you as a datasheet. With the results of your query in front of you, you can then modify the query until it suits your needs and answers your questions. Once it's given you the information you need, you can save the query for future use.

Before you begin using the Simple Query Wizard, you should carefully consider what types of information you would like to receive from your query. It will save you time and energy if you plan ahead, focusing on which fields to select for the data you need. Of course, you can also modify a query at any time.

Create a query

To identify the highest priced bonbons, Mary Culvert needs a list of available bonbons, in order according to the cost of each, from the Bonbons table. In the following exercise, you help her create a simple query to identify the highest-priced bonbons at Sweet Lil's and print the list for future reference.

For a demonstration of how to create a query with the Simple Query Wizard, open the Office 8in1 Step by Step folder on your hard disk. Then open the Access Demos folder, and double-click the Query Wizard icon.

1. In the Database window, click Queries on the Objects bar to display the queries list.

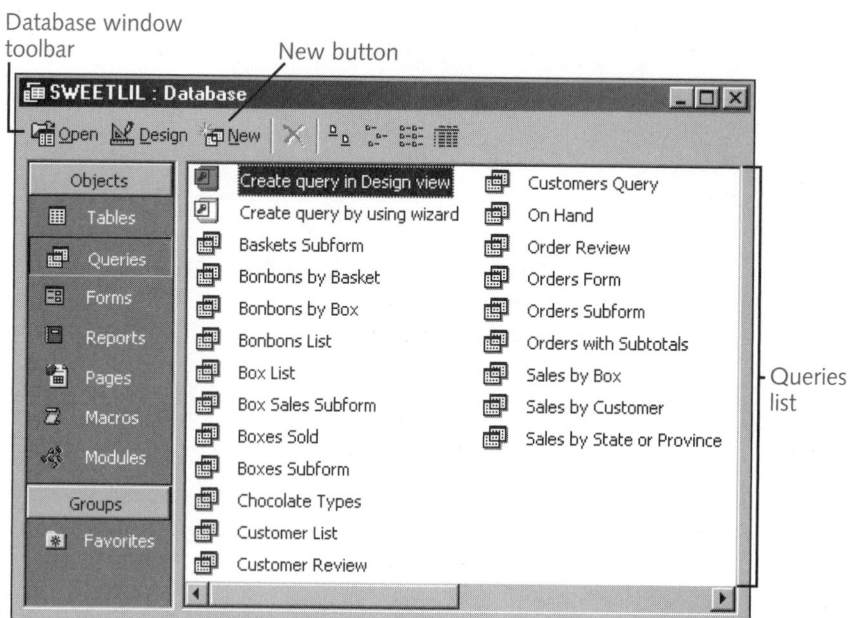

2. On the Database window toolbar, click the New button.
   The New Query dialog box appears.

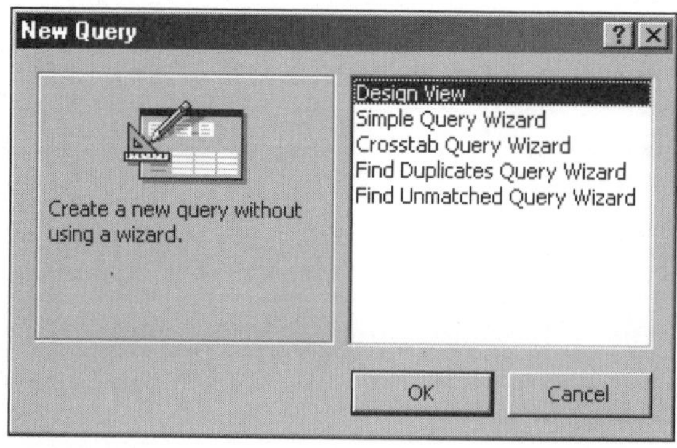

3 Double-click Simple Query Wizard in the list.

The first page of the Simple Query Wizard appears.

4 Click the Tables/Queries drop-down arrow, and then select Table: Bonbons.

The Bonbons fields are displayed in the Available Fields list.

You can also select the field and then click the Select button (>) to add the field to the Selected Fields list.

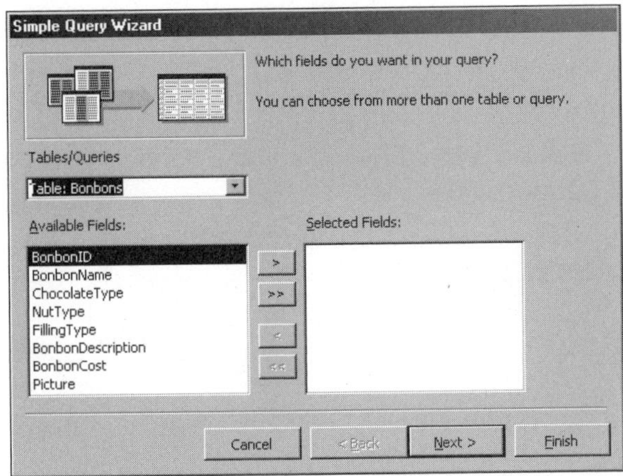

5 In the Available Fields list, double-click BonbonName.

BonbonName moves from the Available Fields list to the Selected Fields list.

6 In the Available Fields list, double-click ChocolateType, NutType, FillingType, and BonbonCost.

The four fields move to the Selected Fields list.

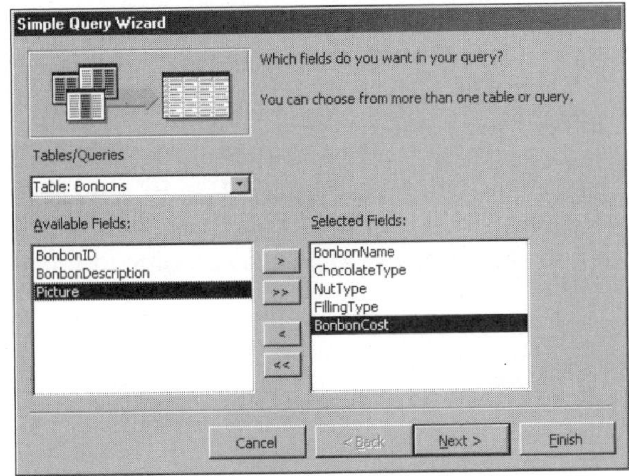

7. Click Next.

   The second page of the Simple Query Wizard appears, asking whether you want a detail or a summary query.
8. If it is not already selected, click the Detail option, and then click Next.

   The third page of the Simple Query Wizard appears, asking you to enter a title for your query.
9. Type **Bonbon Stats For Mary** and then verify that the Open The Query To View Information option is selected.
10. Click Finish.

    The Simple Query Wizard closes, and the Bonbon Stats For Mary query opens in Datasheet view.

Print the query as a datasheet

Print

1. With the Bonbon Stats For Mary query open in Datasheet view, click the Print button on the Query Datasheet toolbar.

   The Print dialog box appears.
2. Click OK.

   The Print dialog box closes, and the query datasheet is printed.
3. Close the query.

Modifying a Query in Design View

With your query open in Query Design view, you can add fields and controls. Query Design view lets you design the layout of your query. This is where you place controls and modify them if necessary. You can also add, rearrange, rename, and remove fields. Most of these tasks cannot be accomplished while the query is open in Datasheet view, which is where you view the results of your query in a simplified row-column format.

In addition, while working in the upper portion of the Query window in Query Design view, you can insert new tables and fields that broaden the scope of the query. These modifications can be made at any time in Query Design view.

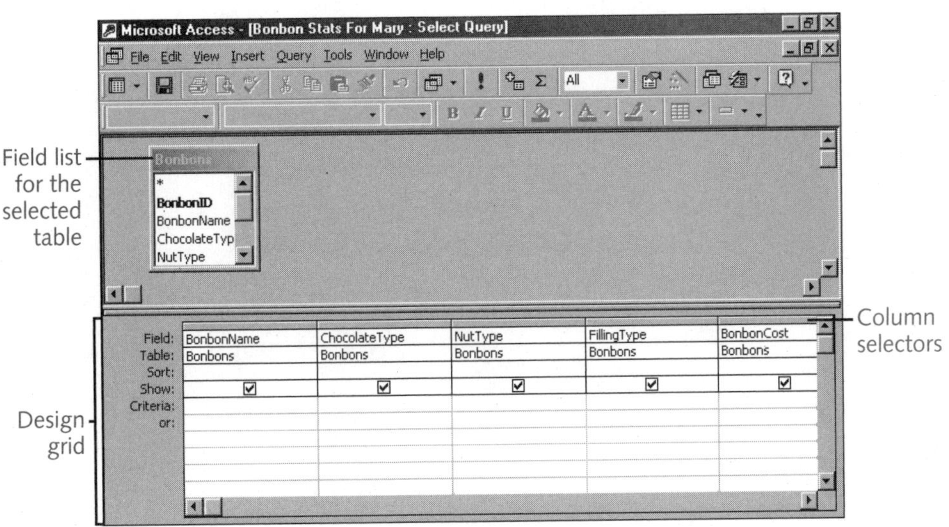

Mary Culvert reviews the query and sees the need for a few changes. She needs a description of each bonbon and, because she places more importance on the cost of the bonbons than the chocolate type, she'd like to shift the BonbonCost field to the left, between ChocolateType and BonbonName.

Add a field to an existing query

1. In the Database window, verify that Queries on the Objects bar is displayed.
2. In the queries list, verify that Bonbon Stats For Mary is selected, and then click the Design button on the Database window toolbar.

   The Bonbon Stats For Mary query opens in Design view.
3. Drag the BonbonDescription field from the Bonbons field list in the upper portion of the window to the empty field at the right of the BonbonCost field in the design grid. You may need to scroll in the field list to find the BonbonDescription field.

   The BonbonDescription field appears in the design grid.

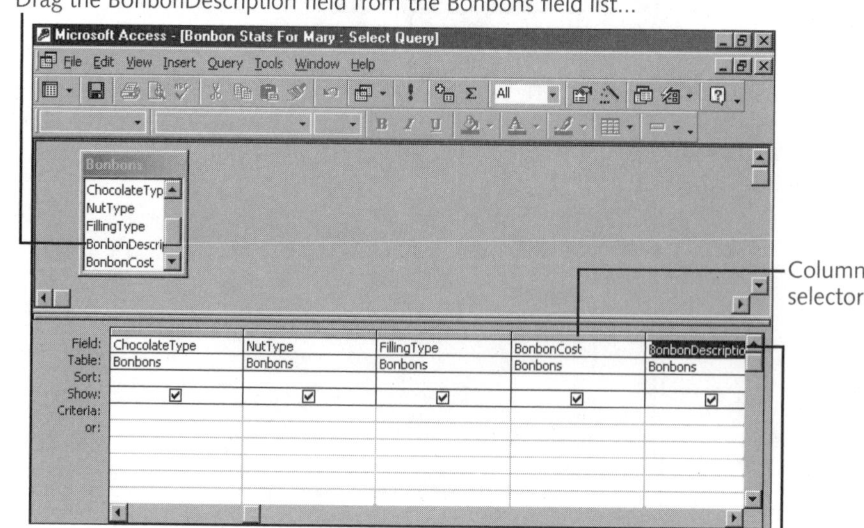

...to the empty field in the design grid.

Rearrange fields within a query

1. Click the BonbonCost column selector at the top of the design grid.

   As you point to the column selector, the pointer changes to a downward-pointing black arrow. The BonbonCost column is selected.

2. Click the column selector again, and drag the column to the left until the border between the BonbonName column and the ChocolateType column is highlighted.

   The BonbonCost column appears between the BonbonName and ChocolateType columns in the design grid.

New position

Field:	BonbonName	BonbonCost	ChocolateType	NutType	FillingType
Table:	Bonbons	Bonbons	Bonbons	Bonbons	Bonbons
Sort:					
Show:	☑	☑	☑	☑	☑
Criteria:					
or:					

Deleting a field in Query Design view does not affect the data itself, just the current view of the data.

Remove fields from a query

Mary realizes that she's primarily interested in fillings, the most variable element of the bonbon product line. She asks that you remove the ChocolateType field altogether.

1. Click the ChocolateType column selector at the top of the design grid.

   The ChocolateType column is selected.
2. Press Delete.

   The ChocolateType field is deleted from the query.
3. On the Query Design toolbar, click the Save button.
4. Close the Bonbon Stats For Mary query.

Save

Refining a Query with Criteria

The results of the current Bonbon Stats For Mary query show the cost of each bonbon, listed by filling type and nut type. Today, Mary Culvert receives news that almond prices are now skyrocketing. Mary wants to identify the bonbons that are already the most costly to produce and, in light of the news, those that contain almonds. She can do both by setting the appropriate criteria for her query.

Access 2000 uses a technique called *Query By Example* (QBE) to set criteria. You select the field that contains the information you want to see. The field and contents you select serve as an example: "Show me records that look like this." In some cases, you may use an expression to match the data against a value that you select.

An *expression* is a mathematical formula used to calculate a value. Expressions can be used to establish criteria for queries. Mary will need to use an expression to find the bonbons that cost more than 25 cents to produce.

Specify criteria

1. In the Database window, verify that Queries on the Objects bar is selected.
2. In the queries list, select Bonbon Stats For Mary, and then click the Design button on the Database window toolbar.

   The Bonbon Stats For Mary query opens in Design view.
3. In the NutType column of the design grid, click the Criteria cell.
4. Type **Almond** and press Enter.

   Quotation marks appear around the text.

Quotation marks appear around new text criteria, but not around numerical criteria.

5. In the Bonbon Cost column of the design grid, type **>0.25** in the Criteria cell, and press Enter.

Find bonbons that cost more than 25 cents to produce...

Field:	BonbonName	BonbonCost	NutType	FillingType	BonbonDescription
Table:	Bonbons	Bonbons	Bonbons	Bonbons	Bonbons
Sort:					
Show:	☑	☑	☑	☑	☑
Criteria:		>0.25	"Almond"		
or:					

...and that contain almonds.

View

6. On the Query Design toolbar, click the View button.

The refined query results appear in Datasheet view.

Bonbon Name	Bonbon Cost	Nut Type	Filling Type	Bonbon Description
Almond Supreme	$0.30	Almond	None	Whole almond hand-dipped
Almond Fudge Mocha	$0.44	Almond	Amaretto	Classic almond in amaretto.

Add more criteria

While examining the results, Mary Culvert notes that many of Sweet Lil's bonbons contain marzipan, and that marzipan is made of almonds. In light of the sudden increase in the cost of almonds, Mary decides that she will have to include the marzipan-filled bonbons in her cost-cutting analysis. You add another criterion to her query.

View

1. With the Bonbon Stats For Mary query in Datasheet view, click the View button on the Query Datasheet toolbar.

   The Bonbon Stats For Mary query reappears in Design view.
2. In the FillingType column of the design grid, click the Or cell.
3. Type **Marzipan** and press Enter.

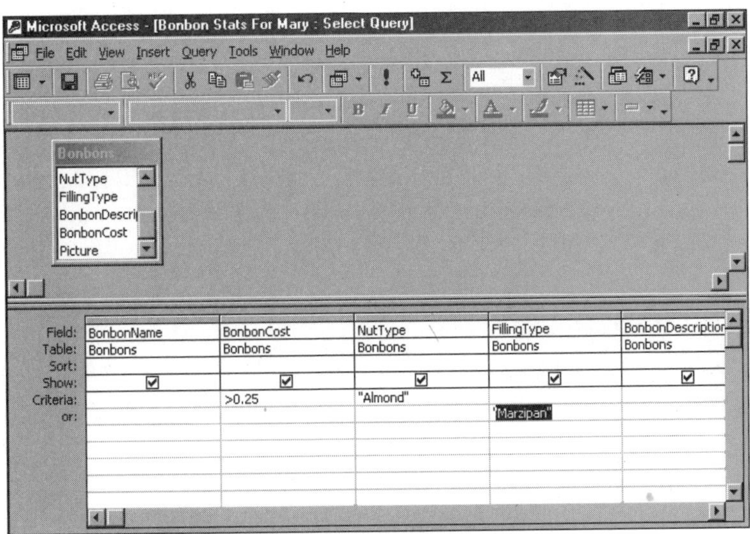

And vs. Or

Typing **Marzipan** in the Or row of the Filling Type column lets your search uncover any bonbons that contain either almonds *or* marzipan. If you type **Marzipan** in the same row as Almond you find only bonbons that contain both almonds *and* marzipan. Access 2000 assumes that all entries on the same row in the design grid of the Query window are additional search criteria.

Save

4. On the Query Design toolbar, click the Save button.
5. On the Query Design toolbar, click the View button.
   The query results reappear in Datasheet view.

Bonbon Name	Bonbon Cost	Nut Type	Filling Type	Bonbon Description
Marzipan Oakleaf	$0.40	None	Marzipan	Marzipan shaped in the form
Almond Supreme	$0.30	Almond	None	Whole almond hand-dipped
Almond Fudge Mocha	$0.44	Almond	Amaretto	Classic almond in amaretto.
Marzipan Delight	$0.38	None	Marzipan	Delicious marzipan with darl
Marzipan Finch	$0.32	None	Marzipan	Finch-shaped marzipan with
Marzipan Maple	$0.37	None	Marzipan	Marzipan shaped in the form
Marzipan Marvel	$0.33	None	Marzipan	Almond-shaped marzipan wi
Marzipan Swallow	$0.34	None	Marzipan	Swallow-shaped marzipan w
*				

6. Close the datasheet.

Presenting a Query More Effectively

A well-designed query can answer not just one but a number of related questions, simply by varying the presentation. The results of a query can be sorted to make it easier to find the information you need immediately. To find a particular bonbon ingredient, for example, you could sort the bonbons alphabetically by filling. To find a specifically priced bonbon, you could sort the records by cost.

For a cleaner presentation, you can also hide unnecessary information. You can hide fields within your query if you don't need them to appear in your current results, but you do require them in order to produce the desired results. For example, you may want to sort the bonbons by their unique ID numbers, but keep those numbers hidden.

Sorting the query results in Datasheet view leaves the original query intact; sorting in Design view is a change to the query itself, allowing the sort to be saved along with the query.

In these exercises, you show Mary how to sort and hide fields in Query Design view.

Sort records alphabetically in Datasheet view

1. Verify that the Bonbon Stats for Mary query results are open in Datasheet view.
2. Click any cell in the Filling Type field.
3. On the Query Datasheet toolbar, click the Sort Ascending button.

Sort Ascending

The records in the query reappear, sorted alphabetically by filling type.

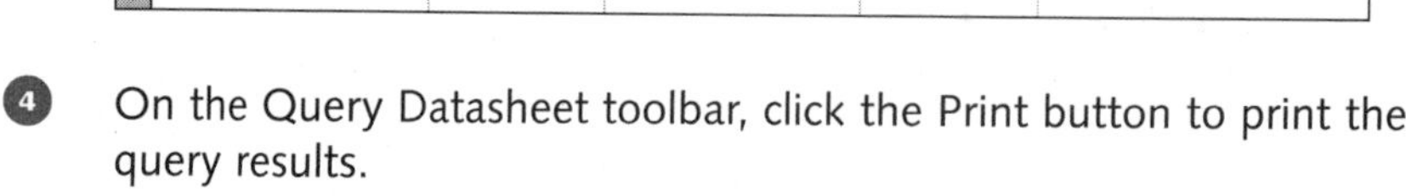

Bonbon Name	Bonbon Cost	Nut Type	Filling Type	Bonbon Description
Almond Fudge Mocha	$0.44	Almond	Amaretto	Classic almond in amaretto.
Marzipan Swallow	$0.34	None	Marzipan	Swallow-shaped marzipan w
Marzipan Marvel	$0.33	None	Marzipan	Almond-shaped marzipan wi
Marzipan Maple	$0.37	None	Marzipan	Marzipan shaped in the form
Marzipan Finch	$0.32	None	Marzipan	Finch-shaped marzipan with
Marzipan Delight	$0.38	None	Marzipan	Delicious marzipan with dark
Marzipan Oakleaf	$0.40	None	Marzipan	Marzipan shaped in the form
Almond Supreme	$0.30	Almond	None	Whole almond hand-dipped

4. On the Query Datasheet toolbar, click the Print button to print the query results.

Print

Sort records by two fields in Design view

Recalling that bonbons containing nuts are nearly always the most expensive types, Mary decides to sort the query by cost and by nut type. This will make it easy for her to identify the higher-priced bonbons, because they'll be ranked first by cost, and then by nut type within each cost level. By setting up the sort in Design view, Mary can save the new sort order as part of the query.

View

1. With the Bonbon Stats For Mary query in Datasheet view, click the View button.

   The Bonbon Stats For Mary query reappears in Design view.

2. In the design grid, click the Sort box of the NutType column.

   A drop-down arrow appears in the Sort box.

3. Click the Sort drop-down arrow, and then select Ascending.

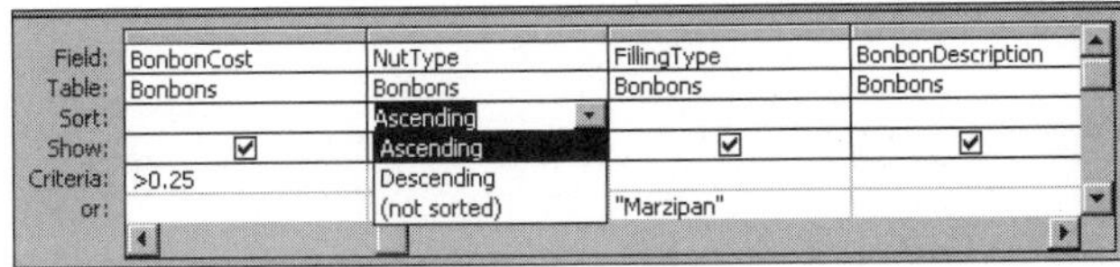

Field:	BonbonCost	NutType	FillingType	BonbonDescription
Table:	Bonbons	Bonbons	Bonbons	Bonbons
Sort:		Ascending		
Show:	☑	Ascending	☑	☑
Criteria:	>0.25	Descending		
or:		(not sorted)	"Marzipan"	

4. Click the Sort cell of the BonbonCost column, click the Sort drop-down arrow, and then select Descending.

View

5. On the Query Design toolbar, click the View button to switch to Datasheet view.

   The query results are now sorted by cost, with the most expensive bonbons first. Any items with the same cost are then sorted alphabetically by nut type.

Bonbon Stats For Mary : Select Query

Bonbon Name	Bonbon Cost	Nut Type	Filling Type	Bonbon Description
Almond Fudge Mocha	$0.44	Almond	Amaretto	Classic almond in am
Marzipan Oakleaf	$0.40	None	Marzipan	Marzipan shaped in th
Marzipan Delight	$0.38	None	Marzipan	Delicious marzipan wi
Marzipan Maple	$0.37	None	Marzipan	Marzipan shaped in th
Marzipan Swallow	$0.34	None	Marzipan	Swallow-shaped marz
Marzipan Marvel	$0.33	None	Marzipan	Almond-shaped marzi
Marzipan Finch	$0.32	None	Marzipan	Finch-shaped marzipa
Almond Supreme	$0.30	Almond	None	Whole almond hand-d

Record: 1 of 8

6. On the Query Datasheet toolbar, click the Print button.

   The query results are printed.

Hide a field

Mary decides that she doesn't really need to see the nut type, just the cost. Since nut type is a factor in determining the cost, it must be included in the query, but it need not appear in the results. Hiding the field will return the desired results without including the field in those results.

View

1. With the Bonbon Stats For Mary query in Datasheet view, click the View button.

   The Bonbon Stats For Mary query reappears in Design view.

2. Click the NutType column to clear the Show check box.

Clear the Show check box to hide the NutType field.

Field:	BonbonName	BonbonCost	NutType	FillingType	BonbonDescri
Table:	Bonbons	Bonbons	Bonbons	Bonbons	Bonbons
Sort:		Descending	Ascending		
Show:	☑	☑	☐	☑	☑
Criteria:		>0.25	Not "almond"		
or:				"Marzipan"	

View

3. On the Query Design toolbar, click the View button to switch to Datasheet view.

   In Datasheet view the NutType field is no longer visible, but the query is still sorted by nut type within cost, and the NutType field has not been deleted from the query.

4. Close the Bonbon Stats For Mary query.
5. Click No to close the message.

Joining Related Tables in the Query Window

Relationships between tables are discussed in Lesson 4, "Managing Database Change."

When you create a query that involves more than one table, Access 2000 needs to know the fields by which the tables are related: the field or fields they have in common. Access 2000 uses these table relationships to combine related data from multiple tables. When fields of more than one table are used in a query, a join line appears between the related fields.

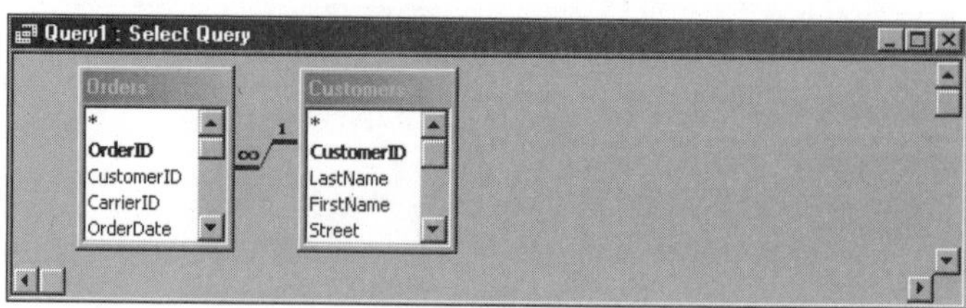

Creating a Query Using Related Tables

The executive staff ask Mary Culvert for a detailed analysis of the company's orders for the first quarter of 1998, to compare with this year's orders to date. Mary decides to include order IDs, customer names, and the date of the orders. Some of this information is contained in the Orders table and some in the Customers table. The two tables are related through the Customer ID field.

Set up a query with two tables

In this exercise, you help Mary create a new query in Query Design view using the Orders and Customers tables, setting criteria to list sales for the last quarter of 1998.

1. In the Database window, click Queries on the Objects bar.
2. On the Database window toolbar, click the New button.

   The New Query dialog box appears.
3. In the New Query dialog box, double-click Design View.

   The Query window opens, and the Show Table dialog box appears.

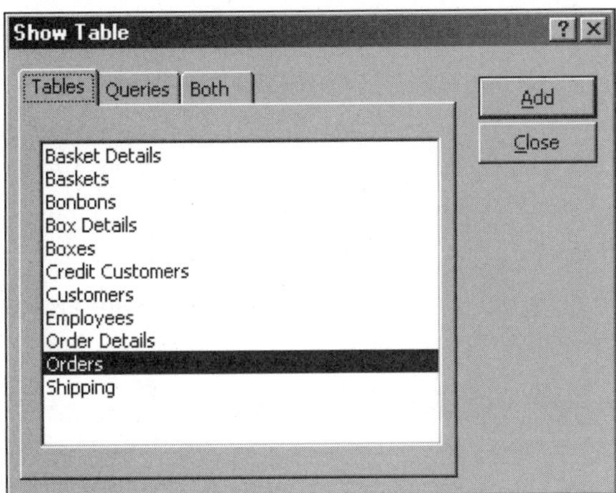

4. In the tables list, double-click Orders, and then double-click Customers.

   The Orders table and Customers table field lists appear in the upper portion of the Query window.
5. Close the Show Table dialog box.

   In the upper portion of the Query window, a join line connects the CustomerID fields of the Orders field list and the Customers field list.

Add fields to a query using multiple tables

1. In the Orders field list of the Query window, double-click CustomerID, OrderID, and OrderDate.

   The three fields appear in the design grid.

2. In the Customers field list, double-click LastName.

   The LastName field is added to the design grid.

Field:	CustomerID	OrderID	OrderDate	LastName
Table:	Orders	Orders	Orders	Customers
Sort:				
Show:	☑	☑	☑	☑
Criteria:				
or:				

Save

3. On the Query Design toolbar, click the Save button.

   The Save As dialog box appears.

4. In the Query Name box, type **Order Information** and then press Enter.

Set criteria for the query

1. In the Criteria cell of the OrderDate column, type **Between 1-Oct-98 And 31-Dec-98** and press Enter.

   Between #10/1/98# and #12/31/98# appears in the OrderDate Criteria cell of the design grid.

2. In the OrderDate column selector at the top of the design grid, double-click the right border of the column selector.

   The right border moves to the right, and the column is resized to show the complete expression.

Field:	CustomerID	OrderID	OrderDate	LastName
Table:	Orders	Orders	Orders	Customers
Sort:				
Show:	☑	☑	☑	
Criteria:			Between #10/1/98# And #12/31/98#	
or:				

3. On the Query Design toolbar, click the Save button.
4. On the Query Design toolbar, click the View button.

View

The datasheet appears, with order IDs, customer IDs, order dates, and last names of the customers who placed orders in the last quarter of 1998.

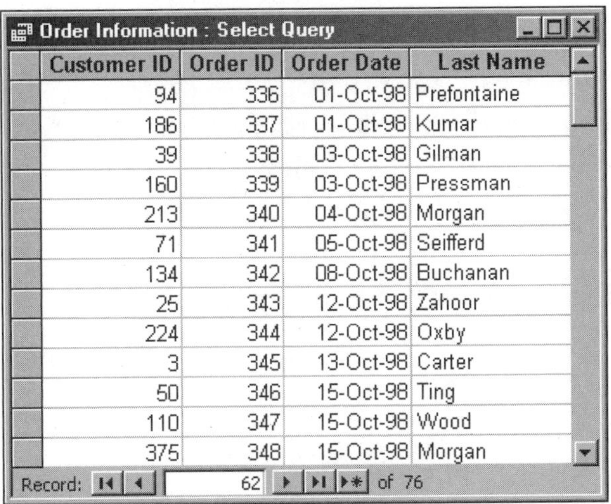

Order Information : Select Query

Customer ID	Order ID	Order Date	Last Name
94	336	01-Oct-98	Prefontaine
186	337	01-Oct-98	Kumar
39	338	03-Oct-98	Gilman
160	339	03-Oct-98	Pressman
213	340	04-Oct-98	Morgan
71	341	05-Oct-98	Seifferd
134	342	08-Oct-98	Buchanan
25	343	12-Oct-98	Zahoor
224	344	12-Oct-98	Oxby
3	345	13-Oct-98	Carter
50	346	15-Oct-98	Ting
110	347	15-Oct-98	Wood
375	348	15-Oct-98	Morgan

Record: 62 of 76

5 Close the Order Information query.

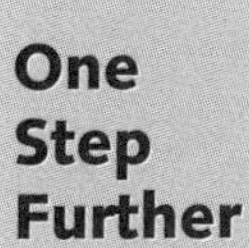

Fine-tuning Queries

Access 2000 provides additional ways to help you refine queries for your intended audience. You can change the field labels to clarify the information within your fields. This assists everyone who sees the query results. For example, an ID field can be given a more informative column heading. And when you want to filter out all but the most significant information, you can use the Show Top filter to limit the available information within each field to the first few rows or a percentage of the rows.

Change a field label

Mary wants to clarify the column headings on some of the field names in her query. In this exercise, you rename a field column heading by setting the Field Caption property for the CustomerID field.

1. In the Database window, verify that Queries on the Objects bar is selected.
2. In the queries list, select Order Information, and then click the Design button on the Database window toolbar.

   The Order Information query opens in Design view.
3. In the CustomerID column of the design grid, click the Field cell.

Properties

4. On the Query Design toolbar, click the Properties button.

   The property sheet for the CustomerID field opens.
5. In the Caption property box, type **Winter Customers**

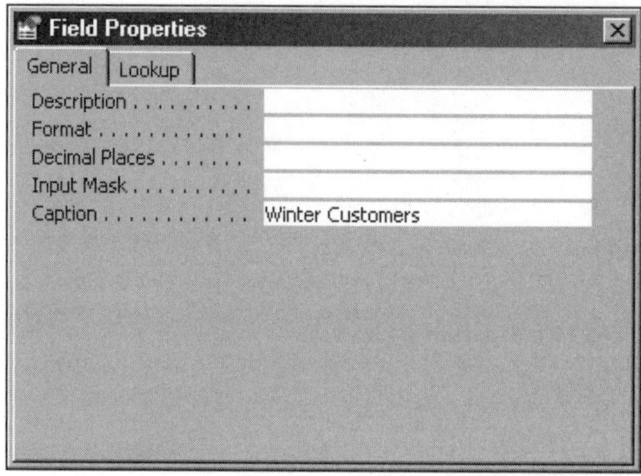

6. Close the property sheet.

View

7. On the Query Design toolbar, click the View button to switch to Datasheet view.

   The CustomerID field is renamed Winter Customers.
8. Double-click the right border of the Winter Customers field selector to view the entire field name.

Display only the top values

After taking another look at the Order Information query, Mary decides that she'd now like to see a list of only the 25 most recent orders. You use the Top Values property to limit the query to the top 25 values in the Order Date column.

View

1. With the Order Information query in Datasheet view, click the View button.

   The Order Information query reappears in Design view.

2. In the OrderDate column, click the Sort row, click the drop-down arrow, and then select Descending.

   The order dates are sorted in descending order, with the most recent dates at the top.

You can also use Top Values to select a given percentage of the available records.

3. On the Query Design toolbar, click the Top Values drop-down arrow, and then select 25.
4. On the Query Design toolbar, click the View button to switch back to Datasheet view.

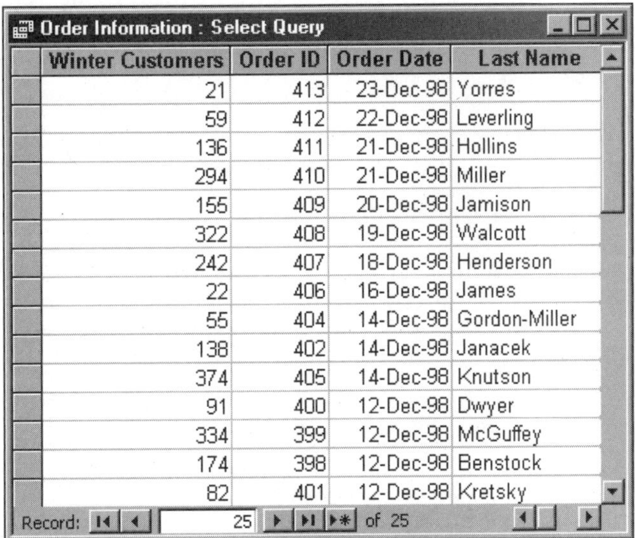

Order Information : Select Query

Winter Customers	Order ID	Order Date	Last Name
21	413	23-Dec-98	Yorres
59	412	22-Dec-98	Leverling
136	411	21-Dec-98	Hollins
294	410	21-Dec-98	Miller
155	409	20-Dec-98	Jamison
322	408	19-Dec-98	Walcott
242	407	18-Dec-98	Henderson
22	406	16-Dec-98	James
55	404	14-Dec-98	Gordon-Miller
138	402	14-Dec-98	Janacek
374	405	14-Dec-98	Knutson
91	400	12-Dec-98	Dwyer
334	399	12-Dec-98	McGuffey
174	398	12-Dec-98	Benstock
82	401	12-Dec-98	Kretsky

Record: 25 of 25

5. Save and close the query.

Finish the lesson

- On the File menu, click Exit.

Lesson 5 Quick Reference

To	Do this	Button
Create a query	In the Database window, click Queries on the Objects bar, and then click the New button on the Database window toolbar. Double-click Simple Query Wizard, and follow the instructions.	
Print a query	With the query open in Datasheet view, click the Print button on the Query Datasheet toolbar, and click OK.	
Add a field to a query	In Design view, in the upper portion of the Query window, double-click the field in the appropriate field list.	
Rearrange fields	In Design view, in the design grid, click the column selector and drag the column to the new position.	
Remove a field from a query	In Design view, in the design grid, click the appropriate column selector, and press Delete.	
Set criteria	In Design view, enter criteria in the appropriate Criteria cells of the design grid.	
Sort records in a query	In Datasheet view, click the field or fields you want to sort, and then click the Sort Ascending or Sort Descending button on the Query Datasheet toolbar.	 
Hide a field in a query	In Design view, in the design grid, clear the Show check box of the field you want to hide.	
Add two tables to a query	In the Database window, click Queries on the Objects bar, and then click the New button on the Database window toolbar. In the New Query dialog box, double-click Design View, and then double-click the two tables in the tables list.	
Set field properties	In Design view, select the field in the design grid. Click the Properties button on the Query Design toolbar. Change the appropriate property in the property sheet.	
Display the top values of a query	In Design view, sort the column whose values you want to display. Click the Top Values drop-down arrow, select the number of values you want, and then switch to Datasheet view to display the top values.	

PART 6

Microsoft Publisher 2000

Using the Microsoft Publisher Catalog

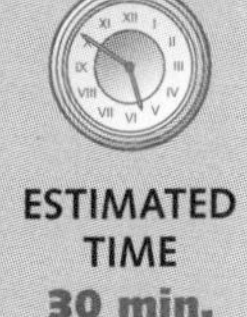

ESTIMATED TIME **30 min.**

In this lesson you will learn how to:

- ✔ *Start Publisher.*
- ✔ *View publication sections in the Catalog.*
- ✔ *View publication types.*
- ✔ *View design sets.*
- ✔ *View blank publication layouts.*
- ✔ *Enter and store personal information.*

It wasn't too long ago when desktop publishing required expensive computer hardware and software and quite a bit of publishing expertise. Today, just about anybody can create high-quality publications and documents with a personal computer and an easy-to-learn desktop software application like Microsoft Publisher 2000. One of the chief benefits of Microsoft Publisher lies in the hundreds of built-in designs that you can use to create eye-catching brochures, newsletters, and other documents. Best of all, you don't have to create publications from "scratch," although you can if you want to.

In this lesson, you will learn how to start Publisher, and use and understand the Microsoft Publisher Catalog. You will also view publication types, design sets, and blank publication layouts. Finally, you will learn how to enter and store personal information that you can use to customize your publications.

Starting Publisher 2000

Microsoft Office 2000 8-in-1 Step by Step will help you learn the features of Publisher 2000 as well as introduce you to many desktop publishing concepts and techniques. You'll find this book useful whether you are completely new to desktop publishing and Publisher 2000, or whether you have some publishing experience or have used a previous version of Microsoft Publisher.

As you read and work through the Publisher chapters in this book, imagine you are a new business partner in a small public relations firm, Impact Public Relations. Part of your job will involve preparing printed materials for your company's clients. In this role, you will be using Microsoft Publisher 2000 to create professional-looking documents. Another business partner who has some experience using Microsoft Publisher will be helping you transition into your new position. You'll begin by starting Publisher and touring its main features.

Start Microsoft Publisher

If you are familiar with earlier versions of Microsoft Publisher, this lesson also serves as a useful guide to the new Publisher 2000 Catalog.

In this exercise, you start Microsoft Publisher and view the main Catalog.

1. On the Windows taskbar, click the Start button.

   The Start menu appears.
2. Point to Programs.

   A menu of available programs appears.
3. Click Microsoft Publisher.

   Microsoft Publisher starts and displays the main Catalog window.

Touring the Publisher Main Window

In publishing, the term "layout" refers to the organization and position of images, text, and other elements on the page.

When you start Publisher, you will actually see two windows, although one is partially hidden by the other. The main window is the Publisher *Catalog*, which provides the many templates and designs that you can use to help build your publications. A *template* is a preformatted publication, such as a newsletter, complete with sample text and graphics that you can use as a pattern to create your own. Selecting a *design* means choosing the layout and color scheme for your publication. There are many different designs for a single publication type. For instance, the newsletter template has dozens of designs, each with different colors and graphics from which you can choose. You can select which design you want to use before you open and use a template to create your publication.

The window behind the Catalog is called the *Publication window*, which is where your new publication appears. You can view the Publication window either by selecting a design from the Catalog or by clicking the Exit Catalog button.

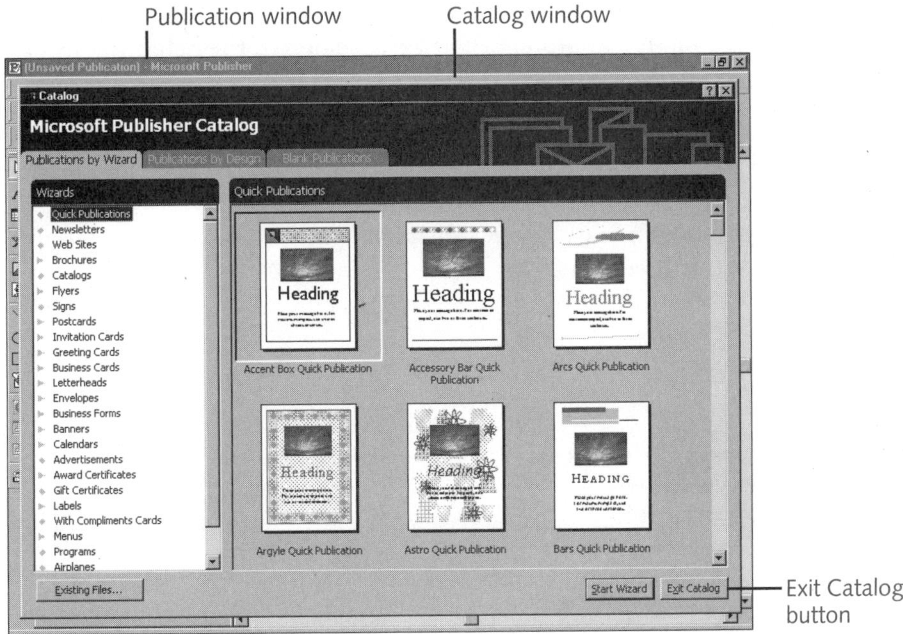

Working with Wizards

Many of the features of Publisher are built around the concept of *wizards*. A wizard is a series of screens that walk you through the task of creating a template. Literally hundreds of wizards are available in Publisher. Each wizard screen asks for specific information from you to aid in creating the publication in a more personalized way. For instance, you might be asked to select a color scheme, a paper size, or possibly to enter some personal information.

Just for Fun

The Publisher Catalog also includes wizards for creating paper airplanes and origami. Kids especially can have great fun with these. After you use one of these wizards to create an airplane or origami shape, you can print out the design along with a set of instructions for cutting and folding the parts into place.

Using the Microsoft Publisher Catalog

Your business partner begins your tour by introducing you to the basic types of publications that are available in the Publisher Catalog. She explains that the Publisher Catalog helps get you started by providing built-in designs for common publication types—such as newsletters, brochures, catalogs, flyers, letterheads, and much more. When you use one of the helpful wizards to build your initial publication, Publisher displays *placeholder* content in different parts of the publication to give you suggestions on how to use the built-in designs tastefully. You can then replace the sample placeholder content with real text and graphics to piece together your own publication quickly and easily.

The following illustration shows the placeholder content that appears for one side of a three-panel brochure:

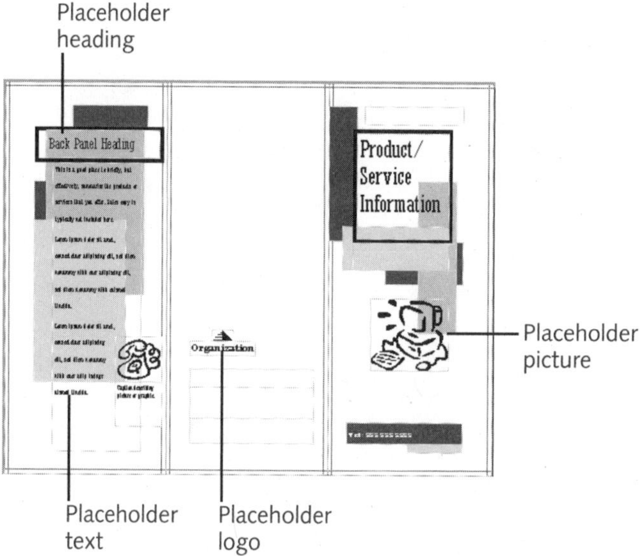

The Publisher Catalog is divided into three sections, indicated by the three tabs near the top of the window: Publications By Wizard, Publications By Design, and Blank Publications. Each of these sections is discussed on the following pages.

Publications By Wizard

You use the Publications By Wizard section of the Publisher Catalog to create designs based on a type of publication. You select the wizard for the type of publication you want to create in the left pane, and then a collection of designs for that publication type appears in the right pane. For instance, if you want to create a brochure, you click Brochures in the Wizards list to display the available brochure designs. You then click the design you want to apply, and click the Start Wizard button. The wizard will guide you through all of the remaining steps.

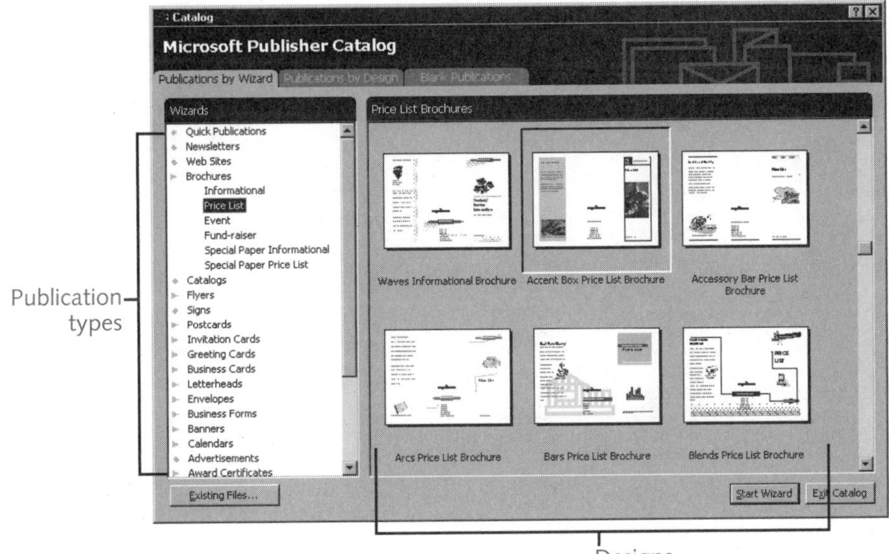

> **tip**
>
> To learn more about the components of the Catalog, you can click the Help button (the question mark symbol) in the upper-right corner of the Catalog window. A help mouse pointer will appear. Then click a part of the Catalog that you would like to learn more about. Publisher will display a description of the feature or component that you have selected.

Publications By Design

You can use the Publications By Design section to create publications based on a particular design style or theme. Each *design set* that appears in the left pane shows sample publication types for that design in the right pane. For instance, if your company decides to use the Arcs design as the theme for its publications, you might begin by selecting the Publications By Design tab, clicking the Master Sets list, and then clicking Arcs in the list. Next you would select a publication type in the right pane, such as a business card, catalog, or report. Then you would click the Start Wizard button to create the publication.

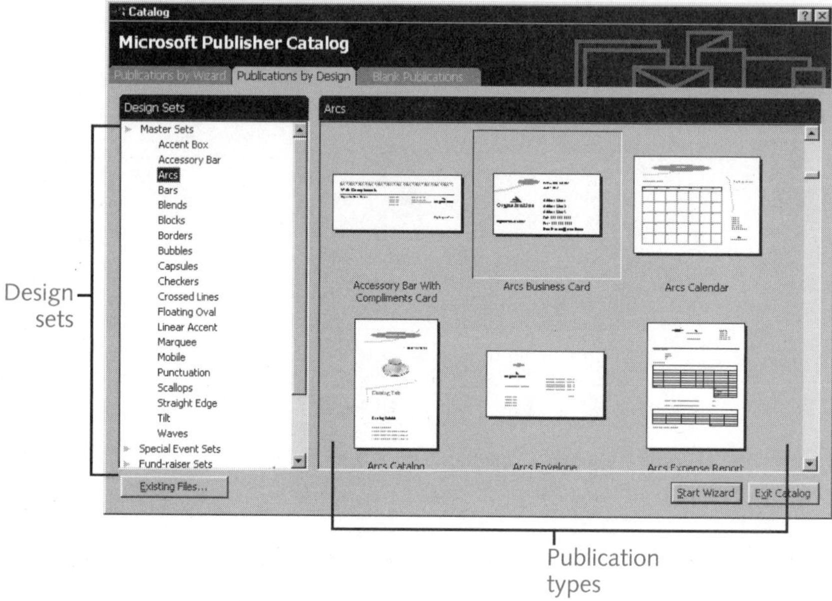

Blank Publications

The Blank Publications section lets you create publications from scratch using a particular page size and layout. You select the Blank Publications tab if you want to create your own design (rather than use one of the built-in designs). The left pane displays blank publication types, such as a Web page, business card, or banner. The right pane provides thumbnails of each blank template. When you select a blank publication type, Publisher displays exactly that—a blank publication window using the format that you've chosen, with no placeholder text or designs included.

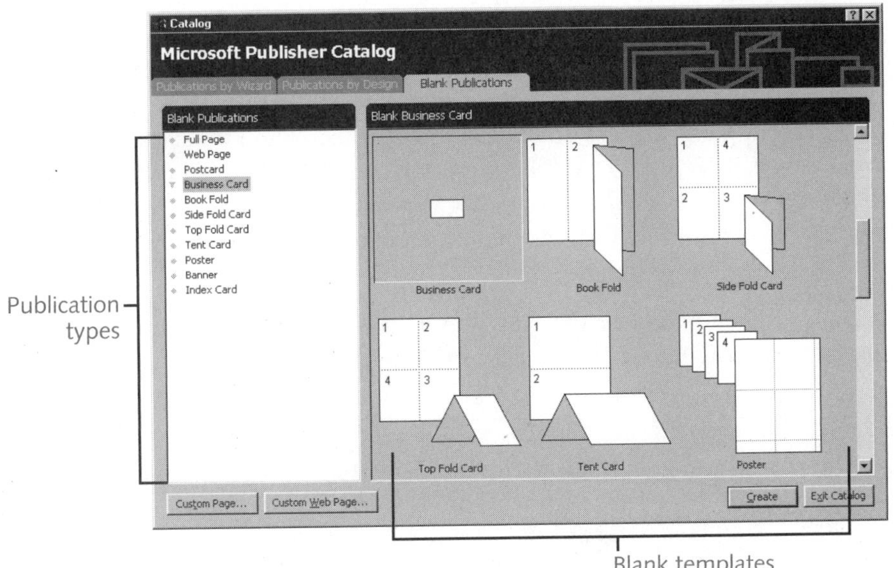

tip

If you want to create a blank publication but don't want to use any of the available designs, you can click the Custom Page button (in the bottom-left corner of the Catalog window) to display the Page Setup dialog box. You can use this dialog box to change the paper fold, change the page dimensions, and to define specially sized mailing labels and envelopes. Similarly, the Custom Web Page button allows you to customize the design of a Web page.

Switch to different Catalog sections

In this exercise, you view the three Publisher Catalog sections.

1. Click the Publications By Design tab.

   A list of design sets appears in the left pane with a thumbnail of each publication type appearing in the right pane.

2. Click the Blank Publications tab.

   A list of blank publication types appears in the left pane with a thumbnail of each blank template in the right pane.

3. Click the Publications By Wizard tab.

   A list of publication types appears in the left pane with design thumbnails for each publication type appearing in the right pane.

Viewing Publications By Wizard

"Thumbnail" is the common publishing term for small graphical page representations (sample designs). In Publisher, these appear in the right pane of each Catalog window.

The next stop on your tour of Publisher is to take a closer look at one of the Publisher Catalog sections—Publications By Wizard. The Publications By Wizard window displays a list of publication types in the left pane. When you click a publication type, design thumbnails for that publication type appear in the right pane. Each thumbnail shows the same content as all of the other samples, but uses a unique design theme.

For instance, when you click the Newsletters publication type in the left pane, you'll see the following set of newsletter design thumbnails in the right pane.

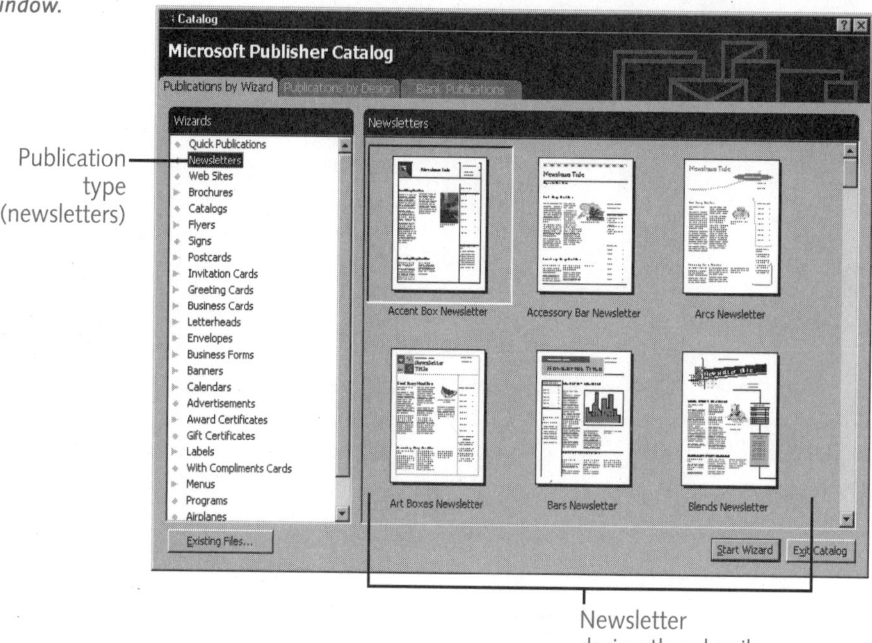

Select publication types

"Quick Publications" are one-page templates that can be used to create a handout, flyer, or cover page. They also can be used for any other purpose that you find useful.

In this exercise, you display design thumbnails for several publication types.

1. Click the Publications By Wizard tab, if it is not already selected.

   The Quick Publications design thumbnails are displayed automatically because they are first in the list of publication types.

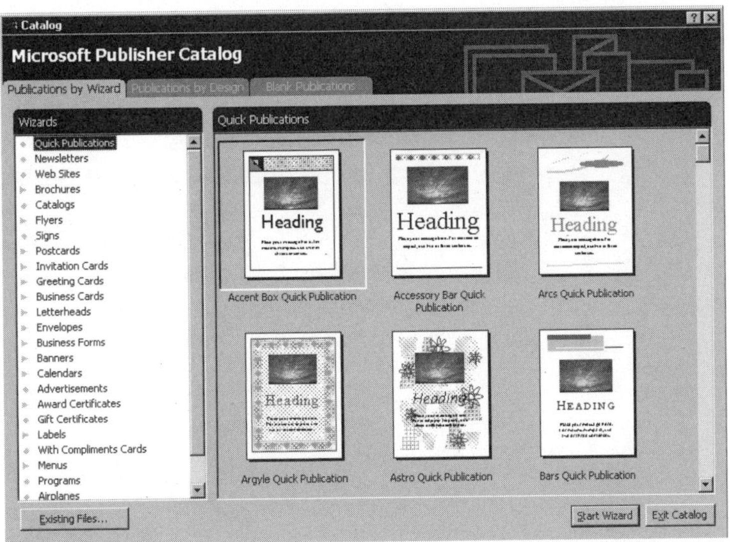

2 In the list of publication types, click Catalogs.

A set of Catalog design thumbnails appears in the right pane.

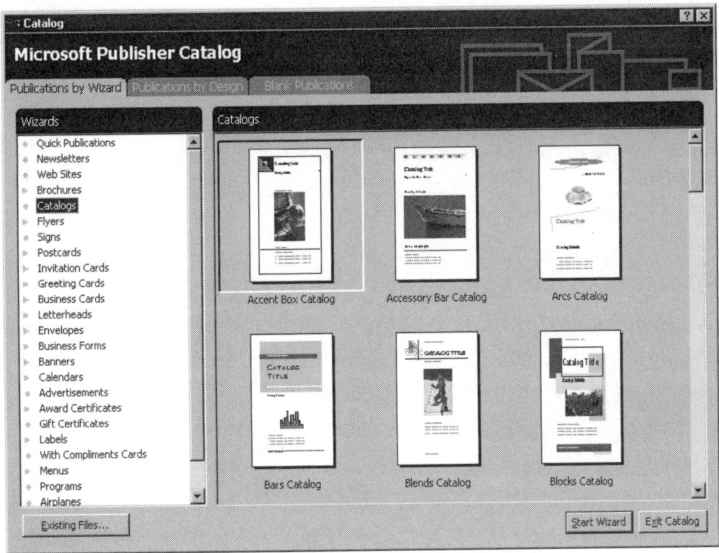

3 In the list of publication types, click Advertisements.

A set of Advertisement design thumbnails (suitable for placement in a local newspaper or magazine) appears in the right pane.

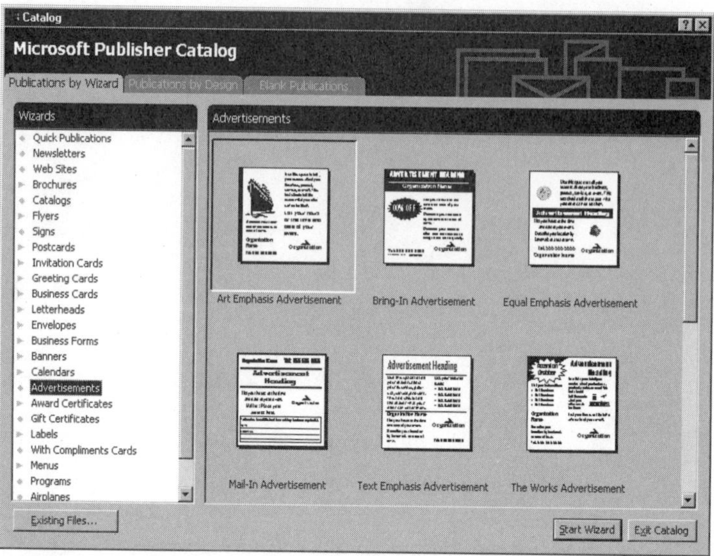

Displaying Additional Publication Types

Many publication types are further broken into subtypes. A publication type that does not include any subtypes has a diamond to the left of its name in the Wizards pane. A publication type that does include additional subtypes has a right-pointing triangle to the left of its name. When you click the name of a publication type that has a right-pointing triangle, the triangle changes to a down-pointing triangle, and the publication type expands to display all of its subtypes.

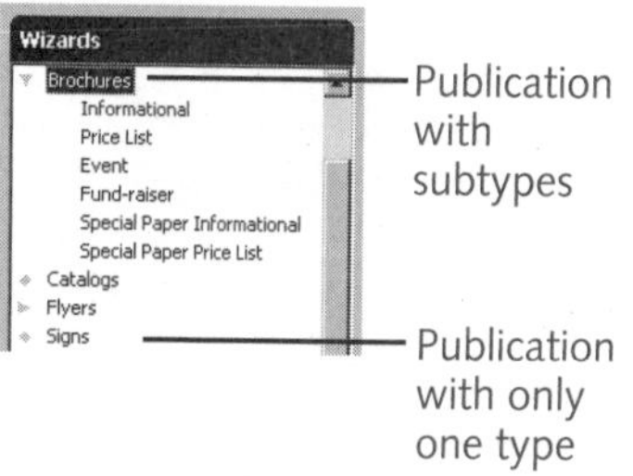

Most publication types display more thumbnails than will fit within the right pane on a single screen. For all publication types, you can view more thumbnails by using the vertical scroll bar on the right side of the window.

You can also scroll quickly through the thumbnails of a publication's subtype by clicking the name of the subtype. The sample thumbnails in the right pane will jump to the subtype that you selected.

Scroll through sample design thumbnails

In this exercise, you practice viewing design thumbnails for a particular publication type by scrolling in two different ways.

1. Click the Publications By Wizard tab, if it is not already selected.
2. Click Brochures in the list of publication types in the left pane.

   A list of brochure subtypes is displayed.
3. In the list of brochure subtypes, click Fund-Raiser.

   The right pane jumps to the start of the fund-raiser section of design thumbnails.

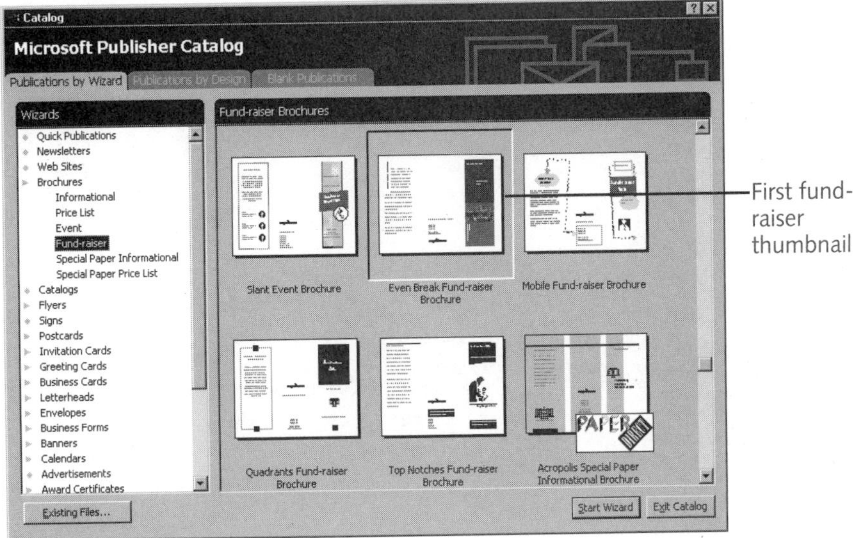

4. Click Special Paper Price List in the list of brochure types.

   The beginning of the Special Paper Price List Brochure thumbnails is displayed.

5. On the vertical scroll bar, click the up arrow and hold down the mouse button.

   Publisher scrolls upward through all the sample brochure thumbnails until the top row is displayed.

Viewing Publications By Design

Your business partner would like to familiarize you with the second section of the Catalog—Publications By Design. The Publications By Design window works almost exactly the opposite of the Publications By Wizard window. That is, when you display the Publications By Design window, a list of design sets appears in the left pane, while publication types for that design set appear in the right pane.

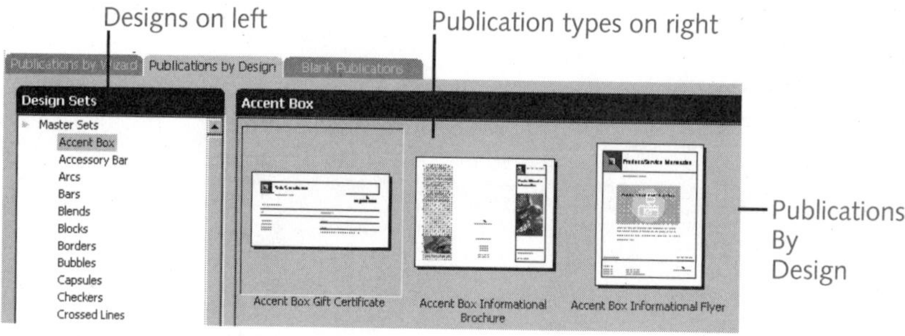

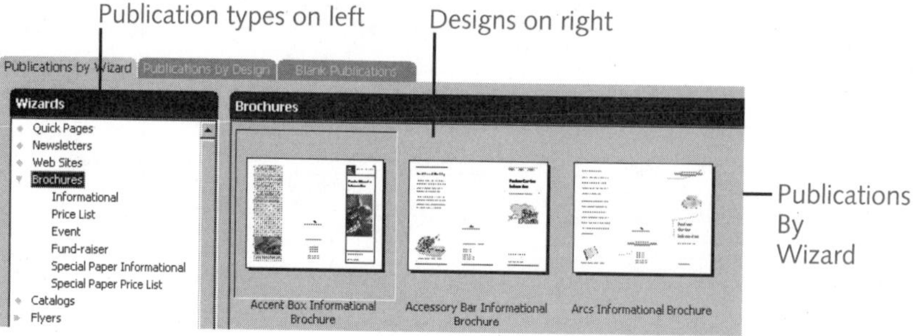

Working with Design Sets

The left pane of the Publications By Design window is organized into design sets. Each set contains several design styles organized around a common theme. *Master Sets* includes design sets that use lines and shapes to create designs and borders for letterheads, calendars, and more. The other sets, such as Special Event Sets and Holiday Sets, are organized around a related event, activity, or type of business—such as holiday greeting cards and restaurant menus.

View Master Sets

In this exercise, you click several design sets to view their themes and publication types.

1. Click the Publications By Design tab.

   The Publications By Design window is displayed with the list of Master Sets expanded.
2. In the list of Master Sets, click Arcs.

   The right pane displays sample thumbnails showing how the Arcs design is applied to different publication types.
3. In the list of Master Sets, click Bubbles.

   The right pane displays sample thumbnails showing how the Bubbles design is applied to different publication types.
4. In the list of Master Sets, click Marquee.

   The right pane displays sample layouts showing how the Marquee design is applied to different publication types.
5. Click Master Sets in the list.

   The subsets are collapsed, or "rolled up," so that they no longer appear.

tip

Although you might need to expand a set to list its subsets, it's also a good idea to collapse subsets when you no longer need to use them. Collapsing subsets helps you focus on the broader list of sets and also reduces the need to scroll through the list to view all available items.

View other design sets

In this exercise, you click several other design sets to see how each might be useful to your business.

1. Click the Publications By Design tab, if it is not already selected.
2. In the list of design sets, click Special Event Sets.

   The set of special event designs is expanded to display three subsets, and thumbnails of special event publication types appear in the right pane.
3. Use the down arrow on the vertical scroll bar to view the other thumbnails in the set.
4. Click Fund-Raiser Sets in the list of design sets.

   The set of fund-raiser designs is expanded to display three subsets, and thumbnails of fund-raiser publication types appear in the right pane.
5. Select and view design sets for Holiday Sets, We've Moved Sets, and Restaurant Sets.
6. Collapse Restaurant Sets so that the subsets no longer appear in the list.

Putting the Office Assistant to Work

The Office Assistant is an animated Help system that lets you find answers to even your most perplexing Office questions. When you want help on a Publisher feature, simply ask the Office Assistant a specific question, and a list of possible answers is offered. Plus, these assistants are as much fun to watch as they are helpful.

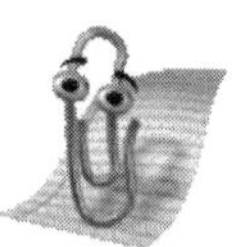

Clippit

One such assistant is Clippit, an animated paper clip who is always ready to help you learn more about Publisher. While Clippit fetches help whenever you make a request, it tries to stay out of your way the rest of the time by jumping to a different part of the screen whenever it's in the way of your cursor or your typing.

To send Clippit off for help, double-click its picture. When the search dialog balloon appears, type in your request, and then click the Search button. The Office Assistant will then retrieve any topics related to your search request. Simply click one of the help topics to find your answer.

(continued)

continued

If you don't want the Office Assistant following you around, you can turn it off by right-clicking it and then clicking Hide on the shortcut menu that appears. After you hide the Office Assistant several times, you'll be asked if you want to turn off the Office Assistant permanently or just hide it again.

By the way, if your Office Assistant isn't activated and you feel like you're missing out on the fun, you can activate it by clicking Help (in the Publication window) and then clicking Show The Office Assistant.

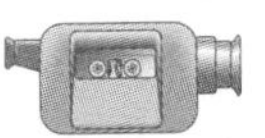

For a demonstration of how to change to a different Office Assistant character, open the Office 8in1 Step by Step folder on your hard disk. Then open the Publisher Demos folder, and double-click the Change the Assistant icon.

Displaying a Publication

At this point, your business partner suggests using one of the built-in designs to create and view a template. She explains that each design template is built by a wizard. Some wizards display several screens, requesting that you provide customized information. Other wizards display only one screen. In any case, your business partner tells you that an easy way to display a design template and bypass the wizard is to double-click the sample layout in the right pane. When you use this approach, the wizard accepts all of the default settings, without prompting you for information, and immediately displays the template.

Display a design template

In this exercise, you bypass a wizard to view a design template.

1. Click the Publications By Design tab, if it is not already selected.
2. In the list of Master Sets, click Checkers.
3. Use the down arrow on the vertical scroll bar to scroll down until you see the thumbnail for Checkers Special Offer Flyer.
4. Double-click the Checkers Special Offer Flyer thumbnail.

   The Checkers Special Offer Flyer design template is displayed, showing placeholder text and graphics for different parts of the flyer.
5. Click the Finish button. Publisher bypasses the other wizard steps.

Viewing Blank Publications

Your business partner is now ready to show you the third section in the Catalog—Blank Publications. She explains that these publication designs provide blank templates without placeholder text, for publications such as Web pages, posters, and business cards. These layouts are popular among experienced Publisher users who want to create their own content from scratch. However, because they are blank and don't contain placeholder information, they also provide a good format in which to practice skills without disrupting existing components—much like practicing your driving skills in an empty parking lot.

View blank publication layouts

In this exercise, you return to the Catalog, display blank publication layouts, and then create a blank tent card.

1. On the File menu, click New.

   The Catalog is redisplayed over the top of your publication window.
2. Click the Blank Publications tab.

   The Blank Publications window appears.

> **tip**
>
> You can also design your own blank page size. To do so, you click the Custom Page button at the bottom of Blank Publications Catalog window, and then specify a layout option and a publication size.

3. Use the down arrow on the vertical scroll bar to view the available publication layouts.
4. Double-click the Tent Card thumbnail in the right pane.

   Publisher asks if you want to save the current publication (the flyer you created) before creating the new publication.
5. Click the No button.

   The flyer publication is closed without being saved, and Publisher now asks if you want to insert the page required to create a tent card.
6. Click the Yes button.

   The tent card blank page is displayed.
7. On the File menu, click Close.

   The publication is closed.

One Step Further Entering Personal Information

A nice feature of Publisher is its ability to store personal information about you, your business, or a customer, and then include this personal information on the new publications you create. Company name and address information can be printed automatically on a brochure, letterhead, or business card.

You enter personal information by using the Personal Information dialog box, which you access by clicking Personal Information on the Edit menu. You can create up to four information sets—a set for your primary business, secondary business, another organization, and your home and family. After you've entered information for a personal information set, you can then redisplay the Personal Information dialog box at any time to make changes.

Enter personal information about yourself and your company

In this exercise, you add name, address, and company personal information.

1. On the Edit menu, click Personal Information.

   The Personal Information dialog box is displayed.

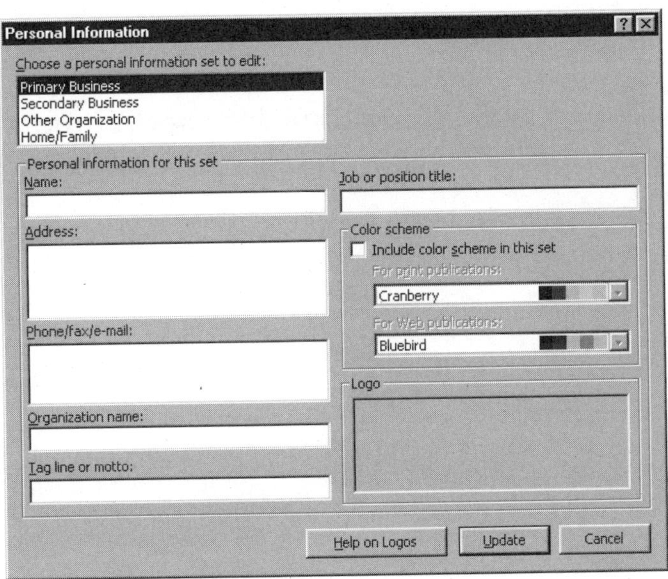

2. Press Tab, type your name in the Name text box, and then press Tab again.
3. Type the following in the Address text box, pressing Enter at the end of each address line. When you have completed typing the address, press Tab.

   2600 Broadway

   San Francisco, CA 94112
4. Using the following information, type your business phone, fax phone, and e-mail address in the Phone/Fax/E-Mail text box, pressing Enter at the end of each line. When you have completed entering this information, press Tab.

   555-5300 (Voice)

   555-3220 (Fax)

   (type your own e-mail address here, if you have one)
5. Type **Impact Public Relations** in the Organization Name text box, and then press Tab.
6. Type **We don't just create media relations, we create media relationships.** in the Tag Line Or Motto text box, and then press Tab.
7. Type **Media Specialist** in the Job Or Position Title text box, and press Tab.
8. Click the Include Color Scheme In This Set check box, and select Cranberry as the For Print Publications color scheme and Bluebird as the For Web Publications color scheme.
9. Click Update.

   You have now completed all of the information that Publisher needs to automatically print your company information on publications.

Create personal information for another organization

In this exercise, you create information for a client's company.

1. On the Edit menu, click Personal Information to display the Personal Information dialog box.
2. Click Other Organization in the Choose A Personal Information Set To Edit list in the left pane.

   A new set of text boxes appears so that you can add information for a client's company.
3. Use the following information to create the information for your client, pressing Tab and Enter as necessary to move between lines and text boxes.

In this box	Type
Name	Amy Isaacson
Address	1345 Mountain View Rd. Lakewood, CA 90035
Phone/Fax/E-Mail	805-555-4323 (Voice) 805-555-4066 (Fax) amyi@LMR.com
Organization Name	Lakewood Mountains Resort
Tag Line Or Motto	We're as close as your imagination.
Job Or Position Title	Guest Relations
Color Scheme	Mulberry (for both Print Publications and Web Publications)

4. Click Update when you have finished, and click No to save your work at another time.

   Information about your key client is ready to be applied automatically to publications that you create.

Finish the lesson

- On the File menu, click New.

  The Catalog reappears.

Lesson 1 Quick Reference

To	Do this
Start Publisher	Click the Start button, point to Programs, and then click Microsoft Publisher.
Display the Catalog	Click the Start button, point to Programs, and then click Microsoft Publisher. Or, click Exit Catalog, and then click New on the File menu.
Switch between Catalog sections	Click the tab of the desired section.
Display a Publications By Wizard item	In the Catalog, click the Publications By Wizard tab. Click the desired publication type in the left pane. Double-click the sample thumbnail.
Display a Publications By Design item	Click the Publications By Design tab. Click the desired item in the left pane. Scroll down to find the desired layout. Double-click the sample thumbnail.
View Master Sets in the Publications By Design window	In the Catalog, click the Publications By Design tab, and then click a design set.
View other design sets	Click the name of the design set that you want to view. Scroll down through the right pane or click a subset in the left pane.
Display a blank publication	Click the Blank Publications tab. Scroll down to locate the desired blank publication thumbnail in the right pane. Double-click the sample thumbnail.
Enter or edit personal information	On the Edit menu, click Personal Information. Click the desired information category in the Choose A Personal Information Set To Edit list. Type the desired information in the appropriate text boxes. Click the Update button.

2

Creating and Editing One-Page Publications

In this lesson you will learn how to:

- ✔ *Use wizards to create business cards, letterhead, and envelopes.*
- ✔ *Select different frames in a publication.*
- ✔ *Change text attributes.*
- ✔ *Move and resize frames.*
- ✔ *Save publications.*
- ✔ *Change the viewing size of publications.*

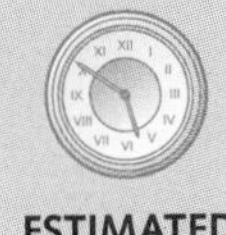

ESTIMATED TIME
40 min.

Your business partner suggests that a good way to develop your Microsoft Publisher skills is by creating some simple business documents. This approach will work out well because your key account, Lakewood Mountains Resort, has requested that Impact Public Relations design new business cards and letterhead for the resort. The task won't be that complex, and Publisher's capabilities will help you create some satisfying results.

In this lesson, you'll learn how to create three of the most common types of documents used in business—business cards, letterhead, and envelopes. The completed publications can then be sent to a copy shop or commercial printer to create preprinted color business cards, letterhead, and envelopes for Lakewood Mountains Resort.

Creating a Business Card

Few things in Publisher are easier than creating a business card. If you have already supplied personal information to Publisher, this information will be used to generate an attractive business card for you. You can then add an existing business logo, or you can allow Publisher to create one for you.

Create business cards

This exercise assumes that you have entered the Personal and Other Organization information sets described in the One Step Further section of Lesson 1, "Using the Microsoft Publisher Catalog.

The workspace includes both the publication page and the empty "scratch" area around the publication page.

In this exercise, you use information that you have already supplied to Publisher to create a business card design for the Lakewood Mountains Resort.

1. Start Publisher, or if it is already started, make sure the Catalog is displayed (on the File menu, click New to display the Catalog) and the Publications By Wizard tab is selected.
2. In the list of publication types in the left pane, click Business Cards.

   A set of business card thumbnails appears in the right pane.
3. Double-click the Bars Business Card thumbnail.

   A business card is created using your default personal information and is displayed in the workspace area of the publication window.
4. Click the Finish button.
5. In the Business Card Wizard section of the left pane, click Personal Information.

   In the bottom of the left pane, the wizard asks you which personal information set you would like to use for this publication.
6. Click Other Organization in the Personal Information section.

   The wizard replaces your personal information with the information for Lakewood Mountains Resort. (You entered this information in the "One Step Further" exercise for Lesson 1.) Although you like the design, you would like to try a different color scheme.
7. In the Business Card Wizard section of the left pane, click Color Scheme.

   A list of color schemes appears in the bottom half of the left frame.
8. Test a few different color schemes by selecting some that look interesting to you. When you have finished sampling the color schemes, return to the Mulberry scheme.
9. Click Design in the Business Card Wizard, and then change the design scheme to Marquee.

Viewing Frames and Frame Content

Your business partner explains that you do not have to use the content that Publisher supplies within a design. She reminds you that, even after you use a wizard, some or all of the text and graphics that appear in your publication are just there to serve as placeholders. You can replace the placeholder content with your own text and pictures.

All of the content in a publication is placed in *frames*, which are rectangles that can be moved and resized. There are basically two types of frames—a *text frame* and a *picture frame*. Although any type of content can go in either type of frame, text frames do in fact work best with text, and picture frames are better suited for holding images. Every frame is defined by a dotted-line border that appears on screen but does not print.

The easiest way to identify the type of frame in a publication is to position the mouse pointer over the frame (but don't click). Within a second or two, a *ScreenTip* will appear, telling you what kind of frame your pointer is positioned on, and often will describe the content of the frame. When you position the pointer on different areas of a frame's border, it changes appearance to let you know that this is a suitable boundary for, say, moving or resizing the frame.

Use the mouse to view frame information

If you are not working through this lesson sequentially, open the file Business Card 2 before you continue.

In this exercise, you position the mouse pointer on different locations within the business card to view information for frames.

1. Position the mouse pointer over the words *Lakewood Mountains Resort.*

   Publisher displays a ScreenTip telling you that this is the Organization Name Text Frame.

2. Position the pointer anywhere over the address, and then position the pointer over one of the phone numbers.

   Publisher displays ScreenTips identifying both frames.

3. View the frame information for the name Amy Isaacson and for the job title Guest Relations.

Viewing Different Mouse Pointers

As you might have already discovered, the mouse pointer in Publisher changes depending on its location in a publication. Publisher provides more than 15 different pointers, but you'll see these basic seven types most frequently.

Use this pointer		To
	Pointer	Select menu items, buttons, tools, and other basic options.
	I-beam	Position the insertion point in text.
	Mover	Move frames and other objects.
	Resizer	Change the size of frames and other objects. You can resize a frame horizontally, vertically, or diagonally.
	Crosshairs	Draw a new frame.
	Hand	Start a wizard or other service indicated by a button adjoining a frame.
	Crop	Trim off a portion of a picture.

Some of the pointers are displayed when you place the mouse pointer over a certain part of a frame. Other pointers will appear only when the frame has been *selected*. To select a frame, you click anywhere within the frame. The dotted-line frame border will be replaced by a solid border with *selection handles*. The handles are the black squares located along the frame border. You use these handles to resize a frame horizontally, vertically, or diagonally.

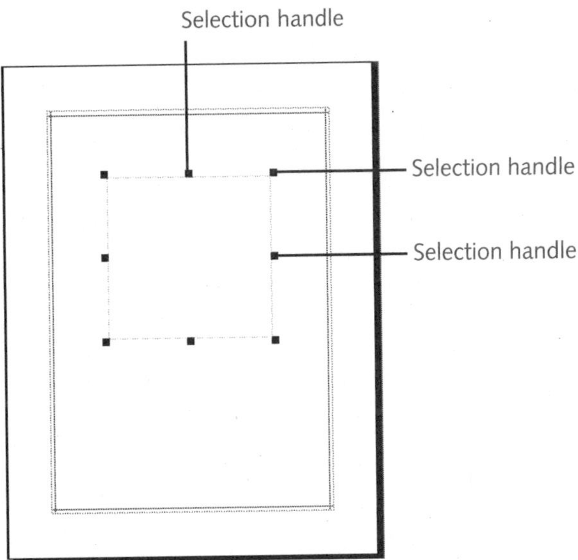

The mover works a bit differently for text frames. When a text frame includes only placeholder content, the mover will appear whenever you position the pointer over the frame. You can then click and drag the frame to a different location. But when a text frame contains real content, the mover will appear only when you position the pointer over the border. You can then click the border and drag the frame to a different location. In a picture frame, the mover appears whenever you position the pointer anywhere on the frame.

Some frames have a special purpose for the particular type of publication you are creating. A good example is the logo frame in the business card you have created. The logo frame actually encapsulates two frames—one for the logo picture and another for the logo text. When you click the logo frame, a Wizard Wand button will appear attached to the bottom of the frame. This button indicates that a wizard is available to guide you through the steps to create and insert a logo.

Display mouse pointers

If you are not working through this lesson sequentially, open the file Business Card 2 before you continue.

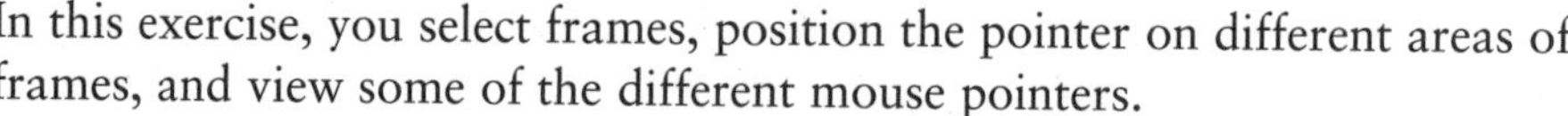

In this exercise, you select frames, position the pointer on different areas of frames, and view some of the different mouse pointers.

1. Position the mouse pointer anywhere over the pyramid picture in the business card.

   The pointer changes to the mover and the ScreenTip reads *Logo Picture*, indicating that this is a picture frame.

2. Click the logo pyramid or the placeholder word *Organization*.

   The frame border changes to a solid line with selection handles. The Wizard Wand button appears at the bottom of the frame.

Wizard Wand

3. Position the pointer on the frame border (but not on a selection handle).

   The Mover appears.

Mover

4. Position the pointer on the selection handle that appears above the top of the pyramid.

   The pointer changes to the Vertical Resizer.

Vertical Resizer

5. Position the pointer over each of the other selection handles, one at a time, to view the other resizers.

6. Position the pointer over the Wizard Wand button.

   The hand pointer appears, and the ScreenTip lets you know that clicking the button will start a wizard (but don't click it yet).

Hand

Using the Logo Creation Wizard

The Logo Creation Wizard is available in any publication that contains a business logo. The wizard walks you through the process of either inserting an existing logo inside the logo frame or creating a new logo. If your company does not have a logo, you can use the wizard to create one for you.

Publisher associates a logo with a particular set of personal information. After you've used the Logo Creation Wizard to insert or create a logo, that logo will be made available in other publications that use the same personal information. For example, you used the Other Organization set of personal information earlier to create a business card for your client. So, after you provide a logo for the business card, that same logo will be made available whenever you create other publications that also use the Other Organization set of information.

Add a logo to a business card

If you are not working through this lesson sequentially, open the file Business Card 2 before you continue.

In this exercise, you insert an existing logo onto the business card.

1. Click the Pyramid icon.

   A Wizard Wand button appears below the logo frames.

2. Click the Wizard Wand button.

   The Logo Creation Wizard pops up in its own window.

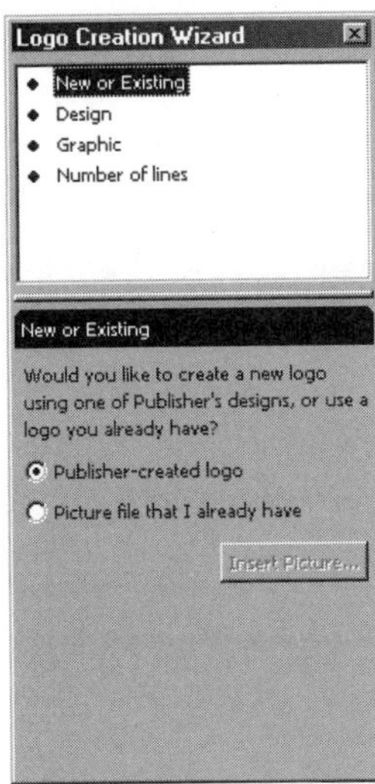

3. Click the Picture File That I Already Have option, and then click the Insert Picture button.

   The Insert Picture dialog box appears.

4. Use the Look In drop-down list to display the contents of the Office 2000 8in1 Step by Step folder on your hard disk drive.

5. Double-click the Publisher Practice folder.

6. Double-click the file named LMR Logo.tif, and then close the Logo Creation wizard window.

   The placeholder graphic is replaced by the actual logo, as shown on the following page.

Close

Moving and Resizing Frames

If you wanted, you could consider the business card complete as it is now. However, maybe you feel that a bit of rearranging is in order to make better use of the space on the card. Your business partner has already explained that you can move a frame by selecting it and then dragging the border of the frame. But in most Publisher templates, much of the space is already occupied by existing frames that contain real or placeholder content. When you drag a frame to a different location, you might find that part of the frame overlaps another frame. Although Publisher allows you to overlap frames, doing so often makes it difficult to determine what content goes with which frame.

A better approach is to resize a frame before you move it so that the border tightly surrounds the content. Or if you are moving a new frame near another frame that has free space within its borders, you can resize the original frame so that the border tightly surrounds the content and thus makes room for the new frame.

Resize and move frames

If you are not working through this lesson sequentially, open the file Business Card 3 before you continue.

You notice that the address lines on the business card take up less than half the vertical space allocated to the frame. In this exercise, you reduce the size of the frame, and then move it to a more appealing location.

1. Click anywhere in the address text frame. (If you want to make sure your pointer is positioned correctly, wait a second or two for the ScreenTip to appear.)

Vertical Resizer

2. Place the pointer on the top-center selection handle until you see the Vertical Resizer, drag the selection handle down until the top border is slightly above the first address line, and then release the mouse button.

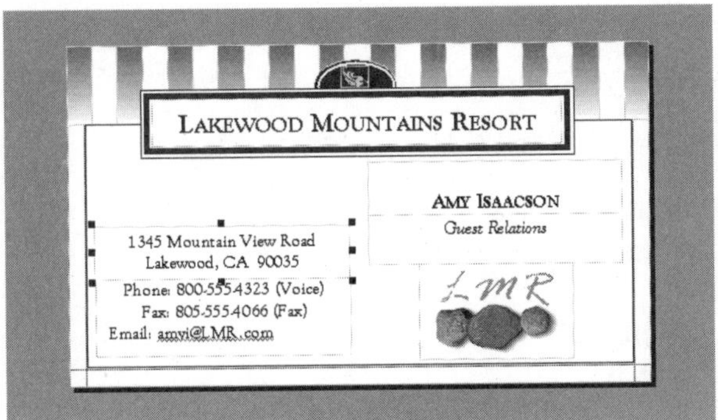

Mover

3. Position the pointer on the top border of the address text frame so that the mover appears.
4. Drag the frame up about one-half inch so that it appears as shown below, and then release the mouse button.

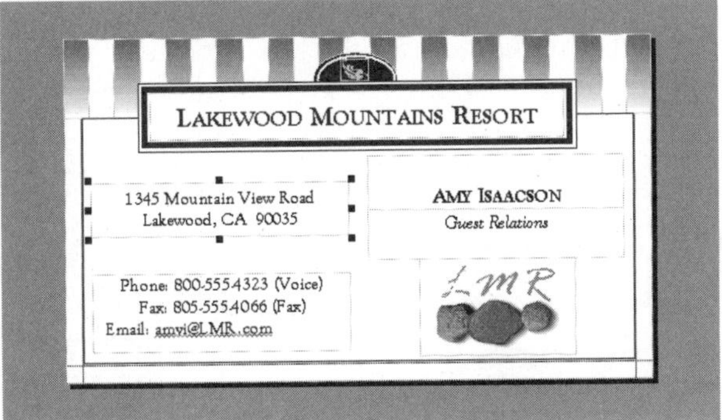

Changing Font Attributes

Sometimes minor changes to the appearance of text can make a big difference in the appearance of a publication. The quickest and often the most effective way to adjust the appearance of text is to change one or more *font attributes*, such as putting text in a bold or italic font, or changing the size of the text altogether. Here are some examples:

Italicizing text for elegance.

Bolding text for emphasis.

Bolding and italicizing for a bit of both.

Enlarging the font to attract the eye.

Changing font attributes works the same in Publisher as it does in all Office 2000 applications. To change attributes to text that has already been typed, you first select the text to be formatted by dragging the I-beam pointer over the text, and then click the text formatting attribute of your choice on the Formatting toolbar.

Apply attributes to text

If you are not working through this lesson sequentially, open the file Business Card 4 before you continue.

In this exercise, you improve the appearance of the business card by bolding, italicizing, and resizing text.

1. Position the pointer in front of the first address line, and then drag down and to the right until all of the text in the address lines has been selected.

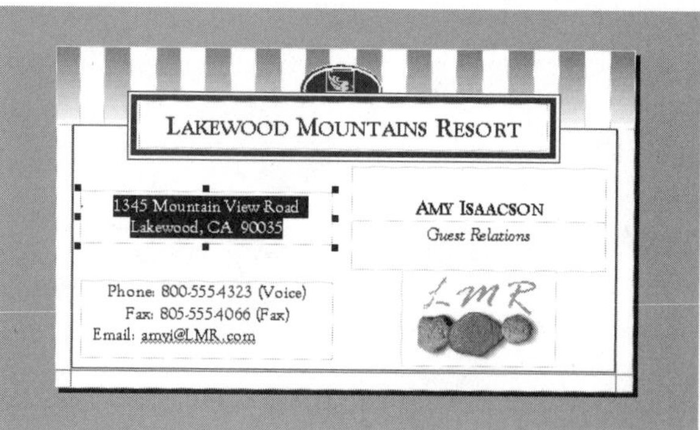

tip

A keyboard shortcut for selecting all of the text in a story (frame) is to press Ctrl+A.

Bold

2. On the Formatting toolbar, click the Bold button.

   The address lines now appear in bold.

3. Drag to select the phone and fax numbers and e-mail address, as shown below.

Italic

4. Click the Italic button on the Formatting toolbar.

   The phone and fax numbers and e-mail address now appear in italics.

5. Triple-click anywhere on Amy Isaacson's name to select it. (Of course, you can also use the dragging method or press Ctrl+A to select the name.)

6. Click the drop-down arrow next to the Font Size box (which currently contains a 9), and click 11.

   The font is enlarged from 9 points to 11 points.

7. Click anywhere outside of the frame to deselect it.

   Your completed business card should match the one shown below.

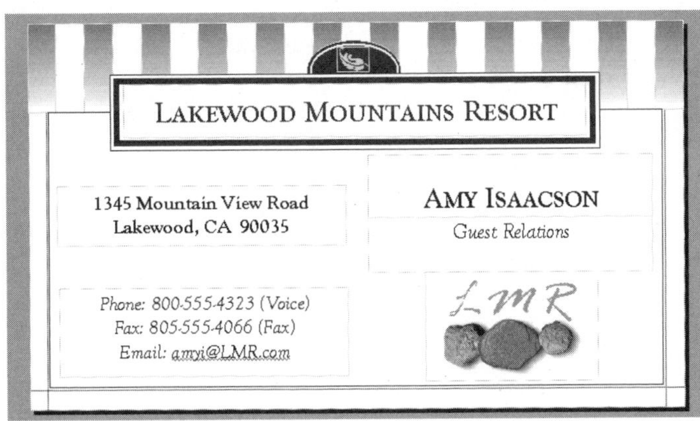

tip

You can make changes to your personal information—such as correcting an address error or adding an e-mail address—at any time. When you click the Update button, Publisher automatically updates the currently open publication with the edited information, if the publication uses that personal information set.

Saving a Publication

If you don't want to be reminded to save your work, you can turn off this option in the Options dialog box, available by clicking Options on the Tools menu.

Saving a publication in Publisher is just like saving a document in any other Office 2000 application. Click Save or Save As on the File menu, and then specify the name and disk location for the publication. By default, Publisher stores your publications in the My Documents folder on the hard disk drive.

If you've had the Office Assistant displayed throughout this lesson, you've already noticed that it reminds you to save your publication every 15 minutes. If you've already done so, that's fine. You can either work through the following exercise or skip to the next section, "Creating Letterhead."

important

Unlike other Office applications, Publisher 2000 allows you to have only one publication open at a time. If you try to create a new publication while you already have one open, Publisher will ask if you want to save your work before closing the current publication.

Save your business card

Step 1 assumes that you are continuing from the previous exercise in this lesson. If you are not continuing from the previous exercise, you should skip this exercise.

In this exercise, you save your business card in the Publisher Practice folder on your hard disk drive.

1. On the File menu, click Save As.

   The Save As dialog box appears.

2. Click the drop-down arrow next to the Save In box, and navigate to the Office 8in1 Step by Step folder on your hard disk drive. Double-click this folder. Then double-click the Publisher Practice folder.

3. Type **LMR Card** in the File Name text box, and then press Enter.

   Publisher saves the publication and then displays a message telling you that you have changed the logo for the Other Organization personal information set. It then asks you whether you want to save this logo for all uses of this information set.

4. Click Yes.

   The logo is now a part of the Other Organization personal information set and will be available when you create publications that use this information set.

Creating Letterhead

Now that you've completed your first publication, your business partner wants to demonstrate how you can use the same design and color scheme to create a consistent "look and feel" for other types of publications that you will create for your client. Because your client also wants you to design letterhead, your next task will be to create letterhead that matches the business card design approach.

As you've seen, a color scheme can be assigned to a personal information set and then reapplied to other publications whenever you use that information set. The color scheme you've specified for the Other Organization information set is Mulberry. However, you need to select a design each time you create a new publication. If you want to apply a consistent design across several publications, you need to remember or jot down the designs that you've selected in previously created publications. For the business card, you selected the Marquee design. So for the letterhead, you will maintain this same design.

Create a letterhead design

This exercise assumes that you have entered the personal and "Other Organization" information described in the "One Step Further" section of Lesson 1.

In this exercise, you create letterhead for Lakewood Mountains Resort.

1. On the File menu, click New.

   The Catalog is displayed.

2. In the left pane, click Letterheads to view the letterhead thumbnails.
3. Scroll through the right pane until you see the Marquee Letterhead thumbnail, and then double-click this thumbnail.

   The Letterhead Wizard starts.

4. Click the Next button.

   The Letterhead Wizard asks you to select a color scheme. You can bypass this step because the color scheme is already defined in the personal information set that you will use.

5. Click the Next button.

   The Letterhead Wizard asks if you would like to include a logo placeholder.

6. Click the Next button.

   Publisher accepts the default answer, Yes, and then asks you which personal information set to use.

7. Click Other Organization, and then click the Finish button.

   The text for Lakewood Mountains Resort replaces the default text, and the company logo is inserted.

Changing the Viewing Size of Your Publications

If you have a Microsoft IntelliMouse, you can also zoom by holding down the Ctrl key and then moving the mouse wheel up or down.

By default, Publisher sizes a publication so that it will fit in its entirety within the workspace (called *whole page* size). For your business card, that approach worked well enough, but for the letterhead and most other publications, this view size is often too small for you to see the content of your publication. Not to worry—Publisher provides several techniques for *zooming* in and out of your publication display. Zooming works like the zoom lens on a video camera: zooming in expands the size of a particular viewing area (and limits your view to only that area), while zooming out reduces the size of the page and increases the viewing area.

Zoom In

Zoom Out

The easiest way to zoom in and out is by using the zoom buttons on Publisher's toolbar. Each time you click the Zoom In button, the page increases in size by 10 to 15 percent (100 percent is actual size). Each time you press the Zoom Out button, the page size decreases by 10 to 15 percent. If you want to zoom to a specific percentage, you can click the drop-down arrow next to the Zoom box and then click a percentage from the list.

If no part of your publication is selected, Publisher zooms in and out from the center of the publication. If you select a particular frame in a publication, Publisher zooms in and out from that region of the publication.

Your business partner explains that as you become more experienced using Publisher, you'll want to zoom in and out of your publication frequently. Zooming in is often necessary to visually inspect, edit, move, or resize a frame. Zooming out is useful so that you can see the overall design of your publication.

Zoom in and zoom out

If you are not working through this lesson sequentially, open the file Letterhead 2 before you continue.

In this exercise, you zoom in on your letterhead publication so that you can read and move content more effectively.

1. On the toolbar, click the Zoom In button.

   Publisher zooms in to a greater percentage.
2. Click the Zoom Out button.

   Publisher zooms out to a smaller percentage.
3. Click the address text frame (located below the logo), and then click the Zoom In button four times.

   Publisher zooms in on the address text frame.
4. Click the Zoom Out button 4 times, and then use the horizontal and vertical scroll arrows to move the page back to the center of the workspace.
5. Click the logo to select it, and then position the pointer over the logo picture so that the mover appears.
6. Drag the logo to the bottom-right corner of the page so that it matches the one shown below.

Zoom In

Zoom Out

Mover

7. Press F9.

   Publisher zooms in on the selected frame at actual size.

8. Press F9 again.

   Publisher zooms out to the previous size.

9. Use the vertical and horizontal scroll bars to reposition the page so that it is in the center of the workspace, and then save the publication with the name *LMR Letterhead*.

One Step Further Creating a Business Envelope

Congratulations! Lakewood Mountains Resort liked the logo and letterhead designs that you created and would like you to use this same design to create a business envelope. The Envelope Wizard allows you to design either a #6 envelope (personal size) or a #10 envelope (business size). The resort manager would like a design for a #10-size envelope.

Create a business envelope

1. On the File menu, click New.

   The Catalog is displayed.

2. Click Envelopes in the list, and then scroll down and double-click the Marquee Envelope thumbnail in the right pane.
3. Click the Finish button.
4. In the Envelope Wizard section of the left pane, click Size, and then click the #10 option button to select the larger envelope size.
5. Click Personal Information, and then click the Other Organization option.

   Publisher adds the Lakewood Mountains Resort mailing information to the return address portion of the envelope.

6. Position the mouse pointer over the mailing address text frame (the rightmost frame) border so that the mover appears, and then right-click and select Delete Object.

   Publisher deletes the frame and the placeholder text.

7. Save the publication to your Publisher Practice folder with the name LMR Envelope.

Finish the lesson

- On the File menu, click New.

  This returns you to the Catalog.

Lesson 2 Quick Reference

To	Do this
Create a business card	Display the Catalog. Click the Publications By Wizard tab. Click Business Cards in the left pane. Double-click the desired business card thumbnail in the right pane, and then work through the wizard prompts or click the Finish button.
Use a different personal information set	Click Personal Information in the top-left pane of the wizard, and then select the desired information set in the bottom-left pane.
Change the color scheme of a publication	Click Color Scheme in the top-left pane of the wizard, and then select the appropriate color scheme in the bottom-left pane.
View frame information	Position the mouse pointer in the frame, and then read the ScreenTip that appears.
Display the Mover	Position the pointer over the frame border until the Mover is displayed.
Display the Resizer	Select the frame and then position the pointer over a selection handle on the frame border to display the Resizer.
Move a text frame	Drag the frame border to move the frame.
Move a picture frame	Click anywhere on the frame and drag it to move the frame.
Resize a frame	Select the frame, and then drag one of the selection handles in the desired direction.

Lesson 2 Quick Reference

To	Do this	Button
Insert a logo from an existing file	Select the logo picture frame, and then click the Wizard Wand button. For existing logos, click the Picture File That I Already Have option, click the Insert Picture button, navigate to the folder that contains the image, and double-click its filename.	
Change font attributes	Select the text that you want to change, and then click the desired font attribute button (bold, italic, or underline) in the Formatting toolbar.	B I U
Change font size	Select the text you want to change. Click the down arrow next to the Font Size text box, and then click a different font size in the list.	
Save a new publication	On the File menu, click Save As, type a name for the publication, and then click the Save button.	
Create letterhead	In the Catalog window, Click Letterheads in the Publications By Wizard list, locate a desired letterhead design in the left pane, and then double-click the thumbnail.	
Zoom in	Click the Zoom In button until the publication size is increased, or select a percentage in the Zoom box drop-down list.	+
Zoom out	Click the Zoom Out button until the publication is reduced, or select a percentage in the Zoom box drop-down list.	–
Toggle between whole page and actual view sizes	Press F9.	

Printing Your Publications

In this lesson you will learn how to:

- ✔ *Print business cards.*
- ✔ *View and navigate through multiple-page publications.*
- ✔ *Print selected pages and ranges in a multiple-page publication.*

ESTIMATED TIME
30 min.

After you've created a publication, you'll naturally want to print it so that you can see the results on paper. Your business partner explains that Microsoft Publisher provides many print options, which vary depending on the type of publication you are viewing and the type of printer you are using. In addition, there are many other publication options available if you want to take your publication to a commercial printer.

In this lesson, you'll print a variety of publications so that you can view and practice using some of the different print options that are available. You'll focus on printing publications at your office, rather than at a commercial printer.

Understanding Your Print Options

Before you begin printing any publications, there are a few common printing terms and features with which you might want to become familiar. While the basics of printing are the same on most printers, printing options will vary from printer to printer. Your business partner at Impact Public Relations uses the analogy of an automobile dashboard. Using all of the knobs, buttons, and dials on the dashboard of your own car has probably become second nature to you. But when you first get behind the wheel of another car, you'll need to spend a few minutes adjusting the different options and features available on the dashboard. You don't need a new driver's license just because you're behind the wheel of a new car; you just need to spend a few moments familiarizing yourself with the different features.

Printing is similar. You might have already become familiar with most of the settings available for your printer at home, but if for any reason you have to print to a different printer, you'll probably find that the options available to you are a bit unfamiliar. Understanding the differences is important for three reasons. First, the printing options that you use at Impact Public Relations might differ from the ones you'll use to print documents at home or at another office. For instance, the printer at your office might allow you to make double-sided publications, while your printer at home might support only single-sided printing.

Second, for high-quality or high-quantity printing, you'll often want to send your publications to a commercial printer. Before you do so, your printer representative might ask you to change the *default printer driver* (the software that controls a specific make and model of printer) that Publisher uses each time you create a publication. Specifying a different printer driver can change the layout of a publication. So, your printer representative might suggest that you specify a printer driver that matches the one used at their shop. That way, what you see on screen as you design your publication will match the results you'll get at the printer.

Third, Publisher often presents you with different printing options based on the size and *orientation* of your publication. Orientation refers to the direction in which text and graphics are printed relative to the horizontal and vertical margins of the paper. Some publications provide better results when they're printed in *landscape* orientation rather than *portrait* orientation. The figure on the following page shows two pages—one printed in portrait orientation and another printed in landscape orientation.

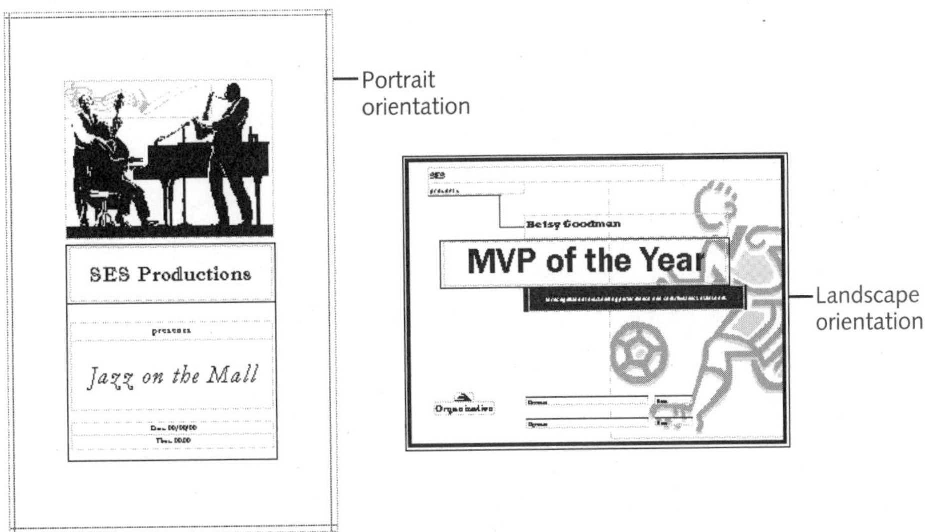

Printing a Business Card

Printing a business card provides some immediate examples of the different print options that are available for a publication that has a unique size. A standard-size business card is only 2 inches by 3½ inches—much smaller than a sheet of 8½-by-11-inch paper. As a result, Publisher gives you the option of printing a single business card in the center of the page or printing multiple cards per page (called *tiling*). You would typically print one card in the center of the page so that you could proof the appearance of your card publication before taking it to the printer. If you were ambitious, you might purchase some heavier-weight paper and then create your own cards, up to 10 per page. Of course, you would also have to trim the cards.

By default, Publisher prints one business card in the center of the page if you click the Print button on the toolbar. The card prints with *crop marks* that define the border of the card so that it can be trimmed to size. You will also see registration marks that a commercial printing service can use to align color separations.

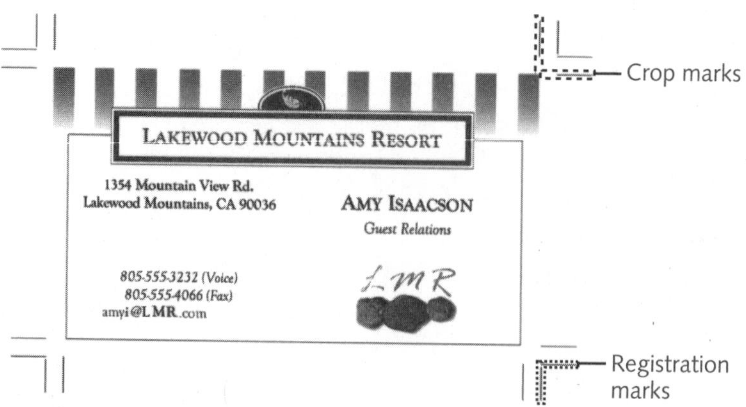

To print 10 cards per page (tile) or to print multiple pages, you use the Print dialog box. The Print dialog box is displayed by clicking Print on the File menu. You can also tile 10 cards per page by clicking Print Tiling in the top-left pane of the Business Card Wizard, selecting the Several Tiled On The Page option button in the bottom-left pane, and then clicking the Print button on the toolbar.

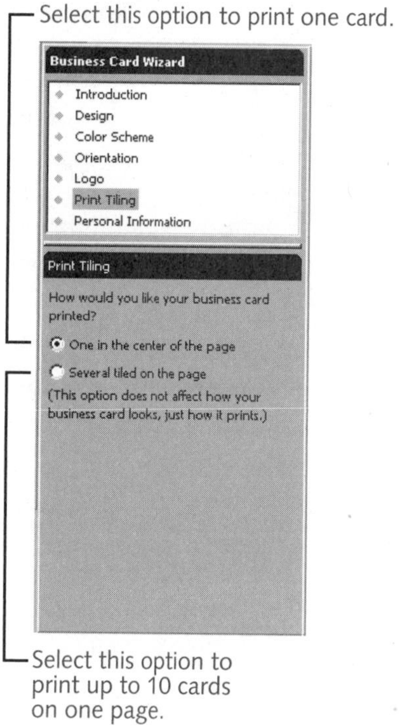

Select this option to print one card.

Business Card Wizard
- Introduction
- Design
- Color Scheme
- Orientation
- Logo
- Print Tiling
- Personal Information

Print Tiling

How would you like your business card printed?

( ) One in the center of the page

( ) Several tiled on the page

(This option does not affect how your business card looks, just how it prints.)

Select this option to print up to 10 cards on one page.

Print a single business card

Before you send Amy Isaacson—your main contact at Lakewood Mountains Resort—her business cards, it would be a good idea to print one copy to proof. In this exercise, you open a business card publication stored in the Publisher Practice folder and then print the card.

1. If the Catalog is currently displayed, close it now. (You can close the Catalog window either by clicking the Close button in the top-right corner of the window or by clicking the Exit Catalog button in the bottom-right corner of the window.)
2. On the File menu, click Open, and then use the Look In drop-down list to navigate to the Publisher Practice folder on your hard disk drive.
3. Double-click the LMR Business Card file.

   The business card is displayed in the publication window.

> **important**
>
> To prevent a printer error message from appearing each time you open a file from the Publisher Practice folder, the default printer for all exercise files has been set to the MS Publisher Color Printer. Before you print any exercise file, you will need to change to your own printer. On the File menu, click Print. Click the Print Name drop-down arrow, and then select your printer from the list.

Print

4. Click the Print button on the toolbar.

   Publisher uses the default printer settings to print one, centered business card on a page.

Print multiple cards per page

If you are not working through this lesson sequentially, open the file LMR Business Card before you continue.

After you're satisfied that the card is correct, you might want to print a sheet of them to provide a guideline for your commercial printer. While you're at it, it might be a good idea to print an extra sheet to keep in your records for when your client needs to reorder. In this exercise, you print two sheets of business cards, with 10 cards printed per page.

1. Make sure the LMR Business Card is displayed.
2. Click Print Tiling in the upper-left pane of the Business Card wizard.

   The Print Tiling options appear in the bottom-left pane.

3. Click the Several Tiled On The Page option in the bottom-left pane.

   Publisher will now print 10 cards on a sheet of paper.

4. On the File menu, click Print.

   The Print dialog box is displayed. The dialog box details that appear on your screen may differ, depending on the type of printer you are using.

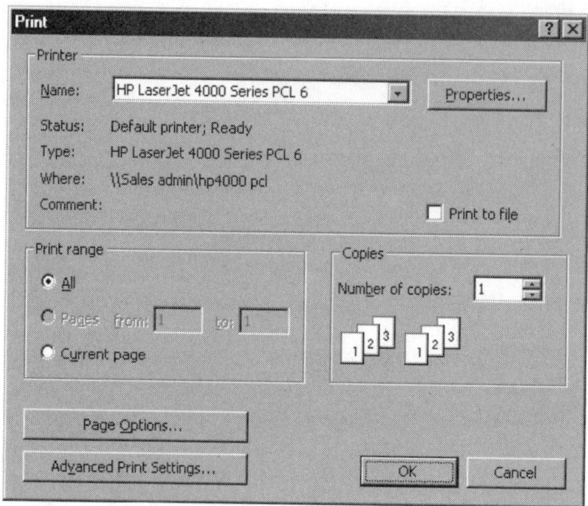

5. Click the Page Options button.

   The Page Options dialog box appears. Notice that the Print Multiple Copies Per Sheet option is already selected, because you just changed this option using the Business Card Wizard.

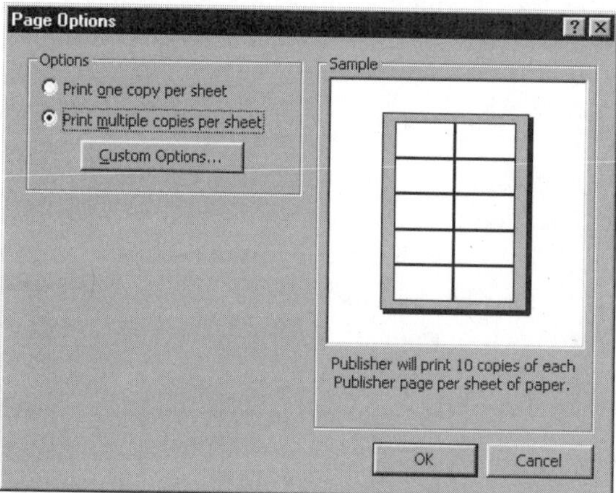

6. Click OK.

   The Page Options dialog box closes and the Print dialog box reappears.

7. Double-click inside the Number Of Copies text box, and type **2**.

8. Click OK.

   Publisher prints two sheets of business cards, 10 per sheet.

Using Expanding Menus in Office 2000

If you've used Microsoft Office applications in the past, you might have noticed that menus are organized a bit differently in Publisher 2000 and in other Office 2000 applications. These new expanding menus are designed to display only the most commonly used commands when you click a particular menu on the menu bar.

The downward-pointing double-arrow at the bottom of a short menu means that other commands are available. You can either position the mouse pointer on this symbol to expand the menu or you can simply wait a few seconds for the expanded menu to be displayed. The menu system will assume that you haven't found what you are looking for in the short menu and will automatically expand the menu to show you all available commands.

If you select a command from the expanded menu, Publisher assumes that you will select this item often or at least occasionally in the future, and moves it up to the short menu. If you don't use that particular command for a while, Publisher will drop it from the short menu and return it to the expanded menu. This approach helps keep the menus looking uncluttered and helps you find what you are looking for a bit faster.

Viewing Multiple-Page Documents

Many publications that you create will contain two or more pages. In Publisher, you can view one or two pages at a time, and you can print all or selected pages. When you create or open a multiple-page publication such as a newsletter or catalog, Publisher displays the publication in *two-page spreads*. Each spread shows how the left and right pages will look together when they are either folded or bound into place.

> **important**
>
> Don't confuse the general Publisher Catalog with the more specific catalog designs that you can use to create product or service catalogs.

In professional publications, page 1 always begins on a right-side page, and pages 2 and 3 then form the left and right pages of the first two-page spread. You can display any spread by clicking either the left or right page number in the Page Navigation bar near the bottom of the publication window.

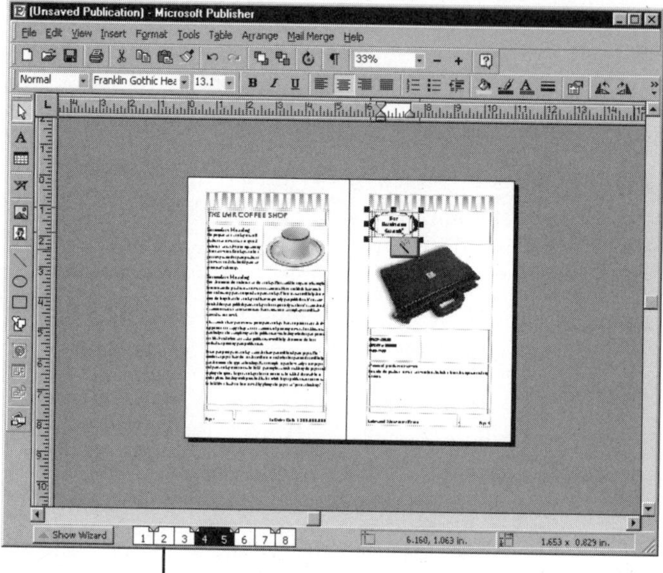

Page Navigation bar

If you want to view only one page at a time, you can easily do so by changing the view. To turn off the two-page spread view, on the View menu click Two-Page Spread. This command is an on/off toggle, so you can turn on the two-page spread view again by following these same steps.

View pages in a multiple-page publication

To introduce you to multiple-page publications, your business partner wants to show you a catalog that Impact Public Relations has created for a client. In this exercise, you open the catalog and view different spreads and pages.

New! 2000

Catalog templates are new in Microsoft Publisher 2000.

1. Open the LMR Gift Shop file stored in the Publisher Practice folder on your hard disk drive. If Publisher asks if you want to save changes to the current publication, click No.

   Publisher displays page 1 of the product catalog.

2. Click either page 2 or 3 in the Page Navigation bar near the bottom of the publication window.

   The spread for pages 2 and 3 is displayed in the viewing area.

3. Click either page 4 or 5 in the Page Navigation bar.

   The spread for pages 4 and 5 is displayed in the viewing area.

4. On the View menu, click Two-Page Spread.

   Publisher turns off the two-page spread view, and now only page 4 is displayed in the viewing area.

5. On the View menu, click Two-Page Spread again.

   Pages 4 and 5 are redisplayed in the viewing area.

Printing a Range of Pages

If you've used other Microsoft Windows applications, you might already be familiar with some basic techniques for printing only selected pages in a multiple-page document. Publisher's options for printing selected pages are similar to those for other Windows applications, and are pretty much self-explanatory: you can print all pages in the publication, print a range of pages in the publication, or you can print only the currently selected page. If you have the two-page spread view turned on and you specify that you want to print the currently selected page, both pages in the spread will be printed.

Printing Page Ranges in Double-Sided Publications

If you are working on a publication that will eventually be printed double sided (duplex) on each sheet of paper, such as a brochure or catalog, and your personal or office printer cannot print double-sided pages, you might be a bit confused the first few times you print. On a printer that can make only single-sided printouts, Publisher will emulate the way pages would be printed front-and-back on a duplex printer. If multiple pages will be printed on a single sheet and then folded and inserted within other sheets, this *imposition* of pages on each sheet will reflect that arrangement. When you print a range of pages, the order of pages on each sheet might seem incorrect to you. However, when they are sent to a copy center or commercial printer, your printer representative should understand the page ordering. (See the illustration on the following page for an example.)

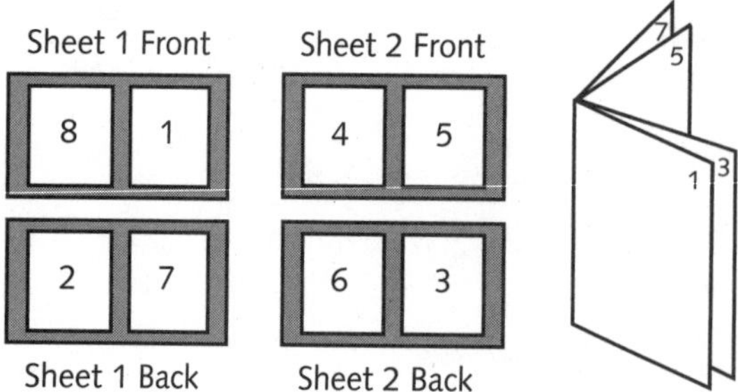

When you select a range of pages to print for any booklet-style publication, Publisher will display the following dialog box (or the Office Assistant—if it is in view—will ask this question).

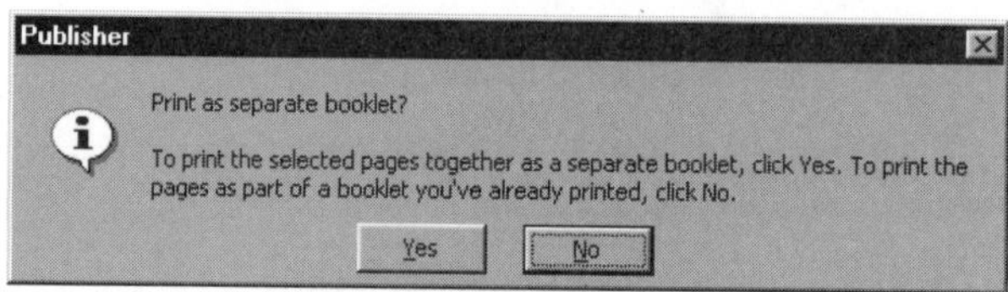

If you want to print the selected page range, including the other pages that will appear on the selected range's spreads (sheets), click Yes. If you want to print only the selected pages on each sheet, click No.

Print selected pages

If you are not working through this lesson sequentially, open the file LMR Gift Shop before you continue.

In this exercise, you print all pages in the catalog, a selected range in the catalog, and then a single page.

> **important**
>
> To prevent a printer error message from appearing each time you open a file from the Publisher Practice folder, the default printer for all exercise files has been set to the Apple Laserwriter Color 12/600. Before you print any exercise file, you will need to change to your own printer. On the File menu, click Print. Click the Print Name drop-down arrow, and then select your printer from the list.

1. On the File menu, click Print.

   The Print dialog box is displayed.

2. In the Print Range section of the dialog box, make sure All is selected, and then click OK.

   Publisher prints four sheets (two pages per sheet) if you have a single-sided printer, or two sheets (four pages per sheet) if you have a double-sided (duplex) printer.

3. On the File menu, click Print.

   Publisher displays the Print dialog box.

4. In the Print Range section of the dialog box, click the Pages option, type **4** in the From text box, press Tab, and then type **6** in the To text box.

5. Click OK.

   Publisher asks if you want to print the selected pages together as a separate booklet or as part of a booklet you've already printed.

6. Click No.

   Publisher prints pages 3 and 6 on one sheet because they are imposed together on one spread in an eight-page booklet and prints 4 and 5 on a single sheet because they are imposed together on one spread in an eight-page booklet.

7. Repeat steps 4 through 6. (The page range from 4 to 6 should already be selected this time.)

   Again Publisher asks if you want to print the selected pages together as a separate booklet or as part of a booklet you've already printed.

8. Click Yes.

   This time, Publisher prints only pages 3 through 6 sequentially. Page 3 is included because it appears on the spread of the selected page range.

9. On the View menu, turn off the Two-Page Spread view, and then select and print only the current page.

   Publisher again asks if you want to print the selected pages together as a separate booklet or as part of a booklet you've already printed.

10. Click either Yes or No (the response will not matter when you print a single page).

    The current page prints separately on a sheet.

Finish the lesson

- On the File menu, click New.

  This returns you to the Catalog.

Lesson 3 Quick Reference

To	Do this	Button
Print a single business card	Open the desired business card file, and then click the Print button.	
Print multiple business cards	Click Print Tiling in the upper-left pane of the Business Card Wizard. In the Print Tiling pane, click the Several Tiled On The Page option. Then click the Print button.	
View different pages	Click the desired page number in the Page Navigation bar.	
Print a range of pages	Open a publication that has multiple pages. On the File menu, click Print, and type the desired page range in the From and To text boxes.	

LESSON

4

Working with Pictures

In this lesson you will learn how to:

- ✔ *Open a blank publication.*
- ✔ *Use the Clip Gallery to insert a clip art picture.*
- ✔ *Create a picture frame.*
- ✔ *Insert a picture from a file.*
- ✔ *Resize a picture frame.*
- ✔ *Recolor a picture and change its border style.*
- ✔ *Create and color shapes.*
- ✔ *Rotate and flip pictures.*
- ✔ *Add a shadow to a picture.*
- ✔ *Import clip art into the Clip Gallery.*
- ✔ *Download clip art from the Clip Gallery Live Web site.*

ESTIMATED TIME
40 min.

Microsoft Publisher 2000 provides you with a lot of flexibility in creating, positioning, formatting, and editing text. As your business partner at Impact Public Relations explains, the text capabilities of Publisher represent only part of the picture. In fact, the ability to insert, position, and size *pictures* in combination with text is the key to creating professional-looking publications.

In this lesson, you use the Clip Gallery to insert clip art into a publication. You then size, recolor, and restore the original color to the picture. You create shapes and then format and color them. You also rotate, flip, and add shadows to manipulate your pictures. Finally, you import a picture to the Clip Gallery and download clip art from the Web.

Opening a Blank Publication

Your business partner would like you to gain some experience working with the pictures available in Publisher. She suggests that you begin by opening a blank page so that you can experiment with some of Publisher's features. She explains that there are two ways to open a blank page.

After you start Publisher, the Catalog window is displayed in the foreground while a publication window is displayed in the background. By default, the publication window displays a blank 8½-by-11-inch page in the workspace. To work with this page, all you need to do is close the Catalog window.

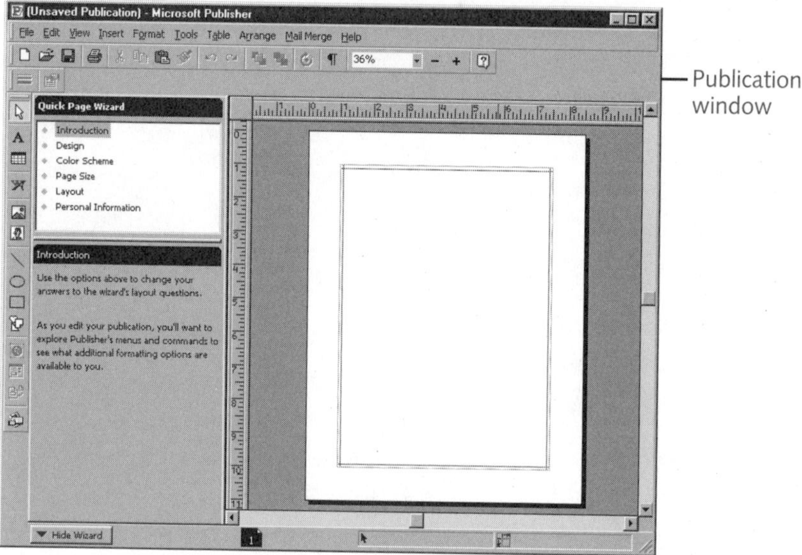

If you already have a publication open, you can display a blank page by first saving the publication and then clicking New on the File menu to display the Catalog. You can then click the Blank Publications tab and double-click the Full Page thumbnail. Your current publication will close and will be replaced by the blank page.

Display a blank page

In this exercise, you use two techniques to display a blank page: first by using the Blank Publications section of the Catalog, and then by restarting Publisher and closing the Catalog window.

1. If the Catalog is not currently displayed, click New on the File menu.

   The Catalog window is displayed.

2 Click the Blank Publications tab, and then double-click the Full Page thumbnail.

Full-size blank page

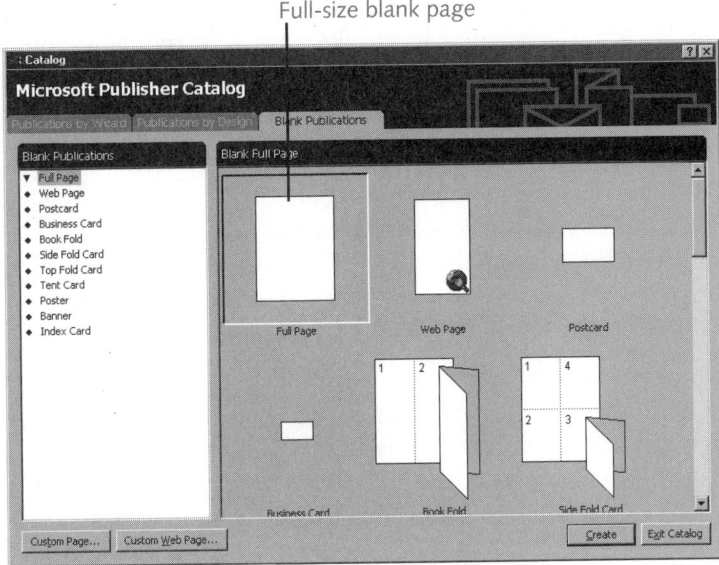

The Catalog closes and a blank page appears in the publication window.

3 Click the Close button at the top-right corner of the publication window.

The Publisher program closes.

4 Click the Start button on the Windows taskbar, point to Programs, and then click Microsoft Publisher.

The Publisher program restarts and the Catalog window is displayed in the foreground.

5 Click the Close button at the top-right corner of the Catalog window.

The Catalog window closes and a blank page is displayed.

Adding Clip Art

You don't have to create your own pictures "from scratch," because Publisher includes thousands of images, called *clip art*, stored either on your hard disk drive or on your Office 2000 CD-ROM. You can insert a picture directly from the Clip Gallery, or you can insert just about any image that you have created, scanned, downloaded from the World Wide Web, or that has been provided to you in an electronic format and stored on disk.

Clip Gallery Tool

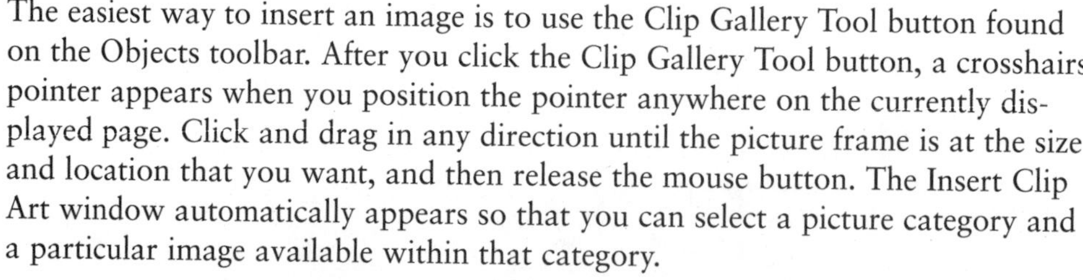

The easiest way to insert an image is to use the Clip Gallery Tool button found on the Objects toolbar. After you click the Clip Gallery Tool button, a crosshairs pointer appears when you position the pointer anywhere on the currently displayed page. Click and drag in any direction until the picture frame is at the size and location that you want, and then release the mouse button. The Insert Clip Art window automatically appears so that you can select a picture category and a particular image available within that category.

For a demonstration of how to insert a clip art picture, open the Office 8in1 Step by Step folder on your hard disk. Then open the Publisher Demos folder, and double-click the Insert Clip Art icon.

The Insert Clip Art window includes three folder tabs: Pictures, Sounds, and Motion Clips. The Sounds and Motion Clips categories are useful for inserting sounds and videos into Web pages that you create. You'll use the Pictures tab to insert pictures into publications that will be printed.

Searching for a Picture

You can browse through the Clip Gallery by selecting one of the category thumbnails, which then displays up to 60 thumbnails relating to that category. If you want to continue browsing through that category, click the Keep Looking button that appears at the end of the thumbnails. To return to the list of categories, you just click the All Categories button on the Insert Clip Art window's toolbar.

You can also use the search text box to enter words or phrases that describe the kind of picture you want. When you use the search feature of the Clip Gallery, it is important to realize that the order in which you enter search words can make a difference. For instance, if you search for "Cats people," the Clip Gallery will first display pictures that have cats *and* people, followed by pictures of cats only, followed by pictures of people only. If you reverse the order of the search by typing "People cats" in the search text box, the Clip Gallery will first display pictures that have cats *and* people, followed by pictures of people only, followed by pictures of cats only.

tip

The Search For Clips text box is not case sensitive, so it doesn't matter whether you type uppercase or lowercase letters. The search result will be the same.

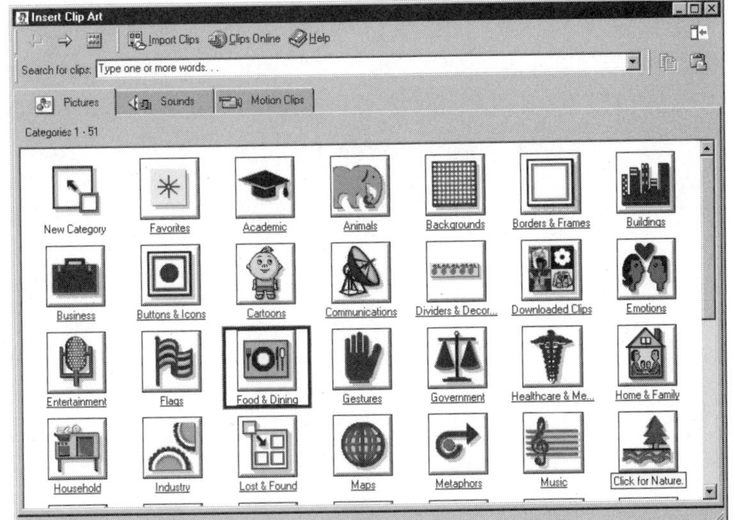

Category thumbnails

If you are not working through the following exercise sequentially, display the Catalog, select the Blank Publications tab, and then double-click the Full Page thumbnail.

Use the Clip Gallery

Your business partner wants you to insert a decorative picture that will be used for several Lakewood Mountains Resort publications. In this exercise, you use the Clip Gallery to browse a library of images, and you insert a picture into a publication.

Clip Gallery Tool

1. Click the Clip Gallery Tool button on the Objects toolbar, and then position the pointer anywhere on the blank page.

   The crosshairs pointer appears.

2. Click near the top-left corner of the page and drag down and to the right until you have created a box about 2 inches wide by 3 inches tall. Release the mouse button.

   Publisher displays the Insert Clip Art window.

3. Scroll down, and then click the Food & Dining category thumbnail.

   The Insert Clip Art window displays pictures related to food and dining.

4. Scroll down to view all of the first 60 pictures in the Food category.
5. At the end of the list of pictures, click the Keep Looking button.

   Publisher displays the next 60 pictures related to food and dining.

To replace an inserted clip art picture, double-click the clip art picture in your publication to redisplay the Clip Gallery, find the new picture, and then double-click it.

6. Click in the Search For Clips text box, type **dogs cats**, and then press Enter.

   Publisher displays pictures of dogs first, followed by pictures of cats.

7. Click in the Search For Clips text box, type **vines**, and then press Enter.

   Publisher displays pictures that contain vines.

8. Click the picture that shows a green vine in a rectangular box.

   Publisher displays a pop-up list of clip art buttons.

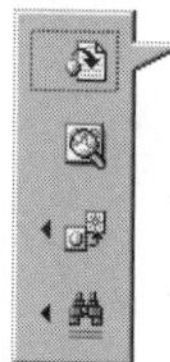

Insert Clip

Close

9. Click the Insert Clip button.

   Publisher inserts the selected picture into your frame.

10. Click the Close button in the upper-right corner of the Insert Clip Art window.

    The Insert Clip Art Window closes.

important

Because the Clip Gallery is a stand-alone application, the Insert Clip Art window will remain open after you insert a picture. You can either close the window on your own (using the Close button) or you can minimize the window if you think you'll want to use it later.

Using Drag and Drop to Insert Clip Art

You can also drag a picture directly from the Insert Clip Art window and into a frame in your publication. If you drag and drop a picture into a portion of your publication that does not have a frame, Publisher will automatically create a frame for the picture.

Change To Small Window

To drag and drop a picture, you first locate the clip art picture that you want to insert. Then, you click the Change To Small Window button located near the top-right corner of the Insert Clip Art window. This will reduce the Insert Clip Art window so that you can view the contents of your publication.

For a demonstration of how to drag and drop a clip art picture, open the Office 8in1 Step by Step folder on your hard disk. Then open the Publisher Demos folder, and double-click the Drag on Clip icon.

Now you can drag the picture into an existing frame or drag it to an empty part of the publication. If you drag the picture into a frame that already contains a picture, Publisher will replace the existing picture with the new one. If you drag the picture into a text frame, Publisher will create a picture frame within the text frame. After you have dragged the picture into your publication, you can either return the Insert Clip Art window to full size by clicking the Change To Full Window button or you can minimize or close the window.

Change To Full Window

Drag a picture into a publication

In this exercise, you drag and drop a picture from the Insert Clip Art window into your publication.

If you are not working through this lesson sequentially, open the file Picture Practice 2 before you continue.

1. On the Insert menu, point to Picture and click Clip Art.

   The Insert Clip Art window opens.

2. Click in the Search For Clips text box, type **picnic**, and press Enter.

   Publisher displays pictures related to picnicking.

3. Click the Change To Small Window button.

   Publisher narrows the size of the Insert Clip Art window and displays it along the left side of your screen so that you can see your publication window.

Change To Small Window

4. Drag the first picture into a blank area of your publication window.

   Publisher places the picture into a picture frame within your publication.

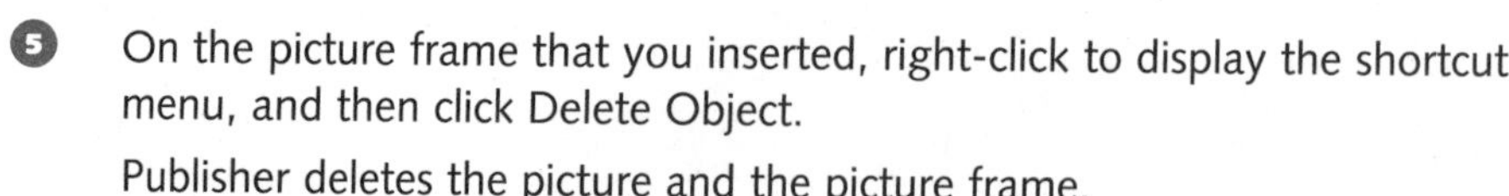

5. On the picture frame that you inserted, right-click to display the shortcut menu, and then click Delete Object.

   Publisher deletes the picture and the picture frame.

Change To Full Window

6. Click the Change To Full Window button.

   The Insert Clip Art window is redisplayed at full size.

7. In the top-right corner of the Insert Clip Art window, click the Close button.

   The Insert Clip Art window is closed.

Size a picture

If you are not working through this lesson sequentially, open the file Picture Practice 2 before you continue.

In this exercise, you resize the picture that you inserted in your publication.

1. Click the vine picture.
2. Position the pointer over the bottom-right corner of the clip art picture until the Resizer appears.
3. Drag down and to the right until the picture is about twice its original size.

   Publisher enlarges the picture.

Undo

4. Click the Undo button.

   The picture is returned to its original size.

Adding a Picture

As huge as Publisher's Clip Gallery is, you aren't limited to the Clip Gallery for images that you want to insert. In fact, you can insert images created or saved by most image-editing programs. When a program saves an image to disk, it saves the image in a particular image *format*. Dozens of image formats are in wide use today, and Publisher supports most of these. Each format saves an image a bit differently. Some formats are optimized so that images are *compressed* or reduced on disk to save space. Compressed images are then uncompressed and displayed at normal size when you insert them into your publications. Other formats are designed to work best with a particular software application. Still other formats are optimized to store color information as efficiently as possible. The following table explains several common image formats, which are usually identified by the filename extensions assigned to them.

Extension	Image format	Use
BMP	Windows bitmap	A Microsoft Windows bitmap image is commonly used for photographs and illustrations. Bitmap images do not always resize well; however, this is a common format recognized by almost all Windows applications.
GIF	Graphics Interchange Format	A GIF is one of three compressed image formats that can be viewed in a Web browser. As a result, GIFs are popular for use in Web pages.
JPG	Joint Photographic Experts Group	A JPG (or JPEG as it is sometimes known) is used to efficiently compress and store images that include thousands or even millions of colors. The JPG format is also supported by most Web browsers and as a result is also a popular format used in Web pages.
TIF	Tagged Image File Format	A TIF (also known as TIFF) is an older format used to compress and store color images. This format is recognized by most Windows applications, but is not recognized by Web browsers.
WMF	Windows Metafile	Like the BMP format, the WMF format is a creation of Microsoft, but it also provides "hinting" information that allows images to be resized without a loss in quality. The WMF format is widely used by Microsoft Office applications, but is not recognized by Web browsers.

Inserting Pictures

If you want to insert a picture that is not included in the Clip Gallery, you can easily do so by first creating an empty picture frame and then pointing to Picture on the Insert menu. Next you click From File to display the Insert Picture dialog box.

Use the Look In drop-down list to select the drive and folder where the desired picture is stored. If you click the picture's filename in the list of files, Publisher will display a thumbnail *preview* of the image in the right side of the Insert Picture dialog box. If the selected picture is the one you want, click the Insert button to insert the picture into the picture frame.

If you are not working through this lesson sequentially, open the file Picture Practice 3 before you continue.

Insert a picture from a file

Your business partner now wants you to insert a photo, which will be used in an upcoming brochure for Lakewood Mountains Resort. In this exercise, you create a picture frame, locate and insert a picture, and then resize the picture.

Picture Frame Tool

1. Click the Picture Frame Tool button on the Objects toolbar, and then position the crosshairs pointer in the center of the publication along the left edge.
2. Drag down and to the right to create a rectangular picture frame that fills most of the bottom half of the page.

   Publisher creates an empty picture frame.
3. On the Insert menu, point to Picture, and then click From File.

   Publisher displays the Insert Picture dialog box.
4. Use the Look In list to navigate to the Publisher Practice folder on your hard disk drive.
5. Click the Beach.jpg filename in the list of files, and then click the Insert button.

   Publisher inserts the picture into the picture frame.

Resizer

6. Position the pointer over the top-right corner of the picture frame until the Resizer appears.
7. Drag down to the left about half an inch.

   Publisher reduces the image size slightly.
8. Save the publication to your Publisher Practice folder using the filename LMR Images.

Recoloring a Picture

Many of the clip art images that Publisher provides in the Clip Gallery contain only one color. You can change the color in these images by using the *Recolor Picture* feature. To recolor a picture, you first click the image that you want to recolor. Then you click Recolor Picture on the Format menu. Publisher displays the Recolor Picture dialog box, which you can use to select a different color for the image.

You should recolor only a one-color picture. If you recolor a color photograph or a multi-colored illustration, it will be changed to a single color. If you do this either intentionally or accidentally and don't like the result, you can click the Restore Original Colors button in the Recolor Picture dialog box.

Publisher displays only those colors used in the current design scheme (which is specified when you use a wizard to create a publication or when you assign a personal information set). If you wanted to view more colors, you would click the Color drop-down arrow and then click the More Colors button. The Colors dialog box would then appear, displaying 84 basic colors.

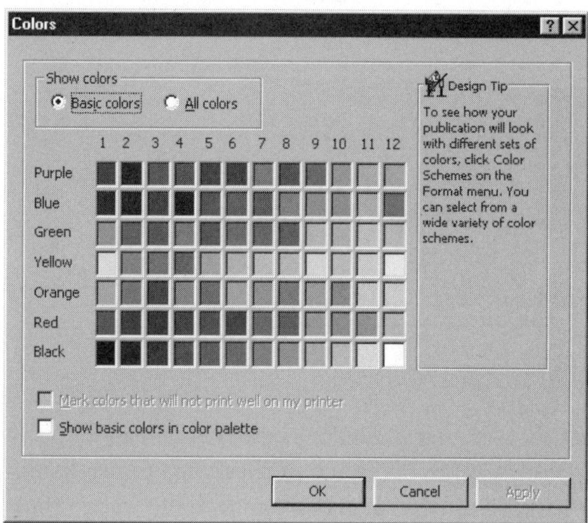

Most monitors and color printers can display or print thousands or even millions of colors by combining the primary colors (red, green, and blue) in different ways. You can expand your color choices by clicking the All Colors option in the Colors dialog box. You can then select a more precise color by clicking inside the color palette and dragging the mouse pointer until the desired color appears in the New color box.

Recolor a picture

If you are not working through this lesson sequentially, open the file LMR Images 2 before you continue.

In this exercise, you change the color of the vine picture to a lighter shade.

1. Click anywhere on the vine picture in your publication.

   The picture is selected.
2. On the Format menu, click Recolor Picture.

   Publisher displays the Recolor Picture dialog box.
3. Click the drop-down arrow next to the Color box.

   Publisher displays a list of colors used in the current color scheme.
4. Click the More Colors button.

   Publisher displays the color palette.

5. Click the second color in the green row, and then click OK.

   Publisher displays a preview of the picture using the selected color.

6. Click the drop-down arrow next to the Color box once again.

   Publisher displays a list of colors used in the current color scheme.

7. Click the More Colors button.

   Publisher redisplays the color palette.

8. Click the All Colors option.

   Publisher displays the color palette of all available colors.

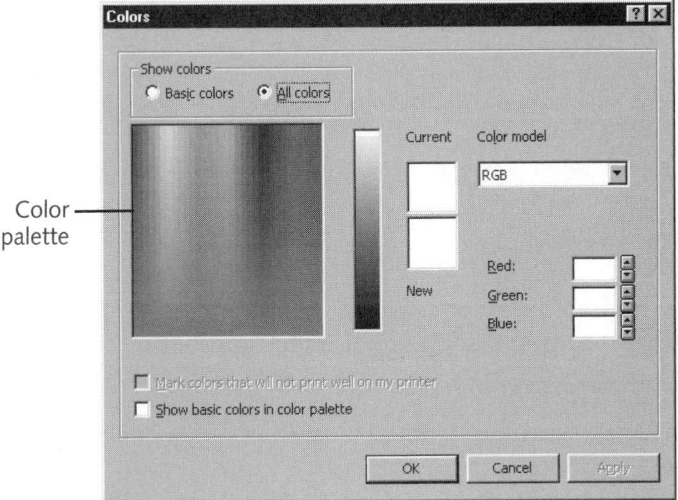

9. Click the color palette, select a color of your own choice (as displayed in the New box), and then click OK.

   Publisher redisplays the Recolor Picture dialog box.

10. Click OK again.

    Publisher recolors the picture using the color that you selected.

Restoring the Original Color of an Image

Whenever you recolor a picture, Publisher stores a record of the original color as well as any other colors that you have selected recently. You can return to a previously used color by displaying the Recolor Picture dialog box, clicking the drop-down arrow to the right of the Color box, and then clicking the desired color. You can return the picture to its original color or colors by clicking the Restore Original Colors button in the Colors dialog box.

Restore the color of a picture

If you are not working through this lesson sequentially, open the file LMR Images 3 before you continue.

In this exercise, you view recent colors that you have selected, and then you restore the vine image to its original color.

1. Select the vine picture, if necessary.
2. On the Format menu, click Recolor Picture.

   Publisher displays the Recolor Picture dialog box.
3. Click the drop-down arrow next to the Color box.

   Publisher displays a list of colors used in the current color scheme, and displays recently used colors in the Recent Colors palette.
4. Click in an empty area of the dialog box.

   Publisher closes the color list.
5. Click the Restore Original Colors button, and then click OK.

   Your picture's original colors are restored.

Creating Shapes

Your business partner explains that Publisher provides several tools that let you create your own shapes and add them to publications. You can create circles, ovals, lines, squares, rectangles, and many other *custom shapes* that Publisher provides for you. All of these drawing features are available from the Objects toolbar.

Drawing tool		Use to
	Oval	Draw ovals and circles. To create a circle, select the Oval Tool, hold down the Shift key, and then drag the pointer. You can also fill an oval or circle with a color.
	Line	Draw lines. You can also change the style, width, and color of a line.
	Custom Shape	Draw a unique shape. Creates a unique shape, such as a starburst, banner, arrow, triangle, bubble, or octagonal or hexagonal shape.
	Rectangle	Draw rectangles and squares. To create a square, select the Rectangle Tool, hold down the Shift key, and then drag the pointer. You can also fill a rectangle or square with a color.

Create shapes

If you are not working through this lesson sequentially, open the file LMR Images 3 before you continue.

In this exercise, you use the Rectangle Tool button to create a rectangle and a square, the Oval Tool button to create a circle, and the Line Tool button to draw a line between two shapes.

1. On the Objects toolbar, click the Rectangle Tool button.
2. Click near the top-right corner of the page, and then drag down and to the left about 1 inch.

   Publisher creates a rectangle of the specified dimensions.
3. Press the Delete key.

   Publisher deletes the rectangle.

Rectangle Tool

4. On the Objects toolbar, click the Rectangle Tool button once again.
5. Hold down the Shift key, click near the top-right corner of the page, and then drag down and to the left about 1 inch.

   Publisher creates a square.

Oval Tool

6. On the Objects toolbar, click the Oval Tool button.
7. Hold down the Shift key, and then drag to create a 1-inch circle underneath the rectangle, but leave about 1 inch of space between the square and the circle.

   Your publication should look similar to the following illustration. If it does not, drag and resize the objects until you have a close match.

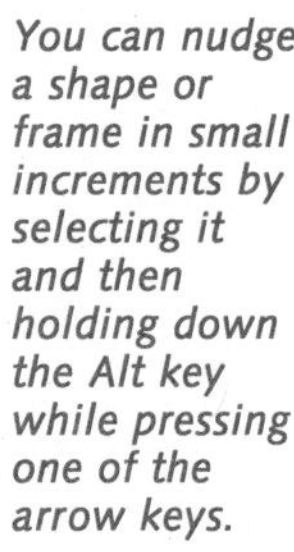

You can nudge a shape or frame in small increments by selecting it and then holding down the Alt key while pressing one of the arrow keys.

Line Tool

8. On the Objects toolbar, click the Line Tool button.

9. Click and drag to form a line from the bottom of the square to the top of the circle, as shown below.

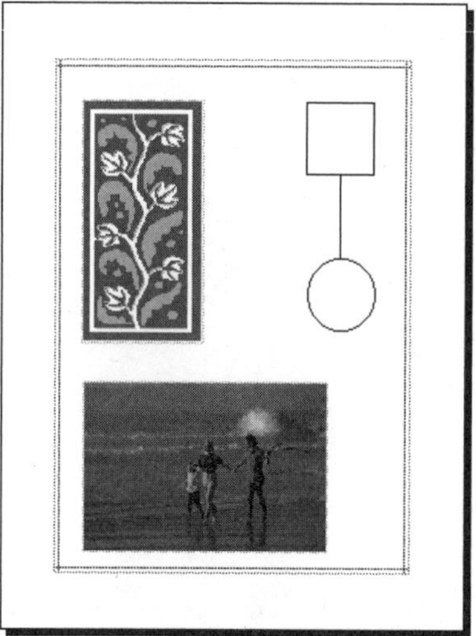

Formatting and Coloring Shapes

Fill Color

Publisher provides a variety of techniques for changing the colors of shapes as well as the border style. To change the color of a shape, you can click the shape, and then on the Formatting toolbar, click the Fill Color button. You can then select an available color in the Scheme Colors section of the list of colors, or you can select More Colors to display and select from additional colors.

tip

You can also change the color of shapes by clicking Fill Color on the Format menu and then selecting a color from the Colors dialog box.

Line/Border Style

To change the border of a shape, click the shape, and then on the Formatting toolbar, click the Line/Border Style button. You can click a different border width, or you can click More Styles to change to a dashed border or to change the border to a different color.

Add/Remove Both Arrows

If you want to add one or more arrowheads to a line without changing other line formatting, you can click one of the Add/Remove Arrow buttons on the Formatting toolbar, such as the Add/Remove Both Arrows button.

Change the color and format of shapes

If you are not working through this lesson sequentially, open the file LMR Images 4 before you continue.

In this exercise, you change the color and format of a square and circle.

1. Click the circle shape.
2. On the Formatting toolbar, click the Fill Color button, and then click a color of your choice from the Scheme Colors palette.

   Publisher fills the circle with the selected color.
3. Click the square shape.

Fill Color

4. On the Formatting toolbar, click the Fill Color button, and then click the More Colors button.

   Publisher displays the Colors dialog box.
5. Click the Basic Colors option, if it is not already selected.

   Publisher switches to the list of basic colors.
6. Click the first color in the Purple row, and then click OK.

   Publisher fills the circle with the selected purple color.
7. Click the line that you drew between the circle and square.

Line/Border Style

8. On the Formatting toolbar, click the Line/Border Style button, and then click More Styles.

   Publisher displays the Line dialog box.
9. In the Line Thickness section, click 4 Pt, and in the Arrowheads section, click the Both option.

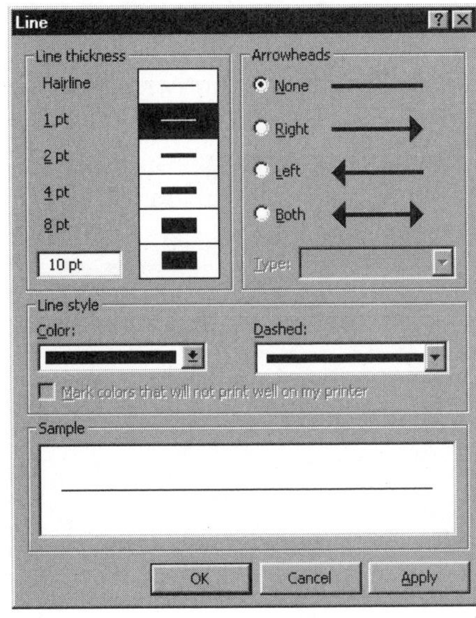

10. In the Line Style section, click the drop-down arrow next to the Color box, and then click the More Colors button. Next click the Basic Colors option, if it isn't already selected, and then click any color in the Blue row.

11. Click OK, and then click OK again to have your changes take effect.

    The line is displayed with the new line thickness, arrowheads, and color.

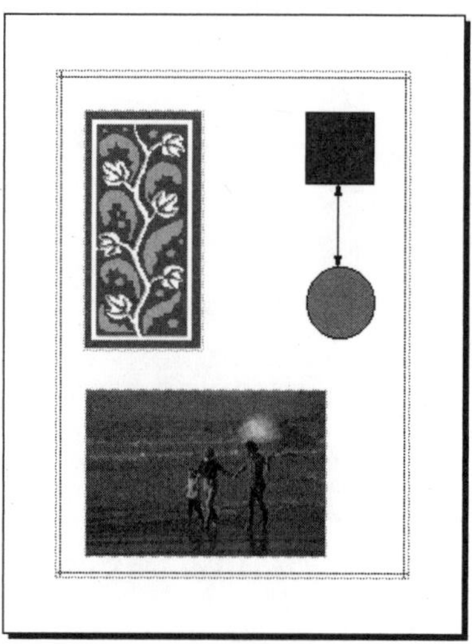

12. Save the publication to the Publisher Practice folder.

Creating Custom Shapes

Custom Shapes Tool

Publisher also provides a palette of custom shapes that you can use to create arrows, banners, starbursts, and a variety of other unique shapes. To create a custom shape, you click the Custom Shapes Tool button on the Objects toolbar. Publisher will display an additional palette of custom shapes. Click the one you want, and then click and drag in your publication to create the desired shape. As is true for basic shapes, you can fill a custom shape with color.

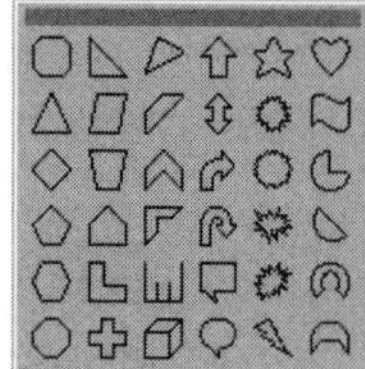

Create a custom shape with a gradient

If you are not working through this lesson sequentially, open the file LMR Images 5 before you continue.

In this exercise, you create a custom shape, fill it with color, and add a gradient.

1. On the Objects toolbar, click the Custom Shapes Tool button.

   Publisher displays a palette of custom shapes.

2. Click the fifth shape (starburst) in the fifth row of the palette of custom shapes, and then drag about one inch in any empty area of your publication to create the shape.

Fill Color

3. On the Formatting toolbar, click the Fill Color button, and then click a color of your choice from the Scheme Colors palette.

   Publisher fills the shape with the selected color.

4. On the Formatting toolbar, click the Fill Color button, and then click Fill Effects.

   Publisher displays the Fill Effects dialog box.

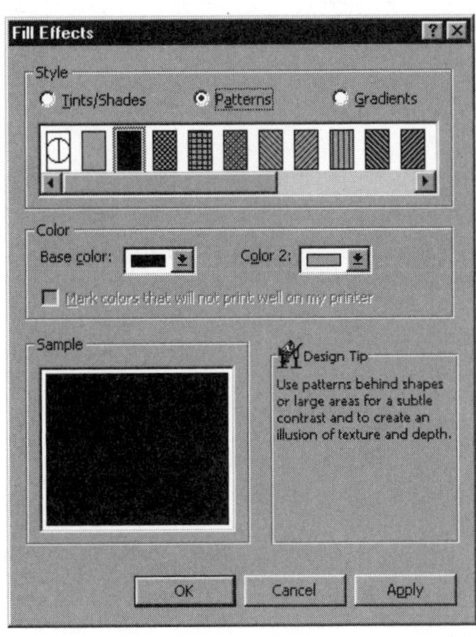

A gradient is a gradual shift in color or grayscale, shifting to the left, right, top, bottom, outward from center, or inward to center.

5. Click the Gradients option, click the drop-down arrow next to the Color 2 box, and then click a color of your choice from the Scheme Colors palette.

   Publisher displays a sample of the picture in the dialog box.

6. Click OK.

   The starburst is displayed with a gradient of the two colors you selected.

7. Save the publication.

Manipulating Pictures

Publisher includes several options that you can use to rotate and flip your pictures, and even to add a shadow to create a heightened effect. The easiest way to rotate or flip a picture is to use the buttons available on the Picture toolbar.

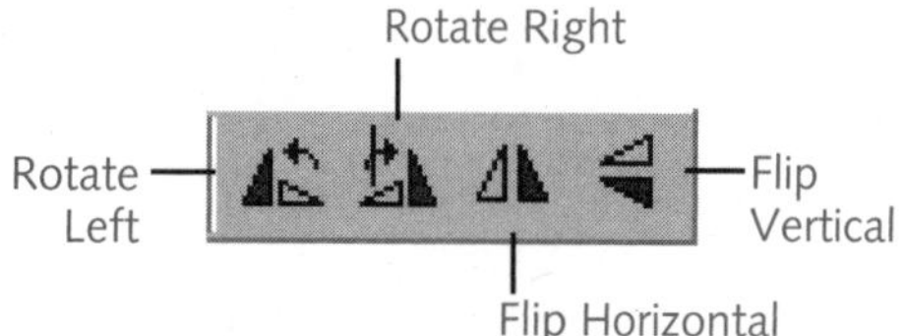

Use this button		To
	Rotate Left	Rotate a picture 90 degrees to the left.
	Rotate Right	Rotate a picture 90 degrees to the right.
	Flip Horizontal	Flip a picture horizontally (so that the right and left sides are reversed).
	Flip Vertical	Flip a picture vertically (so that the top and bottom are reversed).

Custom Rotate

The Standard toolbar also includes a Custom Rotate button that you can use to drag and rotate a picture at a particular tilt. To custom-rotate a picture, select the picture, click the Custom Rotate button, and then select a desired rotation degree. An even easier way to custom-rotate a picture is to click the picture, hold down the Alt key, and then drag one of the corner selection handles in the desired direction.

To add a shadow to a picture, you click Shadow on the Format menu.

Rotate, flip, and add shadows to your pictures

If you are not working through this lesson sequentially, open the file LMR Images 6 before you continue.

In this exercise, you use the toolbar buttons and the Alt key to rotate a picture, and then you flip and add a shadow to a picture.

1. Click the vine picture in your publication.
2. On the Picture toolbar, click the Rotate Left button.

   The picture rotates 90 degrees to the left.
3. On the Picture toolbar, click the Rotate Right button.

   Rotate Right

   The picture rotates 90 degrees to the right, back to its original orientation.
4. Hold down the Alt key, click the top-right selection handle of the vine picture, and then drag down until the picture is rotated about 20 degrees.
5. On the Formatting toolbar, click the Undo button.

   Undo

   The Picture returns to its previous orientation.

tip

The ScreenTip for the Undo button always displays the name of the action that can be undone. Similarly, the Redo button always displays the undone action that can be redone.

6. Click the beach photograph.

   The picture is selected.
7. On the Formatting toolbar, click the Flip Horizontal button.

   Flip Horizontal

   The right and left sides of the photograph are flipped.
8. On the Format menu, click Shadow. (If necessary, wait a few seconds for the Shadow command to appear.)

   A shadow is added to the beach picture.

Zoom In

Zoom Out

9. Click the Zoom In button four times.

   Publisher zooms in on the beach picture so that you can see the effect of the shadow.

10. Click the Zoom Out button four times.

    Publisher zooms back to the original, whole-page size.

11. Save the publication.

One Step Further Adding Pictures to the Clip Gallery

For a demonstration of how to import a picture into the Clip Gallery, open the Office 8in1 Step by Step folder on your hard disk. Then open the Publisher Demos folder, and double-click the Import Clip icon.

Although you can insert a picture from a file located anywhere on your hard disk, this can be tedious if you have to do it repeatedly and have to navigate through several folders. If you have pictures of your own that you will be using in several publications, you can import (add) them to the Clip Gallery so that you can insert them more easily. This is an especially handy feature for pictures that you've scanned in or downloaded from a digital camera.

To import a picture into the Clip Gallery, you begin by clicking the Import Clip button on the Insert Clip Art window's toolbar. When you import a picture, you have the option to either move or copy the picture from its current location into the same folder as all of the other Clip Gallery pictures. You can also specify that you want to leave the picture at its current location and just have the Clip Gallery record the location of the picture file.

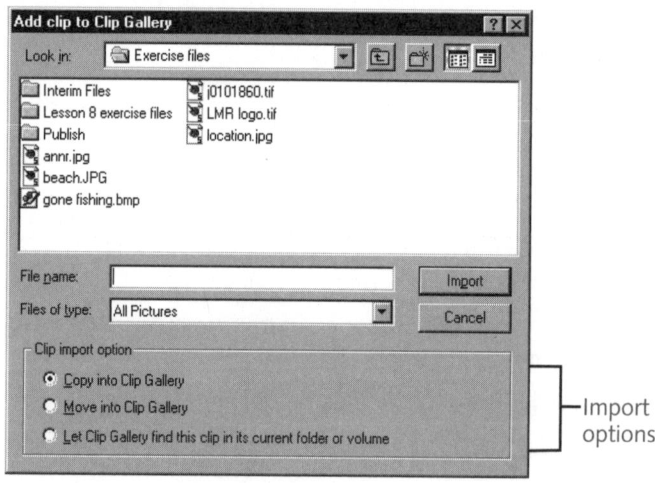

After you locate the file for the picture that you want to import, you can then use the Clip Properties dialog box to create a description for the picture, add it to one of the Clip Gallery's categories, and add key words that you can use to search for and locate the picture quickly.

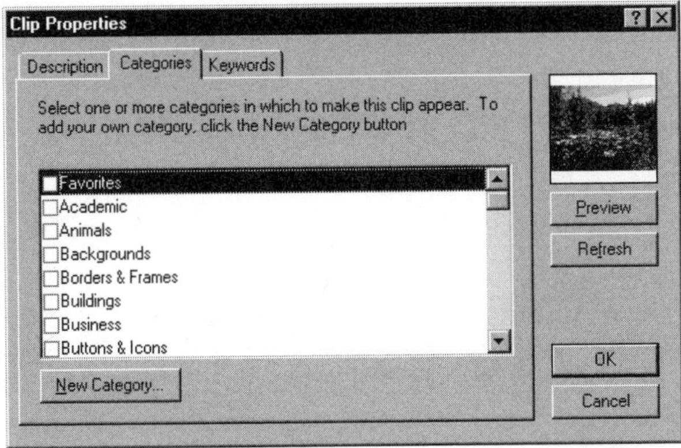

Import a picture into the Clip Gallery

In this exercise, you import a picture into the Clip Gallery and then locate it from within the Insert Clip Art window.

1. On the Insert menu, point to Picture, and then click Clip Art.

   Publisher displays the Insert Clip Art window.
2. Click the Import Clips button.

   Publisher displays the Add Clip To Clip Gallery dialog box.
3. Use the Look In drop-down list to navigate to the Publisher Practice folder located on your hard disk drive, and then double-click the file named Gone Fishing.bmp.

   Publisher displays the Clip Properties dialog box. The Description tab is displayed by default.
4. Type **Fishing vacation**.

   The description is entered.
5. Click the Categories tab.
   Publisher displays the list of existing categories.

tip

You can also use the New Category button to create your own category for pictures that you import. For instance, you could create a new category called My Photos, and then import all your pictures into this folder.

6. Scroll down through the list, and then click in the Photographs check box.

   Publisher will assign the picture to the Photographs category.

7. Click the Keywords tab.

   Publisher displays the Keywords tab of the Clip Properties dialog box.

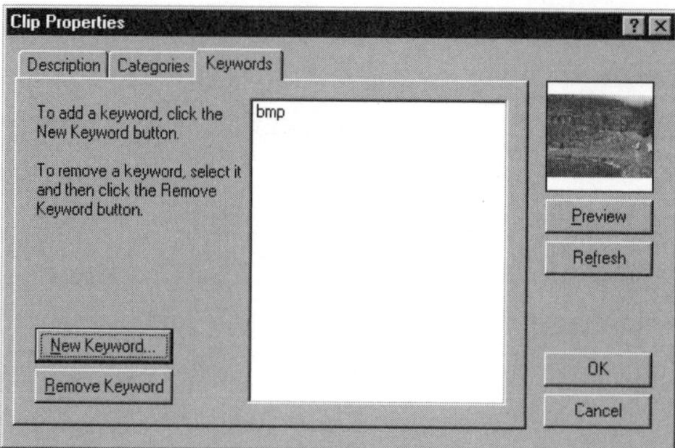

8. Click the New Keyword button.

   Publisher displays the New Keyword dialog box.

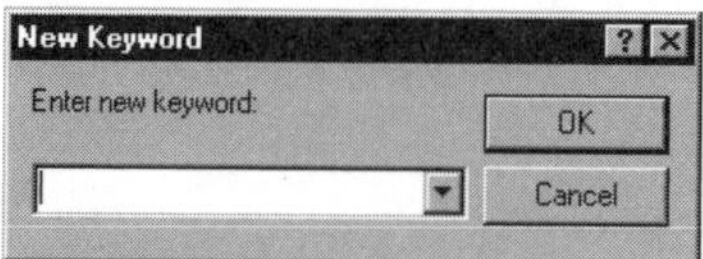

9. Type **fishing** and then click OK.

   Publisher adds this keyword as a search term.

10. Click the New Keyword button.
11. Type **lake** and then click OK.

    Publisher adds this keyword.

12. Click the New Keyword button.

13. Type **mountains** and then click OK.

    Publisher adds this keyword.

14. Click OK.

    Publisher closes the Clip Properties dialog box and displays the picture in the Insert Clip Art window.

All Categories

15. Click the All Categories button.
16. Publisher displays all of the clip art categories.
17. Scroll down and click Photographs.

    Publisher displays pictures in the Photographs category, and displays the imported picture first.

18. Click in the Search For Clips text box, type **fishing**, and then press Enter.
19. Publisher displays pictures related to fishing, and displays the imported picture first.

Downloading Clip Art from the Web

If you want to add to your clip art collection, there are dozens of free clip art collections on the Internet. One such site is Microsoft's Clip Gallery Live. You can access this Web site directly from the Insert Clip Art window. Any clip art that you download from the Web site will be automatically added to the Clip Gallery folder on your hard disk drive. Clip Gallery Live includes standard clip art pictures, plus animated pictures, sounds, and videos.

Download a clip art picture

In this exercise, you download a picture from the Clip Gallery Live Web site.

> **important**
>
> To download a picture from the Clip Gallery Live Web site, you must have an Internet account and a Web browser, such as Microsoft Internet Explorer.

1. If the Insert Clip Art window is not already displayed, on the Insert menu, point to Picture, and then click Clip Art.
2. Click the Clips Online button.

   Publisher displays an alert dialog box notifying you that you must have Web access to continue.

3. Click OK.

   Publisher will start Internet Explorer, dial up to the Internet if you are not already connected, and then display the End User License Agreement Web page.

4. Read the License Agreement, and then click the Accept button if you agree to the licensing terms.

   The Clip Gallery Live home page is displayed. Although the home page is updated frequently, it usually includes links to recently added clip art and seasonal clip art.

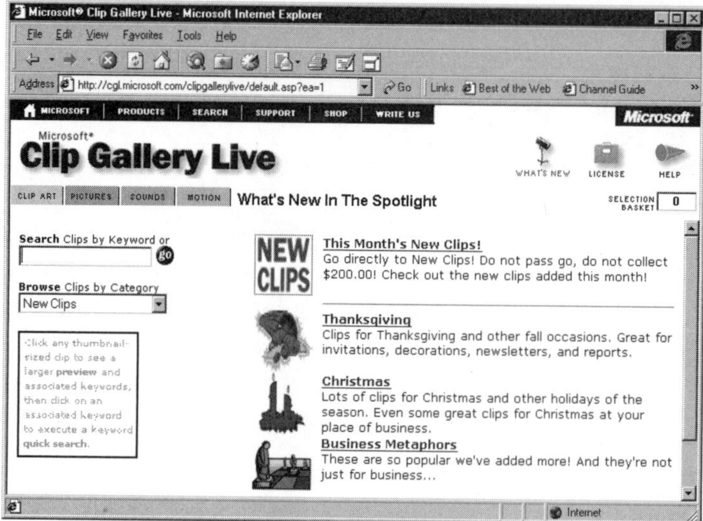

5. Click in the Search text box, type **hotel**, and then click the Go button.

   Thumbnails relating to hotels are displayed.

6. Click one of the thumbnails.

   Publisher displays the picture at its full size.

7. Click the full-size version of the picture.

   The Picture is downloaded to your hard disk drive and then is displayed by itself in the Insert Clip Art window.

Finish the lesson

- Close the Insert Clip Art window, and then close Internet Explorer.

Lesson 4 Quick Reference

To	Do this	Button
Display a blank page	On the Standard toolbar, click the New button.	
Insert a picture from the Clip Gallery	On the Objects toolbar, click the Clip Gallery Tool button, and drag in the publication to create a picture frame. When the Insert Clip Art window appears, type in a description of what you are looking for in the Search For Clips text box, and then press Enter. Scroll through the thumbnails, and click the desired thumbnail. Next click the Insert Clip button, and close the Insert Clip Art window.	
Display the Insert Clip Art window	On the Insert menu, point to Picture, and then click Clip Art.	
Drag and drop a clip art picture onto a publication	Display the Insert Clip Art window, select a category, click the Change To Small Window button, and then drag the image into a frame or onto a blank area of the publication.	
Resize a picture	Select the picture. Position the pointer over a corner selection handle until the Resizer appears, and drag to enlarge or reduce the picture frame.	
Insert a picture from a file	Click Picture on the Insert menu, and click From File. Use the Look In drop-down list to navigate to the folder that contains the desired picture, click the filename, and then click the Insert button.	
Recolor a picture	Click the image that you want to recolor, and then click Recolor Picture on the Format menu. Click the Color drop-down arrow and either select a Scheme Color or click the More Colors button, select a color, and then click OK twice.	
Restore the original color of a picture	Click the picture frame, and click Recolor Picture on the Format menu. Click the Restore Original Colors button, and then click OK.	

Lesson 4 Quick Reference

To	Do this	Button
Create a shape or line	Click a line or shape tool button in the Objects toolbar, and then drag to create the desired shape. To create a circle using the Oval Tool button or a square using the Rectangle Tool button, hold down the Shift key as you drag.	 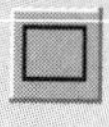
Recolor a shape	Click the shape that you want to recolor. On the Formatting toolbar, click the Fill Color button, and then either select a Scheme Color or click the More Colors button, select a color, and then click OK twice.	
To change a line or shape border	Click the line or shape that you want to change. On the Formatting toolbar, click the Line/Border Style button, and then either select a style or click More Styles to display a dialog box, select the desired options, and click OK.	
Create a custom shape	On the Objects toolbar, click the Custom Shapes button, click the shape that you want to use, and drag in the publication to create the shape.	
Color a shape with a gradient	Click the shape. On the Formatting toolbar, click the Fill Color button, and then click Fill Effects. Click the Gradients option, select the Base Color and Color 2, and then click OK.	
Rotate a picture or shape 90 degrees	Click the picture, and then click either the Rotate Left or Rotate Right button on the Formatting toolbar.	 
Custom-rotate a picture or shape	Click the picture or shape, hold down the Alt key, and then drag one of the corner selection handles either left or right.	
Flip a picture	Click the picture, and click either the Flip Horizontal or Flip Vertical button on the Formatting toolbar.	 

Lesson 4 Quick Reference

To	Do this
Create a shadow around a picture or shape	Click the picture or shape. On the Format menu, click Shadow.
Import a picture into the Clip Gallery	On the Insert menu, point to Picture, and then click Clip Art. Display the Insert Clip Art window, click the Import Clips button, navigate to the folder where the picture file is located and double-click the filename. Add an optional description, category, and keywords, if desired, and then click OK.
Download a picture from the Clip Gallery Live Web site	Display the Insert Clip Art window, click the Clips Online button, and click OK if the alert dialog box appears. Then read the end user license agreement and click the Accept button. Next use the Search text box to search for the desired clip art, click a thumbnail to display the full-size version of the picture, and then click the full-size picture.

LESSON

5

Working with Text

ESTIMATED TIME
40 min.

In this lesson you will learn how to:

- ✔ *Create text frames.*
- ✔ *Define multiple text columns.*
- ✔ *Flow text into the next text frame.*
- ✔ *Disconnect and reconnect text frames.*
- ✔ *Add special effects to text.*
- ✔ *Edit a story in Microsoft Word.*
- ✔ *Create WordArt.*

Microsoft Publisher includes many of the text creation and editing features that you would expect to find in a powerful word processing application, such as Microsoft Word. However, Publisher also includes many other specialized features for improving and arranging text in your publications.

In this lesson, you create text frames and define multiple text columns. You will then flow text into the next text frame and disconnect and reconnect text frames. Finally you will add special effects to the text, edit some text from within Microsoft Word, and create WordArt.

Typing Text in a Text Frame

You've already discovered some of the differences between text frames and picture frames. A picture frame is designed to contain a single graphic image that can be moved and sized easily. By contrast, a text frame is designed to contain blocks of text that can be varied in length, organized into columns, and formatted easily.

Although you can type text directly into a text frame, you'll probably want to do so only for short blocks of text, such as a heading, a caption for an image, or a few sentences that you want to add to a publication. For long sections of text, you'll do better to use a word processing application. You can create text in a Word file and then insert all or part of the file into your Publisher publication. When you create and edit text in a Word file, you can use Word's powerful formatting and display features. After you've formatted the text exactly the way you want it, you can insert the Word file into your publication, with all of Word's formatting features included in your publication.

After you've created or inserted text into a text frame, you can format the text in dozens of different ways. But be warned: there is a tendency to do too much, too soon. If you add too many different text formats to a publication, you can quickly turn an otherwise attractive document into an eyesore.

To format text, you first drag to select the text that you want to format. You can then select a formatting feature available on the Formatting toolbar, or you can click the Format menu to select one of the formatting menu commands. For instance, when you click Font on the Format menu, Publisher displays the Font dialog box. This dialog box includes many of the same formatting features that are available on the Formatting toolbar and allows you to add additional text effects, such as small capital letters (called small caps), shadow effects, and other specialized font attributes.

Type and format text

In this exercise, you open a publication that is still in its early stages of development. The publication will become a one-page insert that will be mailed with other Lakewood Mountains Resort literature to former resort guests. You type text in an existing text frame, and then you apply several formats to the text.

1. If the Catalog is currently displayed, close it now.
2. On the File menu, click Open.

   The Open Publication dialog box is displayed.
3. Click the drop-down arrow next to the Look In box, and then navigate to the Publisher Practice folder on your hard disk drive.

   The contents of the Publisher Practice folder are displayed.
4. Double-click the LMR News publication.

   Publisher opens and displays the incomplete publication in the workspace.

> **tip**
> The publication for this exercise was created using one of Publisher's Quick Publications, a template design that can be used to create a variety of one-page publications.

Zoom In

5. Click inside the text frame to the right of the sunrise picture, and then click the Zoom In button twice.

   Publisher zooms in on the selected frame so that you can more easily read the text that you type.

6. Type **What's New...**

   The text is displayed in the text frame.

You can triple-click to select an entire paragraph of text.

7. Click at the end of the text, and then drag to the left to select the entire text line.

   The text is displayed with a black background to define the selected area. (If you've specified different Windows colors in the Control Panel, the black background might be a different color.)

8. Click the drop-down arrow next to the Font Size box on the Formatting toolbar (which currently displays the number 10).

   A list of font sizes is displayed.

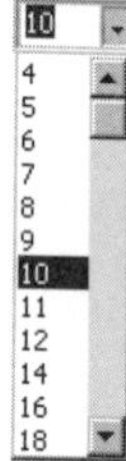

One point is equal to 1/72 of an inch. So, 28-point text is about 1/3 of an inch in height.

9. In the Font Size list, scroll down and click the number 28.

   Publisher displays the text at a larger, 28-point size.

10. Click the drop-down arrow next to the Font box in the Formatting toolbar (which currently displays the font name Times New Roman).

    A list of available fonts is displayed.

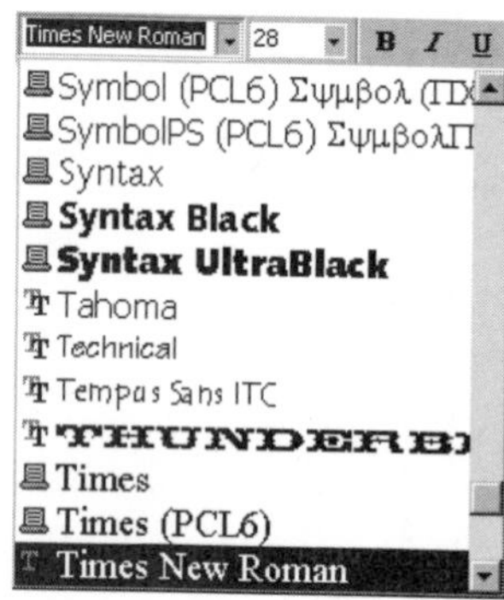

Font Color

If you don't see the Font Color button, click the double arrow at the end of the Formatting toolbar to display it.

11. Scroll up through the list of fonts, and then click to select the font named Goudy Old Style.

    The text is displayed using the selected font.

12. On the Formatting toolbar, click the Font Color button.

    Publisher displays colors that match the current color scheme (Mulberry, which was specified when the publication was created).

13. Click the second color (Accent 1) in the Scheme Colors palette.

    Publisher changes the color.

14. Click in a blank area of the publication.

    Publisher displays the text in the selected color.

15. Triple-click anywhere on the *What's New* text.

    Publisher selects the entire block of text.

16. On the Format menu, click Font.

    The Font dialog box is displayed.

17. In the Effects section, click the Small Caps check box, and then click OK.

    Publisher applies the small caps effect to the text.

18. On the Formatting toolbar, click the drop-down arrow to the right of the Zoom box, and then click Whole Page.

    Publisher displays the page so that it fits within the Publication window in its entirety.

Creating a Text Frame

When you want to add or insert text into an empty area of a publication, you must first create a new text frame. To create a text frame, you click the Text Frame Tool button on the Objects toolbar, and then you click and drag in the publication to size the frame. The text frame will begin where you first click in the publication, and will be sized to match the area that you drag the pointer across. (In other words, the frame will match the starting and ending locations that you specify when you click and drag the mouse pointer.) You can easily resize and move a text frame at any time.

You should create a separate text frame for each block of text that you might later need to format or reposition independently of other frames. If you decide to combine two or more text frames into a single frame, you can do so after you are certain that you want the multiple frames to be treated as a unit. You can also specify that formatting, such as font size, be applied by selecting multiple text frames that are linked.

Create a text frame

If you are not working through this lesson sequentially, open the file LMR News 2 before you continue.

In this exercise, you create a new text frame that you use to type and format new text.

1. On the Objects toolbar, click the Text Frame Tool button, and then position the pointer in the workspace.

   The crosshairs pointer appears.

2. Drag to create an empty text frame beneath the current one, and make it the same size, as shown here.

Zoom In

3. Click the Zoom In button three times.
4. Type **at Lakewood Mountains Resort?**

   The text is entered into the text frame. Notice that Publisher AutoCorrects the lowercase *a* at the start of the phrase.

Picking Up and Applying Existing Formats

A valuable feature of Publisher is the ability to select text that has several formatting attributes and then *pick up* and apply the formats to a different section of text. You can use this feature to avoid having to reapply several formatting attributes (such as font, font size, font color, and so on) individually. Instead, you can specify with the Pick Up Formatting command that you want to apply all formatting attributes from an existing section of text to a new section of text. Even if you want to use most and not all of a text section's formatting, it is often faster to pick up and apply all of the formats, and then turn off the formats that you don't want to use.

Double Arrow

The Pick Up Formatting and Apply Formatting commands are available on the Format menu. However, the first time you display the Format menu, you might not see either of these options. To view them, you can click the downward-pointing double arrow at the bottom of the Format menu to display a complete, expanded version of the menu. When you select a command from the expanded menu, Publisher recognizes that this is a feature you might want to use again, and adds the command to the short menu for future access.

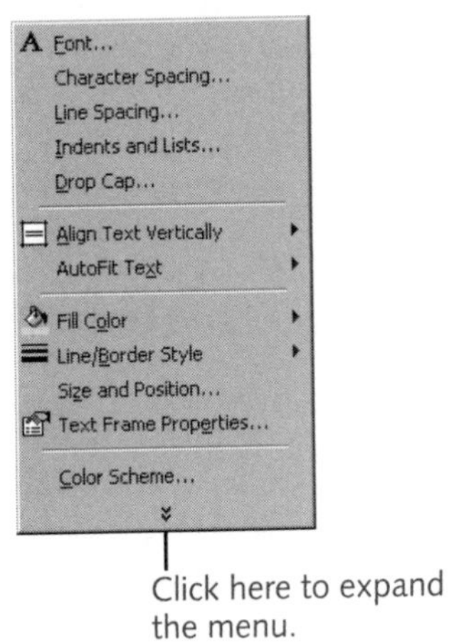

Click here to expand the menu.

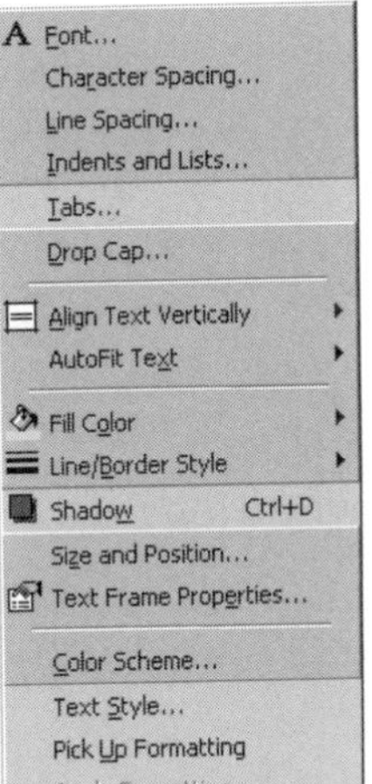

Pick up and apply formats

If you are not working through this lesson sequentially, open the file LMR News 3 before you continue.

In this exercise, you pick up formatting attributes from text in the top text frame and then apply the attributes to the text in the bottom text frame.

1. Click anywhere inside the top text frame (the one that already existed when you first opened the publication).
2. On the Format menu, click the downward-pointing double arrow at the bottom of the menu, if necessary.

   Publisher displays the complete, expanded version of the Format menu.

> **tip**
>
> Another way to display an expanded menu is to click the menu name on the menu bar and then continue to hold the mouse pointer over the short menu. After a few seconds, Publisher recognizes that you haven't found the command you're looking for and automatically displays the expanded version of the menu.

Notice that Publisher has added the Pick Up Formatting command to the short version of the Format menu.

3. Click Pick Up Formatting.
4. Select all of the text in the bottom text frame. (Zoom in, if necessary.)
5. On the Format menu, click the downward-pointing double arrow, and then click Apply Formatting.

   Publisher applies the formatting to the selected text. Notice that the font size is too large for the text frame.
6. While the text is still selected, click the drop-down arrow next to the Font Size box on the Formatting toolbar, and then click 18.

   Publisher changes the font size of the selected text to 18 points, and all of the text now fits within the text frame.

Working with Columns and Autoflow Text

Publisher does not provide any special feature for specifying columns. Instead, you define columns by creating text boxes for each column of text that you want to use, and you specify where you want each column of text to appear.

Your business partner wants you to insert a Microsoft Word file into the publication. The file contains all of the text that should replace the placeholder text in the frame. You're already a step ahead, and realize that you'll probably want to create a new text frame to hold the inserted text. Your partner agrees, but mentions that she would like to place the text in side-by-side columns on the bottom-third of the page. She explains that the inserted text probably will not fit into one column, but if you create two side-by-side columns (text frames), Publisher will offer to *autoflow* the text from the first text frame (column) into the next text frame (column).

Suppose you create only one text frame and all the inserted text won't fit into that frame? Not to worry. Publisher will ask if you want to autoflow the text into a new frame that is automatically created for you. But Publisher creates the next text frame on a new page, using the full width of the current left and right page margins, which might not be what you want. It would be easier to create both frames on your own, and then allow Publisher to autoflow the text from the first frame into the second.

To insert a Microsoft Word file (or any text file from another word processing program) into a text frame, you click Text File on the Insert menu. Publisher will then display the Insert Text dialog box. From there, you use the Look In list to navigate to the folder that contains the desired file, and then double-click to select the file. Publisher will guide you through the remaining steps.

Undo

If you don't like the results, you can easily disconnect the frames to return the flowed text to its original frame. Just click the Undo button to revert to your previous publication layout.

Insert a text file and autoflow text

If you are not working through this lesson sequentially, open the file LMR News 4 before you continue, and ignore step 1.

In this exercise, you create two side-by-side text frames that will serve as columns. First you copy, paste, and move to create an identically sized second text frame. Then you insert a Word file into the first text frame and instruct Publisher to autoflow the text into the next text frame.

1. Click the drop-down arrow to the right of the Zoom box, and then click Whole Page.

Text Frame Tool

2. On the Objects toolbar, click the Text Frame Tool button, and then drag to create a text frame at the location and size of the one shown below.

Copy

Paste

3. On the Standard toolbar, click the Copy button.

   Publisher places a copy of the empty text frame into the Windows Clipboard.

4. On the Standard toolbar, click the Paste button.

   Publisher pastes a copy of the empty text frame overlapping the original text frame.

> **tip**
>
> To copy text or any object to the Windows Clipboard, you can use the shortcut key combination Ctrl+C. To paste the contents of the Clipboard, position the pointer where you want the contents to be pasted, and then press Ctrl+V.

Mover

5. Position the mouse pointer over the right border of the new text frame until the Mover appears, and then drag the frame so that it is at the position of the one shown on the following page.

6. Click inside the left text frame, and then on the Insert menu, click Text File.

   Publisher displays the Insert Text dialog box.

7. Use the Look In drop-down list to navigate to the Publisher Practice folder located on your hard disk drive.

   Publisher displays the contents of the Publisher Practice folder.

8. Double-click the What's New file in the list.

   Publisher briefly displays a dialog box showing that the Word file is being converted to Publisher's text format, and then displays a message notifying you that the text won't fit into the frame and asks if you want to autoflow the text.

9. Click Yes.

   Publisher selects the second frame and asks if you want to autoflow the text into it.

10. Click Yes.

    Publisher flows the text into the second column, which now displays a Go To Previous Frame button at the top of the frame.

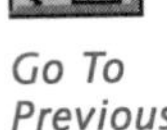

Go To Previous Frame

11. Click the Go To Previous Frame button.

    Publisher selects the previous text frame, which now displays a Go To Next Frame button at the bottom of the frame.

Go To Next Frame

12. Click the Go To Next Frame button.

    Publisher selects the next frame.

tip

The Go To Previous Frame and Go To Next Frame buttons are handy ways to switch between frames, especially if the frames are located on different pages.

Vertical Resizer

13. Click the bottom-center selection handle so that the Vertical Resizer appears, and then drag up until the bottom of the frame is just below the last line of text, as shown below.

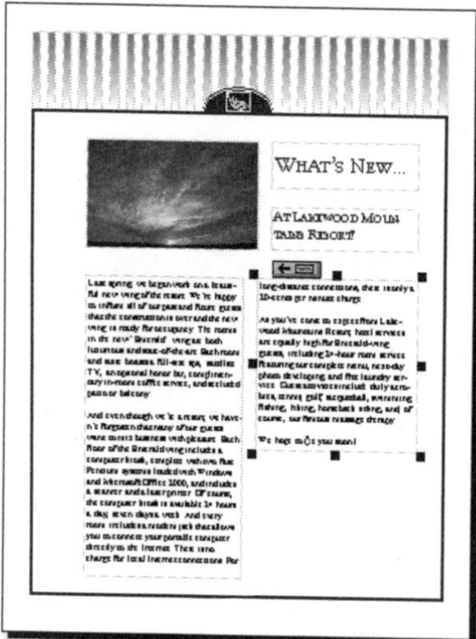

Disconnecting and Reconnecting Frames

You quickly decide to offer your partner an additional challenge. You want to know whether you can rotate only the last line of text—*We hope to see you soon!*—in the second text frame. She says that you can rotate only an object, such as a complete frame. But she mentions that there is an interesting technique you can use to accomplish the desired effect. It involves creating a new text frame and then *connecting* this frame to the previous frame. By connecting frames, you can then autoflow text from one frame into the next frame. This trick will work well for the task at hand, because you can autoflow the last line of text into a new text frame, and then rotate the new frame. If you don't like the results, you can easily disconnect the frames to return the flowed text to its original frame. Just click the Undo button to do so.

Undo

Connecting frames is also useful when you've filled up a page and need to create a new page and a new text frame on the new page. After you've created the new page and a new text frame on the page, you can connect the last frame on the previous page with the new text on the new page. When you connect text frames, *overflow* text (text that is in a frame but can't be viewed because the frame is too small to fit all the text) will flow nicely into the text frame on the new page.

Connect text frames

If you are not working through this lesson sequentially, open the file LMR News 5 before you continue.

In this exercise, you create a third text frame, connect the second text frame to the new text frame, and then flow the last line of text into the new frame.

1. Create a new text frame of the same size and at the same location as the one shown here.

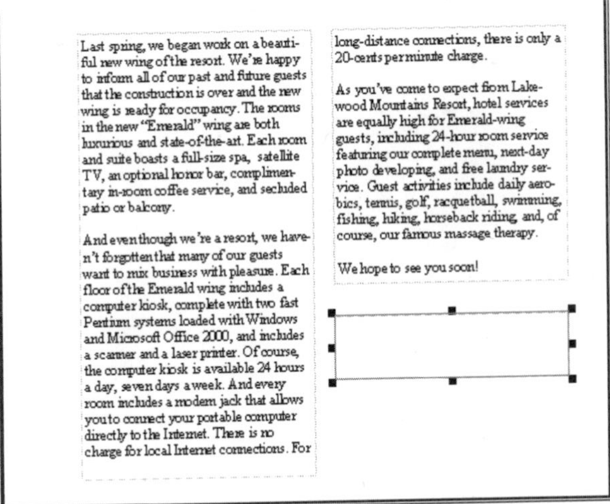

2. Position the pointer on the bottom-center selection handle of the second frame (above the one you just created), and then drag upward until the last sentence, *We hope to see you soon!*, is no longer visible.

   Text In Overflow

   Publisher displays a Text In Overflow icon at the bottom of the frame, indicating that the frame contains more text than will fit in the frame.

Connect Text Frames

3. Click the Connect Text Frames button, and then reposition the pointer on the frame.

   Publisher displays a small bucket, indicating that it is ready to "pour" text into another frame.

4. Position the pointer over the smaller, third frame that you created.

   Publisher now displays a tilted bucket, indicating that it can pour the text into this frame.

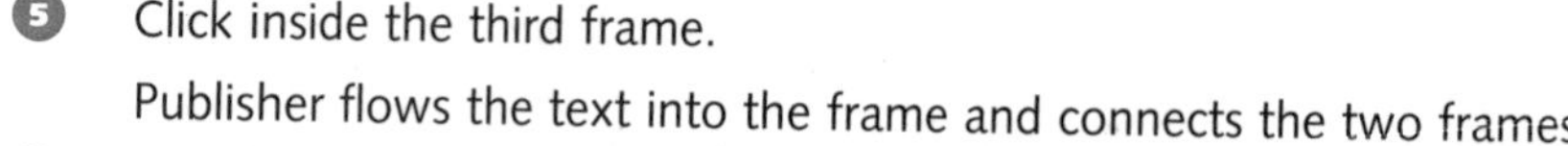

5. Click inside the third frame.

   Publisher flows the text into the frame and connects the two frames.

Disconnect Text Frames

6. Click inside the second frame, and click the Disconnect Text Frames button.

   Publisher disconnects the frames and returns the flowed text back to the second frame.

Connect Frames

7. Click the Connect Frames Button, and click inside the smaller, third frame. The text flows into the third frame and the two frames are reconnected.

Rotating Text

Custom Rotate

Now that you've connected the frames and flowed the last line of text into its own frame, you can rotate the frame separately. One way is to click the Custom Rotate button to display the Custom Rotate dialog box. You can then use this dialog box to specify the degree of rotation either to the left or to the right.

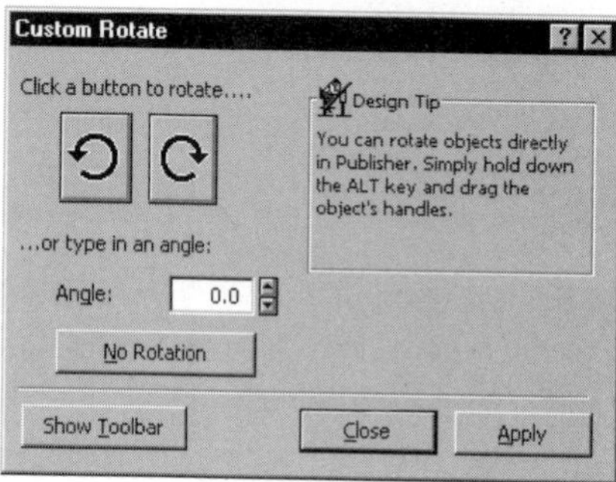

An easier way to rotate a text frame is to hold down the Alt key, click one of the selection handles for the text frame, and then drag right or left to the desired degree of rotation.

Your business partner cautions you about going overboard in using text rotation. Rotated text calls attention to itself, but rotating too large a block of text can make it difficult to read, which your readers probably won't like.

Rotate text

If you are not working through this lesson sequentially, open the file LMR News 6 before you continue.

In this exercise, you format text and resize a text frame, and then drag to rotate the frame.

1. Zoom in as necessary to read the text in the bottom-right text frame.
2. In this text frame, select the line of text *We hope to see you soon!*

3. In the Font drop-down list on the Formatting toolbar, select the Goudy Old Style font.

Font Color

4. On the Formatting toolbar, click the Font Color button.

   Publisher displays a row of colors that match the current color scheme.

5. Click the More Colors button.

   Publisher displays the Colors dialog box.

6. Click the Basic Colors option, if it isn't already selected.

7. In the red row, click the last color box, and then click OK.

   The font color of the selected text changes to a pale shade of red. (You won't see the desired color until you deselect the text, but don't do this yet.)

8. On the Formatting toolbar, use the Font Size drop-down list to change the font size of the selected text to 22 points.

   The text no longer fits on the same line in the text frame.

Text In Overflow

Rotate

9. Position the pointer on the right-center selection handle, and then drag to the right until all of the text is visible on the line.

   The Text In Overflow icon disappears.

10. Hold down the Alt key, position the pointer on the top-right selection handle until the Rotate pointer appears, and then drag up and to the left until the text is rotated to match the following example.

Last spring, we began work on a beautiful new wing of the resort. We're happy to inform all of our past and future guests that the construction is over and the new wing is ready for occupancy. The rooms in the new "Emerald" wing are both luxurious and state-of-the-art. Each room and suite boasts a full-size spa, satellite TV, an optional honor bar, complimentary in-room coffee service, and secluded patio or balcony.

And even though we're a resort, we haven't forgotten that many of our guests want to mix business with pleasure. Each floor of the Emerald wing includes a computer kiosk, complete with two fast Pentium systems loaded with Windows and Microsoft Office 2000, and includes a scanner and a laser printer. Of course, the computer kiosk is available 24 hours a day, seven days a week. And every room includes a modem jack that allows you to connect your portable computer directly to the Internet. There is no charge for local Internet connections. For long-distance connections, there is only a 20-cents per minute charge.

As you've come to expect from Lakewood Mountains Resort, hotel services are equally high for Emerald-wing guests, including 24-hour room service featuring our complete menu, next-day photo developing, and free laundry service. Guest activities include daily aerobics, tennis, golf, racquetball, swimming, fishing, hiking, horseback riding, and, of course, our famous massage therapy.

We hope to see you soon!

11. If you haven't already done so, save the publication to the Publisher Practice folder on your hard disk drive.

Editing Text in Microsoft Word

All of the connected text frames in a publication make up a single *story*—that is, a block of text that is treated as a unit in Publisher. You've already seen how you can insert Microsoft Word files into a text frame or story. But you can also edit a story that's in your publication directly from within Microsoft Word. There are a few good reasons why you might want to do this.

Suppose you want to review the text in a story but the text frames in the story are scattered across different pages and interspersed between graphics. When you click inside a story, and then on the Edit menu click Edit Story In Microsoft Word, Publisher starts the Microsoft Word application. It displays only the text for the story in Word, allowing you to focus solely on the text. Editing a story in Word can also be the preferred method if you know Word quite well and want to use all of Word's formatting and editing capabilities.

Edit a story in Microsoft Word

If you are not working through this lesson sequentially, open the file LMR News 7 before you continue.

In this exercise, you display a story in Word, make a quick editorial change, and then return to Publisher.

1. Click anywhere in the text frame that begins with *Last Spring, we....*

   Publisher selects the text box.

2. On the Edit menu, click Edit Story In Microsoft Word. (You might have to wait a few seconds for this option to appear.)

   Microsoft Word is started, and the text of the story is displayed in Word.

3. Near the bottom of the second paragraph, double-click the word *portable* and type **laptop**.

   Word replaces the word *portable* with *laptop*.

4. On the File menu, click Close & Return To LMR News.

   The document is closed in Word and the edited story is redisplayed in Publisher.

Adding a Drop Cap

Professional publications often employ an interesting element called a *drop cap* that adds an attractive flair to text. A drop cap is an enlarged capital letter, usually applied to the first character at the start of a long section of text, and often in a separate, more decorative font. As is true with rotated text, you should use drop caps sparingly. Too many drop caps can distract the eye. But a well-placed and well-designed drop cap can provide an added dash of professionalism to your publication.

Publisher provides more than a dozen built-in drop cap styles that you can select from. To create a drop cap, select the first character in a block of text, and then click Drop Cap on the Format menu to display the Drop Cap dialog box. You can scroll through the drop cap designs and select one that you like. After you apply a particular drop cap design to your publication, Publisher will move this design to the top of the list so that you can find it easily the next time you want to apply a drop cap.

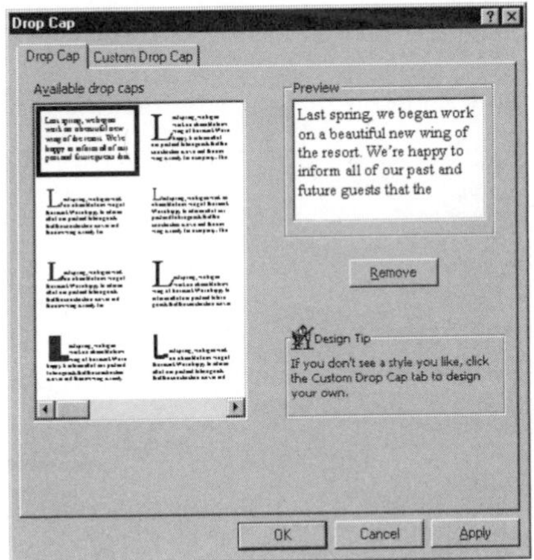

You can also change to a different drop cap style if you decide that the one that you've selected doesn't really fit your publication. To do so, select the drop cap character in your publication, and then click Format on the menu bar. You'll notice that the Drop Cap command has been changed to read Change Drop Cap. You can click this command to display the Drop Cap dialog box. From there, you can select a different drop cap design.

Add a drop cap

If you are not working through this lesson sequentially, open the file LMR News 8 before you continue.

In this exercise, you create a drop cap at the start of the article in your newsletter. You then change the drop cap design.

1. If necessary, click in the top of the text frame that begins *Last Spring, we....*
2. On the Standard toolbar, click the Zoom In button to zoom in to about 75 percent.

   The start of the article is now easier to read, and a single character will be easier to select.
3. Drag to select the first letter in the article (the "L" in *Last Spring*).
4. On the Format menu, click Drop Cap.

   Publisher displays the Drop Cap dialog box.
5. Scroll through the list of drop cap designs, click a design that you like, and then click OK.

   Publisher adds the drop cap design to the selected character, which remains highlighted.
6. Click anywhere in the text frame.

   The drop cap is deselected, and you can now see the effect of the design.

If you don't see a drop cap that you like, you can click the Custom Drop Cap tab, and then design your own.

tip

After you create a drop cap, the enlarged letter might cause text to flow differently into connected frames. If this happens, you might have to make adjustments. For instance, depending on the drop cap you selected in this exercise, it might cause text to flow from the second text frame into the rotated third frame. To adjust for this, you would need to extend the bottom of the second frame so that the desired text is moved back into the second frame and out of the rotated frame.

7. Select the "L" in *Last* again, and then on the Format menu, click Change Drop Cap.

   Publisher displays the Drop Cap dialog box. Notice that your current selection has moved to the start of the drop cap design samples.
8. Scroll through the list of drop cap designs, select a different one, and then click OK.

   Publisher changes the drop cap design.
9. Click anywhere in the text frame to deselect the drop cap.

10. Click the drop-down arrow next to the Zoom box on the Standard toolbar, and then click Whole Page in the list.

    Publisher displays the page at the whole page size. You can now view the results of the drop cap in context with the other elements on the page.

11. Save the Publication in the Publisher Practice folder on your hard disk drive.

One Step Further Creating WordArt

Sometimes changing font size, color, and other text options just doesn't seem to add enough flair to your text. Your business partner mentions, though, that you can add colorful, highly stylized text displays by using a feature called *WordArt,* which not only adds multiple colors and patterns to text, but also can make text appear three-dimensional. To create WordArt, all you need to do is select the WordArt Frame Tool button on the Objects toolbar, and then type your text in the dialog box that appears. Because WordArt stands out on a page, you should limit its use to a few words, such as for a heading or quick message.

Last spring, we began work on a beautiful new wing of the resort. We're happy to inform all of our past and future guests that the construction is over and the new wing is ready for occupancy. The rooms in the new "Emerald" wing are both luxurious and state-of-the-art. Each room and suite boasts a full-size spa, satellite TV, an optional honor bar, complimentary in-room coffee service, and secluded patio or balcony.

And even though we're a resort, we haven't forgotten that many of our guests want to mix business with pleasure. Each floor of the Emerald wing includes a computer kiosk, complete with two fast Pentium systems loaded with Windows and Microsoft Office 2000, and includes a scanner and a laser printer. Of course, the computer kiosk is available 24 hours a day, seven days a week. And every room includes a modem jack that allows you to connect your portable computer directly to the Internet. There is no charge for local Internet connections. For long-distance connections, there is only a 20-cents per minute charge.

As you've come to expect from Lakewood Mountains Resort, hotel services are equally high for Emerald-wing guests, including 24-hour room service featuring our complete menu, next-day photo developing, and free laundry service. Guest activities include daily aerobics, tennis, golf, racquetball, swimming, fishing, hiking, horseback riding, and, of course, our famous massage therapy.

WordArt is displayed in its own window that includes a toolbar providing you with dozens of style, color, shadow, and other format options. You'll notice that each style seems to convey a different "personality" or mood. So using WordArt is a great way to provide a bit of emotional impact to your publications. Like other text, WordArt can be rotated for additional flair.

Add WordArt to a publication

In this exercise, you open a publication, add a WordArt frame, and then design your WordArt text.

1. Navigate to and open the WordArt Sample publication stored in the Publisher Practice folder on your hard disk drive.

WordArt Frame Tool

2. On the Objects toolbar, click the WordArt Frame Tool button, and then drag to create a frame that fills most of the empty area at the bottom of the second column.

   Publisher displays a small Enter Your Text Here dialog box in the WordArt window.

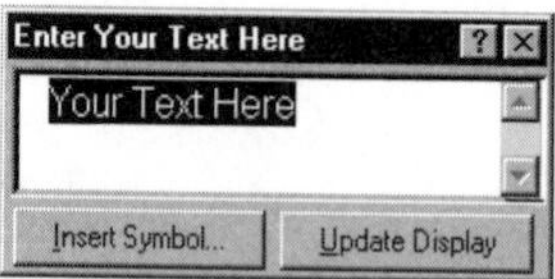

3. Type **Come See Us Soon!**

   Publisher enters the text in the dialog box.

4. Click the Update Display button.

   The text appears in the WordArt frame in the publication.

5. On the WordArt Formatting toolbar, click the drop-down arrow next to the words *Plain Text*.

   Publisher displays samples of different text shapes and movements.

Curve Up

6. Click the Curve Up sample shape.

   The WordArt text is displayed with the Curve Up shape.

Color And Shading

7. On the WordArt Formatting toolbar, click the Color And Shading button.

   Publisher displays the Shading dialog box.

8. In the Foreground drop-down list, click Navy.

9. In the Background drop-down list, click Sienna.
10. In the Style section, click the thick vertical bars tile (sixth row, third column), and then click OK.

    Publisher applies the two-color text style.

Shadow

11. On the WordArt Formatting toolbar, click the Shadow button.

    Publisher displays a list of shadow styles.
12. Click the third shadow style, and then click OK.
13. Click the publication page or click the Close button in the Enter Your Text Here dialog box.

    Publisher closes the WordArt window and displays your WordArt in the publication window.

Zoom In

14. Click the Zoom In button as necessary to see the effects of your changes.
15. Save the publication.

Finish the lesson

- On the File menu, click Close.

Lesson 5 Quick Reference

To	Do this	Button
Create a text frame	On the Objects toolbar, click the Text Frame Tool button, and then drag in the publication to create a text box of the desired size.	A
Add text to a text frame	Click inside the text frame and type the text.	
Format text	Drag to select the text, and then click the desired formatting options on the Formatting toolbar.	
Pick up and apply formats	Select the formatted text that you want to use as a model for formatting other text. On the Format menu, click Pick Up Formatting. Then select the text that you want to format. On the Format menu, click Apply Formatting.	
Insert a text file	Create an empty text frame. On the Insert menu, click Text File, navigate to the folder that contains the desired text file, and then double-click the name of the file to be inserted.	
Autoflow text	After inserting a text file, Publisher notifies you that the text will not fit in the frame. Click Yes to flow all additional text into the next text frame. Publisher asks if you want to connect the next text frame in sequence; click Yes.	
Connect text frames	Select a text frame that has overflow text. On the Formatting toolbar, click the Connect Text Frames button. Click inside the next text frame to flow the text.	
Edit a story in Microsoft Word	Click a text frame in the story. On the Edit menu, click Edit Story In Microsoft Word, make any changes as you would normally in Word, and then on the File menu, click Close & Return To (Filename).	

Lesson 5 Quick Reference

To	Do this	Button
Rotate text	Hold down the Alt key, and then drag a selection handle on the text frame in the direction that you want to rotate the text.	
Add a drop cap	Select the character to which you want to apply a drop cap format. On the Format menu, click Drop Cap. Select a drop cap design, and then click OK.	
Change a drop cap	Select the drop cap in the publication. On the Format menu, click Change Drop Cap, select a different drop cap design, and then click OK.	
Create WordArt	On the Objects toolbar, click the WordArt Frame Tool button, draw a frame, and then type the text for the WordArt. Use the WordArt Formatting toolbar to add effects to the WordArt. Click Update Display to view WordArt changes for new text.	
Change WordArt	Double-click the WordArt text frame, and then use the WordArt Formatting toolbar to make changes. When you have finished, click inside the publication to close the WordArt window.	

PART 7

Microsoft Internet Explorer 5

LESSON

1

Exploring the Web

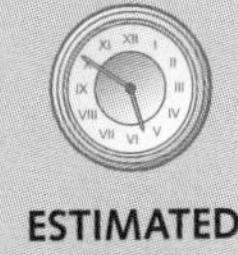

ESTIMATED TIME
30 min.

In this lesson you will learn how to:

- ✔ *Start Microsoft Internet Explorer.*
- ✔ *Browse a Web site.*
- ✔ *Create a desktop shortcut to a Web page.*
- ✔ *Print Web page information.*
- ✔ *Save Web pages.*

Almost everyone has heard of the Internet, and most people know that *www* and *dotcom* have something to do with Web pages. But the Internet is much more than just Web page addresses. With the Internet, you can read up-to-the-minute news reports, reserve plane tickets, listen to music, send and receive electronic messages, get weather reports, shop, conduct research, and much more.

If you want an introduction to the Internet and the World Wide Web, if you need to learn just the latest features of Internet Explorer 5, or if you're switching to Internet Explorer from another product, this part of the book is for you. In this lesson, you'll master techniques for using Internet Explorer and learn some Internet basics along the way.

Before starting to use Internet Explorer, though, a fundamental concept needs to be addressed—the difference between the Internet and the World Wide Web. The *Internet* is a network of computers, cables, routers, and other hardware and software that interconnect and run on a network. The *World Wide Web* consists of documents that are transmitted across the Internet's hardware. The Web is made up of *Web pages* and *Web sites*. A Web page is a specially formatted document that can include text, graphics, hyperlinks, audio, animation, and video. A Web site is a collection of Web pages. Here's where Internet Explorer steps in—before you can view Web pages, you need a *browser* such as Internet Explorer.

Internet Explorer 5 incorporates Microsoft's most advanced techniques for finding, viewing, and managing information on the Internet. The Internet stores millions of Web pages, and your browser is your key to displaying and finding the information you want. The Internet can tell you exactly what you need to know, and it can provide information you didn't even know you wanted. It can also waste hours of your time if you don't know how to manage the data, or if you're using an outdated browser. By using Internet Explorer, you can ensure that you're getting the best return for your Internet time.

Setting the Scene

To demonstrate how the exercises in this book can apply to your day-to-day tasks, a scenario is carried throughout the text. Imagine you are the main contact for a public relations firm, Impact Public Relations, and you're promoting Lakewood Mountains Resort, a luxury resort. In this part, you're using Microsoft Internet Explorer to gather information for your work.

important

The exercises in the Internet Explorer lessons assume that your desktop has the Web Style feature enabled, including the single-click feature. To turn on the Web Style feature, click Start on the Windows taskbar, point to Settings, and then click Folder Options. In the Folder Options dialog box, select Web Style, and click the OK button. If the Single-click dialog box appears, click OK.

Starting Microsoft Internet Explorer

The best way to learn about the Internet is to jump right in. Of course, you must get to the water before you can dive in, so make sure you've configured a connection before starting Internet Explorer.

You can connect to the Internet via a phone line, a modem, and an Internet service provider (a dial-up connection), or you can link to the Internet through a local area network (LAN), such as a company's network.

important

The exercises throughout this book assume you are connected to the Internet through either a LAN or a dial-up connection.

Start Internet Explorer

In this exercise, you start Internet Explorer so you can begin exploring the Web.

Desktop Shortcut

- Click the Internet Explorer icon on your desktop.

  The Internet Explorer window opens and displays your Internet home page.

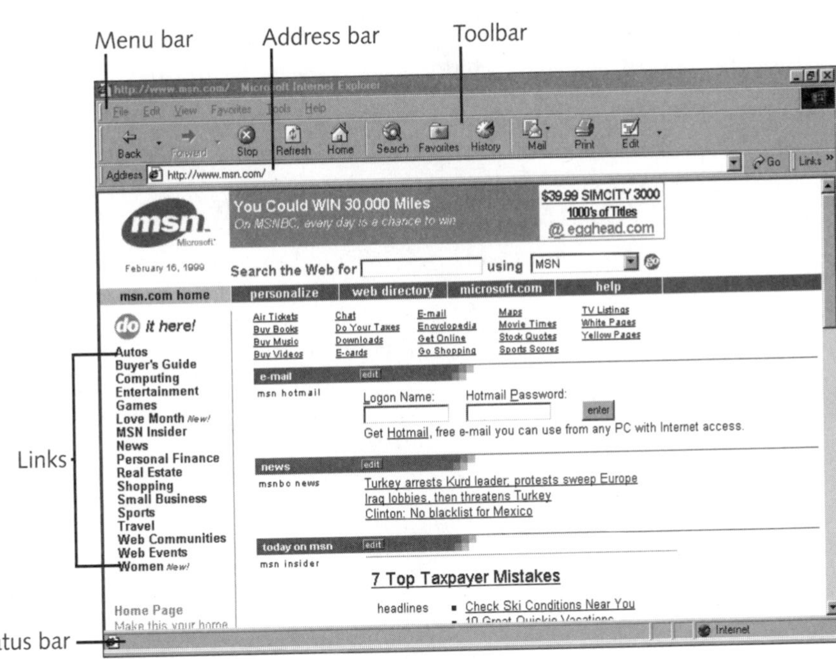

One of the Internet's greatest assets is that it can provide continuously updated content. Therefore, you might notice that the content on the page displayed on your screen is different from the content shown in the illustration.

Browsing a Web Site

After you connect to the Internet and open Internet Explorer, you're ready to start browsing for information. You can access Web pages in two ways: you can type an address in the Address bar, or you can click *hyperlinks* (also called *links)* to move from one Web page to another. Hyperlinks are Web page elements that connect Internet documents. They can appear as text (usually displayed in a different color and underlined) or graphical elements such as buttons. Click a hyperlink to a Web page, and almost instantly, you're there.

Both techniques—typing an address and clicking hyperlinks—use a *Uniform Resource Locator* (URL), or an Internet address. URLs are used to access a particular Internet document. When you enter an address in the Address bar, you manually enter the document's URL. When you click a hyperlink, the browser automatically places the URL in the Address bar and displays the document.

A URL identifies where a document is stored on the Internet. URLs are like street addresses. Just as a street address consists of several parts—number, street, city, state, and postal code—each URL consists of the parts of an Internet address—protocol, domain name, directory path, and filename.

The table below breaks down the following Lakewood Mountains Resort address: *http://mspress.microsoft.com/mspress/products/1349/recreation.htm.*

Example	Component	Definition
http://	Protocol	Indicates that your browser should transfer the document using the Hypertext Transfer Protocol (HTTP). (A *protocol* is a set of rules that one computer uses to "talk" to another computer.) Web documents always use the HTTP protocol.
mspress. microsoft.com	Domain name	Identifies the address of the computer (or *server*) where the document is stored. These are often divided into three parts: *mspress* (indicates that the document is on the Microsoft Press Web); *microsoft* (the name of the computer where the Web is stored, sometimes called the *second-level domain name*); *com* (a two-letter or three-letter extension that identifies the Web page type, also called the *top-level domain*).

Example	Component	Definition
mspress/products /1349	Folder path	Identifies where the document is stored. Similar to your desktop's file and folder organization, URLs can reference folders within folders.
recreation.htm	Filename	Names the specific Web page to be displayed in your browser. If no filename is specified in the URL, the browser displays the Web site's index.htm or default.htm Web page. These pages are generally the main or starting pages (usually called the *home* pages).

Top-Level Domain Names

Many types of organizations maintain Web sites. To make Web addresses easier to understand, they contain an identifier (or top-level Web domain) that classifies the type of organization the name represents. The following are the seven most common top-level domain extensions.

Extension	Organization
.com	Commercial organization within the United States
.edu	Educational institution
.gov	Agency or branch of the government
.int	International organization
.mil	U.S. military site
.net	Networking service (such as an Internet service provider)
.org	Other organizations

In addition to these top-level domain names, a Web address can also supply a country code. For example, .jp is the code for a Japanese Web site and .il is the code for an Israeli Web site. You can view a list of these codes at *www.ics.uci.edu/pub/websoft/wwwstat/country-codes.txt*.

Common Internet Protocols

Occasionally, you'll need to retrieve an Internet file that isn't a Web page and doesn't use the Web's HTTP protocol. The following list provides some of the Internet's more common protocols and their descriptions.

Protocol	Definition
file://	Indicates a path to a file stored on your local hard disk drive or on your network. In Internet Explorer, instead of entering this protocol, you can simply enter your drive letter, such as C:\.
ftp://	Specifies the File Transfer Protocol. This protocol is used to send and retrieve entire documents without displaying the document in your browser. For example, you can use the FTP protocol to send a Microsoft Word document from your computer to another computer connected to the Internet. Then the recipient can open the document in Word.
gopher://	Distributes documents using a menu-based system. Gopher originated at the University of Minnesota (yes, it's named after their mascot), and it has been largely superseded by Web search engines.
http://	Specifies the Hypertext Transfer Protocol. This protocol is used to access Web pages on the Internet and other networks.
https://	Specifies the Hypertext Transfer Protocol, Secure. This is used to access Web pages on the Internet and other networks, using a more secure transmission procedure than the HTTP protocol.
telnet://	Enables you to log on to and work on a remote system just as if the programs and files stored on the remote computer were available on your own computer.
wais://	Stands for the Wide Area Information Server protocol. WAIS is a distributed information retrieval system similar to gopher and the Web.

Internet Explorer offers many helpful features that come into play when you enter a URL in the Address bar. For example, when you access a Web page, you don't need to type in the protocol. Furthermore, you can frequently guess a company's Web page address by inserting the company's name as the second-level domain name. For example, you can retrieve the home page of the Sears Web site by typing *www.sears.com* in the Address bar and pressing Enter. The http:// portion of the Sears URL is automatically inserted by Internet Explorer.

When you enter a URL in the Address bar or click a hyperlink, you spark a series of events. First you tell Internet Explorer which document you want to view. Then Internet Explorer contacts the computer storing the document. After the computer is located, Internet Explorer *downloads* the document to your computer. In other words, Internet Explorer copies and transfers the Web page data from the computer storing the Web page to your computer. Internet Explorer then interprets the data and displays the Web page on your screen.

Back

Forward

After you display a few Web pages, you can quickly navigate among the pages you have visited during the current session. To revisit a previously displayed Web page, you click the Back button on Internet Explorer's toolbar. Likewise, if you've used the Back button at least once, you can use the Forward button to return to a site you visited before going back.

Other times while you are accessing Web pages, you might change your mind about downloading a Web page. Maybe you mistyped the URL in the Address bar, or possibly you elected to open a particular site, only to find that you could rewrite the Constitution during the time it takes to download the graphics. Regardless of the reason, you might need to stop a page from downloading. You can stop a page from downloading by clicking the Stop button on the toolbar.

Stop

Another Web page display technique that you can use on occasion is called *refreshing* a page. Refreshing a page means that you instruct Internet Explorer to re-download the currently displayed page. You might want to do this for a number of reasons: to view updated sports scores, watch breaking news stories evolve, or reload a page you stopped. When you refresh a page, you ensure that you have the most up-to-date version of the Web page. To refresh a Web page, you simply click the Refresh button on the toolbar.

Refresh

In addition to refreshing the current page and moving among visited pages, you can return to your home page at any point during your browsing session.

Home

By default, clicking the Home button displays the MSN home page, or a home page provided by your computer system manufacturer or your Internet service provider. The term *home page* can be confusing because it refers to the Internet home page that is always displayed when you start Internet Explorer, but it also refers to the main starting page at a particular Web site.

The final basic Web surfing skill that you need to learn involves finding specific text on a Web page. You can find text on a Web page just as you find text in a document. The Internet Explorer Edit menu contains a Find command that enables you to search the currently displayed Web page for a particular word or group of words.

You are just starting to represent Lakewood Mountains Resort for your public relations firm. You'll be flying out to visit the resort next week, but for now, your first order of business is to visit the resort's Web site.

Use the Address bar to access an Internet document

In this exercise, you use Internet Explorer's Address bar to display the Lakewood Mountains Resort main page.

1. If necessary, start Internet Explorer, and click in the Address bar (the box next to the word *Address*).

   The currently displayed URL is selected. (If the URL is not selected, double-click it.)

2. Type **mspress.microsoft.com/mspress/products/1349/default.htm** and then press Enter.

   The Lakewood Mountains Resort main page appears.

tip

If you type (in the Address bar) a URL that you've previously entered, Internet Explorer displays a list of addresses that are similar to the one you are entering. If you see the correct address in the list, simply click it. If Internet Explorer does not display the address you want, continue to enter the correct URL, and then press Enter to retrieve the Web page.

The Nature of Frames

Some Web pages are divided into *frames*. Frames enable Web page designers to show more than one Web document in your browser window at a time. Frames are commonly used to show a menu in one frame and the results of clicking menu items in another frame. The Lakewood Mountains Resort main page gives you the option to view the frames version or the no frames version of the Lakewood Mountains Resort home page. Web pages that do not have frames are created as a courtesy to those who use older browsers that cannot support frames.

Click hyperlinks to access Internet documents

In this exercise, you access a Web page by clicking hyperlinks on the Lakewood Mountains Resort main page.

1. On the Lakewood Mountains Resort main page, click the No Frames button.

   The no-frames version of the Lakewood Mountains Resort home page appears with a menu of different hyperlinks.

2. Type **mspress.microsoft.com/mspress/products/1349/default.htm** in the Address bar, press Enter, and then click the Use Frames button.

   The frames version of the Lakewood Mountains Resort home page appears with a menu of different hyperlinks.

3. Click the Recreational Facilities hyperlink in the left frame.

   Internet Explorer downloads the Recreation page. When the Web page is completely downloaded, the status bar displays the word *Done*.

You can tell when your mouse pointer is pointing to a hyperlink, because the pointer changes to a pointing hand.

tip

There might be times when you want to click a hyperlink, but you aren't finished with the currently displayed page. In those instances, you can open the document referenced by the hyperlink in a separate window. That way, you can have two Internet Explorer windows open—one displaying the original document and another displaying the document associated with the hyperlink. To view a linked document in a separate browser window, press the Shift key while you click a hyperlink.

Use the Back and Forward buttons

In this exercise, you use the Back and Forward buttons to redisplay Web pages you've visited during the current session.

If this URL already appears in the Address bar, click at the end of the URL, and press Enter.

1. Type **mspress.microsoft.com/mspress/products/1349/default1.htm** in the Address bar, and press Enter.

   The Lakewood Mountains Resort home page appears.

2. Click the Location hyperlink.

   The Location page appears. Notice that the Back button is now displayed as an available option.

Back

3. On the toolbar, click the Back button.

   The Lakewood Mountains Resort home page appears. Notice that the Forward button is now displayed as an available option.

> **tip**
>
> You can click the drop-down arrows on the Back and Forward buttons to choose sites that you've already visited within a session.

Forward

4. On the toolbar, click the Forward button.

   The Location page appears.

Stop a page from downloading

You can stop a page from downloading if it is taking too long or if you decide you don't want to view the page. In this exercise, you stop loading a Web page.

Stop

- In the left frame, click the On The Town hyperlink, and then click the Stop button before the new Web page appears completely.

  The new Web page stops downloading. Notice the empty placeholders where graphics should appear. (If your Internet access is 128 Kbps or faster, you might not see placeholder text.)

You can also press the Esc key to stop a page from downloading.

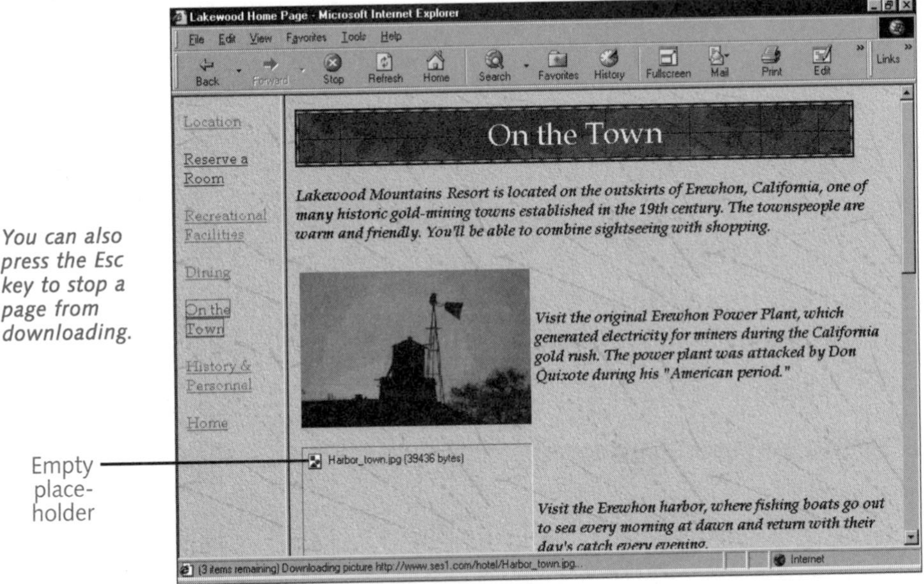

Refresh a Web page

In this exercise, you refresh a partially downloaded page.

Refresh

- On the toolbar, click the Refresh button.

  Internet Explorer reloads the Web page you stopped loading. Notice that the page no longer displays empty placeholders.

> **tip**
>
> Sometimes you will be unable to access a Web page because the computer storing the Web site is too busy. You can click the Refresh button to take a second try at accessing the popular page.

Return to your home page

In this exercise, you return to your Internet home page by clicking the Home button.

Home

- On the toolbar, click the Home button.

  Your Internet home page appears in your browser window.

Find text on a Web page

In this exercise, you find text on a Web page.

You can go to previously viewed Web pages by clicking the drop-down arrow to the right of the Address bar and then clicking the desired URL.

1. In the Address bar, type **mspress.microsoft.com/mspress/products/1349/default1.htm**, and press Enter.

   The Lakewood Mountains Resort home page appears.
2. Click the On The Town hyperlink in the left frame.
3. Click in the right frame.
4. On the Edit menu, click Find (On This Page).

   The Find dialog box appears.

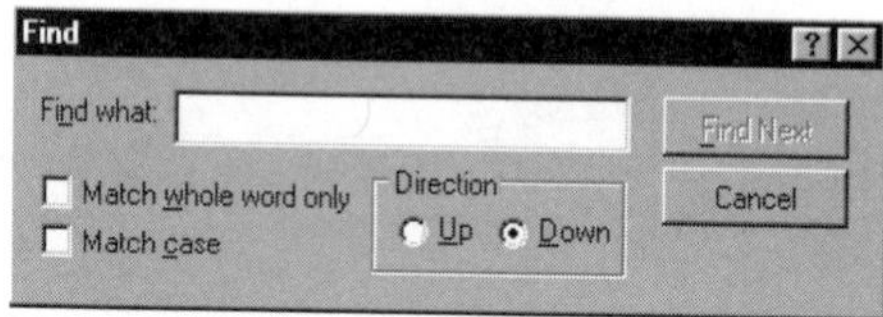

5. Type **Erewhon** in the Find What text box.
6. Click Find Next.

   Internet Explorer highlights the first instance of the specified text.
7. Click Find Next again.

   Internet Explorer highlights the next instance of the specified text.
8. Click Cancel to close the Find dialog box.

You might need to drag the Find dialog box to the left to see the highlighted word.

Creating a Desktop Shortcut to a Web Page

For a demonstration of how to create a desktop shortcut to a Web page, open the Office 8in1 Step by Step folder on your hard disk. Then open the Internet Explorer Demos folder, and double-click the Shortcut icon.

As you probably know from working with Windows, desktop shortcuts let you open files and applications quickly. You can create shortcuts on your desktop that store Internet documents' URLs, which point to Internet pages. These shortcuts will allow you to go directly to a Web page without opening Internet Explorer and typing an address. Internet desktop shortcuts can be clicked, cut, copied, and pasted in the same manner as other shortcuts created in Windows.

As you continue to work on the Lakewood Mountains Resort project, you find that you frequently access the resort's Web page. You learn that you can create a desktop shortcut to a Web page, so you decide to create and use a desktop shortcut for the Lakewood Mountains Resort home page.

Create and use a desktop shortcut

In this exercise, you create a desktop shortcut for the Lakewood Mountains Resort home page. In addition, you use the desktop shortcut and delete it.

1. If necessary, start Internet Explorer.
2. In the Address bar, type **mspress.microsoft.com/mspress/products/1349/default1.htm**, and press Enter.

   The Lakewood Mountains Resort home page appears.
3. On the File menu, point to Send, and then click Shortcut To Desktop.

   A shortcut linking to the Lakewood Mountains Resort home page is created on your desktop.
4. Click the Close button at the top-right corner of the Internet Explorer window.

Close

Desktop Shortcut

Minimize

5. On your desktop, click the Lakewood Home Page shortcut. (The icon is labeled Default1.htm.)

   Internet Explorer opens and the Lakewood Mountains Resort home page is displayed.
6. In the Internet Explorer window, click the Minimize button so that you can view your desktop.
7. Right-click the Lakewood Home Page desktop shortcut.

   A shortcut menu appears.
8. On the shortcut menu, click Delete.

   A message box asks if you want to send the shortcut to the Recycle Bin.
9. Click Yes.

   The shortcut is removed from your desktop.
10. Redisplay the Internet Explorer window.

Printing Web Page Information

Internet Explorer lets you print Web pages in a variety of ways. You can print entire Web pages, selected items, or frames. You can also print linked documents along with the currently displayed page, or you can print a table of links.

When you print an entire Web page, you can display the File menu, and then click Print to display the Print dialog box (as shown in the following illustration). Or you can click the Print button on the toolbar.

Print

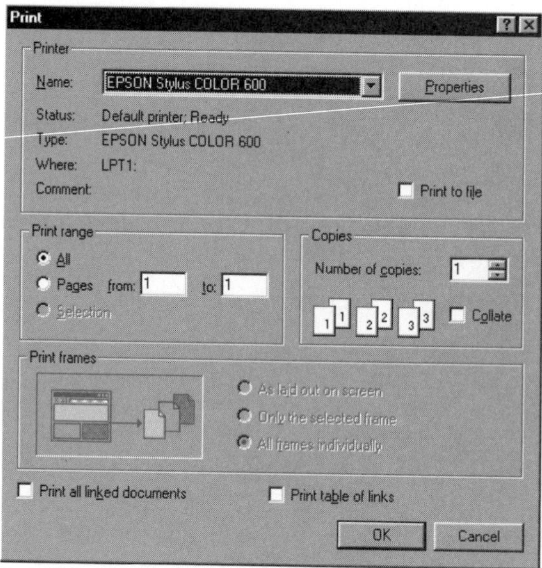

tip

When you print to a black and white printer, you might want to change your hyperlink colors to black before printing. Other colors might not appear when you print, leaving large blank areas in your printed document.

By default, Internet Explorer does not print Web page *backgrounds*. A Web page background is the color, texture, or picture that appears behind the text and graphics on a Web page. For example, the Lakewood Mountains Resort home page has a tan, adobe-textured type of background. Printing Web page backgrounds can waste your time and the printer's ink, as well as produce hard-to-read results. If you want to print a background, you must display the Tools menu, click Internet Options, click the Advanced tab, click the Print Background Colors And Images check box, and then click OK.

important

Your computer must be connected to a printer to complete the exercises in this section. In addition, you should verify that your printer is turned on.

Depending on your screen size, window size, and display settings, you might have to click the double-arrow symbol along the right edge of the toolbar to display the Print button. After you click the double-arrow symbol, Internet Explorer automatically creates a drop-down list (as shown below) if all the toolbar buttons cannot be displayed within the window's size constraints.

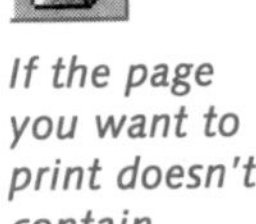

If the page you want to print doesn't contain frames, you can display the page and click the Print button to print the Web page.

tip

Be careful when using the Print button with framed pages. The Print button prints frames based on the previous setting stored in the Print dialog box. To be safe, on the File menu, click Print to display the Print dialog box when printing a framed page. That way, you can specify how you want the frames to be printed. If you want the framed page to be printed as it appears in your window, click the As Laid Out On Screen option.

Another Internet Explorer print option involves links. Internet Explorer gives you the option of printing not just the currently displayed page, but every other page to which it displays a link. This sounds like a handy option, but you should use it with caution. Depending on the number of links on a page, you might end up printing more linked pages than you want. In addition, Web pages are not bound by traditional paper sizes. If you print a single Web page, as many as 20 hard-copy pages could be printed. Instead of printing a Web page and its linked documents, you should consider printing a table of the documents linked to the current page.

You would like to make a hard copy of the Lakewood Mountains Resort Web site for the art department to review in this afternoon's meeting. You decide to print a copy of the Web site.

Beware of Copyrights

Copyright protection on the Internet is a sticky issue. To be safe, assume that all material contained in an Internet document is copyrighted. That means that you can print material for your own private use, but you can't reuse or redistribute the material without permission. If you want to reuse material, such as a photograph from the Lakewood Mountains Resort Web page, obtain permission from the Web site's "Webmaster" or the contact person listed on the page.

Occasionally, you'll run across a site that offers free use of graphics or other material. For example, there are a number of sites that provide icons, background patterns, and custom bullets for use without permission. In those instances, feel free to copy and use the resources you find.

Print a Web page

In this exercise, you print the Lakewood Mountains Resort home page.

1. If necessary, start Internet Explorer.
2. In the Address bar, type **mspress.microsoft.com/mspress/products/1349/default1.htm**, and press Enter.

   The Lakewood Mountains Resort home page appears.
3. On the File menu, click Print.

   The Print dialog box appears.
4. In the Print Frames area, click the As Laid Out On Screen option, and then click the OK button.

   The Lakewood Mountains Resort home page is printed.

Print selected items

In this exercise, you print only the address of the Lakewood Mountains Resort.

1. Select the resort's address (which appears below the picture of the resort).
2. On the File menu, click Print.

   The Print dialog box appears.
3. In the Print Range area, click the Selection option.

4. Click OK.

   The selected text is printed.
5. Click anywhere on the Web page to deselect the text.

Print each frame on a separate page

In this exercise, you print each frame of the Lakewood Mountains Resort home page on a separate page.

1. On the File menu, click Print.

   The Print dialog box appears.
2. In the Print Frames area, click the All Frames Individually option, and then click OK.

   Each frame is printed on a separate page.

Print a single frame

In this exercise, you print the main frame of the Lakewood Mountains Resort home page.

1. Click the right frame of the Lakewood Mountains Resort home page. (This frame contains a picture of the resort as well as address and phone information.)

   Internet Explorer internally marks this as the current frame.
2. On the File menu, click Print.

   The Print dialog box appears.
3. In the Print Frames area, click the Only The Selected Frame option (if necessary).

> **tip**
>
> When you select the Only The Selected Frame option in the Print dialog box, the Print Frames illustration will not indicate which frame is the selected frame.

4. Click OK.

   The selected (right) frame is printed.

Print linked documents

In this exercise, you print the Lakewood Mountains Resort home page and all linked documents.

important

Printing linked documents can result in dozens or even hundreds of printed pages. In one instance, printing an Internet home page along with all its linked documents resulted in sending over 60 separate documents to the printer.

1. Click in the left frame, but not on a link.

   Internet Explorer internally marks this as the current frame.
2. On the File menu, click Print.

   The Print dialog box appears.
3. If necessary, click the Only The Selected Frame option.
4. Click the Print All Linked Documents check box.

   This indicates that you want to print all linked documents as they appear in your browser. Any framed pages will be printed with all frames on one page.
5. Click OK.

   The current frame and all linked pages are printed. Each linked document is treated as a separate printing process. In other words, if four Web pages are linked to the currently displayed page, your printer will process five consecutive documents (of varying page counts, because Web pages do not have to conform to standard printed page sizes).

Print a table of links

In this exercise, you print a table of links for the Lakewood Mountains Resort Web site.

1. Click in the left frame.

   Internet Explorer internally marks this as the current frame.
2. On the File menu, click Print.

   The Print dialog box appears.
3. Click the Only The Selected Frame option if necessary, and click the Print Table Of Links option.
4. Click OK.

   The current page is printed, followed by a two-column table. The left column presents each link's text and the corresponding right column shows each link's complete URL.

One Step Further Saving Web Pages

You do not need to be connected to the Internet to view saved Web pages.

A Web page contains *Hypertext Markup Language* (HTML) formatting tags, graphics, and multimedia files. HTML formatting tags are used to format text, manipulate graphics, add background colors, and customize Web pages. Because a single Web page can consist of a number of *embedded files* (each graphic on a Web page is a separate file linked to the Web page's text document), you can choose to save a Web page in four ways:

- Save a complete Web page. (This saves the HTML file and all additional files, such as images, embedded in the Web page.)
- Save an archive of a Web page. (This saves the entire Web page as a single, uneditable file.)

- Save only the HTML document. (This saves the HTML formatting tags, but does not save embedded files.)
- Save only the text appearing on the Web page.

When you save a complete Web page, Internet Explorer automatically creates a folder with the same name as the saved file. This folder is also placed in the same location as the saved file. When you open the Web page, Internet Explorer opens, and all elements appear in the Web page, just as if you were viewing the page online.

When you save a Web page as an archive file, you save the entire Web page without creating a separate folder to contain the Web page's embedded elements. You can open the archive file to view the entire Web page on your hard disk, but you cannot change the Web page in any way, nor can you access separate components of the saved Web page such as graphics files. Be aware that while an archive file is a single file, it takes up more space on your computer than a Web page saved as a complete Web page.

When you save an HTML file, you leave out the graphics and other embedded elements. You can read formatted text, but you won't be able to view graphics because they're not saved on your hard disk.

Finally, when you save a Web page as a text file, you are only saving the text appearing on the page without any HTML tags. The saved text will not include any formatting, graphics, or other page elements.

You decide that you want to save the no-frames version of the Lakewood Mountains Resort home page to your computer. You aren't sure how you want to save the Web page, so you try all four options. Then you view each option to see which version serves your needs best.

important

If you are saving a Web page with frames, you must save the document as a complete Web page. The other save options do not work with framed Web pages.

Save a complete Web page

In this exercise, you save the Lakewood Mountains Resort home page as a complete Web page.

1. If necessary, start Internet Explorer.
2. Type **mspress.microsoft.com/products/1349/default2.htm** in the Address bar, and press Enter.

   The no-frames version of the Lakewood Mountains Resort home page is displayed.
3. On the File menu, click Save As.

   The Save Web Page dialog box appears.
4. If necessary, click the Save In drop-down arrow, and click Desktop.
5. In the File Name text box, select the current filename, and type **Complete Web Page**.

   The document you are saving will be named Complete Web Page.htm.
6. If necessary, click the Save As Type drop-down arrow; click Web Page, Complete (*.htm,*.html); and then click Save.

   A progress bar shows the progress of the operation as the page's elements are saved. The document and its folder are saved to your desktop.

Save an archived version of a Web page

In this exercise, you save the Lakewood Mountains Resort home page as an archive file.

1. On the File menu, click Save As.

   The Save Web Page dialog box appears.
2. If necessary, click the Save In drop-down arrow, and click Desktop.

3. In the File Name text box, type **Archived Web Page**.
4. Click the Save As Type drop-down arrow, click Web Archive For Email (*.mht), and click Save.

   A progress bar shows the progress of the operation as the page's elements are saved. The document is saved to your desktop as an archive file.

Save only a Web page's HTML file

In this exercise, you save the Lakewood Mountains Resort home page as an HTML file.

1. On the File menu, click Save As.

   The Save Web Page dialog box appears.
2. If necessary, click the Save In drop-down arrow, and click Desktop.
3. In the File Name text box, type **HTML Only**.
4. Click the Save As Type drop-down arrow; click Web Page, HTML Only (*.htm,*.html); and then click Save.

   A progress bar shows the progress of the operation as the page's elements are saved. The document is saved on your desktop as an HTML file.

Save a Web page as a text file

In this exercise, you save the Lakewood Mountains Resort home page as a text file.

1. On the File menu, click Save As.

   The Save Web Page dialog box appears.
2. If necessary, click the Save In drop-down arrow, and click Desktop.
3. In the File Name text box, type **Text File**.
4. Click the Save As Type drop-down arrow, click Text File (*.txt), and then click Save.

   A progress bar shows the progress of the operation as the page's elements are saved. The document is saved as a text file, without HTML formatting.
5. Click the Close button at the top-right corner of the Internet Explorer window.

Close

View saved Web pages

In this exercise, you view saved Web pages.

> **important**
>
> The steps in this exercise assume that you are using the Web pages that you saved in the previous sections. If you didn't save these files, you can still open identical pages from the Internet Explorer Practice folder on your hard disk drive.

You can click hyperlinks on Web pages saved as complete or archived to access the linked Web pages on the Internet.

1. If necessary, display your desktop.
2. Click the Complete Web Page icon on your desktop.

   A complete copy of the saved Web page appears in Internet Explorer with all graphics and other components embedded in the Web page. The local address is displayed in the Address bar.
3. Close the Internet Explorer window.
4. Click the Complete Web_Page Files folder on your desktop.

   The folder's contents are displayed.
5. Click the Main Building file.

   The picture of the Lakewood Mountains Resort appears in Internet Explorer.
6. Close the Internet Explorer window and the Complete Web Page_Files window.
7. Click the Archived Web Page icon on your desktop.

   A complete copy of the Web page opens in Internet Explorer.
8. Close the Internet Explorer window.
9. Click the HTML Only icon on your desktop.

   A modified version of the saved Web page appears in Internet Explorer. The graphics are not displayed, because they are not saved within the file.
10. Close the Internet Explorer window.
11. Click the Text File icon on your desktop.

    A text file is displayed without any formatting. The text file appears in Notepad or another text editor instead of appearing in the Internet Explorer window.
12. Click the Close button at the top-right corner of the text editor.

Close

Finish the lesson

- Drag the icons for any Web page files on your desktop to the Recycle Bin. The saved Web page files are deleted.

Lesson 1 Quick Reference

To	Do this	Button
Start Internet Explorer	Click the Internet Explorer desktop icon.	
Browse to another Web page	Type a Web address in the Address text box and press Enter, or click a hyperlink on the currently displayed Web page.	
Redisplay Web pages viewed during the current session	Click the Back (or the Forward) button.	
Stop downloading a page	Click the Stop button.	
Re-download the current Web page	Click the Refresh button.	
Display your Internet home page	Click the Home button.	
Find text in the current Web page	Click Find (On This Page) on the Edit menu. Type the text you want to search for, and click the Find Next button to find each instance of the search term.	
Create a desktop shortcut	On the File menu, point to Send, and then click Shortcut To Desktop.	
Print a Web page	Click the Print button, *or* click Print on the File menu, select the desired options in the Print dialog box, and then click OK.	
Print selected items	On a Web page, select an item such as a word. Click Print on the File menu. Click the Selection option in the Print dialog box, and click OK.	

Lesson 1 Quick Reference

To	Do this
Print frames on separate pages	Display a Web page that has frames. Click Print on the File menu. Click the All Frames Individually option in the Print dialog box, and then click OK.
Print a single frame	Display a Web page that has frames. Click a frame. Click Print on the File menu. Click the Only The Selected Frame option in the Print dialog box, and click OK.
Print linked documents	Click Print on the File menu. Click either the Only The Selected Frame or All Frames Individually option in the Print Frames section. Click the Print All Linked Documents check box in the Print dialog box, and click OK.
Print a table of links	Click Print on the File menu. Click either the Only The Selected Frame or All Frames Individually option in the Print Frames section. Click the Print Table Of Links option in the Print dialog box, and then click OK.
Save a Web page	Click Save As on the File menu. Use the Save Web Page dialog box to specify how and where you want to save the Web page contents, and click Save.

Finding and Managing Information

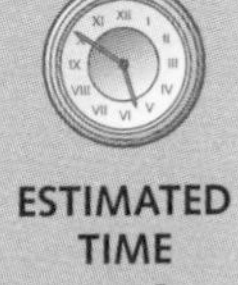

ESTIMATED TIME **30 min.**

In this lesson you will learn how to:

- ✔ *Search for information on the Web.*
- ✔ *Create a Favorites list.*
- ✔ *Use Favorites.*
- ✔ *Manage your Favorites list.*
- ✔ *Use and modify your History folder.*
- ✔ *Manage your temporary Internet files.*

Imagine that you're the account executive for Impact Public Relations' most prestigious client—Lakewood Mountains Resort. The resort's off-season is looming, so you're researching the feasibility of offering package deals to attract business groups and vacationers. You turn to the Internet to research current travel trends, prices, and schedules. Microsoft Internet Explorer 5 offers a number of tools that can help you find and store links to Internet information. As you find sites that interest you, you can create a site list for future reference.

In this lesson, you will learn how to use Internet Explorer to search for information on the World Wide Web. Then you will learn how to create, use, and manage a list of your favorite Internet sites. You'll also see how Internet Explorer keeps tabs on your Internet travels. Finally, you'll learn how you can use and manage Internet Explorer's history feature.

Searching for Information on the Web

The Internet contains so many documents that you'll frequently need help finding specific information. Internet Explorer makes finding Web information easy. You can search for information on the Web by using Internet Explorer's Address bar or by clicking the Search button on the toolbar, which opens the Search Assistant, as shown in the following illustration.

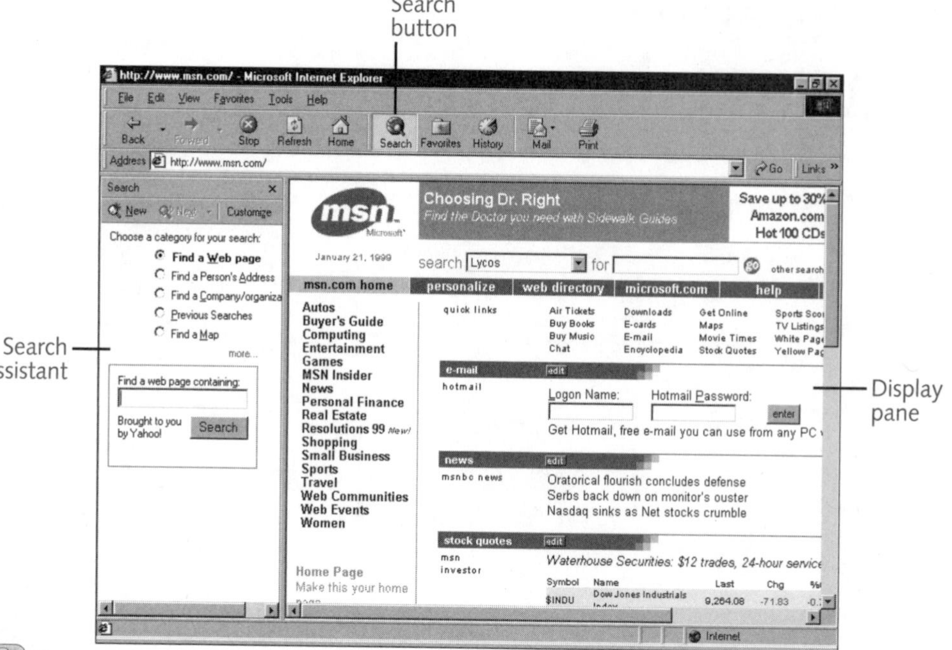

For a demonstration of how to search using the Search Assistant, open the Office 8in1 Step by Step folder on your hard disk. Then open the Internet Explorer Demos folder, and double-click the Search icon.

The Search Assistant is a tool that helps you find information on the Internet. It gives you the choice to search for a subject word, or search for a subject word within a category. Searching by category helps to narrow down what you want to look for. After you type in a subject word and click the Search button, the Search Assistant will display a list of links to Web pages that contain information about your subject word. Just click the link to view the information.

The Search Assistant also gives you the option to choose a *search engine*. A search engine is a Web tool designed to look for Internet information based on subject words (also called *keywords*) or to browse for topics organized by subject groups. You can view other available search engines by clicking the drop-down arrow to the right of the Next button in the Search Assistant.

After you select a search engine, you can type in a keyword or click subject groupings to narrow your search. The more criteria you add to your search the more likely you are to find the type of information you're seeking.

> **tip**
>
> When using a search engine, you can search for multiple terms by including a plus sign between words in the search text box. For example, you can enter *mountain+resort* in the search text box to find Web sites about mountains and resorts. Also, if you want to search for a phrase, you can surround the phrase with quotation marks. For example, you can enter *"bed and breakfast"* to find Web sites about bed and breakfast services. Most search engines include a page dedicated to Internet searching tips and techniques.

You can also search for Web sites using the Address bar. Internet Explorer provides one main Address bar search feature—*Autosearch*. Autosearch enables you to search for Web pages by word or phrase. In the Address bar, type *go*, *find*, or *?* followed by a space and a word or phrase, and then press Enter. The Autosearch Web page will appear with a list of hyperlinks to Web sites. Each Web site will have a short description listed below it. For example, you could type *go fish* to search for information related to fish. The Autosearch Web page will list hyperlinks related to fish. After you read the descriptions of the Web sites, simply click a hyperlink that interests you. The Web site you choose will appear in Internet Explorer.

You will use the Autosearch feature as you gather information for your client, Lakewood Mountains Resort.

Display the Search Assistant

In this exercise, you display and resize the Search Assistant in Internet Explorer.

1. Start Internet Explorer.

Search

2. On the toolbar, click the Search button.

   The Search Assistant is displayed.

3. Click the Search button again.

   The Search Assistant closes.

4. Click the Search button, and position your cursor along the right edge of the Search Assistant.

   The mouse pointer turns into a horizontal double arrow.

5. Drag the right edge of the Search Assistant to the right.

   The Search Assistant appears wider, as shown in the illustration.

The AutoComplete dialog box might appear, asking if you want it to list suggestions of your previous search words as you type search words in the Search Assistant. Click Yes.

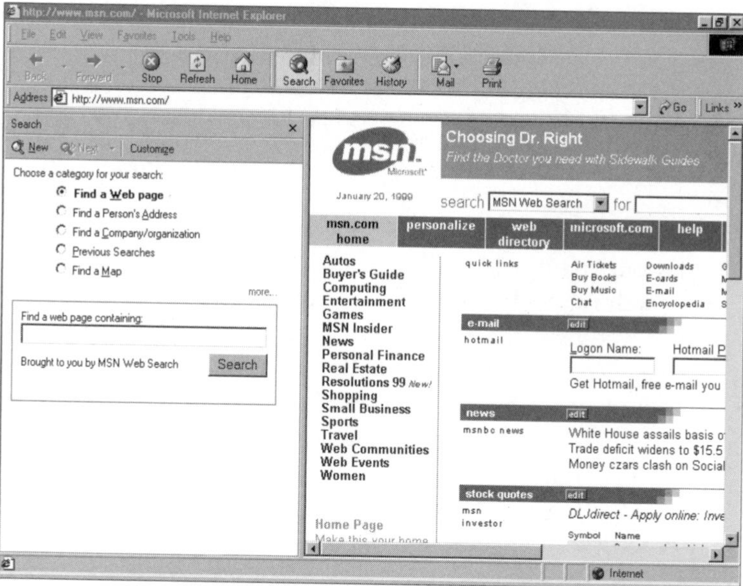

6. Drag the right edge of the Search Assistant to the left until the Search Assistant is close to its original size.

   The Search Assistant becomes narrower.

7. Click the Close button at the top-right corner of the Search Assistant.

   The Search Assistant closes.

Close

Search for a Web site

In this exercise, you use the Search Assistant to do a quick search for the word *airlines*.

1. On the toolbar, click the Search button.

   The Search Assistant is displayed.

2. Type **airlines** in the Find A Web Page Containing text box.

   This indicates that you want to search for Web sites containing the word *airlines*.

You can also start a search by pressing Enter after typing in a word.

3. Click the Search button.

   The search is performed. Links to categories and Web pages containing information matching your search criterion appear in the Search Assistant.

4. Click a link in the Search Assistant.

   A Web page matching your search criterion is displayed in Internet Explorer's display pane.

Your screen will differ from this one if you clicked a different hyperlink.

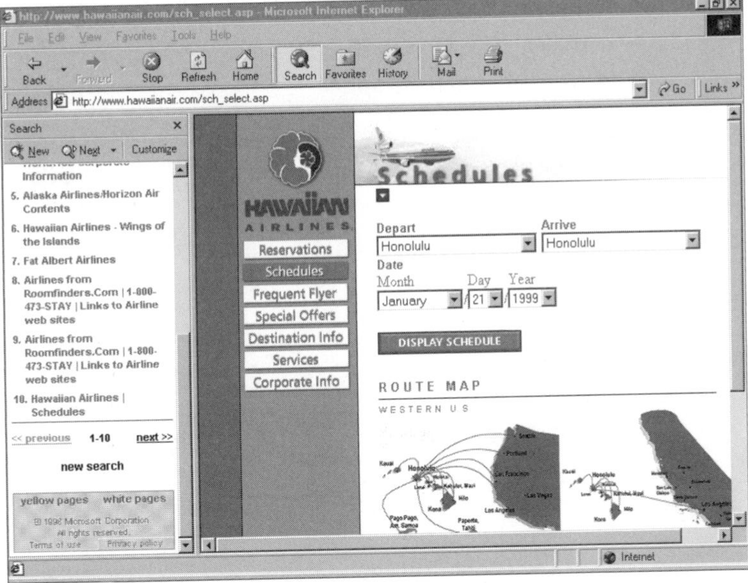

5. In the Search Assistant, click the New button.

   The Search Assistant is now ready for a new search.

6. On the toolbar, click the Search button.

   The Search Assistant closes.

Selecting Your Own Search Engine

There are several search engines (such as Yahoo, Hotbot, and AltaVista) that you can use to find documents on the Internet. You might find over time that you prefer one search engine in particular. Internet Explorer lets you choose which search engine you want to use.

Select a search engine

In this exercise, you conduct a search on restaurants, and then you select a different search engine to conduct a new search on restaurants.

Search

1. On the toolbar, click the Search button.

   The Search Assistant is displayed.
2. If necessary, click the Find A Web Page option.
3. Type **restaurants** in the Find A Web Page Containing text box, and click Search.

   A list of links related to the word *restaurants* appears.
4. In the Search Assistant, click the drop-down arrow to the right of the Next Button.

   A list of search engines appears.
5. Click Yahoo!.

   Yahoo! displays a new list of links related to restaurants.
6. Click the New button.

   A new search can now be conducted.

If you click only the Next button and not the drop-down arrow, the next search engine in the list will conduct a search on restaurants.

tip

You can change the order and content of your search engine list by clicking the Customize button in the Search Assistant. The Customize Search Settings window will appear, and you will see a list of search engines in the Find A Web Page section. Click a search engine in the list box, and then use the up arrow or down arrow button to move the search engine to a different location in the list. You can change the content of the search engine list by deselecting or selecting the check boxes to the left of the search engines. When you are finished making changes, click OK.

Choose a category to narrow your search

In this exercise, you select different categories in the Search Assistant to narrow your searches.

1. Click the Find A Company/Organization option.

   A search for Web pages related to companies and organizations will be conducted.

2. Type **Microsoft** in the Business text box, type **Redmond** in the City text box, type **WA** in the State/Province text box, and click the Search button.

   A list of links related to Microsoft appears in the Search Assistant.

You can select another search engine to conduct the same search by clicking the Next button in the Search Assistant.

3. Scroll down the list, and click one of the Microsoft Corporation links.

   The InfoSpace Web page appears, displaying information about Microsoft.

4. In the Search Assistant, click the New Button, and click the word *More*.

   The list of categories becomes larger.

5. Click the Find In Encyclopedia option.

   The search will be conducted by Encarta.

6. Type **elephants** in the Find Encyclopedia Articles On text box, and click Search.

   Encarta conducts a search on elephants and lists the results.

7. Click the Elephant link.

   The Encarta Web page appears, displaying facts about elephants.

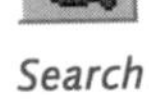
Search

8. On the toolbar, click the Search button.

   The Search Assistant closes.

Use Autosearch

In this exercise, you use Autosearch to find Web pages containing the word *boeing*.

1. Click in the Address bar.

   Internet Explorer selects the current text.

2. Type **go boeing**, and then press Enter.

   The Autosearch Web page appears with a list of hyperlinks related to the word **boeing**.

3. Click any hyperlink on the Autosearch page to display other Web sites related to the word *boeing*.

   Internet Explorer displays the Web site of the hyperlink you clicked.

Creating a Favorites List

Imagine you've been working extensively with your Lakewood Mountains Resort client. You've been visiting the resort's Web site three or four times a day. You're tired of repeatedly typing the Web page address in the Address bar, so you would prefer to create a quicker way to access the page. You learn that you can add an entry to your Internet Explorer Favorites list that will enable you to access the Lakewood Mountains Resort Web page with a single click.

A *Favorites list* is a menu you create that contains a collection of shortcuts to Web pages. Your Favorites list contains at least five folders (you might have additional Favorites folders if you created them in previous versions of Internet Explorer or Windows): Channels (this folder contains *channels,* or Web sites designed to deliver customized information to your computer based on an updated schedule), Imported Bookmarks (this folder contains bookmarks you might have created in other browsers before you installed Internet Explorer 5), Links, Media, and Software Updates.

Your Favorites list can store links to any Web page you choose. The simplest way to add a link is to display the Web page in your browser, and then add the page to your Favorites list.

In addition to placing Web page links in your Favorites list, you can add links to local resources (such as your hard disk or files and folders that you access frequently). Adding a local resource to your Favorites list allows you to quickly display the resource by clicking its Favorites link. To view your Favorites list's contents, click the Favorites button on the toolbar. The Favorites bar is displayed in the left pane of the Internet Explorer window.

Add the current Web page to your Favorites list

In this exercise, you add the Lakewood Mountains Resort home page to your Favorites list.

1. Click in the Address bar, type **mspress.microsoft.com/mspress/product/1349/default1.htm**, and press Enter.

   The Lakewood Mountains Resort home page is displayed.

Favorites

2. On the toolbar, click the Favorites button.

   The Favorites bar is displayed.

3. On the Favorites bar, click the Add button.

   The Add Favorite dialog box appears, as shown in the following illustration.

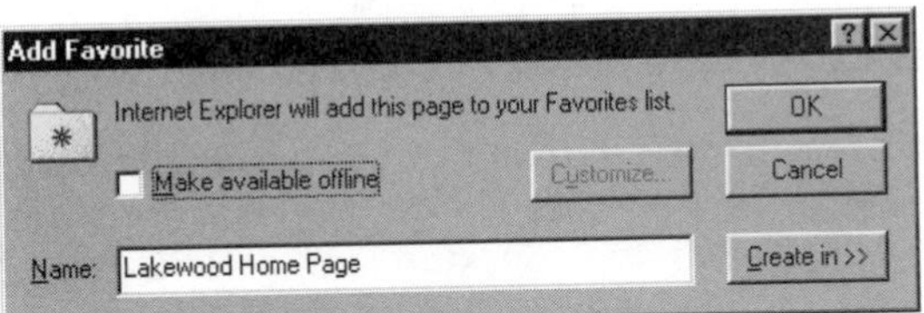

tip

You can also use the menu bar to add Favorites to your Favorites list. Display a Web page. On the Favorites menu, click Add To Favorites, and click OK.

4. In the Add Favorite dialog box, click OK.

   The Favorites list now includes a link to the Lakewood Home Page, as shown in the illustration.

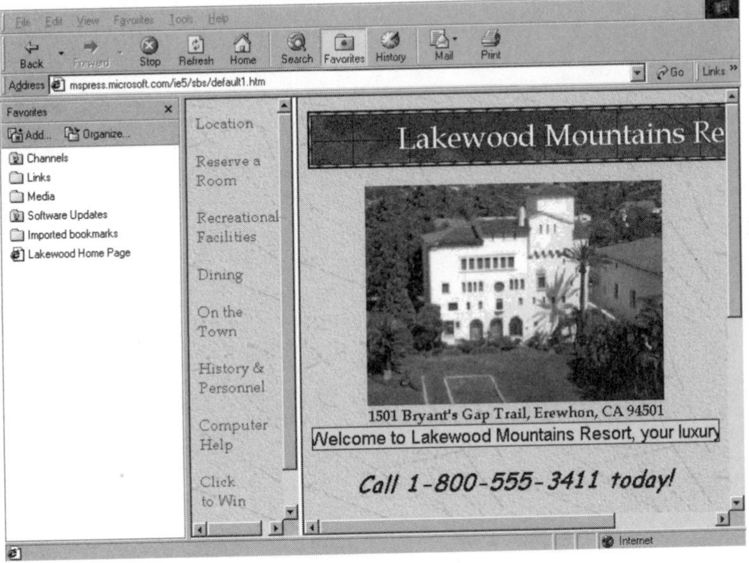

Favorites

5. On the toolbar, click the Favorites button.

   The Favorites bar closes.

Add your desktop to your Favorites list

In this exercise, you add your desktop to your Favorites list.

1. Click in the Address bar, type **desktop**, and press Enter.

   The contents of your desktop appear.

2. On the Favorites menu, click Add To Favorites.

   The Add Favorite dialog box is displayed.

3. In the Add Favorite dialog box, click OK.

   Your desktop is added to your Favorites list.

Back

4. Click the Back button to return to the previously displayed Web page.
5. On the toolbar, click the Favorites button.

   The Favorites bar is displayed. Notice that the Favorites list now includes a link to your desktop.

Favorites

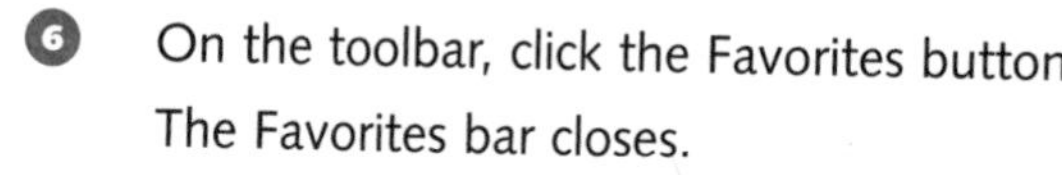

6. On the toolbar, click the Favorites button.

   The Favorites bar closes.

Using Favorites

Creating Favorites means that you can visit Web sites without having to remember the address of a Web page or type a path in the Address bar. Instead, you can display the Favorites bar, find the link that you created, and click it to display the page. You can also access the Favorites list from the menu bar. You can even access the Favorites list without having Internet Explorer open. To do so, click the Start button, point to Favorites, and click a Favorites link.

When you click a Favorites link using the Start menu, Internet Explorer opens and displays the selected Web page.

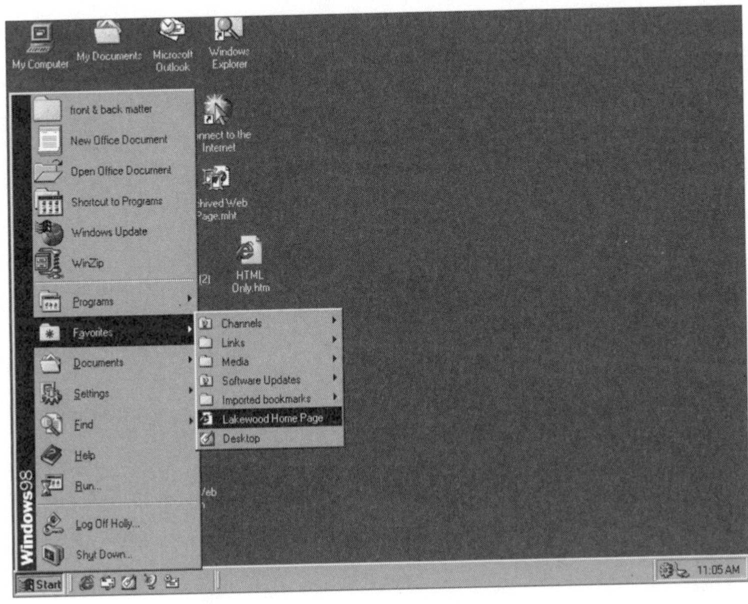

Use the Favorites bar

In this exercise, you add the Expedia Travel site to your Favorites list, and then access the site using the Favorites bar.

1. Click in the Address bar, type **expedia.com**, and press Enter.

   The Expedia Travel site is displayed.

Favorites

2. On the toolbar, click the Favorites button.

   The Favorites bar is displayed.

3. On the Favorites bar, click the Add button, and click OK when the Add Favorite dialog box appears.

   The Expedia Travel site appears as a link in your Favorites list.

Home

4. On the toolbar, click the Home button.

   Your home page is displayed.

5. On the Favorites bar, click the Expedia link.

   The Expedia Travel site is redisplayed.
6. On the toolbar, click the Favorites button.

   The Favorites bar closes.

Use the Favorites menu

In this exercise, you use the Favorites menu to open a Web page.

1. On the Favorites menu, click a Favorites link.

   The Web site is downloaded and appears in Internet Explorer.
2. On the toolbar, click the Back button.

Access Favorites from the Windows taskbar

In this exercise, you use the Windows Start menu to open a Favorites link.

1. On the Windows taskbar, click the Start button, and point to Favorites.

   The contents of your Favorites list are displayed.
2. On the Favorites menu, click a link.

   The Web site associated with the Favorites link downloads and is displayed in Internet Explorer's display pane.
3. On the toolbar, click the Back button.

Managing Your Favorites List

You've decided that you want to create a folder to store links to Web pages associated with your project. Storing these links in a separate folder will help you find the Web pages quickly and to organize links that have a similar topic or purpose. After you create the new folder, you decide to move existing Favorites into the folder. In addition, you want to add a new link directly into the folder.

While moving your Favorites, you notice a site with a long name and find that you can rename the Favorite with minimal effort. Finally, as you organize your Favorites, you realize that you no longer need some of the links, so you delete the links to minimize clutter. To accomplish these tasks, you use Internet Explorer's Organize Favorites dialog box.

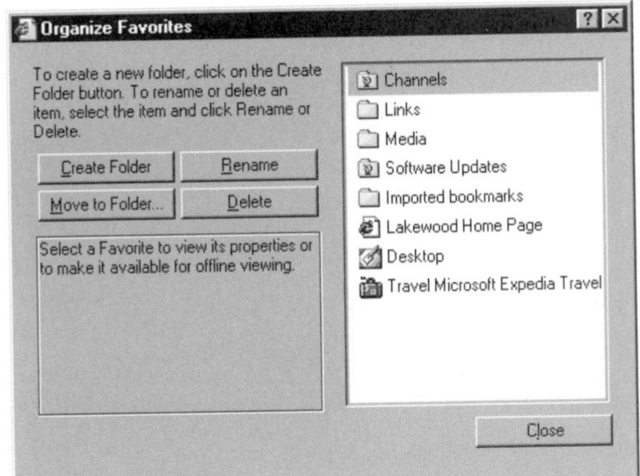

New!

Create a folder within your Favorites list

In this exercise, you create a folder to store Favorites links for your Lakewood Mountains Resort project.

1. On the toolbar, click the Favorites button.
   The Favorites bar is displayed.
2. On the Favorites bar, click the Organize button.
   The Organize Favorites dialog box is displayed.
3. Click the Create Folder button.
   A folder named *New Folder* is added to the bottom of the list.
4. Type **Lakewood Mountains Resort**, and press Enter.
   The new folder is renamed Lakewood Mountains Resort.
5. Click the Close button.
   The Organize Favorites dialog box closes.
6. On the toolbar, click the Favorites button.
   The Favorites bar closes.

Move an existing Favorites link into a folder

This exercise assumes that you have created a Favorites link to the Lakewood Mountains Resort home page. If you have not, follow the steps in the exercise "Add the Current Web Page to Your Favorites List" earlier in this lesson.

In this exercise, you move the Lakewood Home Page Favorites link to the Lakewood Mountains Resort folder.

1. On the toolbar, click the Favorites button.

   The Favorites bar is displayed.

2. On the Favorites bar, click the Organize button.

   The Organize Favorites dialog box is displayed.

3. In the Organize Favorites dialog box, click the Lakewood Home Page link.

   The Lakewood Home Page link is selected.

4. Click the Move To Folder button.

   The Browse For Folder dialog box is displayed.

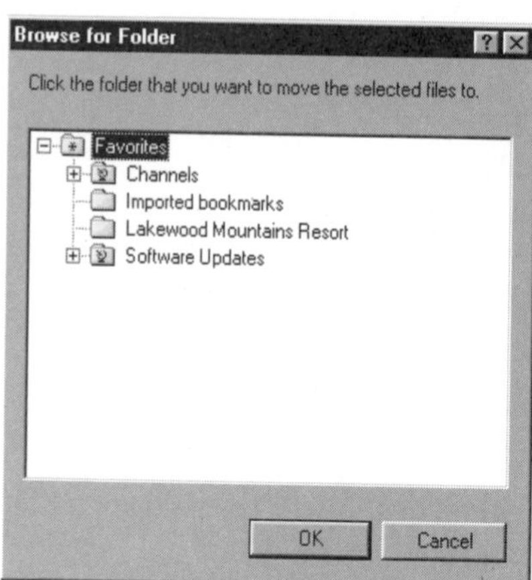

5. In the Browse For Folder dialog box, click the Lakewood Mountains Resort folder, and then click OK.

   The Lakewood Home Page link is now stored in the Lakewood Mountains Resort folder. Notice the Lakewood Home Page link no longer appears in the top level of the Organize Favorites dialog box.

6. In the Organize Favorites dialog box, click the Close button.

   The Organize Favorites dialog box closes.

7. On the Favorites bar, click the Lakewood Mountains Resort folder.

   The Lakewood Home Page Favorites link appears below the Lakewood Mountains Resort folder.

8. Click the Lakewood Mountains Resort folder again.

   The folder closes.

9. On the toolbar, click the Favorites button.

   The Favorites bar closes.

Place a new Favorites link into a folder

In this exercise, you use the Add Favorite dialog box to place the Avis home page into the Lakewood Mountains Resort folder.

1. Click in the Address bar, type **avis**, and then press Enter.

   The Avis home page is displayed.

2. On the toolbar, click the Favorites button.

   The Favorites bar is displayed.

3. On the Favorites bar, click the Add button.

   The Add Favorite dialog box is displayed.

4. If necessary, click the Create In button to expand the Add Favorite dialog box.

5. In the Create In area, click the Lakewood Mountains Resort folder, and then click OK.

   The Avis home page link is stored in the Lakewood Mountains Resort folder.

6. If necessary, on the Favorites bar, click the Lakewood Mountains Resort folder.

   The Avis home page link is displayed below the Lakewood Mountains Resort folder, as shown in the following illustration.

7. On the toolbar, click the Favorites button.

   The Favorites bar closes.

Rename a Favorites link

In this exercise, you create a Favorites link to the Visa International home page, and then you rename the link.

1. Click in the Address bar, type **visa**, and then press Enter.

   The Visa International home page is displayed.
2. On the toolbar, click the Favorites button.

   The Favorites bar is displayed.
3. On the Favorites bar, click the Add button, and then click OK.

   A Favorites link entitled Visa International appears on the Favorites bar.
4. On the Favorites bar, click the Organize button.
5. In the Organize Favorites dialog box, click the Visa International link, click the Rename button, type **Visa**, press Enter, and then click the Close button.

   The Visa International link is renamed *Visa*.
6. On the toolbar, click the Favorites button.

   The Favorites bar closes.

You can also right-click a link in the Favorites list and click Rename to rename a Favorites link.

tip

You can save time by naming your Favorites links as you create them. When the Add Favorite dialog box is displayed, select the current text in the Name text box, type a new name for the Favorites link, and click OK.

Deleting Favorites

The Internet constantly changes, which means that your Favorites links sometimes become outdated. In addition, your needs change over time. You should sort through your Favorites links occasionally to delete outdated and unwanted Favorites links. Otherwise, your Favorites folder could grow unwieldy.

Delete Favorites

In this exercise, you delete the Visa Favorites link.

You can also right-click a link or a folder in the Favorites list and click Delete to delete a Favorites link.

1. On the toolbar, click the Favorites button.
2. On the Favorites bar, click the Organize button.
3. In the Organize Favorites dialog box, click the Visa link.
4. Click the Delete button, and then click Yes to confirm the deletion.

   The Visa Favorites link is deleted from your Favorites list.
5. Click the Close button.

   The Organize Favorites dialog box closes.
6. On the toolbar, click the Favorites button.

   The Favorites bar closes.

Using the History Folder

You just finished surfing the Internet for six hours, looking for information for your Lakewood Mountains Resort project. You realize too late that you forgot to add some helpful sites to your Favorites list. You groan as you wonder how you'll be able to retrace your steps. Fortunately, your partner walks by and notices your dismay. As you explain that you'll never "re-find" some sites, your partner stops you in mid-sentence to ask if you've checked the History folder.

Internet Explorer automatically records a history of each Internet browsing session. This record is in your History folder, which contains links to each site you visit on the Internet. Your History folder also stores other facts, such as the day you visited each Web page.

To view the contents of your History folder, simply click the History button on the toolbar. The History bar appears along the left side of the Internet Explorer window.

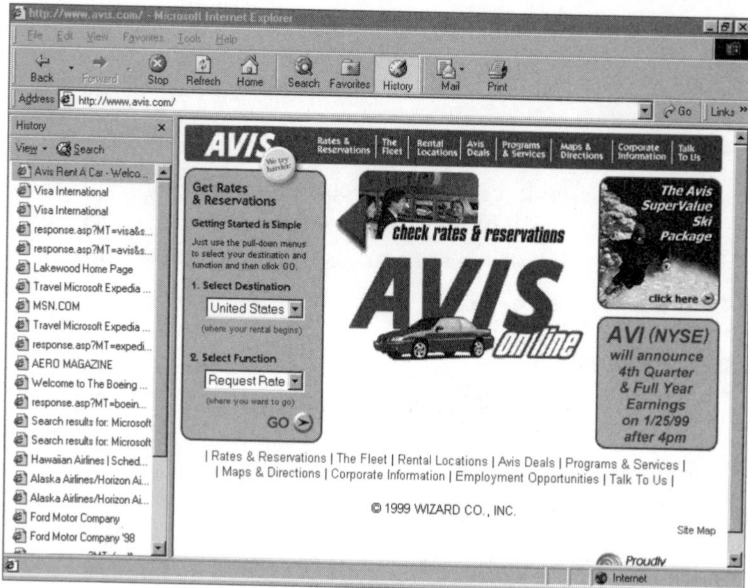

The History bar has a search feature that allows you to type in a search word to locate a site that you visited.

You can specify how long Internet Explorer saves items in your History folder. By default, the History folder stores links to all sites visited within the last 20 days. After an item has been stored for 20 days, it is deleted. For more control, you can manually delete links stored in the History folder. Microsoft refers to deleting all links in your History folder as *clearing* your history.

View your history

This exercise assumes that you have visited the Lakewood Mountains Resort Web site today.

You can view a history of your Internet explorations with a click of a button. In this exercise, you view the contents of your History folder.

1. On the toolbar, click the History button.
   The History bar appears.
2. On the History bar, click the Search button.
3. In the Search For text box, type **lakewood**, and click Search Now.
   A list of Web sites that contain the word *lakewood* appears.

4. Click the View button.

   A drop-down list appears.

5. Click the By Date option.

   A list of folders of Web sites that you visited today appears.

6. On the toolbar, click the History button.

   The History bar closes.

Click a folder to open a list of links, and then click a link to view a Web page that you recently visited.

Configure your history settings

You can change the length of time that Internet Explorer stores your history information. In this exercise, you configure your History folder's settings.

1. On the Tools menu, click Internet Options.

   The Internet Options dialog box is displayed, as shown in the illustration.

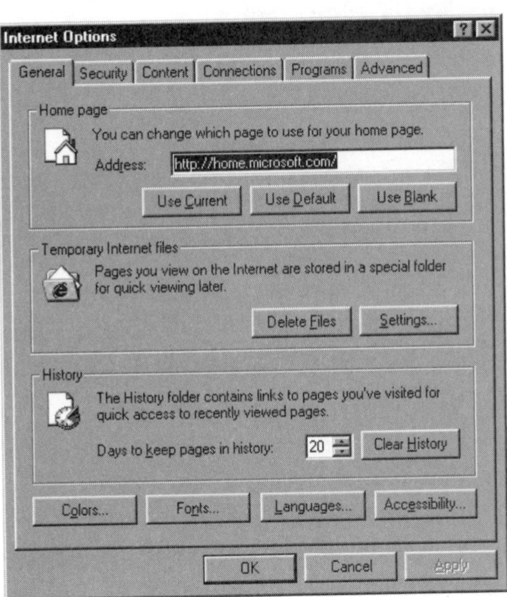

2. On the General tab in the History section, double-click the number in the Days To Keep Pages In History text box.

   The number in the text box is selected.

3. Type **30**.

   The setting changes to 30 days.

4. In the text box, delete 30, type **20**, and click OK.

   The setting returns to 20 days, and the Internet Options dialog box closes.

Clear your History folder

You can manually empty or "clear" your History folder. In this exercise, you clear all of the contents of your History folder.

1. On the Tools menu, click Internet Options.

   The Internet Options dialog box is displayed.
2. On the General tab in the History section, click the Clear History button.

   A message box appears, asking if you want to delete all items in your History folder.
3. Click OK.

   The content of your History folder is deleted.
4. Click OK.

   The Internet Options dialog box closes.
5. On the toolbar, click the History button.

   The History bar no longer displays a list of links.
6. Click the History button again.

   The History bar closes.

One Step Further Managing Your Temporary Internet Files

To help speed up your Internet browsing experience, Internet Explorer saves a "local" copy of every file you view to your hard disk. When you return to a Web site, Internet Explorer first checks to see if a local copy of the Internet site is on your computer. If so, Internet Explorer displays the local files. You can display local files much more quickly than files from the Internet because retrieving a file from your hard disk is much quicker than retrieving it through your Internet connection. This process of saving and displaying local files is called *caching*. Internet Explorer places cached files in the Temporary Internet Files folder. You need to be aware of this because the Temporary Internet Files folder can store a sizable amount of information—and take up a sizable amount of disk space.

Internet Explorer lets you configure your Temporary Internet Files settings. You can set how often Internet Explorer checks the Internet for new versions of Web pages stored in your Temporary Internet Files folder.

You can also dictate the amount of disk space to use for storing cached files. Increasing the size available for your Temporary Internet Files folder can increase how fast previously viewed Web pages are displayed, but large files decrease the amount of space available for other files on your computer.

Updating Stored Web Pages

You can choose from among four Internet Explorer options to check for new content on Web pages stored in your Temporary Internet Files folder.

Select this option	For this result
Every Visit To The Page	Internet Explorer checks for new content on a Web page each time you visit the page.
Every Time You Start Internet Explorer	Internet Explorer checks for new content only on pages you have recently viewed. It does not check for new content each time you view a Web page during the current session.
Automatically	Internet Explorer checks for new content only on pages you have recently viewed. Over time, if Internet Explorer determines that the Web site's files are changing infrequently, it will check for new content less often.
Never	Internet Explorer never checks for updates to stored Web pages. You must click the Refresh button on the toolbar to update a stored Web page.

Configure your temporary Internet files settings

In this exercise, you select how often you want Internet Explorer to check for newer versions of stored files, and you change the amount of disk space allotted for storing your temporary Internet files.

1. On the Tools menu, click Internet Options.

   The Internet Options dialog box is displayed.

2. In the Temporary Internet Files section, click Settings.

   The Settings dialog box appears, as shown in the following illustration.

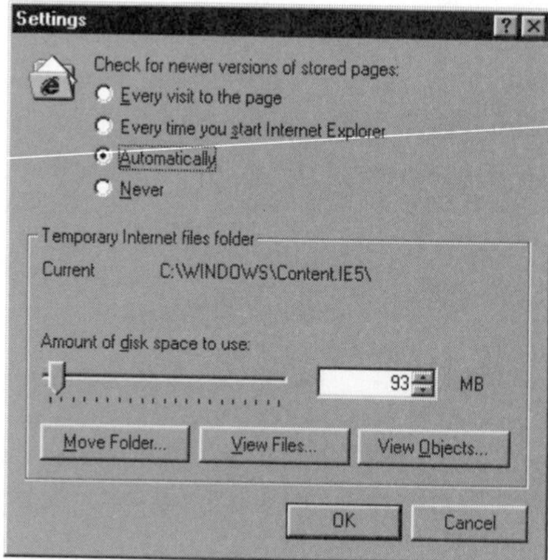

3. Select how often you want Internet Explorer to check for newer versions of stored files. You can retain the Automatically default setting or select one of the other three options.
4. Click the slider (beneath the Amount Of Disk Space To Use section) to the left or right.

   The allocation size for the disk cache changes for the Temporary Internet Files folder.
5. Click OK to close the Settings dialog box, and click OK to close the Internet Options dialog box.

Delete temporary Internet files

As your Temporary Internet Files folder fills up, you might want to delete some of the saved Web page files. In this exercise, you delete temporary Internet files.

After you delete your temporary Internet files, Internet Explorer will download new files when you visit each Web page.

1. On the Tools menu, click Internet Options.

   The Internet Options dialog box is displayed.
2. On the General tab in the Temporary Internet Files section, click Delete Files, and then click OK in the Delete Files dialog box.

   The files stored in your Temporary Internet Files folder are deleted.
3. Click OK.

   The Internet Options dialog box closes.

Finish the lesson

1. If necessary, display your Favorites bar, and delete any links or folders created in this lesson.
2. Quit Internet Explorer.

Lesson 2 Quick Reference

To	Do this	Button
Display the Search Assistant	Click the Search button on the toolbar.	
Search for a Web site	Display the Search Assistant, enter a search word in the text box, and click the Search button.	
Select a search engine	Display the Search Assistant, type a search word in the text box, click the Search button, click the drop-down arrow to the right of the Next button, and select a search engine.	
Choose a category to narrow down searches	Display the Search Assistant, and click a category.	
Use Autosearch	In the Address bar, type **go**, **find**, or **?**, press the Spacebar, type a word or phrase, and press Enter.	
Add the current Web page to your Favorites list	Display a Web page. Click the Favorites button on the toolbar. Click the Add button on the Favorites bar, and click OK.	
Add your desktop to your Favorites list	In the Address bar, type **desktop**, and press Enter. Click Add To Favorites on the Favorites menu, and click OK.	
Use the Favorites bar	Click the Favorites button on the toolbar, and then click a Favorites link on the Favorites bar.	
Use the Favorites menu	Click a Favorites link on the Favorites menu.	
Access Favorites from the Windows taskbar	On the Windows taskbar, click Start, point to Favorites, and then click a Favorites link.	
Create a folder within your Favorites list	Display the Favorites bar, click Organize, click the Create Folder button, type a name for the new folder, press Enter, and click the Close button.	

Lesson 2 Quick Reference

To	Do this	Button
Move an existing Favorites link into a folder	Display the Favorites bar, click Organize, select the item to be moved, click the Move To Folder button, select the folder to store the selected item, click OK, and click the Close button.	
Place a new Favorites link into a folder	Display a Web page. Display the Favorites bar, click Add, click the Create In button (if necessary), click the folder to store the new Favorites link, and click OK.	
Rename a Favorites link	Display the Favorites bar, click Organize, click the link to be renamed, click Rename, type a new name for the Favorites link, press enter, and click the Close button.	
Delete Favorites	Display the Favorites bar, click Organize, select a Favorites link to delete, click Delete, click Yes, and click the Close button.	
View your Web usage history	Click the History button on the toolbar.	
Configure your history settings	Click Internet Options on the Tools menu, make desired changes in the History section, and click OK.	
Clear your History folder	Click Internet Options on the Tools menu, click Clear History, click OK, and click OK to close the Internet Options dialog box.	
Configure your temporary Internet files settings	Click Internet Options on the Tools menu, click Settings, make desired changes, click OK in the Settings dialog box, and then click OK to close the Internet Options dialog box.	
Delete temporary Internet files	Click Internet Options on the Tools menu, click Delete Files, click OK in the Delete Files dialog box, and then click OK to close the Internet Options dialog box.	

PART 8

Microsoft FrontPage 2000

Planning a Web Site

In this lesson you will learn how to:

- ✔ *Plan a Web site.*
- ✔ *Start FrontPage.*
- ✔ *View a Web site in different ways.*
- ✔ *Open and close a Web.*

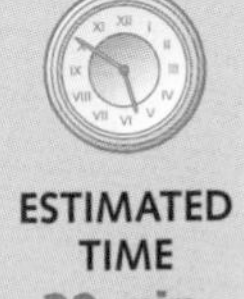

ESTIMATED TIME **20 min.**

Imagine that you are an account executive at Impact Public Relations, an innovative public relations firm that uses the Internet to spread the word about its clients. You've just been assigned to an important new account with Lakewood Mountains Resort, a posh California vacation spot. Your first job will be to create a Web site that spotlights the resort's most attractive features.

There's just one problem. You've been on the World Wide Web, but you don't understand how it works. And the idea of *creating* a Web site—especially for a crucial new account—is very intimidating. But you're in luck. A fellow account executive tells you about a Web tool called Microsoft FrontPage 2000, and volunteers to help you along as you learn to use it.

In this lesson, you will learn how the Web operates and how Web pages make up Webs, or Web sites. You will also learn how to plan your own Web site, complete with hyperlinks. Finally, you will learn how to start FrontPage, use FrontPage views, open and close a Web, and quit FrontPage.

Understanding the World Wide Web

The World Wide Web (or the *Web*) makes it easy to use the *Internet*, a worldwide network of computers created in the late 1960s. Originally, the Internet required you to learn many arcane commands—not only to use it, but also to get data from computers connected to it. If you wanted to get data from a computer that used the UNIX operating system, for example, you needed to know the commands for using UNIX; to get data from a VAX computer that used the VMS operating system, you needed to know the commands for VMS. The Internet worked, but it was difficult to use.

In 1992, however, Tim Berners-Lee and other researchers helped launch the Web, which allowed users to "browse" the Internet without knowing complex commands. In the years that followed, Web *browsers* such as Microsoft Internet Explorer made the Web even easier and more powerful.

> **important**
>
> In this book (and elsewhere), you'll see the word *Web* used in two different ways. Usually, *Web* refers to the World Wide Web. However, it can also refer to a *FrontPage-based Web*, a set of Web pages you create in FrontPage for your Web site. The context should make it clear what *Web* means in each particular case.

The key to creating the Web was *hypertext,* a method for linking blocks, or "pages," of data that was first conceived in the 1960s. It wasn't until the 1990s, however, that Berners-Lee and his coworkers applied the hypertext concept to the Internet, with what they called *HTTP* (Hypertext Transfer Protocol). And with HTTP, the World Wide Web was born.

Today, there are millions of Web sites. You can access information on a wide range of topics, you can run a Web-based business, you can even learn about the Web and its underlying technology.

Understanding Web Pages and HTML

If hypertext and HTTP were the keys to creating the World Wide Web, the key to creating Web pages is *HTML* (Hypertext Markup Language). *HTML* uses codes, called *tags*, to format and define text on a Web page. The Web browser that you use translates these codes into the Web page text and graphics you see on your screen.

HTML tags do more than tell Web browsers how to format text and place graphics. Hyperlinks, for example, tell the Web browser to locate a different

Web page on the Internet and display it on the user's screen. The code for a typical Web page and the page it creates are shown in the following illustrations.

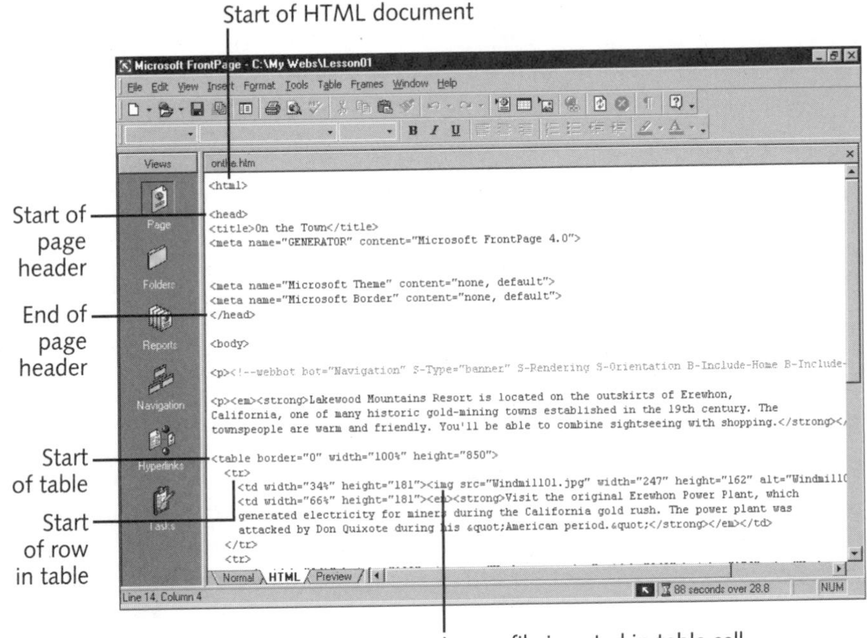

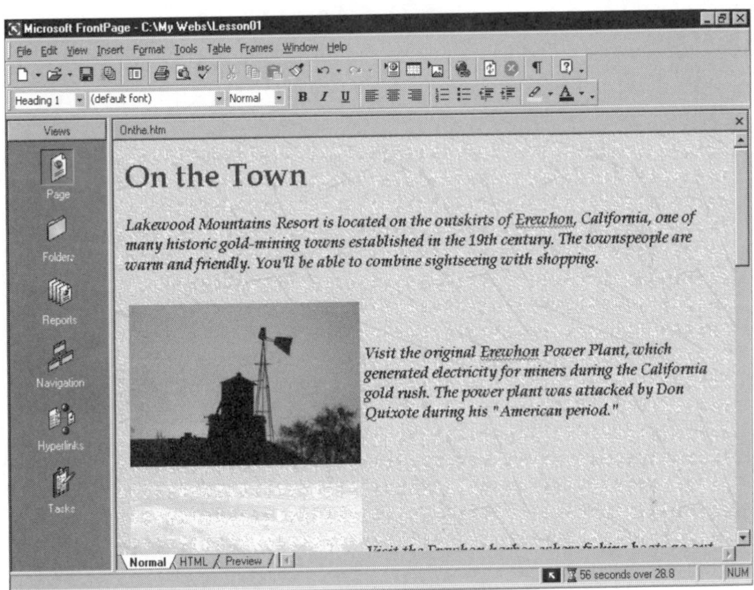

Many Web pages today use *scripts* created with languages such as Microsoft VBScript and JavaScript. These "mini-programs" are embedded in Web pages, where they handle formatting, images, and multimedia display routines much like any other programming language. A new and more advanced way to handle many scripting tasks is to use *Dynamic HTML* (DHTML). With DHTML, you can create simple animations and many other effects.

So, you're feeling overwhelmed by HTML and its many options? Now your coworker gives you the good news. To create Web sites with FrontPage, you don't have to learn anything about HTML, scripts, or DHTML unless you want to. With FrontPage, you simply type the text you want on your Web page, drop in any pictures or sounds you desire, and use FrontPage's features to do anything for which you would normally have to write a script or DHTML. You can still write HTML, scripts, or DHTML if you want, but it's not required.

tip

This book teaches you how to create Web sites for the World Wide Web. You can use the same techniques to create Web sites for an *intranet*—a network that works like the World Wide Web but has security features that restrict parts of it so that only users within your company or organization can access its pages.

Understanding Web Pages and Web Sites

You'll learn more about wizards and templates in Lesson 2, "Creating a Web Site."

A Web *site* is a collection of related Web pages and other files linked together. Web sites usually have a specific purpose, whether it be personal or business-related. FrontPage comes with *wizards*, which walk you step by step through the process of creating a Web site, and *templates*, which are built-in Web pages containing all the formatting required to build and customize your own Web pages. Wizards and templates can help you create several different kinds of Web sites.

A hyperlink is text or an image on a Web page that, when clicked, immediately sends you to another Web page or site.

On each Web site, one page is designated as the *home page*. This is the page that users see first when they visit the Web site. From the home page, users can click *hyperlinks* to jump to other pages on the Web site or to pages on different Web sites. Those hyperlinks might be Web sites on the same computer as the first Web site, or they might be stored on a computer halfway around the world. A typical Web site organization is shown in the following illustration.

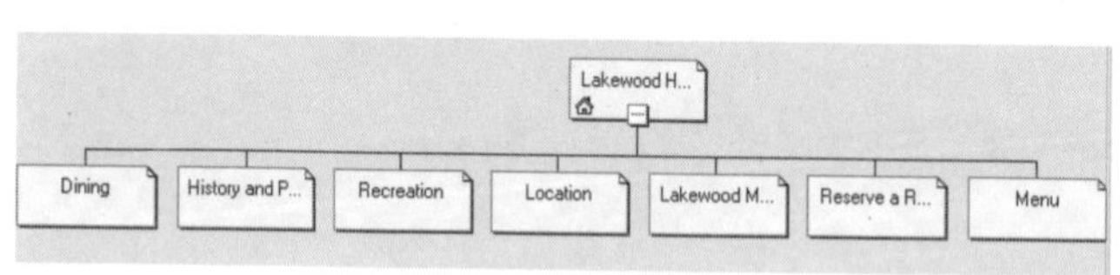

The home page is at the top, with linked pages on the row below it. Usually, each page under the home page—called a "child page" of the home page—contains hyperlinks to the other pages on the Web site, as well as hyperlinks back to the home page. Often, child pages will have hyperlinks to still other pages that are below them in the organization, and so forth.

You can use FrontPage to create and manage Web sites on the Internet or on an intranet.

A Web site resides on a *Web server,* which is a computer dedicated to making Web pages available to people who want to visit the site. (However, with FrontPage, you can create your Web site right in your computer's file system and publish the Web site to a server when you are ready.) Normally, a Web server is connected to the Internet, which makes its Web pages available for viewing on the World Wide Web. Many companies and organizations are setting up Web servers on intranets. These private Web servers are ideal for hosting Web sites that contain project files and other internal data that need to be shared by staff members. Some pages of the intranet Web site are made available to the world, while other pages remain accessible only to users within the organization.

Finding a Web Server

Before you set up the Web site for your client, Lakewood Mountains Resort, you need to find a place to put it: a Web server.

Most Internet service providers (ISPs) offer Web hosting as part of the package when you buy an Internet account. Web hosting simply means that the ISP provides space on a Web server computer for your Web files. Online services such as America Online also offer Web hosting. For simple Webs, an ISP's Web hosting services are often adequate. For larger and more sophisticated Webs, though, an account with a *dedicated* Web host can be a good investment. A dedicated Web host can offer more disk space for your Web files and, often, faster equipment.

Whether you choose an Internet service provider or a dedicated Web host, there's an important question you should always ask: "Do you have the FrontPage Server Extensions?" FrontPage has a slew of extra features to help you create exciting Web sites and put them on the Web with minimal effort. But some ISPs and Web hosts do not have the FrontPage Server Extensions. Some ISPs have them for business Internet accounts but not for the less-expensive personal accounts.

So, where can you find a FrontPage-supporting Web host? On the Web, of course. Navigate to Microsoft's Web Presence Provider site at *microsoft.saltmine.com/frontpage/wpp/list/* to view lists of ISPs and Web hosts that have the FrontPage Server Extensions.

Planning Your Web Site

Let's assume you've found a Web host that has the FrontPage Server Extensions. Now you need to decide what should go into the Web site you present to your client. You must first decide on the purpose of the Web site. In the case of Lakewood Mountains Resort, there are two main purposes.

- To provide information about the resort for prospective customers.
- To enable customers to request room reservations over the Web.

Of course, Web sites can have many additional purposes. One Web site might provide technical support for a computer product. Another might have a catalog and allow customers to place secure orders over the Web. The purpose of a Web site determines its design and the pages it should include.

Like all Web sites, the resort's Web site will start with a home page. From there, it needs at least one page about each of the resort's major selling points. So that customers can request reservations over the Web, the site will also need a form on which customers can enter their name, address, and reservation data.

You call the resort manager to learn about the resort's major selling points. You end up with a list of topics, each of which will get its own Web page.

- The resort's secluded location.
- The resort's recreational facilities.
- The resort's fine food.
- The picturesque town just a few minutes away.
- The resort's colorful history and helpful staff.

Based on this information, you come up with a diagram of the Web site.

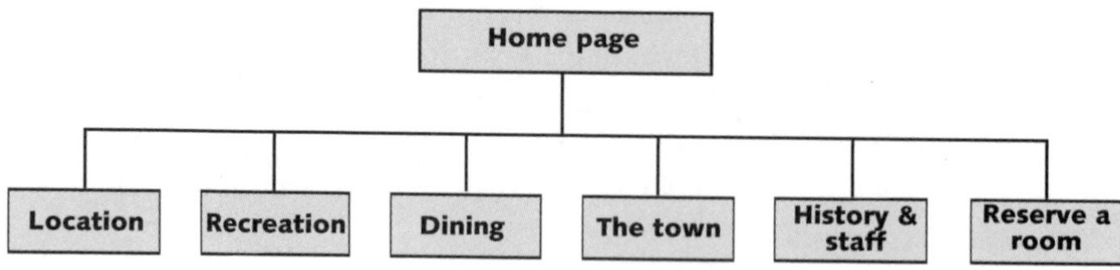

Now is the time to ask how the pages will be linked together. The obvious answer is "by hyperlinks," but FrontPage helps you use hyperlinks in a variety of ways. You can put all your hyperlinks on the home page, or if you're interested in a more high-tech alternative, you can use a *navigation bar,* one of FrontPage's special features. You can also create an *image map*—a picture with "hot spots," or hyperlinks within an image, that users can click to go to the desired pages.

Your coworker suggests a simple yet elegant solution: a menu *frame*. A frame is a pane in a Web site that works independently of the main pane. A frame is displayed continuously even as the user selects other hyperlinks that are displayed in the main pane. As the user moves around the Web site, pages are displayed in the right frame, while a menu of hyperlinks stays constant in the left frame. After considering these options, you decide to use frames in the Web site.

Managing a Web Site with FrontPage

The Views bar now provides an easy way to switch between views of Web structure and pages, and it includes an all new Reports view.

FrontPage makes it easy not only to create Web pages and Web sites, but also to manage them. The FrontPage window is divided into three main sections, each of which gives you a different kind of control over your Web site.

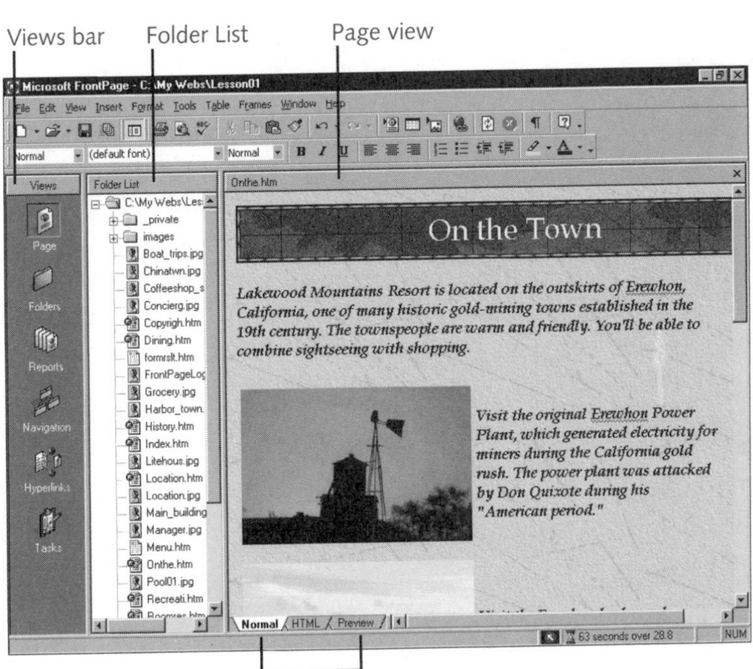

In FrontPage, you can view a Web in several different ways. The Views bar displays icons that let you view and edit different aspects of your Web.

Icon	Name	Description
	Page	Displays a Web page for viewing or editing.
	Folders	Displays a list of folders and files in the current Web.
	Reports	Displays a list of reports on different aspects of the current Web, such as the number of linked files, broken links, and the number of "slow" pages that would take more than 30 seconds to download to a computer over a 28.8-KB connection. (Thirty seconds is the default value, but you can change it.)
	Navigation	Displays a tree diagram of the current Web and makes the Folder List display a list of folders and files in the current Web.
	Hyperlinks	Displays a diagram of hyperlinks to and from the current page.
	Tasks	Displays a list of tasks to be done on the current Web. When you use some of the wizards to create a Web, FrontPage compiles a task list. You can also add tasks on your own.

The Folder List displays all folders and files in the current Web, while the currently selected page is displayed in Page view. At the bottom of the screen, a status bar displays information about the current page or operation. When a page is displayed in Page view, for example, the status bar shows an estimated download time for the page over a 28.8-KB modem connection.

Before you can work with any of the exercise files, you must install the files from the Microsoft Office 2000 8-in-1 Step by Step CD-ROM. For installation instructions, see "Installing the Practice Files" on page xviii.

Import the Lesson 1 practice Web

In this exercise, you create a new Web based on the files in the Lesson01 folder in the FrontPage Practice folder. You will use this Web for all the exercises in Lesson 1.

1. On the Windows taskbar, click the Start button, point to Programs, and then click Microsoft FrontPage.

   FrontPage starts.

If a dialog box appears asking if you'd like to make FrontPage your default HTML editor, click Yes.

2. On the File menu, point to New, and then click Web.

   FrontPage displays the New dialog box.

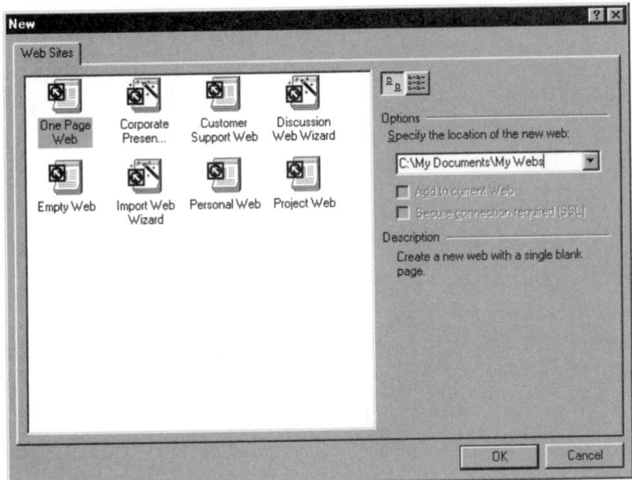

If your hard disk drive is not drive C, substitute the appropriate drive letter in step 3.

FrontPage will create the Lesson01 directory for you.

3. Click the Import Web Wizard icon. In the Specify The Location Of The New Web text box, delete the default text and type **C:\My Webs\Lesson01**, and then click OK.

   FrontPage displays the first Import Web Wizard dialog box.

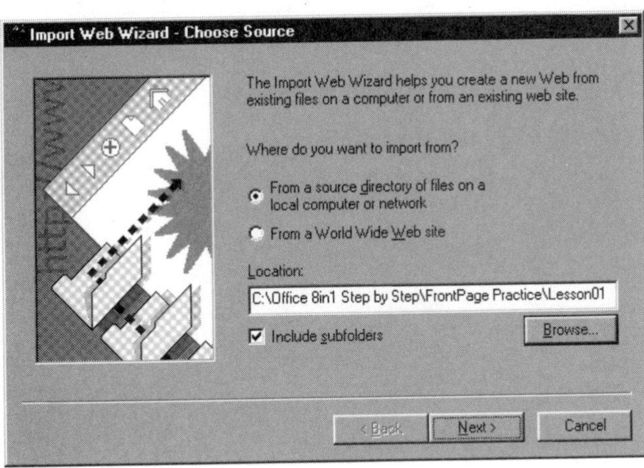

4. Click the From A Source Directory Of Files option, click the Include Subfolders check box, and click the Browse button.
5. Browse to the Lesson01 folder, which is in the FrontPage Practice folder in the Office 8in1 Step by Step folder. Click OK.

6. Click Next twice, and then click Finish.

   FrontPage creates a new Web based on the practice files and places it in the Lesson01 folder.

Explore FrontPage views

In this exercise, you explore different views of your new Web.

In the Folder List, an icon appears next to each filename, indicating the type of file (Web page, image file, and so forth).

1. If your Web is not already displayed in Page view, on the Views bar, click the Page icon.
2. In the Folder List, double-click the file Welcome.htm.

   FrontPage displays the Welcome Web page.

On the status bar, FrontPage estimates the amount of time the current page will take to download over a 28.8-KB modem connection.

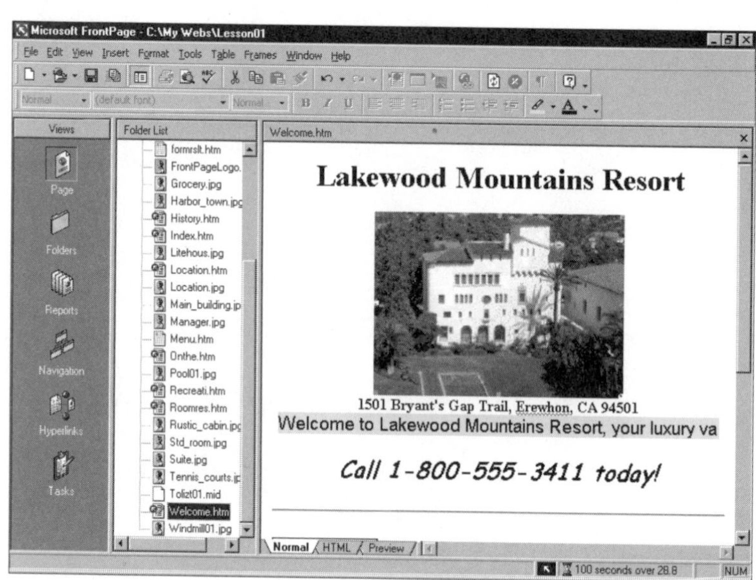

For a demonstration of how to explore FrontPage views, open the Office 8in1 Step by Step folder on your hard disk. Then open the FrontPage Demos folder, and double-click the FrontPage Views icon.

3. At the bottom of the FrontPage window, click the HTML tab.

   FrontPage displays the HTML code for the current page.
4. At the bottom of the FrontPage window, click the Preview tab.

   FrontPage displays a preview of how the page will look in a Web browser.
5. On the Views bar, click the Folders icon.

   FrontPage displays a list of all folders and files in the current Web.

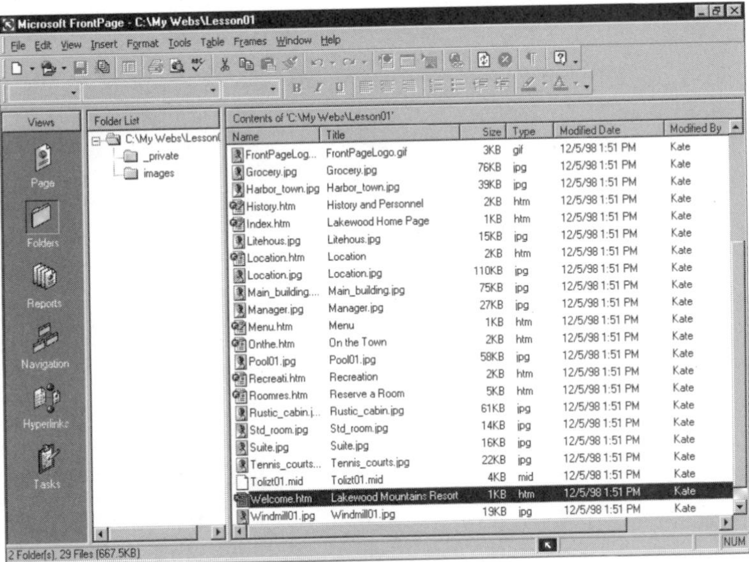

6 On the Views bar, click the Reports icon.

FrontPage displays a list of reports about the current Web.

You can use the Reports toolbar to switch quickly between different report views.

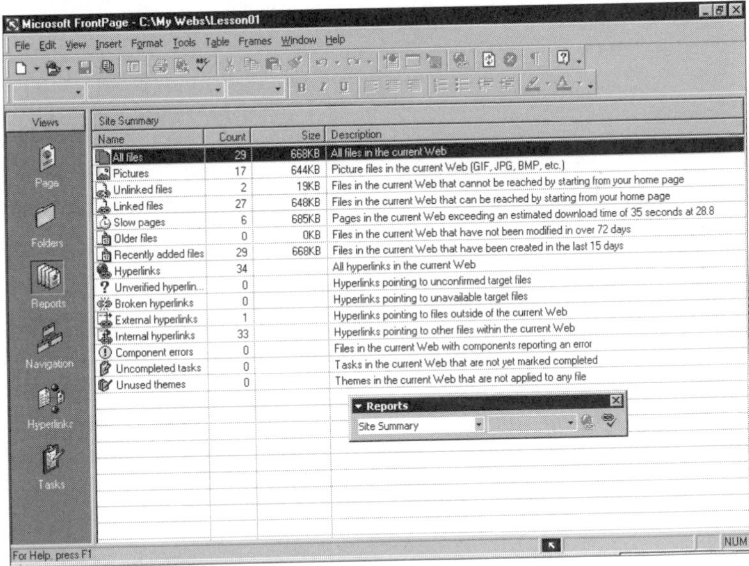

In the Navigation view's tree diagram, you can drag Web pages to restructure your Web.

7 On the Views bar, click the Navigation icon.

FrontPage normally displays a tree diagram of the current Web. However, because you haven't yet created any Web pages, there is no tree diagram to display.

8. On the Views bar, click the Hyperlinks icon.

   FrontPage displays a diagram of hyperlinks going to and from the page.

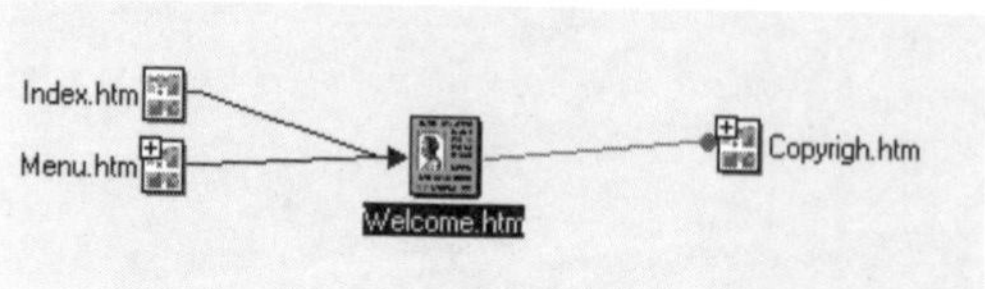

9. On the Views bar, click the Tasks icon.

   Currently, there are no tasks to display.

Understanding FrontPage Folders

When you install FrontPage 2000, it creates a folder called "My Webs." This is the default folder in which FrontPage will store any Webs you create. Each separate Web you create gets its own subfolder in the My Webs folder in which FrontPage stores files specific to that Web.

When FrontPage creates a Web, it also creates at least three different folders in which to store Web pages and files. You don't have to worry about these folders; you can ignore them and your Web will still work perfectly. However, understanding these folders gives you insight into your Web and can help you organize your files.

Folder	Explanation
Main folder	Default folder for your Web page, image, and Java class files.
_private	FrontPage stores files used to organize and manage your Web in this folder. Should be left strictly alone.
Images	Folder into which you can move image files if desired. If you have a large number of image files, this helps remove clutter from your main folder.

(continued)

continued

In addition to the three default folders, you can also create your own folders to hold specific types or groups of files.

Create a folder

1. On the Views bar, click the Folders icon.
2. On the File menu, point to New, and then click Folder.

   FrontPage creates a new folder. The default folder name is New Folder.
3. Delete the default folder name, type the desired name, and press Enter.

   FrontPage renames the folder.

You can create a new folder for any purpose. The only thing you must remember is to use FrontPage—not the Windows Explorer—to move files into the folder. When you use FrontPage to move files, any hyperlinks to those files are automatically updated.

Close and reopen a Web

In this exercise, you close and reopen the Lesson01 Web.

1. On the File menu, click Close Web.

   FrontPage closes the Lesson01 Web.
2. On the File menu, click Open Web.

   FrontPage displays the Open Web dialog box.

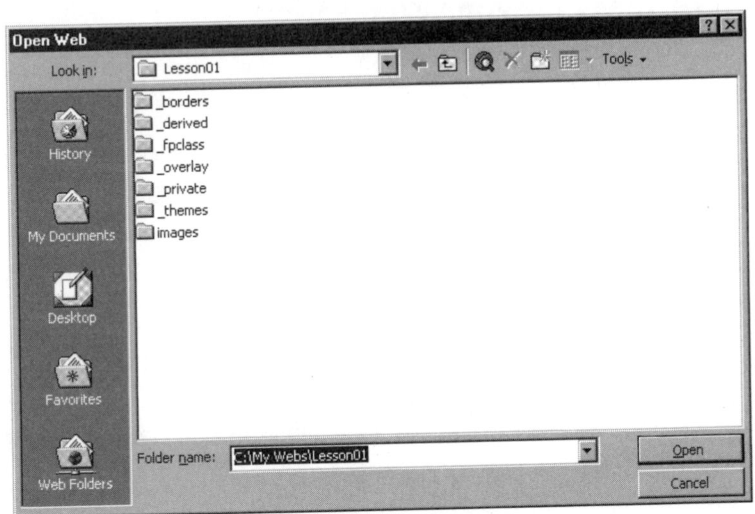

3. If necessary, browse to the Lesson01 Web in the My Webs folder.
4. If necessary, in the file list, click the Lesson01 folder.
5. Click the Open button.

   FrontPage opens the Web.
6. On the Views bar, click the Page icon, and then in the Folder List, double-click the file History.htm.

   FrontPage displays the History and Personnel Web page.

One Step Further

Getting Ideas for a Web Site

You've tentatively decided to use frames in your Web for Lakewood Mountains Resort, but you'd like to get some more ideas for enhancing your Web. Your coworker suggests that the best place to look is the Web itself.

The first and most obvious place to look is Microsoft's own FrontPage Web site at *www.microsoft.com/frontpage*. Another place to look is CNet's Builder.com Web site at *www.builder.com*. This site has tutorials on Web design, HTML, scripting, and many other Web topics.

Finally, you should surf the Web to view as many Web pages as you can. Ideas are everywhere, and as long as you don't just copy the content of someone's Web site, the ideas are free. You'll often find some of the most innovative and appealing Web ideas at some of the most unusual—even bizarre—Web sites.

Get ideas for your Web site

In this exercise, you visit Web pages on the Internet to familiarize yourself with some of the places that offer ideas on Web design.

1. Connect to the Internet, and then double-click the Web browser icon on the Windows desktop.

   Your Web browser opens and displays your Internet home page.
2. In the Address bar, type **microsoft.com/clipgallerylive**, and press Enter.

   The End User License Agreement (EULA) is displayed.
3. Read the license agreement, and then click the Accept button.

   The Microsoft Clip Gallery Live Web page is displayed in your browser. From here you can download clip art, photo images, sounds, and videos.

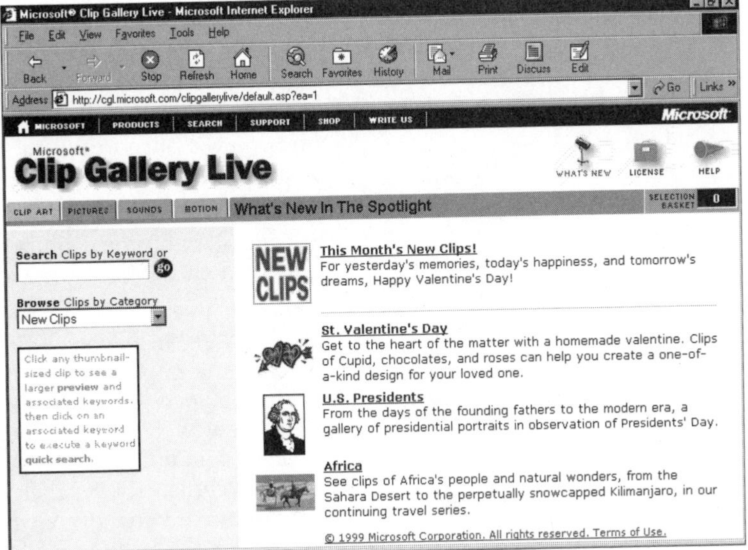

Microsoft's Clip Gallery Live page is continuously updated. If you visit the page on the Web, it will look different from the illustration shown here.

4. In the Address bar, type **microsoft.com/frontpage**

   Microsoft's FrontPage Web site is displayed in your browser.

5. In the Address bar, type **www.builder.com**, and then press Enter.

   The CNet Builder.com Web page is displayed in your browser.

Finish the lesson

Close

1. Click the Close button at the top-right corner of your Web browser window.

   Your Web browser closes and FrontPage reappears.

2. On the File menu, click Close Web.

3. For each page, if FrontPage prompts you to save changes, click Yes.

   FrontPage saves your changes and closes the Lesson01 Web.

Lesson 1 Quick Reference

To	Do this	Icon
Plan a Web site	Decide on the purposes of the Web site, and then decide what Web pages are needed for the site.	
Start FrontPage	Click the Start button, point to Programs, and click Microsoft FrontPage.	
Create a new Web based on Web page files in a folder	On the File menu, point to New, and click Web. In the New dialog box, click the Import Web Wizard icon. In the Specify The Location Of The New Web text box, type the folder containing the files for the new Web. Click OK, click the From A Source Directory Of Files option, click the Include Subfolders check box, and click the Browse button. Browse to the folder that you want to import, click OK, click Next twice, and then click Finish.	
Open a Web	On the File menu, click Open Web. In the Open Web dialog box, browse to the folder containing the Web, and click the Open button.	
View or edit a Web page	Double-click the filename (with an .htm extension) in the Folder List.	
Preview the appearance of a Web page in Page view	Click the Page icon on the Views bar, and click the Preview tab at the bottom of the FrontPage window.	
View a tree diagram of a Web structure	Click the Navigation icon on the Views bar.	
View a diagram of hyperlinks to and from a Web page	Click the Web page filename in the Folder List, and then click the Hyperlinks icon on the Views bar.	
View a list of tasks required to complete a Web site	Click the Tasks icon on the Views bar.	
View a list of folders and files in a Web	Click the Folders icon on the Views bar.	
View reports about a Web	Click the Reports icon on the Views bar.	

LESSON

2

Creating a Web Site

In this lesson you will learn how to:

- ✔ *Create a Web.*
- ✔ *Create a home page.*
- ✔ *Add and format Web page text.*
- ✔ *Add a scrolling marquee to a Web page.*
- ✔ *Preview a Web.*
- ✔ *Add pages to a Web.*
- ✔ *Change Web page properties.*
- ✔ *Organize a Web.*

ESTIMATED TIME **40 min.**

Now that you've defined the purposes of the Lakewood Mountains Resort Web site and determined which pages it should include, it's time to start creating the Web site in Microsoft FrontPage 2000. That's the good news. But your boss just stuck his head in your office and announced that you're meeting with the client tomorrow afternoon. A first draft of the Web site has to be ready for presentation at the meeting.

In this lesson, you will learn about FrontPage tools that can help you create a Web site in record time. You will then create a Web and add a home page. You will enter and format text on the page, add a scrolling marquee, create another page, and import an existing page. You will change the properties of a Web page and preview your Web. Finally, you will learn how to organize your Web.

Creating a Web Site Using a Wizard

There are three ways to create a Web in FrontPage: use a wizard, use a template, or create the Web "from scratch." The method you choose depends on your specific needs and situation.

FrontPage wizards are best used for complex Web sites. Each wizard creates a different type of Web using a series of dialog boxes in which you select the specific options that fit your situation.

When you've made all your selections, the wizard creates the Web site based on your input. FrontPage includes the wizards described in the following sections.

Corporate Presence Wizard

The Corporate Presence Wizard creates a Web site for a company. The Web site includes a home page, a table of contents, a News Release page, a product and service directory, a Web page for each product or service, a Customer Feedback page, and a Web page that lets visitors search your site.

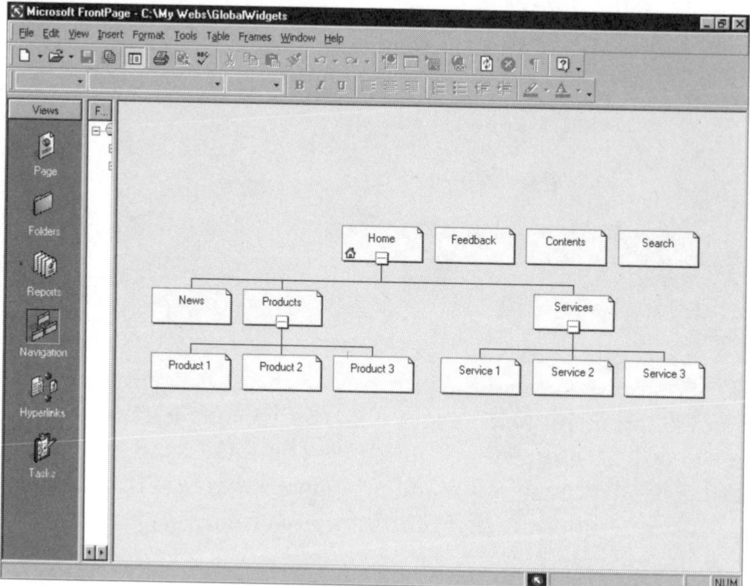

Discussion Web Wizard

The Discussion Web Wizard creates a Web site with a threaded message board, which allows visitors to view, post, and reply to messages on your Web site.

Import Web Wizard

The Import Web Wizard creates a new Web site based on existing Web files on your own computer or on a Web server. You can then modify the Web pages and Web structure as needed. You'll find this wizard especially useful for creating and testing updated versions of your own Web sites.

Create a Web site using a Wizard

In this exercise, you create a Web site using the Corporate Presence Wizard.

1. On the File menu, point to New, and then click Web.

   FrontPage displays the New dialog box.

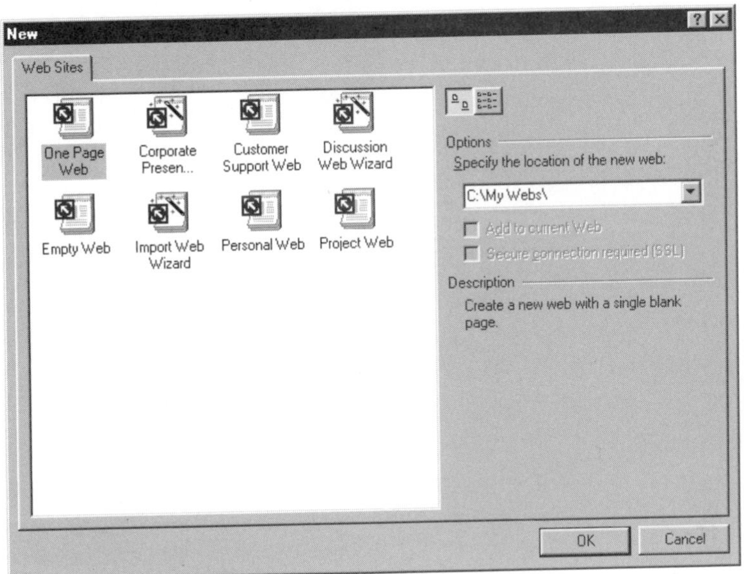

2. In the Web Sites pane, click the Corporate Presence icon.

   FrontPage will use the Corporate Presence Wizard to create the Web.

3. In the Specify The Location Of The New Web text box, delete the default text and type **C:\My Webs\MyWizardDemo**.

   FrontPage will create the C:\My Webs\MyWizardDemo folder. It will put all the Web files in that folder and its subfolders.

If your hard disk drive is not drive C, substitute the appropriate drive letter in step 3.

4. Click OK, and then click Next.

   FrontPage displays the first Corporate Presence Web Wizard dialog box, which explains the purpose of the Wizard. It then displays the second dialog box, in which you can select pages to include in the Web.

The Corporate Web Wizard displays different dialog boxes depending on which pages you select for inclusion in your corporate Web.

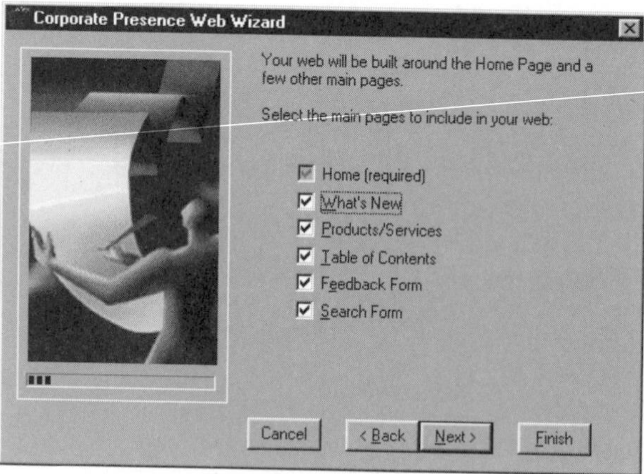

5. Click the What's New check box and the Search Form check box to clear them, and then click Next.

   FrontPage will not include a What's New or a Search Form page in the Web. FrontPage displays the next dialog box, in which you select the information to be displayed on your corporate home page.

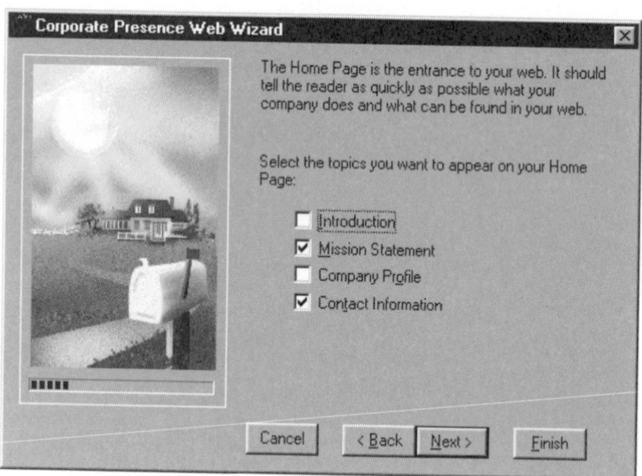

6. Click the Introduction check box to select it, and then click Next.

   FrontPage will display an introduction on your corporate home page. FrontPage displays the next dialog box, in which you select how many pages the wizard should create to show information about products and services.

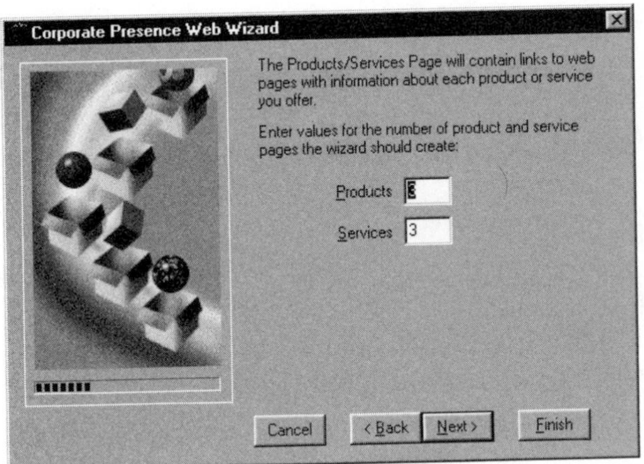

7 Click Next.

FrontPage accepts the default settings of three Product pages and three Services pages and displays a dialog box in which you can select the information you want displayed on each product or service Web page.

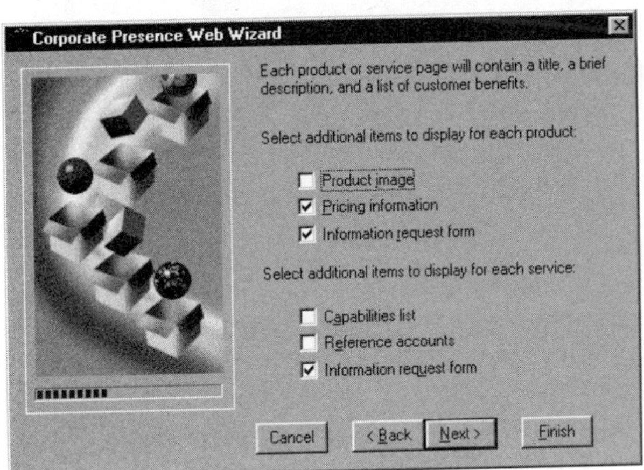

8 Click Next.

FrontPage accepts the default settings and displays a dialog box in which you can select the information you want to collect from Web site visitors who respond on your Feedback page.

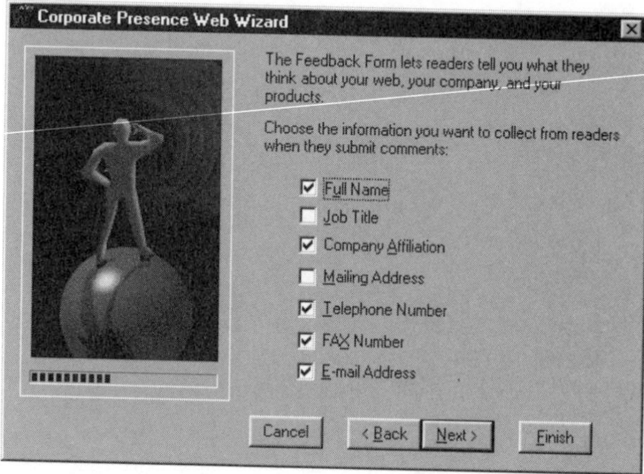

9 Click Next five times.

FrontPage displays a dialog box in which you enter the name and address of your company.

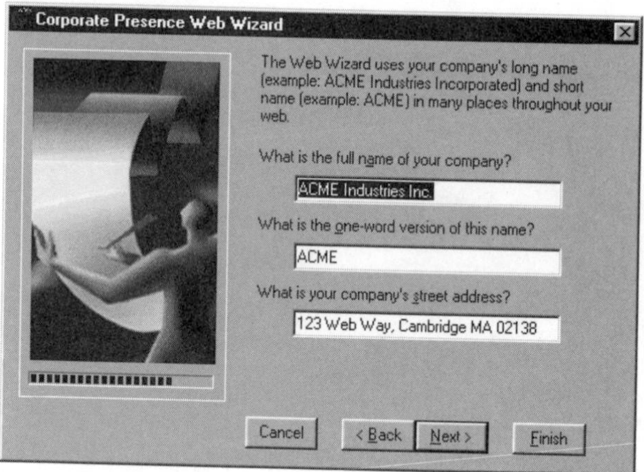

To keep this exercise brief, you skipped several dialog boxes you would normally complete, such as one in which you enter your company's phone number.

10 In the What Is The Full Name Of Your Company text box, type **Lakewood Mountains Resort**. Press Tab, type **Lakewood**, press Tab, type **1501 Bryant's Gap Trail, Erewhon, CA 94501**, and click Finish.

FrontPage creates a corporate presence Web based on the options you selected and the information you entered.

11 On the Views bar, click the Navigation icon, and in Navigation view, double-click the Home Page icon.

FrontPage displays your corporate home page. You can now modify the page by entering additional information.

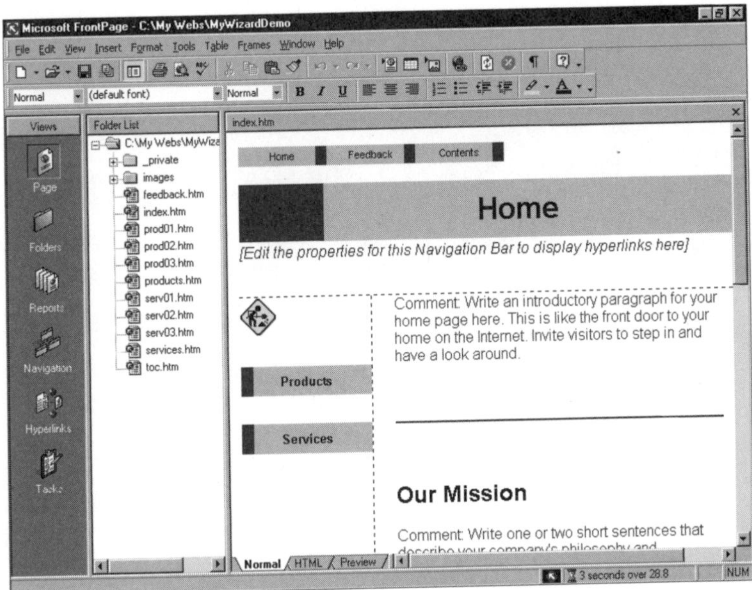

12 On the File menu, click Close Web.

FrontPage closes the Corporate Presence Web you just created.

tip

When you are creating Web filenames, get into the habit of creating names that do not contain spaces. Most Web servers do not recognize spaces in filenames. If you want to keep your Web filenames descriptive, you can separate words and still keep them connected by placing the underscore character (_) between words.

Corporate Presence Web Pages

The Corporate Presence Wizard can include several ready-to-use pages on your Web site. Even if you don't use the Corporate Presence Wizard, you can create these pages individually by using Web page templates. To use a template to create a page, click the Page icon on the Views bar. On the File menu, point to New, and click Page. FrontPage displays the New dialog box with a menu of page templates. Click the icon for the type of page you want to create, and then click OK.

(continued)

continued

Page template	Creates
Home	A home page containing information you specify.
What's New	A page with information about new pages or other updates on the Web site.
Products/Services	One or more pages about products or services offered by your company, with a description of each product or service, benefits, part numbers, and pricing.
Table of Contents	Lists all the pages in the Web site, with a hyperlink to each page.
Feedback Form	Allows Web site visitors to send feedback to an e-mail address you specify.
Search Form	Allows Web site visitors to search the Web site for pages containing words they specify.

Creating a Web Site Using a Template

Unlike wizards, which prompt you for input and then design a Web based on that input, templates are ready-made Web sites that you can modify for your own needs. FrontPage includes the following templates.

This template	Creates
Customer Support Web	A Web site in which a company can answer customer questions and get feedback. It combines a message board with several other features, such as a frequently asked questions list (FAQ), a suggestion form, and an area for downloading information and software.
Project Web	A Web site to share information about a project with members of the project team. It includes a page that lists team members, a schedule page, a project status page, a message board, and a search page.
Personal Web	A Web site to showcase the interests of an individual. It includes a home page, a photo album page, an interests page, and a Web page for links to other Web sites.
One Page Web	A Web site with only a home page.
Empty Web	A Web site that you build from scratch. It does not include any Web pages.

Create a Web site using a template

In this exercise, you create a Web using the Customer Support Web template.

If you completed the previous exercise, notice that FrontPage has suggested MyWizardDemo2 as the name of your new Web because the last Web you created was named MyWizardDemo.

If your hard disk drive is not drive C, substitute the appropriate drive letter in step 3.

Unlike a wizard, which asks you a series of questions about your Web, a template is a blueprint used to create a particular kind of Web. Once you've created the Web, you can then modify it to suit your needs.

1. On the File menu, point to New, and then click Web.

   FrontPage displays the New dialog box.

2. In the Web Sites pane, click the Customer Support Web icon.

   FrontPage will use the Customer Support Web template. This creates a Web site designed to provide help and solve problems for users of a company's products.

3. In the Specify The Location Of The New Web text box, delete the default text and type **C:\My Webs\MyTempDemo**, and click OK.

   FrontPage creates a new Web based on the Customer Support template.

4. In the Folder List, double-click the file Index.htm.

   FrontPage displays the new Web's home page.

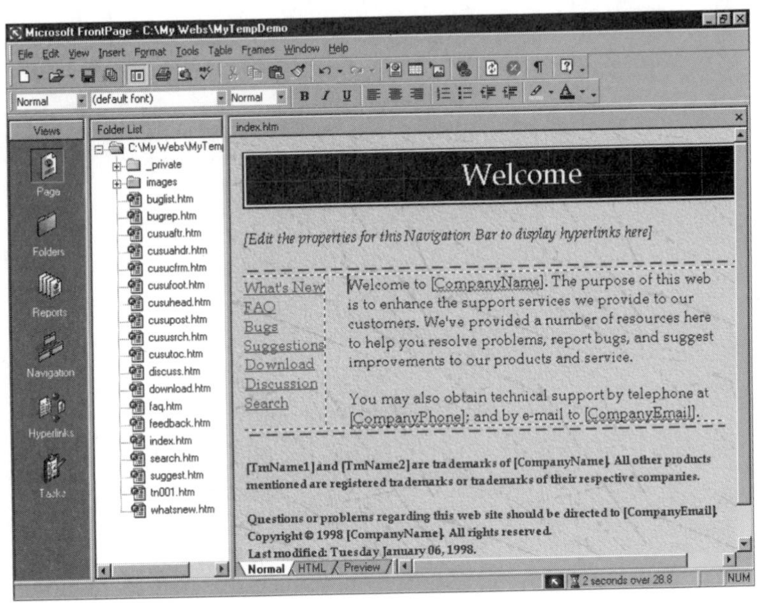

5. On the displayed Web page, select the text *[CompanyName]*, and then type **Lakewood Mountains Software**.

   FrontPage replaces the selected text with the text you typed.

6. On the toolbar, click the Save button.

   FrontPage saves the Web page with your changes.

Save

7 In the Folder List, double-click the file Bugrep.htm.

FrontPage displays the Web page that allows users to report problems in the company's products or services.

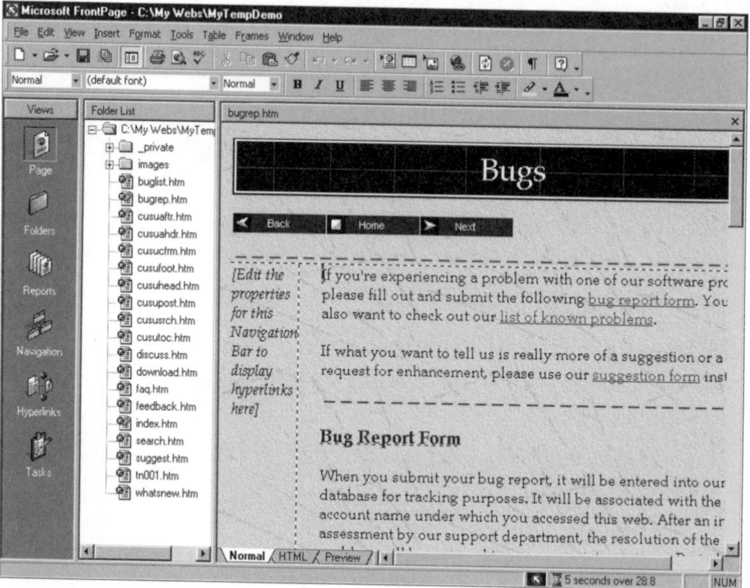

8 In the Folder List, double-click the file Discuss.htm.

FrontPage displays the Web page that allows users to read and respond to messages in a discussion board.

9 On the File menu, click Close Web.

FrontPage closes the Web you just created.

Creating and Importing Webs

Whether you use wizards or templates, there are essentially two ways to create a Web. The first way is to create the Web's pages and other files after you create the Web itself. The second way is to create a new Web based on existing files.

The second approach works especially well when you have a previous version of a Web—whether on your local hard disk drive or on a remote Web server—and you want to create a new version of the Web.

Create an empty Web

In this exercise, you create a new Web using the Empty Web template. You then close the empty Web.

1. On the File menu, point to New, and then click Web.

   FrontPage displays the New dialog box.

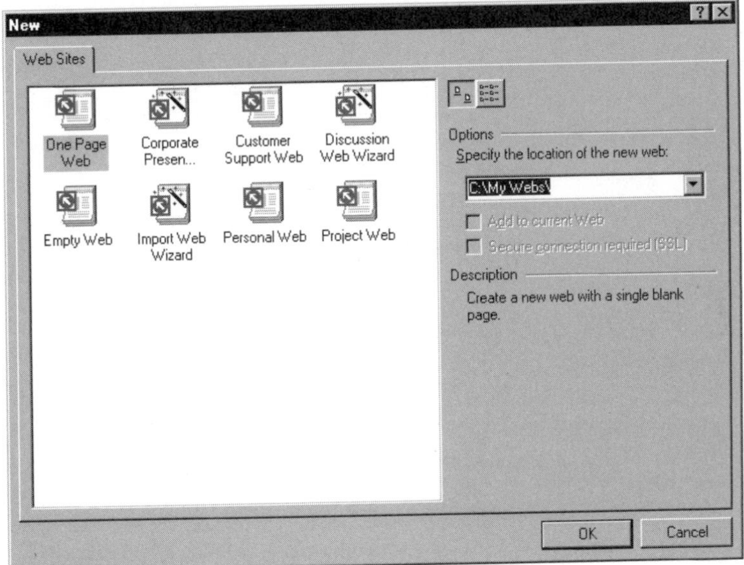

If your hard disk drive is not drive C, substitute the appropriate drive letter in step 2.

2. Click the Empty Web icon. In the Specify The Location Of The New Web text box, delete the default text and type **C:\My Webs\Empty02**, and then click OK.

   FrontPage creates a folder named Empty02 and places a new, empty Web in the folder.

3. On the Views bar, click the Navigation icon.

   FrontPage normally displays a tree diagram of the current Web. However, because you haven't yet created any Web pages, there is no tree diagram to display.

4. On the File menu, click Close Web.

   FrontPage closes the empty Web.

Import the Lesson 2 practice Web

In this exercise, you create a new Web based on the files in the Lesson02 folder in the FrontPage Practice folder. You will use this Web for all the remaining exercises in Lesson 2.

If your hard disk drive is not drive C, substitute the appropriate drive letter in step 2.

1. On the File menu, point to New, and then click Web.

   FrontPage displays the New dialog box.
2. Click the Import Web Wizard icon. In the Specify The Location Of The New Web text box, type **C:\My Webs\Lesson02**, and then click OK.

   FrontPage displays the first Import Web Wizard dialog box.
3. Click the From A Source Directory Of Files option, click the Include Subfolders check box, and click the Browse button.
4. Browse to the Lesson02 folder, which is in the FrontPage Practice folder in the Office 8in1 Step by Step folder, and click OK.
5. Click Next twice, and then click Finish.

   FrontPage creates a new Web based on the practice files and places it in the Lesson02 folder.

Creating a Home Page and Adding Text

Once you've created a Web, the next step is to add Web pages. By default, the first page you add will be treated as your Web's home page. The filename for the home page is either Default.htm or Index.htm, although the Web page title can be anything you choose.

> **tip**
>
> Web servers don't all use the same conventions for naming home pages. Most require this file to be named either Default.htm or Index.htm. If your home page name is different from what the Web server you're publishing to requires, don't worry; FrontPage automatically renames the home page when you publish a Web to a server. (If you're uploading files manually instead of having FrontPage publish them for you—as you must with popular Web sites such as GeoCities or The Globe—you will have to rename the file yourself.)

FrontPage makes it easy to add text and other elements to Web pages. To add text, you simply type it on the page. You can then apply standard Web text styles to the text. You can also format text (and other Web page elements) with FrontPage's own formatting tools and styles for headings or body text. There's even a Formatting toolbar with the same buttons as those in Microsoft Word and other familiar Microsoft Office programs.

Create and title a Web page

If you are not working through this lesson sequentially, follow the steps in "Import the Lesson 2 Practice Web" earlier in this lesson.

In this exercise, you create a home page for Lakewood Mountains Resort.

1. On the Views bar, click the Navigation icon.
2. On the File menu, point to New, and then click Page.

   FrontPage creates a new Web page and displays it as an icon.

You can also click the New button on the toolbar to create a new page.

For a demonstration of how to create a home page, open the Office 8in1 Step by Step folder on your hard disk. Then open the FrontPage Demos folder, and double-click the HomePage icon.

3. In the home page icon, click the text *Home Page* to select it, type **Lakewood Mountains Resort**, and then press Enter.

   FrontPage retitles the Web page.

Add and format text

In this exercise, you open the Lakewood Mountains Resort home page for editing. You then add and format text on the page.

1. Make sure your Web is displayed in Navigation view. Double-click the Lakewood Mountains Resort home page icon.

   FrontPage displays the home page in Page view.

2. Type **Lakewood Mountains Resort** (but do not press Enter).

3. The Text Style box at the left end of the Formatting toolbar currently says Normal. Click the drop-down arrow to expand the list.

   The Text Style list shows available text styles.

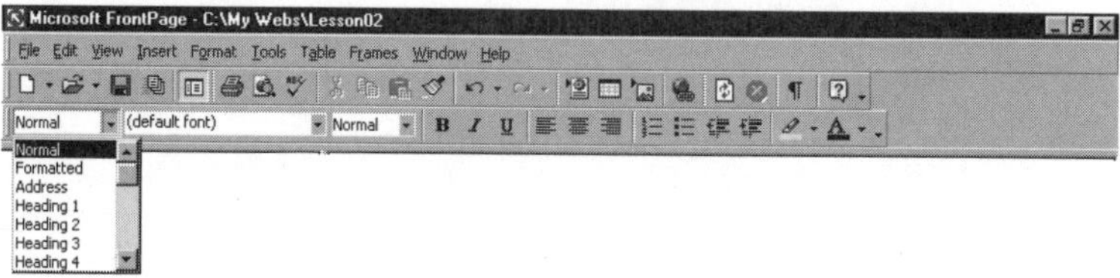

Center

4. Click Heading 1 in the list, and then on the Formatting toolbar, click the Center button.

   FrontPage formats the line in Heading 1 style and centers the heading horizontally on the Web page.

5. Press Enter twice, and type **1501 Bryant's Gap Trail, Erewhon, CA 94501**

tip

Notice that FrontPage underlines the word *Erewhon*. This indicates that the FrontPage spelling checker did not find the word in its word list and that it might be misspelled. However, you know that it is the proper name of a town and is spelled correctly. You'll learn how to use FrontPage's spelling checker in Lesson 5; just ignore the underlining for now.

6. Select the text in the address line.

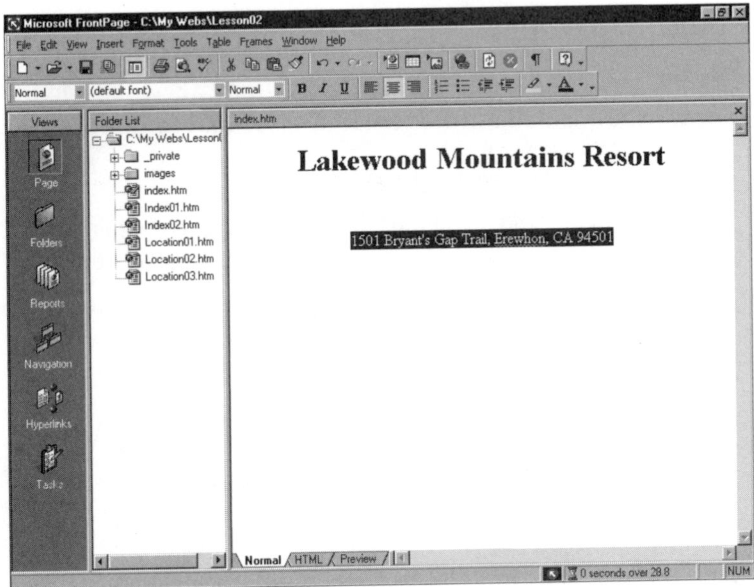

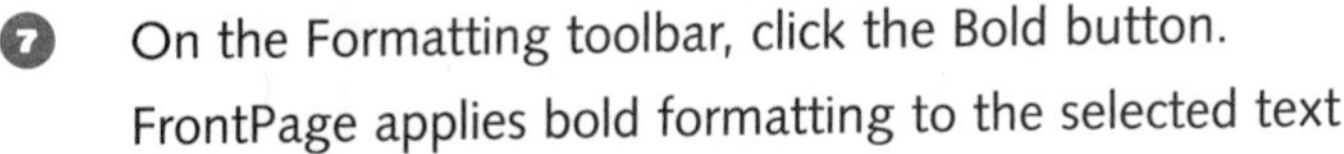

Bold

Save

7. On the Formatting toolbar, click the Bold button.

   FrontPage applies bold formatting to the selected text.

8. On the toolbar, click the Save button.

   FrontPage saves your changes.

Adding, Formatting, and Previewing a Marquee

You can easily add an impressive feature to the Lakewood Mountains Resort home page. A scrolling *marquee* displays text that slowly moves across the screen. This provides an eye-catching way to showcase a marketing message for Web site visitors. But use marquees and other animations sparingly. Numerous studies of Web users have noted that many people find Web sites that have excessive motion, animation, and blinking to be annoying.

You can adjust the speed and direction of a marquee's text movement, as well as the font, size, and style of the text.

Add a marquee

If you are not working through this lesson sequentially, follow the steps in "Import the Lesson 2 Practice Web" earlier in this lesson, drag the file Index01.htm from the Folder List into the Navigation view, and double-click its icon.

In this exercise, you add a marquee to the Lakewood Mountains Resort home page. You then adjust the scrolling speed and format the text.

1. Click the line below the address line.

   FrontPage moves the insertion point to the next line. Notice that the insertion point is now aligned with the Web page's left margin.

2. On the Insert menu, point to Component, and then click Marquee.

   FrontPage displays the Marquee Properties dialog box.

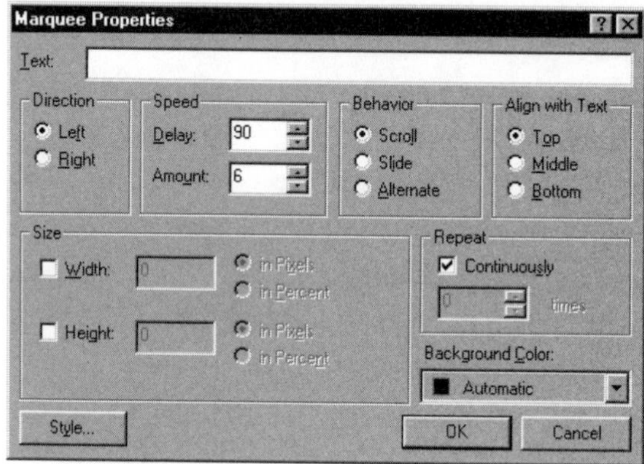

3. Type the following in the Text text box:

   Welcome to Lakewood Mountains Resort, your luxury vacation retreat! Come home to: Spacious rooms. Fine food. Golf. Tennis. Swimming. Boating and fishing. Special programs for kids. And surprisingly low rates!

4. Click OK.

   FrontPage places the marquee on your Web page. Only part of the text is visible, and it isn't scrolling. The text will scroll to the left when the page is displayed in a Web browser. You'll preview the marquee later in this lesson.

Customize the marquee

In this exercise, you change the width and background color of the marquee.

1. Right-click the marquee.

   A shortcut menu appears.

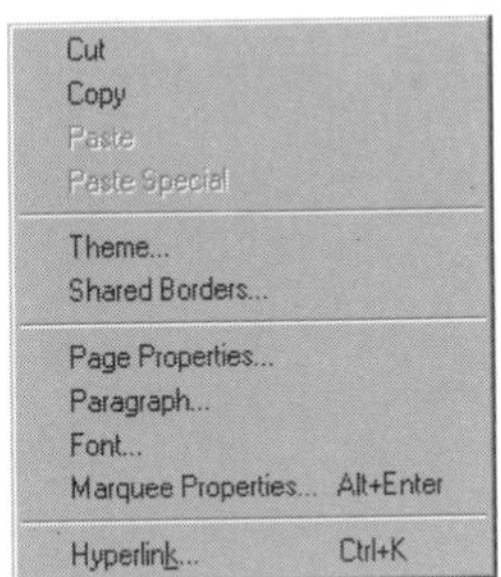

2. On the shortcut menu, click Marquee Properties.

   FrontPage displays the Marquee Properties dialog box.

3. In the Size section of the dialog box, click the Width check box, double-click the Width text box, type **400**, and verify that In Pixels is selected.

   The marquee will now have a width of 400 pixels.

4. Click the Background Color drop-down arrow.

   The Background Color palette expands.

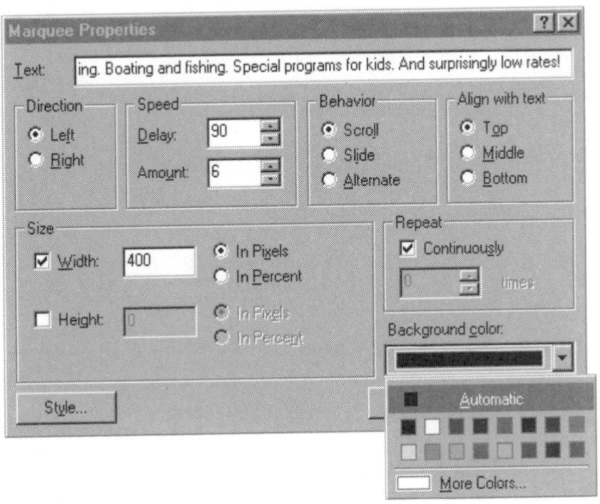

5. Click the Yellow color tile.

   The Background Color palette closes.

6. Click OK.

   FrontPage closes the Marquee Properties dialog box and changes the background color of the marquee to yellow.

Format the marquee text and save your work

In this exercise, you change the font and size of the marquee text.

1. Right-click the marquee, and then click Font on the shortcut menu.

   FrontPage displays the Font dialog box.

In the Font dialog box, you can also click the Character Spacing tab to change the spacing or vertical position of the text in the marquee.

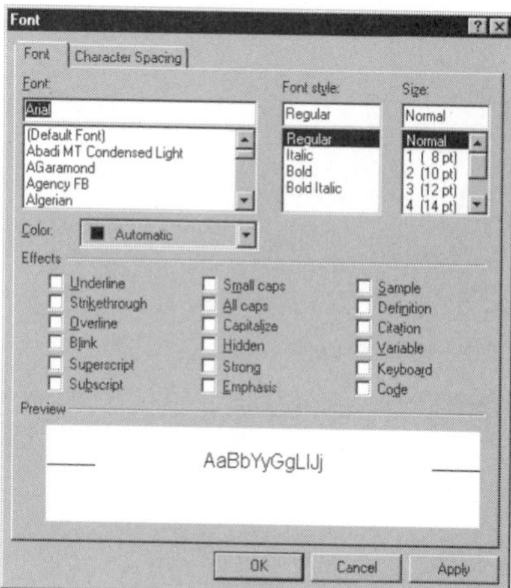

2. In the Font list, click Arial.

   FrontPage displays a sample of the Arial font in the Preview pane.

3. In the Size list, click 4 (14 pt).

   The preview text increases in size to 14 points.

> **tip**
>
> Points measure the height of text characters: there are 72 points per inch. Thus, 72-point type is one inch high, 12-point type is one-sixth of an inch high, and 14-point type is slightly less than one-fifth of an inch high.

4. Click OK.

   FrontPage displays the marquee text in its new font and size.

Save

5. On the toolbar, click the Save button.

   FrontPage saves the Lakewood Mountains Resort home page.

Preview your Web page

In this exercise, you preview the Lakewood Mountains Resort home page.

1. Click the Preview tab at the bottom of the FrontPage window.

   FrontPage displays a preview of the Web page. Although this provides you with a quick look at a Web page's appearance, it doesn't show how the page will look when loaded in a Web browser. Notice that the marquee text scrolls from right to left.

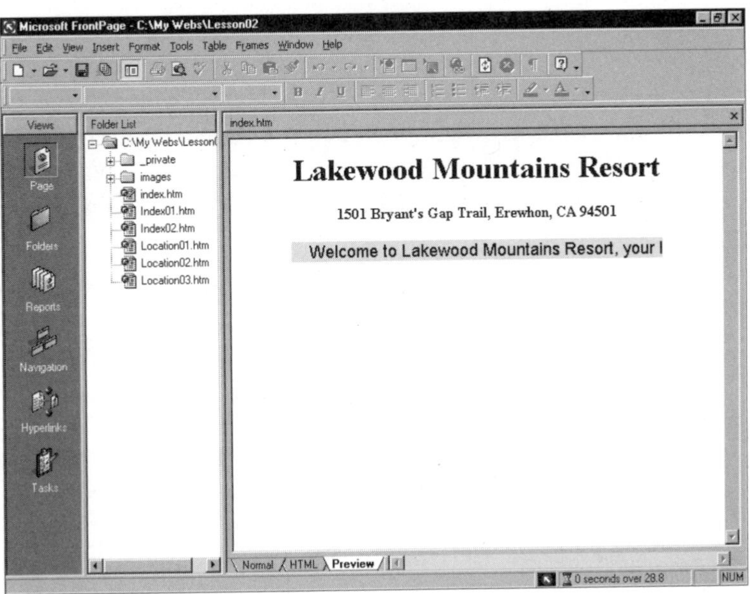

Preview In Browser

Close

2. On the toolbar, click the Preview In Browser button.

   FrontPage displays the Web page in your default Web browser.

3. Click the Close button at the top-right corner of the Web browser window.

   Your Web browser closes and FrontPage is redisplayed.

4. On the Views bar, click the Navigation icon.

   FrontPage displays the Web structure.

Adding Web Pages

A Web can have just a single Web page. For a personal Web, you might consider this. But the Lakewood Mountains Resort Web needs several pages. You'll find that, with FrontPage, adding pages is easy to do.

To add a page, you can either create a new page or import an existing page. If you choose to create a new page, you can do so in most views. If you create a new page with your Web displayed in Navigation view (the view displayed when you click the Navigation icon on the Views bar), FrontPage creates a blank page and adds it to your Web.

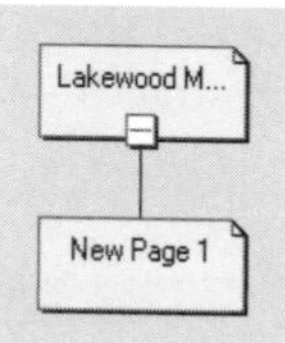

There's an advantage in creating a page while your Web is shown in Page view (the view displayed when you click the Page icon on the Views bar). If you create a page in this view, you can use FrontPage's Web page wizards and templates. If you create a page in other views, it is a new blank page.

Just like the templates for Web sites, the templates for Web *pages* are predesigned Web page blueprints for specific purposes. When you create a page with the Guest Book template, for example, the new page contains features and layout needed for a Web site guest book, as shown in the illustration. You simply add your own text and the page is ready to be used.

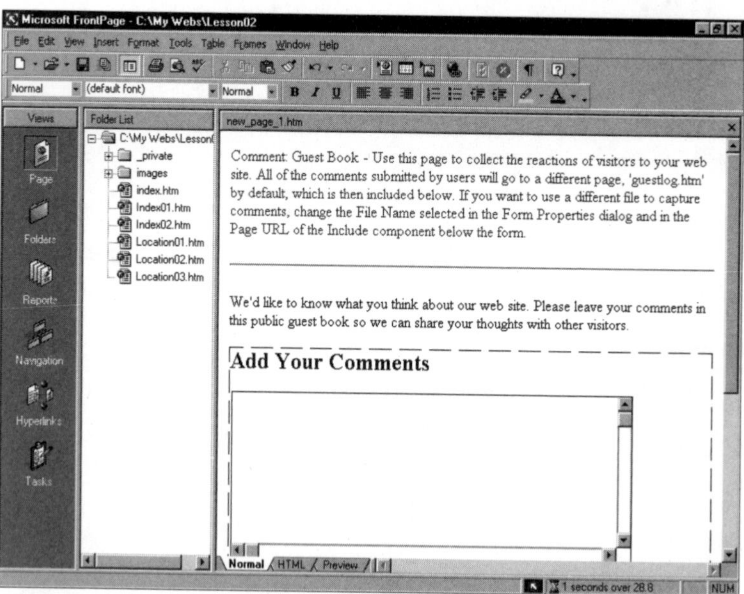

When creating the Web for Lakewood Mountains Resort, you'll create new pages in both Navigation and Page view, and you'll import an existing page.

Add a new Web page in Navigation view

If you are not working through this lesson sequentially, follow the steps in "Import the Lesson 2 Practice Web" earlier in this lesson, and drag the file Index01.htm from the Folder List into Navigation view.

In this exercise, you create a new page in Navigation view, and then delete it from your Web.

1. Make sure your home page is selected in Navigation view. On the File menu, point to New, and then click Page.

   FrontPage creates a new Web page and adds it to the Web's tree diagram as a child of the home page.

2. Click the new page, and then press Delete. If the Delete Page dialog box appears, click the Delete This Page From The Web option, and click OK.

   FrontPage deletes the new Web page and its link to the home page.

Add a new Web page in Page view

FrontPage uses the terms "parent" and "child" to differentiate between upper-level and lower-level Web pages.

In this exercise, you switch to Page view and browse through page templates before creating a new Web page.

1. On the Views bar, click the Page icon.

   FrontPage displays the Web page in Page view.

2. On the File menu, point to New, and then click Page.

   FrontPage displays the New dialog box.

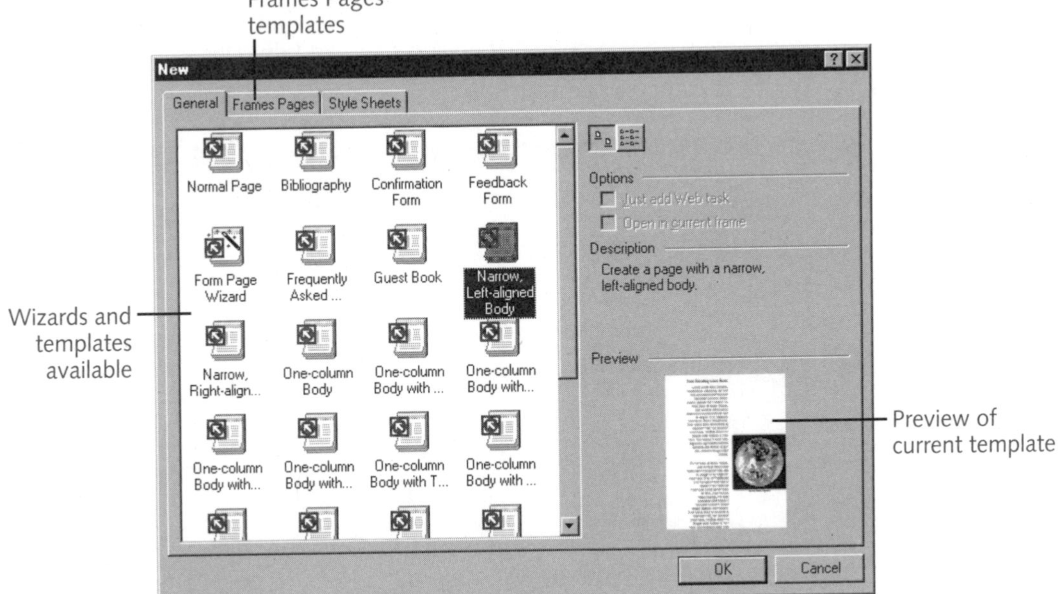

3. Click the icon for the Narrow, Left-Aligned Body template.
   FrontPage displays the Web page layout in the Preview pane.
4. Click the Frames Pages tab at the top of the dialog box.
   FrontPage displays available templates for frames pages.

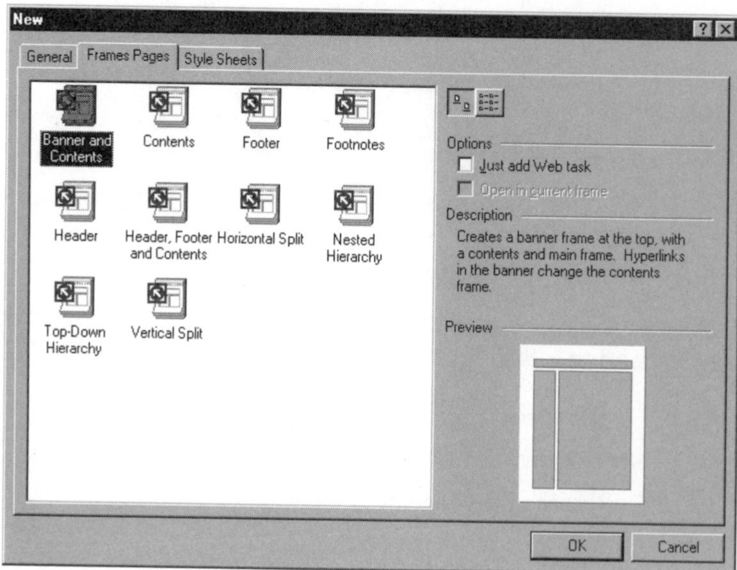

5. Click the General tab, click the Normal Page template, and then click OK.
   FrontPage creates a new, blank Web page and displays it in Page view.

Save

6. On the toolbar, click the Save button to display the Save As dialog box.

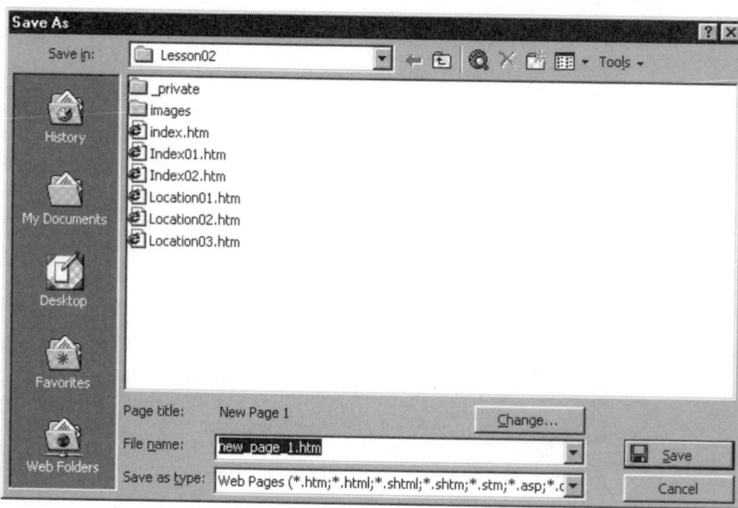

Save

7. In the File Name text box, type **Location.htm**, and then click Save.

   FrontPage saves the new Web page and adds it to the Folder List.

8. On the toolbar, click the Save button.

   FrontPage saves your changes to the Web.

New

> **tip**
>
> You can also create a new page by clicking the New button at the left end of the toolbar. Click the drop-down arrow to view a menu of options, including New Web.

Import a Web page

In this exercise, you import an existing Web page into the Lakewood Mountains Resort Web.

1. On the Views bar, click the Navigation icon.
2. On the File menu, click Import.

   The Import dialog box appears.

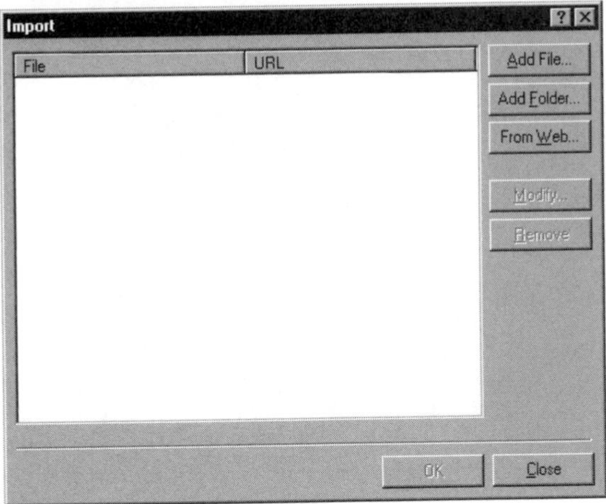

3. Click the Add File button.

   FrontPage displays the Add File To Import List dialog box.

4. Click the Look In drop-down arrow, browse to the Office 8in1 Step by Step folder, and double-click it. Then double-click the FrontPage Practice folder, and finally double-click the Extras folder.

   The Extras folder opens and displays a file list.

5. Click the file named Recreati.htm, and then click the Open button.

   FrontPage adds the file to the import list.

Press Ctrl while you click to select all three files.

6. Use the same method to add the files Boat_trips.jpg, Pool01.jpg, and Tennis_courts.jpg to the import list.

7. Click OK.

   FrontPage imports the Web page and photo files into your Web. Notice that they now appear in the Folder List.

8. In the Folder List, double-click Recreati.htm.

   FrontPage displays the Recreation Web page.

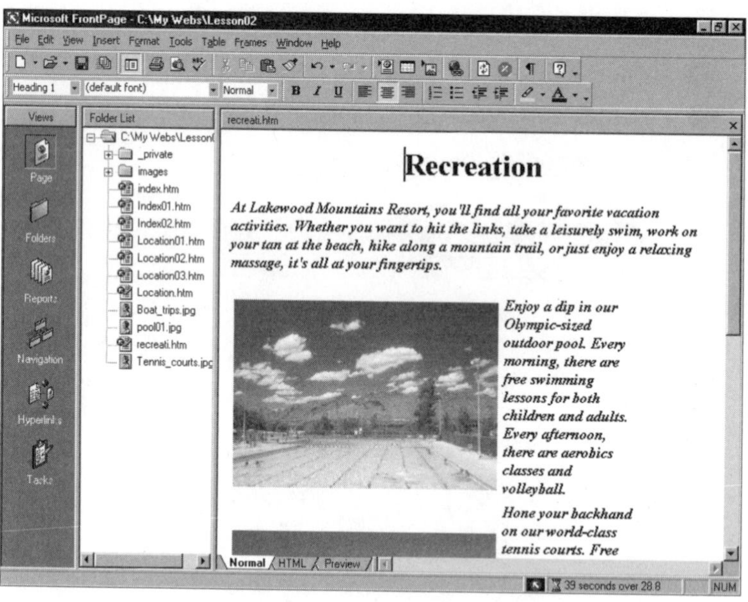

Save

9. On the toolbar, click the Save button.

   FrontPage saves your changes.

Inserting a File into a Web Page

It's easy enough to enter Web page text in FrontPage. But what if you used Microsoft Word to write a description of Lakewood Mountains Resort? Of course, you could print the document and retype the text in FrontPage. But it's easier to insert the Word document's contents directly into a Web page.

Using FrontPage, you can insert the following types of files into Web pages.

- Microsoft Word documents.
- RTF (Rich Text Format) documents.
- TXT (plain text, or ASCII) files.
- Worksheets from Microsoft Excel and Lotus 1-2-3.
- WordPerfect 5.*x* and 6.*x* documents.
- HTML (Web page) files.

Insert a Microsoft Word document into a Web page

In this exercise, you insert the contents of an existing Microsoft Word document into a Web page.

1. In the Folder List, double-click the file Location01.htm.

   FrontPage displays the page (a blank Web page) in Page view.

2. On the Insert menu, click File.

   FrontPage displays the Select File dialog box. Navigate to the Extras folder within the FrontPage Practice folder.

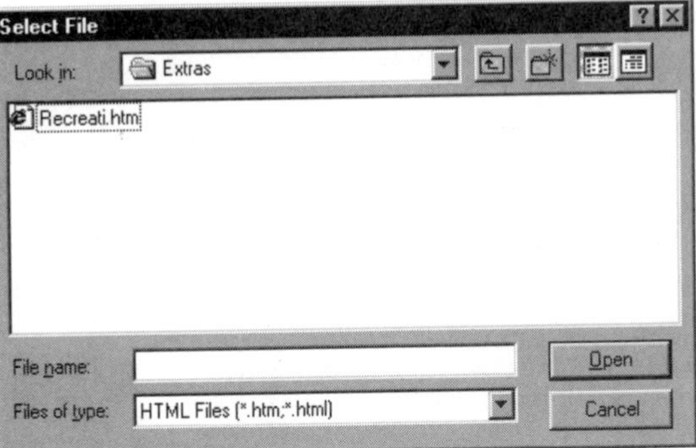

If an alert box is displayed notifying you that this feature is not installed, insert the Microsoft Office 2000 CD 1 in your CD-ROM drive, and click Yes.

3. Click the Files Of Type drop-down arrow, and click Word 97-2000 (*.doc).

   There is only one Word document in the folder: Location.

4. Click Location.doc, and then click the Open button.
5. If an Open File As dialog box appears, click OK to accept RTF as the default selection.

   FrontPage imports the text and inserts it on the Location01.htm page. Notice that the document's formatting, such as the bold type, has been preserved.

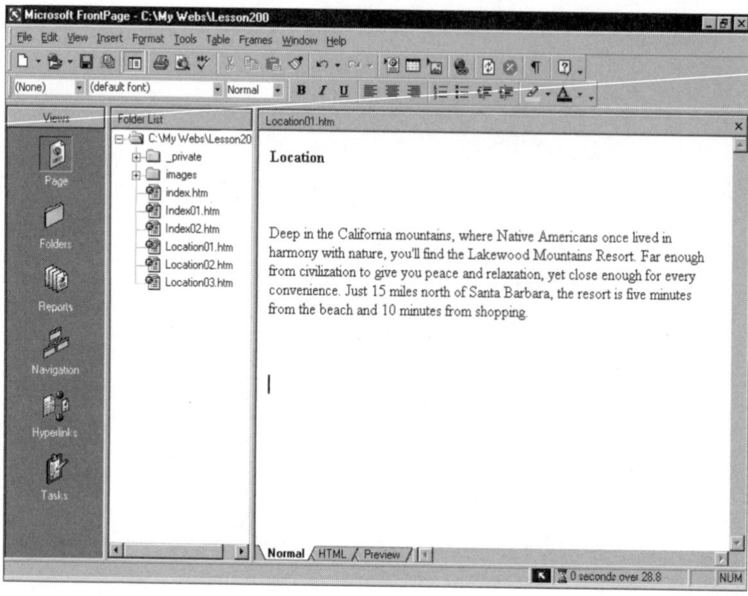

Save

6. On the toolbar, click the Save button.

   FrontPage saves the Web page.

Changing Web Page Properties

Web page properties include a page's title, type, location, and summary. You can change a Web page's properties even after it has been created in FrontPage.

View and change the properties of a Web page

If you are not working through this lesson sequentially, follow the steps in "Import the Lesson 2 Practice Web" earlier in this lesson.

In this exercise, you view and change the properties of the Location Web page.

1. In the Folder List, right-click Location02.htm, and then click Properties on the shortcut menu.

   FrontPage displays the Location02.htm Properties dialog box.

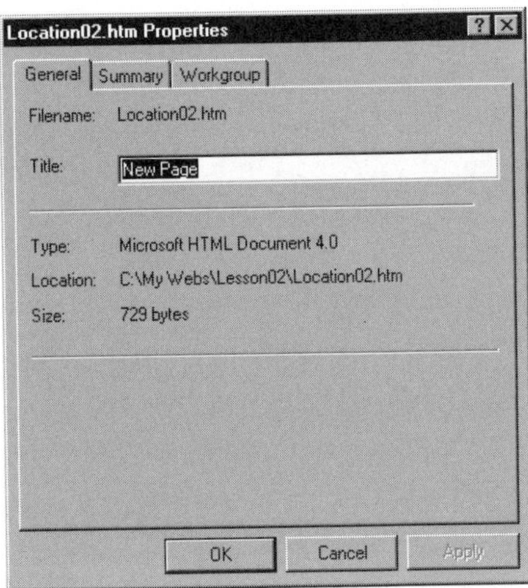

2. In the Title text box, type **Location**, and then click the Summary tab.

   FrontPage displays the Summary section of the dialog box. In the Comments text box, you can type an explanation of the purpose of the current page.

3. Click OK.

   FrontPage changes the title of the Web page.

Save

4. On the toolbar, click the Save button.

   FrontPage saves the Location page with its new title.

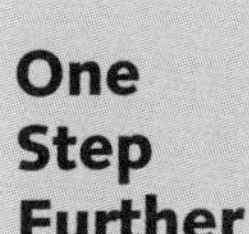

One Step Further Organizing Your Web

Although you now have three pages (the Index page, the Location page, and the Recreation page) in the Web site for Lakewood Mountains Resort, they aren't arranged in any particular structure. You know that the home page is the "starting" page, but beyond that, there's no organization.

In FrontPage, you can structure your Web by dragging Web page files into the Navigation view's tree diagram. There are many good reasons to do this. First, it makes your Web structure easier to understand. Instead of having to remember which Web pages link to which, you can simply look at the tree diagram.

Another reason has to do with designing your site. You can make FrontPage set up navigation bars to link all the pages displayed in Navigation view. Navigation bars use the information in the tree diagram to link pages. If the tree diagram of your Web isn't accurate, navigation bars won't work correctly.

Organize your Web

If you are not working through this lesson sequentially, follow the steps in "Import the Lesson 2 Practice Web" earlier in this lesson.

In this exercise, you create a navigation structure for the Lakewood Mountains Resort Web.

1. On the Views bar, click the Navigation icon.

   Only the home page is displayed in Navigation view.

2. Drag the file Location01.htm from the Folder List into Navigation view below the home page.

   A line connects the home page to the Location page.

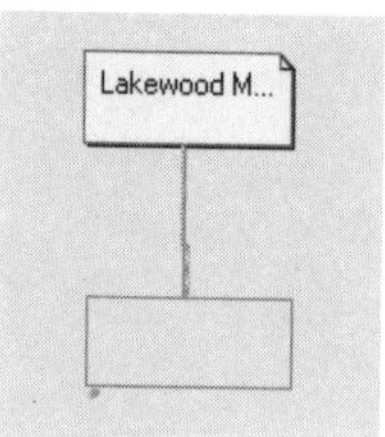

3. Release the mouse button.

   FrontPage makes the Location page into a child page (lower-level page) of the home page.

Finish the lesson

1. On the File menu, click Close Web.
2. If FrontPage prompts you to save changes, click the Yes button.

   FrontPage saves your changes and closes the Lesson02 Web.

Lesson 2 Quick Reference

To	Do this	Button
Preview a Web page	Display the page in Page view and click the Preview tab at the bottom of the FrontPage window. *Or* click the Preview In Browser button on the toolbar.	

Lesson 2 Quick Reference

To	Do this
Create a Web	On the File menu, point to New, and click Web. Click the icon for the desired wizard or template. In the Specify The Location Of The New Web text box, type the name of the new Web and click OK. Use the Next button to work through the wizard dialog boxes, making selections as desired, and then click the Finish button.
Create a blank Web page	Display the Web in Navigation view. On the File menu, point to New, and then click Page.
Create a Web page using a wizard or template	Display the Web in Page view. On the File menu, point to New, and then click Page. In the dialog box, click the wizard or template you want to use, and click OK.
Enter and format text on a Web page	Double-click the Web page in the Folder List. In Page view, type and format text just as you would in Microsoft Word.
Add a marquee	Display the Web page in Page view and click the location where you want the marquee. On the Insert menu, point to Component, and then click Marquee. Type the marquee text, and then click OK.
Change marquee properties	Right-click the marquee and click Marquee Properties on the shortcut menu. Enter new properties as desired, and then click OK.
Change a Web page's properties	Right-click the Web page in the Folder List, and then click Properties. Use the General, Summary, or Workgroup tabs to enter or select new properties as desired. Click OK.
Import a Web page	On the File menu, click Import, and then click the Add File button. Browse to the file, click it, and click Open. Click OK.
Insert a file into a Web page	Display the Web page in Page view, and on the Insert menu, click File. Browse to the location of the file to insert, click the Files Of Type drop-down arrow, and then click the desired file type. Click the file to insert, and then click Open.
Organize a Web	Display the Web in Navigation view. Drag Web pages from the Folder List to form a tree diagram of the Web structure.

LESSON

3

Linking Web Pages

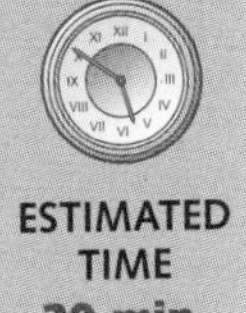

ESTIMATED TIME
30 min.

In this lesson you will learn how to:

- ✔ *Create text hyperlinks between Web pages.*
- ✔ *Link to Web pages on the Internet.*
- ✔ *Create electronic mail links.*
- ✔ *Edit hyperlinks.*
- ✔ *Create Web page bookmarks.*
- ✔ *Create image map hyperlinks.*

Your client meeting with Lakewood Mountains Resort was a success: the resort manager was enthusiastic about the prototype Web site you created in Lesson 2. But she had a question: "Aren't the Web pages supposed to be linked together? I thought a user should be able to jump from one page to another by clicking text on the Web page."

You explain that Web pages can contain *hyperlinks,* which tell a Web browser to jump to another page on the Web site or on the Internet. She seems satisfied with that answer, which is lucky for you. Although you've used hyperlinks while surfing the Web, you have never created any. You'll soon learn that Microsoft FrontPage 2000 makes creating hyperlinks quick and easy.

In this lesson, you will learn how to create several kinds of hyperlinks. You will create text hyperlinks between Web pages, link to pages on the Internet, and create e-mail links. You will learn how to create and use bookmarks on your Web pages. Finally, you will create an image map hyperlink.

Creating Text Hyperlinks

A hyperlink is an HTML instruction embedded in a Web page. The instruction tells a Web browser to display another file or Web page when the visitor clicks the corresponding text or graphic. The newly displayed file can be a Web page on the World Wide Web, a Web page on a corporate intranet, or a file stored locally on the user's computer.

Pointing Hand

Each hyperlink has two parts: the hyperlink itself, and the *target,* which is the file displayed when a visitor clicks the hyperlink. When a visitor moves the mouse pointer over a hyperlink, it changes from its normal shape to a pointing hand. This tells the visitor that the pointer is over a hyperlink. The status bar at the bottom of the visitor's Web browser usually displays the address of the target. Without Microsoft FrontPage, creating hyperlinks can be complicated. But with FrontPage, you hardly need to worry about any of this. To create hyperlinks, you just point and click. FrontPage takes care of the details.

Import the Lesson 3 practice Web

In this exercise, you create a new Web based on the files in the Lesson03 folder in the FrontPage Practice folder. You will use this Web for all the exercises in Lesson 3.

1. On the File menu, point to New, and then click Web.

   FrontPage displays the New dialog box.

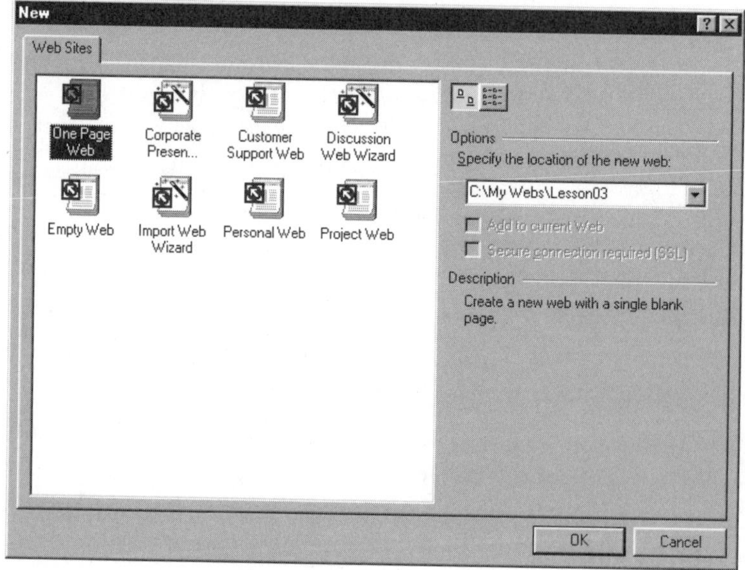

If your hard disk is not drive C, substitute the appropriate drive letter in step 2.

2. Click the Import Web Wizard icon. In the Specify The Location Of The New Web text box, delete the default text and type **C:\My Webs\Lesson03**, and click OK.

   FrontPage displays the first Import Web Wizard dialog box.

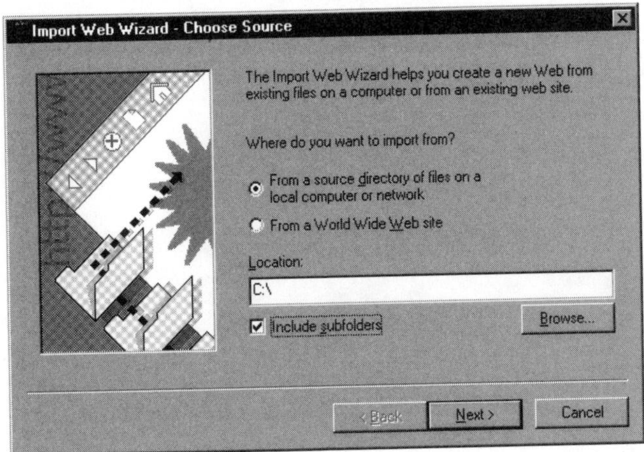

3. Click the From A Source Directory Of Files option, click the Include Subfolders check box, and click the Browse button.
4. Browse to the Lesson03 folder, which is in the FrontPage Practice folder in the Office 8in1 Step by Step folder, and click OK.
5. Click Next twice, and then click Finish.

   FrontPage creates a new Web based on the practice files and places it in the Lesson03 folder.

New! 2000

tip

If you need to quit FrontPage before you finish these exercises, here's a quick way to open the Lesson03 Web again. On the File menu, point to Recent Webs, and then click Lesson03.

Link to a Web page in your current Web

In this exercise, you create a hyperlink between the Lakewood Mountains Resort home page and the Recreation page.

1. In the Folder List, double-click the file Index.htm.

   FrontPage displays the home page in Page view.

2. On the home page, select the word *Recreation*.
3. On the Insert menu, click Hyperlink.

   FrontPage displays the Create Hyperlink dialog box.

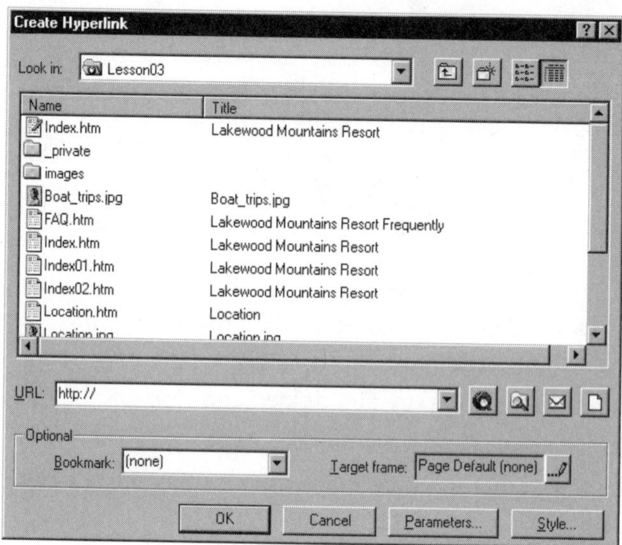

The shortcut key for inserting a hyperlink is Ctrl+K.

4. Click Recreati.htm in the file list.

   FrontPage displays *Recreati.htm* in the URL text box. This is the Web page address for the hyperlink.

5. Click OK. Deselect the word *Recreation* by clicking any blank area of the home page.

   FrontPage creates the hyperlink. Notice that the word *Recreation* is now underlined, indicating that it is a hyperlink.

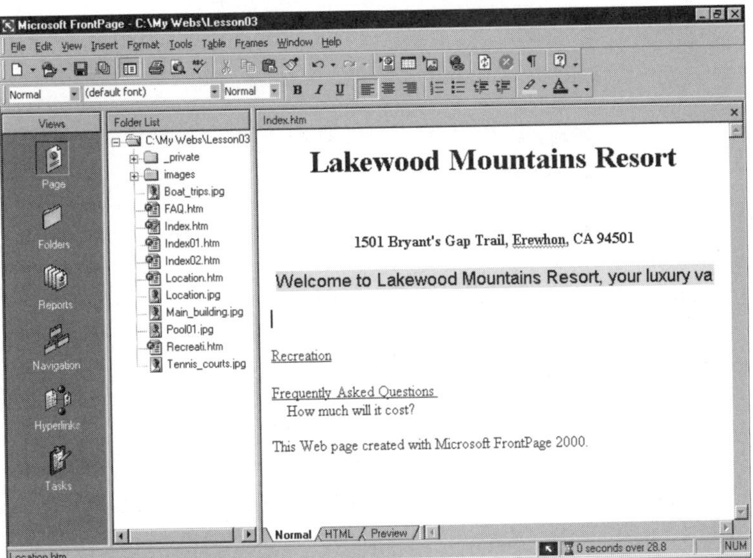

Save

6. On the toolbar, click the Save button.

   FrontPage saves your changes.

tip

When you move the mouse over a hyperlink, FrontPage displays the link target address on the status bar, at the lower-right corner of your screen. You can check the functioning of your hyperlink by holding down Ctrl and clicking the link, whereupon FrontPage displays the target page. In a later exercise, you will preview your links in your Web browser.

Link by dragging

In this exercise, you create a hyperlink by dragging a Web page from the Folder List onto the Web page displayed in Page view.

1. In the Folder List, click Location.htm.
2. Drag Location.htm so that it is just above the Recreation hyperlink, and then release the mouse button.

   FrontPage creates a hyperlink to the Location page.
3. Press Ctrl and click the new Location link.

   FrontPage displays the Location page.

4. In the Folder List, double-click Index.htm.

   FrontPage redisplays the home page.

Save

5. On the toolbar, click the Save button.

   FrontPage saves your changes.

Link to a Web page on the Internet

In this exercise, you create a hyperlink to a Web page on the Internet.

1. If necessary, connect to the Internet, and then switch back to FrontPage.
2. Select the word *Microsoft* in the last line on the home page, and then on the Insert menu, click Hyperlink.

   FrontPage displays the Create Hyperlink dialog box.

Web Browser

3. Click the Web Browser button to link to a Web page on the Internet.

   FrontPage opens your Web browser and instructs you to browse to the Web page you want to link.
4. In the Address bar of the Web browser, type **www.microsoft.com/frontpage** and press Enter.

   Your Web browser connects to the Microsoft Web site and displays the FrontPage home page.
5. Press Alt+Tab on your keyboard to switch from your browser to FrontPage.

   In the URL text box, FrontPage displays the Web address of the Microsoft FrontPage home page, as shown in the illustration.

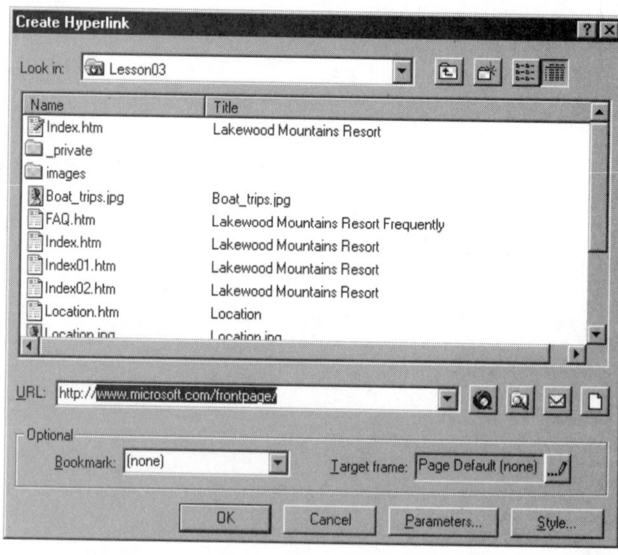

6. Click OK.

   FrontPage creates the hyperlink.

Save

7. On the toolbar, click the Save button.

   FrontPage saves your changes.

Test your hyperlinks

In this exercise, you test the hyperlinks you created on the Lakewood Mountains Resort home page.

1. If necessary, connect to the Internet, and then switch back to FrontPage.

Preview In Browser

2. On the toolbar, click the Preview In Browser button.

   FrontPage displays the home page in your Web browser.
3. Click the *Location* hyperlink.

   Your Web browser displays the Location page.

Back

4. On the toolbar of your Web browser, click the Back button.

   Your Web browser returns to the Lakewood Mountains Resort home page.
5. Click the *Recreation* hyperlink.

   Your Web browser displays the Recreation page.

Back

6. On the toolbar of your Web browser, click the Back button.

   Your Web browser redisplays the Lakewood Mountains Resort home page.

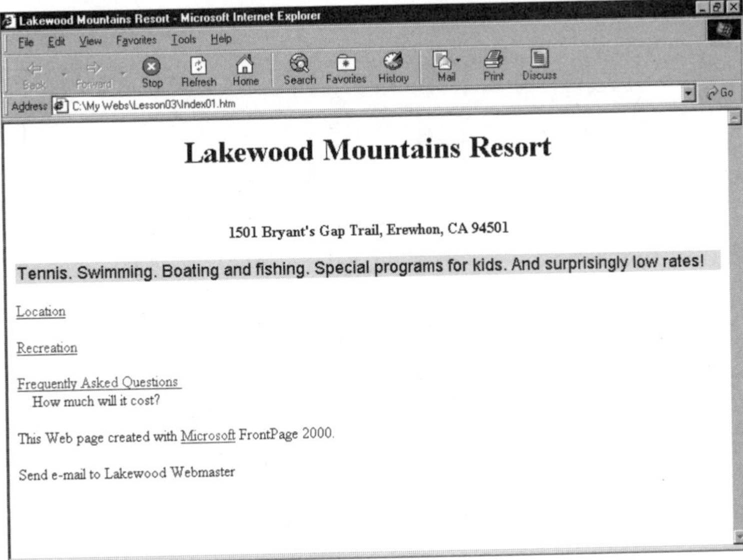

7. Click the *Microsoft* hyperlink.

   FrontPage displays the Microsoft FrontPage home page in your Web browser.

Close

8. Click the Close button at the top-right corner of your Web browser window.

   Your Web browser closes, and FrontPage is redisplayed.

Different Kinds of Hyperlinks

You can create several kinds of hyperlinks in the Create Hyperlinks dialog box.

You can also type the target address of the new hyperlink in the URL text box to create any kind of hyperlink.

Click	Name	To create a hyperlink
A file in the Folder List		To another page in your Web.
	Web Browser	To a file on the Internet.
	Local File	To a file on your own computer.
	E-mail	That sends e-mail.
	New	To a new Web page and link to it.

Creating a Link to an Electronic Mail Address

Hyperlinks can do more than just display a Web page or file. They also provide a way for Web site visitors to send electronic mail to addresses specified in hyperlinks. When a visitor clicks an e-mail hyperlink, the Web browser launches the visitor's e-mail program and displays a message composition window with the e-mail address already entered. The visitor then writes and sends the e-mail message normally.

For the Lakewood Mountains Resort home page, you want to enable visitors to send e-mail to the resort's Web site administrator, so you'll create a link to the Web administrator's e-mail address.

Create an electronic mail link

In this exercise, you create a hyperlink that enables Web page visitors to send electronic mail to the Web site administrator.

If you are not working through this lesson sequentially, follow the steps in "Import the Lesson 3 Practice Web" earlier in this lesson, and in the Folder List, double-click Index01.htm.

E-mail

1. Click the empty line below the Microsoft hyperlink.
2. Type **Send e-mail to Lakewood Webmaster**, and then select the words *Lakewood Webmaster*.
3. On the Insert menu, click Hyperlink.

   FrontPage displays the Create Hyperlink dialog box.
4. In the Create Hyperlink dialog box, click the E-mail button.

   FrontPage displays the Create E-mail Hyperlink dialog box.

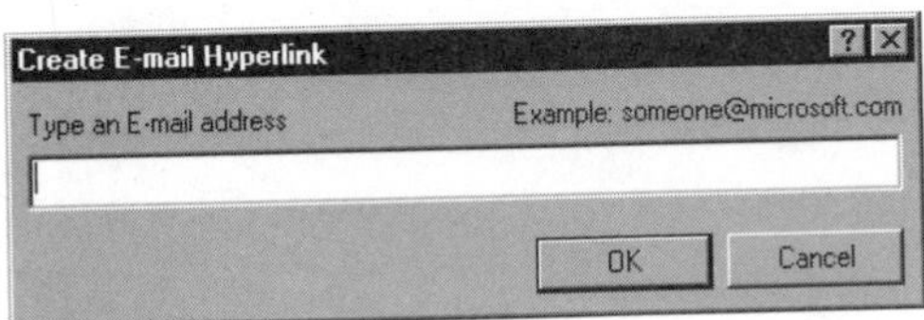

5. In the text box, type your own e-mail address, and then click OK.

   The Create E-mail Hyperlink dialog box closes and the Create Hyperlink dialog box is again visible. Notice that the URL contains the text *mailto:* followed by your e-mail address.
6. Click OK.

   FrontPage creates the new e-mail hyperlink.
7. On the toolbar, click the Save button.

   FrontPage saves your changes.

Save

Editing Hyperlinks

Just like many other things in the modern world, hyperlinks often change. The name of a Web page file might change, it might be moved to a different Web site, or it might be deleted altogether. When such a change occurs, you need to change any hyperlinks that connect to the target file. Fortunately, changing a hyperlink in FrontPage is just as easy as creating it in the first place.

Change a hyperlink

In this exercise, you change the target Web page of the Lakewood Frequently Asked Questions hyperlink and then change the text of the Location hyperlink.

If you are not working through this lesson sequentially, follow the steps in "Import the Lesson 3 Practice Web" earlier in this lesson, and in the Folder List, double-click Index01.htm.

1. Right-click the Frequently Asked Questions hyperlink.

   FrontPage displays a shortcut menu.
2. Click Hyperlink Properties.

   FrontPage displays the Edit Hyperlink dialog box. Notice that the Frequently Asked Questions link has the Location page as its target in the URL text box. The Location page is an incorrect target for this link.

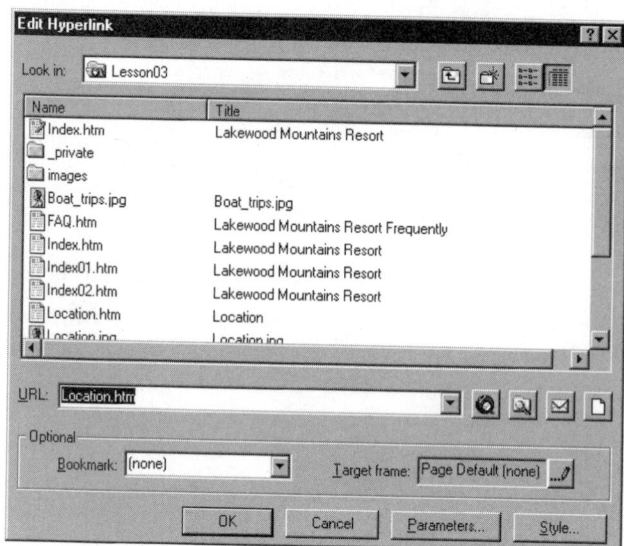

3. Click FAQ.htm in the file list, and then click OK.

   FrontPage changes the target page to FAQ.htm.
4. Click any blank area of the page to deselect the link, and then check the Frequently Asked Questions link by pressing Ctrl and clicking the link.

   FrontPage displays the Frequently Asked Questions page.

Close

5. Click the Close button at the top-right corner of the FAQ page.

   FrontPage closes the FAQ page and displays the Index page.
6. Double-click the Location hyperlink, and then type **Resort Location**.

   The new text replaces the old text, leaving the hyperlink intact.

Save

7. On the toolbar, click the Save button.

   FrontPage saves your changes.

Delete a hyperlink

In this exercise, you delete a hyperlink but leave its Web page text intact.

1. Right-click the Lakewood Webmaster hyperlink.

   FrontPage displays a shortcut menu.
2. On the shortcut menu, click Hyperlink Properties.

   FrontPage displays the Edit Hyperlink dialog box. The URL text is selected.
3. Press Delete.

   FrontPage deletes the URL text from the text box.
4. Click OK.

   FrontPage deletes the hyperlink from the Web page text. Notice that the text is no longer underlined.

Save

5. On the toolbar, click the Save button.

   FrontPage saves your changes.

> **tip**
>
> You can also delete a hyperlink by deleting the text on the Web page that contains the hyperlink.

Creating Bookmarks on a Web Page

Normally, when visitors click a hyperlink to a Web page, their browsers display only as much of the page as will fit in the browser window. If the Web page is longer than will fit on the screen, visitors must scroll down the page to see the rest of its content. For long Web pages, this can get to be a considerable chore.

Bookmarks can help with this problem. In FrontPage, a bookmark is a link to a specific location on a Web page. Lakewood Mountains Resort's Frequently Asked Questions (FAQ) page is very long, so you decide to insert a few bookmarks to make things easier for Web site visitors.

If you are not working through this lesson sequentially, follow the steps in "Import the Lesson 3 Practice Web" earlier in this lesson.

Create bookmarks

In this exercise, you create bookmarks on the Lakewood Mountains Resort's Frequently Asked Questions (FAQ) Web page.

1. In the Folder List, double-click the file FAQ.htm.

   FrontPage displays the FAQ page in Page view.

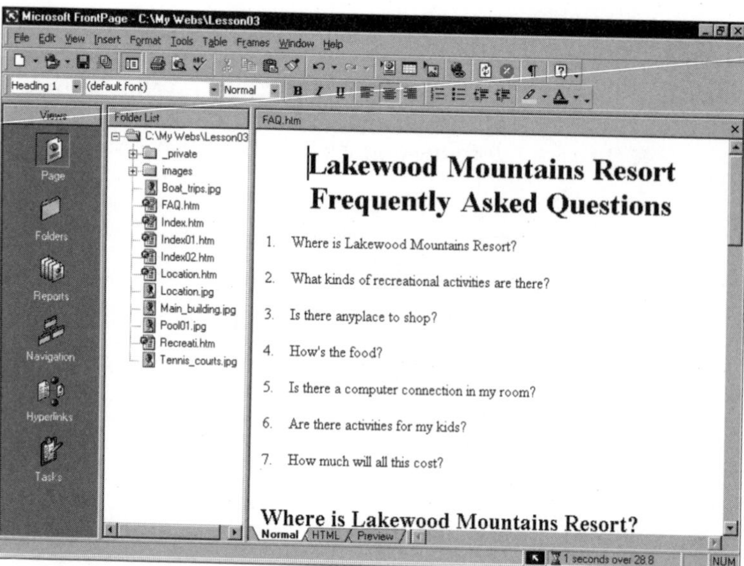

2. Scroll down to the end of the FAQ page.

   FrontPage displays the question *How much will all this cost?* and its answer.

3. Select the question text *How much will all this cost?*

tip

You aren't required to select text for a bookmark. You can simply place the insertion point where you want the bookmark, click Bookmark on the Insert menu, type a name for the bookmark, and click OK.

4. On the Insert menu, click Bookmark.

   FrontPage displays the Bookmark dialog box.

5. Click OK, and then deselect the question text by clicking any blank area of the FAQ page.

   FrontPage creates the bookmark. Notice that the text is now underlined with a broken line. The broken underline distinguishes it from the solid underline displayed by a hyperlink.

6. Scroll up to the paragraph with the heading *How's the food?*, and select the question *How's the food?* On the Insert menu, click Bookmark.

   FrontPage displays the Bookmark dialog box.

7. In the Bookmark dialog box, click OK.

   FrontPage inserts another bookmark on the FAQ page.

Save

8. Deselect the question text by clicking any blank area of the FAQ page, and then on the toolbar, click the Save button.

   FrontPage saves the FAQ page with the new bookmarks.

Link to a bookmark on the same Web page

In this exercise, you link from one location on a Web page to a bookmark at another location on the same Web page.

1. Scroll to the numbered list of questions at the top of the FAQ page.
2. Select the text *How's the food?*
3. On the Insert menu, click Hyperlink, and then click FAQ.htm in the dialog box's file list.
4. Click the Bookmark drop-down arrow, click *How's the food?*, and click OK.

   FrontPage inserts the hyperlink.

Save

5. On the toolbar, click the Save button.

   FrontPage saves your changes.

Link from another Web page to a bookmark

In this exercise, you create a link from a Web page to a bookmark on another Web page.

1. In the Folder List, double-click the file Index.htm.

   FrontPage displays the home page in Page view.

2. Select the text *How much will it cost?*
3. On the Insert menu, click Hyperlink.

   FrontPage displays the Create Hyperlink dialog box.

4. In the file list, click FAQ.htm, and then click the Bookmark drop-down arrow at the bottom of the dialog box.

   FrontPage displays a list of bookmarks on the FAQ page.

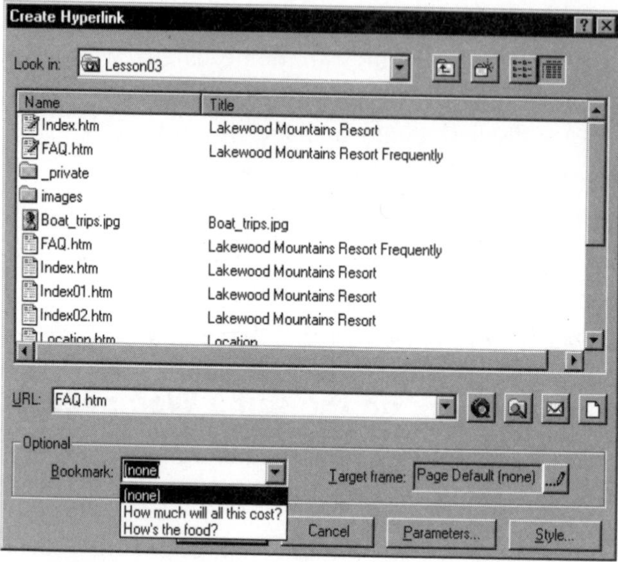

5. In the Bookmark list box, click *How much will all this cost?* and click OK.

   The URL text box displays the target address and FrontPage inserts the hyperlink.

Save

6. On the toolbar, click the Save button.

   FrontPage saves your changes.

Test your bookmarks

In this exercise, you test the bookmarks you created in the previous exercises.

Preview In Browser

1. On the toolbar, click the Preview In Browser button.

   FrontPage opens the home page in your Web browser.

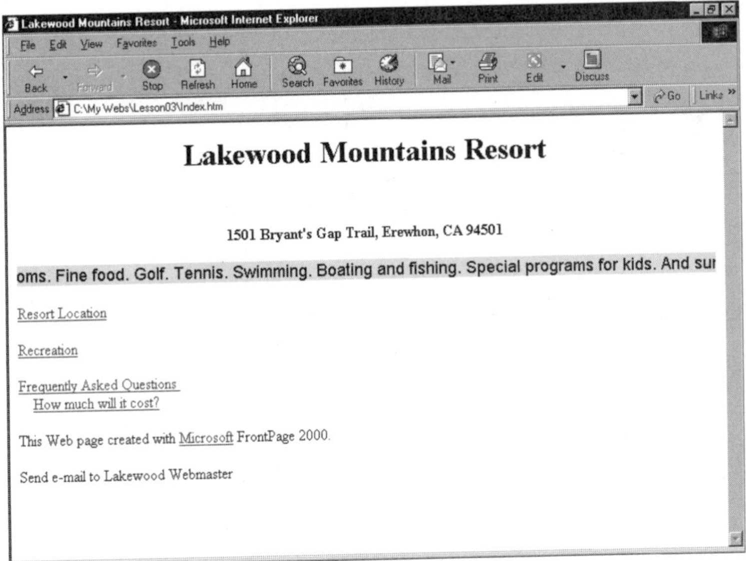

2. Click the *How much will it cost?* hyperlink.

   Your Web browser jumps down to the final question on the FAQ Web page.

3. Scroll to the top of the FAQ page.

4. Click the *How's the food?* hyperlink.

   Your Web browser jumps down to the *How's the food?* bookmark.

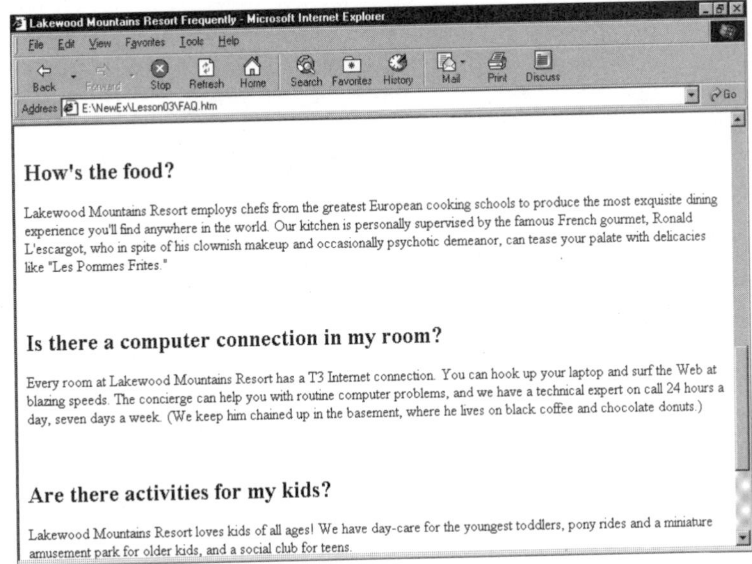

Close

5. Click the Close button at the top-right corner of your Web browser window.

   Your Web browser closes, and FrontPage is redisplayed.

Save

6. On the toolbar, click the Save button.

   FrontPage saves your changes.

Delete a bookmark

In this exercise, you delete a bookmark from the FAQ page.

1. In the Folder List, double-click the file FAQ.htm.

   FrontPage displays the FAQ page in Page view.

2. If necessary, scroll to display the *How's the food?* bookmark (not the hyperlink).

3. Right-click the bookmark text.

   A shortcut menu is displayed.

4. On the shortcut menu, click Bookmark Properties.

   FrontPage displays the Bookmark dialog box.

You can also right-click the bookmark text, click Bookmark Properties, and press Delete to delete a bookmark.

5. In the Other Bookmarks On This Page box, click *How's the food?*, and then click the Clear button.

   FrontPage deletes the bookmark.

Save

6. On the toolbar, click the Save button.

   FrontPage saves your changes.

One Step Further Creating Image Map Hyperlinks

So far, you've created text hyperlinks for the Lakewood Mountains Resort Web site. The resort manager, however, would like the Web site to have more visual excitement. She's seen Web sites in which a visitor can click part of an image and be taken directly to the Web page connected with that part of the image.

You've heard about that feature. It's called an *image map*. FrontPage makes it easy to create image maps. All you have to do is insert an image on a Web page, draw *hotspots*, create a few hyperlinks, and you've got an image map.

Insert an image on a Web page

If you are not working through this lesson sequentially, follow the steps in "Import the Lesson 3 Practice Web" earlier in this lesson.

In this exercise, you insert an image of the hotel building on the Lakewood Mountains Resort home page in preparation for creating an image map.

1. In the Folder List, double-click the file Index.htm.
   FrontPage displays the Lakewood Mountains Resort home page.
2. Click the line below the text *Lakewood Mountains Resort* and above the resort's address.
3. On the Insert menu, point to Picture, and then click From File.
   FrontPage displays the Picture dialog box.
4. In the file list, click Main_building.jpg.
   FrontPage displays a preview of the image in the preview pane.

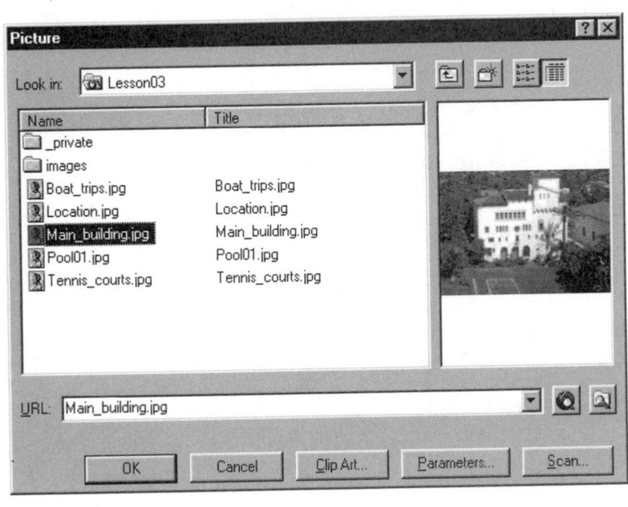

5. Click OK.

   FrontPage inserts the image at the location you selected.

6. On the toolbar, click the Save button.

   FrontPage saves your changes.

Save

Create an image map

For a demonstration of how to create an image map, open the Office 8in1 Step by Step folder on your hard disk. Then open the FrontPage Demos folder, and double-click the ImageMap icon.

In this exercise, you draw hotspots on the resort image to create an image map.

1. Click the resort image to select it.

   FrontPage displays the Image toolbar along the bottom of the screen.

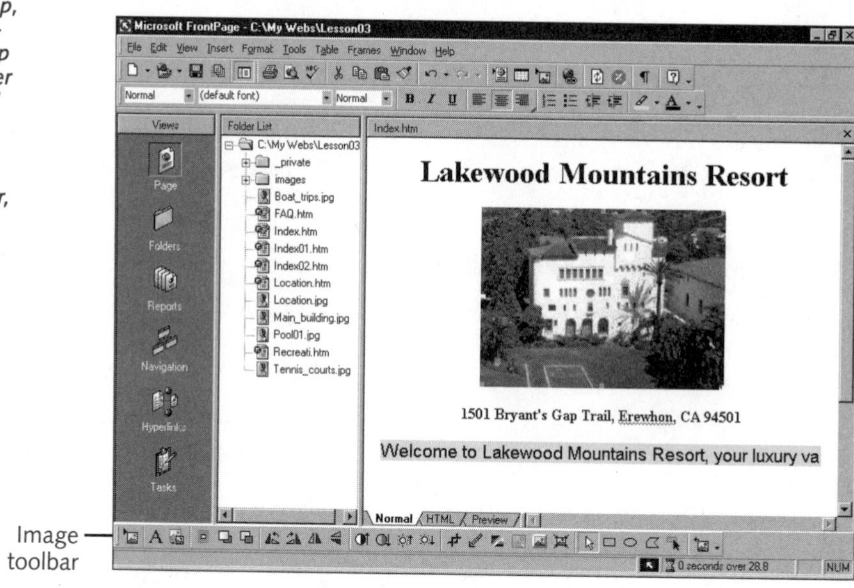

Image toolbar

Rectangular Hotspot

2. On the Image toolbar, click the Rectangular Hotspot button.
3. Hold down the mouse button, drag the mouse pointer to draw a rectangle on the grassy area in front of the hotel building, and release the mouse button.

   FrontPage displays the Create Hyperlink dialog box.

4. In the file list, click Recreati.htm, and then click OK.

   FrontPage inserts a hyperlink for the image area you selected.

5. Click the Rectangular Hotspot button, draw another rectangle on the hotel building, and then release the mouse button.

   FrontPage displays the Create Hyperlink dialog box.

6. In the file list, click Location.htm, and then click OK.

   FrontPage inserts another hyperlink for the image area you selected.

Save

7. On the toolbar, click the Save button.

   FrontPage saves your changes.

Test the image map

In this exercise, you test the image map you created in the previous exercise.

Preview In Browser

1. On the toolbar, click the Preview In Browser button.

   FrontPage displays the home page in your Web browser.

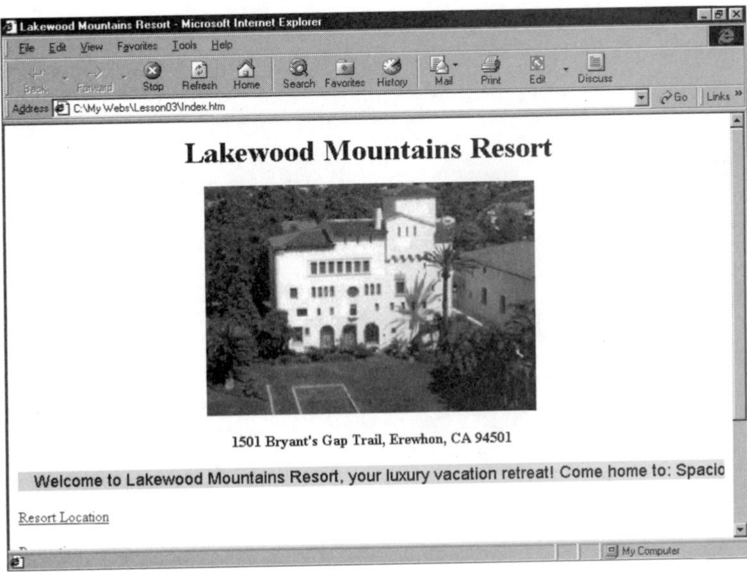

2. Move the mouse pointer over the image.

   Over the hotspots, the mouse pointer turns from an arrow into a pointing hand, indicating the presence of hyperlinks.

Pointing Hand

3. Click the grassy area hotspot.

   Your Web browser displays the Recreation page.

Back

4. On the toolbar of your Web browser, click the Back button, and then click the hotel building hotspot.

   Your Web browser displays the Location page.

Finish the lesson

Close

1. Click the Close button at the top-right corner of your Web browser window.
   Your Web browser closes and FrontPage reappears.
2. On the File menu, click Close Web.
3. For each page, if FrontPage prompts you to save changes, click Yes.
   FrontPage saves your changes and closes the Lesson03 Web.

Lesson 3 Quick Reference

To	Do this
Import a Web	On the File menu, point to New, and click Web. Click the Import Web Wizard icon, type the name of the folder for the new Web, and click OK. Click the From A Source Directory Of Files option to select it, click the Include Subfolders check box, and then click the Browse button. Browse to the folder that contains the files you want to import, and click OK. Click Next, click Next again, and then click Finish.
Create a text hyperlink	Select the hyperlink text, and on the Insert menu, click Hyperlink. If necessary, browse to the target file. Select the target file, and click OK.
Create a hyperlink by dragging	Display the Web page that will have the hyperlink in Page view. Drag a file from the Folder List to the desired location on the Web page and release the mouse button.
Change a hyperlink target	Right-click the hyperlink and click Hyperlink Properties. In the Edit Hyperlink dialog box, select the new hyperlink target, and click OK.
Change hyperlink text	Select the hyperlink text, and type the new text.
Delete a hyperlink	Right-click the hyperlink text, click Hyperlink Properties, and then press Delete. Click OK.
Create a bookmark	Select the bookmark text. On the Insert menu, click Bookmark, and then click OK.
Create a hyperlink to a bookmark	Select the hyperlink text, and then click Hyperlink on the Insert menu. If necessary, browse to the target file. Select the target file, click the Bookmark drop-down arrow, click the desired bookmark, and then click OK.

Lesson 3 Quick Reference

To	Do this	Button
Delete a bookmark	Right-click the bookmark text, click Bookmark Properties, and then click the Clear button.	
Create an e-mail hyperlink	Select the hyperlink text, and then on the Insert menu, click Hyperlink. Click the E-mail button, type the e-mail address, and click OK twice.	
Insert an image on a Web page	Place the insertion point in the desired location. On the Insert menu, point to Picture, and then click From File. If needed, browse to the location of the image file. Click the image file, and then click OK.	
Create an image map	Click the image on the Web page. On the Image toolbar, click the Rectangular Hotspot button and draw a hotspot on the image. In the Create Hyperlink dialog box, select the target file, and then click OK.	

LESSON

4

Adding Multimedia to Web Pages

In this lesson you will learn how to:

- ✔ *Insert photos and clip art on a Web page.*
- ✔ *Create thumbnails of Web page images.*
- ✔ *Edit Web page images.*
- ✔ *Add a background sound to a Web page.*
- ✔ *Add a motion clip to a Web page.*
- ✔ *Create hover buttons on a Web page.*

ESTIMATED TIME **30 min.**

So far, the managers of Lakewood Mountains Resort have been very happy with your work on the resort's Web site. However, you'd like to impress them even more by incorporating pictures, sounds, and motion clips on their Web pages. After all, the Web is a graphically oriented way to send information over the Internet. A state-of-the-art Web site should make use of that feature.

Your coworker tells you that Microsoft FrontPage 2000 makes it simple to put all kinds of multimedia on Web pages, so you decide to give it a try. In this lesson, you will learn how to insert photos and clip art images on Web pages, insert images in table cells on a Web page, and create thumbnails. You will also learn how to add a background sound to a Web page and insert a motion clip on a Web page. Finally, you will learn how to create *hover buttons* that change in appearance when a mouse pointer is positioned over them.

Import the Lesson 4 practice Web

In this exercise, you create a new Web based on the files in the Lesson04 folder in the FrontPage Practice folder. You will use this Web for all the exercises in Lesson 4.

If your hard disk drive has a letter other than C, substitute the appropriate drive letter in step 2.

1. On the File menu, point to New, and then click Web.

   FrontPage displays the New dialog box.
2. Click the Import Web Wizard icon. In the Specify The Location Of The New Web text box, type **C:\My Webs\Lesson04**, and then click OK.

   FrontPage displays the first Import Web Wizard dialog box.
3. Click the From A Source Directory Of Files option, click the Include Subfolders check box, and click the Browse button.
4. Browse to the Lesson04 folder, which is in the FrontPage Practice folder in the Office 8in1 Step by Step folder, and click OK.
5. Click Next twice, and then click Finish.

   FrontPage creates a new Web based on the practice files and places it in the Lesson04 folder.

Using Images on Web Pages

Your first task is to learn how to insert different kinds of images on Web pages. There are essentially two kinds of static images you'll use on Web pages: photo files and clip art. Photo files come in many different file formats, but they're usually either GIF (Graphics Interchange Format) files or JPEG (Joint Photographic Experts Group) files. GIF and JPEG files compress the image, allowing a smaller file size than other formats. This allows GIF and JPEG files to download faster to a Web site visitor's computer.

Likewise, clip art images come in a variety of formats, including GIF, JPEG, BMP (Windows bitmap), and PNG (Portable Network Graphics). However, GIF and JPEG are still the most common formats for clip art files. FrontPage includes an extensive Clip Art Gallery with hundreds of ready-to-use images, including buttons, cartoons, pictures, backgrounds, and many other images. The Clip Art Gallery even includes sound and motion clip files.

Regardless of the file format, you insert photo and clip art images on a Web page in much the same way. In FrontPage, it's just a matter of making a few menu selections. An especially valuable FrontPage feature creates *thumbnails*, which are small versions of images that download very quickly. To create a thumbnail, you first insert a full-sized image file on a Web page. Then you select the image and click the Auto Thumbnail button on the Image toolbar.

On the Web page, FrontPage replaces the original full-sized image with a thumbnail version. By clicking the thumbnail, a Web site visitor can display the full-sized image.

Insert a photo on a Web page

If you are not working through this lesson sequentially, follow the steps in "Import the Lesson 4 Practice Web" earlier in this lesson.

In this exercise, you insert a photo on the Lakewood Mountains Resort Welcome page.

1. In the Folder List, double-click the file Welcome01.htm.

   FrontPage displays the Lakewood Welcome page in Page view.

2. Click the blank line underneath the text *Lakewood Mountains Resort* and above the resort's address.

   The insertion point is centered on the line.

3. On the Insert menu, point to Picture, and then click From File.

   FrontPage displays the Picture dialog box.

For a demonstration of how to insert a photo on a Web page, open the Office 8in1 Step by Step folder on your hard disk. Then open the FrontPage Demos folder, and double-click the InsertPhoto icon.

4. In the file list, click Main_building.jpg.

   FrontPage displays a preview of the image in the preview pane.

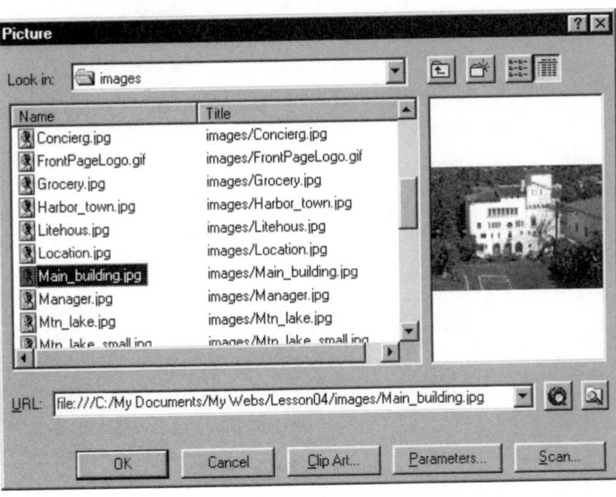

5. Click OK.

   FrontPage inserts the image at the location you selected.

6. On the toolbar, click the Save button.

   FrontPage saves your changes.

Save

tip

By reducing the size of image files, you reduce the time it takes to download them to the Web site visitor's computer. Apart from reducing the size of the image itself, a good way to shrink file size is to use an image-editing program such as Paint Shop Pro or Microsoft PhotoDraw to reduce the number of colors in the image.

Explore the Clip Art Gallery

In this exercise, you explore the FrontPage Clip Art Gallery.

1. In the Folder List, double-click the file Sights01.htm.

   FrontPage displays the Web page.

2. On the Insert menu, point to Picture, and then click Clip Art.

   FrontPage displays the Clip Art Gallery window. On the Pictures tab, you can select clip art to insert on Web pages.

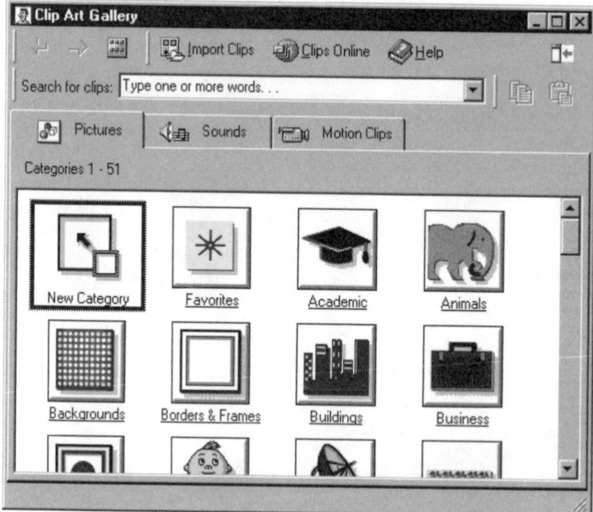

3. Click the Sounds tab.

   On the Sounds tab, you can select sound effects to insert on Web pages.

4. Click the Motion Clips tab.

   On the Motion Clips tab, you can select motion clips and animated GIF files to insert on Web pages.

5. In the Categories pane, click the Academic icon.

   FrontPage displays the motion clips available in this category.

6. Click one of the motion clip pictures.

   FrontPage displays the pop-up menu for the motion clip. The clip is an animated GIF file.

If there are no motion clips displayed, you can download clips from the Microsoft Clip Gallery Live.

An animated GIF file contains a short sequence of images. When a Web site visitor views the GIF file, the images are displayed in rapid sequence, producing an animated picture.

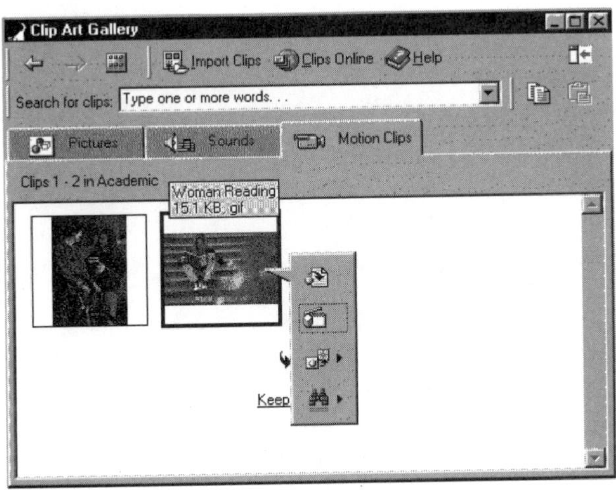

7. On the pop-up menu, click the Play Clip button.

   FrontPage plays the motion clip in the GIF Player window.

8. Click the Close button at the top-right corner of the GIF Player window.

   FrontPage closes the GIF Player window.

9. On the Clip Art Gallery toolbar, click the Back button.

   FrontPage redisplays the Motion Clips tab of the Clip Art Gallery window.

10. Click the Close button at the top-right corner of the Clip Art Gallery window.

    FrontPage closes the window.

Play Clip

Back

The Forward and Back buttons work just as they do in Microsoft Internet Explorer.

tip

To download additional clip art, sounds, and motion clips from the Web, connect to the Internet, and click the Clips Online button on the toolbar in the Clip Art Gallery window. FrontPage connects to the Microsoft Clip Gallery Live site on the World Wide Web, from which you can download additional clip art images for your Web pages. You can also download clip art, sounds, and motion clip files from newsgroups on the Internet, such as *alt.binaries.sounds.midi*.

Search the Clip Art Gallery

In this exercise, you search for clip art in the Clip Art Gallery.

1. On the Sights01 Web page, click the blank line below the heading and above the table.

   FrontPage moves the insertion point to the line below the heading.
2. On the Insert menu, point to Picture, and then click Clip Art.

   FrontPage displays the Clip Art Gallery window.
3. Click in the Search For Clips text box, type **arrow**, and then press Enter.

   FrontPage searches the Clip Art Gallery for arrow images and displays the search results on the Pictures tab.

The window on your screen might differ slightly from the one shown in the illustration.

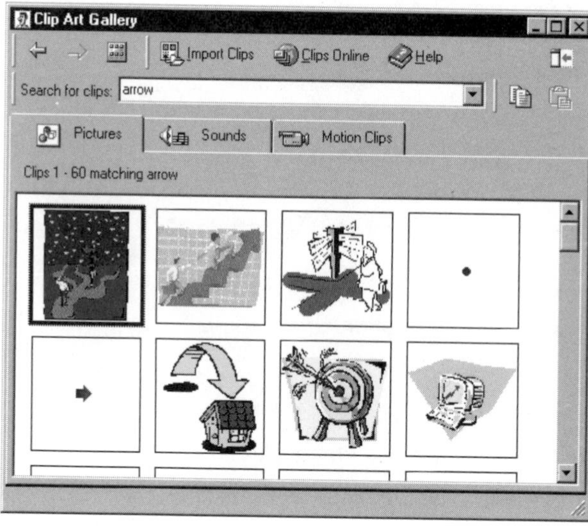

Insert clip art on a Web page

If your window does not contain the globe-arrow image, just use any clip art image you like.

In this exercise, you select a clip art image, insert it on a Web page, and then save the Web page.

1. Click the globe-arrow image.

   FrontPage displays the pop-up menu for the clip art image.
2. On the pop-up menu, click the Insert Clip button.

   FrontPage inserts the globe-arrow clip art at the selected location on the Web page and closes the Clip Art Gallery window.

Insert Clip

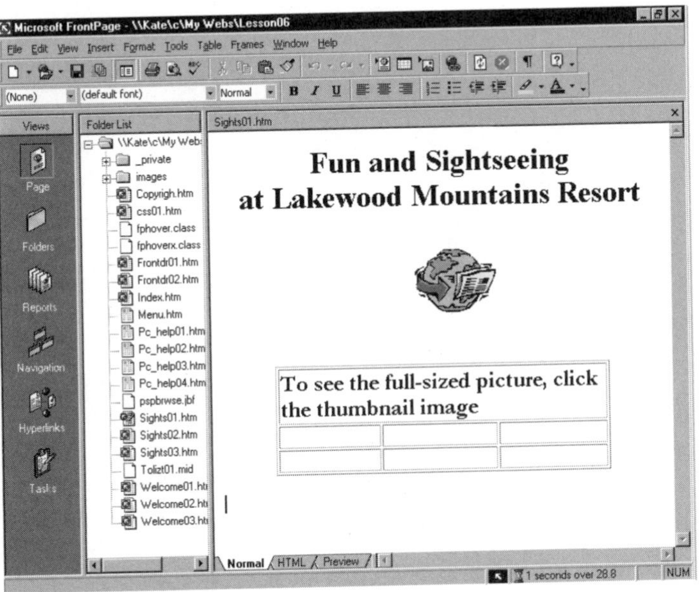

Save

3. On the toolbar, click the Save button, and then click OK in the Save Embedded Files dialog box.

   FrontPage saves the Web page with your changes.

tip

You can make almost any image on a Web page a hyperlink, including clip art. To make a clip art image a hyperlink, right-click the image, and click Hyperlink on the shortcut menu. In the Create Hyperlink dialog box, browse to the file that will be the link target, click the file, and click OK.

Insert images in table cells and create thumbnails

In this exercise, you arrange images on a Web page by inserting them in table cells. You then shrink the images by converting them to thumbnails that link to the full-sized images.

1. In the Folder List, double-click the file Sights02.htm.

   FrontPage opens the Web page in Page view.

2. Click in the top-left cell of the first empty row in the table. On the Insert menu, point to Picture, and click From File.

   FrontPage displays the Picture dialog box.

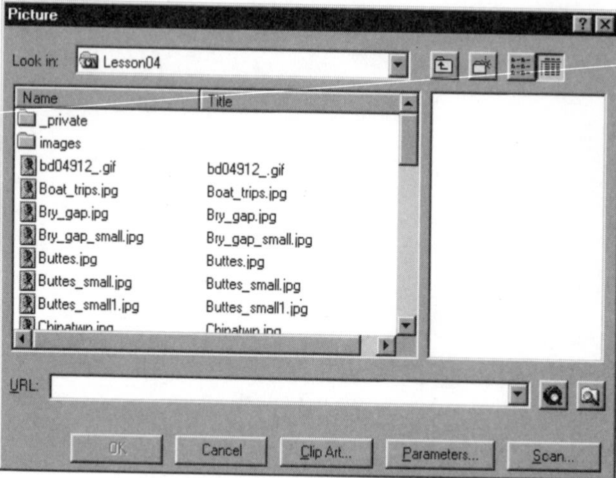

3. In the file list, click Bry_gap.jpg, and then click OK.

   FrontPage inserts the image into the table cell. Notice that the image is too large to fit in the table cell.

4. Click the image in the table cell.

   FrontPage displays the Image toolbar along the bottom of your screen.

Auto Thumbnail

5. On the Image toolbar, click the Auto Thumbnail button.

   FrontPage converts the table image into a much smaller thumbnail that contains a hyperlink to the full-sized image.

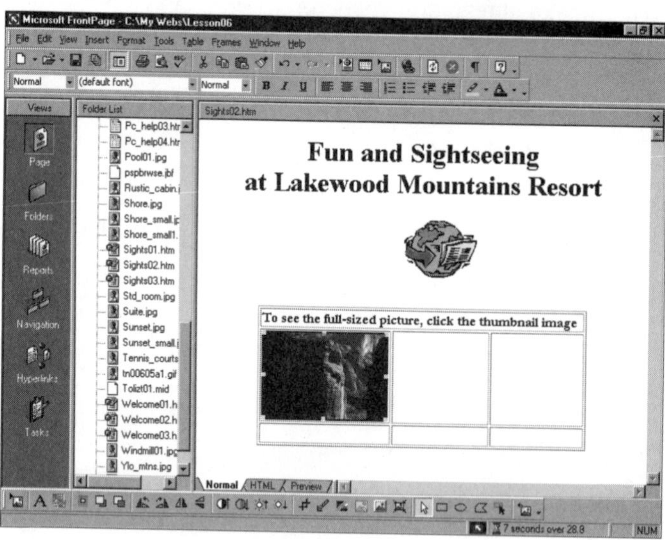

6. Click in the middle cell of the same row. On the Insert menu, point to Picture, click From File, click Shore.jpg, and then click OK.

   FrontPage inserts an image into the middle cell of the row.

Auto Thumbnail

7. Click the image in the middle cell, and on the Image toolbar, click the Auto Thumbnail button.

   FrontPage creates a thumbnail image and links it to the full-sized image.

Save

8. On the toolbar, click the Save button, and click OK in the Save Embedded Files dialog box.

   FrontPage saves your changes.

Move image files to the images folder

When you create a Web, FrontPage automatically includes an images folder. If your Web has a large number of images, moving all image files to the images folder makes your Web easier to manage. In this exercise, you move image files from your Web's main folder to its images folder and observe how FrontPage updates the images' hyperlinks.

1. On the Views bar, click the Folders icon.

   FrontPage displays a list of all files and folders in the Lesson04 Web.

2. Click the Type button at the top of the file list.

   FrontPage displays the files in alphabetical order by type.

If files are displayed in reverse order, click the Type button one more time.

3. In the file list, click Boat_trips.jpg. Scroll down until you see Ylo_mtns_small.jpg, hold down Shift, and click that file.

4. Drag the selected files to the images subfolder in the Folder List.

   FrontPage moves all the JPEG image files to the images subfolder and updates all hyperlinks between Web pages and JPEG files to reflect the files' new location.

5. In the file list, click FrontPageLogo.gif, hold down the Ctrl key, and click any other GIF files.

   The GIF image files are selected.

6. Drag the GIF image files to the Images subfolder.

   FrontPage moves all the GIF image files to the images subfolder and updates the hyperlinks.

7. On the Views bar, click the Page icon, and then double-click Sights03.htm in the Folder List.

   FrontPage displays the Web page in Page view.

8. Right-click the picture in the top-left table cell, and then on the shortcut menu, click Hyperlink Properties.

   FrontPage displays the Edit Hyperlink dialog box. Notice that the hyperlink's target (in the URL text box) has been updated and is in the images folder.
9. Click the Cancel button in the Edit Hyperlinks dialog box.

   FrontPage closes the Edit Hyperlinks dialog box.

Editing Images on Web Pages

Placing an image on a Web page is easy, but often the image is too large or too small to fit properly on the Web page. Moreover, some Web site visitors set up their Web browsers to download Web pages without embedded images: this makes the pages download more quickly, but leaves gaps where images would otherwise appear. FrontPage enables you to specify "alternative text" that is displayed when images aren't downloaded. Instead of the image, visitors see your alternative text description at the page location where the image would have appeared.

Resize an image

If you are not working through this lesson sequentially, follow the steps in "Import the Lesson 4 Practice Web" earlier in this lesson.

In this exercise, you resize an image on a Web page.

1. In the Folder List, double-click Welcome02.htm.

   FrontPage displays the Welcome02.htm Web page in Page view. The hotel image is so large that it pushes the address and phone number off the bottom of the screen.
2. Click the hotel image, and then scroll to the lower-right corner of the image.

   A small square (a resize handle) appears at the corner of the image.
3. Move the mouse pointer over the resize handle.

   The mouse pointer changes into a diagonal double arrow.

Double Arrow

4. Drag the mouse pointer upward and to the left to shrink the image.

   FrontPage resizes the hotel image, retaining the original proportions, as shown in the illustration on the following page.

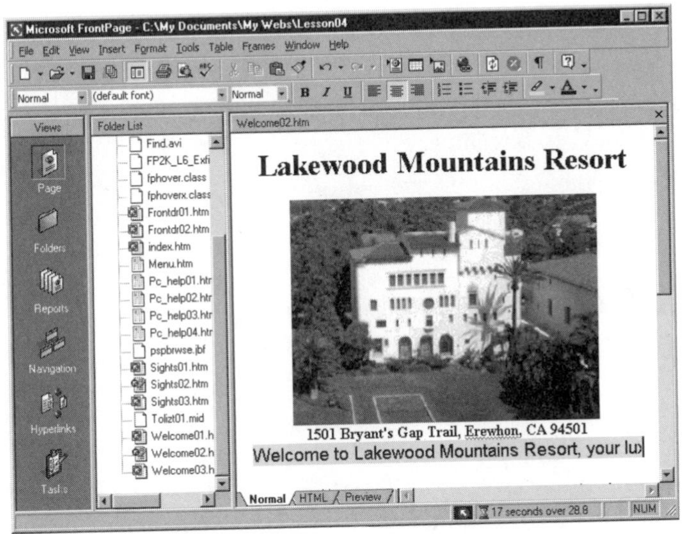

Specify alternative text for an image

In this exercise, you specify alternative text for an image on a Web page.

1. Right-click the hotel image, and then on the shortcut menu, click Picture Properties.

   FrontPage displays the Picture Properties dialog box.

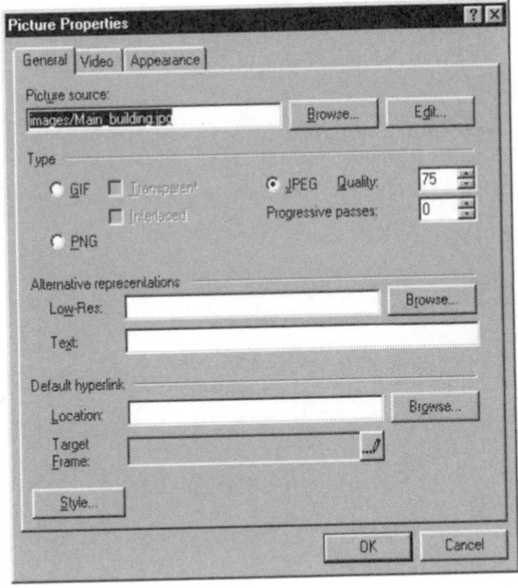

2. Click in the Text text box under Alternative Representations, type **Lakewood Mountains Resort main building**, and click OK.

   FrontPage inserts the text to be displayed if a Web site visitor's browser does not display Web page images.

3. On the toolbar, click the Save button.

   FrontPage saves your changes.

Save

Adding Sound Effects and Music to Web Pages

Most Web page content is informative, but there's more to the Web surfing experience than just getting information. You want the Lakewood Mountains Resort Web site to be a pleasant place to visit. One way to make the site interesting is to add a background sound to the home page. This background sound will play as long as the home page is displayed in a Web browser.

> **important**
>
> When you use these steps to insert a sound file on a Web page, the sound file will play only if the page is loaded in Microsoft's Internet Explorer Web browser—but not if the user loads it into Netscape's Navigator Web browser. Netscape Navigator uses different HTML coding to play a background sound.

Add a background sound

If you are not working through this lesson sequentially, follow the steps in "Import the Lesson 4 Practice Web" earlier in the lesson.

In this exercise, you add a background sound to a Web page and preview the sound in your Web browser.

1. In the Folder List, double-click Welcome03.htm.

   FrontPage displays the Welcome03.htm Web page in Page view.

2. Right-click a blank area of the page, and then click Page Properties.

   FrontPage displays the Page Properties dialog box.

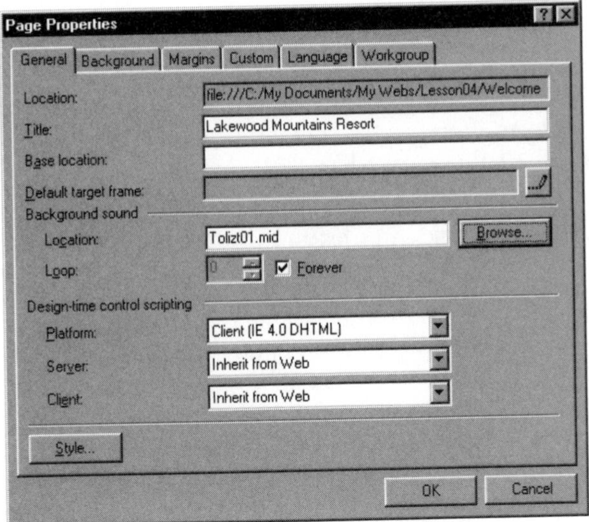

3. Click the Browse button.

   FrontPage displays the Background Sound dialog box.

4. Click Tolizt01.mid, and click OK twice.

   FrontPage inserts the file as a background sound that will play as long as the page is displayed in a visitor's Web browser.

Save

5. On the toolbar, click the Save button, and then click the Preview In Browser button.

   FrontPage saves the page and displays it in your Web browser. If you are using Microsoft Internet Explorer, the background sound plays automatically.

Preview In Browser

6. Click the Close button at the top-right corner of your Web browser window.

   Your Web browser closes and FrontPage reappears.

Close

tip

By default, a background sound continues to play as long as the Web page is displayed in a visitor's Web browser. However, you can specify that the sound play a certain number of times and then stop. In the Page Properties dialog box, clear the Forever check box. In the Loop text box, enter the number of times the background sound should repeat, and then click OK.

Adding Video to Web Pages

So far, you've had great success using FrontPage to insert static pictures on Web pages. What's even more impressive, however, is that you can just as easily insert motion clips on Web pages. When Web site visitors load a page with an embedded motion clip, the video will automatically play both motion and sound. You can also create hyperlinks that lead to motion clip files.

Insert a motion clip

If you are not working through this lesson sequentially, follow the steps in "Import the Lesson 4 Practice Web" earlier in this lesson.

In this exercise, you insert a motion clip on a Web page and preview the video in your Web browser.

1. In the Folder List, double-click Pc_help01.htm.

   FrontPage displays the Web page in Page view.

2. Click the empty line just below the page text. On the Insert menu, point to Picture, and then click Video.

   FrontPage displays the Video dialog box.

The file Pc_help02.htm is the completed version of the page you edit in this exercise.

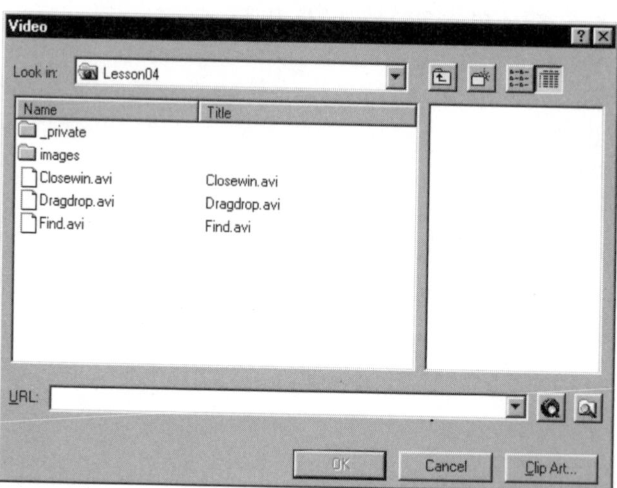

3. Click Closewin.avi in the Lesson04 folder, and then click OK.

   FrontPage inserts the motion clip directly on the Web page. When a Web site visitor displays the page, the video will play once.

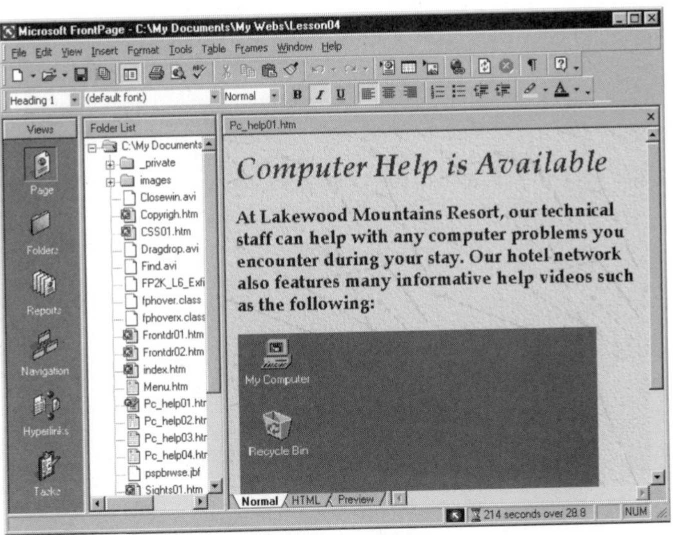

Save

Preview In Browser

Close

4. On the toolbar, click the Save button, and then click the Preview In Browser button.

   FrontPage saves the page and displays it in your Web browser. The motion clip plays automatically.

5. Click the Close button at the top-right corner of your Web browser window.

   Your Web browser closes and FrontPage reappears.

Link to a motion clip

In this exercise, you create a hyperlink to a motion clip file instead of inserting the file directly on a Web page.

1. In the Folder List, double-click Pc_help03.htm.

   FrontPage displays the Web page in Page view.

2. Select the text *How to drag and drop.*

3. Right-click the selected text, and on the shortcut menu, click Hyperlink.

   FrontPage displays the Create Hyperlink dialog box.

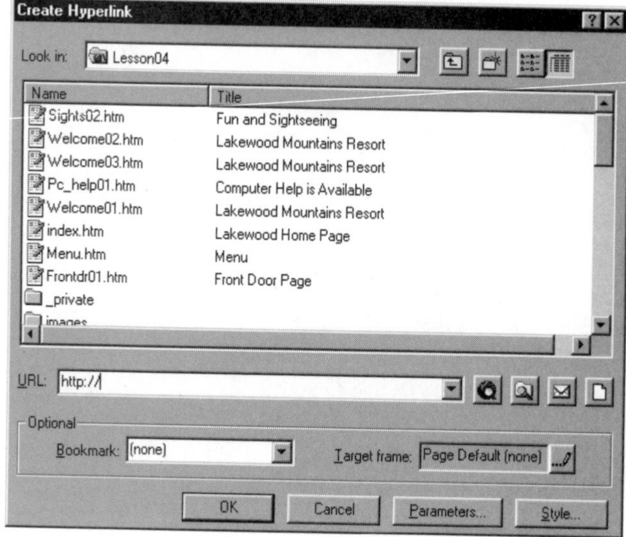

The file Pc_help04.htm is the completed version of the page you edit in this exercise.

4. In the file list, click Dragdrop.avi, and then click OK.

   FrontPage inserts the hyperlink.

Save

Preview In Browser

5. On the toolbar, click the Save button, and then click the Preview In Browser button.

   FrontPage saves the Web page and displays it in your Web browser.

6. Click the hyperlink How To Drag And Drop.

   The Windows Media Player opens and plays the motion clip.

Close

7. Close the Media Player and your Web browser.

   FrontPage is redisplayed.

Using Style Sheets to Position Web Page Items

One of the exciting but somewhat advanced techniques supported by FrontPage 2000 is the ability to use Web page *style sheets* to control the appearance of your Web pages. A Web page style sheet is a separate text file in which you specify how various elements of your Web page should look. Techniques for creating style sheets—called *cascading style sheets* (CSS) because you can apply multiple style sheets to a single Web page—are defined by the World Wide Web Consortium (*www.w3.org*).

FrontPage makes it easy to use one of the most powerful style sheet features to be added in the latest CSS version: absolute and relative positioning of Web page elements. Previously, you've seen how you can use tables to place items in specific locations on your Web pages. That's how it's been done for most of the Web's history. With style sheets, however, you can position Web page items exactly where you want them *without* using tables.

With FrontPage, you don't have to write any style sheet code to position Web page items. You simply use menu choices and dialog boxes to specify the position you want for an item. FrontPage does all the work of creating the style sheet code; you never even have to see it.

Use a style sheet to position an image

If you are not working through this lesson sequentially, follow the steps in "Import the Lesson 4 Practice Web" earlier in this lesson.

1. On the Views bar, click the Page icon.

   FrontPage displays the Web in Page view.
2. On the toolbar, click the New button.

   FrontPage creates a new Web page and displays it in Page view.
3. If the New dialog box appears, click OK to accept the Normal Page.
4. On the Insert menu, point to Picture, and then click From File.

   FrontPage displays the Picture dialog box.

New

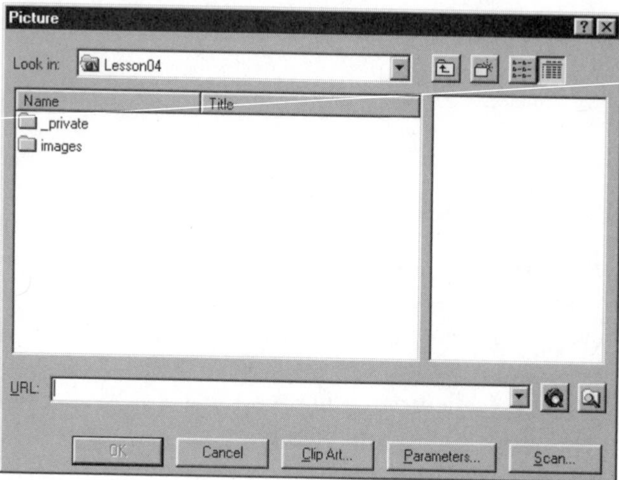

5 Double-click the Images folder, click Bry_gap_small.jpg, and click OK.

FrontPage inserts the picture at the top-left corner of the Web page.

6 On the Insert menu, point to Picture, and then click From File.

FrontPage displays the Picture dialog box.

7 In the dialog box's file list, click Shore_small.jpg, and click OK.

FrontPage inserts the new picture just to the right of the first picture.

8 Right-click the second picture (Shore_small.jpg). On the shortcut menu, click Picture Properties. Click the Style button, click the Format button, and in the drop-down menu, click Position.

FrontPage displays the Position dialog box.

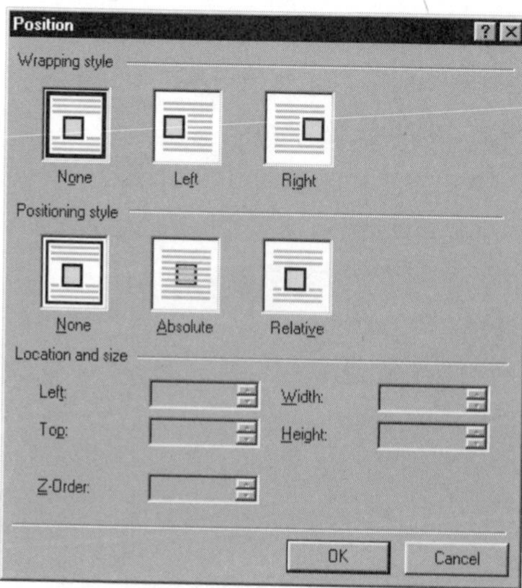

9. In the Positioning Style section of the dialog box, click the Absolute icon. Type **300** in the Left text box and type **50** in the Top text box.

   FrontPage will position the picture 300 pixels from the left edge of the Web page and 50 pixels from the top of the Web page.

10. Click OK three times.

    FrontPage closes all the dialog boxes and positions the picture at the location you specified.

11. Right-click the first picture (Bry_gap_small.jpg). On the shortcut menu, click Picture Properties. Click the Style button, click the Format button, and in the drop-down menu, click Position.

    FrontPage displays the Position dialog box.

12. In the Positioning Style section, click the Absolute icon. Type **50** in the Left text box and type **50** in the Top text box.

    FrontPage will position the picture 50 pixels from the left edge of the Web page and 50 pixels from the top of the Web page.

13. Click OK three times.

    FrontPage closes all the dialog boxes and positions the picture at the location you specified.

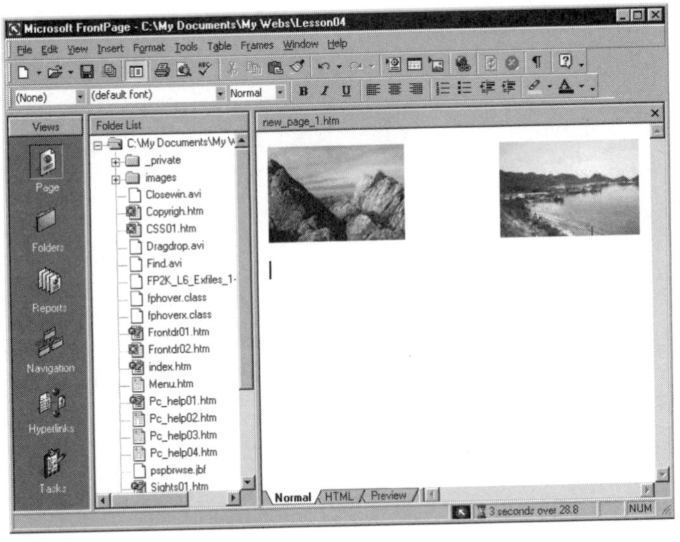

Save

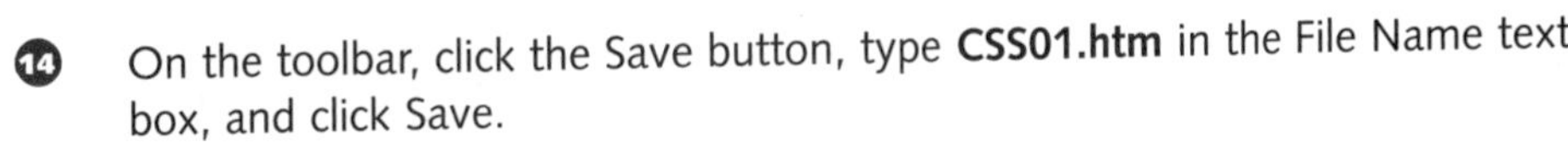

14. On the toolbar, click the Save button, type **CSS01.htm** in the File Name text box, and click Save.

    FrontPage saves your changes.

tip

You can use style sheets to position items on a Web page with *absolute* or *relative* positioning. Absolute positioning, which you used in the previous exercise, places the item at exactly the distance you specify from the top and left edges of the page—even if there's another item in that location. Relative positioning moves the item the specified distance down and to the right from the point at which it would normally appear, not from the edges of the page. Thus, relative positioning is slightly safer but doesn't give you as much control.

One Step Further Creating Hover Buttons

Motion clips aren't the only kind of animation you can create with FrontPage. Another popular multimedia effect is the *hover button*, whose appearance changes if a Web site visitor points to it with the mouse—that is, when the mouse pointer "hovers" over the button.

A hover button is actually a Java applet created by FrontPage. You can use a hover button to link to another Web page. When a Web site visitor points to the hover button, the button displays a hover effect such as changing color or appearing to have been pushed. When a Web site visitor clicks the hover button, the linked Web page is displayed.

Create a hover button

If you are not working through this lesson sequentially, follow the steps in "Import the Lesson 4 Practice Web" earlier in this lesson.

In this exercise, you create a hover button and set its properties.

1. In the Folder List, double-click Frontdr01.htm.

   FrontPage opens the Web page and displays it in Page view.

2. Click the line below the *Welcome* text. On the Insert menu, point to Component, and then click Hover Button.

   FrontPage displays the Hover Button Properties dialog box. The default text in the Button Text box is already selected.

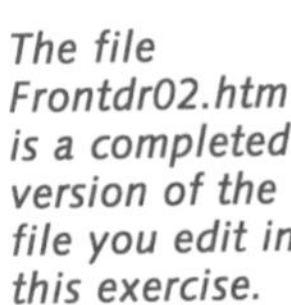

The file Frontdr02.htm is a completed version of the file you edit in this exercise.

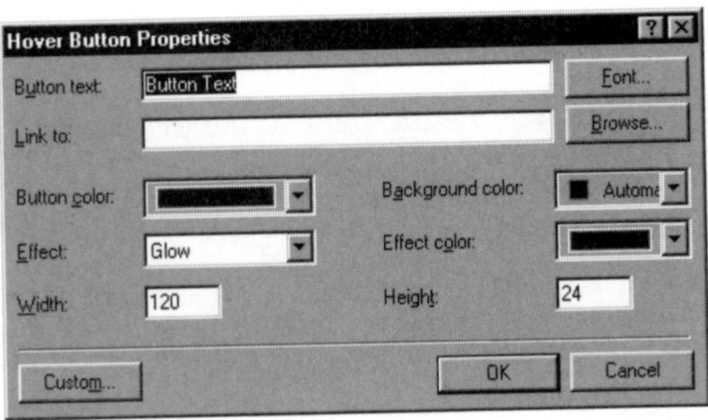

3. Type **Enter the Web Site** in the Button Text text box. Type **300** in the Width text box and **50** in the Height text box.

   FrontPage sets the button caption and size.

4. Click the Effect drop-down arrow.

   FrontPage displays a list of animation effects you can use with hover buttons.

5. Click Bevel In.

   FrontPage sets the button to look as if it has been pressed when the mouse pointer is on it.

6. Click the Browse button.

   FrontPage displays the Select Hover Button Hyperlink dialog box.

7. Scroll down in the file list, click Index.htm, and click OK twice.

   FrontPage creates a hover button with the properties you specified.

Save

Preview In Browser

8. On the toolbar, click the Save button, and then click the Preview In Browser button.

   FrontPage saves your changes and displays the page in your Web browser.

9. Move the mouse pointer over the hover button.

   The hover button text moves slightly, as if the button has been pressed inward.

10. Click the hover button.

    Your Web browser loads the Web's home page.

tip

Another way to create a hyperlink hover button is to right-click the button, and click Hover Button Properties on the shortcut menu. The Hover Button dialog box will be displayed. In the Link To text box, browse to the file that will be the link target, click the file, and click OK.

Finish the lesson

Close

1. Click the Close button at the top-right corner of your Web browser window. Your Web browser closes and FrontPage reappears.
2. On the File menu, click Close Web.
3. For each page, if FrontPage prompts you to save changes, click Yes. FrontPage saves your changes and closes the Lesson04 Web.

Lesson 4 Quick Reference

To	Do this	Button
Insert a photo on a Web page	Click the desired location on the Web page. On the Insert menu, point to Picture, and click From File. Browse to the desired file, click it, and click OK.	
Search the Clip Art Gallery	On the Insert menu, point to Picture, and click Clip Art. In the Search For Clips text box, type the search text, and press Enter.	
Insert clip art on a Web page	Click the desired location on the Web page. On the Insert menu, point to Picture, and click Clip Art. Click a category, click the desired clip art, and click the Insert Clip button.	
Insert an image in a table cell	Click in the desired table cell. On the Insert menu, point to Picture, and click From File. In the file list, click the desired image, and click OK.	
Move image files to the images folder	Click the Folders icon on the Views bar, and click the Type button at the top of the file list. Select the image files, and drag them to the images folder in the Folder List.	
Create image thumbnails	Click the image on the Web page, and then click the Auto Thumbnail button on the Image toolbar.	

Lesson 4 Quick Reference

To	Do this
Resize an image	Click the image to select it, and then drag one of its resize handles to resize the image.
Add a background sound to a Web page	Right-click a blank area of the Web page, and on the shortcut menu, click Page Properties. Click the Browse button, select the desired sound file, and click OK twice.
Specify alternative text for an image	Right-click the image, and on the shortcut menu, click Picture Properties. Click in the Text text box, type the alternative text, and then click OK.
Insert a motion clip directly on a Web page	Click the desired location on the Web page. On the Insert menu, point to Picture, and click Video. Select the desired motion clip, and then click OK.
Link to a motion clip	Select and right-click the text or image for the link. On the shortcut menu, click Hyperlink. Select the desired video file, and then click OK.
Create a hover button	Click the desired location on the Web page. On the Insert menu, point to Component, and click Hover Button. Enter the button text and dimensions, click the Effect drop-down arrow, select an effect from the list box, and click the Browse button. Browse to the file you want the hover button to link to, and click OK twice.

Publishing a Web

In this lesson you will learn how to:

- ✔ *Check spelling on Web pages.*
- ✔ *Publish a Web locally.*
- ✔ *Publish a Web to a Web server.*
- ✔ *Update a Web on a Web server.*
- ✔ *Maintain a Web.*
- ✔ *Delete a Web.*
- ✔ *Publish a Web to a non–FrontPage-compliant Web server.*

ESTIMATED TIME **30 min.**

Your work on the Lakewood Mountains Resort Web site has been a success. Using the tools provided by Microsoft FrontPage 2000, you've created an attractive and useful set of Web pages. There's just one thing left to do: publish your Web to a Web server.

In this lesson, you will learn how to check spelling on your Web pages prior to publishing them on the Internet or on a company intranet, how to publish your Web locally to make a backup copy of your Web files, how to publish your Web to a Web server that has the FrontPage Server Extensions and to a Web server that does not, how to update and maintain your Web on the Web server, how to rename your Web, and how to delete your Web from a Web server.

Import the Lesson 5 practice Web

In this exercise, you create a new Web based on the files in the Lesson05 folder in the FrontPage Practice folder. You will use this Web for all the exercises in Lesson 5.

If your hard disk drive has a drive letter other than C, substitute the appropriate drive letter in step 2.

1. On the File menu, point to New, and then click Web.

   FrontPage displays the New dialog box.

2. Click the Import Web Wizard icon. In the Specify The Location Of The New Web text box, delete the default text and type **C:\My Webs\Lesson05**, and click OK.

   FrontPage displays the first Import Web Wizard dialog box.

3. Click the From A Source Directory Of Files option, click the Include Subfolders check box, and click the Browse button.
4. Browse to the Lesson05 folder, which is in the FrontPage Practice folder in the Office 8in1 Step by Step folder, and click OK.
5. Click Next twice, and then click Finish.

   FrontPage creates a new Web based on the practice files and places it in the Lesson05 folder.

Checking the Spelling on Web Pages

Before you publish a Web—whether on the Internet or on a company intranet—you want to make it as close to perfect as you can. Careless errors make a bad impression that extends beyond the Web site to your company itself.

At Impact Public Relations, your marketing copywriters have a saying: "No wun spels perfecly all the thyme." No matter how carefully you type information on the Web pages for Lakewood Mountains Resort, at least a few spelling errors are inevitable. To catch and correct these errors, you can use FrontPage's spelling checking feature. The spelling checker compares the words on your Web pages to the entries in its own spelling list. If FrontPage doesn't find a word in its list, it flags the word as a possible misspelling.

By default, FrontPage's spelling checker checks words as you type them on a page and underlines any words it doesn't recognize. If you like, you can correct any suspect words as soon as you see the spelling checker underline them. Because proper names and many technical terms are not included in the spelling dictionary, they are often flagged by the spelling checker. Click the Ignore button to continue checking spelling without changing the flagged word.

Most users prefer to check spelling all at once, checking a full page of text or the entire Web. In this section, you'll learn how to check spelling on an individual Web page or on your entire Web.

> **tip**
>
> Running a spelling check is very helpful, but it's no substitute for proofreading Web pages with your own eyes. For example, in the marketing copywriters' adage, the word *time* is misspelled as *thyme*. FrontPage's spelling checker, however, wouldn't catch that error, because *thyme* is a real word—although the wrong word in this particular context.

Check spelling on a single Web page

If you are not working through this lesson sequentially, follow the steps in "Import the Lesson 5 Practice Web" earlier in this lesson.

In this exercise, you check and correct spelling on a single page of the Lakewood Mountains Resort Web.

1. In the Folder List, double-click the file History.htm.

   FrontPage displays the History and Personnel page in Page view.

2. On the Tools menu, click Spelling.

   FrontPage displays the Spelling dialog box. FrontPage has flagged the word *Bromo* because the word doesn't appear in the spelling checker's word list. In this case, you know that Bromo is a proper name and is spelled correctly.

You can also press the F7 function key to check spelling.

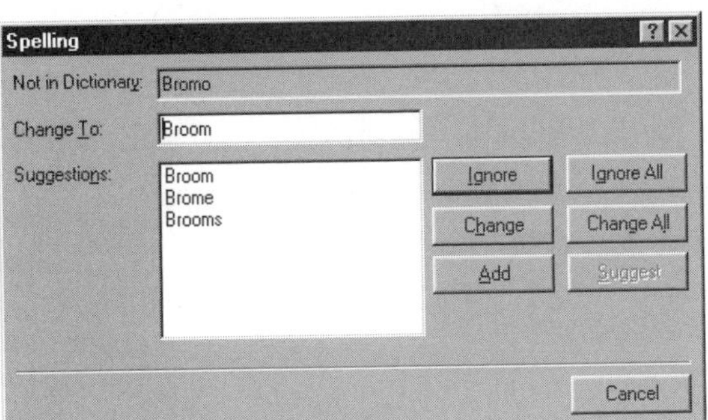

3. Click the Ignore button.

   FrontPage displays the next apparent misspelling. In this case, the word *hotel* has been misspelled as *hotl.*

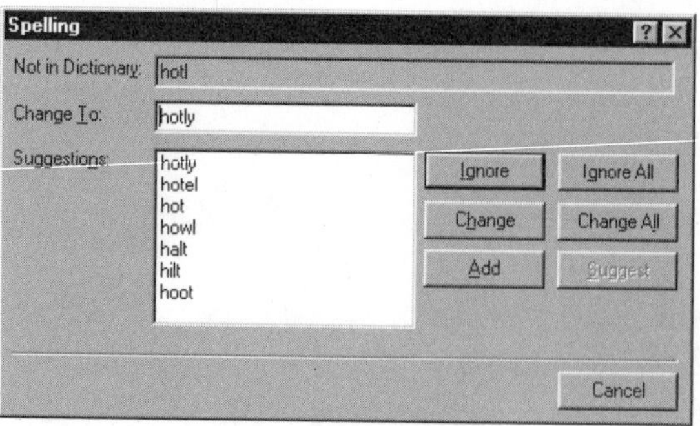

4. In the Suggestions list, click *hotel*, and then click the Change button.

   FrontPage corrects the word on the Web page and displays the next apparent misspelling.

5. In the Suggestions list, click *problem*, and then click the Change button.

   FrontPage corrects the word on the Web page and displays the next apparent misspelling. You know that *M.I.T.* is short for Massachusetts Institute of Technology, so the word is not misspelled.

6. Click the Ignore button.

   FrontPage displays a message box stating that the spelling check is complete.

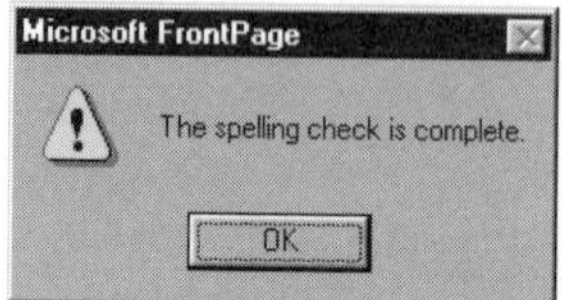

Save

7. On the toolbar, click the Save button.

   FrontPage saves your changes.

8. On the File menu, click Close.

   FrontPage closes the History and Personnel Web page.

tip

If you need to see a word in context to determine if it's misspelled, you can drag the Spelling dialog box to one side of the screen.

Check spelling on an entire Web

In this exercise, you check and correct spelling on the entire Lakewood Mountains Resort Web.

1. On the Views bar, click the Navigation icon, and then on the Tools menu, click Spelling.

   FrontPage displays the Spelling dialog box. The Entire Web option is selected.

2. Click the Start button.

   FrontPage displays a list of pages with apparent spelling errors. In each row, FrontPage lists the page, the number of apparent errors on that page, and the words that seem to be misspelled.

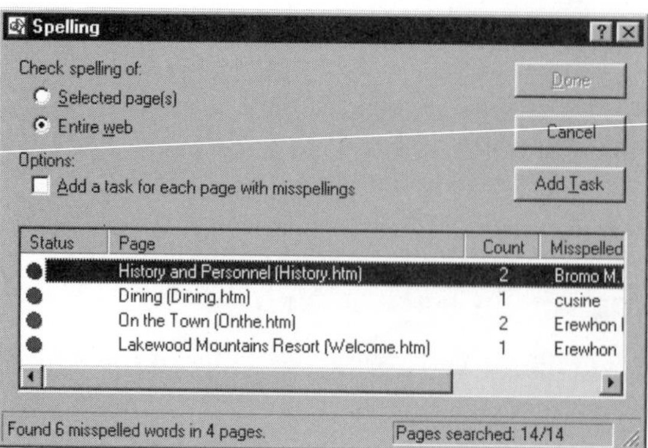

3 In the Spelling dialog box, double-click the file Dining.htm.

FrontPage displays the Dining page in Page view and flags the misspelling.

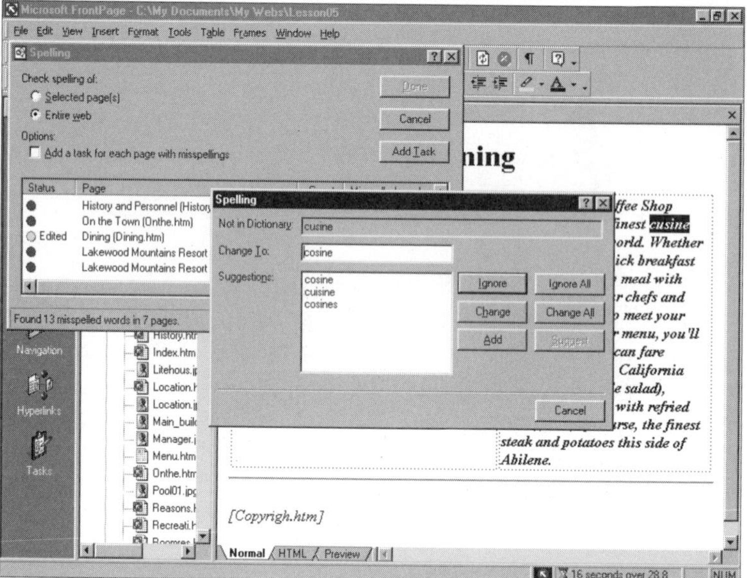

4 In the Suggestions list, click *cuisine*, and then click the Change button.

FrontPage corrects the word and displays the Continue With Next Document? dialog box, as shown on the following page.

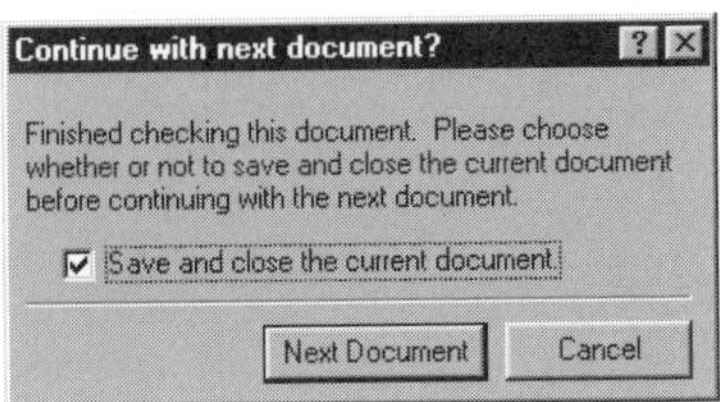

5. Click the Next Document button.

   FrontPage saves your changes to the Dining page, closes the Dining page, and displays the next Web page that contains spelling errors.

6. Click the Cancel button three times to close the dialog boxes.

   FrontPage ends the spelling check.

Publishing a Web

Once you've checked your Web for spelling errors, you're ready to publish it. Publishing your Web is the reason you've worked so hard to create a good looking Web in FrontPage. You should also publish a copy of your Web locally on your own hard disk drive. This local copy serves as a backup. If you make changes to your working copy of the Web (the one you will publish to a server) and then want to undo those changes, you can refer to this original copy of your Web (your locally published copy).

Before you can publish your Web, you should get the following information from your Internet Service Provider (ISP) or system administrator.

- The address of your Web server
- The preferred home page name (index.htm or default.htm)
- The FTP server address (if your Web server does not have the FrontPage Server Extentions)
- Folder information (if your Web server does not have the FrontPage Server Extensions)

Your Publishing Options

Many ISPs offer free Web hosting to their customers. To take advantage of this, you usually have to upload your Web to a subdirectory under the ISP's domain name. If your ISP's server name is isphost.com and your name is Tom Smith, for example, your Web address might be *www.isphost.com/users/tsmith*. Depending on the purpose of the Web, this might be an acceptable option. However, this approach has several drawbacks. First, free Web space is often limited to 5 MB or less—not enough for a complex Web or a business Web site. Second, you have little control over the Web address you're assigned. For a commercial Web site, it's important that the address be easy to remember and type. To create a professional Web site, it is a good idea to register your own domain name, such as ActiveEd.com or HansonBrothers.net, using your company name or some variation, and set up a business Web site with a Web hosting company that can provide the space your site will need (typically 5 MB to 100 MB).

Before you can register a domain name, you must have the following information:

- Administrative contact (information for the person who will manage the registration paperwork).
- Technical contact (information for the person who will manage and update your Web site).
- Billing contact (information for the person who will handle payment for your domain name registration and the ultimate owner of the Web).
- Server names (the primary and secondary domain names of the server that will host your Web; your ISP can provide these to you).
- Net addresses (the IP addresses for your host server names; your ISP can provide these also).

Register your domain name

These steps are subject to change.

1. Start your browser and navigate to *www.internic.net*. Click in the Search text box.
2. Type your desired domain name in the text box and press Enter. Repeat the search, trying different variations of the name, until you receive a No Match Found message.

   You now have an unused domain name that you can register.

(continued)

continued

3. Make sure that your Web hosting service has mapped your domain name to their server names and net addresses.
4. Navigate to *www.internic.net* again, and click the Web Version Step-by-Step hyperlink under the Type column.
5. At the bottom of the page, click the Forms hyperlink. Enter the necessary information. Make sure the New Registration option is selected.
6. Click the Step 1: Organization Information Section button, enter the requested information, and click the Step 2: Technical Contact Information button.
7. Follow the steps to finish registering your domain name.

   InterNIC will send e-mail confirmation. Copy this information and send it to *hostmaster@internic.net*. You will be mailed a printed invoice so that you can make payment.

Publish your Web locally

If you are not working through this lesson sequentially, follow the steps in "Import the Lesson 5 Practice Web" earlier in this lesson.

In this exercise, you publish a copy of your Web to your hard disk drive on your computer.

1. On the File menu, click Publish Web.

   FrontPage displays the Publish Web dialog box.

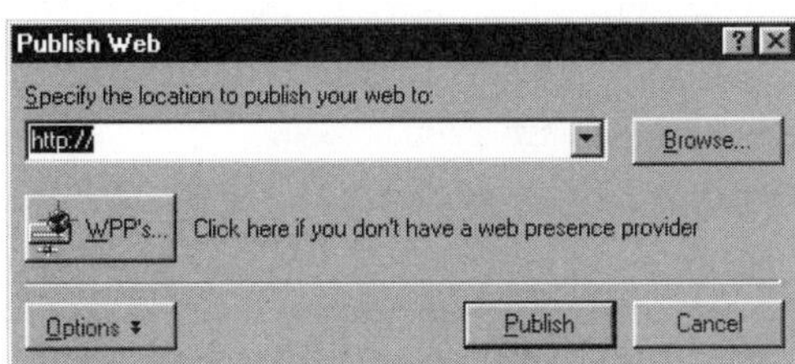

If your hard disk has a drive letter other than C, substitute the appropriate drive letter in step 2.

2. In the Specify The Location To Publish Your Web To text box, type **C:\My Webs\Copy of Lesson05 Web**, and then click the Publish button.

   FrontPage publishes a copy of your Web to your hard disk drive and displays a message box confirming that the Web site was published successfully.

3. If a Publishing FrontPage Components dialog box appears, click Continue.

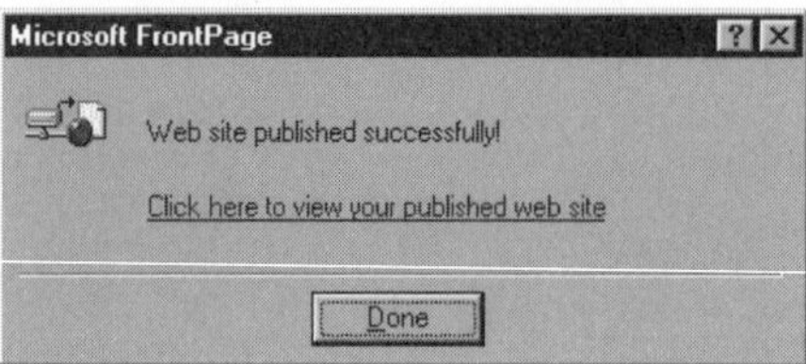

4. Click the Done button.

   FrontPage closes the message box.

Publish your Web to a Web server

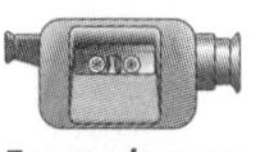

For a demonstration of how to publish a Web to a Web server, open the Office 8in1 Step by Step folder on your hard disk. Then open the FrontPage Demos folder, and double-click the PublishWeb icon.

In this exercise, you publish your Web to a Web server that has FrontPage Server Extensions—what is often referred to as a *FrontPage-compliant* Web server.

> **important**
>
> In order to complete the following exercise, you must have access to a Web server that has FrontPage Server Extensions. On Microsoft's Web site, you can find a list of Web hosting services that support FrontPage extensions. Just navigate to *www.microsoft.com/frontpage* and click the link to the list of FrontPage Web Presence Providers.

1. If necessary, connect to the Internet or to the intranet to which you'll publish your Web.
2. On the File menu, click Publish Web.

   FrontPage displays the Publish Web dialog box.

To find out the URL of your Web server and the folder to which your Web is published, check with your ISP, Web hosting service, or system administrator.

3. In the Specify The Location To Publish Your Web To text box, type the URL of your Web server and the folder to which your Web should be published.
4. Click the Publish button.

   FrontPage connects to your Web server and, for some servers, displays the Name And Password Required dialog box.

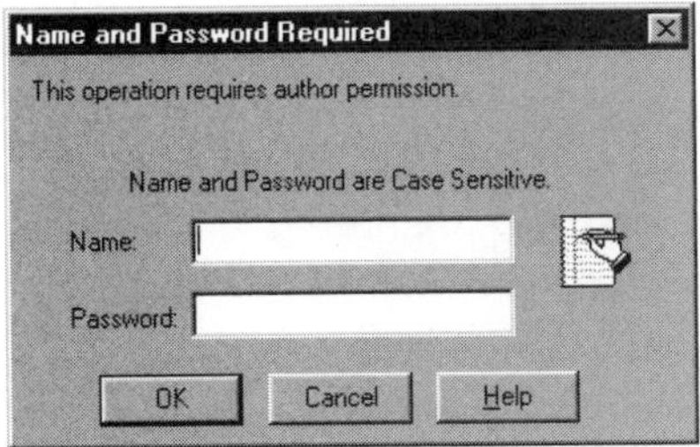

5. If prompted, type your name in the Name text box, type your password in the Password text box, and click OK.

   FrontPage publishes your Web to the selected folder of the Web server and displays a message box confirming that the Web site was published successfully.
6. Click the Done button.

tip

On most Web servers, your user name and password are *case sensitive*, which means that the uppercase version of a letter is treated as a completely distinct letter from its lowercase counterpart. For example, if your password is *microsoft* and you type it *Microsoft*, the password will be rejected. Be sure to type your user name and password exactly as they were created for your account.

Publishing Your Web to Public Web Hosts

The number of ISPs and Web hosting services that support FrontPage is growing rapidly. (If you're not sure whether your ISP or Web hosting service has the FrontPage Server Extensions, its technical support staff can tell you.) However, some Web hosting services—especially free services—do not support FrontPage extensions.

There are two ways to publish your Web to these sites. First, you can use FTP (File Transfer Protocol), discussed later in this lesson. In many cases, however, the Web host has its own method that allows you to upload files to your folder on the Web server. GeoCities, as shown in the following illustration, has a "file manager" that enables you to select files on your hard disk drive, one at a time, and upload them to your GeoCities Web folder.

You can also use the file manager to view and edit your Web page files on the server. Other public Web sites offer similar methods.

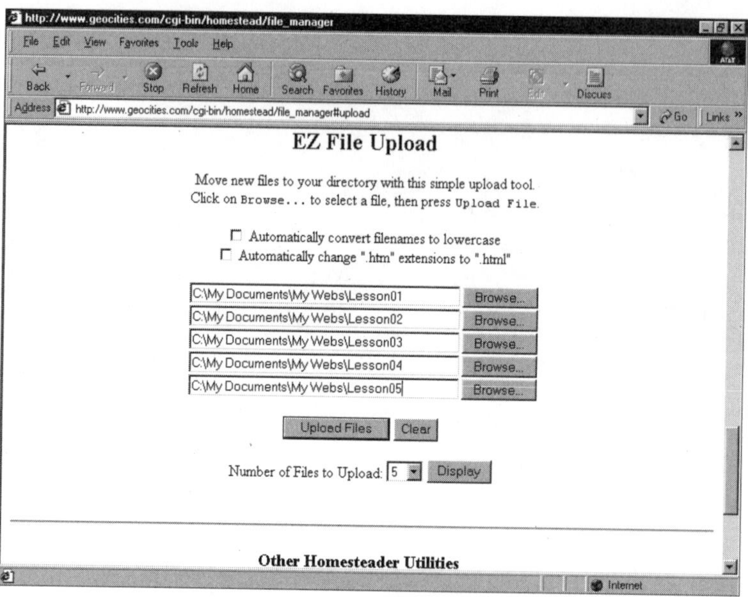

Updating and Maintaining a Web

Once you've published a Web, the job's not over. You'll continually update and improve your Web, both to enhance it with new ideas and to respond to requests from clients, such as the management of Lakewood Mountains Resort.

In this section, you will learn how to update some or all pages of your Web on a Web server, how to open a Web from the server in FrontPage, how to edit and delete your Web files on the server, how to rename your Web on the server, and how to delete your Web from the server.

Open your Web located on the Web server

To complete the following exercise, you must have published your Web to a Web server.

In this exercise, you use FrontPage to open your Web located on the remote Web server.

1. On the File menu, click Open Web.

   FrontPage displays the Open Web dialog box.

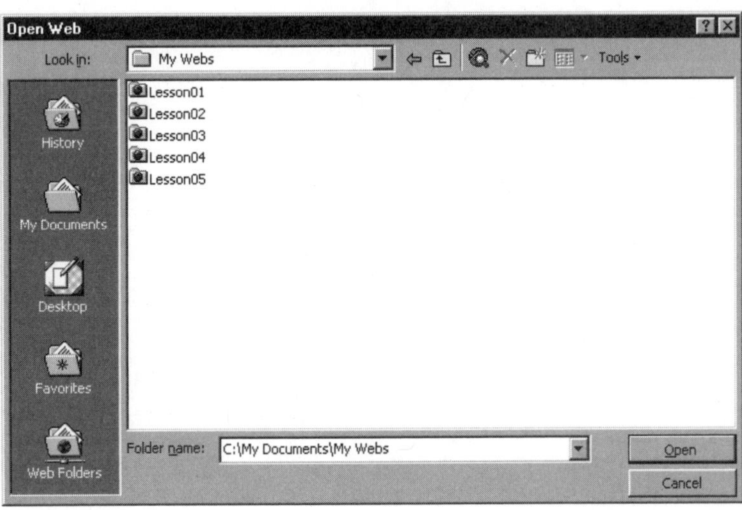

2. Click the Folder Name text box, type the URL of your Web site, and then click Open.

   Your Web server may prompt you for a user name and password.

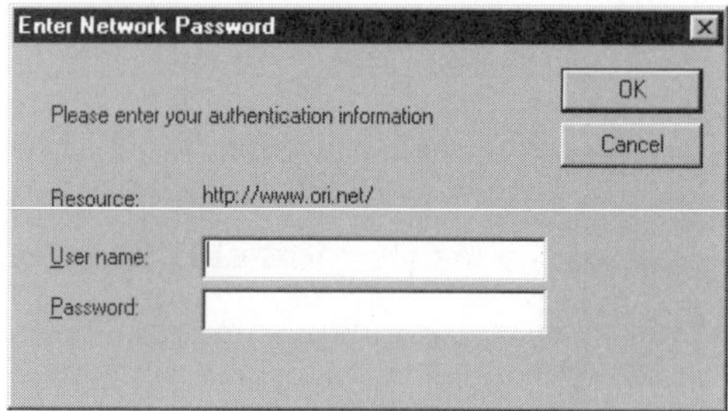

3. If prompted, type your user ID, and press Tab.

   Your user or administrator ID is entered, and the insertion point moves to the Password text box.

4. If prompted, type your password, and then click OK.

   FrontPage displays a list of your Web files on the Web server.

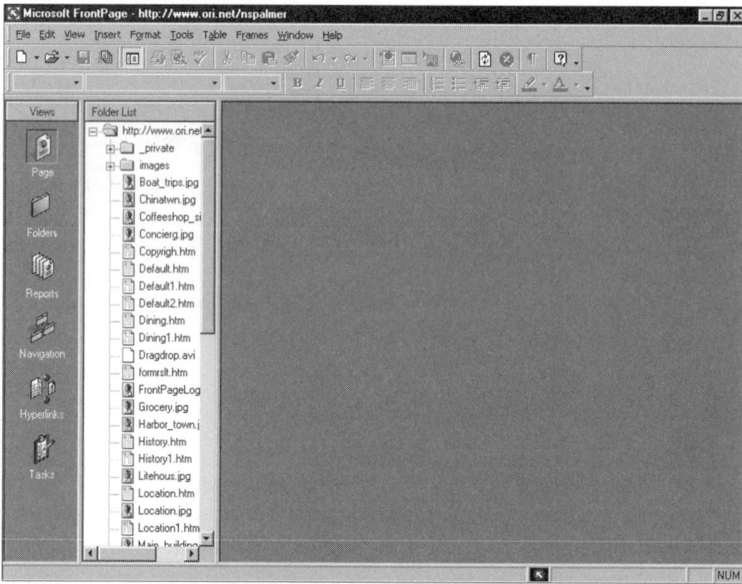

5. If necessary, click the file for the home page (index.htm or default.htm) and click the Open button.

   FrontPage opens your home page in Page view from the Web server.

When you open a file located on the Web server, FrontPage displays it in Page view, just the same as if you had opened a local copy of the file from your hard disk drive.

> **tip**
>
> If you are connecting to your Web server with a dial-up connection, it might take a few minutes for your home page and Web information to download to your computer. While the download is in progress, FrontPage will display the message "Requesting data" in the status bar at the lower-left corner of your screen.

Maintain your Web

The Lakewood Mountains Resort manager has pointed out an error on the Web site that you need to correct. You've also found an unused video file that you want to delete to save space on the server.

In this exercise, you perform routine maintenance on your Web while it resides on the Web server.

1. In the Folder List, double-click the file History.htm.

   FrontPage downloads the page from the Web server and displays it in Page view.

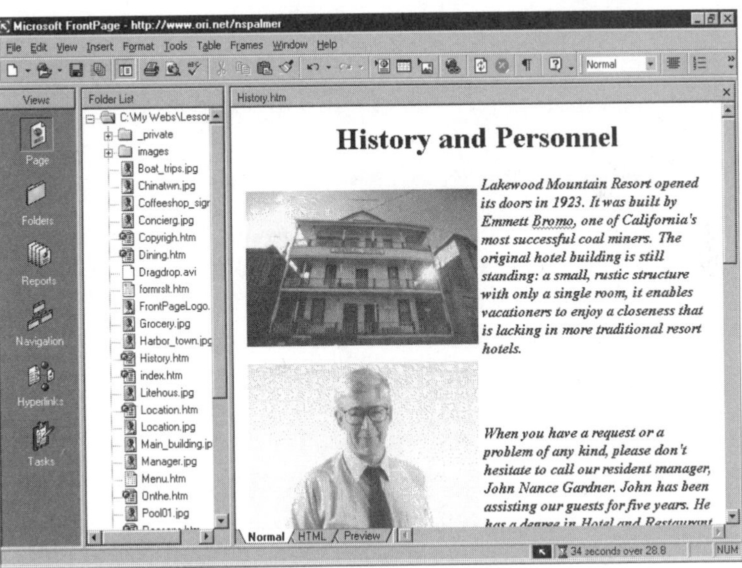

2. In the second line of body text, click between the *2* and the *3* in *1923*.

   FrontPage positions the insertion point in the text.

3. Press the Delete key once, and then type **4**.

   FrontPage changes the date of the resort's founding to 1924.

Save

4. On the toolbar, click the Save button.

   FrontPage saves your change to the History.htm file on the Web server. Because you are updating a file on the remote Web server, it takes a little longer than it would if the file were on your hard disk drive.

5. In the Folder List, click the file Dragdrop.avi.

   FrontPage selects the Dragdrop.avi file on the Web server.

6. Press the Delete key.

   FrontPage displays the Confirm Delete dialog box.

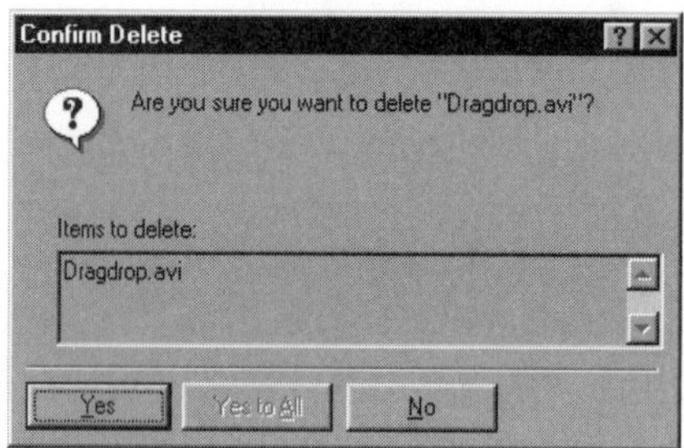

7. Click Yes.

   FrontPage deletes the file from the Web server.

Update your Web on the Web server

In this exercise, you update your Web on a Web server that supports FrontPage Server Extensions. When you update a Web, you upload new Web pages or revised versions of existing Web pages.

1. On the File menu, click Publish Web.

   FrontPage displays the Publish Web dialog box.

2. Click the Options button.

   FrontPage displays the Options section of the dialog box. Notice that the Publish Changed Pages Only option is selected. With this option selected, FrontPage will upload pages to the server only if they've been changed since they were originally published on the server.

3. If you want to upload copies of all your Web page files, not just the ones that have changed, click the Publish All Pages option.

4. In the Specify The Location To Publish Your Web To text box, type the URL of your Web server and the folder to which your Web should be published.
5. Click the Publish button.

   FrontPage connects to your Web server and, on some servers, displays the Name And Password Required dialog box.

If a dialog box asks whether or not to overwrite a file, click Yes.

6. If prompted, type your name in the Name text box, type your password in the Password text box, and click OK.

   FrontPage updates your Web page files on the Web server and displays a message box confirming that the Web site was published successfully.
7. Click the Done button.
8. On the File menu, click Close Web.

   FrontPage closes your Web.

Rename your Web

By default, your Web name is the same as the name of the folder in which your Web is kept—whether on your local hard disk drive or on the remote Web server. For example, if your Web is in a folder named *Lakewood*, FrontPage would title your Web simply *Lakewood*. In this exercise, you rename your Web.

> **important**
>
> The steps for renaming a Web are the same whether you're renaming a Web on your local hard drive or on the remote Web server. However, depending on your access permissions, you might not be able to rename your Web on the Web server. Check with your system administrator if you need help.

1. On the Tools menu, click Web Settings.

   FrontPage displays the Web Settings dialog box.

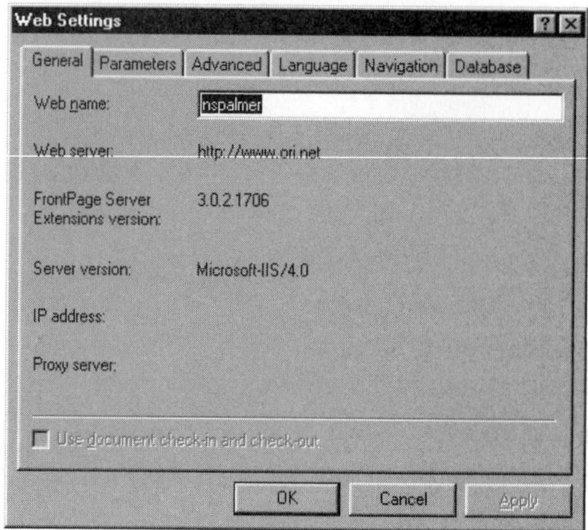

2. In the Web Name text box, delete the default name, type **Lakewood Mountains Resort** or another new name for the Web, and click OK.

   FrontPage renames your Web.

Delete your Web files from the Web server

There are two ways in which you can delete your Web from a remote Web server. First, you can delete all the files in your Web but leave the Web folder intact. Second, you can delete the files and the Web folder. You can easily delete your Web files, but it's best to leave deleting your Web folder to your Web administrator.

To delete individual files from a Web server, simply select only the files you want to delete instead of selecting all the Web files.

In this exercise, you delete your Web files from the Web server.

1. Open your Web on the Web server using the steps described in the exercise "Open Your Web Located on the Web Server," earlier in this lesson.

   FrontPage displays your Web server files in the Folder List.
2. On the Views bar, click the Folders icon.

   FrontPage displays the Web files in Folders view.
3. On the Edit menu, click Select All.

   FrontPage selects all the files in the Web folder.
4. Press the Delete key.

   FrontPage displays a dialog box asking you to confirm the deletion.

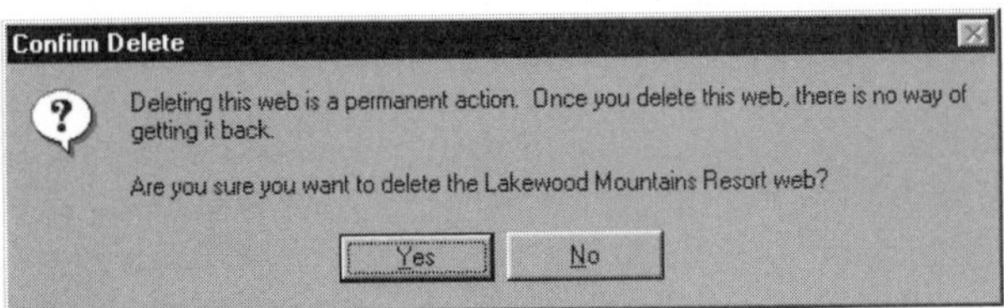

5. Click Yes.

   FrontPage deletes the files from the Web server.

One Step Further Using FTP to Upload a Web

If your Web server does not have the FrontPage Server Extensions, FrontPage uses FTP (File Transfer Protocol) to upload your files to a server. The details of using FTP will vary depending on the Web host, but in general, you follow the same steps as if you were publishing to a Web server that supports FrontPage Server Extensions. When FrontPage connects to the Web server, it recognizes that the server does not have the FrontPage Server Extensions. After getting your user ID and password for the Web server, FrontPage prompts you to type an FTP address to which it can upload files.

Normally, you just enter the name of the Web site's FTP server, and the server automatically routes the files into your private Web folder. Though the files are uploaded to the FTP server, they will be accessible only to you.

important

The following exercise assumes you are using Internet Explorer 5 or later. If you are using an earlier version of Internet Explorer (or another Web browser that does not support FTP), you should obtain an FTP utility program. Many such programs are available on the Web from sources such as *www.download.com*. This exercise also assumes that you are uploading to a non–FrontPage-compliant Web server operated by a Web host that allows FTP uploads.

Use FTP to upload your Web files

If you are not working through this lesson sequentially, follow the steps in "Import the Lesson 5 Practice Web" earlier in this lesson.

In this exercise, you use FTP to publish your Web to a non–FrontPage-compliant Web server.

1. On the File menu, click Publish Web.
2. In the Specify The Location To Publish Your Web To text box, type the FTP address of your Web server, such as *ftp://ftp.mybigcompany.com*.
3. Click the Publish button.

   FrontPage connects to the Web site's FTP server and displays a progress bar. When the connection is established, FrontPage may display the Name And Password Required dialog box.

You must begin the address with ftp:// so that FrontPage knows you want to connect to an FTP server over a network, and not simply publish your Web files locally with "ftp" as part of the Web name.

4. If prompted, in the Name text box, type your user name, and in the Password text box, type your password. Click OK.

   FrontPage uploads your files to the Web host's FTP server.

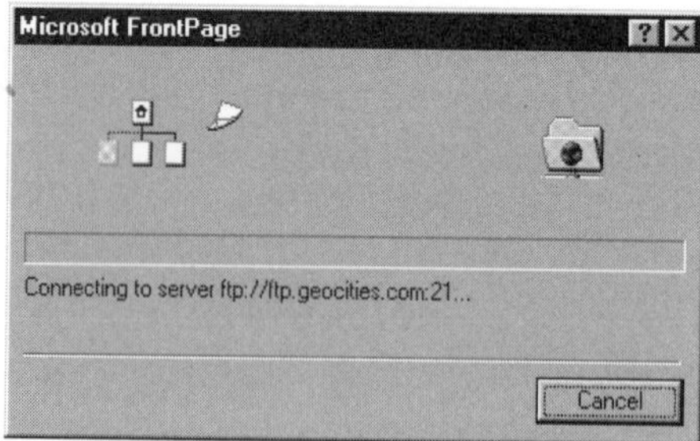

important

Your user name and password for the FTP server might not be the same as your user name and password for the Web server. Check with your Web server's system administrator if you need help.

Finish the lesson

1. On the File menu, click Close Web.
2. For each page, if FrontPage prompts you to save changes, click Yes.

   FrontPage saves your changes and closes the Lesson05 Web.

Lesson 5 Quick Reference

To	Do this
Check spelling on a Web page	In the Folder List, double-click the page you want to check, and on the Tools menu, click Spelling.
Check spelling on an entire Web	Click the Navigation icon on the Views bar. On the Tools menu, click Spelling, and click Start. Double-click pages in the page list to correct spelling.
Publish a Web locally	On the File menu, click Publish Web. In the Specify The Location To Publish Your Web To text box, type a folder name on your hard disk drive, and then click the Publish button.
Publish a Web to a FrontPage-compliant Web server	If necessary, connect to the Internet or company intranet. On the File menu, click Publish Web. In the Specify The Location To Publish Your Web To text box, type the URL of your Web server and your Web folder on the server, and click the Publish button. Type your user name and password, and then click OK.
Open a Web on a Web server	If necessary, connect to the Internet or company network. On the File menu, click Open, type the URL of your Web site, type a user name and password, and click OK.
Edit a page on a Web server	In FrontPage, open the Web on the Web server. In the Folder List, double-click the page you want to edit. In Page view, make the desired changes.
Delete a file from a Web on a Web server	In FrontPage, open the Web on the Web server. In the Folder List, click the file to delete, press the Delete key, and then click Yes.
Update a Web on a Web server	If necessary, connect to the Internet or company network. On the File menu, click Publish Web. Click Options and choose the desired update option. In the Specify The Location To Publish Your Web To text box, type the URL of the Web server and the Web folder on the server, and click the Publish button. Type your user name and password, and then click OK.
Rename a Web	On the Tools menu, click Web Settings. In the Web Name text box, delete the default text, type the new name, and click OK.

Lesson 5 Quick Reference

To	Do this
Publish a Web via FTP	In FrontPage, open a local copy of your Web and connect to the Internet or company intranet. On the File menu, click Publish Web. In the Specify The Location To Publish Your Web To text box, type **ftp://** and the URL of your FTP server, and click the Publish button. If necessary, type your user name and password, and click OK.

Index

Page numbers in italics indicate illustrations.

Symbols

A

D

E

G

H

L

M

N

Q

S

Z

Get a **Free**

e-mail newsletter, updates, special offers, links to related books, and more when you

register on line!

Register your Microsoft Press® title on our Web site and you'll get a FREE subscription to our e-mail newsletter, *Microsoft Press Book Connections.* You'll find out about newly released and upcoming books and learning tools, online events, software downloads, special offers and coupons for Microsoft Press customers, and information about major Microsoft® product releases. You can also read useful additional information about all the titles we publish, such as detailed book descriptions, tables of contents and indexes, sample chapters, links to related books and book series, author biographies, and reviews by other customers.

Registration is easy. Just visit this Web page and fill in your information:

http://www.microsoft.com/mspress/register

Microsoft®

Proof of Purchase

Use this page as proof of purchase if participating in a promotion or rebate offer on this title. Proof of purchase must be used in conjunction with other proof(s) of payment such as your dated sales receipt—see offer details.

Microsoft® Office 2000 8-in-1 Step by Step

1-57231-984-4

____

CUSTOMER NAME

Microsoft Press, PO Box 97017, Redmond, WA 98073-9830

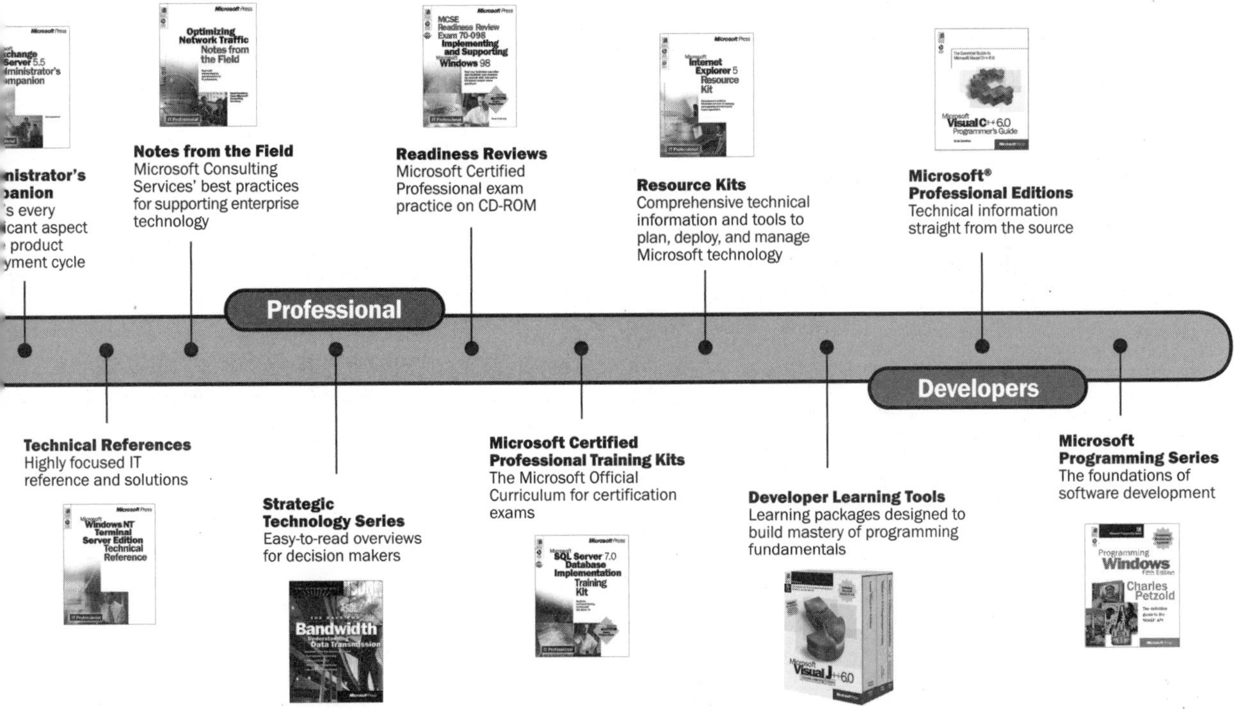

MICROSOFT LICENSE AGREEMENT

Book Companion CD

IMPORTANT—READ CAREFULLY: This Microsoft End-User License Agreement ("EULA") is a legal agreement between you (either an individual or an entity) and Microsoft Corporation for the Microsoft product identified above, which includes computer software and may include associated media, printed materials, and "online" or electronic documentation ("SOFTWARE PRODUCT"). Any component included within the SOFTWARE PRODUCT that is accompanied by a separate End-User License Agreement shall be governed by such agreement and not the terms set forth below. By installing, copying, or otherwise using the SOFTWARE PRODUCT, you agree to be bound by the terms of this EULA. If you do not agree to the terms of this EULA, you are not authorized to install, copy, or otherwise use the SOFTWARE PRODUCT; you may, however, return the SOFTWARE PRODUCT, along with all printed materials and other items that form a part of the Microsoft product that includes the SOFTWARE PRODUCT, to the place you obtained them for a full refund.

SOFTWARE PRODUCT LICENSE

The SOFTWARE PRODUCT is protected by United States copyright laws and international copyright treaties, as well as other intellectual property laws and treaties. The SOFTWARE PRODUCT is licensed, not sold.

1. **GRANT OF LICENSE.** This EULA grants you the following rights:
   - a. **Software Product.** You may install and use one copy of the SOFTWARE PRODUCT on a single computer. The primary user of the computer on which the SOFTWARE PRODUCT is installed may make a second copy for his or her exclusive use on a portable computer.
   - b. **Storage/Network Use.** You may also store or install a copy of the SOFTWARE PRODUCT on a storage device, such as a network server, used only to install or run the SOFTWARE PRODUCT on your other computers over an internal network; however, you must acquire and dedicate a license for each separate computer on which the SOFTWARE PRODUCT is installed or run from the storage device. A license for the SOFTWARE PRODUCT may not be shared or used concurrently on different computers.
   - c. **License Pak.** If you have acquired this EULA in a Microsoft License Pak, you may make the number of additional copies of the computer software portion of the SOFTWARE PRODUCT authorized on the printed copy of this EULA, and you may use each copy in the manner specified above. You are also entitled to make a corresponding number of secondary copies for portable computer use as specified above.
   - d. **Sample Code.** Solely with respect to portions, if any, of the SOFTWARE PRODUCT that are identified within the SOFTWARE PRODUCT as sample code (the "SAMPLE CODE"):
     - i. **Use and Modification.** Microsoft grants you the right to use and modify the source code version of the SAMPLE CODE, *provided* you comply with subsection (d)(iii) below. You may not distribute the SAMPLE CODE, or any modified version of the SAMPLE CODE, in source code form.
     - ii. **Redistributable Files.** Provided you comply with subsection (d)(iii) below, Microsoft grants you a nonexclusive, royalty-free right to reproduce and distribute the object code version of the SAMPLE CODE and of any modified SAMPLE CODE, other than SAMPLE CODE, or any modified version thereof, designated as not redistributable in the Readme file that forms a part of the SOFTWARE PRODUCT (the "Non-Redistributable Sample Code"). All SAMPLE CODE other than the Non-Redistributable Sample Code is collectively referred to as the "REDISTRIBUTABLES."
     - iii. **Redistribution Requirements.** If you redistribute the REDISTRIBUTABLES, you agree to: (i) distribute the REDISTRIBUTABLES in object code form only in conjunction with and as a part of your software application product; (ii) not use Microsoft's name, logo, or trademarks to market your software application product; (iii) include a valid copyright notice on your software application product; (iv) indemnify, hold harmless, and defend Microsoft from and against any claims or lawsuits, including attorney's fees, that arise or result from the use or distribution of your software application product; and (v) not permit further distribution of the REDISTRIBUTABLES by your end user. Contact Microsoft for the applicable royalties due and other licensing terms for all other uses and/or distribution of the REDISTRIBUTABLES.

2. **DESCRIPTION OF OTHER RIGHTS AND LIMITATIONS.**
   - **Limitations on Reverse Engineering, Decompilation, and Disassembly.** You may not reverse engineer, decompile, or disassemble the SOFTWARE PRODUCT, except and only to the extent that such activity is expressly permitted by applicable law notwithstanding this limitation.
   - **Separation of Components.** The SOFTWARE PRODUCT is licensed as a single product. Its component parts may not be separated for use on more than one computer.
   - **Rental.** You may not rent, lease, or lend the SOFTWARE PRODUCT.
   - **Support Services.** Microsoft may, but is not obligated to, provide you with support services related to the SOFTWARE PRODUCT ("Support Services"). Use of Support Services is governed by the Microsoft policies and programs described in the

user manual, in "online" documentation, and/or in other Microsoft-provided materials. Any supplemental software code provided to you as part of the Support Services shall be considered part of the SOFTWARE PRODUCT and subject to the terms and conditions of this EULA. With respect to technical information you provide to Microsoft as part of the Support Services, Microsoft may use such information for its business purposes, including for product support and development. Microsoft will not utilize such technical information in a form that personally identifies you.

- **Software Transfer.** You may permanently transfer all of your rights under this EULA, provided you retain no copies, you transfer all of the SOFTWARE PRODUCT (including all component parts, the media and printed materials, any upgrades, this EULA, and, if applicable, the Certificate of Authenticity), **and** the recipient agrees to the terms of this EULA.
- **Termination.** Without prejudice to any other rights, Microsoft may terminate this EULA if you fail to comply with the terms and conditions of this EULA. In such event, you must destroy all copies of the SOFTWARE PRODUCT and all of its component parts.

3. **COPYRIGHT.** All title and copyrights in and to the SOFTWARE PRODUCT (including but not limited to any images, photographs, animations, video, audio, music, text, SAMPLE CODE, REDISTRIBUTABLES, and "applets" incorporated into the SOFTWARE PRODUCT) and any copies of the SOFTWARE PRODUCT are owned by Microsoft or its suppliers. The SOFTWARE PRODUCT is protected by copyright laws and international treaty provisions. Therefore, you must treat the SOFTWARE PRODUCT like any other copyrighted material **except** that you may install the SOFTWARE PRODUCT on a single computer provided you keep the original solely for backup or archival purposes. You may not copy the printed materials accompanying the SOFTWARE PRODUCT.

4. **U.S. GOVERNMENT RESTRICTED RIGHTS.** The SOFTWARE PRODUCT and documentation are provided with RESTRICTED RIGHTS. Use, duplication, or disclosure by the Government is subject to restrictions as set forth in subparagraph (c)(1)(ii) of the Rights in Technical Data and Computer Software clause at DFARS 252.227-7013 or subparagraphs (c)(1) and (2) of the Commercial Computer Software—Restricted Rights at 48 CFR 52.227-19, as applicable. Manufacturer is Microsoft Corporation/One Microsoft Way/Redmond, WA 98052-6399.

5. **EXPORT RESTRICTIONS.** You agree that you will not export or re-export the SOFTWARE PRODUCT, any part thereof, or any process or service that is the direct product of the SOFTWARE PRODUCT (the foregoing collectively referred to as the "Restricted Components"), to any country, person, entity, or end user subject to U.S. export restrictions. You specifically agree not to export or re-export any of the Restricted Components (i) to any country to which the U.S. has embargoed or restricted the export of goods or services, which currently include, but are not necessarily limited to, Cuba, Iran, Iraq, Libya, North Korea, Sudan, and Syria, or to any national of any such country, wherever located, who intends to transmit or transport the Restricted Components back to such country; (ii) to any end user who you know or have reason to know will utilize the Restricted Components in the design, development, or production of nuclear, chemical, or biological weapons; or (iii) to any end user who has been prohibited from participating in U.S. export transactions by any federal agency of the U.S. government. You warrant and represent that neither the BXA nor any other U.S. federal agency has suspended, revoked, or denied your export privileges.

DISCLAIMER OF WARRANTY

NO WARRANTIES OR CONDITIONS. MICROSOFT EXPRESSLY DISCLAIMS ANY WARRANTY OR CONDITION FOR THE SOFTWARE PRODUCT. THE SOFTWARE PRODUCT AND ANY RELATED DOCUMENTATION ARE PROVIDED "AS IS" WITHOUT WARRANTY OR CONDITION OF ANY KIND, EITHER EXPRESS OR IMPLIED, INCLUDING, WITHOUT LIMITATION, THE IMPLIED WARRANTIES OF MERCHANTABILITY, FITNESS FOR A PARTICULAR PURPOSE, OR NONINFRINGEMENT. THE ENTIRE RISK ARISING OUT OF USE OR PERFORMANCE OF THE SOFTWARE PRODUCT REMAINS WITH YOU.

LIMITATION OF LIABILITY. TO THE MAXIMUM EXTENT PERMITTED BY APPLICABLE LAW, IN NO EVENT SHALL MICROSOFT OR ITS SUPPLIERS BE LIABLE FOR ANY SPECIAL, INCIDENTAL, INDIRECT, OR CONSEQUENTIAL DAMAGES WHATSOEVER (INCLUDING, WITHOUT LIMITATION, DAMAGES FOR LOSS OF BUSINESS PROFITS, BUSINESS INTERRUPTION, LOSS OF BUSINESS INFORMATION, OR ANY OTHER PECUNIARY LOSS) ARISING OUT OF THE USE OF OR INABILITY TO USE THE SOFTWARE PRODUCT OR THE PROVISION OF OR FAILURE TO PROVIDE SUPPORT SERVICES, EVEN IF MICROSOFT HAS BEEN ADVISED OF THE POSSIBILITY OF SUCH DAMAGES. IN ANY CASE, MICROSOFT'S ENTIRE LIABILITY UNDER ANY PROVISION OF THIS EULA SHALL BE LIMITED TO THE GREATER OF THE AMOUNT ACTUALLY PAID BY YOU FOR THE SOFTWARE PRODUCT OR US$5.00; PROVIDED, HOWEVER, IF YOU HAVE ENTERED INTO A MICROSOFT SUPPORT SERVICES AGREEMENT, MICROSOFT'S ENTIRE LIABILITY REGARDING SUPPORT SERVICES SHALL BE GOVERNED BY THE TERMS OF THAT AGREEMENT. BECAUSE SOME STATES AND JURISDICTIONS DO NOT ALLOW THE EXCLUSION OR LIMITATION OF LIABILITY, THE ABOVE LIMITATION MAY NOT APPLY TO YOU.

MISCELLANEOUS

This EULA is governed by the laws of the State of Washington USA, except and only to the extent that applicable law mandates governing law of a different jurisdiction.

Should you have any questions concerning this EULA, or if you desire to contact Microsoft for any reason, please contact the Microsoft subsidiary serving your country, or write: Microsoft Sales Information Center/One Microsoft Way/Redmond, WA 98052-6399.

PN 097-0002296